THE TREATY OF MAASTRICHT

THE <u>TREATY</u> OF MAASTRICHT

From Conception to Ratification:
A Comprehensive Reference Guide

Richard Corbett

LONGMAN
CURRENT
AFFAIRS

THE TREATY OF MAASTRICHT
From Conception to Ratification:
A Comprehensive Reference Guide

Published by Longman Group UK Limited, Westgate House,
The High, Harlow, Essex CM20 1YR, United Kingdom

ISBN 0–582–20906–4

A catalogue record for this publication is available from the British Library

Typesetting by The Midlands Book Typesetting Company, Loughborough.
Printed in Great Britain by BPCC Wheatons Ltd, Exeter.

1000110263

To Tom, Hannah and Laura,
citizens of the European Union

CONTENTS

ANNEXES

DOCUMENTATION SECTION

DOCUMENTS LEADING UP TO THE IGCs

DOCUMENTS DURING THE IGCs

TREATY ON EUROPEAN UNION (the Treaty of Maastricht)

REACTIONS TO THE TREATY OF MAASTRICHT

ABOUT THE AUTHOR

Richard Corbett was head of a "Task Force" dealing with the intergovernmental conference that led to the Maastricht Treaty in the secretariat of the Socialist Group in the European Parliament. In this context he worked closely with Parliament's Vice-President, David Martin, in preparing Parliament's proposals forwarded to the IGCs, and with Socialist Group President, Jean-Pierre Cot, in his meetings with responsible ministers in the national governments, and Jacques Delors during the negotiations. He attended the inter-institutional conferences and played a key drafting role in the parliamentary conference (or "assizes") on the eve of the IGCs.

Previously, he worked as a civil servant of the European Parliament itself, notably on the secretariat of the Committee on Institutional Affairs when it prepared parliament's draft Treaty on European Union under the authority of Altiero Spinelli, and following the IGC which led to the Single European Act. He is now responsible for the issue of enlargement to Austria, Finland, Norway and Sweden.

Richard Corbett has written widely on European affairs and is co-author of *The European Parliament* (Longman, 2nd ed. 1992).

ACKNOWLEDGEMENTS

The author's main acknowledgement as regards the content of this book is to Martyn Quinn, who prepared the sections concerning the proceedings of the IGC on Economic and Monetary Union.

My other main acknowledgements are to Elisabeth Sweeney-Smith and Majella McCone, without whose sterling work in typing the text and helping to track down elusive documents, this book would never have appeared. In this respect, thanks are also due to the people of Denmark for having, in initially rejecting the Treaty, given an extended deadline for producing the book.

Thanks also to David Martin MEP, Vice-President of the European Parliament, for contributing to the conception of this book, for allowing access to his files and documents and, last but not least, for the exhilarating time we had working together on the Martin Reports and following the IGCs.

Finally, the author must emphasize that the views expressed in this book are strictly personal.

The Publishers are grateful to the Directorate-General for Information of the European Parliament and to David Martin MEP, Vice-President of the European Parliament, for supplying material for the Documentation Section of this book.

INTRODUCTION

The Treaty on European Union signed in Maastricht in February 1992 is a milestone in the process of European integration. Its repercussions will be felt for many years to come, and it has already created minor political earthquakes in a number of the Community's Member States. Undoubtedly, it brings the Community forward to a higher level of integration, whilst at the same time placing question-marks over its future development.

This book examines the *process* surrounding the Maastricht Treaty from the initial pressures that led to calls for a revision of the EC Treaties, at first with regard to EMU and then for a wider political union, through the various conceptions and proposals as they were elaborated in the Community's institutions and in the national capitals, via the negotiations themselves to the signing of the Treaty, the ratification procedure in the Member States and the initial implementing measures.

Amidst all the hyperbole that has surrounded debate on the Treaty, the book will attempt to present a realistic account of events, and to enable the reader to judge for him or herself by reprinting, in its documentation section, the key proposals and ideas put forward before and during the negotiations. The full Maastricht Treaty is also included, as well as the conclusions of the Edinburgh Summit and other relevant texts adopted after the Maastricht Treaty was signed.

This is not a legal commentary on each article of the Maastricht Treaty. Instead it analyzes the political processes involved and compares and contrasts the positions taken by the Member States in the negotiations. It traces the origins of the main reforms introduced by the Treaty in what was, despite the formal secrecy of the intergovernmental conferences, a remarkably public process (although public interest was only stirred towards the end).

No book on this subject — even of this size — can hope to be exhaustive. But although the account given in the six chapters of this book does not cover every detail, nor is every relevant text contained in the documentation section, this book nonetheless attempts to provide a comprehensive survey of the conception, negotiation and ratification of the Treaty on European Union.

ACRONYMS

CAP	Common Agricultural Policy
CEAC	Conference of European Affairs committees (of the national parliaments and the EP)
CFSP	Common Foreign and Security Policy
CIP	*See* PIC
COMECON	(East European) Council for Mutual Economic Cooperation
COREPER	Committee of the Permanent Representatives of the Member States
COSAC	French acronym for CEAC
CSCE	Conference on Security and Cooperation in Europe
EAEC	European Atomic Energy Community
EBRD	European Bank for Reconstruction and Development
EC	European Community
ECB	European Central Bank
ECJ	European Court of Justice
ECOFIN	Council, meeting at the level of Economic and Finance Ministers
ECSC	European Coal and Steel Community
ECU	European Currency Unit
EDC	European Defence Community
EDF	European Development Fund (Lomé Convention)
EEA	European Economic Area
EEC	European Economic Community
EES	European Economic "Space" — mistranslation from EEA.
EFTA	European Free Trade Association
EIB	European Investment Bank
EMF	European Monetary Fund
EMI	European Monetary Institute
EMS	European Monetary System
EMU	Economic and Monetary Union
EP	European Parliament
EPC	European Political Cooperation
EPU	European Political Union
ERM	Exchange Rate Mechanism (of the EMS)
ESCB	European System of Central Banks
EURATOM	*See* EAEC
EUROFED	Term for Central Bank system not retained in Treaty
EUROPOL	Proposed European Criminal Investigation Office
GATT	General Agreement on Tariffs and Trade
GDP	Gross Domestic Product
IGC	Intergovernmental Conference
IIA	Interinstitutional Agreement
IMF	International Monetary Fund
JHA	Title VI of Treaty of Maastricht concerning cooperation in the fields of Justice and Home Affairs
MEP	Member of the European Parliament
NATO	North Atlantic Treaty Organization
PESC	French acronym for CFSP

PIC	Parallel Interinstitutional Conference (more usually referred to by its French abbreviation CIP), originally, "Preparatory" Interinstitutional Conference
PU	Political Union
QMV	Qualified Majority Voting
SEA	Single European Act
SMEs	Small and Medium-sized Undertakings (Enterprises)
TREVI	Working party of the EC Member States on Terrorism, Radicalism, Extremism and Violence
UNICE	European Employers' organization
VAT	Value Added Tax
WEU	Western European Union (defence organization of nine countries: EC minus Ireland, Denmark and Greece)
WTO	Warsaw Treaty Organization (or "Warsaw Pact")

CHRONOLOGY

February 1984	EP adopts a draft Treaty instituting European Union (Spinelli Report).
May 1984	President Mitterrand, speaking to EP, undertakes to take up draft treaty and seek intergovernmental negotiations.
June 1984	European Council in Fontainebleau sets up ad hoc committee of personal representatives of heads of government to make suggestions for institutional reform (Chair Senator Dooge).
January 1985	Delors I Commission takes office.
June 1985	European Council in Milan examines report of Dooge committee and, by majority vote, agrees to convene an intergovernmental conference to revise the treaties.
December 1985	IGC reaches climax in Luxembourg meeting of European Council.
February 1986	The Governments of the Twelve sign the Single European Act.
July 1987	Single European Act enters into force (six months later than scheduled) setting 1992 as deadline for completion of single market and for scheduled review of EPC.
February 1988	Extra European Council in Brussels agrees "Delors package" increasing Community budgetary resources and adjusting procedures to take account of new needs arising from SEA.
June 1988	European Council in Hanover charges a Committee including the governors of the Central Banks — chaired by Jacques Delors — with the responsibility of drafting a report on EMU.
April 1989	Delors Committee submits its report.
18 June 1989	European elections. Referendum in Italy produces 89.1 per cent in favour of charging European Parliament with writing a draft Constitution for a European Union with a European Government.
26–27 June 1989	European Council in Madrid examines report of Delors Committee and accepts in principle the idea of holding an intergovernmental Conference on EMU.
27 July 1989	European Parliament calls for the IGC on EMU to examine also the question of institutional reform.
11 November 1989	Berlin wall "falls".
23 November 1989	European Parliament calls for IGC on EMU to have a wider remit and envisages convening "assizes" with national parliaments and a conference with the other institutions to press its demands.

17 January 1990	Jacques Delors proposes in European Parliament the launching of negotiations on Political Union parallel to those on EMU.
14 March 1990	European Parliament adopts MARTIN I report by 213 votes to 19, proposing subjects for negotiation on political union.
21 March 1990	Belgian government Memorandum takes up main points of "Martin" Resolution.
21 March 1990	Italian Chamber of Deputies adopts resolution endorsing the "Martin" Resolution of EP.
19 April 1990	Kohl-Mitterrand letter to Irish Presidency supports idea of a second IGC on political union to "strengthen democratic legitimation", "render its institutions more efficient", "ensure unity and coherence" and to define a "common foreign and security policy".
19–20 April 1990	European Trade Union Confederation (ETUC) adopts submission to IGC on EMU.
28 April 1990	The extraordinary European Council in Dublin asks the foreign ministers to examine the need for other treaty changes and a second IGC on Political Union.
4 May 1990	Spanish government proposes that IGC on Political Union should examine European citizenship (Gonzalez letter).
10 May 1990	Danish Memorandum on points for the IGC on Political Union.
13 May 1990	Commission holds special weekend meeting/"seminar" to reflect on Political Union.
15 May 1990	Greek Memorandum on points for the IGC on Political Union.
17 May 1990	First meeting of Interinstitutional pre-conference brings together the Foreign Ministers, four Commissioners and 12 MEPS in Strasbourg.
19–20 May 1990	Foreign Ministers meet in Parknasilla and discuss possible items for IGC on Political Union.
25–26 June 1990	The European Council in Dublin formally examines the ideas discussed by Foreign Ministers and agrees on the principle of a second IGC on political union to run parallel to that on EMU.
1 July 1990	First phase of EMU (not requiring Treaty amendments) begins: Italy takes over rotating Presidency of Council.
11 July 1990	The European Parliament adopts its detailed proposals for the Intergovernmental Conferences (Martin II) by 217 votes to 38.
13 July 1990	Belgian Senate adopts resolution supporting EP resolution of 14 March.
21 July 1990	Commission holds seminar on integration of foreign and security policy into EC and institutional changes.

2 August 1990	Iraq invades Kuwait.
21 August 1990	Commission publishes its proposals for EMU including draft treaty articles.
1 September 1990	Signing of Treaty on Union between the two Germanies.
3 October 1990	German unification. Former East German territory therefore becomes part of EC.
8 October 1990	2nd meeting of interinstitutional pre-conference (Luxembourg). Pound sterling joins ERM at (high) parity announced unilaterally by UK.
21 October 1990	Commission publishes its "opinion" on Political Union.
23 October 1990	3rd meeting of interinstitutional pre-conference (Strasbourg).
26 October 1990	Dutch government policy document on Political Union presented to the Dutch Parliament.
27–28 October 1990	The European Council in Rome agrees (with UK reservations) that the IGC on EMU should aim to establish a single currency managed by an independent Central Bank, which could be operational in 1997. It fixes 1 January 1994 — for start of phase II of EMU and agrees some main features of EMU.
15–16 November 1990	EPP (Christian Democrats) Congress adopts in Dublin proposals for a European federal constitution.
16 November 1990	Italian Presidency presents initial report on political union for discussion in Council on 4 December and with Parliament in interinstitutional meeting on 5 December.
19 November 1990	CSCE Summit in Paris.
22 November 1990	European Parliament approves draft treaty articles corresponding to its July resolution for submission to IGC (Martin III Report) and gives favourable opinion for convening the IGCs.
23 November 1990	Summit of Liberal Party (ELDR) Leaders in Berlin adopts declaration on Treaty revision.
27–30 November 1990	The Conference of national Parliaments and the European Parliament in Rome ("Assizes") adopts a final Declaration which takes up most of the European Parliament's requests contained in the Martin Reports.
29 November 1990	John Major replaces Margaret Thatcher as British Prime Minister.
5 December 1990	4th meeting of Interinstitutional pre-conference (Brussels).
6 December 1990	Kohl-Mitterrand Memorandum completing their letter of 18 April 1990.
7 December 1990	Memorandum of the Foreign Ministers to the European Council on preparation for the IGC on Political Union.
9 December 1990	Declaration of Socialist Party Leaders meeting in Madrid on the Intergovernmental Conferences.

10 December 1990	Portuguese Government Memorandum on the IGCs.
14–15 December 1990	Rome II European Council meeting indicates wide agenda for Political Union IGC.
15 December 1990	Launch in Rome of the Intergovernmental Conferences on Political Union, Economic and Monetary Union.
1 January 1991	Luxembourg takes over Presidency of EC Council.
17 January 1991	Gulf War begins.
5 March 1991	Interinstitutional conference (Council, Parliament, Commission) in Brussels discusses Parliament's powers.
8 April 1991	Interinstitutional conference in Brussels discusses EMU.
11–12 April 1991	ETUC adopts submission to IGC on Political Union.
15 April 1991	The Luxembourg Presidency presents a "non paper" on Political Union constituting a synthesis of the several hundred specific proposals submitted by national governments, Parliament and Commission.
16 April 1991	Luxembourg Prime Minister Santer meets with Christian Democrat leaders in European Parliament (Klepsch, Tindemans) and Foreign Minister Poos with Socialist Group leaders (Cot, Hänsch, Martin).
17 April 1991	Poos presents Luxembourg draft in European Parliament debate.
21 April 1991	Poos meets Committee on Institutional Affairs of European Parliament to discuss details of draft.
7–8 May 1991	Conference of European Regions adopts resolution on IGCs calling for greater participation of regional authorities in European affairs.
15 May 1991	Interinstitutional conference in Strasbourg discusses powers of Commission and the structure ("pillar" vs unitary) of the Treaty.
2–3 June 1991	Foreign Ministers meet in Dresden to discuss structure of Treaty.
6 June 1991	Luxembourg Presidency presents "non paper" on EMU.
11 June 1991	Interinstitutional Conference in Strasbourg on EMU.
18 June 1991	New version of the Luxembourg "non paper" on political union, now called "draft treaty".
18 June 1991	French *Assemblée Nationale* specialized body adopts report on IGCs accepting orientation of Luxembourg Presidency's text, but calling for its strengthening in a federal direction.
27 June 1991	Belgian Chamber of Representatives adopts resolution criticizing Luxembourg text as regards the structure of the Treaty (intergovernmental pillars) and the insufficiency of the EP's powers. Decides not to ratify any new Treaty if EP rejects it.

28–29 June 1991	The European Council in Luxembourg agrees to take the Luxembourg text as the basis for further intergovernmental negotiations.
1 July 1991	Netherlands takes over rotating Council Presidency.
15–17 July 1991	Western Economic Summit in London.
August 1991	Just after the international crisis of the failed coup in Moscow the Dutch Presidency prepares a draft treaty "towards European Union" which revises certain fundamental points of the Luxembourg text. The Dutch Finance Minister circulates a draft Treaty for EMU which adopts the "two-speed" approach.
5 September 1991	Dutch Presidency (Finance Minister Kok and European Minister Dankert) discuss drafts with Socialist MPs from European and national parliaments attending a Socialist Group conference in Brussels.
9 September 1991	Interinstitutional Conference in Brussels on EMU.
19 September 1991	Dankert meets Committee on Institutional Affairs of European Parliament to discuss details of draft.
21–22 September 1991	"Conclave" of Economic and Finance Ministers in Apeldoorn.
24 September 1991	The Dutch government withdraws the draft of a two-speed EMU and formally adopts a "Draft Treaty towards European Union".
30 September 1991	Dutch text on Political Union is rejected by a majority of the Twelve in Brussels.
1 October 1991	Interinstitutional Conference in Brussels.
21 October 1991	Council reaches agreement on EEA.
31 October 1991	ETUC and employers' organization (UNICE) jointly agree on proposal for Treaty provisions on role of social partners.
5 November 1991	Interinstitutional Conference in Brussels.
7–8 November 1991	NATO Summit in Rome.
8 November 1991	Dutch Presidency presents new draft treaty on Political Union
12–13 November 1991	"Conclave" of Foreign Ministers in Noordwijk.
20 November 1991	Dutch Presidency presents its new draft in debate in European Parliament.
1–3 December 1991	Finance Ministers meet in "conclave" in Scheveningen (Sunday 1st) and Brussels (2nd and 3rd).
9–10 December 1991	Maastricht European Council reaches conclusions on all the outstanding points in the IGCs.
1 January 1992	Portugal takes over rotating Council Presidency for the first time.
January 1992	Mini-IGCs to revise the ECSC and Euratom Treaties.

7 February 1992	Signature of Treaty on European Union in Maastricht by Foreign and Finance Ministers. Ceremony attended by Parliament (Klepsch, Martin) and Commission (Delors).
17 March 1992	Danish Parliament, pending a referendum, approves Treaty by 130 votes to 25.
8 April 1992	European Parliament approves the new Treaty whilst calling for further progress and inviting national parliaments to prepare further reforms.
21 May 1992	UK Commons approves Maastricht Bill in second reading by 336 to 92.
2 June 1992	Danish referendum produces 50.7 per cent No to 49.3 per cent Yes, thereby rejecting Treaty.
3 June 1992	President Mitterrand announces a referendum in France.
4 June 1992	Foreign Ministers of the Member States, meeting in Oslo on the fringe of a NATO meeting, agree to continue with ratification procedures in the other Member States, leaving an open door for Denmark but excluding any possibility to modify or renegotiate the Treaty.
18 June 1992	Irish referendum approves Treaty by 69 per cent to 31 per cent, despite appearance of abortion issue.
23 June 1992	French Congress (National Assembly and Senate in special joint session) approves constitutional amendments needed for Treaty by 592 votes to 73.
26–27 June 1992	European Council meeting in Lisbon "underlines the importance of respecting the timetable laid down for ratification to ensure in any case the entry into force of the Treaty as of January 1, 1993". Delors reappointed to head his third Commission as of January 1993.
1 July 1992	UK takes over rotating Council Presidency.
2 July 1992	Luxembourg Parliament approves Treaty by 51 votes to six.
17 July 1992	Belgian Chamber of Representatives approves Treaty by 146 to 33.
31 July 1992	Greek Parliament approves Treaty by 386 votes to eight.
28 August 1992	Monetary Committee asserts commitment to existing ERM parties.
5 September 1992	Economic and Finance Ministers meet in Bath, UK. Norman Lamont refuses to devalue pound and Germany refuses to make a substantial cut in interest rates or to revalue mark.
13 September 1992	First realignment within ERM since 1987: Lira devalued.
17 September 1992	Monetary crisis. The pound is unable to maintain position and UK government unilaterally withdraws from ERM. The Lira follows. Italian Senate approves Treaty by 176 to 16.

20 September 1992	French referendum approves Treaty by 51.05 per cent to 48.95 per cent.
16 October 1992	Birmingham European Council meeting adopts Declaration on "A Community close to its citizens".
22 October 1992	Seven parties in Danish *Folketing* agree on "national compromise" seeking special interpretation of the Treaty for Denmark.
29 October 1992	Italian Chamber of Deputies approves Treaty by 403 votes to 46. Spanish Congress approves by 314 to three.
4 November 1992	Belgian Senate approves Treaty by 115 votes to 26.
17 November 1992	Portuguese Parliament approves Treaty by 200 votes to 21.
25 November 1992	Spanish Senate approves Treaty by 220 to 0.
2 December 1992	*Bundestag* approves Treaty by 543 to 17.
11–12 December 1992	European Council meeting in Edinburgh agrees package of measures for Denmark and on subsidiarity, transparency and openness in decision-taking. Also approves "Delors 2" package increasing EC budgetary resources.
15 December 1992	Dutch Parliament approves Treaty with unanimous vote in first Chamber.
16 December 1992	Association agreements with Poland, Hungary and Czechoslovakia signed.
18 December 1992	German *Bundesrat* approves Treaty by a unanimous vote.
1 January 1993	Denmark takes over rotating Presidency of EC Council.
6 January 1993	Delors III Commission takes office.
13 January 1993	Schlütter government falls in Denmark. Rasmussen becomes Prime Minister in Social Democrat-led majority government.
14 January 1993	UK Commons resumes consideration of Maastricht Bill (committee stage).
18 May 1993	2nd Danish referendum approves Treaty by 56.8 per cent to 43.2 per cent.
20 May 1993	Commons approves Maastricht Bill (3rd reading) by 292 to 112.
1 July 1993	Belgium takes over rotating Council Presidency.
20 July 1993	UK Lords approves Maastricht Bill (3rd reading) by 141 to 29.
22 July 1993	Commons ties on Labour amendment seeking UK adherence to Social Protocol and rejects government motion approving its position on opt-out.
23 July 1993	Commons approves vote of confidence in government linked to its position on Social Protocol.

I

WHY A NEW TREATY?

When in 1986 the Member States of the European Communities signed the Single European Act (SEA), there were many who thought that they would be unlikely to return to the issue of Treaty amendment before the end of the century. Enormous political effort had gone into the negotiations that led to the Single Act which had in the end agreed only a limited set of modifications and additions to the EEC Treaty and which was ratified in some Member States only with considerable difficulty.[1]

The Single Act did contain a provision requiring Member States to examine whether any revision of Title III (political cooperation in foreign affairs) would be required, but only "five years after the entry into force of the Act" (i.e. in 1992), and it seemed unlikely that Member States would wish to embark on a global process of Treaty revision so soon after the previous one. Yet, not only did they do so, agreeing on a substantial package of reforms, but they also agreed on a further Intergovernmental Conference (IGC) in 1996 which could take the integration process yet further.

What were the processes which led to this dramatic acceleration? They are manifold, involving aspects of all of the following and no doubt others. Let us examine some key components.

1. The general dynamic of unification

The Community is never at a standstill. The whole process of integration from 1950 until the present day has been one of successive steps forward on the basis of compromises negotiated among the Member States. The Community has actually spent more than half of the years of its existence in IGCs or other reviews of its constitutional bases.[2]

The dynamic presiding over such negotiations has usually been the same: a majority of Member States wishing to press ahead with a minority reluctant to do so. The majority sometimes threatens to move ahead without the minority, but would prefer not to. The minority does not want to move very far ahead, but would prefer a compromise to being left out. Usually, a compromise is reached, but negotiations then re-open some years later on some other aspect of integration.

Over time, of course, the respective sizes and the cohesion of each group has changed.

---

[1] The Danish Parliament initially rejected the Single European Act causing the Government to call a referendum which approved it by 56 per cent to 44 per cent. In Ireland, the parliamentary ratification was overturned by the Supreme Court, thereby necessitating a referendum to change the constitution.

[2] Mentioning only the major episodes, one can cite the IGC on the ECSC (1950–51), the IGC on the Defence Community (1950–52), the Spaak Committee (1955), the IGC on the EEC and the EAEA (1956–57), the Fouchet Negotiations (1961–62), the IGC on the Merger Treaty (1964), the two Budgetary Treaties (negotiations in 1969–70 and 1974–75) negotiations on the European Elections Act (1975–76), the Tindemans Report (1975–76), the Report of the Three Wise Men (1979), the Genscher-Colombo Initiative leading to the Stuttgart Declaration (1981–83), the Dooge Committee (1984–85), the IGC that produced the Single European Act (1985–86), the Delors Committee (1988–89) and the most recent IGCs (1990–92).

At times, it has been a minority of just one that has blocked progress. Most States have constantly been in one camp or another, whereas others have swung back and forth. France, notably, with internal divisions, has swung to the reticent camp under De Gaulle, before switching back again under Mitterrand.

These generalizations hide, of course, a multitude of differences on individual subjects and nuances arising from particular political situations. Nonetheless, the overall dynamic stands out clearly. Its consequence is that as soon as one set of negotiations has been finished and the results (if any) entrenched as Treaty amendments or in some other form, then the debate re-opens again in a new phase. From 1965 (De Gaulle's "empty chair" crisis) to 1984 (the Parliament's draft treaty on European Union and the Dooge Committee) the gaps between the steps forward were longer and the steps themselves were smaller, but even then the same pattern could be discerned (1970 and 1975 Budget Treaties, 1976 European Elections Act, 1979 establishment of EMS).

Following the signature of the SEA in 1986, the Community moved straight into a negotiation on its financial and budgetary resources (the Delors package) which resulted, after a year's negotiation involving a failed summit, in an agreement in early 1988 (requiring national ratification) on increasing the Community's financial resources and improving its decision-making procedures with regard to the use of those resources. It was only four months later that the European Council set in motion the process leading to EMU by setting up the Delors committee to investigate and make proposals for progress towards EMU — the Member States were again, and with hardly a pause for breath, involved in talks fundamental to the integration process itself.

2. The implications of the single market

One of several objectives of the SEA was the establishment of a deadline for completing the Community's internal market. This, together with the Commission's "White Book" listing the (nearly 300) legislative measures needed to eliminate all remaining barriers to the internal market, gave a powerful impetus to the Community's institutions and to the Member States to achieve at last this key objective of the original EEC Treaty. But, as the internal market took shape, a growing realization of its implications took place.

In a single market with goods, services, capital and labour circulating freely among Member States (the Single Act even specified that the market should be "an area without internal frontiers"), it becomes impossible — or at least, extremely difficult — for Member States to regulate separately matters such as consumer protection, emission standards and other environmental norms, many social standards, or banking regulations. It becomes very difficult for them to diverge greatly in their rates of indirect taxation without distorting competition. Cooperation in matters of police and customs becomes imperative. Last, but not least, the issue of monetary integration arises: does a single market require a single currency, or can separate currencies co-exist in a single market ?

It was this last issue which was to lead the way. It already had a long history dating back to the Spaak Report in 1956. In principle, the establishment of economic and monetary union (EMU) had been a Community objective since 1969 (Hague Summit of Community Heads of Government). The Werner Report in 1970 proposed the establishment of EMU by 1980 through gradual convergence of economic and monetary policies and progressive narrowing of the margins for exchange-rate fluctuations. The broad substance of this report was agreed by the Heads of Government in 1972 and the Community actually embarked on the first of three intended stages of EMU — the famous "snake in the tunnel" mechanism for exchange rates. However, the effect of the successive shocks of the collapse of the Bretton Woods system of international monetary management and the first oil crisis of

October 1973 led to the effective shelving of the process at the Paris Summit of 1974.

The Member States returned to the issue in 1978 following an initiative from the Commission President, Roy Jenkins. The Bremen Summit agreed to the proposal of Helmut Schmidt and Valery Giscard D'Estaing to set up the European Monetary System (EMS) which was put into operation in March 1979. This established a new system of limited fluctuation margins, known as the Exchange Rate Mechanism (ERM), with realignments of these margins to be agreed by common accord. The European Currency Unit (ECU) was established as a composite currency (basket of currencies), used as the denominator of Community transactions. However, not all the Member States participated in the ERM, the United Kingdom being the most notable absentee until 1990.

Nevertheless, the EMS enjoyed a certain degree of success. Realignments of central exchange rate margins took place with decreasing frequency (seven in the first four years, four in the next four and only one in the last four of its first 12 years' existence up to 1991) and the differentials in rates of inflation and rates of interest have declined. The ECU was being increasingly used as a denominator and value not only by the Community institutions but also by governments and companies.

The Community thus had a lengthy history of seeking to establish EMU and an understanding of the main issues involved, but without ever having managed to reach the point of moving to a single currency. EMU was discussed in the 1985 IGC which produced the SEA, but that IGC only agreed to add a brief reference to EMU to the EEC Treaty which was redrafted simply to refer to it and mention the existence of the EMS and the ECU, specifying that any development would require further treaty amendment. This failure to make progress was partly due to outright opposition from the United Kingdom, whose Chancellor of the Exchequer (Nigel Lawson) stated that "the inclusion of Economic and Monetary Union as a goal in the Treaty is unacceptable and pointless", and partly due to hesitations among other Member States about spelling out steps on a timetable towards EMU in the Single Act. The Act was, after all, the first relaunch of a stagnant Community and to overload it with an ambitious programme whose details would require lengthening the duration of the IGC was felt by several Member States to be too risky. However, besides adding the brief reference to EMU to the EEC Treaty, it was agreed to include in the preamble of the SEA a reference to the 1972 commitment to a progressive realization of EMU and this at least planted a seed for future reference.

It was, indeed, impossible to sideline the issue. After the entry into force of the Act, it became more pressing. This was because the 1992 programme involved the abandonment of controls on capital flows, making the ERM less easy to manage, yet also making the Member States more interdependent in their monetary policy. There was a growing feeling that the full benefits of a single market would not become available if it continued to be based on separate currencies. On this last point, the European Parliament, and later the Commission, made studies estimating the cost to the European economy of maintaining separate currencies at 30 bn ECU per year (transaction costs, hedging costs against exchange rate changes, maintenance of separate reserves and reliance on the dollar for pricing in the international trade). These costs would, of course, only increase as the single market developed and European economies became even more interlinked. A mere four months after finally settling the budgetary consequences of the SEA by agreeing on the "Delors package", the European Council set up in June 1988 a Committee composed of governors of the central banks of the Member States and three independent experts[3] chaired by Jacques Delors, the President of the Commission, to study and propose concrete steps to EMU.

---

[3] Niels Thygesen, Professor of Economics, Copenhagen; Alexander Lamfalussy, General Manager of the Bank for International Settlements in Basle, Professor of Monetary Economics at the Catholic University of Louvain-la-Neuve; Mr. Miguel Boyer, President of Banco Exterior de Espana.

The Committee submitted its report, which became known as the *Delors Report*, in April 1989[4] proposing a three-phase advance to EMU, the last two of which would require a new Treaty. It suggested that the European Council convene an intergovernmental conference to negotiate this Treaty on the basis of the Report. One striking feature of the Report was that the Central Bank Governors were unanimous on the need for EMU, on the basic structure of the system to be established (including the need for regulating national fiscal policy) and on the three-phase approach to EMU. Their governments, however, were to prove less than unanimous.

Because of its huge influence upon the subsequent process, it is worth looking at the findings of the report. They described the structure and content of monetary union in considerable detail. The main *principles* settled by the committee were that:

- A new set of treaty amendments would have to be prepared — the scale of the project considered meant that a simple adaptation of what already existed would prove insufficient.

- The creation of a union should be envisaged as a single process with the decision to start the first stage representing a clear political commitment to undertake the entire process.

- Economic union and monetary union should be treated as a parallel but separate process. Monetary union would consist of the irreversible convertibility of currencies (with a stated preference for a single currency instead of 12 linked ones) and would require the creation of a new Community institution — the European Central Bank (ECB) — which would sit at the centre of a federal system of all central banks participating in the union (the European System of Central Banks — ESCB). Economic union would not require new institutions but would need the close coordination of Member States' economic policies and would imply a degree of supranational control, in particular in the area of setting mandatory rule to govern budget policies with majority decisions over questions relating to budget deficits.

- The ESCB must be free of political control and should have the primary objective of price stability. These conditions are similar to those applying to the German Bundesbank and their inclusion reflects the huge influence of Germany throughout all of the EMU negotiations. The Germans would simply not even consider a European Central Bank with less stringent rules than those of the Bundesbank and therefore these conditions were included from the very beginning.

In addition to setting out the basic principles for EMU, the Delors Report also provided a clear outline for achieving EMU in three stages. Stage One, the preparatory stage, was to consist essentially of a strengthening of what already existed. It was to be a move, "from the implicit to the explicit", but would not involve any significant transfer of power or innovation. In practice this stage would see the use of current texts to the full in making public and open recommendations to Member States in matters of economic and budgetary policy and strengthening the directive on convergence. State Two would be the transition phase and would involve the convergence of Member States' economic policy and performance. This stage would also see the creation of the new monetary institutions which would help oversee the transition period and would act as the embryonic ECB. The third and final stage was to be EMU itself with a single currency and economic policy decided in common.

---

[4] Published by the Office for Official Publication of the European Community, ISBN 92–826–0655–4.

The report was careful to leave the political decisions to the heads of state or government, including the crucial issue of the timetable.

The European Council meeting in Madrid in June 1989 agreed, despite the misgivings of Mrs Margaret Thatcher, then the UK prime minister, to proceed to EMU with phase one to begin on 1 July 1990. An intergovernmental conference to negotiate the necessary Treaty revisions was envisaged to begin at this point (the start was eventually fixed for December 1990 by the Strasbourg European Council of December 1989), and a set of conditions were agreed for the pound sterling to join the exchange rate mechanism (these had more to do with internal difficulties of the British Government with Mrs Thatcher coming under pressure from her Chancellor, Mr Nigel Lawson, and Foreign Secretary, Sir Geoffrey Howe, to join the ERM).

The year and a half between Madrid and the opening of the IGC on EMU were to be used for intensive preparatory work and discussions among the Member States. By the opening of the IGC, 11 Member States had agreed that the beginning of phase two should begin in 1994, that the ultimate objective should be a single currency and that a new monetary institution of independent character should be established.

The issue of EMU had thus prised open the door to a new treaty revision, but other pressures were soon to widen the agenda further. Some of these were the issues mentioned above that also sprung from the single market, but above all there was the fundamental question of the political context of monetary union: in Germany in particular it was felt that full monetary union was only sustainable in a stronger political framework. Monetary union required political union.

3.   The changing international context

1989 was the most dramatic year in the process of rapid change in central and eastern Europe, culminating in the fall of the Berlin Wall on 11 November. This new and changing international context persuaded many that the Community needed to become a stronger actor on the international scene. It was the most significant framework for international cooperation and integration on the continent, and many of the new governments in central Europe were turning towards the Community. The prospect of German unity also persuaded many that such a large state should be firmly anchored in a strengthened Community.

There were also those who took the opposite view: that a break-up of the Eastern bloc should not be met by a strengthening of what many perceived as the core of the Western bloc and that rather than create a tighter Community of 12, wider frameworks for cooperation across the whole of Europe should be created.

The former view tended to have the support of a majority in the Community, in particular as it became clear that this was also the wish of many central and eastern European countries. Germany, too, wanted to ensure that its unification would take place without unduly alarming its partners and the best way to do so was to emphasize the European credentials of Germany and its willingness to operate in partnership with the other Member States. France was particularly anxious to retain its special relationship with Germany, fearing that the latter might well "turn eastwards", seeking new economic ties and political cooperation in that direction.

All these concerns added to the pressure for a broadening of the remit of the IGCs to include "political union", i.e. a general strengthening of the Community and, in particular, of foreign policy cooperation. The European Parliament's initial pleas were reinforced by the Belgian government's memorandum of March 1990 and by the joint statement of

French President François Mitterrand and German Federal Chancellor Helmut Kohl on 19 April 1990 in which they asked the European Council to convene a second IGC to run parallel to that on EMU, with the objective of strengthening the democratic legitimacy of the Union, rendering its institutions more efficient, ensuring unity and coherence of the Community's economic and political action and defining a common foreign and security policy.

The development of a common foreign policy had, of course, been a long- standing objective, but one which had only made gradual and halting progress. In the early days the attempts to set up a European Defence Community (EDC) and the preparations for a European Political Community had envisaged integration of foreign policies, but the rejection by the French National Assembly of the EDC Treaty in 1954 left this as a virtually taboo subject for many years. The Fouchet plan of the early 1960s had envisaged intergovernmental cooperation on foreign policy, but suspicions that the then French President, Charles De Gaulle, wished to subsume the whole Community edifice in this intergovernmental framework was among the reasons which led to the failure of this initiative too. In 1970, the then six Member States embarked on an informal process of consultation and cooperation among the foreign ministers on the basis of the Davignon Report.[5] This cooperation was reinforced in 1973 (Davignon II Report) and 1981 (London Report). Gradually, meetings with Foreign Ministers were synchronized with those of the Community Council, the Commission was able to attend meetings and Ministers agreed to answer parliamentary questions and respond to European Parliament resolutions. These developments were confirmed in the Stuttgart Declaration on European Union in 1983, but were never given Treaty status nor formalized in any legally binding way.

However, in 1984 the European Parliament, in its "Draft Treaty on European Union", proposed to lay down treaty provisions for a common external policy. Although decision-taking would continue to require unanimity and the method would be one of "cooperation" among the Member States, the latter could decide to transfer matters to the field of "common action" where majority voting could apply and the Commission would have an executive role.

In the SEA, the Member States laid down for the first time treaty provisions concerning European Political Cooperation (EPC), and they referred to the objective of a "European Foreign Policy". The Act essentially consolidated the forms of cooperation that had developed up to 1985. It had the merit of solemnly entrenching the EPC procedures in the Treaty, but maintained their separation from the Community legal framework by including them in Title III of the SEA which was not added to the Community Treaties but stood in its own right. This meant, for instance, that there would be no role for the Court of Justice in enforcing decisions or in resolving conflicts, and that there would be a lesser role for the Commission and the Parliament.

This system, which had governed the Community's external relations since the entry into force of the SEA, meant that there were, in fact, two overlapping frameworks for external relations: the Community framework in which matters of trade, commerce, overseas aid, development policy and the external aspects of other Community policies (transport, research, agriculture etc.) were settled, and the EPC framework for matters not coming under the Community treaties (notably the political and diplomatic aspects of external relations — military aspects were specifically excluded by the limitation of EPC to political and economic aspects of security).

In practice, this distinction was becoming more and more difficult to maintain. As the Community's economic importance in world affairs grew, so its decisions could not be taken without reference to wider political considerations. On the other hand, when a

---

[5] Etienne Davignon was at the time political director of the Belgian Foreign Office.

decision was taken under EPC procedures, it seemed obvious and logical to use, where possible, Community instruments to further the proclaimed objectives. Thus, the Foreign Ministers might find it desirable to adopt sanctions against South Africa or Iraq, but a Community legal instrument was needed to impose them. Indeed, in the absence of any prospects for joint military action by the Member States, the only common instruments available to them were the Community's instruments: sanctions or trade agreements, the granting or withholding of financial aid, access or lack of access to the internal market and so on. Yet all these decisions were taken by qualified majority voting and with an important role for the Commission and, in some cases, the Parliament.

The European Parliament had been advocating the merging of EPC into the Community framework, arguing that the maintenance of this artificial distinction was anachronistic. President Delors complained about having to explain to Nelson Mandela, the black South African political leader, the difference between EPC, represented by the Member State having the Presidency, and the Community, represented by the Commission, both acting on behalf of what outsiders perceived to be the same union of states.

The events in central and eastern Europe also led, for the first time, to the USA leaving the leadership role to the European Community for at least some aspects of policy towards central and eastern Europe. First, the Community — indeed the Commission — was given the task of coordinating Western aid towards central and eastern Europe (on behalf of the Group of 24). Later, the USA was to let the EC play the leading role in the initial attempts to solve the Yugoslav crisis. The sheer pressure of events seemed to be driving the Community towards shifting to a higher gear. The disparity of Community Member States in their attitude to the Gulf War of 1991 did not detract from this:– it served as a reminder of how weak the structures were when opinions were divided.

4.   Pressure from the European Parliament

The European Parliament had been the catalyst behind the 1985 IGC which led to the SEA. Its proposal for a Treaty of European Union, put forward in February 1984 at a time of stagnation in the Community, led to the European Council (Fontainebleau, June 1984) establishing a Committee to examine institutional reform and then (Milan, June 1985) convening the IGC.[6] The results of the IGC in the form of the SEA was far from satisfactory to the European Parliament which continued to press for further reform. In the period 1987–89 the European Parliament's Committee on Institutional Affairs produced a series of reports purporting to show why the Single Act was insufficient. These resulted in Parliament resolutions on:

– the cost of "non-Europe" (Catherwood Report 17 July 1988)
– the democratic deficit (Toussaint Report 17 July 1988)
– the procedures for consulting European citizens on European political unification (Bru Puron Report 17 July 1988)
– the first year of application of the Single European Act (Graziani Report 27 October 1988)
– Fundamental Rights and Freedoms (De Gucht 12 April 1989)

---

[6] For a full account of that IGC, see "The 1985 IGC and the Single European Act" (R.G. Corbett) in *Dynamics of European Union*, Editor, Roy Price (Croom Helm 1987).

These were then brought together in a final report on the strategy for achieving European Union (Herman report) adopted in February 1989 in which Parliament called for further reforms and itself undertook to prepare proposals following the 1989 European elections. These proposals would be based on its 1984 draft Treaty and on the experience of the Single Act, as well as on discussions that Parliament intended to pursue with national parliaments.

A recurring theme in European parliamentary debates was that European Union had popular support in most Member States, thwarted partly by the inertia of national administrations. It therefore sought to appeal over the heads of national governments to national parliaments and to public opinion.

As regards national parliaments the European Parliament obtained explicit support in a number of cases, even before the entry into force of the Single Act. The Belgian Senate and the Belgian Chamber of Representatives adopted identical resolutions on 10 July 1986 and 24 July 1986 respectively, stating that the scope of the Single European Act was insufficient to meet the needs of further European integration and calling for the European Parliament to "prepare, in agreement with the other Community institutions, a draft Treaty for the Union to be submitted to the national Parliaments for ratification."

The Italian Senate on 1 October 1986 approved a resolution in which it affirmed that the "Single European Act is quite incapable of producing the European Union to which the Heads of State and of Government of the Member States have repeatedly and solemnly pledged themselves" and called on the Government "to support the European Parliament in its efforts to accelerate the process of European unification and ensure that an explicit mandate is given to the European Parliament to be elected in 1989, also authorizing it to hold an opinion poll among the citizens of the Member States, if necessary"; The Italian Chamber of Deputies approved a resolution in similar tone on 17 December 1986.

In the Irish parliament, the report of the Joint Committee (of the two Houses) on the Single Act stated that the "principles of democracy are not served if the European Parliament's role is restricted to a consultative one".

The Dutch parliament in November 1986 reconfirmed "its support for the draft treaty adopted by the European Parliament on 14 February 1984" and considered "that the Single European Act fails to meet the real requirements". It considered it "essential and urgent to encourage appropriate measures to reactivate the fight for European Union" and considered "that there must be adequate support for the strategy recommended by the European Parliament's Committee on Institutional Affairs to ensure that the Assembly elected in 1989 is entrusted with the task of preparing the draft of an act of union for subsequent ratification by the national parliaments".

The Belgian parliament took the initiative of organizing an interparliamentary conference on European union in May 1987 in which the parliaments of all the Member States except Ireland[7] participated along with MEPs. The conference did not formally adopt any declaration or resolution, but the general thrust of its discussions was that the SEA was insufficient and that further reform was necessary in the coming years, and the majority of participants subscribed to a text supporting "the idea of holding public consultation on the feasibility of strengthening European democracy by reinforcing the European Parliament's legislative powers".

This last point was taken up by the European Parliament in a paragraph of the Herman report in which it called for the principle of Parliament drafting a constitution for European Union to be submitted to the electorate in a referendum, either at European level "or failing that in the Member States where possible". One Member State was to react to this

---

[7] Ireland was holding its referendum on the ratification of the Single European Act at that time.

invitation, namely Italy, which held a referendum in conjunction with the 1989 European elections. A majority of 89.1 per cent committed its government to seeking constitutional reform at European level, to be based on proposals of the European Parliament.

Parliament initially considered that 1992 was likely to be the crucial year in forcing a further step forward, as this was the year in which the Single Act envisaged the possible revision of foreign policy cooperation, the year in which the budgetary perspectives agreed in 1988 would run out, and last but not least, the year in which the single market was due for completion and its consequences would be apparent. The convening of an IGC on EMU by the European Council in 1989 meant that events were moving somewhat faster than Parliament had envisaged, albeit only in the field of EMU.

When the new Parliament convened after the 1989 elections, it was, of course, pleased that the Member States had agreed to convene this IGC, but it was concerned to ensure that the scope of the negotiations and the Treaty revision should not be limited to EMU alone. It immediately called for the mandate of the IGC to be extended to include institutional reform (Resolution of 27 July 1989), a position which it elaborated further in a Resolution on the IGC adopted on 23 November 1989, spelling out an agenda for institutional change which it asked the IGC to address. This included an enlargement of Parliament's powers, insertion of fundamental rights into the Treaty, strengthening social policy provisions, strengthening regional cohesion and more majority voting in Council.

Parliament undertook in this Resolution to prepare its own proposals and laid down the first markers for a strategy for building support for them, envisaging (1) "an *interinstitutional conference* at the beginning of 1990" in which "an equal number of representatives of the Commission, the Council and the European Parliament will take part and which will draw up specific proposals for the necessary reform of the Treaty", and (2) inviting the Parliaments of the Member States to participate in "European *Assizes*" — an Assembly of the Parliaments of Europe — to "discuss the next stages in the implementation of European Union". We shall examine the impact of these events — both of which eventually took place — in the next chapter.

Parliament began this work at a time when there was no agreement on a wider agenda or a second IGC, and even the Commission was reticent, fearing that it might overload the EMU process. Parliament's pressure for a wider agenda for the IGC eventually began to elicit a response during the last few months of 1989 and the first few of 1990, when first the Commission (in the form of Delors, speaking in a Parliament debate in December 1989, accepting the idea of a second IGC on European Union "at the same time or a couple of years later" as that on EMU), then the Belgian government (Memorandum of 20 March 1990), the Italian Parliament (resolution of 21 March 1990), the French and German governments (Joint Letter in April 1990) and the Dutch and Greek governments all began to advocate a wider agenda for the IGC or a second IGC; the latter was eventually agreed in principle by the Member States at the European Council meeting in Dublin on 26 June 1990. The Belgian government, indeed, prepared its proposals (in the form of a Memorandum to the other governments) in consultation with key MEPs. We shall return to these various initiatives in the next chapter.

5.   The perspective of enlargement

An additional pressure for reform which was not particularly pressing when the IGC on EMU was first agreed, but which became more important as the process evolved, was the perspective of a substantial enlargement in the number of the Member States of the Community. Before the IGCs had been convened, Turkey, Malta and Cyprus had applied to join. The Commission's opinion on Turkey's application had been negative, but those of Malta and Cyprus had not yet been examined and were still on the table. In 1989, Austria applied to join and this application immediately raised two sets of problems. First, it was the first time that a constitutionally neutral state had applied, drawing attention in its application to its neutral status. This automatically raised the whole question of widening versus deepening and whether, if the Community were to let in neutrals, it would be shutting the door towards further development of a common foreign and security policy. Secondly, the Austrian application seemed motivated largely by economic reasons and this despite the negotiations to establish a European Economic Area (EEA) which would have allowed the European Free Trade Area (EFTA) countries to participate in the Community's internal market without needing to apply for full membership. Austria's application showed that this half-way house was not satisfactory for at least one of the EFTA countries, and that it might not prove satisfactory for others too. Indeed, the growing economic interdependence of the EFTA countries and the EC, which the EEA could only accentuate in the long run, left the EFTA states in a situation in which they would have to adjust to more and more Community decisions, without being full participants in that decision-taking. There was bound to be pressure within their countries for accession.

As the IGCs began, it became clear that this was indeed a trend. Sweden moved towards applying and submitted its formal application on 1 July 1991. Debate in Finland began to move in the same direction. Norway began cautiously to reopen the painful debate which had split the country in 1972. Even in Switzerland, the Congress of the Swiss Socialist Party called for Swiss accession to the Community. All these countries except Norway practised one or another form of neutrality, and all eventually applied to join.

The events of central and eastern Europe alluded to above lent extra weight to this process. Poland, Hungary and Czechoslovakia all announced that they aspired to Community membership by the turn of the century. Later, during the IGCs, similar noises emerged from the Baltic states, from Slovenia and Croatia and from other south east European states.

The prospects of a greatly enlarged Community acted as a spur to the revision process. It was clear that the institutional framework of the Community as it stood was incapable of functioning effectively in a Community of 18, 24 or 36 Member States. The Commission in particular took the view that a process of deepening was necessary in order to enable widening. The Commission, Parliament and several Member States were of the view that the Community should clearly state its federal vocation, including its ambitions for a common foreign and security policy, before it let in Member States who might otherwise be tempted to oppose such a development.

6.   Other factors

There can be no doubt that there were also a host of other motivations which led to the Member States embarking on a revision of the Treaties. The multiple consequences of the Single Market, referred to in Section 2 above, created a host of particular desires by individual Member States for the strengthening or modification of Community provisions in particular fields beside those of economic and monetary reform. It also generated widespread debate about the nature of European integration and the democratic structure of a Community that would, in the widely reported view of President Delors, be responsible for adopting up to 80 per cent of the economic and social legislation applicable in the Member States by the mid 1990s. The robust reaction to this prospect by Mrs. Thatcher in a speech made in Bruges in 1988 stimulated further debate on this, but in most Member States the reaction was not to seek ways of halting the ongoing development of the Community but to seek ways of making that development more democratic.

The personal commitment of some key actors should not be underestimated. The role of President Mitterrand was crucial. Had, say, Jacques Chirac been President of the French Republic, he would have been subjected to many of the same pressures (and the evolution of the Gaullist Party's position on Europe bears testimony to this) but it is unlikely that he would have been willing to go so far or to have taken as many initiatives as President Mitterrand did. Mitterrand's involvement in European affairs stretched back to the 1948 Congress of the European Movement in The Hague, and it was his positive reaction to the European Parliament's Draft Treaty on European Union of 1984 which paved the way to the negotiations that established the Single European Act. Chancellor Kohl, too, was a strongly committed European, as were most Belgian, Dutch, Italian and Spanish leaders: but in France the differences between various leaders and parties was more pronounced and the importance of who held office perhaps greater.

In one key Member State, the Prime Minister changed immediately before the opening of the IGCs. Indeed, Thatcher was ousted partly because of the European issue. Assessments differ as to how this would have affected the outcome: her acceptance of the convening of the IGCs is taken by some to show that she would have negotiated a compromise which might not have been very different from the actual outcome. Her successor, John Major, changed the tone but not the substance of the UK's negotiating position. For all the protestations of the Thatcherites at the result of the IGC, it is possible that Thatcher would have accepted, under external and internal pressure, much the same compromise if she could have obtained the same opt-out clauses.

In terms of personalities, mention must be made of Jacques Delors. No President of the Commission since Walter Hallstein has played such a prominent role on the European scene, nor held office for such a long period. His ability both to set the agenda by raising issues and to broker compromises was outstanding.

Finally, it is striking that no fewer than eight of the heads of government (plus Delors) had all been members of the European Council during the previous IGC in 1985. They all knew exactly what sort of process they were embarking on and had a good knowledge of all the issues. Only John Major (UK), Constantine Mitsotakis (Greece), Anibal Cavaco de Silva (Portugal) and Charles Haughey (Ireland) lacked this experience.

II

SETTING THE AGENDA

Agreeing to call IGCs to revise the Treaties was one thing. Agreeing on exactly what items they should discuss and what areas of the Treaty needed revision was another. This chapter will examine the period in the run-up to the IGCs in which proposals, suggestions and ideas were floated and subjected to preliminary examination. The two IGCs were somewhat different in this respect.

1. Towards the EMU IGC

The IGC on EMU already had the blueprint drawn up by the Delors Committee of Central Bankers which, as we have seen, specified all the issues needing negotiation in the IGCs. For 11 states it was quite clear that EMU meant the establishment of irrevocably fixed exchange rates (with the probable option of a single currency), a common monetary policy, free circulation of capital and the establishment of a central banking system. Negotiations would therefore be about the timetable for achieving these targets, conditions that needed to be fulfilled for transition to the final stage of monetary union, the provisions for external relations of the monetary union, and filling out the economic side of EMU. The UK did seek to redefine what EMU meant, first by floating a proposal for competing currencies (i.e. that all national currencies should be legal tender throughout the EC, competing for usage) and then by putting forward its "hard ECU" proposals (i.e. that the ECU should be "hardened" by making it impossible to devalue against the strongest national currency, and that it should become a 13th currency in parallel to national currencies). These were looked at politely by the other Member States, but the UK was unsuccessful in persuading the others that monetary union meant anything less than the ultimate establishment of a single currency.

Before the IGC started, preparations began in the monetary committee, the Committee of Central Bank Governors and in a high-level working group chaired by Elizabeth Guigou, then a member of the Secretariat of the Elysée, and later to become French European Affairs Minister. The work revealed some differences of emphasis among the 11 Member States supporting monetary union.

These initial differences included a split over the role of the ECU, with most member states foreseeing a central role while Germany argued that once currencies were in the process of being irrevocably fixed, the ECU (whose present success the Germans saw as resting upon a lack of confidence in existing national currencies) would begin to lose its appeal.

Germany was initially isolated (although it did receive support from the Luxembourg government) in its insistence upon very strict convergence criteria being met before any transition to EMU could proceed. Germany, and the Bundesbank in particular, were not prepared to accept any form of EMU that might endanger the highly valued monetary stability of the Deutsche Mark.

The work of the Committee of Governors deserves a special mention since they produced (as they had been instructed to do at the Madrid summit meeting) the draft statute for the proposed European Central Bank. This was eventually to be attached, only slightly amended, as a protocol to the eventual Maastricht Treaty revisions. This statute was a detailed and comprehensive body of work which explicitly concerned itself with the realization of the European monetary body which lay at the heart of the Delors Report's envisaged EMU. The Committee's main proposals were that for the final stage of EMU, a European System of Central Banks (ESCB) would be necessary — this would consist of a European Central Bank (ECB), endowed with its own legal personality, and the Central Banks of participating Member States. Reflecting German pressures, the absolute primacy of monetary stability and the independence of the ESCB were enshrined as sacrosanct principles in the Committee's final report. This work was produced in spite of the stated position of the UK government that it did not accept the case for a single currency and monetary policy. The Governor of the Bank of England nevertheless participated fully in all of the Committee's discussions.

The final contributor to this pre-IGC phase of preparation was the European Parliament through its reports and through the Inter-Institutional Conference. Parliament was a long-standing advocate of EMU which had featured in its 1984 draft Union treaty and in several reports before and since then. In view of the IGC, it defined specific proposals in the shape of reports drawn up by its Committee on Economic and Monetary Affairs, which followed the same three- phase approach as the Martin Reports (see below) on political union (principles, details, legal form). The rapporteur was Fernand Herman, Christian People's Party (EPP), (Belgium).

The European Parliament defined monetary union as "the circulation of a single currency, the conduct of a single external and internal monetary policy and the establishment of a European System of Central Banks including an autonomous European Central Bank". The Bank's autonomy would be guaranteed by a requirement that it "may not request or receive instructions", but it would have to "support the economic and social policy guidelines" of the Community. Its Governing Council would consist of the national Central Bank governors and the Board of Directors, the latter being the Governor, Deputy Governor and between three and five others appointed by Council on a proposal from the Commission with Parliament's assent for a five-year term. EMU would be phased in by New Year 1996, but "certain Member States may be granted at their request and in light of their specific situation, longer time-limits". As with the Martin Reports, Parliament's position was approved by a large majority achieved by negotiations among the main political groups and supported even by MEPs from countries displaying reticence towards the EMU proposal.

By the time of the Rome I meeting of the European Council in October 1990, all Member States except the UK were able to agree that the IGC should aim for an *independent* Central Bank (this guarantee of independence was important in terms of securing Germany's commitment to EMU) and that the three-phase timetable contained in the Delors Report should be followed, with the second phase beginning in January 1994 and the third phase some three years later.

This growing consensus among the 11 on fundamental principles of EMU made the UK's isolation more and more apparent. On 5 October, Thatcher, under pressure from her cabinet, agreed to allow sterling to join the ERM, but the UK remained alone in arguing that EMU was not necessary to achieve the full benefits of the single market. Any hopes that the gesture of joining the ERM might gain more sympathetic treatment of the UK's position and its "hard-ECU" plan, at least on the part of the Germans, were dashed by the Rome I Summit. The UK's gesture was, in fact, considered long-overdue and the unilateral announcement of the (over-valued) rate at which the pound would join further ruffled feathers. When the Rome I Summit (confirming the views of the Christian Democrat pre-summit a few days before) essentially decided to proceed without the UK, Thatcher was furious.

Her criticisms of the other Member States, her accusations against the other leaders for having "ambushed" her, her assertions that EMU proposals were in "cloud cuckoo land" and the isolation — yet again — of the UK, provoked the resignation of Sir Geoffrey Howe as Deputy Prime Minister and the challenge to her leadership of the Conservative Party which led speedily to her own resignation on 22 November after failing to obtain the necessary majority for re-election. The most prominent opponent of EMU was sidelined, and although the attitude of her successor John Major was not yet clear, it was apparent that the other Member States were determined to press ahead on the basis agreed in Rome.

The EMU IGC was therefore well prepared when it started, and participants had a clear idea of exactly what they would be negotiating. Furthermore, there was only a limited number of precisely defined issues.

2.   Political union: the skeleton

The situation for the political union IGC was almost the opposite: the agenda was open-ended, comprising potentially any subject not covered by the EMU IGC. Although some "headlines" were known — such as foreign and security policy, institutional reform, and economic and social cohesion — the details still needed to be filled in and it was clear too that any subject could be put on the agenda, if it was pushed for sufficiently strongly. Although this was no guarantee as to the final outcome of the IGCs, considerable effort was made by the Member States, the Commission and the European Parliament in this period to ensure that particular items were firmly on the agenda.

First among those with an interest in influencing the agenda of the IGC on political union was the European Parliament. As we saw in Chapter I the Parliament had been the first to press for a conference on political union in the first place and had defined as early as November 1989 — well before such a conference had even been proposed by any government — both a list of subjects which it wished to see pursued and a strategy for building up support for them.

During 1990, Parliament gradually substantiated its positions. It appointed Labour MEP David Martin, a Vice-President of the European Parliament, as rapporteur and, on his suggestion, agreed to three phases of work. The first phase (Martin I report), prepared by the committee from December 1989 to February 1990, which led to a parliamentary resolution adopted on 14 March 1990, laid down general principles and guidelines of Parliament's approach, listing the subjects which Parliament asked the IGC to address (at a time when Member States had still only agreed on an IGC on EMU alone). The second phase (Martin II report), which led to a parliamentary resolution adopted on 11 July 1990, spelt out Parliament's proposals in detail (by which time the Member States had just agreed to the principle of calling a second IGC on political union). The third phase consisted of "translating" this resolution into the legal language of draft Treaty amendments (Martin III) which were duly adopted by Parliament on 22 November 1990, just before the opening of the IGCs[8], and consisting of the only draft treaty articles to be tabled before the opening of the political union IGC.

---

[8] This three-step approach was similar to that used in 1982-84 for the adoption of the draft Treaty establishing European Union (Spinelli Report).

In devoting the whole of 1990 to the gradual formulation of specific proposals, and at the same time beginning a dialogue with the other institutions, with national parliaments and, at the level of its political groups, with national political parties, the European Parliament was able to help formulate much of the preliminary thinking that went into the preparation of the IGCs. Parliament's suggestions for a pre-conference with Council and Commission and for the European "Assizes" with national parliaments met with positive responses. The pre-conference met four times in the course of 1990 with the participation of all the Member States and the Commission. The parliamentary assizes took place in Rome in November 1990 just a week after the adoption of the Martin III Report. As we shall see below, both were useful vehicles for Parliament to canvass support for its views and indeed a final declaration adopted by the assizes by 150 votes to 13, endorsed almost all the main proposals that Parliament had put forward in the Martin report. For the rest, the European Parliaments's influence was more indirect, though none the less significant. As the meeting place of all of Europe's major political parties, and the forum in which discussions on the future of the Community took place at party-political level (rather than at the level of Ministers and officials), the European Parliament's deliberations played an important role in shaping the climate of opinion of the political classes in the Member States, albeit in some more than others. In terms of shaping the agenda for the forthcoming negotiations, the European Parliament, through these various means, was strikingly successful.

What were the issues for whose inclusion in the Treaty revision the Parliament pressed, and what were its precise proposals? The first Martin Resolution of March 1990 established a shopping list of demands, aiming to transform the Community into a "European Union of Federal Type". Besides monetary union, Parliament advocated the full integration of EPC into the Community framework, more extensive treaty provisions in the social and environmental sectors, incorporation into the treaties of fundamental rights, the provision for systematic majority voting in Council, a strengthening of the Commission's executive powers, a reform of the budgetary resources system, and, last but not least, increasing the powers of the European Parliament (specifying co- decision with Council on Community legislation, assent for all major international agreements entered into by the Community and for constitutional decisions requiring national ratification, involvement in the appointment of the Commission and the right to initiate legislative proposals).

Parliament, whilst emphasizing that this was far from being its only pre- occupation, was naturally particularly concerned with its own powers. The rapporteur's report drew attention to the fact that legislation "that has been rejected by Members that the electorate has chosen to represent it at European level can nevertheless come into force" in the Community context. He therefore proposed building a co-decision procedure such that Parliament's explicit approval would be required for all Community legislation. This would not be done through the existing crude form of co-decision brought in by the Single Act in the Assent procedure, which does not allow each Institution to consider the others' amendments, but by adjusting the cooperation procedure.

In the parliamentary debate, Parliament's proposals received strong support from the President of the Commission Jacques Delors, who added only the point that security should become a full part of foreign policy considerations of the Community. The Commission thus swung around behind Parliament's proposal to deal with these issues in the current round of Treaty revision, whereas previously it had been reluctant to do so, preferring to concentrate on EMU before moving on to other things.

The Italian Parliament immediately backed the European Parliament, adopting a resolution on 21 March 1990 which specifically endorsed the European Parliament's Resolution. At the same time it offered to co-host the "assizes" that the European Parliament had suggested. This Resolution bound the Italian Government to supporting the European Parliament's initiative.

The Belgian government was the first national government to give backing to this strategy. It published a memorandum in March 1990, which it had drawn up after following closely the preparation of the Martin Report in Committee and the debate on it[9], and had produced a remarkably similar set of conclusions. The Belgian government memorandum argued, like Parliament, for an extension of qualified majority voting in Council to all the policy areas, for Parliament to elect the President of the Commission and subject the whole of the Commission to the approval of the Parliament, to modify the cooperation procedure by giving Parliament a right to reject by a majority of its members legislation adopted by Council in its second reading and to extend the assent procedure to revisions of the Treaty, own resources and all major international agreements. It supported the entrenchment of human rights in the Treaty and supported Parliament's definition of subsidiarity. Concerning political cooperation, however, it proposed only to bring this closer to the Community domain, and not fully to integrate it. It was open on the issue as to whether there should be a second IGC or whether these issues should be dealt with together with EMU in a single IGC.

The European Parliament, the Commission, the Italian parliament and the Belgian government thus placed firmly on the agenda a whole series of further treaty reforms, notably constitutional changes, that they wished to be dealt with alongside EMU. Although UK Foreign Minister Douglas Hurd made a sarcastic remark to the effect that Belgium had been the first to dive into the swimming pool, even if there was no water in it, decisive support was forthcoming from Chancellor Kohl and President Mitterrand in their joint letter to the Heads of Government of the other Member States in April 1990, before the meeting of the European Council that month in Dublin. In this letter they called for a second IGC on political union "to be held parallel to the conference on economic and monetary union", intending it to enter into force at the same time on 1 January 1993 after ratification by national parliaments. They proposed that the IGC should deal with democratic legitimacy, the efficiency of the Community institutions, the unity and coherence of the Union's economic and monetary and political action, and the definition of a common foreign and security policy. This was an agenda, albeit in headline terms, which matched that of Parliament.

When the first Dublin meeting of the European Council of 28 April 1990 considered the issue, it agreed to study the need for treaty amendments in the terms outlined in the Kohl/Mitterrand letter. The Foreign Ministers were entrusted with this examination and were asked to report back in June to the second Dublin European Council which would decide on whether a second IGC parallel to that on EMU would be necessary.

Between the two meetings of the European Council two new governmental statements added to the numbers pressing for reform. First, the Spanish Prime Minister, Felipe González, wrote to his colleagues backing the idea that European citizenship should also be dealt with during an IGC on political union. Second, the Greek government published a memorandum on 15 May which backed most of the proposals contained in the Martin I Report.

The Foreign Ministers considered the issues at an informal meeting in Parknasilla on 19/20 May. They cautiously produced a report which consisted of a list of questions and issues to investigate. It fell short of putting forward specific items for treaty revision. It took up all the issues listed in the European Parliament's March Resolution, putting them in the form of questions: should the field of competence of the Community be enlarged? Should citizen's rights be entrenched? Should foreign policy come under the Community method? What should be the role of the Commission in foreign policy? It listed a number

---

[9] The Belgian Permanent Representative also met David Martin during this period.

of points to be examined concerning the powers of the European Parliament, including co-decision, strengthened powers of control, and participation in the designation of the President and Members of the Commission. It also stressed the need to examine the extension of majority voting in the Council and the powers of the Commission.

The meeting of the European Council in Dublin on 25/26 June 1990 was able to reach agreement on the basis of this report on convening an IGC on political union running parallel to that on EMU.

3. Putting flesh on the bones

(1) The European Parliament's proposals

By fortunate timing, the European Parliament was able to adopt its detailed proposals for treaty reform within one month of the European Council having examined the list of subjects proposed by the Foreign Ministers and having agreed to an additional IGC. Parliament's Committee on Institutional Affairs was already working on elaborating detailed proposals to fill in the "headlines" put forward by Parliament in March. The Committee's Report (Martin II) was submitted to plenary in July 1990 and Parliament adopted the Resolution setting out in detail proposals for treaty reform. Parliament was therefore ahead of the governments and the Commission in terms of spelling out detailed proposals. It was thus able to shape the agenda to a considerable degree, and its proposals are therefore worth examining in detail.

Parliament's resolution first provided definition of European Union. According to Parliament this would comprise:

- "economic and monetary union with a single currency and an autonomous central bank;
- "a common foreign policy, including joint consideration of the issues of peace, security and arms control;
- "a completed single market with common policies in all the areas in which the economic integration and mutual interdependence of the Member States require common action notably to ensure economic and social cohesion and a balanced environment;
- "elements of common citizenship and a common framework for protecting basic rights;
- "an institutional system which is sufficiently efficient to manage these responsibilities effectively and which is democratically structured, notably by giving the European Parliament a right of initiative, of co-decision with the Council on Community legislation, the right to ratify all constitutional decisions requiring the ratification of the Member States also and the right to elect the President of the Commission;"

The Resolution then spelled out the particular treaty changes, except as regards EMU which was dealt with in a separate resolution (Herman Report, see p. 13). A large number of changes were sought by Parliament, but they can be broadly grouped under three headings: (1) enlargement of Community *competences*, (2) making the Community's decision taking more *efficient* and (3) rendering it more *democratic*.

Enlargement of the field of *competences* of the Community was considered necessary in three main areas and a number of small ones. The main fields were economic and monetary union (as we have seen), common foreign and security policy (CFSP) and citizenship.

Concerning the CFSP, Parliament felt that the time had come to integrate EPC into the Community framework, although it acknowledged that specific decision- taking procedures, protecting Member States' interests, would continue to be necessary in this field. It envisaged a system of qualified majority voting, but with the possibility of granting derogations to individual Member States or, in exceptional circumstances, the right of individual states to opt out. The Commission, rather than just the presidency of Council, would take on a role in external representation for all areas of foreign policy not just for the economic areas as now.

Concerning citizenship, Parliament advocated the granting of voting rights in local and European elections in the Member State of residence and the entrenchment of basic human rights in the Treaty. Citizens of Member States would become at the same time citizens of the Union.

Parliament also advocated the strengthening of existing Community competences in the fields of the environment, social matters, economic and social cohesion, development policy, education, culture and transport. In all these areas it was felt that the existing Treaty provisions were inadequate or, in some cases, were totally absent and that the addition of new articles to the Treaty would serve a useful purpose.

At the same time, and in order to demonstrate that, despite this large increase in the field of Community competence, it was not advocating a centralized superstate, Parliament also advocated the entrenchment in the Treaties of the principle of subsidiarity. This principle was often quoted by federalists as the basis for allocating competencies between different tiers of government. It had been mentioned in Parliament's 1984 draft Treaty of European Union, since when its use in the English language had blossomed. However, as the interpretation of the principle is always a matter of judgement, it was perfectly possible for opponents of European integration to use this principle to advocate minimal or no competence to the Community. Indeed, Thatcher and the "Bruges Group" began to do precisely this. Parliament's Committee on Institutional Affairs, when preparing the Martin Report, therefore decided to draw up a special report on this matter and charged former French President Valéry Giscard D'Estaing to be its rapporteur. This was dealt with in parallel to Martin II Report (and, indeed, its translation into proper legal language in parallel with the subsequent Martin III Report). Giscard, who was leader of Parliament's Liberal Group at the time, had been pressing for a role in the institutional debate, and the other groups were willing to involve this former President of the European Council by giving him this report, albeit on just one aspect. There was broad agreement on the idea of spelling out the principle of subsidiarity in the Treaty, but in view of the highly divergent interpretations given to the term, the exact formulation became a matter of controversy. Some Members advocated a "positive" definition ("the Union shall carry out those tasks . . .") whilst others felt that a "negative" definition ("the Union shall carry out only those tasks . . .") was more reassuring to the Member States in what would in effect always be a political judgement. In the end, Parliament opted for the "negative" definition, but specified that the Community should act wherever more effective.

There was also controversy over the procedures invoking the principle of subsidiarity in front of the European Court. Giscard had proposed allowing a preliminary reference to the Court of any Commission proposal to check whether it conformed to the principle of subsidiarity, but this would have opened the door to filibustering and delaying tactics. A majority of Parliament felt that this was not necessary, the existing procedures for bringing matters post facto to the Court being sufficient (though they were willing to accept a suspensive effect on the entry into force of the final decision if the Court ruled by urgent procedure). Indeed, bringing a Commission proposal to Court would have been futile as these can be changed considerably during the legislative procedures. The Giscard Resolution was heavily amended along these lines before being adopted by Parliament. The Martin Report duly took up the principle.

The second main area of Parliamentary proposals related to the *efficiency* of the Community's institutions. This concerned primarily the issue of qualified majority voting (QMV) in the Council of Ministers. Parliament argued that the extension of QMV to new areas by the SEA in 1987 (which had broadly coincided with the demise of the practice of always seeking unanimity even where QMV could be applied) had led to an anomalous situation. Single Market liberalizations, most of which could be adopted by QMV, were proceeding far more rapidly than the laying down of minimum social and environmental standards to apply in that market, most of which required unanimity. It was not that Member States were frequently resorting to voting in Council, but the dynamics of negotiations within Council were completely different when there was the possibility of a vote being taken. Member States were more willing to compromise than face the prospect of being outvoted. Where unanimity was required, however, this was not the case and negotiations tended to drag on, reaching at best a compromise based on the lowest common denominator — hardly satisfactory when minimum environmental or social standards were at stake. Some matters were blocked entirely as a result of the opposition of a single national government. The Martin Report called this "the dictatorship of the minority".

Parliament advocated the use of QMV for all areas where the Treaties give the Community competence. Unanimity would be retained only for constitutional matters — that is Treaty revisions, accession of new Member States, enlargement of Community competencies or increasing budgetary resources. In addition, as we saw above, special provisions would apply in the field of foreign policy.

Extending QMV in Council was not the only way of increasing the efficiency of the Community system advocated by the European Parliament. It also called for a strengthening of the Commission's executive powers, criticizing a system whereby committees of national civil servants are able to review and even block the Commission's implementation of Community policies. The number and variety of such committees had given rise to the term "comitology" to describe their proliferation. Most such committees have the power to refer Commission decisions to the Council (by-passing the Parliament) where, in some cases, Council can then hold up the implementing measure indefinitely — even where this is a matter of applying policies that have already been agreed. In practice, matters are usually settled by an accommodation between Commission bureaucrats and national bureaucrats. This means that the whole process of implementing agreed Community policies is subject to delays and pressures from vested national interests at all stages, and emerges from meetings of officials with little clarity in overall accountability. Parliament argued for the Commission to be given less restricted implementing powers, subject, where major political problems occurred, to recall to the full legislative authority (i.e. Council and Parliament, at either's request).

Parliament also advocated strengthening the Court of Justice by giving it the right to impose penalties on Member States failing to comply with its judgments.

The third main area of parliamentary concern was *democracy*. As regards its own powers, the European Parliament put forward proposals for specific procedures that would meet its two main requests: co-decision with Council on legislation and involvement in the appointment of the Commission. Regarding co-decision, Parliament's proposal built on the cooperation procedure that had been introduced by the SEA. It proposed to modify this procedure and to extend its application to all areas where Council acted by QMV (i.e. all except constitutional matters where Council would act by unanimity with the assent of the European Parliament). The procedure would be modified to provide that legislation could only be approved with the explicit approval both of Council and of Parliament. To facilitate agreement, Parliament envisaged using the conciliation procedure (first introduced by a joint agreement of the three institutions in 1975 for legislation with budgetary consequences) in order to thrash out compromises where Council and Parliament did not initially agree. Parliament proposed that conciliation come in after its second reading if it fails to approve Council's position (if Council approved Parliament's initial position, no second readings would be necessary at all). It also envisaged changing the practice whereby the Commission has discretion as to whether or not to accept parliamentary amendments, by providing that any amendment approved by a majority of MEPs would *have* to be incorporated into the Commission's proposal at first reading. It also simplified the cooperation procedure by providing that where Parliament and Council agree at an early stage (i.e. through Council adopting the same position as Parliament in its first reading, or through Parliament in its second reading approving Council's position) for the procedure to be successfully concluded at that stage, thus obviating the need for further readings where both branches have already agreed.

This procedure differed from the co-decision procedure that Parliament had put forward in its 1984 draft treaty, but did so in a way intended to build on the intervening experience of the cooperation procedure. It could thus be presented as a further step in a process of evolutionary change. Indeed, Parliament presented it as a moderate proposal, pointing out that it would not give the European Parliament the right to impose anything on national governments that they did not want, as Council's approval would continue to be necessary, but that it would mean that the decisions taken by Ministers behind closed doors in Council meetings would only become law if they were also explicitly approved in a public vote in the assembly chosen by the electorate to act at Community level. This would be an additional democratic safeguard and would resemble the bi-cameral systems that function in many countries. Indeed, structurally it would be remarkably similar to the system applicable in Germany, where most legislation requires the approval both of the elected *Bundestag* and of the body composed of Ministers from State Governments, the *Bundesrat*, with a conciliation procedure to reconcile differences.

As regards the appointment of the Commission, Parliament went further than it had in its 1984 Draft Treaty where it simply provided for a vote of confidence by Parliament in the Commission as a whole. Parliament now took up President Mitterrand's proposal that the President of the Commission should be elected by the European Parliament and proposed a two-stage procedure in which Parliament would first elect the President of the Commission on a proposal of the European Council and, secondly (once the full team of Commissioners has been settled by agreement between the President designate and the national governments) would hold a debate and a vote of confidence in the Commission as a whole before it could take office.

The vote of confidence had become an established Community practice even without any basis in the Treaty, since Parliament began to organise such debates on its own initiative in the early 1980s. Indeed, the last two Commissions had waited until they had obtained the vote of confidence from the European Parliament before they took their oath of office at the Court of Justice. Entrenching this in the Treaty would, Parliament hoped, be a mere formality. Electing the President, however, was more ambitious, though here too Parliament could point to the precedent of the Assembly of the Council of Europe which elects the Secretary-General of that organization on a proposal of the Committee of Ministers, the Committee sometimes submitting one and sometimes more than one candidate.

The prominence of the position of Commission President had been restored by Jacques Delors and there was a strong argument for a greater democratic element in its appointment. It was also a job in which there was no "buggin's turn" among the Member

States, and was normally sorted out by agreement by Heads of Government in which national parliaments were not and could hardly be involved. Parliament felt that its case was good.

Besides these "big two" there were a number of other items on Parliament's shopping list. Parliament proposed to formalize in the treaties various rights that it had acquired in legislation or in practice. This included the right to set up committees of inquiry in order to investigate cases of maladministration or alleged contravention of Community law; the obligation of the Commission to respect Parliament's requests in the budgetary discharge procedure; recognition in the Treaties of the rights of members of the public to petition the European Parliament; and Parliament's right to bring cases to the European Court for annulment of Community acts. It also sought the right to initiate legislative proposals where the Commission fails to do so.

Parliament did not consider that adjusting its own powers was the only way to improve democratic accountability in the Community. It also proposed that Council should meet in public when adopting legislation, that national parliaments should have better access to information (a separate resolution, based on the report by Maurice Duverger but heavily amended, was adopted on relations between the European Parliament and national parliaments), that a consultative committee of Regions should be set up to allow regional authorities a direct input into the Community system, and that the EC should entrench fundamental rights in the treaty and accede to the Council of Europe's Convention on Human Rights.

Parliament's Resolution was adopted by an overwhelming majority reflecting the consensus achieved among the major political groups in the Parliament. On institutional matters, the European Parliament always sought to reach broad agreement in order to maximize its impact on the various governments of diverse political colours. It meant that broadly the same points would be made by MEPs within all the main political parties of the Member States and towards the national governments and parliaments.

This is not to say that the European Parliament was monolithic, even among the majority supporting the Martin proposals. There were, naturally enough, differences of emphasis on a left-right scale on, for instance, the degree of emphasis to be given to economic and social cohesion, social policy, environmental policy and so on. There were different views as to the best way of increasing the powers of the Parliament. There were differences over strategy, with some who believed that Parliament should threaten to use its various negative powers (e.g. its right to reject the budget, to delay legislation and to block association agreements or accession by new Member States) as a means of exerting pressure on the governments. There were different approaches to federalism. Finally, the co-existence within Parliament of rival political families naturally led to occasional friction and jealousies.

On this last point, the European People's Party (Christian Democrats) found themselves in a particularly awkward position. The Christian Democrats portray themselves, especially at election time, as *the* European federalists "par excellence". However, just as in 1984–87, when Spinelli had been the driving force behind Parliament's proposal for a new Treaty and Mitterrand had been the most prominent in ensuring that the governments then embarked on the reform process that led to the Single European Act, Christian Democrats seemed again to be concerned that the leading figures in this reform process were from other parties. Parliament's rapporteur, David Martin, was a socialist, as was its President, Enrique Baron, who had the important task of speaking for Parliament at ministerial and European Council meetings. Three successive presidencies of Council during the IGCs were socialist: Gianni De Michelis (Italy), Jacques Poos (Luxembourg) and Piet Dankert (Netherlands, — Minister for European Affairs; the Netherlands Foreign Secretary was largely embroiled on behalf of the Community in the Yugoslav crisis). Finally, the President of the Commission, Delors, was also Socialist.

The Christian Democrats therefore wished to highlight their own role and, if possible, to outflank all others in the "European" stakes. They saw their chance with the issue of a European "Constitution". The Committee on Institutional Affairs had agreed that it would be appropriate for Parliament to draft a "constitution" on European Union in response to the referendum held on this subject in Italy at the time of the 1989 elections. Emilio Colombo, former Italian Prime Minister, had been appointed rapporteur. However, once the Member States agreed to call IGCs to revise the treaties, it was clearly inappropriate to start drafting constitutions. Unlike 1984, when the drafting of a new Treaty had started off a process of reform, this time the Member States had already agreed to embark on a Treaty revision and Parliament was already preparing proposals in that context. To put forward specific proposals to amend the existing constitution (i.e. the Treaties) and at the same time a separate global proposal for a new constitution — even if contradictions could be avoided — would be a confusing and time-consuming exercise. Parliament therefore decided to leave the drafting of a proposal for a global constitution until after the IGCs, when such a process could be used either to relaunch the reform process if the IGCs were unsuccessful or to consolidate the results if they were successful.

However, in order to raise their profile, Colombo and the Christian Democrats insisted on producing "interim reports" on the draft constitution. Furthermore, Colombo timed the submission of his drafts to coincide with consideration of the Martin reports. It was difficult for the other groups to prevent this without causing a dangerous row with the Christian Democrats, who were very insistent. But, in allowing this to happen, Parliament created unnecessary confusion by adopting, at the same time as Martin II and Martin III reports, completely different resolutions on what might be included in a future constitution. In some circles, and in particular, some countries such as Italy, these proposals inevitably achieved as much if not more publicity as what was supposed to be Parliament's own submissions to the IGCs.

Apart from this tension between rival political groups, Parliament was largely successful in maintaining a broad consensus among its main groups and therefore in submitting the same arguments on the same key points within most national political parties and towards most governments. Being the first to put such detailed and specific proposals on the table, the European Parliament was in this way again at the forefront of agenda-setting for the IGC.

(2) The inter-institutional preparatory conference

Parliament was able to bring its proposals direct to the national governments in the inter-institutional preparatory conferences that met four times before the start of the IGCs. On two occasions Parliament's delegation met the General Affairs Council (Foreign Ministers) to discuss political union and on two occasions it met the Finance Ministers to discuss EMU. The first of these meetings took place just after the April meeting of the European Council in Dublin had envisaged the possibility of calling a conference on political union, before the Foreign Ministers had finalized their report to the subsequent European Council meeting in June. Indeed, the Foreign Ministers had their key meeting in this process at a special "gymnich-type" meeting in Parknasilla on the following two days. This first interinstitutional meeting consisted largely of exhortations by MEPs to the Foreign Ministers to ensure that the scope of an eventual IGC on political union be as broad as possible.

Parliament's delegation was a high-level one. Besides Parliament's President, it included the chairmen of the five largest political groups (Jean-Pierre Cot, Egon Klepsch, Giscard

D'Estaing, Sir Christopher Prout, Adelaide Aglietta), the Chairman of the Institutional Affairs Committee (Marcelino Oreja), the rapporteurs on European Union generally and EMU in particular (Martin, Herman) and three prominent members of the Institutional or Social Affairs Committees (Klaus Hänsch, Colombo, Karl von Wogau, Buron). Thus, the delegation included one former Head of State, a former Prime Minister, two former Foreign Ministers and a former Finance Minister. This remained the basis of Parliament's delegation for all subsequent meetings, though the individuals were replaced by others from the same political group for particular meetings where individual expertise was required (e.g. when discussing social affairs or EMU).

The meetings were an opportunity for MEPs to confront all the Ministers participating in the IGCs directly. Each conference lasted half a day and were usually accompanied by opportunities for informal dialogue. The conferences at least ensured that Ministers were not only aware of Parliament's demands in general terms but also had to listen to detailed argument and explanation by MEPs, and, to a certain extent, to respond to them. For instance, the German government representative announced at the first meeting that it supported the co-decision formula contained in the Martin Report, and the Dutch government announced that it would not accept increased responsibilities for the European Community without an increase in its democratic legitimacy.

Following the first meeting on 17 May at which MEPs were still arguing in favour of a second IGC with a broad remit, three other ones took place after the principle of two IGCs had been agreed at the second Dublin Summit. These took place on 8 October 1990 in Luxembourg (on EMU), on 23 October 1990 in Strasbourg (on political union) and on 5 December 1990 in Brussels (on Parliament's involvement in the IGCs and on co-decision).

At this last meeting, the pre-conference reached an understanding on Parliament's involvement in the forthcoming IGCs. Parliament had been pressing to be allowed to participate in the IGCs, arguing that although the procedure foreseen in Article 236 did not envisage this, neither did it envisage participation by the Commission, which, however, was present. There was therefore no formal reason why another European institution, namely the Parliament, could not be present as well. Parliament also pointed out that in the previous IGC in 1975, its President, accompanied by Altiero Spinelli, had participated in two of the five Ministerial-level meetings, and that IGC had agreed to "submit its results" to Parliament. To press Parliament's case, its committee on institutional affairs went so far as to suggest that Parliament should vote against convening the PU IGC.

This argument was not fully accepted by the national delegations. There was some reluctance by Ministers to accept a participant which might make agreement among governments more difficult and create, from their standpoint, an undesirable precedent. Instead, an understanding was reached that the President of Parliament would be invited to address IGC Ministerial-level meetings at their openings, that there would be a "trialogue" consisting of the Presidents of the three institutions and that the inter-institutional pre- conference would be transformed into an "inter-institutional parallel conference" meeting during the course of the IGCs. Indeed, they were to meet virtually monthly, alternating between political union and monetary union. Finally, it was understood that sufficient time would be available between the conclusion of the IGCs and the beginning of national ratification to allow the European Parliament to pronounce on their results, which would be particularly important in view of the linkage that some national parliaments had made between their positions and that of the European Parliament.

(3) The Parliamentary Assizes of November 1990

Never before has a major international negotiation been preceded by a conference of the very parliaments that would later have to ratify the outcome of the negotiations. The fact that they did so and concluded with a Declaration approved by an overwhelming majority (150 to 13) in which their expectations of the IGC were clearly expressed, was highly significant.

It was President Mitterrand, in a speech to the European Parliament, on the 25 October 1989, who launched the term "Assizes". He asked "Why should the European Parliament not organize assizes on the future of the Community in which, alongside your Assembly, delegations from national parliaments, the Commission and the governments would participate?". The European Parliament later seized upon this idea and linked it to the IGCs, conceiving of the "Assizes" as a joint parliamentary preparation for the IGCs.

After the European Parliament had taken up the idea, it was discussed in the regular meetings held by the Presidents of all the national parliaments and of the European Parliament. The Italian *Camera dei Deputati* offered to host the meeting. Details of the preparations were also discussed in the meetings of the chairmen of the specialized organs in national parliaments that deal with European affairs who had begun to meet regularly in 1989, but most preparation was done via the offices of the respective presidents.

It was agreed that approximately two-thirds of the participants would be from national parliaments and one-third from the European Parliament (a compromise between those who thought there should be an equal number of European and national parliamentarians and those who thought that the European Parliament should have a delegation of similar size to those of the largest national parliaments). Each national parliament would have a number of delegates equal to one-third the number of MEPs it had in the European Parliament, rounded to the nearest whole number (but with a slight adjustment for the smallest three parliaments leading to the national parliaments having, in fact, more than two-thirds of the total number of delegates: 173 to 85). For various reasons of protocol, the question of who formally convened the conference was left ambiguous, with most parliaments considering that it was "self-convened" by all the parliaments collectively. Although the meeting was formally entitled "Conference of the Parliaments of the European Community", the term "Assizes" soon gained usage in ordinary conversation despite its ambiguous meaning in the English language at least.

Most national parliaments (though not necessarily each chamber: in the UK for instance only the House of Lords) prepared written submissions to the Assizes, usually consisting of any resolutions adopted by that parliament on the matter or else of reports from the specialized committee. The European Parliament's contribution consisted of its proposed Treaty amendments.

Debates took place on the floor of the *Camera dei Deputati* over a four-day period. Besides the actual participants, speeches were made by the President of the Italian Republic, Francisco Cossiga, the President of the European Commission, Jacques Delors, and the President of the Council, Giulio Andreotti. Debates were presided over by a triumvirate consisting of the presidents of the two Italian Chambers (Nilde Iotti and Giovanni Spadolini) and the President of the European Parliament (Enrique Baron Crespo).

The final Declaration was prepared by a drafting committee consisting of the chairmen of the 18 specialized committees in national parliaments that deal with European affairs together with eight MEPs. Originally, it had been agreed (by the preparatory meeting of presidents) that five MEPs only would take part in the drafting committee, but this was changed at the opening plenary meeting of the Assizes in order to achieve roughly the same proportion of national and European MPs as in the Assizes as a whole. Under the rules agreed beforehand by the presidents, and approved by the plenary at the opening, the drafting committee would submit a text which could be approved by the plenary only by an absolute majority of participants. Amendments could also be tabled in plenary, but would similarly require an absolute majority of participants in order to be adopted.

The issue of seating arrangements in the Assizes was a matter of some controversy. The initial seating arrangement consisted of each national parliamentary delegation sitting together as a block, with the European Parliament delegation in the centre part of the hemicycle, divided into its political groups. At the opening of the first session of the Assizes, however, participants voted by a large majority to sit instead according to political affiliation, based on the political groupings of the European Parliament. It was argued that this was a more "European" arrangement and that differences of point of view were more on a political basis than a national basis.

The decision to sit and operate in transparty political groupings had not met with universal approval. The British Conservatives — not then part of any Europe wide grouping — had opposed it. Laurent Fabius, then President of the French *Assemblée Nationale* but also an MEP and member of Parliament's Committee on Institutional Affairs, had initially also opposed the idea, but following a dinner of Socialist delegation leaders organized by Jean-Pierre Cot, the evening before the Assizes, at which almost all leaders spoke in favour of sitting by political family, he not only accepted the idea but agreed to Cot's proposal that he, given his unique position as MEP and President of a national parliament, should formally move it in the plenary the following day.

This decision was to prove important for the whole dynamics of the Assizes. The political groupings met before or after the daily sittings of the Assizes in order to consider jointly their position on different questions, not least the final declaration and amendments thereto. The secretariats of the political groups in the European Parliament provided facilities for these meetings, and the core of MEPs within each grouping, having the best international contacts and, frequently, the best linguistic skills, were often among the key actors in such meetings.

Some of the political groups in the European Parliament organised pre-meetings with their counterparts in the national parliaments the day before the Assizes in Rome. This was the case for the Socialist, Christian Democrat, Liberal and Green groups. Indeed, the Socialists' meeting adopted a "declaration" of Socialist participants in the Assizes, equipping Socialist participants — both national and European — with a set of positions before entering the Assizes. This text was negotiated by consensus among the various Socialist party delegation leaders, with more cautious parties being encouraged to shift position. The acceptance by the Labour Party delegation of full economic and monetary union, for instance, was endorsed two days later by the party's national executive committee.

The drafting committee worked on the basis of an initial draft prepared by Charles Ferdinand Nothomb, President of the Belgian Chamber of Deputies (and former Foreign Minister and MEP). As Chairman of the Belgian Chamber, he was ex-officio chairman of its mixed committee on European Affairs, composed on a parity basis of Belgian MEPs and MPs, and was therefore the one person present both at meetings of Presidents of Parliaments and of the meeting of chairmen of the specialized committees (CEAC), both of which had been involved in the preparation of the Assizes. A keen European, his offer to chair the drafting committee and to submit a first draft was accepted by the others.

Nothomb submitted his first draft to the drafting committee only on the evening of the first full day of the Assizes (27 November). He had used the previous 24 hours to hold informal consultations with delegation leaders. The draft was then examined by the drafting committee which fixed a deadline of 10 o'clock for that same evening for its members to submit amendments. These amendments were then examined and voted on the next day by the drafting committee, a simple majority being enough to adopt them. Some 80 amendments were submitted, about half of which were adopted.

Within the drafting committee, there were naturally differences of opinion. The chairmen of the national parliamentary committees largely reflected the position of the majority in their parliaments and were therefore closest to the position of their respective governments, but sometimes the differences went beyond this. The UK House of Commons committee, for instance, was chaired by Nigel Spearing (Labour), a long-standing anti-marketeer. The French Senate's Committee was chaired by Jacques Genton, a Gaullist Euro-sceptic. The committee of the *Assemblée Nationale* was chaired by Charles Josselin who, whilst generally a mainstream French Socialist pro-European, was among sponsors of a proposal to establish a "Congress" of national parliamentarians at European level, an idea which in the end did not receive majority support at the Assizes.

The text of the drafting committee was submitted to the plenary, where it had been agreed that five or more members could table amendments. Some 222 amendments were submitted, largely as a result of discussions in meetings of the political groupings, but also by some national delegations (though some were later withdrawn).

The final sitting on Friday morning was given over almost entirely to the votes on the amendments and the text. By this time many members had left. Absences at this stage particularly affected German delegates (who were a few days away from a general election) and Italians (who were particularly prey to domestic political distractions). As a result, the requirement that, to be adopted, an amendment secure a majority of participants (i.e. 130 votes) meant in practice some three-quarters of those present. As a result, only 25 amendments were adopted. When it came to the final vote only 189 members were present and the text was adopted by 150 votes to 13. However, it can safely be said that were it not for the early departures, it would have been adopted by an even larger majority.

The Declaration endorsed the objective of re-modelling the Community into a European Union on a federal basis and backed a single currency governed by an autonomous central banking system, taking the view that this required stronger instruments of economic and social cohesion. It supported the incorporation of EPC into the Community structures and the inclusion of European citizenship and fundamental rights in the Treaties. It backed extension in Community competences in the social and cultural fields, and also endorsed the institutional requests of the European Parliament concerning co-decision on legislation, appointment and term of office of the Commission, right of initiative, scrutiny powers and assent procedure for Treaty modifications. It called for the European Parliament and the national parliaments to prepare a constitution, with the Commission becoming the executive and Parliament and Council exercising legislative and budgetary functions.

Thus, the Assizes also served to re-emphasize a number of key issues and to help build a body of support for them on the eve of the IGCs.

4. The Commission's Opinion

The Commission produced its "Opinion", required under the treaties in order to convene the IGC on political union, on 21 October 1990. It confirmed that the Commission had now swung firmly behind the holding of a second IGC, no longer fearing that this might undermine the EMU process, and showed that the Commission backed a substantial agenda for reform which matched largely that put forward by the European Parliament, though diverging subtly on some crucial points.

The Commission argued for a single Community with a common institutional structure, albeit with flexibility with regard to decision-taking procedures. This treaty would not see the final shape of European Union, but should leave the door open to developments in a federal direction. QMV should apply in foreign policy matters in areas determined unanimously by the European Council.

It favoured extending Community competence to largely the same fields as those proposed by the European Parliament as well as introducing the notion of Community citizenship (free movement, voting rights in local and European elections) and incorporating a reference to the European Convention on Human Rights. Extensions of competence would be balanced by incorporating the principle of subsidiarity which it would link notably to Article 235. Within the areas of Community competence, QMV would apply to all except constitutional issues and a restricted number of sensitive issues such as taxation, social security or treatment of nationals of third countries.

Institutionally, it favoured strengthening the Commission's executive powers in the way that Parliament had proposed (i.e. only advisory and management committees to constrain the Commission), but opposed undermining the exclusive right of initiative of the Commission. It supported giving the Court of Justice the right to impose sanctions.

As regards Parliament's powers, it did not support co-decision, but merely an extension of the cooperation procedure and its modification such that the Commission's second reading proposal, taking account of Parliament's amendments, would stand unless rejected by a simple majority in Council. It supported giving Parliament the right to confirm the appointment of both the President and the College of Commissioners.

5.   The preparatory work among governments

Faced with this flood of proposals and ideas coming from all directions, the governments (Foreign Ministers) discussed their approach to the political union IGC at an informal meeting of Foreign Ministers in Asolo on 6/7 October; the General Council in Luxembourg on 22 October and in Brussels on 5/6 November, and in the European Council meetings of Rome I and Rome II of 27/28 October and 14/15 December 1990 respectively, held similar discussions.

At the same time further memoranda or position papers emerged from national governments. The Danish government, already supporting EMU, approved a memorandum on 4 October which many felt was rather encouraging, showing how far one of the traditionally reticent countries was willing to go. Denmark's memorandum, approved by the market committee of the *Folketing*, called for the extension of qualified majority voting in environmental, social and research matters, an extension of Community competence in the fields of indirect taxation, consumer protection and development aid, health education, energy, telecommunications and cultural cooperation and exchanges. It supported giving the European Parliament the right to initiate legislation where the Commission fails to act and called for the extension of the cooperation procedure to all areas of internal policy decided by QMV. It proposed the creation of an ombudsman. It advocated greater powers of scrutiny for the Parliament over the Commission and backed the proposal to create a Committee of the Regions. It called for some Council meetings to be held in public. It called for strengthening foreign policy cooperation, but not its extension to military cooperation. In this area, unanimity should remain the norm, but it favoured merging the EPC secretariat and Council.

At the other end of the spectrum, the Dutch government published a paper on 26 October stating that the Netherlands was "quite prepared to be pragmatic provided that the ultimate aim of a federal Europe remains intact". It stated that "democratic legitimacy" was the key issue for the Netherlands: "new steps were impossible without simultaneously extending the powers of the European Parliament". In this context it was in favour of extending and strengthening the cooperation procedure in the way proposed by the Commission in its opinion, but reinforced by combining it with the conciliation procedure. It supported an extension of the assent procedure to Articles 113, 138, 201 and 236 and giving the European Parliament a "right to request" form of initiative. It supported giving the Parliament the right to appoint and censure *individual* Commissioners. On the policy front, it had reservations regarding the intergovernmental approach favoured by some other states concerning CFSP and JHA, as well as on strengthening the role of the European Council. It supported extending QMV and expanding the list of Community competences.

Some national parliaments again took position between the second Dublin and Rome European Councils. The Belgian Senate on 13 July gave explicit backing to the European Parliament resolution (Martin report), called for integration of EPC into the EC system and backed the creation of a Committee of the Regions. The UK House of Lords European committee adopted a report on 30 October, the conclusions of which pleaded in favour of constructive UK participation in the process, drawing attention to the benefits of a single currency (which outweighed the loss of national control), for a limited extension of QMV and of the cooperation procedure and for making EPC more efficient and effective. It preferred to avoid debate on federalism, arguing that "the constitution of the Community is unique and will remain unique". The Italian *Camera dei Deputati* (Committee III) adopted a position on 20 November such that Italian ratification of the new treaty would depend upon its approval by the European Parliament, a position accepted by the Italian government.

During this period, first ideas were exchanged among the governments at Permanent Representative level. Italy put forward a paper on 18 September proposing that the competences of the Western European Union (WEU) be transferred to the future European Union. The UK submitted proposals for technical improvements in EPC, for improving budgetary control, and for allowing the Court of Justice to fine Member States failing to respect its judgments. Germany took up the idea of an organ to represent the regions at Community level. Germany also put forward a formulation for inserting the principle of subsidiarity in the treaty. Spain followed up Felipe Gonzalez's letter on citizenship with a more detailed paper.

The deliberations of the Foreign Ministers culminated in the two Roman European Council meetings. It is a measure of how far the debate was carried forward by the various contributions made during this whole period that the conclusions of Rome II — less than seven weeks later — was already far more extensive than Rome I, which, in its turn, was already more forthcoming than Dublin.

In Rome I, the European Council "confirmed the will progressively to transform the Community into a European Union by developing its political dimension . . ." but references to extending European Community powers, developing the European Parliament's role in the legislative sphere, defining European citizenship, the objective of a common foreign and security policy and the need to go beyond the present limits with regard to security were all subject to UK reservations in what was to be Thatcher's last summit. The conclusions recorded that "on these points the United Kingdom delegation prefers not to preempt the debate in the intergovernmental conference". The conclusions made no specific reference to extending QMV, nor to involving the European Parliament in the appointment of the Commission.

The Rome II conclusions saw the European Council agree to a long list of issues that should be on the agenda for the IGC, asking the latter to give them "particular attention". This was the culmination of all the agenda-setting exercises of the European Parliament, the assizes, the inter-institutional conference, the Commission and national governments and parliaments. The European Council's list began with the heading "democratic legitimacy" where it asked the conference to consider extending and improving the cooperation procedure, extending the assent procedure, involving the Parliament in the appointment of the Commission and its President, increasing Parliament's powers of budgetary control and financial accountability and consolidating the right of petition to the Parliament and the latter's powers of inquiry as regards Community matters. It also asked the conference to consider developing a co-decision procedure for acts of a legislative nature. It noted the support for creating arrangements enabling regional and local authorities to be consulted.

Under the heading of a common and foreign security policy, it asked the IGC to examine an institutional framework based on one decision-making centre, namely the Council, a unified secretariat (EPC and Council), a reinforced role for the Commission, adequate procedure for consulting and informing the European Parliament and procedures ensuring that the Union speaks with one voice towards the outside. Decision-taking would be based on the rule of consensus for "defining general guidelines" (with abstention or non-participation to be encouraged to facilitate consensus) and QMV for "the implementation of agreed policies".

On security, the European Council emphasized that the prospective role for the Union in defence matters should be considered, including the idea of a commitment by Member States to provide mutual assistance (as in Article 5 of WEU Treaty). It committed the IGC to examine the future of WEU, without going as far as the Italian Presidency which had proposed the gradual absorption of WEU by the European Union by the 1998 expiry of the WEU Treaty.

Under the heading of European citizenship, the IGC was asked to consider voting rights in European and municipal elections, joint consular protection and freedom of movement, as well as the creation of an ombudsman.

Under the heading of extending and strengthening Community action, the European Council noted that there is "a wide recognition of the need to extend or redefine the Community's competence in specific areas" citing notably the social dimension, cohesion, environment, health, research, energy, infrastructures and cultural exchanges. The IGC was asked to examine the means of bringing intergovernmental matters in the field of justice and home affairs into the Union framework. It emphasized the importance of the principle of subsidiarity without specifying that this should be incorporated into the treaties.

Finally, under the heading of "effectiveness and efficiency", the European Council "emphasized that extending the responsibilities of the Union must be accompanied by a strengthening of the Commission's role and in particular its implementing powers" and asked the IGC to examine the extension of majority voting in Council, with a view to "making it the general rule with a limited number of exceptions".

Thus it can be seen that from a few sketchy headlines in the early months of the year, the agenda for the IGC had been thrashed out to cover a wide series of potentially important reforms. Almost all of the points initially listed by the European Parliament, and subsequently spelt out in its specific proposals, had found an echo and were supported either by particular governments, or were backed by the conference with national parliaments or by the Commission in its opinion, or else taken up directly by the Foreign Ministers via the interinstitutional conferences. Placing issues on the agenda of the IGC was, of course, no guarantee as to the final result. Nevertheless it was an essential first step. With such a wide agenda, the IGC on political union could no longer be seen as a mere appendage of that on EMU. Potentially it was even more important.

III

THE CONDUCT OF THE IGCs

1. Procedures and methods

The IGCs began simultaneously in December 1990, immediately after the second Rome European Council. From the beginning, it was agreed that they should conclude in time for the Summit due under the Dutch Presidency of the Council at the end of the following year, which was eventually held in Maastricht. In the end, some legal work was necessary after the Summit which meant that the IGC, technically, only finished early in 1992 under the Portuguese Presidency. Politically, however, Maastricht can be seen as the final point of the negotiations.

The IGCs thus took place under three successive presidencies: the Italian, whilst only for the first meetings, also included the final preparatory phase for the IGC and the two Rome Summits (De Michelis, Foreign Minister chairing the Political Union IGC and Guido Carli, Finance Minister chairing the European Monetary Union IGC); Luxembourgish (Poos, Foreign Minister chairing Political Union and Jean-Claude Juncker, Finance Minister chairing EMU) and Dutch (Hans Van den Broek, Foreign Minister chairing Political Union, but with Dankert, European Minister — and former EP President — in practice playing the major role while Van den Broek was involved in the Yugoslav crisis, and Kok, Finance Minister chairing the EMU IGC).

The general pattern throughout the IGCs was for monthly ministerial meetings except for the August break, which intensified in the run-up to the Maastricht Summit. In all there were some 10 formal and two "informal" ministerial sessions each on EMU and on political union before the final Maastricht Summit. In between times, the detailed work was carried out in weekly meetings of the "personal representatives" of the Ministers. For the most part these comprised the Permanent Representatives of the Member States in Brussels. The Ministers also met nine times (alternating monthly EMU and political union) with the delegation of 12 MEPs in the parallel inter-institutional conference.

As we have seen, the nature of the two IGCs was somewhat different. Whereas the EMU IGC dealt with a specific subject, most participants had a clear idea of what issues were to be negotiated and a blue-print existed in the form of the report of the Delors Committee of the Central Bank Governors, the same was not the case in the political union IGC. Here, there was no limitation as to the number of subjects that might be raised, there was no jointly prepared blueprint (although there were the comprehensive submissions of the Parliament, the Commission and the Belgian, Dutch and Greek governments) and the objectives of the Member States were divergent on a great number of points. The EMU IGC was therefore able to get to grips relatively quickly with the key issues, whereas the political union IGC first went through a three-month phase of collecting and studying a multitude of individual proposals for treaty amendments.

It was agreed at the outset that the results of both IGCs should be sent for ratification together, which implied a parallelism in their work. Coordination and cohesion of the two IGCs was the responsibility of the Foreign Ministers, and for this reason their Personal Representatives were allowed to attend EMU IGC meetings as well.

All matters in the PU IGC were prepared by the same group at the level of officials, unlike the 1985 IGC where one working party (again, mainly the permanent representatives) prepared modifications to the Community treaties and another (the political directors in each foreign ministry responsible for EPC) prepared the provisions on political cooperation. Not too much should be read into this exclusion of the political directors — it would have been impossible to sideline figures so close to Ministers' ears — but it did mean that the overall approach was likely to be more cohesive and, as regards foreign policy, less wedded to EPC practices. Indeed, since the first months of the IGC took place while ministers (and political directors) were preoccupied with the Gulf War, the "personal representatives" were left with considerable leeway at the early stages.

This early phase in the political union IGC was an opportunity for Member States to table formal treaty amendments reflecting their approaches to European Union or anticipating already possible compromises. Altogether, some 2,000 pages of draft treaty articles were submitted by the Member States and the Commission, additional to the submissions already made by Parliament.

Following this phase of presentation and discussion of the numerous treaty amendments submitted, the Luxembourg Presidency undertook to prepare a global "non-paper" which, taking what appeared to be a majority viewpoint on each of the issues discussed so far, constituted a global draft treaty as regards political union. This was submitted to the Foreign Ministers on 15 April and communicated at the same time to the European Parliament, with Foreign Minister Poos participating in a debate in Parliament on 17 April, using the opportunity for informal discussions with leaders of the Socialist Group, whilst his coalition partner Ministers did likewise with the EPP Group.

This non-paper was subject to intense discussions over the next few weeks both within the IGC and outside. The Commission and the European Parliament were particularly critical of the "pillar" structure introduced whereby new treaty provisions in the field of foreign affairs and internal police matters would not be added to the EC treaty but would be carried out in a separate legal framework. The European Community as such would only be one element of a wider European Union, the other elements being largely intergovernmental. These issues shall be examined in more detail in the next chapter. It was, however, the intimate conviction of the Luxembourg Ministers that their approach was the only one capable, at the end of the day, of reaching the necessary unanimity. The Commission, the Parliament and some governments including those of their Benelux partners, were strongly critical of this approach, arguing that it was too early in the IGC to offer compromises to the reticent Member States and that it was better first to put pressure on for a more satisfactory solution.

Following the special meeting of Foreign Ministers in Dresden which examined the main criticisms that had been made to the non-paper, the Luxembourg government produced a new "draft treaty" in June in good time for the June meeting of the European Council. This paper was only slightly different from the non-paper, taking some account of the criticisms, as we shall see in the next chapter. The June European Council, as planned, did not enter into detailed discussions on the IGCs, merely taking note of developments so far, conducting an informal exchange of views and concluding that the Luxembourg document was a good base for negotiations.

The appearance of the non-paper, the controversy surrounding it and the European Council meeting, however, all served to bring the IGCs into the public domain. Indeed, it was when the media highlighted certain aspects of the drafts such as references to the "federal character" of the Union, that some ministers of national governments began to adopt more outspoken and less flexible positions.

The Dutch Presidency, no doubt due partly to the Yugoslav crisis, only gradually got to grips with the IGCs. It too produced a global non-paper or draft treaty, but only in September — over two months into its Presidency. Despite the crisis and the summer holiday, this was universally considered to have been a mistake, leaving too little time before Maastricht to begin again on a new basis. The Dutch paper, indeed, made substantial changes from the Luxembourg text which the European Council had considered to be a good basis for further negotiations. In particular, it had brought foreign policy and internal affairs into the Community framework, producing a unitary structure for European Union albeit with modulated decision-making procedures. It also took a different approach to increasing the legislative powers of the European Parliament, proposing a smaller increase across the board instead of a large increase in a limited area.

A draft version of the Dutch document had been circulated informally at the very beginning of September and had even been discussed by Dankert with the spokesmen on European affairs of the Socialist parties in all the national parliaments who were attending a Socialist Group conference in Brussels. Despite support from these quarters, it met outright hostility from the UK government and a number of others. Although the final version published later in September was a watered down version, it nevertheless did not get very far. At a meeting of Foreign Ministers on 30 September which became known in the Netherlands as the "black Monday" of Dutch diplomacy, the text was rejected as a basis for further negotiations. Only Belgium lent it further support. The other pro-federalist countries felt that it was technically very difficult to switch texts at this stage. Although the Dutch text reflected the majority opinion on most issues it would clearly never be the subject of consensus and now was the wrong time to accentuate the divisions between the majority and the reluctant minority. Even those who thought that the Luxembourg text should have been more advanced felt that it was too late at this stage of the IGC to try to regain lost ground.

The IGC thus proceeded with the Dutch Presidency submitting, on an issue-by- issue basis, modifications of the Luxembourg text. These were examined in the regular meetings of the permanent representatives, culminating in new global text examined in a "conclave" of the Foreign Minsters in Noordwijk on 12/13 November. This was intended to iron out the main remaining divergences before the Maastricht Summit. In fact, it only managed to tackle a proportion of them despite reconvening in Brussels two weeks later. By then, however, the number of issues remaining for settlement at the Summit itself had been narrowed down to fewer, albeit crucial, matters.

Similarly, in the IGC on EMU, steady progress had led, as we shall see, to agreement on most of the main issues, with only a handful needing settlement at the Summit. Among them were those where the outlines of a settlement were clear, but where there was a reluctance to finalize them before a global agreement was reached at the Summit.

The Dutch Presidency, like the Luxembourg Presidency, reported on developments to the European Parliament not only through the Inter-institutional conference but directly to plenary. Indeed, the European Parliament held a debate almost monthly on one aspect or another of the IGCs. Minister Dankert also appeared before Parliament's Committee on Institutional Affairs, and the respective Socialist and Christian Democrat Ministers were in contact with their corresponding groups in the European Parliament. As a result, there was no danger of the issues of major concern to the Parliament, including the issue of its own powers, being forgotten or sidelined in the last few weeks.

The Maastricht Summit or European Council Meeting was held on 9/10 December. Most participants arrived in Maastricht on 8 December, to be confronted by large international rallies and demonstrations in favour of European Union. Indeed, the rally organized by the Union of European Federalists included several thousand participants from central and eastern Europe as well as from the Community. Sir Norman Fowler, MP, chairman of the Conservative Party's European committee, who had accompanied the British delegation to

Maastricht, was howled down in the pedestrianized streets of Maastricht when recognized by the public.

The atmosphere was therefore electric in this small town that had been entirely taken over by the Summit. Last-minute lobbyings and briefings went on late into the night, each night. Agreement was far from certain when the Summit opened with the traditional address from the President of the European Parliament, and even when it embarked on its final session of the evening of the second day. Only in the early hours of the morning of 11 December was it announced that a final compromise had been reached. At the price, notably, of special provisions to apply to the UK for EMU and for social policy, the Summit agreed on the establishment of a European Union including, notably, the notion of Union citizenship, the principle of a common foreign and security policy, a single currency, and an increase in the powers of the European Parliament. These and other key issues in the negotiations will be examined in the next chapter.

2. External influences

Throughout the IGC there were of course attempts to influence it from the outside. Among others, these included statements and actions by non- governmental organizations, pressure from governments of third states, national parliaments, political parties or factions thereof and, as we have seen, the European Parliament.

Indeed, the latter was the only external body to be given a permanent and formal channel of communication to the IGCs. As we saw in the preceding chapter, the governments agreed to continue the Inter-institutional conferences that had been held in the preparatory stage of the IGCs. As a result, a total of 10 meetings were held between the IGC Ministers and the delegation of parliamentarians, generally alternating monthly between EMU and Political Union subjects.

Parliament's delegation to the Inter-institutional conference also embarked on a tour of the national capitals where they met successively each of the Prime Ministers or Heads of Government. These meetings were important not so much in terms of presenting Parliament's arguments to the more reluctant Heads of Government as in terms of putting pressure on those Heads of Government who were on record as being in agreement with Parliament's requests, in order to ensure that they lived up to their public statements and felt obliged to fight on the Parliament's behalf. Thus the meetings with Chancellor Kohl and Prime Ministers Gonzalez, Andreotti, Martens and Lubbers were perhaps the most important.

Besides these contacts Parliament's President spoke at a number of the Ministerial meetings of the IGCs, notably at the conclave in Noordwijk, as well as at all the European Council meetings held during this period.

Pressure from national parliaments was largely directed towards their individual participants in the IGCs. There were no new parliamentary Assizes during the IGCs to permit a collective approach, although this had been suggested just prior to Maastricht by a number of parliamentarians. Generally, it was felt that the Declaration adopted, just before the IGC started, by the Assizes in Rome was sufficient as a collective statement. However, the Presidents of seven national parliaments and the European Parliament met on 6 December, just before the summit, in Brussels, under Dutch chairmanship. On the initiative of Laurent Fabius, Rita Süssmuth and Charles Ferdinand Northomb (Presidents of the French *Assemblée*, the German *Bundestag* and the Belgian Chamber), they issued a statement recalling the "Assizes" Declaration and calling on the heads of government to be particularly attentive to the democratic dimension of the envisaged reforms. The text was signed, apart from by the above-mentioned, by the Presidents of the Italian, Luxembourgish and Portuguese parliaments.

Separate pressure towards each individual government in a domestic political context would clearly not be as coherent as that produced by the Assizes. National parliamentary debates tended to throw up a host of reservations on particular subjects and to warn governments of potential difficulties in ratification. In France, for instance, it showed that although the Gaullist party was no longer as hostile to Europe as in the past, it would, for the most part, oppose any supranational development. Even part of the Socialist Party (the faction around Jean-Pierre Chevènement) was also likely to oppose the new Treaty. The most spectacular parliamentary debates were in the UK, where attention focused on the divisions within the Conservative Party with former Prime Minster Thatcher joining with the traditional anti-European elements to send warning shots over the bows of John Major. With an election pending this limited Major's margin for manoeuvre with his overriding preoccupation becoming the unity of the Conservative Party. It would be difficult to steer any course that would satisfy all the currents in his party, but it became clear that was what he would attempt to do — whatever the cost to the rest of the Community.

Third-country governments naturally took an interest in the IGCs. Governments of the EFTA countries negotiating the European Economic Area Agreement with the Community, especially those who were expecting to apply for full membership, were particularly interested but were not in a strong position to influence the negotiations lest they jeopardize their future credibility as a full member. Thus, although the Austrian and Swedish governments may well have had misgivings on the concept of a common security policy, they nevertheless did not seek to block this development, although they did let it be known that they were happy with the idea for subcontracting security matters to WEU, to which not all members of the Community belonged.

Non-governmental organizations were also active. The ETUC issued further statements in the course of the IGCs, dwelling in particular on the social chapter. The employers' organization, UNICE, did the same. ETUC and UNICE jointly negotiated a series of draft articles on the involvement of the social partners in preparing social legislation. This was taken up by the Commission and served as a basis for negotiation on this subject in the IGC, despite the UK's Confederation of British Industry (CBI) repudiating what its representative in UNICE had agreed.

The party political federations — Confederation of Socialist Parties of the EC (CSP); European Liberals, Democrats and Reformists (ELDR); and the European Peoples' Party (EPP) — all met regularly before and during the IGCs, often at the level of party leaders and prime ministers. These "summits" each issued declarations, normally quite federalist in inclination — their internal dynamics tended to put pressure on the more doubting or cautious parties to move forward. Members of the Commission belonging to the corresponding political grouping, and the Chairmen of the corresponding Groups in the European Parliament also participated in such "summits". However, the UK governing party did not belong to any of these political families, and remained outside these circuits.

IV

THE SUBSTANCE OF THE NEGOTIATIONS

This chapter will examine the substance of the negotiations, focusing on 11 key subjects. Before examining the proceedings of the IGC, however, it must be pointed out that at a general level one important feature overshadowed the whole process. This was the contrast in attitude between the majority of Member States and United Kingdom. As Ambassador Philippe de Schouthete de Tervarent (Belgian Permanent Representative to the EC, and personal representative of the Foreign Minister in the political union working party) put it: "It seems that most Member States shared these preoccupations [for strengthening integration], to various degrees. In the negotiations, France and Germany focused on foreign policy and security, Spain on citizenship and cohesion, Italy and Belgium on the powers of the Parliament and majority voting, Denmark on the environment. . . But it is important to underline that one of the principal partners was convinced by none of these arguments. The United Kingdom had participated with reluctance in the first analyses concerning EMU [and for political union]; the whole exercise seemed to it to be pointless, even. [. . .] The final result cannot be correctly appreciated if one ignores the fact that one of the principal participants had no objectives and was seeking no results. This was without doubt the principal difficulty in this negotiation which can, in a way, be analyzed as debate between supporters of movement and supporters of the status quo".[10]

1. Structure of the Treaty and the federal objective

The 1950 Schuman Declaration had already referred to the ultimate federal objective of European integration. Indeed the EC displays a number of federal characteristics such as its legal system, with the supremacy and direct applicability of Community law, its independent executive branch (Commission), its elected Parliament and majority voting among Member States in significant areas of policy. These federal characteristics were sufficiently important to make some Member States wary about giving the Community full competence in the sensitive area of foreign policy, and, especially, security. As described in chapter I, foreign policy cooperation eventually started outside the legal framework of the EC on an informal and intergovernmental basis. This "European Political Cooperation" (EPC) developed during the 1970s and 1980s and gradually included the Commission in its activities, with ministers also answering questions from the European Parliament. The SEA gave treaty status to EPC for the first time, but without incorporating it into the Community treaties — it remained a separate framework, though linked to the Community.

In practice, the two frameworks were becoming increasingly difficult to separate. The

---

[10] Paper delivered to the Institut d'Etudes Européennes of the Université Libre de Bruxelles on the occasion of their study day on "European Union after Maastricht" (Brussels, 21 February 1992). Published by them: D/1992/2672/27. Author's translation.

Community's own instruments of external relations (trade, financial aid, diplomatic accreditations) increasingly and inevitably had major political implications. At the same time, many EPC decisions (e.g. sanctions) could only be implemented through a Community legal instrument. Many therefore felt that the time had come fully to integrate EPC into the Community framework, albeit with appropriately modulated decision-taking procedures. This view was reflected in Parliament's proposals to the IGCs[11] and in the memoranda of the Belgian and Dutch governments. When the IGC got under way, the Commission tabled a specific proposal to the effect that foreign policy, along with development policy and external trade, were to become chapters of the EC Treaty.

Early discussions in the IGC, however, showed that this view was far from obtaining unanimous support. The UK in particular objected to bringing EPC fully into the Community framework. However, it was not alone on this. France, although in the integrationist camp on most issues, also had misgivings.

There were similar reservations in another context, equally sensitive from the viewpoint of national sovereignties. This was cooperation in the field of justice and home affairs (JHA). Over the years a number of intergovernmental frameworks for cooperation had emerged, notably TREVI which had an elaborate structure of its own. These procedures were often criticized as being secretive (partly inherent to their subject matter) and not being subject to any parliamentary scrutiny be it national or European.

The definition of the internal market in the Single Act as an "area without internal frontiers" had given cooperation in these areas greater importance, and linked the subjects more directly to the Community as such. Again, there was a feeling that these practices should be given treaty status, codified, linked to the Community and subjected to at least some scrutiny by the European Parliament. However, there was a marked reluctance to bring these matters fully into the Community's legal framework, where no one could predict the possible interaction of Community law and judicial cooperation in these fields. In particular, the case law of the Court of Justice, with its evolving concepts of due process, proportionality, non-discrimination on the grounds of nationality etc., might have unforeseen consequences, the nature of which might appeal to the wider public, but was not likely to appeal to interior ministries.

Consequently, the Luxembourg "non-paper" of April 1990 proposed a similar structure to the SEA, with EPC and JHA kept outside the Community framework under separate treaty provisions not part of the EC legal system, with no legal review by the Court and with the Commission enjoying a lesser role in initiating proposals and in implementing policies. The European Union would thus be founded on three "pillars", coordinated by the European Council. This structure was therefore baptized as the "Greek temple" approach.

Nonetheless, the CFSP would be more "communautaire" than EPC. Council (rather than a separate meeting of Foreign Ministers) would be primarily responsible for determining policy. The EPC secretariat would be absorbed by Council. Even the language changed, referring to "Member States" rather than the "High Contracting Parties" and to "common policy" rather than "cooperation". At the same time, the Community "pillar" itself was strengthened, even in the field of external relations (where development policy was made a new chapter of the EEC treaty rather than a matter for CFSP) and given more federal characteristics such as the notion of common ("Union") citizenship and the objective, under the EMU provisions (which might instead have been made a fourth pillar), of a single currency. The name of the EEC treaty was changed to EC treaty, to indicate its political, not just economic, finality.

---

[11] See Martin reports and EP resolutions of 11 July (paras. 8-12) and 22 November 1990, Articles 130u-130v.

This "pillar" structure was immediately criticised by the European Parliament, the Commission and the more federalist-minded governments. The Commission tabled a set of amendments to it, designed to ensure a unitary structure of the treaty, by providing for the European Union to "take the place of the European Communities" and by adding provisions on foreign policy cooperation and internal affairs to the modified Community treaties. This corresponded to the Commission's original proposals, but this time the Commission took over the operational details of the Luxembourg draft regarding foreign policy, thus setting out a stronger role for the Council and its Presidency and a lesser role for the Commission than in its initial proposals. The Commission attached an explanatory memorandum in which it stated that the IGC "should be guided by the basic thinking which has been behind the construction of Europe for 40 years now, namely that all progress made towards economic, monetary, social or political integration should gradually be brought together in a single Community as the precursor of a European Union. This being so, it is somewhat paradoxical that the current trend [. . .] would depart from this general unification process and keep the Community no longer as the focal point but simply as one entity among others in a political union with ill-defined objectives and a variety of institutional schemes". The Commission argued that, like EMU, the CFSP provisions would have particular characteristics, but that this should not preclude their integration into the Community framework. This model was baptized the "tree" approach.

The foreign ministers discussed the issue at several meetings in May and June. A majority of Member States (Belgium, Germany, Greece, Ireland, Italy, Spain, the Netherlands) supported the "tree" approach rather than the "temple" approach. The Luxembourg Presidency, however, was not convinced that the majority view was capable of gaining the necessary consensus at the end of the day.[12] Nevertheless, the Luxembourg Presidency did make some adjustments in its new text "Draft Treaty on the Union" of 20 June. These were designed to reassure the majority that the pillar structure would not be the beginning of the end of the Community system but, on the contrary, could represent a step towards communautarization of the two non-Community pillars, described as "half-way between the Community and the intergovernmental domain". The main changes were as follows:

– to specify that the Union "shall be founded on the European Communities *supplemented* by other policies and cooperations established by this treaty": this indicated a priority to the Community system, with the other pillars being merely "supplements";

– adding two separate specifications to the effect that the "acquis communautaire" could not be undermined by the new pillars but, on the contrary, should develop further;

– to specify that "the Union shall be served by a single institutional framework" thus ensuring an *institutional* merger of EPC with the Community (i.e. it would be run by the Community institutions, albeit predominantly the Council), even if it would remain *legally* separate;

– to state that the treaty "marks a new stage in the process leading gradually to a Union with a federal goal";

– to include a revision clause specifying that a new IGC would be convened in 1996 "in the perspective of strengthening the federal character of the Union";

– transferring some "constitutional" clauses of the EC treaty (concerning treaty revision and accession of new Member States) to the final provisions of the Union treaty, thus assuring the unity of the whole in these respects;

---

[12] A view supported after the IGCs by the Belgian Permanent Representative, who was one of the most fervent supporters of the "tree" approach (See De Schouthete, op. cit.).

– to specify that the Union was responsible not just for relations among its Member States but also among its "peoples": this again to underline that the process was not merely intergovernmental.

These changes did not fully satisfy the federalist camp. The Belgian Chamber of Deputies adopted a resolution on 27 June 1991 in which it recalled "that European integration must lead to a Union with a democratic system and a federal structure; rejects the tripartite structure proposed by the Presidency of the EC Council". The European Parliament also called (14 June) for "the unicity of the Community's legal and institutional system [to] be safeguarded and extended to other sectors which currently enjoy inter-state cooperation such as foreign policy". But nor was the other camp satisfied, the UK and Denmark objecting in particular to the reference to the federal goal.

Although the European Council meeting on 28/29 June in Luxembourg agreed that "the Presidency's draft forms the basis for the continuation of negotiations", it also considered "that the Union should be based on the following principles: [. . .] full maintenance of the acquis communautaire and development thereof, [and] a single institutional framework". This seemed to endorse the Luxembourg Presidency's revised approach, but the Dutch Presidency, which took over on July 1, nevertheless made another attempt to reopen the issue, circulating a new "Draft Treaty Towards European Union" which took up the unitary ("tree") structure, adding all new policy areas to the EC treaty. Indeed, it abandoned the term "European Union" (except in the title), using the term European Community throughout.

An informal draft of this text was circulated to Member States and the European Parliament at the beginning of September, but the official version (slightly modified to take account of comments received) was only circulated on 24 September — almost three months into the Dutch Presidency and less than three months from Maastricht. Partly for this reason, and partly because most Member States did not believe it was realistic to reopen these questions at such a late stage, the text was withdrawn after an overwhelmingly hostile reaction (only Belgium gave some support) by the Foreign Ministers on 30 September, dubbed the "Black Monday" of Dutch diplomacy.

October saw discussions in the IGC take place on the basis of revisions of individual extracts of the Luxembourg text. The next global text was distributed on 8 November in view of the Noordwijk "conclave" of Foreign Ministers of 12/13 November. This text reverted to the Luxembourg structure. However, visa policy was transferred from the JHA pillar to Community competence, and an evolutive clause provided for the possibility of subsequent transfers to be made by Council, acting unanimously. The new text also spelled out that a number of EC treaty articles (those defining the composition of the institutions and certain of their prerogatives) would apply directly to CFSP and JHA, and that administrative expenditure would (and operational expenditure could) be charged to the Community's budget. All these changes enmeshed the CFSP and JHA further into the EC.

The specific reference to the "federal goal", however, continued to be contested by the UK government, which maintained that it would not sign a treaty containing such a reference. Most of the other Member States insisted on keeping the reference, as part of the compromise on the structure of the Treaty. Indeed, the UK's focus on the word, rather than on substantive "federal" developments such as citizenship, convinced many that the term had become a fetish for reasons to do with internal divisions within the UK Conservative Party. Its removal could best be left to the Maastricht Summit itself, thus allowing Prime Minister Major to claim victory on that point, leaving the substance intact.

Indeed, this was what occurred. The pillar structure was maintained, but with the federal reference replaced by a reference to the new Treaty marking "a new stage in the process of creating an ever closer union among the peoples of Europe in which decisions are taken as closely as possible to the citizens". Although it was pointed out that an "ever-closer Union" must logically imply a more centralized Union than a federal one, this text satisfied the UK delegation. In exchange, a reference was incorporated into Article B to the effect that the 1996 IGC should review the pillar structure.

2.   Economic and Monetary Union

While the intensive preparation which led up to the EMU IGC meant that by December 1990 work on the project was already very advanced, Member States were still anxious to gain the edge in the negotiations. As a result, the first months of the IGC saw a flurry of position papers being published as most of the major players made their opening negotiating gambits and outlined their preferred vision of EMU, although the Commission's draft treaty of December 1990 remained the basis for negotiations.

The first of these position papers was released by the Bundesbank actually just before the IGC began. It reflected the Bank's cautious and pragmatic approach to EMU and was presented in a singularly clear, forceful and direct manner. The German Chancellor, Helmut Kohl, was a strong (political) supporter of EMU and the paper did not challenge the idea of Union in principle. However, it did reflect the strand of German thinking, held by the Bundesbank in particular, that the disappearance of the Deutschmark and the transfer to a Community institution of the powers of the Bundesbank itself would only be acceptable if the alternative "was at least as good" as what already existed. In light of this the Bundesbank stated that EMU could only be the result of a slow and careful process which avoided any measures which might upset Member States' economies during the transition period; that any future ESCB would have to be fully independent and have the absolute priority of fighting inflation; that very strict convergence criteria would have to be met before any union could be considered; and that monetary union would have to be accompanied by an economic union.

In reality, much of what was being demanded was already contained in the Delors Report (for example, an independent ESCB geared to fighting inflation) but the Bundesbank was in effect double underlining these points just in case any doubts persisted. In the words of its paper these demands were "indispensable, not optional requirements". Most of these demands were to be satisfied during the following negotiations, reflecting the strength of the German position as Europe's monetary superpower. That said, it is interesting to note that over the key issue of setting a timetable for EMU (the Bundesbank was adamantly opposed to this, stating that EMU should only begin once clearly measurable convergence criteria had been met) political considerations won the day and a timetable was drawn up. This was to leave the Bundesbank less committed to EMU.

The next, and most radically different, position paper was submitted by the British Government on 10 January 1991. The paper elaborated, in treaty format, the British proposals for a "hard-ECU" which had been first outlined in a speech by the UK Prime Minister, John Major, to the German Industry Forum in July 1990. It represented the main (indeed the only) departure from advancing an EMU of the style devised by the Delors Committee. As the paper's introduction clearly stated, the British Government was "not able to accept the imposition of a single currency and a single monetary policy" — a position which the government was to repeat many times (even though others responded that an agreed EMU was no "imposition"). Instead, the UK proposed an intergovernmental approach aimed at the "progressive realization of EMU". A new institution, the European Monetary Fund, was to be set up and charged with establishing and then supervising a new 13th European currency (the hard-ECU). This would co-exist with the existing 12 currencies and was not intended to replace them (although this was accepted as a long-term possibility).

The Commission gave the proposal a suitably diplomatic welcome, recognizing it as a significant advance upon the previous British position (hostility to any supranational monetary policy). In as far as this new proposal recognized the need for a new Treaty, a common monetary institution, a common policy vis-à-vis third countries, and that the ECU *could* eventually become Europe's single currency, it was supported. But the Commission went on to note that the proposal did not fit into the generally agreed concept of what EMU would consist of, and in addition criticized it for being simultaneously too complex and too limited.

The President of the Bundesbank, Karl Otto Poehl, was less diplomatic. He called the proposal "inadequate" and went on to state that the impression that the proposal had received considerable support was entirely false. According to him, the unpublished deliberations at the recent Rome summit meeting (October 1990) revealed that the idea of a hard-ECU was rejected by "practically all member countries, central banks and also the governments in the Community". However, Poehl did recognize some virtue in the element of the proposal which proposed "hardening" the ECU (i.e. permanently fixing the basket of currencies which set the value of the ECU instead of, as was the practice, re-adjusting the weighting every five years). This idea was taken up by the Germans within the IGC (and was eventually agreed to at Maastricht).

Poehl summarised the UK proposal as a "detour on the road to EMU" and consequently rejected it. It would be fair to say that this view was shared by his own government and by the vast majority of the other Member States. The UK was unwilling to advance any further along the Delors Report road to EMU and the other countries were not prepared to settle for anything less. For the rest of the negotiations the UK, although involved throughout, would be mainly concerned with securing an acceptable "opt-out clause". France and Germany remained the big two players for the rest of the negotiations.

The role of the ECU also formed a central part of a detailed Spanish position paper which devoted itself exclusively to the questions of how to manage the new Community monetary institution in stage two of EMU and how best to strengthen the ECU during the same period.

The final position papers were those of the French government (February 1991) and the German government (March 1991). Both countries had been consistently strong supporters of EMU and both recognized the Delors Report and the subsequent work which had been carried out upon it as their preferred basis for such a union. Bearing this in mind, it is no real surprise that neither of these papers contained any radical challenges to the ongoing EMU process. Instead they tended to deal with details and restated their governments' main concerns (for example, the German paper once again laid great emphasis upon the independence and anti-inflation role of any ESCB).

However, the papers did contain several points of interest. The most significant aspect of the French position was its attempt to limit the role of the Commission and the EP in the EMU process. The EP was only to be consulted and Council would act upon Commission recommendations.[13] The French also proposed to force the Commission to share its previously exclusive right of initiative with Member States in certain circumstances. This position of the French government hardly tallied with its commitment to a "supranational federal entity"[14], but the government, and in particular the Ministry

---

[13] A "recommendation" could be changed by QMV in Council, whereas under the treaties, Commission "proposals" can be approved by QMV but only changed by unanimity.

[14] Statement of Foreign Minister Dumas to French Parliament. Debates of the *Assemblée Nationale*, 27.11.91.

of Finance and Economy, wanted Council to act as a strong economic counterweight to the autonomous monetary powers of the Central Bank. As we shall see, the French were largely unsuccessful in these aspects.

The German proposal reflected many of the previously stated German concerns about an EMU being established before Member States' economies were fully prepared for it. A very cautious and detailed approach was taken and many of the conditions insisted upon by Germany would eventually find their way into the Treaty (for example, sanctions could be levelled against any member of the Union who disobeyed decisions on budgetary discipline). However, in several cases German caution was overruled. For instance, directions for a future economic policy such as "Member States shall attempt to privatise public enterprises" were not included in the final Treaty revisions.

With the principles of EMU and its three stages outline already settled by the preceding meetings of the European Council, most of the IGC's actual work was confined to sorting out the details of how to make EMU work. How long should the term of office be for members of the ECB Executive? (eight years, non- renewable, was agreed). What should be the precise terms of the convergence criteria which must be met before any country could be allowed to participate in the Union? How would derogations to these criteria be decided upon?

In fact, the Finance Ministers and their representatives managed to resolve all the outstanding issues either before Maastricht (on the basis of the Dutch Presidency's revised draft EMU treaty of 28 October) or at a final meeting which was held alongside the European Council itself. At no stage did the Heads of State or Government have to intervene directly in the negotiations, and the Dutch Presidency actually decided to rearrange the agenda of the summit, placing EMU first, to ensure that it started with a success and to create a positive mood for what was to follow. All of this is a reflection of the length, care and success of the whole negotiating process.

One major issue settled in the autumn was that of the role of the central monetary authorities during phase II. Germany caused some consternation in the early months of the IGC by arguing that the Central Bank should only be established with the introduction of a single currency in phase III, and not in phase II as argued in the Delors' report, lest this create confusion over the responsibility for monetary policy in the intermediate phase. By the autumn, agreement was reached on a Dutch Presidency proposal that phase II should see the establishment of a "Monetary Institute" (EMI) charged with strengthening the coordination of national monetary policies, to develop the role of the ECU and to prepare for the establishment of the Central Bank. The EMI would be wound up with the transfer of monetary sovereignty to the Central Bank in phase III.

Another issue was that of the competence to deal with external exchange rate policy. On this, Germany did not get its way. It had argued that this was such an important aspect of monetary policy that the Central Bank should have ultimate competence for this aspect too. The IGC reached agreement, however, that the Council would take final decisions in this field. It would act by QMV except when concluding formal agreements with third countries on exchange rate systems where unanimity would apply.

Of the big issues which remained until last, the most important were the questions of the UK's opt-out clause and that of the conditions necessary to move to the final stage of EMU. Both of these questions would have to wait until Maastricht itself before satisfactory solutions could be found.

After the rejection of the British "hard-ECU" proposal it became clear that the UK government would find whatever version of EMU the other 11 adopted unacceptable. The UK therefore pressed for a general opting-out clause (covering the stage before the final move to EMU) to be included in the Treaty, rejecting the idea of a UK-specific clause appended to the Treaty. The Commission was strongly opposed to such a general clause, believing that it would undermine the credibility of the whole process if a clear and irrevocable pledge was not given by all parties of their intent to go all the way with EMU. This opinion was shared by all the other Member States except Denmark.

Jacques Delors himself referred to the idea of a general opt-out clause as "a sword of Damocles" suspended over the credibility of EMU. However, he also recognised the danger of repeating "the sad story of the Luxembourg compromise on majority voting and essential national interests". Instead, the Commission advocated some form of compromise solution and offered its services as a consensus finder.

At the "marathon" meeting of Finance Ministers, held at Scheveningen and Brussels during the week before the Maastricht summit, a draft protocol was circulated between the Presidency and the British delegation. This protocol, largely inspired by Jacques Delors, was to be attached at the end of the Treaty and would only apply to the UK. It would allow the UK parliament to decide, independently of the European Council, on whether or not it was going to take part in stage three of EMU.

The Danish delegation was the only other supporter of a general opting-out clause. At the marathon meeting the Danish Finance Minister had indicated his country's intention to hold a double referendum of the EMU Treaty: the first to take place before ratification by the *Folketing* (the Danish Parliament) and the other before transition to the final stage. Unlike the UK the Danes were prepared to consider the idea of a country-specific opt-out, but they made it clear that they did "not want the same protocol as the United Kingdom as the reasons (requiring it) are not the same".

The UK held out against this formula even when it was being actively endorsed by all of the other Member States, and it had to be resolved by Finance Ministers at the Maastricht summit itself. Dutch Finance Minister and president of the IGC, Wim Kok, called this "one of the most important subjects at Maastricht". The UK did eventually back down over this issue — it was, after all, hard to insist that everyone else should have an opt-out clause when nobody else wanted it! — and two protocols were attached to the EMU Treaty, one for the British (following the lines described above) and a separate one for the Danes.

The other major question concerned how to get to the final stage of EMU. Along with the issue of opting out, this dominated the Scheveningen/Brussels marathon meeting. The decision of whether or not a country should be allowed to join phase III would be based upon objective economic (convergence) criteria whose principles would be included in the body of the Treaty and whose exact details would be annexed to the Treaty as a protocol. In fact, this condition had long been accepted and was supported by most of the Member States (in particular Germany). The criteria laid down in the convergence protocol (which Council, acting unanimously, may replace with new provisions) specify four elements:

- price stability with an inflation rate no more than $1\frac{1}{2}$ points higher than the average of the best three Member States;
- no "excessive deficit" as decided by Council which must make an assessment where a Member State has a persistent deficit of over 3 per cent GDP;
- participation without severe tensions or devaluations in the ERM for at least two years;
- nominal long-term interest rates of no more than two points above the average of the three Member States performing best in terms of inflation.

These are to be examined in conjunction with the balance of payments situation, wages, price levels and market integration, in deciding which countries fulfil the necessary conditions for moving to a single currency. In addition to this, the critical mass (the number of states required to proceed with the Union) was gradually being settled at "more than half" (i.e. at least seven) although some Member States were still advocating a numerically precise seven or eight members.

However, the discussions really centred on finding a way of preventing the decision of moving to the final stage being subject to continued postponements because decision by unanimity is the norm within the European Council (the body charged with the responsibility to move to EMU). France suggested that the decision of moving to the final stage be taken by simple majority in 1998 if there proved to be no consensus in 1996 (the date selected for the Member States' first attempt at EMU). This would mean that a Member State fulfilling the convergence requirements at this stage would no longer be able to back out of EMU and would provide EMU with a timetable for not only Stage Two (January 1994, as had already been agreed at the Rome I summit) but also for the final transition (the beginning of 1999 at the very latest). According to this proposal the irreversibility of the process would be assured. There were some doubts expressed over this proposal from Member States which felt that setting an automatic date would take the pressure off Member States to make a real effort to reach the convergence criteria, but the basic principle attracted general support.

The Dutch Presidency then pushed this proposal a little further by proposing that the vote in 1996 should be made by QMV and that no Member State not fulfilling the necessary conditions could prevent the accord. While most of the Member States agreed with the need to make the EMU process irrevocable, certain countries (Spain, Greece, Portugal and the UK) had problems with this wording. The Greeks expressed fears over the creation of a two-speed Europe and the Spanish Prime Minister, Felipe Gonzalez, emphasized the difficulties his country would face in meeting the convergence criteria.

In the end, the desire to set a concrete date for EMU so as to underpin the commitments made at Maastricht was to win the day. The final agreement reached was that in 1996, based upon the reports of the Commission and the EMI on the achievement of the convergence criteria, the Council would decide by QMV whether a majority of Member States met the stipulated conditions. It would then forward its recommendation to the Heads of State and Government (meeting as the Council) who will decide by QMV whether it is appropriate to enter the third stage. If no decision is reached in 1997, then EMU will definitely come into force on 1 January 1999 among those Member States meeting the convergence requirements.

The importance of solving the questions of transition to stage three and the opt-out clause cannot be understated. As Padoa Schippoa, Deputy Director General at the Banca d'Italia observed, they moved the Treaty from being one of "procedure and intent" to being a Treaty of "effective commitment". Without the questions of who (no general opting-out clause), and when (a firm date for entry into the final stage) being decided, the Treaty would have carried very little credibility and consequently much less worth.

The IGC also settled the other remaining issues. The most important of these was the economic counterpart of monetary union. The Werner report in 1970 had been quite elaborate on the restrictions and rules to be imposed on national economic policies. The Delors Report had considerably watered this down, and Maastricht did so still further. Economic policy would, as far as possible, be left to the Member States. Nevertheless, there would be some commonly agreed rules: no monetary financing of deficits, no bailing out, no excessive deficits or public debt (whether an excessive deficit or debt exist would be decided by Council — QMV — which would examine a Commission report on countries whose deficit went higher than 3 per cent GDP or whose debt went beyond 60 per cent of GDP). Council would lay down economic policy guidelines, but on these guidelines there would be no sanctions. "Multilateral surveillance" and the coordination policies within the Council would be the prescribed means of achieving economic union.

Sanctions were provided, however, in the case of Member States failing to correct persistent excessive deficits. These sanctions were to follow a scale: Council to make confidential recommendations to the Member State, followed by public recommendations, followed by notice to take the necessary measures, followed by a requirement to publish additional information before issuing bonds and securities; inviting the European Investment Bank to reconsider its lending policy towards the Member State concerned; to require the Member State to make a non-interest bearing deposit or, finally, to impose fines. Decisions would be taken by a two-thirds majority of the weighted votes of the Member States excluding the votes of the Member State concerned.

The institutional issues were also settled. The rights of initiative of the Commission were preserved, except to the extent that it would share its monopoly with the Central Bank itself when it came to proposals to change the statute of the Central Bank. However, for some decisions, Council would act on a Commission recommendation rather than a Commission proposal (i.e. Council could change it by a qualified majority). As to the European Parliament, its assent would be required for changes to the statute of the Central Bank, and for the granting of specific tasks to the Central Bank and the cooperation procedure would be used when it came to adopting rules for the multilateral surveillance procedure, for implementing the article on sanctions or for taking measures concerning the circulation of coins. For the rest, Parliament would simply be consulted. The new co-decision procedure would not be used in the EMU framework. Thus Parliament's role was more than just consultative, as some governments had wanted, but fell short of Parliament's aspirations.

Finally, Parliament would be consulted on the appointment of the President, Vice-President and the four members of the Executive Board. In this case, however, "consultation" amounts to a public vote on an individual, possibly after public hearings and questioning. It is unlikely that a negative vote by Parliament would be ignored, so the procedure is tantamount to a confirmation.

3.   Common Foreign and Security Policy (CFSP)

Apart from the issue of having a separate "pillar" for CFSP as opposed to full integration into the EC framework, examined above, discussions on this aspect of the IGC revolved around four other, though related, issues: how to go beyond simple cooperation and coordination by consensus of national (and Commission) foreign policies (with the related issue of introducing QMV); how much the CFSP should include defence policy; the relationship with WEU and the relationship to the Atlantic Alliance.

Member States were divided not only on the degree of integration they wanted but also as to whether they saw the Atlantic framework as being supreme in security matters. These cleavages were not identical. Thus the Netherlands, generally in the integrationist camp, was firmly Atlanticist. Ireland, not keen on integration in this field, was equally reticent about links to NATO. NATO itself was going through a major reassessment of its role in response to the changes in eastern Europe (though this was before the collapse of the Soviet Union), culminating in a NATO summit held in Rome in November 1991. It was clear that, for many Member States, these processes were linked and no definitive conclusion could be reached in the IGC until after the NATO summit, a point confirmed by the Luxembourg European Council mid-way through the IGCs.

Despite this, key aspects of the final package emerged very quickly. Already before the IGC began, the Rome I European Council of October 1990 "recorded consensus on the objective of a common foreign and security policy" (a term already more ambitious than "political cooperation") and that "no aspect [. . .] will in principle be excluded [and there is] consensus to go beyond the present limit with regard to security". The Rome II European Council of December 1990 agreed that there should be "one decision-making centre, namely the Council"; a "unified secretariat"; a "reinforced role for the Commission"; "adequate procedures for consulting and informing the European Parliament"; "detailed procedures [for speaking] with one voice on the international stage, in particular in international organisations and vis-à-vis third countries"; and that the IGC should consider introducing QMV "for the implementation of agreed policies", and a future "role for the Union in defence matters". Thus, traditional reticences (Ireland, Denmark) towards dealing with defence appeared to be overcome, and all Member States were willing to go beyond EPC, to reinforce procedures and to merge the EPC secretariat into the Council.

In the opening weeks of the IGC, the Commission put forward a set of draft treaty articles on foreign and security policy, as part of its proposal for a new title in the EC treaty on a common external policy. Taking an approach very similar to that of the European Parliament, it proposed that for matters that were "vital common interests" (to be defined by the European Council, acting unanimously), Council should act by QMV to define the principles of common policy and on action to be taken to implement it, though dispensations could be granted to individual states. For matters not deemed to be of vital common interest, positions would still be coordinated for items of "general interest", more or less as in EPC. In all matters the Commission would be granted a non-exclusive right of initiative. The Commission and the Council Presidency would be jointly responsible for external representation, assisted where appropriate by the previous and following Presidencies (the Troika thus becoming a "Quadriga"). Security would come under this dual system, with the issues of arms control, CSCE and UN security matters, peace-keeping operations, and technological cooperation already defined as vital common interests. However, for security policy, Council could decide to refer implementation to WEU. This would be provisional, as the Union would "promote the gradual integration of WEU into the Union". The "long-term objective" of "a common European defence" would be "in full compliance with commitments entered into in the Atlantic Alliance", but Member States in NATO "would express the Union position there".

The Commission considered that the two key aspects were a move towards QMV in some significant areas of joint concern (failing which there would be little difference from existing procedures) and an extension in scope to cover security and defence (which the Commission recognised would have to be based on WEU, notably given Ireland's reluctance on military matters and the UK's reluctance to change existing structures, but which it hoped to link firmly into the European Union process).

The Commission approach was not shared by all. The UK tabled a proposal to revise Title III of the SEA, keeping the CFSP outside the Community framework, though granting the Commission a non-exclusive right of initiative. Cooperation would be extended to security matters, but if "an issue relating to defence arises, any further European consultation or cooperative action shall take place within the framework of WEU" which, in the UK conception, was not part of the Union. It was also specified with regard to NATO that "nothing in this Title shall impede such cooperation". No provisions were envisaged for QMV in the CFSP, even for implementing measures, a position shared by Denmark. In its reluctance to allow military matters to be discussed in the CFSP, the UK obtained some sympathy from the Netherlands, Portugal and Denmark. The Netherlands, however, diverged enormously from the UK in supporting QMV (if based on a Commission proposal, otherwise unanimity) for implementing measures on ordinary CFSP matters. Germany, France, Italy, Spain, Belgium, Greece and Luxembourg considered that WEU could be the instrument for applying the Union's defence policies, but that it should become part of the Union's institutional system and eventually (1996/98) absorbed by the European Union. The UK, the Netherlands, Portugal and Denmark felt WEU should be equidistant between NATO and the European Union, and that NATO should remain predominant in the field of defence. The UK, the Netherlands, Italy, France and Germany all submitted memoranda or proposals regarding CFSP corresponding to these positions (the latter two jointly).

Faced with this divergence of views, confirmed by the responses to a questionnaire it sent out on CFSP, the Luxembourg Presidency incorporated into its "non-paper" of 12 April 1990 provisions on CFSP which built on the Commission proposals but attenuated some of the effects. It too envisaged two tiers of policy: **cooperation**, where Member States "inform and consult one another" on any matter "of general interest" with Council in these areas, defining common positions "wherever necessary" on which "Member States shall base their policies and actions"; and **joint action** where, once Council has decided the subject and defined the objectives, "each Member State shall be bound by the joint line of action in the conduct of its international activity" and where no national action could be taken without first allowing for prior discussion in Council, except "in cases of urgent need". National measures would in any case have to be "in accordance with the objectives of the joint line of action". External representation would be in the heads of the Council Presidency "assisted" by the Troika (where appropriate) and by the Commission. Parliament would be informed and consulted "on the main lines" of policy. "Principles and general guidelines" of the CFSP would be defined by the European Council. COREPER and the Political Committee of heads of Foreign Office Departments would be responsible for preparation of meetings and monitoring. Security matters "which have defence implications" could ("may") be referred to WEU "wholly or partly" (where it was envisaged that a Declaration of WEU Member States, annexed to the Treaty, would be drawn up to specify detailed arrangements), but security decisions would "not effect" obligations under the NATO or WEU treaties. The "eventual framing of a common defence policy" was contained in square brackets.

Thus the difference between "cooperation" and "joint action" appeared to be very little in terms of instruments available, preparation, potential scope, implementation or even decision-making procedure. Whereas the latter was crucial in the Commission's proposal, the "non-paper" provided only that Council "may" stipulate that "detailed arrangements for carrying out" a joint action could be carried out either by QMV or "by a majority to be "defined" (the two being offered as alternatives in square brackets).

The Luxembourg Presidency's "draft treaty" some two months later contained only a few modifications of substance to the non-paper as regards the CFSP. It plumped for "QMV" rather than "a majority to be defined" as the option Council could choose for implementing joint actions. It removed the square brackets around the "eventual framing of a common defence policy", and specified that CFSP "includes all questions relating to security of the Union". It added a new paragraph allowing closer cooperation among two or more Member States provided that it "does not conflict or impede" the CFSP (this as a result of Franco-German concerns). It transferred to the EEC treaty an article allowing Council to break off economic relations with third countries.

In September the Dutch Presidency presented its draft which, as described in section 1, sought to overturn the pillar structure. Even this, however, preserved a two-tier approach. It provided for Community competence in the areas where the Luxembourg text had provided for joint action, but for other areas Article 30 of the SEA would continue to provide for cooperation among Member States, though this too would be amended. As regards the actual decision-taking procedures, in each case the Dutch text retained the Luxembourg proposals except that the Court of Justice would be competent to rule on procedural matters (only) of joint action. As regards security, however, the Dutch, reflecting their Atlanticist outlook, departed considerably from the Luxembourg text, providing that the Community's security policy should "complement the security policy resulting from [the NATO and WEU treaties] whilst observing the powers peculiar to each of those organizations". No question of WEU subordination to the Community!

Following the rejection of the general approach of the Dutch draft treaty, discussions continued on the basis of revisions of the Luxembourg text. At this point, several Member States made attempts to shift the debate in their direction, whilst at the same time giving some ground. This was done on the occasion of some of the numerous bilateral summit meetings that punctuated the whole IGC.

First, on 4 October, Italy and the UK issued a joint declaration. In it, the UK accepted for the first time that "political union implies [. . .] the longer-term perspective of a common defence policy", albeit qualified as needing to be compatible with what it called "the common defence policy we already have with all our allies in NATO". The Declaration envisaged WEU being "entrusted with the task of developing the European dimension in defence [. . .] as the defence component of the Union and as a means to strengthen the European pillar of the Alliance". WEU ministerial organs would be moved to Brussels and it would "take account in its activities the decisions of the European Council" as well as "positions adopted in the context of the Alliance". A WEU "European reaction force" would be set up. The Declaration was presented as a synthesis and possible compromise, reached by one of the most federalist countries and the UK, on the eve of a Foreign Ministers IGC meeting in Utrecht devoted to security and defence.

Second, on 11 October the French, German and Spanish Foreign Ministers (Roland Dumas, Hans-Dietrich Genscher and Francisco Fernandez Ordoñez) met in Paris and issued a short communiqué reaffirming their support for a Union "with federal vocation" which should "include all the questions relating to security and defence, with the long-term prospect of common defence" and with QMV "over the modalities in setting up" the CFSP.

Third, on 16 October, France and Germany made public some draft treaty articles and related draft documents which were circulated to other Member States with a covering letter (dated 11 October) from Kohl and Mitterrand. The emphasis remained different from the Anglo-Italian Declaration in a number of respects. WEU would be an *optional* way of *implementing* Union decisions ("decisions and measures taken by the Union in this area may be developed and implemented entirely or in part by the WEU"), rather than being fully responsible in its own right. Instead of NATO being "reinforced", NATO obligations would be "not affected", and Member States would coordinate their positions within NATO. However, the similarities with the Anglo-Italian text were also striking, with the details of moving WEU to Brussels and institutional cooperation envisaged being very similar.

This convergence of positions — or, at least, a shift in the UK's position — was taking place against a rapidly developing background. The Gulf War at the beginning of the year, followed by the Kurd crisis and then the Yugoslav crisis, had shown clearly both the limits of current European cooperation and its potential. In the Gulf, the Community had acted decisively where there was a formal Community competence — it was the first to apply sanctions against Iraq — but when military action was taken, the Member States scattered in all directions. The Kurd and Yugoslav crises, in contrast, had seen Community initiatives and, indeed, in the latter case Community leadership in the West's initial management of the crisis, with the USA content to take a back-seat role. The EC observers sent to Yugoslavia may not have been successful on the ground, but they were a first "joint action" in the field of security. These events no doubt helped shift perceptions in the more reluctant Member States as to the potential usefulness of a CFSP with a defence dimension, not least in areas where NATO was an inappropriate instrument.

On 8 November the Dutch introduced a new global text containing new provisions on CFSP. It was based on the last Luxembourg text but with a new order of Articles and with some small but important changes of substance, designed to strengthen the procedures. Thus the new draft provided that Council "stipulate as a general rule" that measures implementing joint action should be adopted by QMV. The Commission would be "fully associated" with (instead of simply able to "assist") the Council Presidency and the Troïka in external representation. Member States could take unilateral measures in areas of joint action only in the case of "imperative need" (not "urgent need"). Additional provisions were added concerning the cooperation of diplomatic missions and a special annual debate in the European Parliament. On security, it reverted to the Luxembourg approach.

The text was now close to what would be the final consensus, but the two key issues of security (the nature of the relationship to WEU) and majority voting on implementing joint action, continued to be the subject of intense negotiations, which resulted in further modifications. By Maastricht, the final version reached a compromise on the position of WEU, stating that the "Union requests WEU to elaborate and implement decisions", thus leaving it ambiguous as to whether *all* decisions in the defence field had to be referred to WEU. It specified that WEU was "an integral part of the development of the Union" and reverted to the formula that policies "shall be compatible with NATO". The definition of joint action was modified to specify that these could take place wherever Member States have "important" (rather than "essential") interests in common, but at the same time it was specified that there would be no joint action in the field of defence. As regards the decision-taking for implementing joint action, a more neutral formula was used, stating that Council shall "define those matters on which decisions are to be taken by a qualified majority", and a Declaration was annexed to the Treaty stating that "Member States will, to the extent possible, avoid preventing a unanimous decision where a qualified majority exists in favour of that decision". The reference to an eventual common defence policy was moved from the general definition of the CFSP and moved to the Article on security, but it was also strengthened by specifying that this common defence policy "might in time lead to a common defence" — a still more far-reaching concept. A completely new point was added providing an obligation for Member States of the United Nations Security Council to defend the positions of the Union and to keep the other Member States fully informed.

4.   Justice and home affairs (JHA)

Member States had collaborated for a number of years at intergovernmental level, and largely outside the Community framework, on a number of matters in the field of responsibility of interior ministries. This included the TREVI Group, dealing with terrorism, police cooperation, trans-frontier crime and drug trafficking (holding ministerial meetings every six months and with a number of working parties); the ad-hoc group on immigration; the judicial cooperation working party; the group of coordinators on free circulation of people; four working parties among the Schengen Member States, a drugs working party within EPC and five working groups in the framework of the Council of Europe. The IGC on Political Union had to consider whether, and if so how, to integrate the forms of cooperation that existed among the 12 Community States into the European Union framework.

The Luxembourg Presidency put forward a paper on 10 January containing four options: (1) continue to develop cooperation outside the Community/Union framework; (2) putting a brief reference in the Treaty to the principle of cooperation, leaving it to Council to work out details later; (3) elaborating a full set of treaty provisions defining the fields to be covered and the decision-taking procedures; or (4) full communautarization (i.e. dealing with these matters entirely according to standard Community procedures and within the EC legal framework). The initial reaction from the other Member States was mixed. The Netherlands, Belgium, Italy and Spain preferred option 4. France and Germany preferred option 3 in the immediate term, with a future transition to option 4. Portugal supported option 3, the UK, Ireland and Greece preferred option 2 and Denmark could accept either options 1 or 2.

The Luxembourg Presidency chose option 3 and prepared a text included in its non-paper of April which, as regards its substance, remained virtually intact for the remainder of the IGC. The only significant changes of substance between April and December were the addition of the proposed European Police Office (as a result of a German initiative); the addition of the reference to compliance with the European Convention on Human Rights (ECHR) and the 1951 Convention on the status of refugees; making optional rather than mandatory both the use of majority voting for implementing measures and the granting to the Court of Justice of power to rule on disputes regarding the implementation of conventions; providing for the European Parliament to be consulted; moving visa policy into the Community framework and providing, in an annexed declaration, that asylum policy might also be so moved before the end of 1993.

Few Member States had submitted detailed proposals of their own. The UK had done so in March, providing for Interior and Justice Ministers to cooperate, as directed by the European Council, by mutual information, consultation and coordination of national policies. The Commission would have no right of initiative and Parliament would merely be informed. A structure of working groups would take over the functions of TREVI and other intergovernmental frameworks. Belgium submitted on 23 May a sharp note expressing scepticism regarding the Luxembourg approach, arguing that many of the matters would, under Court of Justice case-law, fall under Community provisions in any case. It pointed to the Benelux experience showing that freedom of movement inevitably requires a common visa policy. Belgium's argument was heeded in so far as visa policy was transferred to the Community "pillar".

5. Social policy

Under the original treaties, social policy was not given a high priority. Article 118 of the Treaty of Rome required the Commission to promote close cooperation between Member States in the field of social policy, but only by making studies, delivering opinions and arranging consultations. No legislative tools were available (except indirectly under Article 100, legislative harmonization for the common market, by unanimity), although the social fund did enable the Community to intervene with budgetary means in certain areas.

As part of the SEA package, a new Article 118A was added to the social chapter of the Treaty, providing for Community legislation, by QMV, for harmonizing conditions for the health and safety of workers. Outside the field of health and safety, however, unanimity would continue to apply, and the new Article 100A (internal market harmonizations) specifically excluded from its scope the rights and interests of employed persons.

The SEA also added a new Article 118B which stated that the Commission would work to develop the dialogue between the social partners at European level which could, if the two sides agreed, lead to agreements. This text was not very specific as to the nature of such agreements nor the procedures for enforcing them.

Article 118A did lead to the adoption of a series of measures in the health and safety field. However, the Commission, the Parliament and most Member States, as well as the

European trade unions were strongly critical of the imbalance in the completion of the internal market following the SEA. The lack of treaty provisions and the restriction of the scope of QMV, meant that social policy was lagging well behind market liberalizations. In an attempt to build up momentum, Commission President Jacques Delors put forward the European Social Charter, which, after lengthy negotiations, was approved by 11 of the 12 Member States at the Strasbourg Summit in December 1989. On this basis, the Commission then drew up the Social Action Programme to implement the Charter. This consisted of some 45 items of proposed legislation or action.

Nevertheless, implementation of the Social Action Programme remained unsatisfactory, despite the Commission resorting to the tactic of using Article 118A even for measures which were only partly concerned with health and safety, such as the regulation of working time.

Meanwhile, the use of Article 118B to promote social dialogue at the European level between employers and industry began on a range of subjects, some joint positions being agreed at the sectoral level. In some cases, such as in the retail trade and railways, this led to agreements on developing common training standards. It was now proposed to go further and strengthen these newly developed practices.

The European Parliament advocated a considerable strengthening of the Community's competences in the social sphere, by, among other things, deleting the restriction of scope of Article 100A and by enlarging the scope of Article 118A beyond health and safety to include living conditions, social protection and training, whilst providing further in Article 118 that common policies and cooperation should extend to labour law and working conditions, social security, collective bargaining and the right of association. It called for Article 118B to provide for a legal framework for collective conventions at Community level between management and labour. This view obtained qualified support from a majority of Member States. Proposals were tabled in the IGCs by Belgium (25 January), supporting the enlargement of the scope of Community competence to social security and employment matters, the application of QMV throughout the social field for adopting minimum standards and for strengthening the social dialogue by providing for legislative follow-up to agreements; Italy (19 February) for a wider definition of competences and QMV throughout; France (25 March) for enlarging competence to include working conditions and bargaining and for extending QMV to all except social protection and social security. Denmark and the Netherlands had made similar proposals in their memoranda before the IGCs started. The UK, however, remained opposed entirely to any change to the social chapter. Spain (28 February) proposed extending competences to include social security of migrant workers, employment, right of association and collective bargaining, working conditions and working time, but QMV would apply only within the framework of unanimously agreed "stages" and "action programmes", and not at all as regards working conditions and working time: Spain clearly wished to retain its competitive edge in some of these matters — precisely the reason for the opposite view taken by some northern European countries.

In an effort of compromise, the German delegation proposed (20 February) to introduce for the social field "reinforced QMV" such that a text would be adopted only if it achieved a minimum of 66 (instead of 54) favourable votes in Council out of a possible 76. This was supported by Portugal (10 April) but gave rise to misgivings as creating a dangerous precedent.

The Commission put forward a proposal for a revised social policy chapter of the EEC treaty which would enlarge the scope of Community action notably to include living and working conditions, basic rights of workers, information, consultation and participation of workers and the functioning of the Labour market. In these areas the EC could "complement and support the action of the Member States". This would be done through laying down minimum standards. QMV would apply except for harmonization of social security systems, right to strike or employment of third country nationals. However, before proposing legislation, the two sides of industry would always be given a chance of negotiating a "framework agreement" applying "throughout a trade or industry at European level". Only if no such agreement could be reached within a reasonable time, or if an agreement was reached but management and labour requested the Commission to make its application mandatory, would the Community act by legislation.

Negotiations proceeded with great difficulty. Eventually, a text emerged taking up the Commission proposal (and as regards agreements between the social partners, taking up a proposal agreed between ETUC and UNICE) but making it less effective (mainly by restricting QMV). The UK, however, remained adamant that it would accept no change to the social chapter of the treaty. Yet it was also clear that the absence of any strengthening of social provisions was equally unacceptable to several other Member States. The result in Maastricht was the social protocol pulled out of a hat by President Delors to avoid deadlock, whereby 11 Member States can use the EC structure (with 44 votes instead of 54 votes necessary for a qualified majority) to adopt measures that will not apply to the UK. This unprecedented solution showed the determination of the 11 not to be blocked by the one. However, the continued existence of the social chapter of the treaty, will, in many cases, allow action at the level of the 12 provided the UK is willing. Where it is not, the 11 can proceed without the UK.

6. Other extensions of Community competence and the principle of subsidiarity

The PU IGC considered a whole range of proposals to add further titles to the EEC Treaty extending the Community's competence to new areas, or further extending the scope of existing competences. Such an operation had taken place during the 1985 IGC, leading to new provisions in the EEC Treaty on social policy, cohesion, research and environmental policy.

In many cases, Community action in the fields concerned was already under way using Article 235 or even Article 100A as a legal basis. The advantage of writing a specific title or chapter in the Treaty was the greater legitimacy that this provided for Community action. Action based on Article 235 was, by definition, a fallback solution, was linked to the functioning of the common market, and was only possible by unanimity. Writing specific provisions into the Treaty permitted a more detailed specification of objectives and could, within these limits, allow for QMV.

The IGC received proposals for new provisions on **trans-European networks** (proposals from Spain and Germany); **transport safety** (Germany, Luxembourg); **public health** (Portugal, Ireland, Spain, Italy, the Netherlands, Denmark and Germany); **development policy** (the Netherlands and Denmark); **education** (Greece, Italy, Spain, Ireland, Germany and Denmark); **culture** (France, Spain, the Netherlands, Denmark and Germany); **energy** (Belgium, Denmark and Ireland); **consumer protection** (Spain and Denmark); **industrial policy** (Belgium); **tourism** (Greece and Italy); **civil protection** (Italy); **youth** (Spain and Italy); and **animal protection** (Germany). Proposals were also put forward to strengthen existing Community provisions concerning **economic and social cohesion** (Ireland, Spain and Greece); **environmental policy** (the UK, the Netherlands, Germany, Greece and Denmark); **research** (Germany, Greece, Belgium, Spain and Denmark); and **social policy** (Denmark, France and Belgium). In most of these areas, the Commission too submitted proposals, often in response to those from the Member States. For its part, the European Parliament had not been particularly pressing as regards extension of Community competence (beyond CFSP and social affairs mentioned above), contenting itself with advocating new provisions on culture, transport and cohesion. However, besides new policy areas, it had called for the incorporation into the treaties of **fundamental rights** and freedoms and for Community accession to the ECHR, as well as the development of common forms of **European citizenship** through "such measures as voting rights for Community citizens in municipal and European elections in their Member State of residence"[15]. This was largely backed by the parliamentary assizes, and the Commission also came up with proposals.

Some of these proposals aroused little controversy. This was the case, for instance, with development policy where there was a long tradition of Community activity. In other areas there was some discussion as to the scope of the new policy. This was the case, for instance, for culture, where Member States were cautious, especially having regard to the national and regional sensitivities in this field. In this area, as for industrial policy (where there was a long history of divergent approaches among Member States), the IGC agreed to incorporate new titles in the Treaty but provided for decision-taking only by unanimity. It also specified that harmonization of national legislation was excluded in these areas, as in the areas of education, vocational training and public health.

Finally, there were some areas which proved controversial or unexpectedly complex due to overlap with other provisions. Thus, for energy, civil protection and tourism, no new titles were added to the EC Treaty, though the three subjects were added to the list of Community activities defined in Article 3 of the Treaty thus facilitating recourse to existing treaty provisions. Declaration No. 1 annexed to the Maastricht Treaty provides for the 1996 IGC to examine whether to draft new titles for these three areas. Consumer protection was also subject to some controversy, having been dropped by the Dutch Presidency in its initial Draft Treaty of September. It was reinstated by the November version. Again, overlap with existing legal bases appears to have been the main difficulty, the Community already being active in this field on the basis of Article 100A.

A key issue was **economic and social cohesion**, where the less prosperous Member States were eager to see a stronger commitment to cohesion to balance the feared effects of EMU. Ireland, Spain and Greece all submitted specific proposals. However, potential financial contributors were quick to point out that this was not necessarily a matter for treaty amendment: the Community already had the necessary instruments, and was likely to re-examine the financial system in the following year. Nevertheless, the less prosperous states insisted on some degree of commitment as part of the overall package, and this was done by reinforcing the provisions of the Single Act and providing for a **cohesion fund** to help finance environmental and transport projects in the least prosperous Member States. A protocol annexed to the treaty committed the Community to reviewing the own resources system in order to make it more sensitive to individual Member States' ability to pay. It was agreed that the Commission would bring forward proposals for a new financial and budgetary package during 1993.

The European Parliament proposals concerning **citizenship** were taken up in the new treaty, but largely made subject to implementing provisions to be adopted by unanimity before 1995. Much therefore remains to be settled, but the inscription of the principle of common citizenship in the treaty was a notable achievement. Although referring to "Union" citizenship, the provisions were incorporated into the EC treaty and will thus be part of Community law. Besides voting rights in local and European elections it provides for consular protection abroad. The Ombudsman and the right to petition the EP (see below) were also mentioned in this context.

---

[15] Paras. 18 & 19 Martin II Resolution op. cit. footnote.

In order to balance the extension of Community competences, or at least to show that it did not imply centralization of all powers in these areas in the Community institutions, it was agreed to enshrine the **principle of subsidiarity** in the Treaty. Taking up the European Parliament's suggestion, this was done by adding a new article (3B), as desired by Germany, the Netherlands and the UK. (Other Member States would have preferred it to be in the preamble of the Treaty.) The principle is, however, defined with a slightly different wording from that proposed by Parliament, referring to Community action "only if and in so far as" the objectives can be better achieved by the Community, whereas Parliament's definition referred to Community action "wherever" objectives can be undertaken more efficiently by the Community[16]. Furthermore, the principle of **proportionality** was added to this article, specifying that action "shall not go beyond what is necessary to achieve the objectives of the Treaty". Whether this difference in wording will have any practical effect will depend on how far the Court of Justice is willing to get involved in what is, essentially, a political judgement to be made on a case-by-case basis.

As we shall see the issue became a crucial one during the ratification of the new treaty, and the Community institutions adopted procedures to encourage themselves to take greater account of subsidiarity. However, Member States continued throughout to have radically different views as to the implications of the principle.

7.   Extension of qualified majority voting (QMV)

The EEC Treaty originally laid down that decision-taking in the Council required unanimity in certain areas, qualified majority voting (QMV) in others and, for a small area (notably procedural points) simple majority voting.

In practice, in the years following the "Luxembourg compromise", very little QMV took place in Council. This was partly due to a reluctance to force a new crisis with France, but was reinforced in 1973 by the accession to the Community of new Member States who essentially shared the French view on these matters. Together, France, the UK and Denmark constituted a sufficiently large minority to prevent decisions even by QMV: in other words, if a matter were put to the vote against the wishes of any Member State, it would not get through, as these countries would not vote for a proposal in such circumstances. It therefore became habitual to negotiate on all texts, virtually line by line, until all Member States agreed before putting the matter to a vote in Council.

By the 1980s, this working method was coming under increasing strain. A number of negative consequences were becoming increasingly apparent. These were notably:

- the inefficiency of such a decision-taking procedure (it took, for instance, 17 years to agree on a directive on the mutual recognition of architects' qualifications);
- the fact that virtually any Community policy or action could only be the lowest common denominator acceptable to all Member States;
- the resulting reduced significance of the Commission's right of initiative, and the role of the European Parliament;
- bureaucratization of the whole Community system, since such detailed and time-consuming negotiations could only be carried out by national civil servants.

---

[16] In the 1984 Draft Treaty, Parliament had used the words "only if". The UK argued in the IGC for "shall not go beyond the minimum necessary". The "Assizes" backed "to the extent that".

Above all, however, it became apparent that unanimity when agreeing on *new* Community policies was one thing, but unanimity for the management or revision of *existing* policies was another. In these cases, the Community as a whole had a vital interest in ensuring that it could take rapid decisions, and the blocking power given to individual Member States was a threat to the continued existence of Community policies. It was clear that national ministers were quite capable of deeming almost anything to be an important national interest when the status quo was to the advantage of their state. Reforms in the CAP, for instance, were all too easy to block by any Member State gaining from particular aspects, even when this was at huge expense to the Community as a whole. This applied to varying degrees to all Community policies and to all Member States. The right of veto proved to be the dictatorship of the minority.

The first major crack in the practice of unanimity came in 1982, when the UK attempted to block the annual package of farm prices (to the details of which it had already agreed) in order to extract concessions in separate negotiations on the Community's budget. This was perceived by other Member States to be almost a form of blackmail: the Community *had* to decide urgently on the agricultural prices for that year, and the UK was not objecting to the contents of the package but was merely using its supposed right of veto to extract concessions on another matter. This attitude provoked a sufficient number of Member States — including France — to take part in a vote to put the UK in a minority.

A shift in the attitude of some Member States gradually took place, and by 1985 they were ready to change both their practice and the treaties. In the SEA, they increased by 10 the number of articles which required QMV. This increase was linked to certain agreed objectives, such as most of the legislative harmonizations necessary for completing the internal market by 1992, and for decisions that follow up unanimously agreed framework decisions (e.g. for individual research programmes following the adoption of the multi-annual framework for research and for regional fund decisions following the adoption of the overall structural fund regulation).

This change in the treaties did not in itself effect the Luxembourg compromise, as the compromise was a political statement with no legal basis, let alone treaty basis. Indeed, Thatcher declared to the House of Commons that it remained in place. However, such a change to the treaties, duly ratified by all national parliaments, changed the constitutional framework within which the decisions concerned would be taken and signified at least a willingness to take votes more frequently. There would, after all, be little point in modifying the treaties if this were not the case.

Council followed up this treaty change with an amendment to its internal rules of procedure. After a year of negotiations, it agreed to change its rules to oblige the President-in-office to move to a vote upon the request of the Commission or the representative of any Member State, provided that the request is supported by a simple majority of Member States.

The context was also changed by the accession of Spain and Portugal, which meant that it was no longer clear that states seeking to invoke the Luxembourg compromise would have sufficient support in Council to constitute a blocking minority.

The upshot of all these developments was that, for the areas now subject to QMV, there has been a reluctance by Member States to try to block majority votes. Interestingly, there have been cases in which Member States in the minority have challenged a vote in the Court of Justice on the grounds of an incorrect legal base (arguing that an article requiring unanimity should have been used) rather than invoke the Luxembourg compromise during the vote.

These changes resulted in considerable improvement in Council's decision- taking in the areas to which majority voting applied. Important votes were taken on subjects as varied as emission standards for car pollution, a ban on hormones in meat and the permitted radioactivity levels in foodstuffs. Even where no votes were taken, governments tended to reach consensus more quickly in areas where, if they stuck to a rigid position, they might be outvoted.

By contrast, those areas in which the treaty continued to require unanimity remained subject to extremely lengthy negotiations and even blocking by individual Member States. It also meant that some essential Community policies continued to be subject to the rule of the lowest common denominator, not least in the fields of environmental protection, many aspects of social policy, harmonisation of indirect taxation (allowing "tax haven" countries to dictate policy to the rest), the framework programme for research, monetary integration, most aspects of foreign aid, etc.

The European Parliament therefore proposed to generalize QMV for all matters other than constitutional (e.g. treaty amendments, accession of new Member States). The Commission supported Parliament's line with a slight nuance, stating in its Opinion that QMV "should apply to all areas of Community competence except constitutional questions, and with possible restrictions in the areas of taxation, social security and the status of non-Community nationals".

In the IGC most Member States agreed with this approach, but with a wide definition of what were "constitutional matters" and, in almost every case, a list of further exceptions. By the end of May the Presidency had established that constitutional matters remaining subject to unanimity would include Treaty Articles 138(3), 149(1), 157(1), 165(4), 166(3), 168A(2 & 3), 188(2 & 3), 194–196(2), 201–206(4), 217–223(2 & 3), 235, 236, 237 & 238. Concerning the exceptions in "non-constitutional" areas, Belgium wished exceptions for Articles 93, 100 & 159, Germany for Articles. 57(2), 93, 99, 100, 149, 147(1) and 168(3), Greece for Articles 57, 75(3), 84(2), 93(2), 99, 158, 159 and 209; Luxembourg for several matters, notably Article 99; the Netherlands for Articles 93(2) and 159 and, as regards the fixing of general principles only, Articles 99, 121, 57(2) and 235. Italy listed no exceptions. The UK, at the opposite extreme, wanted no extension at all in QMV.

The Luxembourg Presidency considered that this matter would be one of the last to be settled in the IGC and left it largely up to the Dutch Presidency. The issue inevitably arose, however, in the context of discussions relating to each policy area where modifications to Community competences were proposed, or where changes in the European Parliament's powers were being considered.

The final result was not very substantial, as a result of the opposition of individual States to particular changes or the UK to any change. In the new Treaty, QMV is extended to environment policy (except fiscal, land-use, water and energy aspects), some aspects of social policy under the protocol applicable to 11 Member States, and to some of the new policy areas added to the EC Treaty (incentive measures in the field of education and vocational training; health; trans-European networks; development policy; consumer protection, the approval of regulations governing the ombudsman and various EMU measures). A switch to QMV is scheduled for 1 January 1996 for determining which third country nationals require visas. Council will be able to decide unanimously on switching to QMV for the remaining areas of environmental policy, and for measures under CFSP or JHA.

A new category of two-thirds majority of the weighted votes in Council has also slipped into the Treaty. This is provided for in relation to EMU if not all Member States join phase III, which, at least initially, is highly likely. Rather than calculate various possible permutations for different scenarios, it was agreed that a two-thirds majority — less than the current QMV which is about 71 per cent of the votes — should apply. Similarly, a two-thirds majority is provided for under the EMU provisions (Article 104C) for voting among other Member States on recommendations and sanctions against a Member State failing to take action on excessive deficits (on which the Member State in question does not vote). A two-thirds majority is provided for the implementation of JHA conventions.

Finally, the Social Protocol provision for a qualified majority consisting of 44 out of 66 votes (without the UK) also just happens to be a two-thirds majority.

8.   The legislative powers of the European Parliament

The IGC faced a situation in which a majority (Belgium, Netherlands, Germany, Italy, Greece, Spain and, to a certain extent, France) accepted, in principle, the European Parliament's request for co-decision powers with Council on the adoption of Community legislation, whereas two (the UK and Denmark) were strongly against and two (Portugal and Ireland) were far from enthusiastic.

As we have seen, Parliament proposed a procedure whereby if, after two readings, Parliament and Council still diverged, a conciliation committee (12 Ministers and 12 MEPs) would be convened to negotiate a compromise. The compromise would have to be approved by both institutions. Texts would then be signed into law by the President of Parliament and the President of Council jointly. The German government tabled a proposal that was virtually identical. The Italian government proposed one that was similar and the German and Italian Foreign Ministers issued a joint public statement emphasizing the importance they attached to increasing Parliament's powers. The Commission, however, which had initially been against giving co-decision powers to the European Parliament (in its opinion on the convening of the IGCs) came up with a proposal superficially similar to that of Parliament, but differing in a number of details, notably in maintaining the Commission's discretion in whether or not to accept Parliament's amendments, whatever the majority by which they are adopted. The parliamentary amendments the Commission rejects can only be adopted by unanimity in Council, as is the case with Member States' amendments. The Commission argued that this was fundamental to the equilibrium of the Community and was supported by Belgium, Germany, Ireland, Portugal and the UK — an unusual coalition!

The Luxembourg Presidency non-paper contained a proposal for a "co-decision procedure" that would apply only to a few items of Community legislation, (environment, research, development cooperation and economic and social cohesion). Furthermore, it would be used only to adopt a new category of Community "laws" which would, in these fields, lay down the framework for subsequent Community action that would take the traditional form of regulations or directives adopted pursuant to existing procedures.

This, of course, was a long way from satisfying the European Parliament, whose members were quick to point out that this would amount to Parliament dealing, on average, with about one co-decision procedure each year. Parliament was also critical of the precise procedure put forward because it provided that if the conciliation procedure failed to find an agreement between Council and Parliament, Council could then adopt its own text — choosing if it wants some of the amendments proposed by Parliament — and this text would become law unless Parliament rejected it within two months by a majority of its members.

Parliament felt that this weighted the procedure in favour of Council. Council would not be obliged to negotiate in good faith in the conciliation committee, as it could simply wait for the deadline, adopt its own text and challenge Parliament to reject it. Parliament would be unlikely to make frequent use of its right to reject, not simply because this requires a majority of members to do so, but because it would leave Parliament with a perceived negative role, being blamed for blocking Community action.

The Dutch Presidency took a different approach. Instead of an important step forward in Parliament's powers in a highly limited number of areas, it proposed a limited extension of Parliament's powers that would apply to a wider area. The Dutch proposed to take the existing cooperation procedure, to use it in almost all cases in which Council adopted legislation by a qualified majority vote and strengthen it by giving Parliament the right to reject the final outcome of Council's second reading.

A first draft of the Dutch text (circulated informally for consultation in September but never formally tabled in the IGC) had envisaged a second modification to the cooperation procedure such that when the Council considered the Commission's revised proposal in second reading, it would be deemed to have *approved* it if it failed, by the three-month deadline, either to amend it (by qualified majority) or to change it (by unanimity). (At present, if Council fails to do either by the deadline, the text falls.) It was soon clear that this second modification stood no chance of being accepted by the IGCs — it would, after all, mean that the Commission's reviewed proposal, taking up Parliament's amendments, could become law if only one Member State agreed with it and was willing to prevent a decision in Council before the deadline.

Thus, the text eventually tabled by the Dutch Presidency envisaged simply giving Parliament a right of rejection or veto of Council's decisions at the end of the cooperation procedure. Whilst this would undoubtedly reinforce Parliament's bargaining position in the procedure, it would place Parliament under the same constraints regarding the rejection of texts as were described above in relation to the Luxembourg proposal, and without any provision for a conciliation procedure. On the other hand, the proposal applied to virtually all Community legislation and not to a small category only (though the Luxembourg proposal reappeared too in this version of the Dutch text, for the four areas that the Luxembourgers had envisaged).

As we saw above, the whole of the Dutch draft treaty was withdrawn after two weeks. In October and early November, the Dutch proceeded to produce new texts, based largely on the old Luxembourg text, for each and every subject that came up for discussion in the IGCs, leaving the issue of how the various elements would be put together to a later stage. Concerning the powers of the European Parliament, they produced a new text which took the old Luxembourg text as its basis, but which applied the co-decision procedure more widely, to all the areas that had since the SEA been subject to the cooperation procedure, multi-annual programmes for the environment, the framework programme for research, and indicative programmes for trans-European infrastructures.

Discussions in the IGC then revealed opposition by different Member States to different items on this list — and by the UK to all of them. Spain and Portugal opposed co-decision for the research framework programme and for the environment; Luxembourg for Articles 100a and 100b; France and Spain regarding the objectives of the structural funds; France as regards development cooperation programmes; and even the Commission expressed reservations with regard to the application of the co-decision procedure to Articles 100a and 100b (internal market harmonizations) arguing that these articles were sometimes used for highly technical matters.

This list of objections was, however, gradually whittled away, notably at the Noordwijk Conclave of 13 November. The Commission, in particular, having been strongly criticized by MEPs, withdrew its opposition to the use of co-decision for Articles 100a and 100b, without which the scope of the procedure would have been minimal. In the end, some 15 items were accepted for co-decision — a number higher than those previously falling under the cooperation procedure (see table p. 92).

The IGC also returned to Parliament's objections to the provisions allowing Council to act unilaterally in the event of conciliation failing. Italy, Spain, Greece, Germany, Belgium and the Commission all supported Parliament's view that the negotiation of an agreement in conciliation should be the *only* way forward when positions diverge, but this view did not reach consensus. Council's right to act unilaterally, provided Parliament does not subsequently reject the text outright, was preserved. As to the Commission's right to vet Parliament's amendments (those that it rejects would need unanimity to be accepted in Council), this too was maintained, except in the context of the conciliation committee where Council's delegation can accept Parliament's amendments by QMV, irrespective of the position of the Commission.

Interestingly, part of the compromise among the governments was to avoid calling the new provisions the "co-decision procedure". The UK government, which had been vocal in its opposition to co-decision, hoped to camouflage its concession by avoiding the term. The treaty therefore refers only to "the procedure laid down in Article 189B", though the UK government tried using the term "negative assent procedure" [sic] when describing it to the UK parliament! Similarly, the term "cooperation" procedure is deleted in the treaty, with reference now to the "189C" procedure. This will now apply to most of the areas not covered by co-decision where Council acts by qualified majority. The main exceptions are agriculture and trade, where Parliament, as before, will simply be consulted.

Finally, the IGC examined Parliament's request to extend the **assent procedure** (single reading, no amendments, Parliament's approval necessary) to further categories of inter-national agreements than at present, to treaty revisions and to constitutional matters where Council acts by unanimity. The Dutch Presidency proposed in October that it should be extended to cover measures concerning the right of residence of Union citizens (this was initially opposed by Luxembourg and the UK); rules for the structural funds and the creation of new funds (opposed by the UK and the Commission); the uniform electoral system; and further categories of international agreements. Other delegations proposed to add the definition of own resources (supported by Italy, Spain, Greece and Germany), Article 235 and treaty revisions (supported by Italy, Spain, Greece, Germany, Belgium, the Netherlands and the Commission), and the introduction of the final phase of EMU (supported by Italy, Greece and Belgium). Only the proposals of the Dutch Presidency were incorporated into the final package, the other four falling. However, two areas from EMU were added at the end: amendments to the Protocol of the Central Bank and conferral of special tasks on the Central Bank.

The overall outcome is a substantial step forward for the European Parliament's powers in the Community's legislative procedures. However, it is an uneven one, leaving a confusing variety of procedures (assent, co-decision, cooperation, consultation) mostly complicated and with variants (QVM, unanimity). It is certainly not easy for MEPs to explain their powers to the public!

9.   The Parliament and the Commission

While Parliament has always enjoyed the right to dismiss the Commission by a vote of censure obtaining a two-thirds majority, the treaties did not involve it in the appointment of the Commission. As we have seen, Parliament proposed to the IGC that the term of office of the Commission should be linked to that of Parliament and that, following each European parliamentary election, the President of the Commission should be elected by Parliament on a proposal of the European Council. Once he/she together with the Council had agreed on the rest of the College of Commissioners, they should be subjected to a collective vote of confidence by Parliament before taking office (as Parliament had done without treaty provision since 1980).

Parliament received early support from Germany which tabled a similar proposal (but proposing that the Commission President be reconfirmed after 2½ years), and the formali-zation of the vote of confidence in the treaties appears to have met with early acceptance in the IGC despite initial Danish and UK resistance. Even Member States not enthusiastic about increasing Parliament's powers were prepared to accept this change, which could be presented as being little more than entrenching existing practice.

The proposal that Parliament should also elect the President of the Commission on a proposal of the European Council was, however, more problematic. Several Member States (the UK, Ireland, Portugal, Denmark and the Netherlands), considered that this "dual investiture" of both the President and the College was too much. The Commission itself, supported by Germany, Belgium, Italy and Spain, was prepared to accept the proposal. As to the suggestion that the term of office of the Commission should be changed from four to five years to coincide with that of Parliament, this met initially with support only from Germany, Italy and Spain, and hostility from Ireland, France, Greece, Portugal and the UK. Nevertheless, Parliament continued to press the point, which featured prominently in the discussions held in the interinstitutional conference and in the discussions held by Parliament's delegation touring the national capitals to meet the various heads of government. The point was finally included in the text at Maastricht itself, not having achieved even majority support at the Noordwijk meeting of the foreign ministers the previous month. This was, perhaps, one of the clearest examples of Parliament's involvement in the IGC producing a specific result.

The new Treaty thus takes up Parliament's proposal almost entirely. The term of office of the Commission is linked to that of Parliament and the Commission as a whole can only take office following a vote of confidence from the European Parliament. Instead of electing the President of the Commission on a proposal of the European Council, Parliament will only be "consulted". But "consultation" in such circumstances — a public vote on an individual politician by an elected Parliament — is surely tantamount to an election or confirmation, as it is inconceivable that any politician would wish to proceed should Parliament reject his or her candidacy.

A more serious departure from Parliament's original proposal is that the President-designate is not given a stronger role in the choice of Commissioners. Member States will be obliged to *consult* the President of the Commission, but not, as Parliament proposed, to choose the rest of the Commission in *agreement* with the President. Such a change would have strengthened the collegiate nature of the Commission and its cohesion as a team.

This new procedure will begin after the 1994 European elections. The autumn months will be used to go through the procedures so that the new Commission takes office in January 1995 for a five-year period. (This means that the Commission appointed in January 1993 will serve only a two-year term of office.) Any Commission censured by the European Parliament would be replaced by a Commission which would only serve out the term of office of the previous Commission.

The IGC declined to take up a Dutch proposal to give Parliament the right to dismiss individual Commissioners — a right which Parliament had not requested, supporting the doctrine of collective responsibility. The IGC did agree provisionally (Noordwijk Conclave) to reduce the number of Commissioners to one per Member State and to allow the Commission, with the approval of Council acting by QMV, to appoint up to five "junior Commissioners", but this did not survive the Maastricht Summit which instead agreed to review the issue in the course of 1992.

10. Other powers of the Parliament

As well as an increase in its legislative powers and its involvement in the appointment of the Commission, Parliament had asked for a number of its powers of scrutiny and control to be reinforced, and to be given a limited "right of initiative" (i.e. the right to submit legislative proposals to Council).

On this last point Parliament had asked "to be given the right to initiate legislative proposals in cases where the Commission fails to respond within a specified deadline to a specific request adopted by the majority of Members of Parliament"[17], a request which received the support of the parliamentary assizes in Rome. Such a formula would have preserved the Commission's right, in normal circumstances, to initiate legislation, but would have provided a safeguard should it refuse to do so. Within the IGC, the Commission strongly opposed this watering-down of its monopoly on the right of initiative. It was already facing an erosion of this monopoly in the CFSP and JHA pillars as well as in the field of EMU, and did not wish this to be added to in the traditional Community fields. Although Parliament's proposal met with some sympathy, the Commission was able to persuade other Member States to oppose it. The resultant compromise was to add a new Article 138B to the EEC Treaty allowing Parliament to "request the Commission to submit any appropriate proposal" but without providing Parliament with a right to act itself should the Commission fail to respond. Presumably, Parliament would have to have recourse to its right of censure should it be sufficiently dissatisfied with the Commission's response.

Concerning the reinforcement of scrutiny and control powers, Parliament had asked in particular for a treaty right "to establish committees of inquiry to investigate alleged contraventions of Community law or instances of maladministration with respect to Community responsibilities"[18]; for its rights of information in the budgetary control procedure to be enhanced; for the observations it makes in the discharge decisions to be binding; the right to request the Court of Auditors to carry out investigations and to submit reports; for the right to take the other institutions to Court for annulment and for the right of Community citizens to petition the European Parliament to be enshrined in the treaties. Most of these requests related to the entrenchment in the treaties of existing practice or of provisions laid down in secondary legislation. Most of them were backed by the parliamentary assizes in Rome.

Agreement was reached quickly on all these points. Member States opposed to increasing Parliament's legislative powers were quick to endorse this increase in its scrutiny powers in order to divert pressure in this direction. The IGC also reached rapid agreement on the principle of Parliament electing a Community ombudsman, something which Parliament had not asked for. The first Luxembourg non-paper incorporated provisions on these points that remained virtually unchanged throughout the IGCs. Only on the number of MEPs needed to request a committee of inquiry (changed from one-half to one-quarter of Parliament, to bring it into line with Parliament's current rules) and the reporting requirements of the ombudsmen were there any further changes. On the right to bring cases for annulment, however, Parliament was only given the right to do so to protect its own prerogatives, not a general right.

11. Other institutional changes

A number of other proposals to reform the institutions were also considered. The IGC provided for the *Court of Justice* to impose "a lump sum or penalty payment" on Member States that have not complied with its judgements. This was one of the few European Parliament proposals that obtained wholehearted backing from the UK (at least, until the controversy over the Winchester by-pass arose). The Commission had backed the proposal, but only half-heartedly, submitting only a memorandum and not a specific

---

17   Martin II Resolution, para. 34.
18   Martin II Resolution, para. 40.

proposal to the IGCs. The new treaty also allows further competences to be transferred from the Court of Justice to the Court of First Instance, thus potentially increasing the efficiency of the Community's judicial system.

The IGC took up Parliament's proposal[19] to establish a *consultative committee of regional and local authorities* whose status would be comparable to the Economic and Social Committee. Parliament's proposal had received strong backing from those Member States with strong regional or federal structures, notably Belgium and Germany, but met with some resistance from Spain, France and the UK. Nevertheless, as a consultative committee with members nominated by national governments, it proved acceptable to the IGC.

Also of interest to regions is a change in the definition of the *composition of the Council* agreed at Maastricht. In response to concerns expressed by the Belgian and German governments, it is no longer necessary for Member States to be represented by a minister from the national government: representatives from regional governments may attend instead, provided they have the title of minister (in practice, only in Germany or Belgium) and provided they are authorized to commit the national government.

The *Economic and Social Committee* had been campaigning for a enhanced status. It received limited support from the European Parliament and from most of its own members, notably from trade unions and employers' organizations, who argued vis-à-vis their respective governments in favour of these changes. In the end, the Maastricht Treaty allows the Economic and Social Committee to adopt its own Rules of Procedure without reference to Council, to meet on its own initiative and to issue opinions on its own initiative. It also increased the minimum time limit for ESC opinions from 10 days to a month.

Some attempts were made to examine the *hierarchy of Community legislative acts*. Unlike most national contexts, there is no separation in the Community between basic legislation and implementing provisions. Frequently, technical measures that, in most national contexts, would be left to the executive have to go through two readings each in Parliament and Council. There is a degree of delegation of implementing measures to the Commission, but subject to scrutiny by a myriad of committees of national civil servants (hence the term "comitology" to describe the situation), but the system has been criticized strongly. Parliament put forward proposals for a greater degree of delegation of powers to the Commission, subject to a right of retrieval for Council and Parliament. The Commission brought forward a far more comprehensive proposal for a complete revision of the hierarchy of Community acts, with a large degree of delegation but only limited possibilities of retrieval. The complex interrelation of the issues proved too much for the IGC to handle in the time available, and the issue has been left over to the 1996 IGC.

Proposals were also brought forward, originating with some members of the French National Assembly, for a "*congress*" of national parliamentarians, later modified to being a conference of national parliamentarians and MEPs. The proposal gained support from the UK, Portugal, Spain and Greece. It was strongly opposed by the European Parliament, which considered that the creation of an additional body, alongside the Council (representing national governments) and the Parliament (representing the electorate) was superfluous and would render the decision-making procedures even more complex. The parliamentary assizes in Rome did not take up the French proposal and it ran out of steam in the IGCs, though the French government persisted until the very end. Finally, it was agreed on the basis of a UK proposal, to add to the Maastricht Treaty a simple Declaration encouraging national parliaments and the European Parliament to cooperate with each

---

[19] Martin II, para. 22.

other and another Declaration inviting them to meet as a conference of parliaments of the European Community on appropriate occasions to discuss the main features of European Union.

12. Overall results

Douglas Hurd, the UK Foreign Secretary, in presenting the Maastricht Treaty to the House of Commons[20], stated that "Maastricht was an important step away from an increasingly centralized — and potentially arthritic — Community". He and the Prime Minister drew attention to the new "pillars" that were not incorporated into the Community treaties and claimed that Europe had turned its back on the federal model.

Such an interpretation stretches the bounds of credibility. The sphere of competence of the European Community as such was extended by the Treaty of Maastricht, and within those competences an extended use of qualified majority voting has been provided for. The powers of the supranational Parliament have been enhanced. The Commission, with its extended term of office and with its greater dependence on the Parliament for its appointment, has become more independent from national governments. Even the CFSP and JHA "pillars", although still separate from the more federal Community, have been drawn closer to it than before. They will be managed through the Community institutions, financed partially under its budget, and be subject to the same revision clauses. To the extent that there is conflict or overlap in their competences, Community provisions prevail, and the JHA "pillar" contains a clause allowing further transfers of competence to the EC. In 1996, a new IGC is to examine whether to go further down this road.

Yet those who fear a "centralized super-state" are equally off the mark. The Union/Community still requires a basic consensus of its component states to function. This is not so much because Member States can still exercise individual responsibility for coercive force, but because even the basic operation of the EC requires consensus, for instance, to appoint a new Commission, to modify the Community's budgetary resources, to fix the seat of institutions or to appoint a new judge to the Court. A single state could cause the Community to grind to a halt as regards its very functioning, let alone as regards the several policy areas that still require unanimity.

The Community is still far from even a federal system, let alone a centralized state, in other respects too. Its budget is still scarcely more than 1 per cent of GDP. The "Brussels bureaucracy" is smaller than most local authorities, with fewer than 9,000 civil servants (after taking away linguistic and related staff) serving 350 million inhabitants. The bulk of public policy-making remains at national or sub-national level, including most issues which continue to gain the bulk of public attention, such as health, schooling, law and order, local and regional transport, taxation, housing and social security.

The Treaty of Maastricht can best be seen as another milestone in the long and complex process of incremental integration in Europe. Again, a compromise was reached between the integrationist majority (itself more consciously and more outspokenly federalist in intent than for a long time) and the more reluctant minority. Again, a new round of negotiations will not be long in coming — indeed has been scheduled for three years hence, though could well come about earlier. Again, the compromise reached contains ambiguities and can be presented with different nuances to different audiences or constituencies. Again, it will disappoint many and arouse fears in others. Yet, the Treaty on European Union is potentially the most significant step forward since the treaties of

---

[20] Report of the debate in the *Independent*, 22 May, 1992.

Rome. In terms of sheer volume, it extends or amends more than 150 articles of the original treaties and in addition contains some 35 articles relating to areas not covered by them. In terms of its vocabulary it breaks new ground with concepts of Union citizenship, and a common foreign and security policy. In terms of its objectives, it contains an element of extraordinary importance for integration, namely the single currency. In terms of the powers of the European Parliament, it makes a significant breakthrough. In terms of the determination of the majority, it demonstrates their will to press ahead, allowing the minority a limited opt-out of key areas.

The first challenges and battles over the significance of the Treaty began within weeks of its signature, in the ratification procedures and in the first follow-up measures. These we shall examine in the next two chapters.

V

RATIFICATION OF THE MAASTRICHT TREATY

1. From initial complacency to the Danish shock

When the signing ceremony of the Treaty took place in Maastricht on 7 February 1992, few anticipated the problems that lay ahead with its ratification. The countries that were traditionally reticent about the integration process seemed content with the compromise. Criticisms emanated mainly from those who felt it was too timid a document, lamenting in particular the "pillar" structure, the lack of explicit commitment to the federal objective and the insufficient increase in the powers of the European Parliament. These criticisms came in particular from the Benelux countries, Germany, Spain and Italy. The Italian and Belgian parliaments stated that they would not ratify the Treaty if the European Parliament did not accept it.

There was indeed a possibility that the European Parliament would reject the Treaty. Its Committee on institutional affairs produced a report[21] listing a number of "shortcomings" of the Treaty, notably its pillar structure, the retention of Council unanimity in a large number of areas (including two where codecision would apply), the imbalance towards Council in the codecision procedure, the limited field of application of the latter and the variety of complex legislative procedure making public understanding of the Community system even more difficult. The report also highlighted some 16 "positive elements", which had originally been proposed by Parliament itself, and two other elements which had not. Following its committee, Parliament itself came out by 235 votes to 64 on 14 April 1992 in favour of ratification, which it recommended to the Member States, whilst resolving, as it had done six years earlier concerning the SEA, to "exploit to the very limit the possibilities offered by the Treaty", and also to "pursue its endeavours to obtain a democratic and effective European Union of federal type".

Potential federalist opposition to the Maastricht compromise thus failed to materialize, and until the Danish referendum of June 1992 there was little sign of the anti-European camp gaining in support. In the UK, opponents of Maastricht in both main parties kept a low profile in the run-up to the April general election, and even after the election the second reading of the Maastricht bill in the House of Commons obtained a comfortable majority of 244. In Ireland, where a referendum was required, early polls showed a consistent lead in favour of the Treaty. In Denmark, the Treaty sailed through the *Folketing* which approved it on 12 May by a majority of 130 to 25 with 20 abstentions.

This contrasted with the situation in 1986 when the Single European Act was ratified. At that time the *Folketing* had initially rejected the SEA, but allowed the government to appeal to the people in a consultative referendum. This gave a majority in favour of ratification and the *Folketing* duly changed its mind. This time, with such a large majority

---

[21] Martin Report IV on the results of the intergovernmental conferences A3–123/92.

supporting the Treaty in the *Folketing*, and with both the Conservative-Liberal coalition government and the main Social Democrat opposition party supporting ratification, few expected the Danish to reject the Treaty. Indeed, early opinion polls showing a potential no vote quickly gave way to polls showing a majority in favour.

Nonetheless, the Danish people rejected the Treaty on 2 June by 50.7 per cent to 49.3 per cent. The recent evolution of Danish political and parliamentary views in favour of Europe had not been matched by a similar evolution among the wider public. On the contrary, traditional Danish reticence about European unification was found to be as strong as ever when faced with such concepts as European citizenship and the prospect of a future common defence.

In many ways, this was not surprising. Faced with a divided public opinion ever since Danish accession to the EC, successive governments had presented steps forward in Europe in minimalist terms, downplaying losses of sovereignty and aspirations for European Union, emphasizing an intergovernmentalist view of the European "cooperation" (*"samarbeid"*). The 1986 referendum on the SEA had been won with the government using the argument that it did *not* set up the European Union that others had wanted. A recent policy document of the Social Democrats was entitled "Yes to the EC, no to the European Union". It was inevitable that a treaty with European Union in its title and clearly going a number of steps down the integrationist road would not be acceptable without considerable explanation and a shift in public opinion.

The yes campaign was complacent, particularly among the key social-democratic voters, with the party at that time preoccupied with the preparations of a difficult congress following a bruising leadership struggle. At the same time, there was the same anti-establishment mood which seemed to be sweeping other countries at this time (notable in the Belgian and Italian elections and in the Ross Perot phenomenon in the USA), a protest vote against a government that had been in office for a decade, and a reaction against the recently agreed CAP reforms by Danish farmers, traditional supporters of the EC.

The results sent shock-waves throughout the Community. In the UK, consideration of the Maastricht bill in the Commons was suspended. In France, Mitterrand announced a referendum on ratification. The Foreign Ministers of the Member States organized a hasty meeting on the 4 June in Oslo, on the fringe of a NATO meeting that most of them were attending. They all agreed that the ratification procedures should be continued in the remaining Member States and excluded any renegotiation of the Treaty.

This decision was crucial. Any attempt to renegotiate the Treaty at that stage would have been an open invitation to opponents of particular aspects of the Treaty in all Member States to seek renegotiation of the points they disliked. Furthermore, Denmark had to be given time to analyze the reasons for the Treaty's rejection and propose a way forward. But above all, it was a signal of the determination of the majority to press ahead, if necessary without Denmark, though it avoided the question of how this could be done legally (it would have required negotiating a new treaty along the lines of Maastricht among those states wishing to proceed in such a way and either seeking a two-tier relation with Denmark or else effectively killing off the old EC). Although the UK let it be known that it was unwilling to proceed without Denmark, the signal from the overwhelming majority of Member States was clear: adjustment, if necessary, but no backtracking from the Maastricht process.

2. Ten ratifications

Although the UK suspended its parliamentary consideration of Maastricht and postponed it until the autumn, all the other Member States continued with their ratification pro-

cedures. The immediate hurdle was the **Irish** referendum on 18 June. Here, opposition
came from largely the same groups who had opposed the SEA, voicing fears for Irish
neutrality and the further insertion of a small peripheral economy into the wider European
one. The Danish result gave them a filip and they also argued against attempts to corner
a fellow small state. But it was the abortion issue which gave greatest cause for alarm
when, following an Irish court ruling prohibiting a juvenile pregnant rape victim from
seeking abortion in the UK, both extreme opponents of abortion (arguing that the EC's
provisions on free circulation and freedom to provide services would ultimately undermine
the ban on abortion in Ireland) and some supporters of a liberal abortion law (arguing that
the protocol in the Maastricht Treaty which explicitly recognized Ireland's right to maintain
its own constitutional position on these questions would introduce the possibility for Irish
governments to derogate from free circulation and freedom to provide services), opposed
ratification of Maastricht. On 1 May, the Irish government obtained a Declaration from all
Member States clarifying that the protocol was not intended to derogate in this way, but
this clearly did not convince everybody. Nonetheless, the referendum result was almost
identical to that in the 1987 referendum on the SEA: 69 per cent in favour.

This result seemed to put ratification back on its tracks. The **Luxembourg** parliament
approved the Treaty by 51 votes to six on 2 July and on 31 July **Greece** approved it by the
largest majority ever obtained for a European treaty in the Greek parliament (286 votes
to eight). Attention now turned to **France**, where Mitterrand had called a referendum, as
we have seen, in response to the Danish result, hoping to show popular support for the
Treaty was as strong in other countries as it was weak in Denmark. He may also have had
domestic policy in mind, on an issue that would divide the opposition parties. Nonetheless,
it was a high risk strategy.

It should not be forgotten that France has always been the most reluctant of the original
six Member States and it frequently held up, or only grudgingly accepted, steps forward in
European integration. The ECSC and EEC treaties were only ratified by small majorities
and the EDC Treaty was rejected, bringing the integration process to a halt for a number
of years. Under de Gaulle, France had provoked the "empty chair" crisis which led to the
so-called Luxembourg compromise. Direct elections to the European Parliament were only
approved through the government of the day making it a confidence motion.

This reticence has been because, internally, France has been divided on Europe, and the
political cleavage has remained remarkably similar over the years with the Communists on
the left and most Gaullists and the populist right (formerly Poujadists, now supporters of
Le Pen) opposing each step in European integration. Together, these elements of French
politics, although divided on other issues, have always had more than 40 per cent of the
vote — a solid base for a "no" vote even in the best of circumstances.

Yet, it was the worst of times to organize a referendum. Europe was facing an economic
downturn, tensions in the EMS and dismal failure in the former Yugoslavia. Racist attacks
in Germany stimulated memories of the past. The CAP reform, though long overdue, was
proving highly unpopular among farmers.

It was also the worst of times domestically. The French Parliament, in Congress in
Versailles, had approved the Maastricht constitutional amendments by an overwhelming
majority — 89 per cent — and the referendum was unnecessary. It was inevitably
portrayed by the opposition as a domestic political manoeuvre, intended to boost the
flagging popularity of the Socialist government and to divide the opposition. Mitterrand
had been in power for over 12 years and the government was at a record low in opinion
polls. Strikes and road blocks during the summer brought the country to a standstill, the
"no" campaign rose to lead for a while in the polls, and turmoil hit the exchange markets,
causing the withdrawal of two currencies from the ERM and jeopardizing EMU.

The anti-Maastricht campaign was fought on a curious mixture of domestic issues combined with European fears that had little to do with Maastricht but more to do with longstanding European problems or issues arising from the SEA and the single market: the reform of the CAP, the "technocratic" nature of the EC, potential influx of immigrants, criminals and drugs in a single market without border controls. Genuine Maastricht issues such as monetary union, the powers of the EP, or even voting rights scarcely featured. Polls showed that 40 per cent of the electors voted according to domestic considerations. The pro-Maastricht campaign thus faced on uphill struggle, unable to set the agenda and, as in Denmark, finding it difficult to explain a complex political compromise, now formulated as an even more complex legal text, to a sceptical public. A televized debate between President Mitterrand and Philippe Seguin, a leading no-campaigner, helped turn the tide, but the yes-campaign ultimately had to rely on very general and non-specific public support for "Europe". In the circumstances, the 51.05 per cent "yes" vote on 20 September was a remarkable success, and can be seen as an acceptance of continued European integration, capable of winning a majority even in the worst possible circumstances, and winning over a proportion of the Gaullists.

Ratification then proceeded rapidly and smoothly in most other countries. In **Italy** the Chamber of Deputies approved the Treaty on 29 October by 403 votes to 46 with 18 abstentions, the Senate having previously approved it on 17 September by 176 votes to 16 and one abstention. **Belgium** completed its parliamentary procedures on 4 November when the Senate approved the Treaty by 115 votes to 26 and one abstention, the Chamber having approved it on the 17 July by 146 votes to 33 and three abstentions. In **Spain**, the *Cortés* first modified the constitution, then approved ratification: the Congress on 29 October by 314 to three with 8 abstentions and the Senate on 25 November by 220 votes to 0 with 3 abstentions. In **Portugal**, the parliament approved the necessary constitutional amendments on 17 November and the Treaty on 10 December by 200 votes to 21. The **Netherlands** completed its procedures on 15 December by a formal vote in the First Chamber, the Second Chamber having approved a text on 13 November by 137 to 13. Thus, in most Member States, ratification was easy and non-controversial: a point easily forgotten when concentrating on the difficulties encountered in some countries.

In **Germany**, procedures were somewhat complicated. After some initial hesitation the government agreed with the SPD that ratification required a constitutional amendment and therefore the approval both of the *Bundestag* and of the *Bundesrat* (each by a 2/3 majority). Through the *Bundesrat*, the governments of the German *Länder* were able to press for the involvement of the Länder in defining Germany's position in those areas of European Union competence that were, domestically, a matter for them. They wanted the constitutional amendment to oblige the federal government in future to consult the *Bundesrat* in the formulation of European policy.

None of this concerned the substance of the Treaty — only its national implications. Nonetheless, it took place against a background of relative public unease about the future loss of the Deutschemark — both a key instrument and a symbol of German economic success. As Germany entered a recession, provoked partly by the effects of German unification, including monetary unification, concern about the economic effects of EMU grew. The Danish referendum result boosted the doubts, and some less than pleasant remarks made about Germany in the French referendum campaign also gave rise to misgivings. Concerns were also expressed that the Treaty did not go far enough as regards political union, notably the powers of the European Parliament. But, despite some sensationalist press articles, parliamentary ratificiation was never really in doubt. It was finally achieved on the 18 December when the *Bundesrat* unanimously approved the treaty, the *Bundestag* having done so on 2 December by 543 votes to 17 with eight abstentions.

The constitutional amendments adopted on this occasion provided for a new Article

23 ("Europe") in the Basic Law, authorizing transfers of sovereignty to the European Community and specifying that Germany supported the creation of a united Europe based on respect for the principles of democracy, rule of law, a social and federal state, the principle of subsidiarity and a protection of fundamental rights comparable to that of the German constitution. It laid down that further transfers of sovereignty would require the approval of the *Bundesrat* as well as the *Bundestag*. It specified that the *Bundesrat* must be consulted in all areas where the interests of the *Länder* are affected, and in those areas which are the exclusive competence of the *Länder* the government could delegate its right to sit in the Council to a representative of the *Länder* appointed by the *Bundesrat* (as allowed in the Maastricht Treaty reformulation of the composition of Council). The constitutional amendment also dealt with voting rights and the participation of the Bundesbank in the European Central Bank. It was also agreed that the government would consult the *Bundestag* when taking the decision on moving to the third phase of EMU, without this amounting to a back-door ratification procedure.

The ratification has been challenged in the German constitutional court. The applicants, which include some Green MEPs and the former *Chef de Cabinet* of Commission Vice-President Bangemann, argue that the Maastricht Treaty is not compatible with the fundamental principles of the Basic Law, despite the constitutional amendment adopted.

3.   Britain delays

Meanwhile, in the UK, the ratification procedure was on a rollercoaster. Ratification as such did not need specific authorization from Parliament, but it did need the prior incorporation into UK law of those parts of the Maastricht Treaty which modified Community provisions laid down in the 1972 European Communities Act. It also needed, under the terms of the 1978 European Elections Act, approval of the increases in the powers of the European Parliament. The government therefore put forward a one-page Bill, the aim which was to incorporate Titles II – IV of Maastricht into the European Communities Act and approve the increase in the powers of the European Parliament. The Maastricht Titles on CFSP and JHA were not mentioned in the Bill.

The Bill was introduced to the House of Commons after the British General Election of April 1992 in which ratification of Maastricht had not featured prominently, being supported by all three main parties, with Labour however criticizing the social opt-out. The Maastricht Bill was approved in second reading on 21 May by 336 to 92: a pro-Maastricht majority of 244. Labour abstained because of the social protocol, but 22 Conservatives and 59 Labour members defied their party line to vote against.

This comfortable majority belied a growing opposition to the Treaty by the "Thatcherite" right-wing of the Conservative party in particular. This came out into the open following the Danish referendum, which caused John Major to suspend the committee stage of the Commons' procedures until the autumn. Over the summer, the rebellion grew further with Thatcher herself, and former party chairmen Tebbit, Baker and Parkinson playing leading roles. In the Labour Party too, traditional anti-marketeers such as Peter Shore and Brian Gould were joined by those critical of the EMU provisions (notably the convergence criteria and the independence of the Central Bank). The Labour revolt faded at the annual party conference in September, the one casualty being the resignation of Brian Gould from the shadow cabinet. The Conference overwhelmingly endorsed Maastricht as "the best agreement that can currently be achieved". The Conservative Party conference, however, was dominated by bitter debates over Maastricht and unusually explicit criticisms of the party leadership.

When the government brought the Maastricht Bill back to parliament on 4 November after the party conference season, it sought to face down the rebels head on by introducing a "paving motion". This was a resolution, procedurally unnecessary, seeking to endorse the government's approach to Maastricht. As such, it attracted the hostility of the Labour Party which could scarcely endorse the government's approach (given the social opt-out) nor vote for a motion which it felt was a de facto vote of confidence in the government (and at a time of considerable unrest following the pit closure dispute). With 26 Tory "rebels" voting against the motion, the government was only able to carry the day by a majority of three (319 to 316) with the support of the Liberals and after persuading a number of Tory rebels to back down, either through pressure or by virtue of a last-minute concession promising to defer consideration of the Bill, with the final vote only after a new Danish referendum the following year. This latter concession caused considerable controversy, as the government had previously rejected a Labour amendment to postpone consideration by a mere few weeks until after the Edinburgh Summit. It also went back on an undertaking made at the Lisbon European Council to ratify by the end of the year. Above all, it meant that the UK would be tied to the Danish timetable and, possibly, the Danish decision.

4. Finding a solution for Denmark

Events in the UK and Denmark were watched with consternation in the other capitals and in the Community institutions. Naturally, there was a desire to facilitate Danish and British ratification, but without re-opening the Maastricht text. Like the Foreign Ministers in Oslo, the European Parliament adopted a resolution on 10 June, hoping that respect for the wishes of the Danish people could be reconciled with the need to continue with the ratification process, excluding any attempt to re-open negotiations on the Treaty. Parliament referred explicitly to seeking ways of allowing the Treaty, if necessary, to enter into force among those countries which did ratify. The European Council meeting in Lisbon on the 26/27 June confirmed this view, underlining the need to "ensure *in any case* the entry into force the Treaty as 1 January 1993" (my emphasis). It stated that enlargement negotiations would only begin after ratification of Maastricht. At the same time, it began to edge forward in other areas which might help Denmark reconsider: a section of its conclusions entitled "A Union close to citizens" emphasized the need for greater transparency in decision-making and for reinforced dialogue with citizens. It emphasized those parts of Maastricht that brought Europe "closer to the citizens" and recalled the important role of the principle of subsidiarity. Indeed, this latter point met with favour on various sides as a way forward.

By the Birmingham European Council on 16 October, called initially in response to the turmoil on the currency markets, it was clear that the Treaty would not be ratified by the end of the year but "as soon as possible". The European Council noted that the Danish government had brought forward a white paper hoping to reach a broad agreement in the *Folketing* on a package of proposals to solve the Danish problem. It adopted a "Birmingham Declaration" on "a Community close to its citizens" which reaffirmed commitment to Maastricht, but stated that the Member States were "determined to respond to the concerns raised in recent public debate". It emphasized the need for better information, greater respect for cultural traditions, better information for national parliaments and the introduction of procedures to make a reality of the principle of subsidiarity. All these elements were designed to appeal in Denmark, but also to reticent backbenchers in the UK.

After Birmingham, negotiations among the Danish political parties proceeded on the basis of the government's white paper and an alternative paper put forward by the Social Democrats. Eventually seven of the eight parties in the *Folketing* agreed on 22 October on a "national compromise", later approved by the appropriate *Folketing* committee. According to this compromise, Denmark would not take part in any common defence policy, would not enter the third phase of EMU, would not be bound by the provisions concerning Union citizenship, would not accept transfers of sovereignty in the field of Justice and Home Affairs (JHA) (which would have to remain at the intergovernmental level), and all this to take the form of a "legally binding" arrangement concluded for an unlimited period. Curiously the only aspect which appeared to require a change to the text of the Treaty was the citizenship aspect — where Denmark anyway applied domestically most of what Maastricht envisaged, and which it had supported in the IGC.

It thus fell to the Edinburgh European Council of 11–12 December to respond and to negotiate a package of measures which would enable the Danish government to submit Maastricht to a new referendum, with a chance of success. It was no doubt hoped that some of these measures might also facilitate ratification in the UK, as well as begin to address some issues of wider public concern that had been highlighted during the ratification procedures generally. The European Council agreed in this context:

- a set of conclusions including a "decision" and declarations on "Denmark and the Treaty on European Union";
- guidelines to implement the subsidiarity principle;
- measures to increase transparency and openness in decision-making procedures of the Community;
- some other measures that might facilitate ratification.

Let us look at these in turn.

(a) The specific arrangements for Denmark

The European Council agreed on a set of arrangements which it considered were "fully compatible with the Treaty", but which included a European Council "decision" for which the treaties make no provision. The decision in fact consisted largely of an interpretation of the Treaty. It specified (Section A) that the citizenship provisions of the Union Treaty confer additional rights and do not in any way take the place of national citizenship, Member States remaining solely responsible for their nationality laws. It noted (Section B) that the Union Treaty (protocol on certain provisions relating to Denmark) gives Denmark the right not to participate in the third stage of EMU, and noted that Denmark intended to make use of that right (though it would participate in stage 2). It noted (Section C) that nothing in the Treaty commits Denmark to become a full member of WEU and that Denmark would not take part in the implementation of Union decisions having defence implications. It noted (Section D) that Denmark will participate fully in cooperation on JHA on the basis of the provisions of Title VI of the Treaty, implying that Denmark would not participate in such cooperation were it transferred to the Community pursuant to Article K9. Finally, it stated that the duration of this "decision" would be governed by Articles Q and N2 of the Union Treaty, i.e. the articles which refer to the unlimited duration of the Maastricht Treaty and the article referring to renegotiation thereof in 1996. It also stated that Denmark could at any time inform the other Member States that it no longer wishes to avail itself of all or part of this decision (Section E).

In separate "declarations", the European Council noted that the Treaty does not prevent any Member State from maintaining or introducing more stringent protection measures compatible with the Treaty in the fields of working conditions and social policy, consumer protection, or the environment. The Treaty allows Member States to pursue their own policy with regard to distribution of income and welfare benefits. Another declaration noted that Denmark will renounce its right to exercise its Presidency of Council for the elaboration and implementation of decisions having defence implications. In such a case the "normal rules" for replacing the President would apply, also with regard to external representation.

The third element of the Danish arrangements were two unilateral declarations by Denmark of which the 11 other Member States took cognizance. The first of these spelt out further that citizenship of the Union was a different concept from citizenship of a nation state. It pointed out that nationals of other Member States already have the right to vote and to stand in municipal elections in Denmark and that Denmark intends to extend this to the European elections. This implied that it was a matter of national policy rather than a Community obligation. It pointed out that any additional rights of Union citizenship required the unanimous agreement of Member States and possibly constitutional amendments in Denmark. The second declaration further spelt out that any transfer of a matter from the sphere of cooperation in JHA to the Community's sphere would require unanimous agreement and national ratification, possible involving constitutional amendments in Denmark.

Although these arrangements merely spelt out what was already inherent in the legal situation under the Treaty of Maastricht, and in that sense did not modify the Treaty, it nevertheless represents a serious prejudice on future developments. In specifying already that Denmark will not participate in stage 3 of EMU it renders inevitable the establishment of a two-tier system of the single currency countries operating a Central Bank and the others remaining in an EMS-type relationship with the single currency. It seems to preclude any transfer of matters from the JHA pillar to the Community. It puts a damper on any blurring between the WEU and the European Union, with Denmark clearly recoiling from the prospect of WEU membership and even refusing to preside Council meetings at which defence matters are discussed in the Union framework.

Rather than blows to the Maastricht system, however, it seems likely that the Danish arrangements are a blow to the 1996 IGC, scheduled to re-examine among other things the "pillar" structure of the Treaty and the defence policy provisions in view of the impending expiry of the WEU Treaty. The Danish arrangements and the general difficulties in ratifying Maastricht in some countries will make it more difficult to envisage full absorption of WEU by the Union or the merger of the three pillars into a single legal structure.

The European Council did make some attempts at damage limitation: it specified that these arrangements "apply exclusively to Denmark and not to other existing or acceding Member States". It also noted "that Denmark does not intend to make use of the following provisions in such a way as to prevent closer cooperation and action among Member States". Nonetheless, it is difficult to imagine that such a precedent will never be invoked by any other current or future Member State.

(b) Subsidiarity

The European Council took note of an "overall approach to the application by the Council of the subsidiarity principle" which had been prepared by the Council (Foreign Ministers) on the basis of a detailed Commission memorandum,[22] and invited the Council, the

---

[22] Bulletin EC N⁰ 10 – 1992, pp. 116–126.

Parliament and the Commission to seek an interinstitutional agreement on this matter, welcoming the draft for such an agreement presented by the European Parliament.

The overall approach spelt out in no less than 11 pages of the summit's conclusions how Council intended to ensure respect for subsidiarity when considering proposals for Community legislation. In each case, it would examine whether the Community is entitled to act, the extent to which it is desirable to do so, and the nature and extent of Community action which should be proportionate to the objective to be achieved and as simple as possible. On the other hand, the document pointed out that the principle of subsidiarity cannot call into question the powers conferred on the EC by the Treaty, that it is a dynamic concept to be decided on a case-by-case basis, that it must respect the *acquis communautaire*, and not call into question the primacy of Community law, nor affect Community obligations spelt out in the Treaty.

At the end of the day, as before, appreciation of subsidiarity will be a question of political judgement, made in the Council by national ministers who are not of nature predisposed to surrendering national competences to the Community. The new procedures in Council imply that it will consider subsidiarity more deliberately and thoroughly than hitherto, but the result is unlikely to be markedly different. The new Treaty provision does allow judicial review, though experience in other federal-type systems shows that the courts are generally reluctant to make what are essentially political judgements.

As a "selling point" of the Maastricht Treaty, the declaration and the high-profile emphasis given to subsidiarity no doubt helped to smooth the ratification process in the UK and Denmark. The submission by the Commission of a list of examples of existing or pending proposals which might be reviewed or repealed, subject to approval by Community procedures, was clearly intended to add to the credibility of the exercise in this respect.

(c) Transparency

The European Council approved a series of measures designed to make the Community more open and transparent. It agreed that some meetings of the Council could be held in public (i.e. with television cameras present). This would not include, as the European Parliament had been pressing for, public meetings when adopting legislation, but rather public orientation debates on work programmes or major new legislative proposals. A decision to hold an open debate would require unanimity. It was agreed to publish voting records of Member States when a formal vote is taken in Council and to improve press briefings and information material. Council's secretariat, and notably its legal service and jurist-linguist group, were instructed to improve the drafting of legislation to make it more simple and clear. Finally, the text provides for speedier and more organized use of unofficial consolidation or official codification of Community legislation that has been the subject of frequent amendment.

(d) Other measures

The Edinburgh Council also approved other measures with a bearing on the ratification problem. The decision to open enlargement negotiations before completion of ratification, but nonetheless on the basis of Maastricht, meant that they would be under way by the time of the second Danish referendum, thereby emphasizing that a second rejection would jeopardize the prospects for rapid accession of other Nordic countries. The Council also approved a Commission proposal for an economic recovery programme involving the coordinated use of national and Community instruments, including the creation of new Community instruments (two new lending facilities and the Cohesion Fund). This would help rebuff criticisms that the Community did too little to organize a joint approach to growth and employment.

5. The second Danish referendum

The Edinburgh package was welcomed by the seven Danish Parties which had negotiated the "National Compromise" in October. Crucially, this included the Socialist People's Party which had opposed Maastricht in the first referendum, and although the party leadership's decision was challenged in a special party congress, a majority backed it.

On 13 January the Conservative-Liberal coalition fell on an unrelated matter and, after 10 years in office, Paul Schlütter resigned as Prime Minister. A new Social Democrat-led coalition, providing Denmark with a majority government for the first time in over a decade, came to power with Paul Nyrup Rasmussen as Prime Minister and Niels Helveg Petersen of the Radical Party as Foreign Minister. It fell to this new team to lead the referendum campaign, a factor generally welcomed by supporters of the Treaty, as one element of the first referendum had been the anti-government vote of 60 per cent of the Social Democrat supporters.

The date for the referendum was fixed on 18 May, leaving ample time for a lengthy campaign and explanation rather than trying to cash in quickly on the euphoria of the Edinburgh agreement. During the final weeks, the television channels carried two hours of debate and discussion every evening, carefully balanced between Yes and No supporters instead of between political parties which would have given an overwhelming majority for the Yes side. Newspaper coverage, meetings, leafleting and so on were intense. One feature of the second referendum campaign was the intervention of non-Danish politicians, particularly British opponents of Maastricht. Lord Tebbit and other anti-Maastricht activists visited Copenhagen and British billionaire publisher Goldsmith paid for full page advertisements in Danish newspapers.

One aspect of the campaign was the likelihood of the other states proceeding, in one way or another, without Denmark in the event of a new rejection of Maastricht. Opponents of the Treaty claimed this was unlikely, pointing to Britain's refusal to corner Denmark and its decision to wait for the Danish result before completing its own ratification procedures. To avoid the British position actually helping the "No" side, Foreign Secretary Douglas Hurd stated on 25 April that Britain might, after all, take part in negotiating new arrangements among the 11 if the Danes voted "No" again. This statement was the subject of much comment in Denmark.

On 18 May, the Danish people voted by 56.8 per cent to 43.2 per cent to accept the Maastricht Treaty and the Edinburgh Agreement.

6. The UK resumes consideration

Meanwhile, the procedures in the UK resumed in January, but with the clear commitment that the final vote would only be after the Danish referendum.

The parliamentary situation was complex, despite the large majority in favour of the Treaty. The number of Tory "rebels" opposing Maastricht was greater than the government's majority and they were organized as a party within the party, with their own de facto leader (William Cash), Whips (James Cran and Christopher Gill), office (the poet Shelley's old house 100 yards from the Palace of Westminster), finance (partly from Lord McAlpine, former Treasurer of the Conservative Party) and staff. But the government could not simply count on Labour and Liberal support as these parties opposed the UK opt-out on social policy negotiated by Major, and were, in the British adversarial style of Parliament, more than happy to embarrass the government, enhance divisions in the Tory ranks, and use up parliamentary time that would otherwise have been used on other legislative items in the government's post-election timetable. In effect, there was a minority government on this issue.

The committee stage of the Bill began on 14 January 1993 in a committee of the whole House. It was to last nearly four months and take up 163 hours on the floor of the House — only four hours short of the 1972 Accession Bill. Over 600 amendments were tabled by the opposition parties and the Tory rebels. Procedurally, amendments that changed the wording of the Treaty were out of order, but this still left scope for amendments adding provisions for the UK that did not conflict with the Treaty or amendments seeking to delete particular provisions which would then not be incorporated into UK law.

The Labour amendments were mostly "probing amendments" to ensure that each particular aspect of the Treaty would be debated. Any amendments that would render the Treaty unratifiable were withdrawn before the vote. This approach was challenged by Labour's anti-Maastricht minority, but the PLP voted by 112 to 46 not to press wrecking amendments, even on restricting the independence of the Central Bank where Tory rebels might have provided a majority on an issue that was an important Labour Party policy. The strategy of not endangering ratification was therefore assured, although not announced,[23] as it was in the party's interest to keep the government guessing. None the less, most Members of the left-wing "Campaign Group" of MPs opposed Maastricht throughout the proceedings, and the Tribune Group published a pamphlet "The Left and Europe" which, whilst attacking the nationalism of Benn and the Campaign Group, came down in favour of a "no ratification without re-negotiation" position, critical especially of the EMU provisions. However, this view was not universally shared within the Tribune Group and the Tribune MEPs responded with their own pamphlet "Building on Maastricht — A Left Agenda for Europe" which argued for ratification.

Where Labour did press its amendments was on "improvements" to the Bill and, especially, on trying to reverse the UK "opt-out" from the social protocol of the Treaty. It was able to gain a majority for no less than seven amendments in committee or at report stage, thereby more than doubling the length of the Bill.

The "improvements" were :

- a specification that UK members of the Committee of the Regions must be chosen from the ranks of elected members of local authorities [amendment 28, committee stage: adopted on 8 March by majority of 22, despite Welsh and Scottish Nationalist support for government];

- an obligation to provide for the Governor of the Bank of England to make an annual report to Parliament which will be subject to approval by resolution [committee stage new clause 1, now clause 3];

- a requirement that the government report to Parliament on how, within ECOFIN, it is working in pursuit of the objectives of Article 2 of the Treaty (i.e. employment, social protection, sustainable growth respecting the environment, etc.) [committee stage amendment 420];

- a requirement to submit to the Commission data on UK economic performance in real terms (growth, investment, employment, etc.) and not just the nominal terms

---

23 Confidential letters reassuring Labour continental socialist partners were sent to leading Socialist MEPs.

(inflation, deficits) provided for by the Treaty [committee stage new clause 2, now clause 4];

- a requirement to submit to Parliament any data forwarded to the Commission on deficits and to set it in the context of the objectives of Article 2 [report stage, new clause 1, now clause 5];

All these amendments were embarrassing for the government, but the most controversial and hard-fought battles were over the *Social Protocol*. Here, Labour sought to corner the government by making it necessary for them to agree to accede to the protocol in order to be able to ratify the Treaty. However, this could only be done with the support of the Tory rebels whose motives were precisely the opposite, hoping that if the government were so cornered, it would not ratify.

The first problem for the government in this context was an amendment which proposed the deletion from the Bill of the reference to the social protocol. Initially, the government had announced that such a deletion would make it impossible to ratify the Treaty as domestic law would no longer conform to the Treaty. Desperate but unsuccessful attempts were made by the government to pursuade opposition parties and Tory rebels to climb down. Then, in what the *Financial Times* called an "ignominious climb-down" the government announced on 15 February that it had received new legal advice from its Attorney General (which it did not publish) that, as the social protocol was designed so as not to impose legislation on the UK, it was not actually necessary to incorporate it into domestic law. The announcement caused uproar and, later, a challenge in the Courts, but its immediate effect was to let the government off the hook.[24]

Labour then returned with a new attempt to corner the government, based on an amendment conceived by Geoff Hoon (both a new MP and an outgoing MEP). It became known as the "time-bomb", as it provided that the Act should only come into force (and therefore the Treaty only ratified) after each House of Parliament had come to a resolution on the question of adopting the Social Protocol. This guaranteed a separate debate and vote on that issue after the Maastricht Bill was adopted and therefore, as we shall see, fresh opportunity to force the issue.

With these amendments the Bill obtained its third and final reading in the Commons, approved by 292 to 112, (a majority of 180) on 20 May, and was passed on to the House of Lords.

The proceedings in the Upper House were completed in less than one month, despite the participation of an unusually high number of Peers (a record 130 put their names down to speak in the second reading debate, including many of the "heavyweights" of the Thatcher governments of the 1980s). Attention focused on an amendment in favour of holding a referendum, as it was unlikely that the Lords would otherwise amend or reject the Bill passed by Commons. Opinion polls had shown support for a referendum, but only about 800 people had turned up to a rally in Trafalgar Square in favour of one (as against the 10,000 expected by the organizers, Lord Blake's "Campaign for a British Referendum") earlier in the year. An amendment in favour of a referendum had also been rejected in the Commons.

Ignoring pleas by Lady Thatcher and Lord Tebbit, the Lords voted against a referendum by 446 to 176 — a vote in which for the first time in decades more than half of the membership of the Lords took part. They finally approved the Maastricht Bill on 20 July by 141 to 29. It received Royal Assent the same day.

---

[24] The amendment was, in fact, only approved at report stage on 5 May (without a vote), as it was controversially ruled out of order on 30 March by the Deputy Speaker at committee stage, but accepted by the Speaker at report stage.

The government then returned to the Commons for the debate on the Social Protocol. It had to settle the matter before the summer recess, but this also meant that it was on the eve of a by-election in which the Conservative Party looked like losing a normally safe seat.

In a dramatic debate on 22 July, a Labour amendment that the Treaty should be ratified only after the government "has given notification to the European Community that it intends to adopt the Agreement attached to the Protocol on Social Policy" was put to the vote in the Commons and received 317 votes for to 317 against,[25] 15 Tory rebels having joined with the Labour, Liberal, Welsh and Scottish Nationalist parties, and the SDLP, but with the Ulster Unionists rallying to the government at the last minute (with allegations of a deal over Northern Irish issues). In accordance with precedent, the Speaker's casting vote caused the amendment to fall.

The unamended government resolution ("taking note" of the government's stance - a neutral wording designed to appeal to all sides) was then put to the vote. Supporters of the Social Protocol maintained their position but were joined by 23 Tory rebels, defeating the motion by 324 to 316, making it impossible for the government to ratify the Treaty without coming back again to the Commons with a new resolution on the Social Protocol.

The Prime Minister immediately announced that he would table a motion the following day, which would again endorse the government's stance on the social Protocol, but this time making it a confidence motion in the government. A new government defeat would then mean a general election which all Conservatives, including the rebels, were anxious to avoid with their party in third place in recent opinion polls. It was also hinted that any Tory MP failing to support the government would have the Conservative whip removed, the first step towards exclusion from the party. All but one of the rebels duly backed down, despite their previous protestations that this was a matter of principle more important than their party, and the resolution was approved by 339 to 299, a majority of 40.

Could the government have accepted the Social Protocol? Common sense says "Yes", given that its significance was far less than portrayed and that every other government in the EC (and the applicant states), including conservative governments, accepted it. But the "opt-out" had become a symbol, made initially to help pursuade reluctant right-wingers of the virtue of the Maastricht compromise, and it could only be abandoned with great loss of face. Furthermore, at least three Ministers, referred to by Major in an off-guard comment as "bastards", would have resigned had he accepted the protocol. While this would not have made it impossible, especially if the alternative was the even greater climb-down of losing the Treaty (and whereas acceptance of the Protocol would have had a clear majority in the House of Commons), it would have deepened still further the already serious divisions in the Conservative Party.

Thus the national procedures for approving the Maastricht Treaty were completed in all 12 Member States. Only a legal challenge in the Courts in Germany still holds up final ratification at the time of writing, a similar challenge in the UK brought by Lord Rees-Mogg, former editor of *The Times*, having failed at the first hurdle with no appeal being attempted.

---

[25] It was later announced that there had been a mistake in counting the votes and that the amendment had really been defeated by 317 to 318. One can only imagine the pandemonium in the House of Commons had the original result produced a majority in favour of the amendment and the announcement sought to reverse it! (In the House of Lords, the amendment was rejected by 88 to 295.)

VI

INITIAL FOLLOW-UP

A number of important matters were scheduled for negotiation during 1992, either because there was no agreement to include them in the Treaty and the issue was postponed until 1992, or because the Treaty itself required implementing measures to be taken during that year. The main such issues were: the number of MEPs and Commissioners per Member State, the seats of various institutions and organs, adaptation of the WEU, the Delors II Financial Package, preparation of enlargement negotiations, and general preparation of new policies and procedures.

Work on many of these points began in the early months of 1992, but were delayed by the result of the Danish referendum. It is fruitful to go through these points in turn.

1.   Number of MEPs and Commissioners per Member State

During the Noordwijk conclave of the IGC before the Maastricht Summit, provisional agreement had been reached on increasing by 18 the number of German MEPs to take account of German unification and also, in view of enlargement, to reduce the number of Commissioners to one per Member State with the creation of five "junior Commissioners". This was taken out of the package in Maastricht itself, where it was agreed to return to this issue in the course of 1992. Among the reasons for removing it were a French reluctance to move away from parity representation with Germany in Parliament and a realization that there were other distortions in the representation of MEPs.

Although changing the number of Commissioners per Member State does not necessarily require a treaty change (as the treaties specify a minimum of one and maximum of two per Member State), no agreement was reached on this before the procedures were well under way to appoint the next Commission. The matter will therefore be left over until the procedure for appointing the next Commission in 1994, by which time the progress of enlargement negotiations will have shed some further light on the issue.

On the other hand, adjustment of the number of MEPs, although requiring the equivalent of treaty modification, could not be held over as German unification had already taken place. The EP itself, which had made the original proposal for 18 extra German members, returned to the issue following the Maastricht Summit and adopted a proposal for a more comprehensive revision (the De Gucht Report adopted in plenary on 10 June 1992). This proposal was adopted without modification by the European Council in Edinburgh. It envisages 18 extra seats for Germany, making a total of 99, six extra for the other "big" Member States, four extra for Spain, six extra for the Netherlands which was curiously under-represented hitherto, and one extra each for Belgium, Greece and Portugal, giving a grand total of 567.

The new allocation will make the membership of the EP somewhat more proportional to the populations of the Member States without taking away entirely the bias in favour of smaller countries, especially Luxembourg. It is perhaps curious that this will increase the size of the European Parliament on the eve of enlargement, but the De Gucht resolution included proposals for the number of MEPs from the then applicant states: Austria 20, Sweden 21, Finland 16, Switzerland 18, Malta four and Cyprus six. After Norway applied, Parliament proposed 15 seats for that country. Parliament's total size would be 667 if all these countries were to join, or 649 without Switzerland. This is comparable to the size of the House of Commons (651), the *Bundestag* (662), or the Italian *Camera* (630), but leaves little scope for further accessions without a new adjustment of the number of seats per country.

2.   Seats of institutions and organs

The Maastricht Treaty envisaged a decision being taken on the seat of the future Monetary Institute and Central Bank during the course of 1992. However, it was impossible to treat this in isolation from the wider question of seats of Community institutions which had been a running sore for many years. The Member States had never managed to fulfil the obligation placed upon them in the original treaties to agree on a single seat for the institutions. The provisional allocations of 1965 spread them over three towns: Luxembourg, Brussels and Strasbourg. The EP in particular was dissatisfied with this situation, but its attempts to get around this through the gradual concentration of parliamentary activities and staff in Brussels gave rise, over the years, to a number of Court cases. The construction of the new parliamentary chamber in Brussels, allowed by the Court, caused a strong reaction from France which blocked any decisions on the seats of new organs (such as the trade-mark office, and the environment agency) — until it gained satisfaction on the seat of the Parliament. Clearly, it was prepared to do the same concerning the crucial monetary institutions.

   In the negotiations it became clear that this matter was not a priority for any Member State other then those with a direct interest in having the institutions on their territory. The European Parliament's request (and the Treaty obligation) for a single seat might have the sympathy of some Member States, but none were willing to go to the stake on this issue. France continued to press hard, and Belgium felt rather weak at a time at which the Commission had been forced to move out of the Berlaymont building, and scattered in several buildings across Brussels, due to the need to remove dangerous asbestos, which was already taking far longer than expected.

   The result was that France largely gained satisfaction at the Edinburgh summit of having Strasbourg declared the seat of the European Parliament and the normal venue for its monthly part-sessions. The decision recognized the right of the European Parliament to hold additional plenary sessions in Brussels, where its committees would also meet. The secretariat, however, would remain based in Luxembourg! Belgium gained the satisfaction of seeing the seats of the Council and the Commission fixed officially in Brussels, recognizing the de facto situation. Luxembourg similarly saw a formalization of the de facto seats of the Court of Justice, Court of First Instance, Court of Auditors and the European Investment Bank in Luxembourg. Indeed, except for the arrangements concerning Parliament, the decision remained faithful to the provisional decision of 1965.

   The European Parliament immediately declared (resolution December 1992) that it does not feel bound by this decision, questioning its legality. Indeed, not only does the decision not respect the Treaty requirement for a single seat, but it also enters into extraordinary detail about the internal organization of the Parliament, specifying that there should be 12 monthly session periods, including "the budget session"(sic), and that they should be in Strasbourg. Until now, the Court has always ruled that Parliament is entitled to arrange its own internal organization, including the length of what the treaties refer to as an annual session and how this is broken down into part-sessions. It is also doubtful whether a decision imposing such a spread of its activities and secretariat is compatible with the duty of loyal cooperation spelt out in the case law of the Court. The "agreement" nonetheless clears the way for negotiations on the seat of the EMI, due to start work in January 1994, and the Central Bank, as well as other agencies.

3. Adaptation of the WEU

As envisaged in the Maastricht Treaty, Community states not yet members of WEU had the opportunity of joining it. In November 1992, Greece duly joined as a full member and Denmark and Ireland as observers. European members of NATO that were not members of the Community became associate members of WEU (Turkey and Norway).

The WEU secretariat was moved to Brussels, where it occupies premises not immediately adjacent to those of the Community institutions (but much nearer to them than to NATO). As for the development of WEU's own role, the foreign and defence ministers of WEU countries, meeting in Bonn on 19 June 1992, adopted the "Petersberg Declaration" in which the Member States declared that they were "prepared to make available military units from the whole spectrum of their conventional armed forces for military tasks conducted under the authority of WEU". They could be employed for the common defence of the allies, humanitarian tasks, peace-keeping, tasks of combat forces in crisis management or peace-keeping operations. A planning cell in Brussels will be responsible for preparing contingency plans for the deployment of forces under WEU auspices.

Among the units made available to WEU will be the Franco-German brigade (or "Eurocorps"). Kohl and Mitterrand had announced in October 1991 in a letter to the President of the Council their intention to step up Franco-German military cooperation. The proposal was clarified further in May 1992 during the Franco-German summit in La Rochelle. The intention was to make the Franco-German brigade the nucleus of a European unit, and in May 1993 Belgium annouced its intention to join it.

4. Delors II Package

Straight after the Maastricht Summit the Commission put forward a new proposal for future finance of the Community, which became rapidly known as the "Delors II Package", inviting comparison with the "Delors I Package" that had been approved following the adoption of the Single European Act. In both cases, the Commission was seizing the opportunity provided by a new Treaty to argue that the budgetary means to implement it must also be provided by the Member States. In both cases, however, a revision of the Community's budgetary system was required in any event, this time because the financial perspectives agreed in 1987 ran out in 1992. Furthermore, the creation of a Cohesion Fund and the increase in the structural funds implicit in the Maastricht Treaty meant that the current ceiling on Community resources would be reached within a few years.

The Commission proposed that the ceiling for the Community's own resources be raised from 1.20 per cent of GDP in 1993 to 1.37 per cent in 1997, and put forward a breakdown into the various categories of expenditure that this should cover, envisaging a notable increase in structural actions (including the new Cohesion Fund), other internal policies and external action (reflecting the recent trend for the Community budget to be used for foreign policy purposes). In Edinburgh, the European Council agreed, at the end of a lengthy process of negotiation among the Member States, to increase the ceiling to 1.27 per cent of GDP in 1999. This was done by cutting the Commissions's estimates notably for internal policies and external policy, not adjusting the agricultural guideline for the incorporation of the former East Germany into the Community and cutting the margin for unforeseen expenditure from 0.3 per cent to 0.1 per cent of GDP.

There are doubts as to whether this perspective can be held to, especially as it extends so far into an unpredictable future. Even at the time of its adoption, the failure to adapt the agricultural guideline seemed questionable (notably with the recent monetary realignments) to the extent that the European Council conclusions themselves referred to the possibility of agricultural expenditure exceeding the guideline. Similarly, the building commitments of the various Community institutions mean that the guideline for administrative expenditure will be almost impossible to keep, having regard also to the increased size of the European Parliament agreed at the same summit, and the need to establish the Committee of the Regions and the Ombudsman.

The conclusions of the European Council go into great detail about the breakdown of different categories of expenditure — matters which in the past had been left to interinstitutional agreements between Council and Parliament. Certainly, Parliament considers this to be an opening position on Council's side in the negotiation of a new IIA, which the European Council agreed should be negotiated. Indeed until such an agreement is reached, the European Parliament remains free to use its powers under the treaties to allocate spending of "non-compulsory" expenditure (about 40 per cent of the budget), and it could, should it wish, exceed the ceilings envisaged by the European Council for certain categories. The detailed figures may therefore not be definitive, all the more so as the European Council appears to have confused appropriations for commitments and appropriations for payments at different parts of its text.

5. Enlargement

It had been agreed at Maastricht that, whilst 1992 could be used to prepare for the enlargement negotiations, these would only begin after ratification of the Maastricht Treaty and agreement on the Delors II package. This was confirmed at the Lisbon Summit, but relaxed at the Edinburgh Summit as described above.

Faced with applications from Austria, Sweden, Finland and Switzerland (all EFTA countries), Turkey, Malta and Cyprus, the Lisbon meeting of the European Council in June agreed to open negotiations with the EFTA applicants only. It was argued that the EEA Agreement had paved the way and negotiations with these countries could be concluded rapidly. On the other hand, misgivings that were not spelt out in the European Council conclusions regarding the Mediterranean applicants precluded their inclusion in the foreseen negotiations. Turkey had already been subject to a negative opinion from the Commission and, although Member States did not wish to damage their relations with Turkey at a sensitive time in Middle Eastern politics, its candidature nonetheless posed questions of human rights and the occupation of northern Cyprus. Cyprus posed the problem of its division and the Maltese application was from a government enjoying a majority of one in parliament over an opposition party opposed to the application. It also raised the problem posed of the insertion of micro-states into the institutional system.

By the time of the Edinburgh European Council, Norway had added its name to the list of EFTA applicants, but a question-mark hung over Switzerland's application following the narrow rejection in a referendum of the EEA Treaty. The Swiss government let it be known that, while it was not withdrawing the application, it did not expect negotiations to be opened in the near future. Thus, it was agreed at Edinburgh to begin negotiations only with Austria, Sweden and Finland, to be joined by Norway as soon as the Commission's official opinion on the Norwegian application was ready.

The European Parliament, whose approval of an accession treaty is necessary, had stated in April 1992 (resolution on Maastricht) that enlargement of the Community required further institutional reforms. This "no widening without deepening" position was spelled out further in a resolution approved on 20 January 1993 (Hänsch Report) but the European Council maintained its view that the institutional provisions of the Maastricht Treaty were a sufficient basis for a Community of 16. Parliament therefore proposed, after the Danish referendum and at the beginning of the Belgian Council Presidency, that certain institutional changes be made in the Accession treaties, such as extending the use of QMV in Council and lowering the threshold needed to obtain one (a new threshold has to be negotiated in any case for the enlarged EC), reorganizing the Commission, and extending the codecision procedure.[26] A major institutional conflict is possible if there is no response to Parliament's proposals, but some support has been forthcoming and Member States may find it easier to agree to some institutional changes as part of the enlargement package than in the 1996 IGC.

6. Ombudsman and committees of inquiry

The Maastricht Treaty provided for the European Parliament to adopt the regulations governing the duties of the Ombudsman, with the approval of Council acting by a qualified majority. It also specified that the rights of parliamentary committees of inquiry shall be determined by common accord of the Parliament, the Council and the Commission. In both these areas the European Parliament therefore adopted a set of proposals to discuss with the other institutions in interinstitutional conferences (Bindi Report on Ombudsman and Musso Report on Inquiry Committees, adopted by Parliament on 17 December 1992).

Concerning the Ombudsman, Parliament proposed that he/she should have the right "to conduct all enquiries or investigations which he deems necessary to clarify any suspected maladministration in the activities of Community institutions or bodies", while Member State authorities would be obliged to provide all the necessary documentation and information, failing which Parliament will take "appropriate action". As to the requisite qualifications for appointment as Ombudsman, the candidate must "offer every guarantee of independence, and meet the conditions required for the exercise of judicial office in their country or have the acknowledged competence and experience to undertake the duties of Ombudsman"; he/she would receive the same remuneration as a judge of the Court of Justice.

Concerning the committees of inquiry, Parliament proposed that their requests for information and documentation shall be addressed as appropriate to the Presidents of the Community institutions or to the Permanent Representatives of the Member States, and that "officials and other persons employed by the authorities in question shall be automatically authorized to give evidence or testify to the committee". A form of *sub judice* rule is also laid down, in accordance with Article 138c of the Treaty, precluding the setting up of a committee to inquire into a matter already before a court of law, though the suspension of an ongoing investigation because legal proceedings are initiated would be a matter of Parliament's discretion.

---

[26] Resolution of 15 July 1993.

The Commission and the Council subsequently adopted their own positions on these matters and talks began with Parliament, initially through the "trialogue" of the Presidents of the three institutions and then in a full Interinstitutional Conference with the whole of Council and a delegation of 12 MEPs. On 7 June in Luxembourg this conference, although making progress on a number of points, broke up without agreement on the access of the Ombudsman to documents that Member States have transmitted confidentially to the Commission. Parliament was willing to accept that documents classified as "secret" pursuant to the relevant legal provisions would not be available to the Ombudsman, but was insistent that he/she should have at least confidential access to confidential documents that the Member States had already given to the Commission. Failure to provide such access would make it too easy to hinder the Ombudsman's investigations.

Until agreement is reached on this point and similar arguments over the powers of committees of inquiry, no implementing legislation can be adopted. The incoming Belgian Council Presidency has announced that it is confident that agreement can be reached in the autumn of 1993, thereby hinting that Council may adopt a more flexible attitude.

7.   Subsidiarity, transparency and democracy

The Edinburgh European Council had welcomed Parliament's draft of an interinstitutional agreement on subsidiarity and invited Council, Commission and Parliament to complete such an agreement. Parliament, however, continued to insist that such an agreement should be only part of a wider agreement on democracy, openness and transparency in Community decision-taking. Parliament envisaged such issues as the public meeting of Council when adopting legislation and the respect by Council of parliamentary rejection of legislation being addressed. Council has so far (July 1993) been reluctant to go beyond subsidiarity, notably at the above-mentioned Interinstitutional Conference, and here too an agreement is unlikely before the autumn.

Meanwhile, Council has still not implemented the European Council conclusion that the result of votes in Council should be published. On subsidiarity, the review of existing and pending legislation is also proceeding slowly as Council seems reluctant to follow the full legislative procedure in considering each case.

For its part, the European Parliament prepared a thorough revision of its own internal Rules of Procedure designed to take full advantage of the new Maastricht procedures and to re-vamp its own structures.

8.   Other preparations for implementing Maastricht

Council also began to prepare other aspects of the implementation of Maastricht, and, indeed, the foreign ministers decided to continue the mandate of their "personal representatives" who had prepared their work during the IGC on political union. This group began the preparatory work on the new procedures, on the preparation for the Committee of Regions (where two national governments appeared to consider that it should be possible to nominate officials rather than elected local or regional representatives to this body), and foreign policy procedures.

On this latter point, a report was prepared by the foreign ministers and endorsed by the European Council in Lisbon on "the likely development of the common foreign and security policy with a view to identifying areas open to joint action vis-à-vis particular countries or groups of countries". This report spelt out that the CFSP should be seen as the "successor" to EPC, representing a *"saut qualitatif"* giving the *acquis* of EPC greater potential "principally by means of joint action, an additional instrument which implies a strict discipline among Member States". It aimed to be a more active rather than reactive policy. The report proposed a number of geographical areas and horizontal domains for joint action as a first and non-exhaustive indication of areas in which the CFSP should develop. The geographical areas mentioned were central and eastern Europe, the CIS, the Balkans, the Mediterranean (in particular the Maghreb) and the Middle East. In each case a number of objectives and issues for joint action were defined. Furthermore, and for the first time, a number of security issues were listed as a suitable object for joint action, namely the CSCE process, arms control, nuclear non-proliferation issues and economic aspects of security (including arms and technology exports). An ad hoc working group on security was created under the responsibility of the Political Committee.

Despite these preparations, the delays in the ratification of Maastricht combined with the Community's continued failure, along with the UN, to take effective action in former Yugoslavia, cast doubts as to whether the CFSP would amount, in practice, to much more than a grander name for EPC.

9.   Towards EMU?

Although the technical preparations for EMU proceeded in 1992–93, with the Central Bank Governors preparing common procedures for implementing a single monetary policy and even initial preparations for introducing the new bank notes of the single currency, serious question-marks were placed over the timetable for EMU. As noted in Chapter 1, the liberalization of capital movements actually made the management of the ERM potentially more difficult. This did not lead to immediate difficulties, as the ERM was perceived to have been a success. However, the lengthy period without realignments had meant that economic divergences — which had not yet been eliminated — were not adjusted for. Yet, a new and major divergence was appearing as a result of German unification. German monetary union at the rate of 1 to 1, and unification financed initially from borrowing rather than from taxation, had increased inflationary pressures in Germany, causing the Budesbank to raise interest rates. This had a knock-on effect throughout the ERM, although most other countries were in a situation where interest rate cuts were required. As we have seen, the Bundesbank was not necessarily disposed to go out of its way to save EMU.

Despite this growing vulnerability, ECOFIN failed to realign ERM parities at its meeting in Bath on 5 September 1992, with the UK resisting suggestions that it should devalue and Germany resisting suggestions that it should cut interest rates or revalue. With no pressure let off, and with fears of a potential no-vote in the French referendum, following the Danish set-back, the system suffered a first crisis on 13 September, when the lira devalued. Still no other country accepted the need to adjust its own parity. Five days later, with tremendous speculation against the overvalued pound, and with successive interest rate rises failing to stem it, the UK unilaterally withdrew the pound from the ERM. The lira followed.

Recriminations over the attitudes of the British government during the crisis masked the fact that the system as a whole had now lost credibility. In the following months, the Irish, Danish, Spanish and French currencies came under speculative pressure. Further devaluations and recriminations took place. Eventually, in August 1993, the exchange-rate margins of the ERM were fixed at 15 per cent, virtually a floating system.

Although this left the Community in greater monetary disarray than before it had embarked on phase 1 of EMU, it also underlined the difficulty and cost of maintaining separate currencies in a single market. The chances of some countries moving *more rapidly* to EMU could not be ruled out, and the formal preservation of the ERM through wider margins, rather than its abandonment, was indicative of this desire, as well as making it easier for Member States formally to meet the criteria for proceeding to phase 3. With phase 2 on 1 January 1994, the *legal* capacity to move to a single currency among a majority of Member States, if the political will exists, would be in place.

Annex 1: RATIFICATION OF THE MAASTRICHT TREATY

Belgium	17 July 1992: 4 Nov. 1992:	Chamber of Representatives approved by 146 to 33 Senate approved by 115 to 26	Opposition from most Greens, extreme right and most Flemish autonomists
Denmark	12 May 92: 2 June 92: 18 May 93:	Parliament approved 130 to 25 Referendum rejected 50.7 per cent to 49.3 per cent 2nd Referendum accepted by 56.8 per cent to 43.2 per cent	Opposition from Socialist People's Party (1st referendum) and Progress Party (extreme right)
Germany	2 Dec. 92: 18 Dec. 92:	*Bundestag* approved by 543 to 17 *Bundesrat* approved unanimously	Opposition from former Communists of East Germany (PDS)
Spain	29 Oct. 92: 25 Nov. 92:	Congress approved by 314 to 3 Senate approved by 222 to 0	Opposition from extreme Basque nationalists (*Herri Batasuna*)
Greece	31 July 92:	Parliament approved 286 to 8	Opposition from Communists and one Green MP
France	23 June 92: 20 Sept. 92:	Congress (*Assemblée* & Senate) approved constitutional amendment by 592 to 73 (89 per cent) Referendum approved by 51.05 per cent to 48.95 per cent	Opposition from Extreme Right, Communists and about half of the Gaullists and half of the Greens
Ireland	18 June 92:	Referendum approved 69 per cent to 31 per cent	Opposition from nationalist groups and extreme anti-abortionists
Italy	17 Sept. 92: 29 Oct. 92:	Senate approved by 176 to 16 Chamber of Representatives approved by 403 to 46	Opposition from extreme right (MSI) and *Rifondazione Communista*
Luxembourg	2 July 92:	Parliament approved by 51 to 6	Opposition from Communists and some Greens
Netherlands	13 Nov. 92: 15 Dec. 92:	2nd Chamber approved 137 to 13 1st Chamber approved by acclamation	Opposition from Calvinists, extreme right and some Greens

Portugal	10 Dec. 92:	Parliament approved 200 to 21	Opposition from Communists and CDS
UK	21 May 92:	Commons approves principle (2nd reading) by 336 to 92	Opposition mainly from Conservative right wing, Labour left wing and Ulster Unionists. Support for social protocol from Labour, Liberal, SNP, PC and SDLP
	20 May 93:	Commons approves in 3rd reading by 292 to 112	
	20 July 93:	Lords approves 3rd reading by 141 to 29	
	22 July 93:	Vote on resolution concerning social protocol:	

- amendment for UK adherence to protocol: defeated by 317 to 318
- resolution as a whole (accepting non-adherence): defeated 316 to 324

	23 July 93:	New vote on resolution and confidence in government: approved 339 to 299

Annex 2: PROCEDURES RESULTING FROM THE MAASTRICHT TREATY

A. Legislative Procedures

The *assent procedure* applies to:

- measure facilitating right of residence and freedom of movement of European citizens (Article 8a)
- definition of tasks, objectives, organization and coordination of the structural funds (Article 130d)
- creation of Cohesion Fund (Article 130d)
- uniform procedure for European elections (Article 138)*
- international agreements with certain institutional, budgetary or legislative implications (Article 228 (3))
- accession of new member states (Article 0 of common provisions)*
- amendments to the protocol of the European System of Central Banks (Article 106 (5))
- special tasks to be entrusted to the Central Bank (Article 105 (6))

* EP assent by majority of its members (i.e. absolute majority, currently 260 votes)

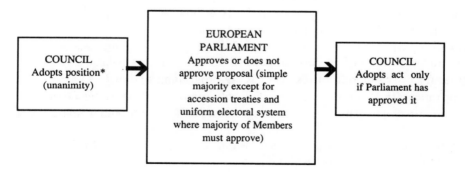

* Council acts on a proposal of

- the Commission (Articles 8a, 105(6), 130d, 228(3))
- the Parliament (Article 138)
- the Central Bank[1] or the Commission (Article 106 (5))
- applicant states, after consulting the Commission (Article 0, Maastricht Treaty)

---

[1] in which case Council may act by a qualified majority

2. The *co-decision procedure (Article 189b)* applies to:
- free movement of workers (Article 49)
- right of establishment (Article 54)
- treatment of foreign nationals (Article 56)
- mutual recognition of diplomas (Article 57 (1))
- provisions for the self-employed (Article 57 (2))
- services (Article 66)
- internal market harmonizations (Article 100A)
- internal market mutual recognitions (Article 100B)
- education (incentive measures) (Article 126 (4))*
- trans-European network guidelines (Article 129d)
- incentive measures in field of public health (Article 129 (4))
- incentive measures in field of culture (Article 128 (5))
- consumer protection (Article 129a (2))
- multiannual Framework Programme for Research & Technology (Article 130 (i))*
- enviroment programmes (Article 130s (3))

* In these areas, Council must act unanimously

3. The *cooperation procedure (Article 189c)* applies to:
- rules prohibiting discrimination on grounds of nationality (Article 6, formerly Article 7)
- transport (Article 75)
- Social Fund implementing decisions (Article 125, formely Articles 126 & 127)
- other measures in field of vocational training (Article 127 (4))
- Trans-European networks (interoperability & finance) (Article 129d)
- Regional Fund implementing decisions (Article 130e)
- Rules for participation of undertakings, research centres and universities in Community research & technological development (RTD programmes) (Article 130j)
- Rules for dissemination of results of RTD programmes (Article 130j)
- Supplementary RTD programmes with only some Members States (Artcle 130 k)
- Community participation in RTD programmes of several Member States (Articles 130 l)
- Environment (except fiscal, land use, water & energy) (Article 130 s (1))
- Development policy (Article 130 w)
- Social policy (health & safety at work) (Article 118a)
- Social policy pursued by 11 Member States re. working conditions, information & consultation of workers, equal treatment and integration into labour market (Protocol of the Member States minus the UK, Art. 2 (2))
- Rules on multilateral surveillance (EMU) (Article 103 (5))
- definition of conditions for access to financial institutions by public authorities (Article 104a)
- definition of access to debt with central banks by public authorities (Article 104b)
- denominations and specifications of coins (EMU) (Article 108 (3))

4.   The *consultation procedure* applies to:

- *common policies*: agriculture (Article 43), private sector competition (Article 87), regulations for state aids (Article 94) certain aspects of EMU (Articles 104c(14), 106(6), 109(1), 109e(6), 109e(7), 109i(2), 109i(3), 109i(4), 109j(2), certain social policy matters (Articles 126 and 127), co-ordination of structural funds (Article 130d), multi-annual framework programmes, for research and development policy and setting up of joint undertakings (Article 130q(1)) enviromental policy (fiscal, land use, water and energy) (Article 130s), further measures to attain one of the Community's objectives (Article 235), abolition of restrictions on the freedom of establishment and on the provision of services (Article 63), taxation (Article 99) harmonization of national provisions which affect the common market (Article 100), determination of which third country nationals require visas (Article 100c(1)), uniform format visas (Article 100c (2)), international agreements other than those requiring Parliament's assent, except Article 113 (3) agreements (Article 228), specific supplementary actions on economic & social cohesion (Article 130b), specific research programmes (Article 130 i (4)), specific measures supporting industrial policy (Article 130 (3)), and energy and radiation (11 articles in Euratom treaty);

- *institutional matters*: appointment of President and members of the Board of the Central Bank (Article 109a (2)) and President of Monetary Institute (Article 109f), framework decision on implementing powers for the Commission (Article 145, third indent), appointment of President of Commission (Article 158), setting-up of the Court of First Instance (Article 168a), amendments to Title III of the Statute of the Court of Justice (Article 188), appointment of the members of the Court of Auditors (Article 206(4)), adoption of the Staff Regulations (Articles 212), and the calling of an intergovernmental conference to modify the Treaty (Article 236);

- *budgetary matters*: decision on the Community's own resources (Article 201), and Financial and other Regulations (Article 209);

- *citizens' rights*: Voting in European and local elections (Article 8b), and other rights (Article 8f).

N.B. For any matter with financial implications the conciliation procedure may also apply.

B.   Other Provisions affecting Parliament

- Union citizens' right to petition EP (*Arts. 8e & 137c*)
- EP to initiate legislation by requesting Commission to submit a proposal (majority of members needed) (*Art. 137a*)
- Detailed provisions governing EP's right of enquiry to be "determined by common agreement of the EP, Council & Commission" (*Art. 137b*)
- EP to appoint Ombudsman (*Art. 137d (2)*)
- EP to lay down "after seeking opinion from the Commission and with the approval of Council acting by a qualified majority" the regulation and conditions governing the Ombudsman's duties (*Art. 137d (4)*)
- EP to approve Commission as a whole (*Art. 158 (2)*)
- Budgetary control powers of the EP strengthened by placing new treaty obligations on Commission to submit information and respond to discharge observations (*Art. 206, replacing 206b)*)

- EP acts able to be challenged in European Court of Justice by Commission, Council or Member States and EP able to challenge acts by other institutions that fail to respect its prerogatives (*Art. 173a*)
- Council able to repeal international agreements to which EP had given its assent without obtaining agreement of Parliament (*Art. 228a*)
- EP & WEU Assembly encouraged to cooperate (*Declaration No. 29 of Annex 2 (WEU Member States), para 4*)

C. New Provisions for Qualified Majority Voting (QMV) in Council

- education (incentive measures and recommendations) (*Art. 126 (4)*)
- vocational training measures (*Art. 127 (4)*)
- health (incentive measures & recommendations) (*Art. 129*)
- enviroment (except fiscal, land use, water & energy) (*Art. 130 s*)
- trans-European networks (*Art. 129d*)
- development policy (*Art. 130w*)
- consumer protection (*Art. 129a (2)*)
- approval of EP regulations governing Ombudsman (*Art. 137 c*)
- some aspects of social policy among the 11 (*protocol No. 14*)
- various items of EMU provisions

Change to QMV on 1 January 1996:

- determination of which third country nationals require visas (*Art. 100 C (3)*)

Two-third majority

- implementation of conventions in field of cooperation in Justice & Home Affairs (*Art. K3 2c thereof*)
- recommendations and measures taken against Member States running an excessive deficit (*Art. 104 c(13)*)
- EMU matters that would otherwise be settled by QMV where one or more Member States have a derogation after introduction of single currency (*Art. 109 K (5)*).

Potential change to QMV (to be decided by Council acting unanimously)

- environment (fiscal, land use planning, water resources & energy) (*Art. 130 s (2)*)
- implementation of joint action in field of common foreign & security policy (*CFSP Art. J3 (2)*)
- measures to implementing joint action in field of cooperation on Justice & Home Affairs (*Art. K3 2b thereof*)
- matters transferred to Community competence from field of cooperation on Justice & Home Affairs (*Art. K9 thereof*)

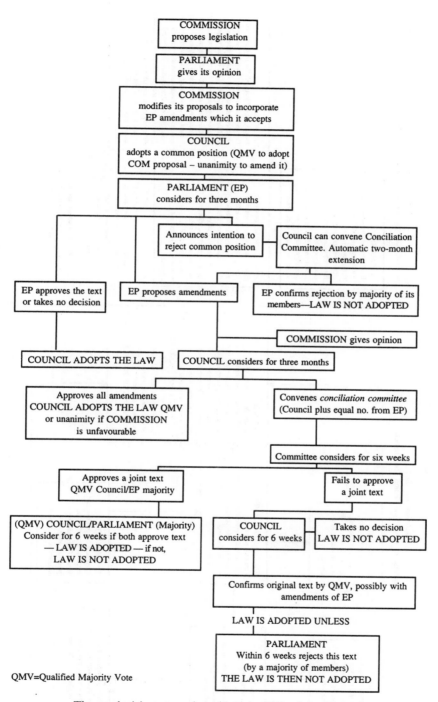

COMMISSION
proposes legislation

PARLIAMENT
gives its opinion

COMMISSION
modifies its proposals to incorporate
EP amendments which it accepts

COUNCIL
adopts a common position (QMV to adopt
COM proposal – unanimity to amend it)

PARLIAMENT (EP)
considers for three months

Announces intention to
reject common position

Council can convene Conciliation
Committee. Automatic two-month
extension

EP approves the text
or takes no decision

EP proposes amendments

EP confirms rejection by majority of its
members—LAW IS NOT ADOPTED

COMMISSION gives opinion

COUNCIL ADOPTS THE LAW

COUNCIL considers for three months

Approves all amendments
COUNCIL ADOPTS THE LAW QMV
or unanimity if COMMISSION
is unfavourable

Convenes *conciliation committee*
(Council plus equal no. from EP)

Committee considers for six weeks

Approves a joint text
QMV Council/EP majority

Fails to approve
a joint text

(QMV) COUNCIL/PARLIAMENT (Majority)
Consider for 6 weeks if both approve text
— LAW IS ADOPTED — if not,
LAW IS NOT ADOPTED

COUNCIL
considers for 6 weeks

Takes no decision
LAW IS NOT ADOPTED

Confirms original text by QMV, possibly with
amendments of EP

LAW IS ADOPTED UNLESS

PARLIAMENT
Within 6 weeks rejects this text
(by a majority of members)
THE LAW IS THEN NOT ADOPTED

QMV=Qualified Majority Vote

The co-decision procedure (Article 189b of the Treaty)

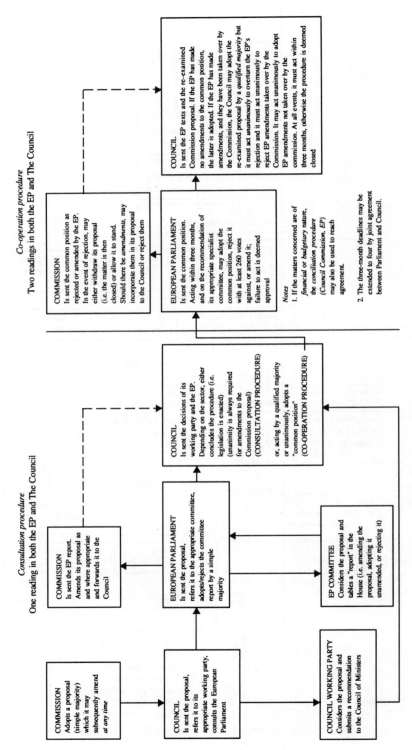

Stages in the consultation and co-operation procedures

Annex 3: POST-MAASTRICHT DEADLINES

1993

Early 1993   Harmonization of asylum policies of the Member States
Enlargement negotiations begin in earnest

By 31 December   Adoption of arrangements for right to vote in country of residence in European elections
Adoption of Rules for common diplomatic protection
Creation of Cohesion Fund
Commission Report on European citizenship, possibly leading to further provisions on citizenship
Commission Report on right of access to information
Council to decide on transfer to Community of competence to deal with right of asylum

1994

on 1 January   Beginning of Phase II of EMU

June   European elections

By 31 December   Adoption by the Council of the conditions concerning the right to vote for all the citizens of the Union in local elections

By 31 December   Report on and possible extension of police cooperation
Appointment, with vote of confidence by European Parliament, of new Commission to take office in January for five-year period

1995

January   New Commission (1995–1999) takes office

31 December   Abolition of derogations authorizing restrictions on capital movements

1996

Before 1 January   Introduction of a uniform format for visas
From 1 January   Introduction of majority voting in the Council for visa policy

By 31 December   Specification by the EMI of the administrative framework for the ESCB
Report to the Council with a view to revision in the context of Article 12 of the WEU Treaty
Possible decision on the beginning of the third stage of EMU

during 1996   Report to the Council with a view to revising the part of the Treaty concerning security
Revision of the Treaty –IGC to consider:
- Article B (revision of the "pillar structure" of the Treaty)
- Article 189 B, 8 (widening the scope of the co-decision procedure)
- Article J 4 and J 10 CFSP (revision of the provisions of the CFSP and on defence)
- Introduction of specific titles in the Treaty to cover civil protection, energy and tourism
- Classification or hierarchy of Community acts

1998

1 July   Decision on which Member States may go on to the third stage of EMU, even if only a minority are ready

December   Expiry of WEU Treaty

1999

1 January   Beginning of the third stage of EMU among Member States that are ready

June   European Parliament Elections

by 31 December   Appoint new Commission with vote of confidence by European Parliament

2000

January   New Commission (2000–2004) takes office

DOCUMENTS LEADING UP TO THE IGCs

1. Extracts of conclusions of European Council (or "Summit") meetings

A. Conclusions of the European Council held in Madrid on 26–27 June 1989 (Extract)

Economic and monetary union

The European Council restated its determination progressively to achieve economic and monetary union as provided for in the Single Act and confirmed at the European Council meeting in Hanover. Economic and monetary union must be seen in the perspective of the completion of the internal market and in the context of economic and social cohesion.

The European Council considered that the report by the Committee chaired by Jacques Delors, which defines a process designed to lead by stages to economic and monetary union, fulfilled the mandate given in Hanover. The European Council felt that its realization would have to take account of the parallelism between economic and monetary aspects, respect the principle of subsidiarity and allow for the diversity of specific situations.

The European Council decided that the first stage of the realization of economic and monetary union would begin on 1 July 1990.

The European Council asked the competent bodies (the Council (Economic and Financial Affairs, and General Affairs), the Commission, the Committee of Central Bank Governors and the Monetary Committee):

(a) to adopt the provisions necessary for the launch of the first stage on 1 July 1990;

(b) to carry out the preparatory work for the organization of an Intergovernmental Conference to lay down the subsequent stages; that Conference would meet once the first stage had begun and would be preceded by full and adequate preparation.

B. Conclusions of the European Council held in Strasbourg on 8–9 December 1989 (Extract)

At the beginning of its meeting, the European Council heard a statement by Mr Baron, the President of the European Parliament, in which he set out the Parliament's position and priorities with regard to the main Community topics in the light of the current situation.

The European Council thanked Mr Baron for his address which made a valuable contribution to the ensuing discussions.

I. Towards European union

The European Council is conscious of the responsibilities weighing on the Community in this crucial period for Europe. The current changes and the prospects for development in Europe demonstrate the attraction which the political and economic model of Community Europe holds for many countries.

The Community must live up to this expectation and these demands: its path lies not in withdrawal but in openness and cooperation, particularly with the other European States.

It is in the interest of all European States that the Community should become stronger and accelerate its progress towards European Union.

The European Council adopted the following conclusions to this end:

II. Making the Single Act a reality

(. . .)

III. Economic and monetary union

1. The European Council examined the work carried out since the European Council meeting in Madrid with a view to a meeting of the Intergovernmental Conference.

    It noted the agreement reached in the ECOFIN Council and the initiatives of the Governors of the Central Banks with a view to strengthening the coordination of economic policies and improving collaboration between Central Banks. It notes that these decisions will enable the first stage of EMU as defined in the report from the Delors Committee to begin on 1 July 1990.

2. It took note of the report from the High Level Working Party, which identified the main technical, institutional and political issues to be discussed with a view to a Treaty on Economic and Monetary Union.

    On this basis, and following a discussion on the calling of an Intergovernmental Conference charged with preparing an amendment of the Treaty with a view to the final stages of EMU, the President of the European Council noted that the necessary majority existed for convening such a conference under Article 236 of the Treaty. That conference will meet, under the auspices of the Italian authorities, before the end of 1990. It will draw up its own agenda and set the timetable for its proceedings.

3. The European Council emphasized, in this context, the need to ensure the proper observance of democratic control in each of the Member States.

    With a view to the new term of the European Parliament which will begin in 1994, it calls for Economic and Monetary Union to comply fully with this democratic requirement.

4. The European Council also took note of the Commission's intention to submit before 1 April a composite paper on all aspects of the achievement of Economic and Monetary Union which will take into account all available analyses and contributions.

    The European Council emphasized the need for the Council (General Affairs) and the ECOFIN Council to use the period prior to the opening of the Conference to ensure the best possible preparation.

    The proceedings as a whole will be examined by the Council (General Affairs) in preparation for the European Council meeting in Dublin.

C. Conclusions of the special meeting of the European Council held in Dublin on 28 April 1990 (Extract)

Political union

The European Council discussed the proposal of President Mitterrand and Chancellor Kohl on political union, and the paper submitted by the Belgian Government on the same subject.

In this context the European Council confirmed its commitment to political union and decided on the following steps:

(i)   A detailed examination will be put in hand forthwith on the need for possible Treaty Changes with the aim of strengthening the democratic legitimacy of the union, enabling the Community and its institutions to respond efficiently and effectively to the demands of the new situation, and assuring unity and coherence in the Community's international action;

(ii) Foreign Ministers will undertake this examination and analysis, and prepare proposals to be discussed at the European Council in June with a view to a decision on the holding of a second intergovernmental conference to work in parallel with the conference on economic and monetary union with a view to ratification by Member States in the same time-frame.

D.   Conclusions of the European Council held in Dublin on 25–26 June 1990 (Extract)

The European Council reviewed the preparation of the forthcoming intergovernmental conference. It noted that all the relevant issues are now being fully and thoroughly clarified, with the constructive contribution of all Member States, and that common ground is emerging in a number of fields. In these circumstances the European Council decided that the intergovernmental conference will open on 13 December 1990 with a view to establishing the final stages of economic and monetary union in the perspective of the completion of the internal market and in the context of economic and social cohesion. The conference should conclude its work rapidly with the objective of ratification of the results by Member States before the end of 1992.

The European Council asked the Economic and Social Affairs Council and the General Affairs Council, assisted by the competent bodies, to carry out their work in such a way that negotiations on a concrete basis can be entered into as soon as the conference opens.

Political union

The European Council had an extensive exchange of views on the basis of the examination and analysis conducted by the Foreign Ministers and the ideas and proposals put forward by the Member States and the Commission.

On this basis, and following a discussion on the calling of an intergovernmental conference on political union, the President of the European Council noted the agreement to convene such a conference under Article 236 of the Treaty. The conference will open on 14 December 1990. It will adopt its own agenda, and conclude its work rapidly with the objective of ratification by Member States before the end of 1992.

Foreign Ministers will prepare the conference. Preparatory work will be based on the results of the deliberations of Foreign Ministers . . . and on contributions from national governments and the Commission, and will be conducted in such a way as to permit negotiations on a concrete basis to begin from the start of the conference.

Close dialogue will be maintained with the European Parliament, both in the preparatory phase and in the conference phase on political union as well as on economic and monetary union.

The European Council considered that the necessary coherence in the work of the two conferences should be ensured by the General Affairs Council.

E.   Conclusions of the special meeting of the European Council held in Rome on 27–28 October 1990 (Extract)

Progress towards European union

At this crucial time for Community integration, the European Council has decided to take a further step towards European unity.

The European Council held a detailed discussion, on the basis of the reports submitted by the Presidency, on the state of preparation of the two Intergovernmental Conferences on Political Union and Economic and Monetary Union to open in December of this year and to proceed simultaneously, in accordance with the timetable set in Dublin.

Conference on political union

The European Council expressed its appreciation of the report from the Presidency and of the Commission's opinion pursuant to Article 236 of the Treaty, which constitute substantial contributions to future proceedings.

The European Council confirmed the will progressively to transform the Community into a European union by developing its political dimension, strengthening its capacity for action and extending its powers to other supplementary sectors of economic integration which are essential for convergence and social cohesion. European union will be the culmination of a progressive process agreed by common accord among the Member States; it will evolve with due regard being paid to national identities and to the principle of subsidiarity, which will allow a distinction to be made between matters which fall within the union's jurisdiction and those which must remain within national jurisdiction.

In accordance with the democratic tradition of all Member States, and to increase the democratic legitimacy of the union, the progress of the Community towards European union must be accompanied by the development of the European Parliament's role in the legislative sphere[1] and with respect to the monitoring of the activities of the union, which, together with the role of the national parliaments, will underpin the democratic legitimacy of the union. This same requirement will be met by defining European citizenship,[1] to be additional to citizenship of a Member State, as well as by taking account, in accordance with appropriate procedures, of the particular interests of the regions.

At the same time, efforts will be made to strengthen the other institutions within a balanced framework by developing the instruments and procedures which have hitherto guaranteed the Community's success. The tasks of the European Council and of the General Affairs Council will also be adjusted in line with these new responsibilities.

In the sphere of foreign policy, the European Council recorded consensus on the objective of a common foreign and security policy[1] to strengthen the identity of the Community and the coherence of its action on the international scene, both of which must be capable of meeting new challenges and commensurate with its responsibilities. The Community's international action will be open to the world and will give a significant role to development policy. The Community will also strengthen its links with the other European countries for which ever-closer cooperation structures must be sought, geared to their individual circumstances.

The European Council noted the need to review the procedures and mechanisms for preparing, adopting and implementing decisions where foreign policy is concerned, so as to increase the coherence, speed and effectiveness of the Community's international action.

The European Council considers that no aspect of the union's external relations will in principle be excluded from the common foreign policy. The European Council noted that there was a consensus to go beyond the present limits in regard to security.[2] The content and detailed rules for the role of the union in the security sphere will have to be defined gradually in the light of the various aspects covered by this concept and without prejudice to the obligations arising out of the security arrangements to which Member States are party.

The European Council requests the Foreign Affairs Ministers to continue the preparatory work leading up to the opening of the Intergovernmental Conference. The Presidency will report on this work and will take account of the opinions of the European Parliament and the Commission.

Conference on economic and monetary union

The European Council in Madrid fixed the date for the start of the first phase of economic and monetary union; in Strasbourg and Dublin it set the timetable for the Intergovernmental Conference and the ratification of its results. It now notes with satisfaction the important developments that have occurred in the wake of these decisions.

The European Council takes note of the results of the preparatory work that constitutes the basis for the Intergovernmental Conference.

For the final phase of economic and monetary union 11 Member States consider that the work on the amendment of the Treaty will be directed to the following points:

(i) for economic union, an open market system that combines price stability with growth, employment and environmental protection and is dedicated to sound and sustainable financial and budgetary conditions and to economic and social cohesion. To this end, the ability to act of the Community institutions will be strengthened;

(ii) for monetary union, the creation of a new monetary institution comprising Member States' central banks and a central organ, exercising full responsibility for monetary policy. The monetary institution's prime

[1,2] On these points the United Kingdom delegation prefers not to pre-empt the debate in the Intergovernmental Conference.

task will be to maintain price stability; without prejudice to this objective, it will support the general economic policy of the Community. The institution as such, as well as the members of its council, will be independent of instructions. It will report to the institutions which are politically responsible.

With the achievement of the final phase of economic and monetary union, exchange rates will be irrevocably fixed. The Community will have a single currency — a strong and stable ecu — which will be an expression of its identity and unity. During the transitional phase, the ecu will be further strengthened and developed.

The second phase will start on 1 January 1994 after:

(i) the single market programme has been achieved;

(ii) the Treaty has been ratified; and, by its provisions:

(iii) a process has been set in train designed to ensure the independence of the members of the new monetary institution at the latest when monetary powers have been transferred;

(iv) the monetary financing of budget deficits has been prohibited and any responsibility on the part of the Community or its Member States for one Member State's debt precluded;

(v) the greatest possible number of Member States have adhered to the exchange-rate mechanism.

The European Council recalls that, in order to move on to the second phase, further satisfactory and lasting progress towards real and monetary convergence will have to be achieved, especially as regards price stability and the restoration of sound public finances.

At the start of the second phase, the new Community institution will be established. This will make it possible, in particular, to:

(i) strengthen the coordination of monetary policies;

(ii) develop the instruments and procedures needed for the future conduct of a single monetary policy;

(iii) oversee the development of the ecu.

At the latest within three years of the start of the second phase, the Commission and the council of the monetary institution will report to the Economic and Financial Council and to the General Affairs Council on the functioning of the second phase and in particular on the progress made in real convergence, in order to prepare the decision concerning the passage to the third phase, which will occur within a reasonable time. The General Affairs Council will submit the dossier to the European Council.

The Treaty may lay down transitional provisions for the successive stages of economic and monetary union according to the circumstances of the various countries.

The United Kingdom is unable to accept the approach set out above. It agrees, however, that the overriding objective of monetary policy should be price stability, that the Community's development should be based on an open market system, that excessive budget deficits should be avoided, and that there should be no monetary financing of deficits nor the assumption of responsibility on the part of the Community or its Member States for one Member State's debt. The United Kingdom, while ready to move beyond Stage I through the creation of a new monetary institution and a common Community currency, believes that decisions on the substance of that move should precede decisions on its timing. It would, however, be prepared to see the approach it advocates come into effect as soon as possible after ratification of the necessary Treaty provision.

Organization of Conferences

Both Intergovernmental Conferences will open on 14 December 1990.

Annex I

Organization of the Conferences

I.14. The composition of national delegations will be decided on by the respective governments. The Commission will be invited to take part with its own representative.

In accordance with the conclusions of the Dublin European Council of 25 and 26 June 1990 the necessary coherence in the work of the two Conferences will be ensured by the Foreign Ministers. The Foreign Ministers will be assisted by their personal representatives at the Conference on Political Union and those representatives may also participate in the work of the Conference on Economic and Monetary

Union. The President of the Commission will also designate his own representative. Consistency and parallel progress will also be ensured by means of regular contacts between the President of the Commission and the Presidency of the two Conferences (Conference on Political Union and Conference on Economic and Monetary Union).

Interinstitutional meetings will be held during the Conferences. In addition to the regular contacts between the Chairman of the Conference, the President of the Commission and the President of the European Parliament, the latter may ask to address the Conference before the start of some of its meetings.

The Secretary-General of the Council will take the necessary steps to provide secretarial services for the two Conferences.

F. Conclusions of the European Council Meeting held in Rome on 14–15 December 1990 (Extract)

Political union

The European Council notes with satisfaction all the preparatory work which is to serve as a basis for the Intergovernmental Conference on Political Union.

The Union will be based on the solidarity of its Member States, the fullest realization of its citizens' aspirations, economic and social cohesion, proper balance between the responsibilities of the individual States and the Community and between the roles of the institutions, coherence of the overall external action of the Community in the framework of its foreign, security, economic and development policies and of its efforts to eliminate racial discrimination and xenophobia in order to ensure respect for human dignity.

Without prejudice to other subjects raised by Governments or by the Commission in the preparatory work, the European Council asks the Conference to give particular attention to the following:

1. Democratic legitimacy

In order to strengthen the role of the European Parliament, the European Council asks the Conference to consider the following measures:

(i) extension and improvement of the cooperation procedure;

(ii) extension of the procedure for assent to international agreements which require unanimous approval by the Council;

(iii) involvement of the European Parliament in the appointment of the Commission and its President;

(iv) increased powers on budget control and financial accountability;

(v) closer monitoring of the implementation of Community policies;

(vi) consolidation of the rights of petition and enquiry as regards Community matters.

The European Council also discussed further-reaching reforms on the role of the European Parliament and asks the Conference to consider developing co-decision procedures for acts of a legislative nature, within the framework of the hierarchy of Community acts.

Consideration should be given to arrangements allowing national parliaments to play their full role in the Community's development.

The European Council notes the particular importance which some Member States attach to:

(i) the adoption of arrangements that take account of the special competence of regional or local institutions as regards certain Community policies;

(ii) the need to consider suitable procedures for the consultation of such institutions.

2. Common foreign and security policy

The European Council welcomes the broad agreement on basic principles concerning the vocation of the Union to deal with aspects of foreign and security policy, in accordance with a sustained evolutive process and in a unitary manner, on the basis of general objectives laid down in the Treaty.

The common foreign and security policy should aim at maintaining peace and international stability, developing friendly relations with all countries, promoting democracy, the rule of law and respect for human rights, and encouraging the economic development of all nations, and should also bear in mind the special relations of individual Member States.

To this end, the Conference will in particular address the Union's objectives, the scope of its policies and the means of fostering and ensuring their effective implementation within an institutional framework.

Such an institutional framework would be based on the following elements:

(i)   one decision-making centre, namely the Council;

(ii) harmonization and, where appropriate, unification of the preparatory work; a unified Secretariat;

(iii) a reinforced role for the Commission, through a non-exclusive right of initiative;

(iv) adequate procedures for consulting and informing the European Parliament;

(v)   detailed procedures ensuring that the Union can speak effectively with one voice on the international stage, in particular in international organizations and *vis-à-vis* third countries.

The following elements should be considered as a basis for the decision-making process:

(i)   the rule of consensus in defining general guidelines; in this context, non-participation or abstention in the voting as a means of not preventing unanimity;

(ii) the possibility of recourse to qualified-majority voting for the implementation of agreed policies.

As regards common security, the gradual extension of the Union's role in this area should be considered, in particular with reference, initially, to issues debated in international organizations: arms control, disarmament and related issues; CSCE matters; certain questions debated in the United Nations, including peacekeeping operations; economic and technological cooperation in the armaments field; coordination of armaments export policy; and non-proliferation.

Furthermore, the European Council emphasizes that, with a view to the future, the prospect of a role for the Union in defence matters should be considered, without prejudice to Member States' existing obligations in this area, bearing in mind the importance of maintaining and strengthening the ties within the Atlantic alliance and without prejudice to the traditional positions of other Member States. The idea of a commitment by Member States to provide mutual assistance, as well as proposals put forward by some Member States on the future of Western European Union, should also be addressed.

3. European citizenship

The European Council notes with satisfaction the consensus among Member States that the concept of European citizenship should be examined.

It asks the Conference to consider the extent to which the following rights could be enshrined in the Treaty so as to give substance to this concept:

(i)   civil rights: participation in elections to the European Parliament in the country of residence; possible participation in municipal elections;

(ii) social and economic rights: freedom of movement and residence irrespective of engagement in economic activity, equality of opportunity and of treatment for all Community citizens;

(iii) joint protection of Community citizens outside the Community's borders.

Consideration should be given to the possible institution of a mechanism for the defence of citizens' rights as regards Community matters ('ombudsman').

In the implementation of any such provisions, appropriate consideration should be given to particular problems in some Member States.

4. Extension and strengthening of Community action

The European Council notes that there is a wide recognition of the need to extend or redefine the Community's competence in specific areas.

It asks the Conference to bear in mind, *inter alia*, the following areas:

(i)   the social dimension, including the need for social dialogue;

(ii) economic and social cohesion among the Member States;

(iii) improved protection of the environment in order to ensure sustainable growth;

(iv) the health sector and in particular the combating of major diseases;

(v) a research effort commensurate with the development of the Community's competitive capacity;

(vi) an energy policy aiming at greater security and efficiency, bearing also in mind cooperation in the whole of Europe;

(vii) providing the Community with major infrastructures, in order also to permit the completion of a trans-European network;

(viii) safeguarding the diversity of the European heritage and promoting cultural exchanges and education.

It should also be considered whether and how activities currently conducted in an intergovernmental framework could be brought into the ambit of the Union, such as certain key areas of home affairs and justice, namely immigration, visas, asylum and the fight against drugs and organized crime.

The European Council agrees on the importance of the principle of subsidiarity, not only when considering the extension of Union competence but also in the implementation of Union policies and decisions.

The European Council stresses the fact that the Union must have at its disposal all the necessary resources to achieve the objectives that it sets and to carry out the resulting policies.

5. Effectiveness and efficiency of the Union

The European Council discussed how to ensure the effectiveness and efficiency of the Union's institutions.

It agreed that the essential role that the European Council has played over recent years in creating fundamental political momentum will continue. The Conference will consider whether the Community's development towards the Union necessitates an accentuation of this role.

Regarding the Council, the extension of majority voting will be examined by the Con-

ference, including the possibility of making it the general rule with a limited number of exceptions.

Regarding the Commission, the European Council emphasized that extending the responsibilities of the Union must be accompanied by a strengthening of the Commission's role and in particular of its implementing powers so that it may, like the other institutions, help to make Community action more effective.

As for the Community's other institutions and organs, the Conference will examine the question of how to improve their effectiveness and efficiency in the light of the suggestions presented by those institutions and by Member States.

Economic and monetary union

The European Council takes note of the Report by the Committee of Governors of the Central Banks, of the draft statute and of the draft Treaty on Economic and Monetary Union submitted by the Commission.

The European Council notes that the Intergovernmental Conferences on Political Union and Economic and Monetary Union will open in Rome on 15 December 1990. The Conferences will take due account of the opinions given by the European Parliament and by the Commission under Article 236 of the Treaty.

The European Council confirms that the work of the two Conferences will proceed in parallel and should be concluded rapidly and at the same time. The results will be submitted for ratification simultaneously with the objective of ratification before the end of 1992.

The European Council takes note of the President's report on his discussions with the European Parliament concerning, inter alia, the contacts between the Conferences and the European Parliament.

The European Council decides to take the fullest account of the European Parliament's views during the Intergovernmental Conferences and at the time of their conclusion.

2. European Parliament Resolutions preceding the IGCs

A. Resolution on the intergovernmental conference decided on at the European Council in Madrid, 23 November 1989

The European Parliament,

– having regard to the final communiqué of the Madrid Summit,

A. whereas the Member States founded the European Community with the aim of creating an ever closer union between the peoples of Europe based on strengthening parliamentary democracy, not weakening it,

B. whereas when the original Community statute was laid down in the founding Treaties the only form of representation was at national level and was of necessity based on intergovernmental negotiations, a situation that prevailed until the election of the European Parliament by universal suffrage,

C. whereas by virtue of its election by direct universal suffrage, the European Parliament's legitimate role is to express the will of the peoples of the Community,

D. whereas in the present state of the Community, the direct democratic mandate takes two different forms: first, that of the direct European mandate embodied by the European Parliament elected by direct universal suffrage, and second, by the direct national mandates expressed according to the various national constitutions,

E. whereas this implies that any modification of the founding Treaties and of Community legislation, particularly the drawing up of the constitutional bases of the European Union, requires a joint decision by the Member States, meeting in the Council of Ministers, and the European Parliament,

F. having regard to its repeatedly expressed belief that the democratic structure of the Community will remain incomplete until Parliament possesses joint decision-making rights on an equal footing with the Council in all important policy decisions, in particular in legislation, and has a decisive say in the appointment of the Commission,

G. convinced that Parliament must have acquired joint decision-making powers on an equal footing with the Council on legislative matters at the latest by the next elections in 1994,

H. recalling that, although Article 236 of the EEC Treaty refers to an intergovernmental conference to agree to modifications to the Treaty, such conferences have in the past never been restricted to representatives of governments but have always included representatives from at least one Community institution, namely the Commission, and that nothing in the Treaty precludes the governments concerned from including representatives from other Community institutions or from seeking to reach agreement with such representatives,

I. recalling its dissatisfaction with the procedures followed during the drafting and adoption of the Single European Act, which failed to meet its demands for democratic reforms,

J. whereas the Community must equip itself with the means to defend its legitimate interests and play its rightful international role, notably in establishing a lasting peace in Europe and, in particular, in fulfilling its historic task vis-à-vis the peoples of Central and Eastern Europe and guaranteeing the individual and social rights of European citizens,

K. whereas the objectives of the draft treaty establishing the European Union, adopted by Parliament on 14 February 1984, remain in force as guidelines and whereas Parliament, in its resolution of 16 February 1989, claimed responsibility for implementing these objectives,

L. whereas the upsurge of democracy in Central and Eastern Europe calls for a swift and significant strengthening of the democratic and political nature of the Community, both as a guarantee of its political cohesion and as a model of credible political democracy and of genuinely democratic institutions,

M. whereas economic and monetary union must be accompanied by a social dimension which must keep pace with the economic and monetary aspects,

1. Calls on the Member States, in the light of the decision of the European Council in Madrid to convene an intergovernmental conference in 1990, to take full account of the aforementioned dual representation so as to enable Parliament to take part on equal terms in both the preparatory stages and the intergovernmental conference itself;

2. Accepts the successive proposals of Felipe Gonzalez and François Mitterrand and proposes the convocation of a preliminary conference at the beginning of 1990 in which an equal number of representatives of the Commission, the Council and the European Parliament will take part and which will draw up specific proposals for the necessary reform of the Treaty; Instructs its President to invite the Commission and the governments to this conference; Invites the parliaments of the member countries to the "European Assizes", an assembly of the parliaments of Europe, to discuss the next stages in the implementation of the European Union;

3. Instructs its Committee on Institutional Affairs to draw up a report in preparation for an assembly of the parliaments of Europe, the "European Assizes", which should begin in the second half of 1990;

4. Calls on the Heads of States or Government to confirm the decision to hold an intergovernmental conference when they meet at the European Council on 8 and 9 December in Strasbourg, to enable it to be opened immediately after the implementation of the first stage of economic and monetary union, since amendments to the Treaties need to be drawn up for this purpose;

5. Calls for the mandate of the intergovernmental conference to include the revision of the Treaties to provide for more efficient and more democratic decision-making in the Community, including more majority voting in Council (especially in environmental and social matters), a strengthening of the Commission's powers to implement Community policies and the enlargement of the power of the European Parliament;

6. Calls for these amendments to the Treaties to confer on the European Parliament the following powers:

– co-decision with the Council on Community legislation;
– right to initiate legislative proposals;
– right to give its assent to the appointment of the Commission, the Court of Justice and the Court of Auditors;
– right of inquiry;
– ratification of all constitutional decisions which also require ratification by the Member States;
– ratification of all important international agreements and international conventions requiring ratification, before their entry into force in the Community;

calls also for the Declaration on fundamental rights and freedoms to be incorporated in the Treaty;

7. Calls on the Member States to ensure that the construction of European Union goes hand-in-hand with a strengthening of regional autonomy according to the principle of subsidiarity;

8. Asks that the next intergovernmental conference should also consider the social dimension of Europe and in particular provide for the extension of qualified majority voting and the cooperation procedure to all social policy matters, so that clearly-defined fundamental social rights secured by procedures before the Community's judicial authorities may actually be established;

9. Points out that European economic and monetary union and the completion of the single market are likely to exacerbate the present disparities between the various regions and will make it necessary to ensure the overall consistency of all Community policies with a view to the balanced development of the regions of Europe;

10. Affirms that its acceptance of the results of the intergovernmental conference will be subject to respect for the conditions regarding procedure and substance referred to above and calls on the national parliaments to support the European Parliament's position as regards the results of this conference;

11. Decides to begin immediately to formulate the constitutional bases of the European Union on the basis of the principles of the draft treaty adopted on 14 February 1984 (subsidiarity, effectiveness and democracy) and of the political and legal consequences ensuing if a small minority of Member States did not join the European Union;

12. Calls on the Commission fully to support the demands made by Parliament regarding the preparations for, the holding of and the mandate of the intergovernmental conference;

13. Instructs its President to forward this resolution to the Council, the Commission and the national governments and parliaments.

B. Resolution on the Intergovernmental Conference in the context of Parliament's strategy for European Union, 14 March 1990 (Martin I Report)

The European Parliament,

- having regard to the Treaties establishing the European Communities and the Single Act amending them,

- having regard to the Solemn Declaration of the Stuttgart European Council of 19 June 1983,[1]

- having regard to its draft Treaty establishing the European Union, adopted on 14 February 1984,[2]

- having regard to its resolution of 16 January 1986 on the Single European Act, in particular paragraph 4 thereof,[3] and its resolution of 11 December 1986 on the Single European Act,[4]

- having regard to its reports demonstrating the insufficiencies of the treaties as amended by the Single European Act and notably its resolutions of:
    - 17 July 1988 on the cost of "non-Europe",[5]
    - 17 July 1988 on the democratic deficit,[6]
    - 17 July 1988 on the procedures for consulting European citizens on European political unification,[7]
    - 27 October 1988 on the first year of application of the Single European Act,[8]
    - 12 April 1989 on Fundamental Rights and Freedoms,[9]
    - 10 October 1988 and 15 December 1989 on the annual reports of the Council on progress towards European Union;

- having regard to various resolutions adopted by national parliaments at the time of ratification of the Single Act or subsequently,

- having regard to the contacts and discussions between its Committee on Institutional Affairs and Delegations from the National Parliaments,

- having regard to its resolution of 16 February 1989 on the strategy of the European Parliament for achieving European Union,[10]

- having regard to the results of the European elections and of the referendum held in Italy on the occasion of the European elections on the granting of a constituent mandate to the European Parliament,

- having regard to the agreement reached at the European Council to convene an Intergovernmental Conference to revise the Treaty with a view to the final stages of EMU,

- having regard to its resolution of 14 April 1989 on the process of European monetary integration,[11] and to its resolution of 25 October 1989 on EMU,[12]

- having regard to its resolution of 18 November 1988 on Community regional policy and the role of the regions,[13] and the attached Community Charter for Regionalization,

- having regard to its resolution of 23 November 1989 on the proposed Intergovernmental Conference called for by the European Council in Madrid,[14]

---

[1] EP Bulletin No. 26 of 28 June 1983.
[2] OJ No C 77, 19.3.1984, p. 33.
[3] OJ No C 36, 17.2.1986, p. 144.
[4] OJ No C 7, 12.1.1987, p. 83.
[5] OJ No C 187, 18.7.1988, p. 244.
[6] OJ No C 187, 18.7.1988, p. 229.
[7] OJ No C 187, 18.7.1988, p. 231.
[8] OJ No C 309, 5.12.1988, p. 93.
[9] OJ No C 120, 16.5.1989, p. 51.
[10] OJ No C 69, 12.3.1989, p. 145.
[11] OJ No C 120, 16.5.1989, p. 331.
[12] OJ No C 304, 4.12.1989, p. 43.
[13] OJ No C 326, 19.12.1988, p. 289.
[14] OJ No C 323, 27.12.1989, p. 111.

- having regard to the report of its Committee on Institutional Affairs and the opinion of the Committee on External Economic Relations (Doc. A3-47/90),

A. reaffirming that Member States have an absolute duty to abide by the judgments of the Court and to implement directives on time; and that failure on their part to create a single market by 31 December 1992 will have grave implications for the future development of the Community into a European Union;

B. whereas it is increasingly necessary rapidly to transform the European Community into a European union of federal type and going beyond the single market and economic and monetary union; whereas this is desired by a substantial majority of the public, as indicated by recent public opinion surveys,

C. whereas progress is particularly urgent in reforming the treaties to provide for a balanced and equitable development of the Single Market and the Monetary Union, notably by providing the Community with clearer and more effective responsibilities in the field of social and environmental policies on the basis of the principle of subsidiarity,

D. whereas the Single European Act itself requires a review of European political cooperation procedures by 1992 and whereas this review is becoming all the more urgent in view of the need for a united foreign policy in face of momentous events outside the Community,

E. whereas progress towards a citizens' Europe has been extremely limited, notably due to the lack of provisions of the treaties enabling progress to be made in this field,

F. whereas even the current level of responsibilities entrusted to the Community require more effective and more democratic institutions,

G. whereas greater effectiveness of the institutions can be achieved notably by providing for systematic majority voting in the Council and the strengthening of the Commission's right to exercise executive powers independently from committees of national civil servants (Comitology),

H. whereas fundamental democratic principles require that Community legislation should only enter into force with the explicit approval, not only of the Council representing national governments, but also of the European Parliament, representing the electorate as a whole,

I. whereas the appointments made to Community bodies exercising important responsibilities and above all, the appointment of the European Commission and in particular its President, should be subject to the scrutiny and consent of the European Parliament,

J. whereas such changes should themselves be negotiated and agreed jointly by the representatives of the Member States and the European Parliament,

K. having regard to the statement by President Delors to the EP on 17 January 1990 on a single Intergovernmental Conference with two parallel themes, economic and monetary union as well as the institutional reforms of the European Community,

L. whereas Parliament has accepted the proposals made by the Presidents-in-Office of the European Council to organize an interinstitutional pre-Conference, which should take place early in 1990, and "assizes" with Members of national parliaments,

M. whereas the rapid changes on the international and European political scene require the Community to speed up its institutional development and the construction of the European Union,

1. Reaffirms that the agenda of the Intergovernmental Conference must be enlarged beyond economic and monetary union; notes that a number of national parliaments as well as the President of the Commission have lent their support to this view; considers that economic and monetary union constitutes only one of many areas of further development in the Community and that the Intergovernmental Conference should therefore consider a range of related issues and take the necessary decisions to avoid jeopardizing the balanced and uniform development of the Community in accordance with Parliament's proposals;

2. Reiterates its view that the Intergovernmental Conference should use as essential criteria in its deliberations the principles of subsidiarity and conferred powers, on the basis of which those powers not specifically conferred on the European Union remain within the Member States;

3. (a) Confirms its decision to convene a pre-Conference involving the European Parliament, the Commission and the Council, for the purpose of:

- preparing the mandate of the Intergovernmental Conference;
- establishing the nature of Parliament's participation in the Intergovernmental Conference;

(b) Decides, in accordance with the above-mentioned resolution of 23 November 1989 and its resolution of 14 December 1989 on the European Council in Strasbourg and the French Presidency's six months in office,[15] and given the need for all Council members to participate in the pre-Conference, that the Parliament delegation shall consist of twelve members;

(c) Decides to invite the Economic and Social Committee to send an observer to the inter-institutional pre-conference;

(d) Calls for this pre-Conference to commence by Spring 1990 and to continue its work until the parties attending the pre-Conference have reached a joint agreement;

4. Instructs its representatives at the pre-Conference to press for the following items to be included on the agenda of the Intergovernmental Conference:

(a) the creation of economic and monetary union in accordance with a specific, automatic and mandatory timetable, between the twelve Member States of the European Community or, if appropriate, between those willing;

(b) a rationalization of the Community's instruments for external relations, notably the full integration of EPC into the Community framework including the granting to the Commission of powers akin to those it possesses in other areas of Community policy in view of ultimately achieving common foreign and security policies in the service of peace;

(c) better treaty provisions in the social and environmental sectors to ensure that the Community is able to develop and manage more effective policies in these fields, so that the single market works to the benefit of all Community citizens and contributes to a better environment;

(d) incorporation into the treaties of the Declaration on Fundamental Rights and Freedoms adopted by Parliament on 12 April 1989 and of provisions promoting a citizens' Europe and the preservation of Europe's cultural diversity;

(e) further improvements in the decision-making capacity of Council, notably by providing for systematic majority voting;

(f) a strengthening of the Commission's powers to implement Community legislation and execute its programmes and policies;

(g) the reform of the system of Community own-resources;

(h) recognition at Community level of the dual legitimacy conferred to the Council on the one hand and the European Parliament on the other, by conferring upon Parliament the powers listed in its resolution of 23 November 1989:

- co-decision with Council on Community legislation,
- right to initiate legislative proposals,
- right to elect the President of the Commission and to give its assent to the appointment of the Commission, the Court of Justice and the Court of Auditors,
- right of inquiry within the framework of the Community's powers,
- ratification of all constitutional decisions which also require ratification by the Member States,
- co-decision in external agreements and international conventions through the parliamentary assent procedure to be extended to all agreements of major importance, including trade agreements,

Finally, it should also consider the institutional future of Europe with a view to instructing the European Parliament to finalize the draft constitution of the European Union, and how best to ensure the cooperation of the national parliaments in the "assizes" in connection with the forthcoming Intergovernmental Conference; in the future construction of the European Union; and in particular in the work of the European Parliament;

---

[15] See Minutes of that day's sitting — Part II, Item 1.

5. Reiterates the demand contained in its resolution of 23 November 1989 that the Intergovernmental Conference proposals be submitted to the European Parliament and the governments acknowledge its right to amend and adopt them; if the European Parliament's position differs from that of the Intergovernmental Conference, a suitable procedure should be initiated with a view to reaching agreement to be submitted to the Member States for ratification; requests that the President of the Parliament, on the same basis as the President of the Commission, should be invited to the ministerial level meetings of the IGC;

6. Undertakes to adopt its opinion on the convening of the Intergovernmental Conference as soon as possible following agreement in the interinstitutional pre-Conference;

7. Requests the Commission to contribute to the success of the interinstitutional pre-Conference; accordingly expects the Commission, throughout the Intergovernmental Conference, to defend Community interest and, in particular, the demands of Community citizens as expressed through their representatives in the European Parliament;

8. Reaffirms its commitment to draw up a draft European constitution and to discuss its proposals with the national parliaments;

9. Reiterates its commitment to have its proposals adopted by all democratic means, in particular by mobilizing European public opinion and its democratically elected representatives;

10. Recalls its position that, while participation in European Union cannot be imposed upon any state against its will, on the other hand, no single State can block the will of the majority to achieve European Union and, if necessary, such a Union should be set up without the initial participation of all the Member States of the Community;

11. Instructs its President to forward this resolution to the Commission, the Council, the governments and parliaments of the Member States and the Economic and Social Committee.

C. Resolution on Economic and Monetary Union, 16 May 1990 (Herman Report)

The European Parliament,

- having regard to its resolution of 14 April 1989[16] on the process of European monetary integration and its resolution of 25 October 1989[17] on Economic and Monetary Union,

- having regard to the Commission's working document of March 1990 which rules out both a system based on competition between monetary policies and any system which does not provide for closer economic union since these two systems do not offer any guarantee of stability and do not reflect political trends in the Community,

- having regard to the interim report of the Committee on Economic and Monetary Affairs and Industrial Policy (Doc. A3-99/90),

A. whereas Economic and Monetary Union is a declared aim of the Community voiced on repeated occasions after 1969 until it was finally enshrined in the EEC Treaty by virtue of the Single Act and explicitly reaffirmed by the Hanover, Madrid and Strasbourg European Councils,

B. whereas the harmonious achievement of this objective depends to a great extent on the acceleration of the political union of the Community with a revision of the Treaties involving a greater role for the European Parliament; and whereas this political union is made all the more necessary by the unification of Germany and the present developments in the Eastern European countries,

C. whereas completion of the single internal market cannot afford all the lasting, permanent advantages which the public expects unless it is rapidly cemented by means of Economic and Monetary Union in which the basic objective of a single cur-

16 OJ No C 120, 16.5.1989, p. 331.
17 OJ No C 304, 4.12.1989, p. 43.

rency will be attained via the progressive use of a common currency (the ecu),[18]

D. whereas the advantages of Economic and Monetary Union for the public, as well as for the governments of the Member States, are greatest when that Union is carried to the ultimate degree, namely a single currency; whereas, conversely, the constraints weighing on the national governments are heaviest when the latter commit themselves to maintaining permanent fixed exchange parities,

E. whereas the beneficial effects that Economic and Monetary Union will have on economic growth and employment are likely to afford the Member States and the Community considerable scope for intensifying their policies in the social, regional and ecological spheres and for giving more meaningful expression to solidarity with the countries of Eastern Europe and the Third World; furthermore, these policies must be implemented actively and pursued with determination,

F. whereas on account of their interplay, economic convergence and cohesion and monetary unification must go hand in hand and whereas, in this connection, the Treaties must be amended in order to enable the Community to consolidate Economic Union and Monetary Union alike,

G. whereas Monetary Union must bring about monetary stability and promote economic and social progress and whereas these objectives can be guaranteed by means of a European central bank system (ECBS) whose autonomy has been secured in advance on the basis of clear legal bases,

H. whereas the ECBS must be given sole power to expand the money supply and the associated power, without requiring prior authorization, to use all the instruments which the leading modern central banks now have at their command to influence the money markets,

I. whereas the above autonomy is situated in the context of concerted action and cooperation with the Community institutions and the national authorities and implies a duty to lend active support to the general economic policy objectives laid down by the Community's political authorities,

J. whereas, in a democratically ordered society, the above autonomy must be counterbalanced by being made subject to public accountability and whereas the leaders of the ECBS must consequently be called to give an account of their stewardship before the European Parliament,

K. whereas the central bank of a federative system must be invested with a twofold legitimacy, that conferred by the people and that conferred by the Member States, and whereas the procedure in our Community legal system which accords most closely with that twofold legitimacy is the one which requires the Council and Parliament each to give their assent, acting on a proposal from the Commission, for determining the statute and operating procedures of the ECBS,

L. whereas to prevent the emergence of a centralized and bureaucratic monetary institution the European central bank should abide by the subsidiarity principle and entrust as many tasks and roles as possible to the existing central banks, its role being primarily one of coordination,

---

[18] For the purposes of this resolution:

A common currency is understood to be a currency circulating in parallel with the national currencies with which a fixed exchange parity has been established and which, without being legal tender, may be accepted and held freely in each of the Member States. The ecu already constitutes such a common currency, its value being determined by the weighted value of the currencies contained in the basket making up the ecu.

A single currency presupposes a single issuing authority, common management of foreign currency reserves, interest rates and exchange rates vis-à-vis third currencies, i.e. the abolition of the monetary powers of the national central banks.

In such a case, the national currencies can exist only as accounting currencies. Their relationship with the single currency would be established irrevocably and their value expressed as a multiple or percentage of the single currency. Such a single currency could circulate in the form of banknotes printed with the ecu value on one side and the national currency equivalent on the other. Notes and coins in circulation account for less than 10% of the money supply.

M. whereas, in order to avoid any prejudice by national authorities to the objective of monetary stability and the convergence of the Member States' macroeconomic policies, strict rules should be fixed strictly limiting the monetary financing of public deficits and banning the automatic bailing-out by the Community of any Member State in budgetary difficulties,

N. whereas the Community must provide itself with the intervention machinery and means required to ensure that the beneficial effects of Economic and Monetary Union are felt in all its regions,

O. whereas, although Community monetary policy can only be a single entity, the diversity of the national economies is still such that there is no option but to continue to apply economic policy measures on a case-by-case basis; whereas that diversity may, in addition, dictate a form of monetary integration which varies according to the Member States and is phased over time according to the degree of their economic convergence,

1. Emphasizes the urgent need to complete the single market by 31 December 1992 and to complement it by establishing Economic and Monetary Union at the earliest opportunity with a view to introducing a single currency as soon as possible;

2. Takes the view that adequate instruments to implement a Community economic policy should be created at Community level;

3. Considers that Economic and Monetary Union cannot be regarded as a realistic prospect unless at the same time the Community provides itself with the legal, budgetary and institutional means of ensuring greater coordination and convergence between the Member States' respective economic policies with a view to greater economic and social cohesion within the Community;

4. Cannot imagine that such a system would work unless budgetary policies are closely coordinated to ensure they are consistent with a monetary policy aimed at promoting stability and with other policies geared towards various other objectives such as balanced growth, full employment and a clean environment; this will involve strengthening the role of the Community budget with a view to promoting the social and economic cohesion of the Member States;

5. Welcomes the decision of Member States' authorities to avoid monetary financing of public deficit and the automatic bailing-out by the Community of any Member State in budgetary difficulties;

6. Agrees, however, with the Commission that direct rules placing upper limits on national budget deficits are neither necessary nor enforceable;

7. Considers that Economic and Monetary Union must be based on a European system of central banks entrusted with the task of autonomously pursuing a common monetary policy aimed at promoting price stability and based on criteria designed to further the balanced economic and social development of the Community and implemented, in accordance with the principle of subsidiarity, by means of a substantial delegation of powers to the national central banks;

8. Considers it essential for the principles of monetary stability and the autonomy of the European central banking system and the need to support general economic policy objectives to be enshrined in the Treaties, and for the mechanisms establishing this autonomy to be the subject of legal guarantees;

9. Considers that a European central banking system should be created that decides autonomously how to implement the monetary policy objectives agreed by the Council and approved by the European Parliament, while ensuring price stability and supporting the objectives of the general economic policy formulated by the Council and the European Parliament; in order to avoid any prejudice by national authorities to the objective of monetary stability and the convergence of the Member States' macroeconomic policies, strict rules should be fixed strictly limiting the monetary financing of public deficits and banning the automatic bailing-out by the Community of any Member State in difficulty, the authorities in charge of the ECBS must report annually on their management of the system to the Council and the European Parliament;

10. Believes that the authorities in charge of the ECBS should give an account of their activities at least once a year to the European Parliament; if and when special economic or currency conditions so require, they shall also make additional reports;

11. Calls for a system of cooperation relationships to be established between the central bank and those responsible for the Community's economic policy to help ensure that internal monetary policy is consistent with external exchange rate policy and to promote coordi-

nated economic policies on the understanding that the general guidelines on exchange rate policy are determined at political level;

12. Calls for monetary integration to be brought very rapidly to the stage where a single currency, the ecu, can be introduced to ensure that the potential advantages of the single market and Economic and Monetary Union are fully exploited, it being understood that a single currency can circulate alongside other currencies, particularly existing national currencies;

13. Calls on the Commission to examine the budgetary and financial measures and the instruments needed to ensure a reasonable spread among the regions of the welfare gains arising from inplementation of common policies, the internal market and Economic and Monetary Union;

14. Urges all the Member States simultaneously to use their best endeavours to achieve Economic and Monetary Union while anticipating that some countries might be granted longer deadlines for embarking on the various stages of integration provided such delays are justified; regards it as unacceptable, however, for formal commitments to be reneged on and the interests of 320 million citizens thwarted by a minority;

15. Declares its willingness to propose precise amendments to the treaties relating to Economic and Monetary Union;

16. Reaffirms that the next intergovernmental conference must consider what changes are needed to the Treaties to extend the Community's possibilities for action in the social area and environmental matters;

17. Instructs its President to forward this resolution to the Commission, the Council, the governments and parliaments of the Member States and the Economic and Social Committee.

D.   Resolution on the Intergovernmental Conference in the context of Parliament's strategy for European Union, 11 July 1990 (Martin II Report)

The European Parliament,

- having regard to its resolution of 14 March 1990 on the Intergovernmental Conference,[19]
- having regard to the Community Charter for Regionalization attached to its resolution of 18 November 1988,[20]
- having regard to the second interim report of its Committee on Institutional Affairs and the opinion of the Committee on Youth, Culture, Education, the Media and Sport (Doc. A3-166/90),

A. Whereas there have been a number of significant developments since, and partly in response to, the adoption of Parliament's resolution, notably:

  - the aide-memoire of the Belgian Government of 20 March 1990, which supports most of the key points in the Parliament's resolution;
  - the three resolutions adopted by the Italian Parliament on 21 March 1990

explicitly supporting the European Parliament's resolution and agreeing to host with the European Parliament the "assizes" of national parliaments and the European Parliament in October 1990;

  - the letter sent by President Mitterrand and Chancellor Kohl to the President-in-Office of the European Council calling for a second intergovernmental conference on political union in order to 'strengthen the democratic legitimacy of the union, render its institutions more efficient, ensure unity and coherence of the union's economic, monetary and political action and to define and implement a common foreign and security policy', this letter following on from the desire expressed on 25 March 1990 by President Mitterrand to see European political union completed by 31 December 1992;
  - the initiative of Felipe Gonzalez, the Spanish Prime Minister, for a citizens' Europe;

[19] OJ C 96, 17.4.1990, p. 114.
[20] OJ No C 326, 19.12.1988, p. 296.

- the ETUC declaration on the political union of Europe;
- the special meeting of the European Council in Dublin on 28 April 1990 at which the European Council "confirmed its commitment to political union" and charged the foreign ministers with preparing "proposals to be discussed at the European Council in June with a view to a decision on the holding of a second intergovernmental conference to work in parallel with that on EMU with a view to ratification in the same time-frame";
- the aide-memoires of the Greek, Dutch and Danish Governments, most aspects of which also support key points in Parliament's resolution;
- the discussions that took place at the first meeting of the interinstitutional preparatory conference held in Strasbourg on 17 May 1990;
- the informal meeting of the Foreign Ministers of the Community's Member States at Parknasilla on 18 and 19 May 1990 and the meeting of the General Affairs Council in Luxembourg on 18 and 19 June 1990;
- the meeting of the European Council of 25 and 26 June 1990 in Dublin which agreed to convene the two intergovernmental conferences,

1. Welcomes the fact that the agenda of the forthcoming reform of the Treaties is to be widened beyond economic and monetary union; underlines, however, its grave concern at the emergence of some positions within the Council defining "political union" as merely a reinforcement of the intergovernmental level of cooperation among the governments of the Member States of the EC;

2. Recalls its preference for a single intergovernmental conference possibly with two working groups, but accepts the proposal for two intergovernmental conferences provided that they are closely coordinated and that they aim for a single coherent package for ratification;

3. Considers that the term "political union" refers to the same aspirations as those which lay behind Parliament's draft Treaty on European Union of February 1984; reaffirms the essential elements of such a political union to be:

- economic and monetary union with a single currency and an autonomous central bank;
- a common foreign policy, including joint consideration of the issues of peace, security and arms control;
- a completed single market with common policies in all the areas in which the economic integration and mutual interdependence of the Member States require common action notably to ensure economic and social cohesion and a balanced environment;
- elements of common citizenship and a common framework for protecting basic rights;
- an institutional system which is sufficiently efficient to manage these responsibilities effectively and which is democratically structured, notably by giving the European Parliament a right of initiative, of co-decision with the Council on Community legislation, the right to ratify all constitutional decisions requiring the ratification of the Member States also and the right to elect the President of the Commission;

with these responsibilities being exercised on the basis of the principle of subsidiarity, which will enable the Union to develop dynamically;

4. Believes that a reform of the Treaties that would achieve these objectives would bring the European Community closer to the "European Union of federal type" advocated by the European Parliament in its resolution of 14 March 1990 and considers, therefore, that such changes should be consolidated in a "constitution" which the European Parliament should prepare; recalls its resolution of 11 July 1990[21] on this draft, which is based on its draft treaty of European Union of 1984, and which should become the basis for the transformation of the Community into a genuine union of federal type;

5. Regards it as essential, at the intergovernmental conference, to amend in a coherent manner all the Treaties establishing the European Communities, in particular the ECSC, EEC, EURATOM and Merger Treaties;

6. Reaffirms the areas in which it would like to see treaty reform, namely those listed in

[21] Part II, Item 10(a) of these Minutes.

paragraph 4 of its resolution of 14 March 1990, and spells out as follows the precise changes that it would seek to achieve for each of the areas listed in that resolution;

Economic and monetary union

7. Economic and monetary union should be established in accordance with a specific, automatic and mandatory timetable, between the 12 Member States of the European Community or, if appropriate, between those willing, in accordance with the criteria spelt out in Parliament's resolutions of 25 October 1989[22] and 16 May 1990[23] on economic and monetary union;

Community foreign policy

8. Considers that Article 30 of the Single European Act should be revised in order to provide for matters currently dealt with under EPC to be dealt with in the Community framework with appropriate procedures; believes that the current division between external economic relations handled by the Community institutions with the Commission acting as the Community's external representative, and political cooperation handled by EPC with the EPC President acting as external representative, is increasingly difficult to maintain in practice; considers that any genuine attempt "to assure unity and coherence in the Community's international action" must abolish this increasingly artificial distinction;

9. Calls therefore for the Council (rather than a separate framework of foreign ministers) to be given the prime responsibility for defining policy; for the Commission to have a right of initiative in proposing policies to Council and to have a role in representing the Community externally, including appropriate use of its external missions in third countries; and for the functions of the EPC secretariat to be absorbed by the Commission and Council; and for the Community's foreign policy to be subject to scrutiny by the Community's elected Parliament;

10. Calls for the scope of the Community's foreign policy to include issues of security, peace and disarmament, with a close coordination of national security policies, and to respect the principle of solidarity and the inviolability of the external borders of Member States;

11. Considers that in all these areas, the Community should aim to have common policies on all matters in which the Member States share essential interests;

12. Considers that membership of international organizations should be adjusted accordingly, with the Community as such seeking membership and representing the Member States in those areas where Community competence has been established, and it should therefore belong notably to the Council of Europe;

Better treaty provisions in the social, environmental, research and cultural sectors

13. Considers that, in order to ensure a balanced development of the internal market, the social and environmental provisions of the treaties should be among those in which majority voting in Council applies; believes this could be best achieved in the context of the improved legislative procedure outlined below;

14. Considers that the objectives of social policy, as defined in the treaties, should be extended, improved and completed, notably by:

- adding to Article 3 EEC the objective of common action in the field of social affairs and employment, which implies the affirmation of the right of workers to be informed and consulted before any decision affecting them;

- deleting paragraph 2 of Article 100a EEC and including social protection in matters concerned by paragraph 3;

- adding to Article 8a EEC that the completion and further evolution of the internal market necessarily imply provisions to secure the convergence, at a higher level, of living and working conditions;

- adding to Article 101 EEC the possibility of Commission intervention in cases where Community action in Member States causes serious economic or social distortion or where the intervention of the structural funds is insufficient;

- adding to the objectives of Article 117 EEC improved training and working conditions, equal opportunities, and access to education and culture, to be granted to

[22] OJ No C 304, 4.12.1989, p. 43.
[23] See Minutes of that sitting, Part II, Item 2.

all citizens of the Member States and to all persons legally resident in the Community;

- adding to the first paragraph of Article 118 of the EEC Treaty the indication that the Commission's task in the social sphere is to implement the common policy in the social affairs and employment sphere and to promote collaboration between the Member States;

- adding to the objectives of Article 118a EEC the continual improvement of living standards and social provisions, equal opportunities, training, minimum levels of social security and welfare, minimum provisions for union law and collective bargaining, covering also workers from third countries;

- amending Article 118b of the EEC Treaty by indicating that the Community must adopt a legal framework which enables the dialogue between the two sides of industry to develop so that European collective bargaining may be undertaken;

- adding to the objectives of Article 119 EEC, concerning equal pay for men and women, the objective of equal opportunities at work and in society;

- establishing, through Article 128 EEC, a common policy providing for all persons in the Community to have access to appropriate vocational training throughout working life;

- modifying the last words of Article 130a EEC to refer to least-favoured regions and population groups;

- strengthening or establishing objectives which are increasingly recognized as being urgent and necessary in the areas of education policy, the mass media, information, research and culture to promote a greater volume of exchanges, cooperation and joint programmes, which respect and enhance the pluralism and diversity which characterize European society;

15. Considers that the objectives of environmental policy, as defined in the Treaties, should be extended, improved and completed, notably by:

- adding to Article 130r(1) of the EEC

Treaty the objective of contributing to international action against the dangers threatening the ecological equilibrium of the planet;

- amending Article 130r(4) of the EEC Treaty in order to specify the Community's concrete contribution to achieving the objectives set out in Article 130r(1) through the establishment of a European Environment Fund;

16. Considers, further, that the Community must ratify the Council of Europe's Social Charter and the International Labour Organization's Conventions on fundamental social rights and the areas covered by Community law;

17. Regards the competences transferred to the Community in the environmental sphere as adequate on condition that their exercise is subject to the joint decision-making procedure set out below;

Fundamental rights and freedoms and a citizens' Europe

18. Calls for the incorporation into the Treaties of the declaration of fundamental rights and freedoms approved by the European Parliament on 12 April 1989;[24] calls for the incorporation into the Treaties of the Declaration against racism and xenophobia adopted by Parliament on 11 June 1986; calls for the Court of Justice to have jurisdiction for the protection of these fundamental rights vis-à-vis the Community with the possibility of direct access to the Court of Justice for Community citizens after national appeal procedures have been exhausted; considers furthermore that the Community should accede to the European Convention on Human Rights of the Council of Europe in order for the Community's procedures protecting fundamental rights to be subject to appeal to an external body at least in the areas covered by the Convention (in the same way as individual States, even those with charters of rights of their own, are subject to the European Convention);

19. Calls for provisions to be incorporated into the Treaties providing for the development of common forms of European citizenship through such measures as voting rights for Community citizens in municipal and European elections in their Member States of residence;

24 OJ No C 120, 16.5.1989, p. 51.

Improving the decision-taking capacity of Council

20. Believes that unanimity should no longer be required for decision-taking in Council, except for constitutional matters (revision of the treaties), accession of new Member States and extension of the field of Community responsibilities (Article 235); considers that the requirement for unanimity for ordinary Community legislation and policies is tantamount to the dictatorship of the minority; considers that the experience of the recent extension of the field of majority voting shows that a significant improvement in the decision-taking capacity of the Council can be achieved by this means;

21. Considers that Council should hold its meetings in public when adopting Community legislation, in order to allow more openness and better scrutiny;

22. Considers it essential to ensure the participation of the regions by means of a body consisting of representatives of the regional authorities in the Member States, whose function would be comparable to that of the Economic and Social Committee in its specific field;

23. Is aware that many national parliaments are seeking to improve their scrutiny over their country's member of Council; expresses its readiness to assist the parliaments of the Member States with access to information; will continue to cooperate with the parliaments of the Member States in the now regular meetings that take place at various levels between these parliaments and the European Parliament; considers, however, that it would not be useful to set up a new institution or "chamber of national parliaments" alongside the European Parliament, as:

- experience of the European Parliament prior to direct elections shows the practical limitations of such a body;
- Community institutions already include a body representing Member States (the Council) and a body representing the electorate directly (the European Parliament);
- decision-taking would become even more complex and therefore less transparent;

and instructs its Committee on Institutional Affairs to prepare practical proposals for improving cooperation with national parliaments;

Strengthening the Commission's implementing powers

24. Considers that the amendment of Article 145 EEC by Article 10 of the Single European Act has not been properly implemented and Declaration No 1 annexed to the Single Act has not been respected;

25. Calls for an amendment to Article 155 of the EEC Treaty and a corresponding deletion in Article 145 of the EEC Treaty in order to clarify that implementing powers should in all cases be conferred on the Commission which, for this purpose, may be assisted by an advisory committee (purely consultative) or a management committee (able, by a qualified majority, to suspend Commission decisions and refer them to the legislative authority (Parliament and Council));

26. Considers that democratic scrutiny of Commission implementing provisions should be ensured by means of an obligation on the Commission to inform Parliament and Council immediately of any such measures and to discuss them with the appropriate organ of Parliament or Council when requested, and that Parliament should have a period of one month after publication of such provisions in which to decide whether it wishes to subject them to the legislative procedure;

27. Believes that the Commission's responsibility to implement the budget as adopted should not be fettered by any committees other than advisory committees;

Strengthening the Community's ability to enforce application of its law

28. Believes that in order to be in a position to check on the implementation of Community law, the Commission must be reinforced by the creation of European Inspectorates working with or within it, most notably and urgently in the field of the environment, and that such Inspectorates should have the task of checking that national authorities are properly applying EC law;

29. Considers it necessary for the Court of Justice to be given powers, to be written into the Treaties, to impose sanctions, including financial sanctions, on Member States which fail to apply Community legislation or implement Court judgments;

Reforming the financial arrangements and in particular the system of own resources

30. Considers that, with the achievement of economic and monetary union and political union, the financial arrangements laid down in the Treaties are no longer adequate; considers, therefore, that there is a need for an overall review of those financial arrangements on the basis of a greater balance between the two branches of the budgetary authority and, in particular, that:

- Article 199 of the EEC Treaty should cover the financial activities of all the Communities, including those (e.g. EDF, ECSC) which have for various reasons not hitherto been included in the budget, and should also cover borrowing and lending operations;

- Article 201 should outline a full own resources regime which would ensure complete financial autonomy and sufficient financial resources for the Community; at all events, in order to ensure coverage of all budget expenditure, Article 200 should be updated,

- the multiannual financial estimates, as drawn up and periodically updated by the Council and Parliament, should form the basis of the budgetary procedure;

- in Article 203, all the special rules concerning compulsory expenditure should be deleted; the maximum rate rule should be replaced by a multiannual and annually rolling expenditure plan, to be determined jointly by Parliament and the Council;

- Articles 204 to 209 should be adapted in accordance with the plan to increase the powers of Parliament;

Recognizing the duality of Community legitimacy: Council and Parliament

31. Considers it to be absolutely essential that Community legislation should be adopted by a procedure of co-decision between Parliament and Council;

32. Believes that the proposal contained in the memorandum of the Belgian Government represents a significant step towards a co-decision procedure, but considers that such a method gives too much weight to the final possibility for the Parliament to reject legislation in what amounts to a third reading and a simple veto power might cast Parliament in

a negative light, as holding up the progress of the Community and causing interinstitutional conflict;

33. Calls for Parliament and the Council to be given equal rights and equal weight in the legislative process, provision being made for a mechanism to settle disputes with the following procedure:

(a) Commission proposals should be forwarded to Parliament which would have the right to approve, amend or reject them; amendments rejected by the Commission would require the support of a majority of the Members of Parliament;

(b) Council could then approve, amend or reject such proposals; it could approve by a majority any text in the form adopted by Parliament; it could amend such texts by a qualified majority where the Commission approved of such amendment or by unanimity where the Commission disapproved; it would require unanimity to approve a proposal rejected by Parliament;

(c) At first reading, flexible deadlines should be set to permit either of the two branches of legislative power to request application of the urgency procedure to a proposal which is being blocked by the other;

(d) If the text approved by Council conformed to that of Parliament, it would be definitively adopted; where it differed from that of Parliament, Council's position would be referred back to Parliament for a second reading;

(e) Parliament, in its second reading, could, by simple majorities, either approve Council's text, or request the opening of the conciliation procedure; should a proposal not be approved within 3 months, it would be referred to the Conciliation Committee;

(f) The Conciliation Committee would comprise an equal number of members of both institutions; members would not be bound by instructions;

The Commission would participate in the work of the committee;

The text agreed on by the committee would be forwarded to the Council and to Parliament for their decision. No further amendments would be admissible;

Should it not secure a majority in one of the two institutions, the legislative procedure would be closed;

(g) Proposals adopted by both Council and Parliament would become law upon the signature of the Presidents of the two institutions;

34. Calls for Parliament also to be given the right to initiate legislative proposals in cases where the Commission fails to respond within a specified deadline to a specific request adopted by a majority of Members of Parliament to introduce proposals; in such cases a Parliament proposal adopted by a majority of Members would be the basis for the subsequent stages of the legislative procedure described above;

35. Calls for Parliament to be given the right to elect the President of the Commission on a proposal from the European Council; the President should, with the agreement of Council, choose the Members of the Commission; the debate and the vote of confidence in a new Commission, which Parliament has held since 1981, should now be formalized in the Treaties;

36. Considers that the procedure whereby Parliament gives its opinion on each nomination to the Court of Auditors should be modified to provide for Parliament to give its approval by a simple majority to nominations to the Court of Auditors and that the same procedure should apply to nominations to the Court of Justice;

37. Calls for the budgetary control powers of the European Parliament to be enhanced and democratic control reinforced, and in particular:

(a) calls for the principle that the observations made in the discharge decisions are binding on all the institutions to be enshrined in the Treaty;

(b) calls for the discharge authority's right to ask the Court of Auditors to carry out investigations and submit reports to be enshrined in the Treaty;

38. Calls for the essential right to go to the Court of Justice for annulment should be explicitly granted to the European Parliament in the Treaties;

39. Demands that each of the three other institutions be entitled to consult the Court of Justice in respect of any matter regarding the interpretation of the Treaties;

40. Considers that Parliament should have a right, enshrined in the Treaties, to establish committees of inquiry to investigate alleged contraventions of Community law or instances of maladministration with respect to Community responsibilities; the Treaties should pro-

vide for an express obligation on Community institutions and other Community and Member State authorities to cooperate with such an inquiry;

41. Calls for Articles 216(EEC), 77(ECSC) and 189(EAEC) to be amended to give the European Parliament the right to fix its own seat unless, within two years, the Member States can finally agree (after a delay of over 30 years) to exercise their power and responsibility "to determine the seat of the institutions of the Community" under the existing Articles;

42. Believes that the assent procedure should be extended to include Treaty amendments (Article 236 EEC and its equivalents in the other Treaties), the uniform electoral system and all significant international agreements entered into by the Community;

43. Undertakes to submit appropriate drafts of Treaty articles and amendments conforming to the above requests in due time before the beginning of the intergovernmental conferences as part of its formal opinion required under Article 236(EEC) for the convening of the conferences; expects the intergovernmental conferences to examine Parliament's requests and either to incorporate them as such in the Treaty revision or to agree with Parliament on alternative possibilities, in accordance with the procedure put forward in paragraph 5 of its resolution of 14 March 1990;

44. Confirms its decision to deliver an opinion pursuant to Article 236 of the EEC Treaty on the convening of the Intergovernmental Conference on political union, on the basis of the results of the preparatory interinstitutional conference and in particular the consensus reached with the governments of the Member States and the Commission on the agenda for the conference and the role of the European Parliament;

45. Calls for a move from the present Community based on Treaties to a Union of federal type on a constitutional basis and demands therefore the amendment of Article 236 of the EEC Treaty, the new version of which should provide for approval of constitutional amendments by the two legislative arms (Council and Parliament) and their subsequent ratification by the Member State parliaments;

46. Considers in any event that such a major revision of the Treaties should be elaborated and agreed jointly by the representatives of the Member States and the representatives elected by the citizens of Europe to the European Parliament;

47. Instructs its President to forward this resolution to the Commission, the Council, the Court of Justice, the Court of Auditors, the Economic and Social Committee, the governments and the parliaments of the Member States and Applicant States and the consultative committee of local and regional authorities and to use this resolution for his submissions to preparatory meetings of the IGC, to "the Assizes" and to European Council meetings.

E. *Resolution on the principle of subsidiarity, 12 July 1990 (Giscard d'Estaing Report)*

The European Parliament,

- having regard to the ECSC, EEC and EURATOM Treaties and the Single European Act,
- having regard to the Draft Treaty establishing the European Union,
- having regard to the future development of the Community, in particular its commitment to draw up a draft constitution for European Union and the fact that this process of transforming the European Community requires a clear distinction to be made between the competences of the Union and those of the Member States,
- having regard to the special nature of the Community, which is based on the principles of democracy, the precedence of Community law over national law, respect for the individual character of the Member States and a unique institutional pattern,
- having regard to the Draft Treaty establishing the European Union which defines the principle of subsidiarity in its preamble and in Articles 12 and 66,
- having regard to the interim report of the Committee on Institutional Affairs and the opinion of the Committee on Youth, Culture, Education, the Media and Sport (Doc. A3-163/90),

1. Notes that the principle of subsidiarity is already implicit in the Treaties, that express reference is made to it there as a result of the Single European Act and that the European Parliament was at pains to give prominent and unequivocal political endorsement to that principle in its Draft Treaty establishing the European Union;

2. Recalls that the Treaties already provide certain important safeguards preventing any undue extension of Community competences, most notably:

- that the Community may act only on the basis of provisions laid down in the Treaties,
- that any extensive interpretation of the Community's objectives, to permit action where the Treaties have not provided an explicit power, may only occur with the unanimous approval of the governments of the Member States in Council (Article 235 EEC and equivalents in ECSC and EAEC Treaties),
- that any extension of Community competence requires modification of the Treaties, which involves unanimous approval of all the Member State governments and ratification by all the Member State parliaments;

3. Notes that the Court of Justice of the European Communities, which is responsible for ensuring respect for the law, has the role of guardian of the division of competences between the Community and the Member States;

4. Is aware of the importance of the principle of subsidiarity in the context of European Union and advocates respect for the "acquis communautaire", but holds the view that the division of tasks, spheres of activity and competences must make allowance for the stage reached at present, as well as the inevitable evolving of the Union, so as to promote and safeguard the interests of all the citizens of the Union and the specific nature of the regions;

5. Believes that ceding the Member States' legislative competences to the European Community, on the basis of the principle of subsidiarity, would worsen the democratic deficit in the Community, if the European Parliament failed to secure the legislative powers and powers to exercise democratic oversight lost by the parliaments of the Member States; elimination of the democratic deficit, in particular by reinforcing the powers of the European Parliament, is the additional element that is

vital for putting the principle of subsidiarity into practice;

6. Considers that the amendments to the Treaties announced by the governments in the context of the Intergovernmental Conference should make provision for specifically enshrining the principle of subsidiarity, so as to ensure the dynamic development of European integration and the greatest possible clarity with regard to the division of competences between the Community and the Member States;

7. Points out that there are very few areas in which the Community has been given exclusive competence (i.e. Member States may no longer act unilaterally in the field concerned, such as for customs tariffs) and that most areas of Community competences are in matters where Member States may also act ("concurrent competence", also known as "shared", "parallel" or "overlapping" competence); considers, therefore, that the principle of subsidiarity should be a guide not just to determine legally the areas in which the Community may act (which has been done in the Treaties) but also, and especially, as a political guide to the extent of Community action in the fields of concurrent competence;

8. Instructs its Committee on Institutional Affairs to look closely into the distribution of competences between the Community and Member States, with due regard for the constitutional structure of each Member State, in accordance with the provisions on this subject contained in the Draft Treaty establishing the European Union (1984);

9. Notes that when the principle of subsidiarity and the criteria mentioned in paragraph 7 are applied, far-reaching competences will remain with the Member States in the fields of economics, taxation, education, culture, social security, health, family policy, the organization of local government, public transport, infrastructure, police, penal code, private law, religion and many other areas;

10. Considers it indispensable for a European Union on a federal model to possess the competences already entrusted to the European Community and the competences essential, in particular, for the achievement of economic and monetary union, common foreign and security policies and the establishment of a People's Europe;

11. Believes that the principle of subsidiarity is important not only as a means of clearly defining the respective competences of the Community and the Member States, but also in respect of the way those competences are exercised;

12. Considers that political and judicial guarantees must be given with regard to respect for the principle of subsidiarity but that effective democratic procedures must be devised to enable the Union to exercise the competences it needs to carry out its tasks, without the risk of an institutional deadlock which might jeopardize the interests of Europe;

13. Confirms that by virtue of the need for unanimity (in the context of Article 235 of the EEC Treaty, Article 95 of the ECSC Treaty and Article 203 of the EURATOM Treaty) the Council (Chamber of States) remains the co-guarantor of respect for the principle of subsidiarity;

14. Considers that the Court of Justice should be given jurisdiction as a constitutional body, with the task of ensuring in particular that the division of competences between the European Community and the Member States is respected; with regard to respect for the principle of subsidiarity, it could have matters referred to it either on a consultative basis — when the Commission or the other institutions enjoying initiative submit the initial proposal — or on an a posteriori basis by the Member States, the Community institutions or the supreme courts of the Member States;

15. Instructs its President to forward this resolution to the Council, the Commission and the Governments of the Member States.

3. Belgian Government

Memorandum of 20 March 1990

Several considerations combine to suggest that the European Community be given a new stimulus towards political union.

(a) Firstly, the transformation of the political scene in Europe is creating a climate of uncertainty and giving rise to speculation. It is time to point out that:

   - the European Community has shown an example of reconciliation and prosperity to the whole continent;

   - this anchor point, far from disintegrating must, in a changing continent, be strengthened and developed in the interests of all Europeans;

   - the Community's political purpose, which has always been present in the European Treaties, now becomes essential for guaranteeing its credibility as a major actor on the European stage.

(b) Secondly, the internal development of the Community, in particular the completion of the internal market and economic and monetary union, highlights the growing "democratic shortfall" in the current institutional framework and requires reform involving a transfer of political power at Community level and a better definition of the principle of subsidiarity.

(c) Thirdly, the special responsibility which the Community is generally thought to have for seeking solutions to the problems of Central and Eastern Europe requires a capacity to take effective and consistent external action, at least in that part of the world.

In that situation, it is necessary in the first place to abide by the aims which the Community has already set itself:

   - completion of the internal market by adopting the legislative programme in the White Paper between now and the end of 1992;

   - introduction of economic and monetary union in accordance with a plan to be laid down by the Intergovernmental Conference called for the end of 1990;

   - development of the Community's social dimension along the lines indicated by the Social Charter adopted in Strasbourg in December 1989.

These aims must be energetically pursued but for the reasons set out above, should be accompanied by a corresponding effort in the institutional and political fields.

The aim of the proposals which follow is to:

   - strengthen the existing institutional machinery in order to make it more effective;

   - increase the democratic component of the institutional machinery by reinforcing the powers of Parliament and developing the Community's social dimension;

   - developing convergence between political cooperation and Community policy; here, the policy towards Central and Eastern Europe could be the first opportunity to put this into practice;

I. Institutional machinery

1. The Council

In order to make the Council more effective as a decision-making forum, the *qualified majority* should become the rule for all decisions taken in the area covered by the Treaties. If exceptions are unavoidable, they should be very few in number. A preliminary list of the relevant Articles in the Treaties is appended.

Unanimity would still be required to extend the range of subjects over which the Community has jurisdiction (Article 235) and for constitutional provisions (revision of the Treaties, accessions).

2. The Commission

(a) In order to reinforce the Commission's implementing powers it will be necessary to return to the spirit of the Single Act and in practice to restrict as much as possible the requirements for delegation and the specific cases in which the Council reserves the right to exercise power itself (see Article 145 - 3rd indent).

(b) In order to increase the Commission's effectiveness as Community executive, it will be necessary to:

- *strengthen the role of the President*

  The President should be elected by the Parliament by a qualified majority of its component members on the basis of a nomination submitted by the European Council before the other members of the Commission are appointed. It would be understood that the elected President plays a decisive role in allocating responsibilities among the Commissioners. This would no doubt enable him to exert real influence over the selection by Member States of the candidates presented for Commissioners;

- *reduce the number of Commissioners (P.M.)*

3. The Court

The authority of the Court is beginning to be undermined by the failure of Member States to take the necessary action on certain Judgments. Ways should be sought, and possibly incorporated in the Treaties, to ensure that Judgments are more fully enforced.

II. Democratic shortfall

1. The Parliament

There is no doubt that the Parliament should become more efficient in operation (in particular in order to cope more effectively with the additional tasks arising from completion of the internal market and from the Single Act), but that is essentially for Parliament itself to decide. The way to reduce the democratic shortfall is not by increasing efficiency but by increasing the powers of the Parliament, mainly in the legislative sphere (although changes might also be considered in the budgetary sphere).

The Parliament's main demand is for a *share in decision-making*. The following reforms would entail a form of joint decision-making:

- extending the *cooperation procedure* to all legislative decisions taken by the Council by a qualified majority (e.g. Articles 63 and 75);
- stipulating that legislative decisions (adopted by the Council on a second reading on completion of the cooperation procedure) may be annulled within three months of

their adoption if Parliament votes by an absolute majority of its component members. In this case the procedure should be begun again with a new Commission proposal.

This would do away with one of the main criticisms of the current practice, which enables the Council to adopt on a second reading Directives which are contrary to the wishes of a majority in the Parliament. Henceforth, every legislative provision would therefore presuppose a Council decision and at least tacit agreement by a majority in the Parliament;

- extending the assent procedure to amendments to the Treaty (Article 236), to own resources (Article 201) and important international agreements (extension of Article 238) and to the uniform procedure for elections to the European Parliament (Article 138(3)).
- conferring on the Parliament the responsibility for electing the President of the Commission (see above). The other members of the Commission (and the judges of the Court of Justice) would continue to be appointed by the Member States but would be subject to a Parliamentary approval procedure (as the members of the Court of Auditors are now).

Amendments of less importance might also be considered:

- strengthening the powers of committees of inquiry
- right of petition in Parliament
- right to take the legislative initiative where the Commission fails to act.

2. A People's Europe/Human Rights

- It will be difficult to achieve a People's Europe, which is directly linked with free movement of persons in the context of the single market, without introducing the qualified majority (see above and Annex).
- To strengthen the democratic nature of the institutional apparatus, it would be desirable for a provision on human rights to be written in to the Treaty and for the Community as such to accede to the Strasbourg Convention on Human Rights and to certain agreements relating to social rights.
- The Parliament should be encouraged to

draw up a uniform procedure for the European elections: this would also enable all Community citizens living in the Community to take part in the elections whatever their nationality.

- Subject to certain residence conditions, the right to vote in local elections, which has been included in a proposal for a Directive, should be phased in for Community citizens throughout Community territory.

III. Subsidiarity

At a time when the development of the European enterprise is leading to a major transfer of legislative power at Community level, it is essential that the principle of subsidiarity be formally written in to the Treaty, for example in the form in which it was expressed in the draft Spinelli Treaty: "The Union shall only act to carry out those tasks which may be undertaken more effectively in common than by the Member States acting separately, in particular those whose execution requires action by the Union because their dimension or effects extend beyond national frontiers."

This broad provision should be supplemented by more precise details of respective powers in sensitive areas in which national traditions frequently differ.

Since the principle of subsidiarity is an ongoing concept, the provisions of the Treaty should be so formulated as to enable a Member State to appeal to the Court of Justice if it considers that a Community decision exceeds the Community's powers as defined by the principle.

IV. Political cooperation

The political challenge constituted by developments in Eastern Europe has shown up more clearly the limitations of the existing machinery of political cooperation. The new international context calls more than ever for truly joint foreign policy. If it is true that the Twelve regard themselves as a focal point for future pan-European integration, the only logical course of action is for them to take part in the discussions as a political entity. This applies not only to a common "Ostpolitik", but also to new relations with the great powers and also when taking up a position in international bodies such as the Council of Europe or the CSCE. We will be taken seriously only insofar

as we assert ourselves. A share in the major decisions of the time has to be earned.

Since answers are now expected without any more delay, there can be no question at this stage of spending time on a hasty revision of Article 30 of the Single Act. It must be hoped, however, that the constraints forced on us by events will encourage us in the not too distant future to amend rules which no longer meet the requirements of the action which it is our ambition and duty to take. In the meantime, in view of the special situation which has been brought about by liberalization in the East, the Twelve must at least adopt a practical attitude and pragmatic approach to problems awaiting a solution. This might take the following form:

1. The Ministers for Foreign Affairs should work together to define and organize a set of principles and guidelines for political cooperation and cooperation by the Member States in relation to Eastern and Central European countries which would serve as a common framework for the activities of the Communities. To be consistent, the framework must cover all aspects: economic and political, bilateral and multilateral (CSCE). For this purpose the Ministers should adopt the custom of meeting regularly, both in the Council and in political cooperation. The General Affairs Council should once again become the Community's political decision-making centre. It must endeavour to pursue a policy rather than produce endless declarations. Similarly, it is conceivable that COREPER and the Political Directors (Political Cooperation) might together prepare the decisions on which would be based a global approach to the questions arising out of developments in Central and Eastern Europe and that the role of the Commission should be better defined, so as to secure the desired consistency.

2. It might also be desirable to obtain a better mix between expertise and diplomatic information from the Member States and the Commission's experience. Without changing the institutional framework and with due regard for the respective powers of each party, it would be possible to conduct an initial experiment in synergy by setting up a "specialized task force" made up of some diplomats specializing in Eastern European countries, who would be seconded by the Member States, and

by some Commission officials. This nucleus would serve as a centre for analysis, study and coordination on Eastern Europe to the benefit of both the Council and the Commission.

3. With a view to political union and, more particularly, to actual participation in the discussions which are about to take place in the CSCE, it is both desirable and necessary that it should be possible to discuss security issues in the broadest sense without restriction in political cooperation. Without prejudice to the powers of other institutions, which are themselves destined to change, the Member States have no cause to deprive themselves everlastingly of the opportunity to discuss this essential aspect among themselves.

Final remarks

1. From a procedural point of view, the European Council might decide:

– either to call a special Intergovernmental Conference;

– or to enturst the dossier to the Intergovernmental Conference called by the Strasbourg European Council.

There are advantages and disadvantages to both solutions and in practice the difference between the two options does not seem very significant, as long as the timing is the same.

2. The aim of these proposals is to bring the Community nearer to political union. They therefore tend to favour an "intensive Europe". They do not constitute a barrier to the building of an "extensive Europe" within which the Community and its Member States would maintain political, economic and institutional relations of another type with other European countries.

Annex

Sectors now subject to unanimity to which the qualified majority rule might be applied.

1. *Internal market*: Article 100a(2) lays down *three exceptions* to the qualified majority rule.

1.1. *Fiscal provisions*: it is conceivable that major fiscal decisions (for example on levels of taxation) could be taken unanimously, but that decisions relating to the basis of assessment and the methods of taxation could be taken by a qualified majority.

1.2. *Free movement of persons*: the qualified majority rule should be introduced along with a declaration (similar to the one in the Single Act) reserving the right of the Member States to act (and their duty to cooperate) in matters relating to immigration and measures to combat terrorism and crime.

1.3. *Rights and interests of employed persons*: the right to act by a qualified majority on social questions is one of the European Parliament's main demands; it might be accompanied by a precise definition of the principle of subsidiarity in this sector.

2. *Research*: Article 130q lays down *two exceptions* to the qualified majority rule: establishment of the framework programme and the setting up of joint undertakings. These two exceptions ought to be abolished. The qualified majority and cooperation with the Parliament could also be introduced for EURATOM research programmes (Article 7 of EURATOM Treaty).

3. *Environment*: Article 130s lays down *unanimity* as the rule: the rule should become the qualified majority.

4. *Coal and Steel*: introduce into the ECSC Treaty a provision corresponding to Article 113 of the EEC Treaty so that matters of common commercial policy in the coal and steel sector cease to be subject to unanimity.

4. Italian Chamber of Deputies

Resolution adopted on 21 March 1990, (384 votes out of 411 in favour)

Extracts

The Chamber of Deputies,

– recalling and reiterating the support of the Italian parliament for the transformation of the EEC into a political union on a federal basis;

(. . .)

Requests the Italian government to support, as of the extraordinary meeting of the European Council on 28 April in Dublin, and in view of its preparations for the Italian Presidency of the Council:

1. The immediate beginning of a gradual process of full integration of the GDR into the Community (. . .).

2. The beginning of intergovernmental negotiations for the achievement of EMU which should begin at the start of the Italian Presidency (. . .). Confirms its support for the request of the European Parliament to be associated with the negotiations on a basis of equality with the governments, and requests the Italian government to propose a working method that conforms to this principle on the occasion of the interinstitutional preconference that will be convened at the initiative of the European Parliament.

3. The need to enlarge the reform of the EEC beyond EMU and its institutional consequences.

Considers that the Italian government should propose, during its Presidency, the holding of two parallel intergovernmental conferences:

(a) The first negotiation must concern a draft treaty on EMU which should enter into force before 31 January 1992.

(b) The second negotiation must prepare an institutional reform of the EEC beyond EMU in view of attributing to the European Parliament a mandate to draft a European constitution which should enter into force before the next European elections in June 1994.

(. . .)

Shares fully the request formulated by the European Parliament in its resolution of 14 March 1990 (Martin Report) (. . .).

Shares, in this spirit, the request — supported by the European Parliament in the above-mentioned resolution — that the following points should be included in the institutional reform of the Community:

(a) Rationalization of the Community's instruments for external relations, notably the full integration of EPC into the Community structure, including the granting to the Commission of similar powers to those which it holds in other sectors of Community policy in order to put into place a common foreign and security policy at the service of peace.

(b) An improvement in the terms of the Treaty concerning the social and environmental sectors so that the Community is able to elaborate and to administer a more effective policy in these fields so that the internal market functions for the benefit of all Community citizens and contributes to an improvement in the environment.

(c) The incorporation into the Treaties of the declaration on fundamental rights and liberties that the European Parliament adopted on 12 April 1989 and of other provisions promoting a Europe of the citizens whilst preserving cultural diversity.

(d) A reinforcement of the means of which Council disposes to take decisions, notably by more frequent recourse to majority voting.

(e) A reinforcement of the powers of the Commission to apply Community law and to carry out its programmes and policies.

(f) A reform of the system of own resources of the EEC.

(g) A recognition, at Community level, of the dual legitimacy represented, on the one hand, by the Council of Ministers and, on the other hand, by the European Parliament.

(In a separate resolution, the Chamber of Deputies offered to host the "assizes" or parliamentary conference that the European Parliament had put forward.)

(Author's translation)

5. Kohl–Mitterrand letter

20 April 1990

"In the light of far-reaching changes in Europe and in view of the completion of the single market and the realization of economic and monetary union, we consider it necessary to accelerate the political construction of the Europe of the Twelve. We believe that it is time "to transform relations as a whole among the member states into a European Union . . . and invest this union with the necessary means of action", as envisaged by the Single Act.

"With this in mind, we would like to see the European Council deciding as follows on 28 April:

(1). The European Council should ask the competent bodies to intensify the preparations for the intergovernmental conference on economic and monetary union, which will be opened by the end of 1990 at the invitation of the Italian Presidency, as decided by the European Council in Strasbourg.

(2). The European Council should initiate preparations for an intergovernmental conference on political union. In particular, the objective is to:- strengthen the democratic legitimation of the union, — render its institutions more efficient, — ensure unity and coherence of the union's economic, monetary and political action, — define and implement a common foreign and security policy.

"The Foreign Ministers should be instructed to prepare an initial report for the meeting of the European Council in June and to submit a final report to the European Council meeting in December. We wish the intergovernmental conference on political union to be held parallel to the conference on economic and monetary union.

(3). Our aim is that these fundamental reforms — economic and monetary union as well as political union — should enter into force on 1 January 1993 after ratification by the national parliaments.

"The Foreign Ministers of the French Republic and the Federal Republic of Germany, Roland Dumas and Hans-Dietrich Genscher, will present these ideas for discussion at the forthcoming informal meeting of the Council of Ministers (General Affairs) on 21 April."

6. Dutch Government 1st Memorandum, May 1990

Possible Steps Towards European Political Union

Introduction

In the course of the debate on Economic and Monetary Union and decision-making on the holding of an intergovernmental conference (IGC), it has become clear that there is a desire for amendments to Community rules going beyond EMU. Firstly, there is the long-standing lack of a democratic dimension within the Community. Over the years, significant improvements have been made (direct elections to the European Parliament, greater budgetary powers and more direct involvement in the laying down of regulations on the internal market), but as the integration process advances, and Community legislation therefore affects the citizens of Europe more directly, it is becoming increasingly clear that a democratic deficit has arisen. This must not be accepted. Respect for the principle of democracy has been won in many different ways in all the member states and is a cornerstone of modern societies. A transfer of powers to a supranational authority must therefore be accompanied by guarantees of sufficient democratic control at this level.

Secondly, developments are taking place in Central and Eastern Europe which not only call for an immediate and active response from the Community but also make it necessary to strengthen the European edifice itself in order to ensure that the Community does not gradually become absorbed into Pan-European structures. Recent history has shown that the Western European integration model is in fact now the only workable one and it is therefore not surprising that it is very attractive to the countries of Eastern Europe. If the Community is to be able to enter into a range of different types of cooperation with the countries of Eastern Europe — and at the same time with the EFTA countries — it must do so from a position of internal strength.

The reunification of Germany is also a good reason for seeking to add a new dimension to the integration process. While the inclusion in the Community of a unified Germany is already an "acquis", this does not provide future generations with a sufficient guarantee that a united Germany will not pursue a course separate from that of the Community. This can only be ensured by so strengthening the Community that the avenue of national "Alleingang" is closed for good.

Lastly, it should be observed that the number of countries seeking accession to the Community is increasing. For a Community which began with six members and now has 12, a further increase before the year 2000 will be possible only if it first strengthens its institutional structure in such a way that expansion does not affect its ability to act.

Against this background, it is certainly desirable to consider carefully whether the existing rules and procedures are still adequate to cope with the far-reaching changes which have already begun or which are impending.

The EMU process is now well under way, and there is a danger that if the IGC–EMU (which will be referred to below as IGC I) were to be charged with institutional non-EMU matters this would delay or even block progress in EMU consultations. There is now a virtual consensus that non-EMU topics should be dealt with by a separate IGC II.

Belgium has already presented an aide-mémoire concerning possible subjects and the approach to be adopted, and President Mitterrand and Chancellor Kohl have called for a "Political Union". The latter term could cause confusion, as the brief explanation which they supplied made it clear that what was envisaged was not the "finalité politique" of European Union but a new step to follow the Single European Act. Partly on account of the term "Political Union", the wish is sometimes expressed that the ultimate aim of union be defined within the framework of the Community and European Political Cooperation. However, it does not seem expedient for the Twelve to embark on a discussion of this.

Whether we should make internal progress towards such union is a different matter. The Netherlands has pursued a consistent line in this respect over the years, starting with the negotiations on the EC treaties in the 1950s, continuing with the discussions about the Fouchet Plan, the conflict over the Luxembourg Agreement, the Spierenburg Report and most recently the consultations on the Single European Act. The Netherlands saw a federal structure as the ultimate objective for Europe. This was based not on pure idealism but on the clearly perceived interests of the Netherlands. Intergovernmental procedures embodied in the Council may at first sight appear to serve the interests of the individual Member States best, but in practice history has shown that this is not the case, even where decisions are taken unanimously. There is no reason, therefore, to adopt a different position now.

It does not seem necessary to define the objective in advance, as we have always seen European union as a process in which the individual steps can be evaluated in the light of an objective formulated in fairly general terms (cf. Article 2 of the EEC Treaty). It can however be said on the basis of experience that in a little under 40 years steps have been taken, through trial and error, in the right direction and that the results of this are certainly in accordance with our wishes and interests. As the process continues, we must be careful not to cooperate in any steps which would block options relating to an ultimate federal structure. This notably means that attempts to increase the importance of the Council (especially the European Council) must be resisted.

It is clear that the unique form of cooperation which was established in the 1950s has been strikingly successful and that, for all its defects, nothing to rival it exists anywhere else in the world. It is therefore essential to keep this structure intact in principle and to strengthen it by eliminating imbalances and defects and adding to it in specific areas.

At this early stage it is difficult to say how far we should go in this direction. However, we should not adopt too modest or limited an aim in advance. Otherwise there is a danger of a minimalist, "à la carte" approach, which would seriously limit our influence on the discussion and reduce the likelihood of a balanced and valuable result being achieved. The latter point also means that we shall have to accept results in certain sectors which are not to our liking. What is important is the overall result of European integration, and this is something from which the Netherlands has always benefited.

An additional reason for not adopting too limited an aim in strengthening European institutions is the tendency of the larger member states to dominate decision-making.

In order to be systematic, it seems appropriate to state here the approach arising from the first round of consultations between the Permanent Representatives. Four main questions were formulated:

- the democratic legitimacy of the Union

- effective decision-making
- unity and coherence in international action
- subsidiarity.

This approach is similar to that which was agreed at the informal European Council in Dublin (at the end of April), except that "subsidiarity" has now been accorded a more prominent place, as a separate point. There is no objection to this.

In the rest of this paper, the topics which could be dealt with by an IGC II will be indicated in greater detail.

I   Increasing the democratic content of the Community decision-making process

There is no genuine parallel at Community level to the role played by parliaments in the legislative process at national level in the member states. As the integration process advances, the absence of genuine parliamentary influence makes itself felt more acutely. The legitimacy of the Community, in the eyes both of its own citizens and of the outside world, is being called into question. All the Member States now recognize that the situation is unsatisfactory. The idea that it would be sufficient for national parliamentary control within individual Member States to be stepped up is losing ground. The way seems to be free for decisions to be taken to increase the involvement of the EP in Community legislation. Simply adopting a national model would not be the appropriate course, as to do so would be to disregard the specific institutional structure of the EC. Democratic control over the institution which is primarily responsible for initiating and implementing Community legislation — the Commission — also calls for special attention. At present the only power which the EP has is that of dismissing the Commission as a whole. This power requires refinement, and, as a natural complement to it, the EP should have a measure of involvement in the appointment of the Commission.

A.   Joint legislation by the EP

A1.   Cooperation procedure

The EP's involvement in the legislative process could be increased by:

- reinforcing the cooperation procedure;
- increasing the number of fields to which this procedure applies.

Reinforcing the cooperation procedure: consideration could be given to amending and supplementing the article 149 procedure as follows:

- paragraph 2f could be amended in such a way that if no decision were taken within three months, the Commission's proposal would be deemed to have been accepted;

- if, in the course of its decision-making, on second reading, the Council took a decision pursuant to paragraph 2c (decision-making by unanimous vote if the EP has rejected the common position of the Council in its entirety), or deviated from the amendments proposed by the EP and accepted by the Commission, the EP could rescind the Council's decision within two months, by a two-thirds majority of the votes cast, with the proviso that a majority of the members must vote.

- in either of the above procedures, a "concertation" procedure could be set in motion between the EP, the Commission and the Council, at the request of one of the three.

The scope of the cooperation procedure: The cooperation procedure could be used in all cases in which the EP currently consults, with the proviso that a distinction should be made between Community decision-making of a legislative nature and subordinate decision-making. The cooperation procedure applies only to decisions of a legislative nature. This aspect calls for attention, as the existing legal structure of the Community does not provide for separate instruments for legislative and executive functions. Regulations and directives, in particular, are used for both purposes. The annual fixing of agricultural prices (an executive function) and the laying down of the basic principles and structure of the CAP (a legislative function) are both carried out by means of the same legal instrument. The situation is further complicated by the fact that it is impossible to make any clear distinction between the Council and the Commission as regards the allocation of legislative and executive responsibilities.

The (shared) right of initiative: Granting the EP the shared right of initiative would accord with the desire to give the EP the powers which a legislature should have. However, it should also be borne in mind that it would assume these powers at the Commission's expense, given that the latter currently enjoys the sole right of initiative. This would entail a fundamental change in the structure of the Community.

A2. The EP's power of approval

The EP already enjoys this power under article 237 (expansion of the Community) and article 238 (association agreements). It is suggested that it be extended to:

- article 113 (trade agreements): a possibility would be to institute a procedure under which the EP would be deemed to consent unless a majority of its members expressly rejected an agreement within two months.

- article 235 (decisions not provided for in the Treaty), in view of the fact that this is a question of decision-making without any specific legal basis, which therefore lies in the grey area between national and Community powers, so that strict democratic control is desirable.

- article 236 (amendments to the Treaty): here too, the EP's consent should be required.

- article 201 (Own Resources Decision): here too, the EP's consent should be required.

- article 138 (procedure for elections to the EP, for which it already has the right of initiative): ditto; thus the EP should have the right of de facto autonomous decision-making.

B. Budgetary procedure

The budgetary procedure laid down in article 203 could be amended so that:

- the distinction between compulsory and non-compulsory expenditure is eliminated; the procedure for non-compulsory expenditure would apply;

- the budgetary procedure would end with a joint decision by the Council and the EP.

Consideration would have to be given to whether, and if so how, this idea could be implemented, while at the same time avoiding the creation of a power vacuum. A new interinstitutional agreement (perhaps a stronger one) could play an important role.

C. Powers over the Commission

1. The influence of the EP over the appointment of the Commission could be strengthened in the following ways:

    – after the appointment of the President-designate of the Commission, the latter should present himself to the EP to discuss his intentions with regard to the membership of the Commission;

    – the newly formed Commission should present itself to the EP in an investiture procedure.

2.   Article 144 (collective dismissal) could be amended to enable the EP to adopt motions rejecting individual members of the Commission. Consideration could also be given to the possibility that if a collective motion of rejection is adopted, elections should also be held for the EP.

3.   The EP ought to have the right of inquiry, which should enable it to question members and officials of the Commission and third parties.

NB Two aspects of paragraph 3 above require further attention:

- Should it also be possible for members of the Council to be questioned, in view of their accountability to national parliaments?
- What powers should the EP be given to enable it to use its right of inquiry?

4.   The possibility of promulgating regulations on public administration at Community level could also be investigated.

D.   *Instituting a Senate*

There are those who advocate that a Senate be instituted to represent the national element in parliamentary control. The EP has likewise made proposals to this effect (sic), which would entail the establishment of a Chamber consisting of national parliamentarians to coexist with the present EP. It seems unlikely that this would be in the interests of the EP itself. If the main responsibility for decision-making were retained by the Council (for the time being), a special relationship would inevitably grow up between the Council and the Senate (national ministers and national parliamentarians!), so that the EP in its present form might well find itself in a vacuum.

It would be more appropriate for a Senate to be based on the existing Council and for it to review Community decision-making in the light of the interests of the member states; such a body should be set up in the longer term.

E.   *The relationship between the EP and national parliaments*

Members of the EP feel that they are operating in something of a vacuum because they have little control over the Council, while national parliaments for their part are seeing their role reduced as a result of increased Community decision-making. A desire for more structural contacts between the two parliamentary levels is therefore growing. This is of course primarily a matter for the parliaments themselves (*assizes*), but it seems worthwhile for governments to consider it too. Perhaps consideration should be given to lifting the prohibition on dual membership of national parliaments and the EP, either wholly or partially. It is true that the objections to dual membership are as strong as ever: in order properly to carry out the duties involved, members would need a 48-hour day. Perhaps some kind of link could be established with membership of an Upper House of Parliament.

II Strengthening the position of the Commission

The Commission constitutes, in effect, the driving force behind the process of integration while at the same time acting as the guardian of the general interests of the Community. In addition, executive power in the Community is vested in the Commission. With regard to this latter point in particular, it must be said that in practice the Member States — i.e. the Council — are ambivalent about delegating tertiary legislation (primary legislation refers to the treaties and secondary to regulations of a general nature). The position on this matter should be clarified.

As far as its executive responsibilities are concerned, the Commission is being assigned a large number of additional duties but, on the other hand, is not equipped with the machinery to carry out these tasks effectively. For that reason, the Commission makes use of national government agencies. However, it has too little manpower even to ensure that the executive powers it delegates are exercised correctly and it is at too great a distance from the level to which these powers have been delegated. This situation should be changed. If the above analysis is generally accepted, there would seem to be grounds for considering the following changes.

The Commission would retain its key role in

the legislative process (with the sole right to initiate legislation and unanimity being required to modify its proposals). Its position in this regard would be strengthened de facto if the qualified majority vote were applied to a greater extent in Council decision-making (see III).

The Commission's executive powers should be increased in the following ways:

1. Given that the use of committee procedures has been unsatisfactory to date, there are grounds for amending article 145 to indicate the conditions subject to which the Commission exercises its executive powers. Limited differentiation should be possible, though with clear criteria governing which procedure should be used in particular situations.

2. Where executive powers have been delegated to national agencies, the Commission's monitoring powers should be strengthened. It is proposed that federal offices be established in every Member State which would liaise closely with the relevant national agencies. Such offices should have a clearly defined role, both to optimize their monitoring powers and to bring "Brussels" closer to the individual member of the public. Their specific supervisory responsibilities could lie, for example, in the following fields:

    (a) collection of the Community's own resources;

    (b) implementing Community regulations relating to, for example, the Common Agricultural Policy, regional policy and social policy. In general, this means the expenditure of Community funds at national level, although it might also involve monitoring the implementation of Community regulations in such fields as the environment and security;

    (c) supervising the implementation of Community legislation (in particular the directives) with regard to both procedure (observance of time limits on implementation) and substance (compliance with Community rules).

Lastly, the number of members of the Commission should be reduced from 17 to 12. Consideration could be given to a further reduction, taking into account, of course, the requirement that the Commission must be able to carry out its responsibilities in a proper manner. A possible interim solution would be that a limited number of Commissioners could be assisted by a number of junior commissioners.

III   Improving decision-making

For many years the Netherlands has cherished the hope that the unanimity requirement in Council decision-making would be abandoned. This hope stems from the Netherlands' belief that such a change would bring about the hoped-for increase in the speed and effectiveness of the Community decision-making process while at the same time elevating the interests of the Community above what are often conflicting national interests. In addition, there are many cases where it would be wrong to think that the unanimity requirement is the best guarantee that national interests will be adequately protected. Firstly, the requirement affords fewer safeguards to the smaller Member States than to the larger, as smaller states have less resistance to pressure than larger ones. Secondly, in cases where the unanimity requirement hinders decision-making, the larger Member States will be more readily inclined than the smaller ones to fill the resulting vacuum with unilateral national measures, an example being road pricing in the Federal Republic of Germany (*Strassenbenutzungsgebühr*).

Experience with the Single European Act can generally be described as positive. The time has now come to consider whether it is possible to abandon the unanimity requirement in respect of other provisions of the Treaty. In principle, as argued above, such a move must be regarded as being in the interests of the Netherlands.

The present situation is as follows:

(a) under article 148, paragraph 1, an absolute majority is officially the rule in decision-making but in fact it is exceptional;

(b) as a rule decisions are taken by qualified majority vote;

(c) the unanimity requirement still applies in many — indeed perhaps in too many — cases. The areas in which this is the case are listed below. (The provisions on unanimity in the ECSC Treaty and the EURATOM Treaty will be examined at a later stage).

The document goes on to list the 30 EEC Treaty Articles requiring unanimity.

The following proposals are put forward:

1. The qualified majority vote should be made the rule, though the absolute majority vote should be maintained in those cases where it already applies.

2. The unanimity requirement should be permitted by way of an exception. It is as yet too early to indicate precisely where this should be the case. To take one example, unanimity might still be required to increase the Community's own resources (with the approval of national Parliaments). On the other hand, it should be possible to take decisions on the harmonization of social security by qualified majority vote in cases where the aim of such harmonization is to raise the general level of provision.

3. Article 235 should be amended such that the unanimity requirement is maintained for decisions whereby the Community enters new areas of government activity, with the proviso that further decision-making in these areas should be done by qualified majority vote. Consideration could be given in this connection to making specific reference to the subsidiarity principle, which should be incorporated into the Preamble.

IV European Court of Justice

The Court of Justice continues to play a vital role in the process of integration. It supervises the application and uniform interpretation of Community law. However, two developments would appear to be undermining its position:

(a) the Court is burdened with an ever-increasing workload which leads to a corresponding increase in the duration of proceedings. The situation has slightly improved with the setting up of a court with jurisdiction to hear and determine at first instance cases brought by natural or legal persons, but further steps would appear to be required. For example, the powers of the court might be extended to other areas. Furthermore, the establishment of six regional courts of first instance competent to hear certain classes of action might be considered. Appeal would then lie to the Court of Justice in Luxembourg;

(b) an increasing number of penalties imposed by the Court are not being carried out. There are few sanctions under EC law which can be imposed on Member States which contravene Community legislation. This constitutes a serious threat to the rule of law in the Community and the position of the Court. We must therefore seek to establish the legal means to enforce the observance of Community law, a need which is also currently felt in connection with Economic and Monetary Union. It might also be possible to impose fines, the proceeds from which would become part of the Community's own resources. Finally, the existing sanctions provided for in the ECSC Treaty (articles 88–92) merit further study.

V The European Court of Auditors

There is an increasing degree of frustration felt within the Court of Auditors regarding the effectiveness of its monitoring of the Community's revenue and expenditure. Particular problems arise with regard to the implementation of Community policy by national agencies on behalf of the Commission and at its expense. One cause of the problem is the fact that the Commission itself has little control over such national bodies. A solution to this problem has already been suggested above.

Problems also arise in the relationship between the Court of Auditors and the Commission whose nature and extent require further examination. The Court of Auditors itself argues that its status should be elevated to that of a Community Institution in order to increase its moral authority and to enable it to apply to the Court of Justice in cases where it receives insufficient cooperation in carrying out its responsibilities. The latter could also be achieved by reinforcing the discharge procedure, thereby creating a route to the Court of Justice via the European Parliament.

VI Strengthening the political dimension

The full integration of EPC within the Community cannot be seen as a realistic objective in the foreseeable future. Strengthening the political dimension will be a step-by-step process in which, by analogy with current Community policy with regard to Eastern Europe, the demarcation between EPC and external EC policy will gradually fade.

This process can be speeded up by closer linkage of the EC and EPC. Steps to this end may be taken in the near future where no amendment to the Treaty is required. For example, sessions of the General Affairs Council and the Ministerial EPC might be combined. This must not of course detract from normal Community decision-making procedure, nor from the proposals made above to strengthen it. In practice, this process of linkage is already taking place in connection with the issue of Eastern Europe. In principle, however, no element of foreign policy should be excluded *a priori* from this new approach.

The meeting in Dublin of the European Council in June should decide to instruct IGC–II to proceed with a revision of Title III of the Single European Act (article 30:12 currently provides for such a decision five years after the Act enters into force, i.e. 1 January 1992). It has become clear that the legally binding nature of this title requires reinforcement. Furthermore, the Commission should become an equal partner in political cooperation.

The present provisions in the Act governing security require strengthening, although the political aspects of security will first have to be dealt with.

VII New policy areas

The question arises of whether IGC-II should further be charged with adding to the Treaty new policy areas in which the Community would be empowered to enact certain regulations, just as the European Act has extended its powers to cover the environment and scientific and technological research. In addition, greater activity in policy areas which already fall under the scope of the Treaty, either wholly or partly, could also be considered. It would appear that caution is required in answering this question.

In the first place, care must be taken to ensure that Community regulations do not harm the pluralist nature of the societies which make up the Community, unless this is necessary for the proper functioning of the Internal Market or in order to achieve other specific objectives of the Treaty.

In the second place, and in relation to the foregoing, the principle of subsidiarity should be taken into account.

This implies that when decisions are to be taken at Community level the question of whether this constitutes a more effective way of fulfilling the responsibilities of government towards individual citizens must first be answered affirmatively. The principle of subsidiarity needs working out in greater detail, but this will continue to be a difficult task as long as the final objective of the integration process has not been defined. As long as we are still on the road to integration, the principle can only be applied in a flexible manner which at each step compels us to consider whether the benefits achieved have an added value which more than compensates for the further distancing of the public from the decision-making process.

In concrete terms, this has the following consequences for the policy areas listed below in random order:

(a) where cultural policy is concerned, an independent Community policy would not appear to be justified, since priority in this field must be given to the objective of pluralism. However, restrictions on the implementation of various national policies will have to be accepted, notably when the limits of what Article 36 and other similar articles can reasonably be taken to mean are exceeded;

(b) in the field of industrial policy a Community policy or increased coordination of national policies might be considered. This has a direct relationship with common trade policy, which is coming under increasing pressure as the absence of Community measures leads to distorted growth;

(c) the question of whether a Community policy on development cooperation should be formulated, notably with regard to structural aspects, alongside the Community's direct involvement in the form of the Lomé Conventions, the cooperation with Mediterranean countries and aid to non-associated countries;

(d) where social legislation is concerned, the aim should be to preserve the level of social provision achieved by Member States. The Treaty contains provisions to this effect. Extension of the areas covered through amendments to the Treaty seems unlikely at this time;

(e) the question of whether decision-making in the area of the free movement of persons should take place at Community level is a very topical one. At present this is principally regulated by international agreements, which hinders the achievement of at least one of the objectives of Article 8A.

7. Danish Government

"Provisional" memorandum of 10 May 1990

Below are the provisional Danish comments on the main points for inclusion in the conclusions of the informal meeting of the European Council on 28 April 1990 in Dublin.

The democratic basis for political union

There must be greater democratic control over and openness in EEC cooperation, notably by introducing principles of transparency in EEC cooperation, including in particular an insight into the administration of the EEC institutions.

Effective operation of the Institutions

Legal acts on the environment and the employment market should be adopted by majority decision, so that minimum guarantees can be laid down for environmental protection and workers' rights.

Unity and cohesion in the Community's action on the international scene

New forms of decision-making and patterns of cooperation shall be established in order to ensure greater unity and cohesion in the Community's action on the international front. In particular, the way should be opened, through a rapid and comprehensive EEC/EFTA agreement for closer cooperation with the EFTA countries and with Central and Eastern European countries which are carrying out democratic reforms.

It is the Danish Government's opinion that strengthening EEC cooperation in the above mentioned areas will contribute to the Community's maintaining its role as the central forum in European cooperation.

The Danish Government considers that one of the goals for the discussions at the Governmental Conference on political union must be to strengthen EEC cooperation in such a way that the Community becomes the basis for the political and economic unity of Europe. As part of that process German unity should be achieved in a broad European context with extensive cooperation within the EEC and a continuing North American commitment to security in Europe. That would also secure growth and employment in the Community, which must moreover be the basic objective of the completion of economic and monetary union. In that connection it should be emphasized that there must be continuing respect for Member States' independent distribution policies.

134

8.   Greek Government

Aide-mémoire of 15 May 1990

Contribution to the reflections on the path towards Political Union

1.   Analysis of the situation — necessity of reform

1.1 The beginnings of the Community responded to an approach adapted to the immediate post-war situation, consisting of fixing objectives and achieving them step by step, the first of these achievements being the ECSC in 1952. This path has been followed with success ever since and, today, it must necessarily lead to the achievement of goals which have been fixed, such as the achievement of the internal market, economic and monetary union, economic and social cohesion.

1.2 Today however, after all these years, the institutional organization of the Community displays disequilibria, tensions and disfunctions which tend to be aggravated by the weight of the problems that have to be dealt with.

The relations between the institutions bear witness to an unstable imbalance, the origin of which is the "democratic deficit" of the Community. The European Parliament, even elected by universal suffrage, sees its powers limited considerably by the treaties, and the Court of Justice of the European Community, for its part, is unable to enforce its judgements.

1.3. But independently from these aspects, the international political scene has been radically transformed away from the situation of confrontation between two blocs. The changes in Europe are particularly radical with the current fall of the Eastern regimes. The new regimes put in place in these countries, but also some other countries in Europe (EFTA), hope to see their relations with the Community strengthened. The Community is considered a unique factor of stability and prosperity in Europe. It is therefore imperative to preserve its achievements and correct its weaknesses.

1.4 Greece considers that political union is an objective at the end of a process of dynamic evolution which must now accelerate and widen by achieving the objective of economic and monetary union and that of a high degree of internal cohesion on the territory of the Community, as well as the development of a common foreign and defence policy.

From the Greek point of view, progression towards political union presupposes an enlargement of the democratic basis on which the functioning and the constitution of the Community rest; it must also be accompanied by an upgrading of the European Parliament which must be the essential organ of scrutiny and of legislation. In other words, the process of political union, and its final expression, require a restructuration of the powers that would enable the Union to take form with full legality and representativity (Parliament). The process of political union therefore requires a remodelling and reinforcement of the institutions.

2.   Reinforcement of the democratic basis of the Community

2.1 Political Union, towards which we are going, requires a correction of the democratic deficit, which arises from the fact that the one institution of the Community that is directly elected by universal suffrage plays a role that is proportionally far too restricted. It is indispensable to upgrade the role of the European Parliament, both by reinforcing its participation in the legislative procedures of the Community and in allowing it a greater degree of democratic scrutiny over the executive.

2.2 Reinforcement of the EP's legislative powers.

- Extension of the assent procedure to articles 236 (treaty revision), 138 (uniform electoral system), 201 (own resources), 235 (new policies) and for certain important international agreements concluded under article 113. The EP must have the right to submit proposals to modify the Treaties.

- Granting to the EP of a right of legislative initiative by a majority of its members in those cases where the Commission refuses to bring forward a proposal or delays in doing so.

- Extension of a cooperation procedure to all acts of legislative nature. The final decision of the Council can be rejected by a majority of the members of the EP within a fixed deadline.

2.3 Reinforcement of democratic control. The EP must participate in the designation of the President and the members of the Commission and have a right of scrutiny over their acts.

- Adoption of an action programme for the Commission at the beginning of each year by a majority of members of the EP.
- The possibility to table motions of censure on individual members of the Commission.
- Extension of judicial control over acts of the European Parliament (modification of article 173 EEC).

3. Reinforcement of the efficiency of the Council of Ministers

3.1 The procedure for drawing up policies and taking decisions must be simplified, but at the same time it is important to make it more coherent, more stable, and to ensure a better coordination of the various Councils. Two principal means can be used to reinforce the efficiency of Council, namely a limitation of the principle of unanimity and an extension of qualified majority voting. The rule of unanimity must remain only for the application of articles 138, 149, 157, 223, 236, 237 and 238 of the Treaty.

3.2 Limitation of the number of Councils to 4. This reform does not require a modification of the Treaty but a simple decision of Council.

- "Political questions" Council:
  Composed of the Foreign Ministers it would deal with political questions, foreign policy and defence as well as institutional matters. It would also ensure general coordination and the preparation of European Council meetings.
- "Economic policy" Council:
  Composed of Ministers of the Economy, it would be competent to deal with macroeconomic policy and monetary affairs.
- "Internal integration" Council:
  Composed of Ministers responsible for Community questions, it would be competent to deal with all the matters currently dealt with by specialized Councils in view of achieving the internal market and common policies, with the exception of agricultural policy.
- "Agriculture" Council.

3.3 It is also indispensable to restructure COREPER on the model of the above Councils in order to improve their preparation.

- COREPER I   :   Political questions (ambassadors)
- COREPER II   :   Economic policy (Deputy permanent reps.)
- COREPER III   :   Internal integration (Deputy permanent reps.)
- Special Committee on Agriculture.

3.4 In certain cases at least, the possibility of holding public meetings of Council should be examined.

(Author's translation from a French version)

9. Report of the Foreign Ministers on the need for treaty changes for political union

Presented to Dublin II European Council, 25–26 June 1990

The European Council agreed at its meeting on 28 April 1990 that a point had been reached where the further dynamic development of the Community had become an imperative not only because it corresponds to the direct interest of the 12 Member States but also because it has become a crucial element in the progress that is being made in establishing a reliable framework for peace and security in Europe. The European Council confirmed in this context its commitment to political union and decided that Foreign Ministers should carry out a detailed examination of the need for possible Treaty changes and prepare proposals for the European Council.

Written contributions have been submitted by Member States and ideas and suggestions compiled. Foreign Ministers carried out an examination and analysis of the issues at meetings in May and June with a view to the debate in the European Council on the convening of an intergovernmental conference on political union to define the necessary framework for transforming relations as a whole among the Member States into a European union invested with the necessary means of action.

The result of this work is set out below.

The overall objective of political union

Political union will need to strengthen in a global and balanced manner the capacity of the Community and its Member States to act in the areas of their common interests. The unity and coherence of its policies and actions should be ensured through strong and democratic institutions.

The union will remain open to membership by other European States who accept its final goals, while developing closer relations with other countries in the spirit of the Rhodes Declaration.

The transformation of the Community from an entity mainly based on economic integration and political cooperation into a union of a political nature, including a common foreign and security policy, raises a number of general questions.

Scope

(i) To what extent does the union require further transfer of competence to the Community along with the provision of means necessary to achieve its objectives?

(ii) How will the union include and extend the notion of Community citizenship carrying with it specific rights (human, political, social, the right of complete free movement and residence, etc.) for the citizens of Member States by virtue of these States belonging to the union?

(iii) To what extent will other areas currently dealt with in intergovernmental cooperation be included, such as aspects of free circulation of persons, the fight against drugs, and police and judicial cooperation?

Institutional Aspects

(i) To what extent will new or changed institutional arrangements be required to ensure the unity and coherence of all the constituent elements of the European union?

(ii) How should the role of the European Council, as defined in the Solemn Declaration on European Union and in the Single European Act, be developed in the construction of the union?

General principles

The following questions should be considered with regard to certain general principles which have been advanced:

(i) In the context of ensuring respect for national identities and fundamental institutions, how best to reflect what is not implied by political union?

(ii) In the context of the application of the principle of subsidiarity, how to define it in such a way as to guarantee its operational effectiveness?

Democratic legitimacy

It is necessary to ensure that the principle of democratic accountability, to which all Member States of the Community subscribe, should be fully respected at Community level. The ongoing transfer of tasks to the Community and the corresponding increase in the power and responsibilities of its institutions require a strengthening of democratic control. This objective should be pursued through a range of measures, among which could be the following:

- increased involvement for the European Parliament:

(i) in the legislative process, possibly including forms of co-decision,

(ii) in the field of external relations;

- increased accountability through reinforced control by the European Parliament over the implementation of agreed Community policies;
- a reinforcement of the democratic character of other institutions (e.g. specific role of the European Parliament in the nomination of the President and Members of the Commission, greater transparency and openness in the working of the Community);
- greater involvement of the national parliaments in the democratic process within the union, in particular in areas where new competences will be transferred to the union.

Efficiency and effectiveness of the Community and its institutions

The adequacy of the Community's response, and of that of its institutions, to the needs arising from the new situation as well as from the implementation of the internal market, the attainment of EMU, the achievement of the aims of the Single European Act, the development of new policies and the enhancement of the Community's international role (including its capacity to respond to the aspirations of countries who wish to see their relations with the Community strengthened) should be examined from two angles; firstly, how to meet the challenges which the Community faces in an overall and balanced way; secondly, from the angle of the functioning of the institutions.

The question of the functioning of the institutions should be examined at several operational levels, while respecting the general balance between institutions:

(i) the European Parliament: (see "Democratic legitimacy" above);

(ii) the Council: improving the decision-making process *inter alia* by enlarging the field covered by qualified majority voting; central coordination through the General Affairs Council; concentration and rationalization of Council work in general;

(iii) the Commission: the number of its Members and strengthening of its executive role with regard to implementing Community policies;

(iv) the Court of Justice: *inter alia* automatic enforceability of its judgments, where relevant;

(v) the Court of Auditors: the strengthening of its role in ensuring sound financial management;

(vi) Member States: ensuring the implementation and observance of Community law and European Court judgments.

In addition, consideration should be given to a review of the different types of legal instruments of the Community and the procedures leading to their adoption.

Unity and coherence of the Community's international action

In accordance with the conclusions reached by the European Council in Dublin on 28 April 1990, the Community will act as a political entity on the international scene.

The proposal for a common foreign and security policy which takes account of the common interests of the Member States, acting with consistency and solidarity, and which institutionally goes beyond political cooperation as it currently functions, raises a number of questions, in particular the following:

Scope

(i) the integration of economic, political and security aspects of foreign policy;

(ii) the definition of the security dimension;

(iii) the strengthening of the Community's diplomatic and political action *vis-à-vis* third countries, in international organizations and in other multilateral forums;

(iv) the evolution of the transfer of competences to the union, and in particular the definition of priority areas where transfer would take place at an initial stage.

Decision-making

(i) use of the Community method (in full or in adapted form) and/or a *sui generis* method, bearing in mind the possibilities offered by the evolution over time of the degree of transfer of competence to the union, referred to above;

(ii) the Commission's role, including the faculty of launching initiatives and proposals;

(iii) establishment of a single decision-making structure; central role of the General Affairs Council and the European Council in this context; preparatory bodies; the organization and strengthening of the Secretariat;

(iv) modalities aimed at ensuring the necessary flexibility and efficiency to meet the requirements of formulation of foreign policy in various areas; consideration of decision procedures including the consensus rule, voting practices involving unanimity with abstentions, and qualified majority voting in specific areas.

Implementation

There is a recognized need for clear rules and modalities for the implementation of the common foreign policy; the following are to be examined in this context:

(i) role of the Presidency (and of the "Troika"), and of the Secretariat;

(ii) role of the Commission;

(iii) role of national diplomatic services in a strengthened collaboration.

10. Belgian Senate

Resolution on the achievement of European Union and preparation of the parliamentary Assizes on the future of Europe, 13 July 1990

The Senate,
- Recalling and reiterating the Belgian Parliament's support for the transformation of the EC into a political union with a federal structure,
- Recalling, in particular, the resolution of 24 May 1984 in favour of the draft treaty establishing the European Union, and the resolutions of 10 July 1986 (Chamber) and of 24 July 1986 (Senate), stressing the need to give the European Parliament a brief to draw up a draft for European Union to be submitted to the national parliaments for approval,
- Stressing its conviction that the political upheavals in the countries of Central and Eastern Europe, and the opening of new negotiations on disarmament bring even closer the prospect of an encounter in a common democratic framework, between countries separated for decades by the Iron Curtain;
- Aware that the current developments in the GDR and its new relations with the FRG constitute a special case in the context of relations between the EC and the countries of Central and Eastern Europe,
- Whereas a balanced solution, which must take into account the interests and the security of all neighbouring countries, and a solution to the many political, economic, monetary, social and environmental problems, can only be found if the GDR is integrated into a European Community which has been strengthened politically,
- Stressing once again the need to speed up the process of Community unification, to allow it to develop into a federal structure, bearing in mind that the unification process must be accompanied by political democratization and an effective social policy.

1. Asks the Belgian Government to:

I (. . .)

II. Initiate intergovernmental negotiations on the achievement of EMU, and propose the formal convening of the Conference and its detailed preparation at ministerial level, during 1990, so as to ensure that this intergovernmental conference can effectively start work in December 1990;

Stresses the importance of defining clearly, in the terms of reference of the Conference, the final objectives of EMU, the details of the transitional stages, and the principle of establishing a firm timetable for the completion of EMU;

Confirms its support for the request by the European Parliament that it should be a regular partner, in the negotiations of the Conference, on an equal footing with the governments;

III. Promote the need to broaden the debate on reforming the EC beyond EMU and its institutional implications;

Considers that the Belgian Government must ensure that the two sets of intergovernmental negotiations (the International Conferences agreed in Dublin on 25 June 1990) should take place at the same time;

(a) The first negotiations must be aimed at drafting a treaty establishing EMU, to enter into force by 31 December 1992;

(b) The second set of negotiations must relate to the institutional reform of the EC beyond EMU with the aim of substantially enhancing the democratic nature of the European institutions by giving full legislative powers to the European Parliament;

Emphasizes the major role which must be played by Belgium in establishing European Union in view of the fact that the Belgian Government will hold the Council Presidency during the second half of 1993, i.e. on the eve of the preparations for the fourth European elections, to be held in June 1994;

Lends its support to the idea that the second set of negotiations should be prepared on the basis of proposals by an ad hoc committee, chaired by the President of the Commission of the European Community, Mr Jacques Delors;

Fully supports the demand made by the European Parliament in its resolution adopted on 14 March 1990 (Martin Report) that the intergovernmental conference should consider the institutional future of Europe with a view to instructing the European Parliament to finalize the draft constitution of the European Union;

Therefore backs the demand — supported by the European Parliament in the above-mentioned resolution — that a series of points should be included in the institutional reform of the EC;

Stresses, in this connection, the need to:

(a) rationalize the instruments available to the Community in the area of external relations, in particular by fully integrating European political cooperation in the Community's structures, with the ultimate objective of establishing a common foreign policy;

(b) integrate the social, cultural and environmental spheres in Community policy, to enable the Community to act effectively in these areas, and make a meaningful contribution to the establishment of social justice and equality beyond the internal borders of the EC and to the protection, conservation and enrichment of the whole of Europe's cultural and natural heritage;

(c) make room for the regional dimension within the institutional framework of the Community;

(d) strengthen, to this end, the Council's decision-making powers, particularly by having more frequent recourse to majority voting;

(e) strengthen the Commission's powers in implementing Community legislation and its programmes and policies;

2. Calls on the Belgian Government to support and promote the convening and preparation of the parliamentary Assizes on the future of Europe, proposed by the President of the French Republic, François Mitterrand, on 25 October 1989; voices its support for the Italian Parliament, which has offered to organize the first session of the Assizes in Rome in October 1990; declares its readiness, if the first meeting of the Assizes proves to have been very useful, to organize a second plenary session of the Assizes in Brussels in 1991; stresses the need for the elected representatives of the citizens at Community and national level to take the opportunity of the Assizes to draw up a joint strategy for transforming the EC into a European Union with a federal structure, on the basis of a draft constitution drawn up by Parliament in close collaboration with the national parliaments.

3. Calls on its President to take the necessary steps to ensure that the Assizes are held before the Intergovernmental Conference in December 1990.

11. European Commission

Proposal for a draft treaty amending the Treaty establishing the European Economic Community with a view to achieving economic and monetary union, 21 August 1990

Explanatory memorandum

1. Need for coherence between the two Intergovernmental Conferences

The European Council's decision to convene two Intergovernmental Conferences running in parallel, one on economic and monetary union and the other on political union, reflects a desire to integrate moves to achieve apparently different but, in practice, intimately linked objectives into the framework of the existing institutions.

Political union enriches the Treaty of Rome by adding a new dimension to the venture launched more than 30 years ago. EMU very much follows in the direction of that venture. As a natural extension to implementation of the Single European Act, EMU, far from being an end in itself, is both a more effective and a more demanding means of fulfilling the mission assigned to the Community by the Treaty. Effectiveness must be accompanied by the solidarity needed for economic and social cohesion to be achieved, but within the framework of a policy taking full advantage of price stability and the strength of the single currency. EMU and political union alike aim to give the Community a new capacity for action and a genuine external identity. Both are aspects closely linked to one and the same movement: the advance towards European union.

These two approaches are intended to complement the Community's achievements to date — and primarily the creation of an area without internal frontiers by 31 December 1992 — by means of closer economic and monetary integration and the development of the political dimension. They draw inspiration from the same institutional philosophy and are based on the need to reconcile more democracy and greater efficiency.

In view of the complementary nature of the objectives to be achieved within a single Community, and in order to maintain a balance, the work of the two Intergovernmental Conferences calls for parallel progress as regards institutional development, with this alone permitting the osmosis necessary between the political, social, economic and monetary spheres.

Without it being possible or necessary to indicate at this stage the final content and shape of European union, care must be taken to ensure that the conditions for transferring new powers to the Community — however important they may be — do not jeopardize the existing institutional framework, which has a proven dynamism.

The main asset of the Treaty of Rome is the relationship of positive synergy between the three institutions: Parliament, the Council and the Commission. The cooperation between the Council and Parliament works by dint of the intervention of a third institution, the Commission, whose essential task is to attempt to safeguard the general interest while bringing closer together the often diverse positions of the Member States.

The joint exercise of new powers in areas which reach to the very heart of sovereignty — such as currency matters and foreign policy — will require the existing institutional framework to be adapted to a higher degree of Community integration.

It will be for each of the two Intergovernmental Conferences, in exercising the mandate they will have been given, to ensure that a dynamic balance is struck between the new decision-making centres and the existing institutions, which will continue to be in charge of implementing all common policies with due regard to the two criteria of democratic legitimacy and efficiency.

The Parliament will be called on to play an increasingly important role, not only through its being closely involved in the decision-making process but also as a result of the indispensable strengthening of its position in terms of democratic accountability.

It will be for the Council of Ministers for Economic and Financial Affairs to take, on the basis of Commission proposals, the decisions within the competence of the Council.

As for the Commission, it will have to continue to perform the tasks assigned to it by the Treaty as an initiator and executor of Community decisions. Its accountability to the European Parliament satisfies in part the requirement of greater democratic accountability.

Finally, the European Council will have to provide the necessary impetus, the very role for which it was originally set up, and to ensure the overall coherence of economic and monetary policy in terms of the broad guidelines which it lays down.

2. The march towards economic and monetary union

The march towards economic and monetary union, which has been a Community objective since 1969, gained fresh momentum in June 1988 with the decision of the Hanover European Council to entrust a committee of experts, chaired by Mr Delors, with the task of studying and proposing concrete stages leading to this union.

This was prompted by the realization that, with the creation of the single market forging ahead, considerable gains were to be expected from economic and monetary union, and in particular the adoption of a single currency.

Over and above the direct gains associated with the elimination of transaction costs are the indirect or dynamic gains, which are potentially much greater although certainly difficult to quantify.

These dynamic gains will stem from price stability, enhanced economic efficiency, itself conducive to growth, and more efficient management of public finances owing to a reduction in the real burden of interest and in the size of deficits. This should have a positive impact on employment and on the balanced development of the regions and, finally, should give the Community a greater role to play in the world economy.

On the basis of the Delors Committee's report and the work carried out by the Community institutions, each meeting of the European Council has provided fresh impetus.

In Madrid, the main principles were laid down:

(i) implementation of EMU in stages, with Stage I to begin on 1 July 1990;

(ii) parallelism between the economic and monetary aspects;

(iii) subsidiarity;

(iv) diversity of specific situations.

In Strasbourg and Dublin, a link was established between EMU and the strengthening of the Community's political dimension, a decision was taken to convene two intergovernmental conferences, and a timetable envisaging the ratification of the Treaty amendments before 1 January 1993 was adopted.

Finally, in Rome, agreement among 11 Member States was reached on the overall conception of EMU, involving the adoption of a single currency (the ecu) and the fixing of 1 January 1994 as the date for transition to Stage II and of the general conditions for the transition leading from Stage I to Stage III. The conclusions of the European Council constitute, in a way, the mandate given to the relevant Intergovernmental Conference.

The preparatory work has now been completed. It is for the Conference that will open on 15 December to agree on amendments to the Treaty of Rome. It will have less than a year in which to do so, given the time needed to complete ratification of the fruits of its work in 1992.

Consequently, and in order that the negotiations can begin on a sound basis as soon as the Conference opens, as the Dublin European Council requested, the Commission is presenting a draft treaty amending the Treaty establishing the European Economic Community with a view to achieving economic and monetary union.

In the spirit of its document of 21 August 1990, and out of a concern to draw the various points of view together, the Commission has striven to combine the main contributions which have been made, namely:

(i) the report of the Delors Committee, which was regarded by the European Council — or at least by 11 of its members — as the outline for establishing EMU;

(ii) the report of the high-level working party on EMU, chaired by Mrs Guigou, which has drawn up a list of essential questions for the Intergovernmental Conference;

(iii) the work of the European Parliament, and in particular the resolution adopted on the basis of the report presented by Mr Herman;

(iv) the reports drawn up by the Commission: the communication to the Council of 21 August and the report on the costs and benefits of EMU;

(v) the work of the Council, based on reports presented by specialized committees;

(vi) the work of the Committee of Central Bank Governors, which has led to the presentation of a draft statute for the new monetary institution (the links between the draft statute and the forthcoming treaty should be emphasized).

3. Points of agreement and remaining differences of approach

The draft treaty, presented by the Commission in accordance with the method employed in drafting the Treaty of Rome, establishes in legal form:

(i) the basic principles of EMU, which are designed to supplement the provisions on the "principles" of the Community (in particular Articles 2, 3 and 4 of the Treaty of Rome); the latter principles will also be enriched by the amendments to be proposed by the Intergovernmental Conference on political union;

(ii) the rules relating to EMU (economic and monetary policies, institutional arrangements), the powers of the new monetary institution, Eurofed (made up of the national central banks and the European Central Bank), the principles governing its operation, and its relations with the Community institutions;

(iii) the principles, rules and procedure relating to the transitional period and the transition to the final stage.

The Conference will centre its deliberations not only on the Treaty but also on the Eurofed Statute, which will take the legal form of a protocol annexed to the EEC Treaty and will constitute an integral part thereof (see Article 239). However, some provisions will have to be amended according to a different procedure and one which is more straightforward than that laid down for the Treaty.

The Commission has taken note of the draft statute drawn up by the Committee of Central Bank Governors: it notes that there is a great deal of common ground between the draft statute and the opinion which it formulated on EMU pursuant to Article 236 of the Treaty.

The Commission is of the opinion that the essential tasks and elements of the system's structure, in particular the principles relating to the balance and relations between the institutions, must be incorporated into the Treaty, whereas the actual operation of the system — essentially that of the new monetary institution — must be dealt with by the Statute, even though the latter may, for reasons of clarity, include certain of the Treaty's provisions.

The draft treaty sets out in legal terms the principles and operating rules of EMU, on which there is already a broad measure of agreement.

This will cover a large part of the agenda of the Intergovernmental Conference, and particularly:

(i) on the economic side:

(a) the tools which must be available to the Community in order to achieve better coordination of economic policy, on the basis of commonly-agreed targets, and an improved measure of convergence;

(b) the minimum rules with which Member States will have to comply in the budgetary sphere in order to prevent the appearance of imbalances which might compromise monetary stability;

(ii) on the monetary side:

(a) the principles which underlie the creation of Eurofed: the priority objective, which must be price stability; its structure, which must be federal; its complete independence, which must be reflected in rules enshrined in the Treaty; and democratic responsibility, which is the corollary to Eurofed's necessary independence;

(b) the tasks, organization and main operating rules of Eurofed.

In general the economic and monetary aspects should be tackled in parallel, as the Delors Committee report emphasized. Since the model that has been chosen does not seek to create new institutions in the economic sphere, but rather to give greater responsibilities to the Council (Economic and Financial Affairs), the draft treaty seeks to provide a mechanism for relations between the existing institutions and the new Eurofed based on the two criteria of effectiveness and democratic legitimacy.

Lastly, the draft treaty lays down procedures for movement from one stage to the next, and foresees the possibility of a period of adaptation for any Member State ratifying the Treaty and thus accepting the ultimate goal of EMU.

In addition to giving legal form to the general agreement which exists, the Commission felt it would be useful for the draft to include provisions dealing with the few questions still open, in order to make it easier for the Conference to concentrate on these questions and to settle them. As is its proper role, however, the Commission has tried to propose solutions which it feels will facilitate the necessary compromises, even where those solutions do not exactly reflect its own initial position.

There are only a few of these questions; they relate essentially to economic union:

(i) *The final shape of economic union.* There is unanimity that certain rules (no monetary financing, no automatic bail-outs) and a principle (the avoidance of excessive budget deficits) should be enshrined in the Treaty. These rules will have to be complied with, but the way in which the principle is to apply can be made more or less binding — sanctions might even be envisaged. The Commission would prefer a system of incentives in a framework of tight multilateral surveillance. An important factor in the success or otherwise of the procedures adopted will be transparency, given its impact on political life in each of the Member States.

(ii) *The relationship between EMU and economic and social cohesion.* This question is central to the future of the Community, and will also have to be considered in the negotiations on political union; it has obvious budgetary implications. For the time being, however, as suggested by the analyses that have been carried out so far, the Commission takes the view that practical discussion of this question will not be possible at the Intergovernmental Conference. Only in 1991, when a progress report has been made on the structural policies, can a review of the February 1988 agreement be envisaged and improvements be made to the mechanism applied since 1989.

(iii) *Democratic responsibility in economic union.* Alongside the European Council, which provides the impetus, the main lines of economic and social policy will continue to be set by Council, Commission and Parliament, the institutional triangle set up by the Rome Treaty. The roles of each of these institutions are strengthened and spelt out in the draft treaty, and the balance between them is clarified. Not only will the Council (Economic and Financial Affairs) see a development of its role as multilateral surveillance is tightened; it will also have to take, in collaboration with the new monetary institution (Eurofed), the main decisions on exchange-rate policy. The Commission will have an important role to play in economic union, and it should accordingly be clearly and directly responsible before the Parliament; this will foreshadow the role the Parliament will play when the building of the Community is complete, that is to say when European union has been achieved.

(iv) *The nature of the transition.* Debate on the duration of the transitional period has obscured its nature. The Commission has taken the side of those favouring a short transitional period, and the reasons which led it to take this position are as strong as ever. Stage I, which began on 1 July 1990, has a vital role to play here. Its success or failure will determine not only the success or failure of the process as a whole but also the duration of Stage II. This can be shorter if Stage I achieves its objectives rapidly, with the Committee of Governors operating as the centre for the elaboration and guidance of monetary policy, while on the economic union side progress is being made on consultation and policy convergence. Stage II represents the introduction of the final mechanism. The Commission is therefore in favour of a transitional stage with a substantial content. In the economic field it is proposing that the final outcome should be anticipated, more in the spirit than in the letter, from the beginning of Stage II. In the monetary sphere, too, the Commission is proposing that Eurofed should be given the task of actively preparing its future role from the day it is set up, and indeed of prefiguring that role. The establishment of an institution and its governing bodies before it takes up its full powers is in line with the thinking and practice of the Rome and Paris Treaties. It allows the institution to make preparations and to take measures necessary for its proper operation while creating a climate of confidence among its members before it enters into full operation. The same thing was done for the introduction of the Rome Treaty and the Community institutions.

(v) *the role of the ecu in the transition.* The nature and role of the ecu in the dynamics of EMU are currently at the heart of a debate which is not simply about method. It is the very essence of the EMU undertaking which is under discussion. In response to those who state that they wish — and are able — to make the ecu an instrument of convergence by "hardening" it, the Commission takes the view that only a strengthening of the ecu is capable of giving it a central position in the EMU process. But this will not come about simply as a result of its being sanctioned by the market but only if the Community and the 12 Member States adopt a series of decisions to promote the use of the ecu and to make it increasingly attractive. Convinced that convergence can and should proceed with the help of the instruments established at the beginning of the first stage, the Commission has chosen this approach, which involves the decision to entrust to Eurofed, once it is set up, the task of managing the ecu.

4. The Community's responsibilities and the creation of appropriate instruments

By adopting a single currency, the ecu, as a replacement for national currencies, the Member States are transferring to the Community an area of competence in which it currently exercises responsibility only very indirectly.

This is the principal change introduced by the draft Treaty. A new institution is to be set up to administer the Community's monetary policy. It will have at its disposal the whole range of instruments necessary for conducting a market-based monetary policy: open-market operations, repurchase agreements, intervention rate, compulsory reserves, etc. It will be for it to equip itself with those instruments and to use them.

At the same time, economic policy instruments will have to be reinforced. The field of economic policy is very wide and cannot be reduced to budgetary policy. The range of instruments to be used goes far beyond those required for simply coordinating economic policies, even since the Community embarked on the first stage of EMU. In some areas, the Treaty already gives the Community a major role which has a clear economic dimension, even if there is not always awareness of this. Whatever fields are involved — whether competition (Articles 85 to 89), the opening up of public procurement (Article 130f(2)), research and development (Article 130f et seq.), European infrastructures (Article 74 et seq.), labour markets (Articles 49 and 118), the environment (Article 130r et seq.) or taxation (Article 99) — Community policies will have to be reinforced in order to improve the general efficiency of the internal market and to increase the competitiveness of the Community economy, which is essential if the basic objectives of European union are to be achieved.

The coordination of economic policies, which is already an area for which the Community has responsibility, will have to be reinforced in particular. The instruments required for the conduct of economic policies will remain the prerogative of the Member States. For the purposes of coordination, however, various additional instruments and procedures will have to be set up:

(i) multiannual economic policy guidelines which will define general objectives for the Community and indicate means of achieving those objectives;

(ii) reinforced multilateral surveillance of economic policies, which will cover all aspects of policy and performance likely to have a significant impact on economic and social objectives. This will lead to the necessary economic policy adjustments as a result of the discussions which will take place in the Council of Ministers, the peer pressure that may be exerted at such meetings and, if necessary, formal recommendations which could be published. Observance of the budgetary rules referred to above forms part of these arrangements. The transparency of these procedures gives promise of their impact;

(iii) a specific financial support mechanism which will be brought into operation in the event of major economic difficulties in one or more Member States or where economic convergence calls for a special Community effort to be made alongside national adjustment strategies. Such support will be conditional; it will take the form of special Community grants or loans as part of a comprehensive programme.

Arrangements need to be made to ensure day-to-day coordination of economic and monetary policy: the participation, without the right of vote, of the President of the Council and of a Member of the Commission in the meetings of the Eurofed governing body (and, in return, the participation of the President of Eurofed in the multilateral surveillance exercises) and the possibility open to the Commission to comment on progress towards EMU in order, where it considers it necessary, to instigate discussion in the various Community institutions.

Cooperation between institutions will be particularly necessary in order to define exchange-rate policy, ultimate responsibility for which will lie, as is the case in the Member States, with the institutions responsible for economic policy. The Council Ministers will have a special role to play, in close collaboration with the new monetary institution, in defining the Community's position in international monetary and financial bodies.

At the same time — and this task is also one for the Conference on Political Union — it will be necessary to amend and rearrange the Treaty provisions on external economic policy in order to reinforce the Community's capacity to act and the way in which it is represented in all international bodies.

Democratic accountability in EMU will take

three practical forms: first of all, the Commission, alone responsible to the Parliament, will have to give it an account of the way in which it is fulfilling its duties, i.e. the way in which it is carrying out its task of coordinating economic and monetary policy. Secondly, Eurofed will explain its policy and report to Parliament. Finally, Parliament itself will hold a general debate on the multiannual guidelines and specific recommendations, during which it will express its view.

All of these arrangements and instruments will ensure that, in addition to there being a clear division of roles between each institution, there is a satisfactory balance of powers, that the need for democratic accountability is satisfied and that the system works effectively.

DRAFT TREATY

Note to the reader: For ease of reference, the sections of the EEC Treaty amended by the new Treaty have been shown in consolidated form, incorporating the amendments.
The amendments are shown in italics.

The EEC Treaty as amended is to read as follows:

Part one: Principles

Article 1
By this Treaty, the HIGH CONTRACT-ING PARTIES establish among themselves a *EUROPEAN COMMUNITY.*

Article 2
The Community, having due regard to the personality of the States it unites and working on the basis of its achievements to date, shall have as its task progressively to achieve economic and monetary union, which shall be based on a single currency, the ecu, social development and the pursuit of a common policy with regard to external relations and security.
It shall be founded on respect for democracy and fundamental rights and on the principle of subsidiarity.
In carrying out its tasks, it shall seek:

(i) to promote within its ambit a harmonious development of economic and social activities, growth, a high level of employment and cohesion in conditions of stability, an accelerated raising of the standard of living and closer relations between the States and peoples it unites;

[(ii) to speak with one voice on the international scene and to act with cohesion and solidarity in order more effectively to defend its common interests and its independence.[1]]

Article 3
For the purposes set out in Article 2, the activities of the Community shall include, subject to the conditions and within the time-limits laid down therein:

(a) the elimination, as between Member States, of customs duties and of quantitative restrictions on the import and export of goods, and of all other measures having equivalent effect;

(b) the establishment of a common customs tariff and of a common commercial policy towards third countries;

(c) the abolition, as between Member States, of obstacles to freedom of movement for persons, services and capital;

(d) the adoption of a common policy in the sphere of agriculture;

(e) the adoption of a common policy in the sphere of transport;

(f) the institution of a system ensuring that competition in the common market is not distorted;

(g) the institution of a common economic policy based on the definition of common objectives, close coordination of Member States' economic policies, and the implementation of the other common policies;

(ga) the definition and pursuit of a single monetary policy whose primary objective shall be to maintain price stability and, without prejudice to that objective, to support the common economic policy;

(h) the approximation of the laws of Member States to the extent required for the proper functioning of the common market;

(i) the creation of a European Social Fund in order to improve employment opportunities for workers and to contribute to the raising of their standard of living;

(j) the establishment of a European Investment Bank to facilitate the economic expansion of the Community by opening up fresh resources;

(k) the association of the overseas countries and

---

[1] To be reviewed in the light of the proceedings of the Intergovernmental Conference on political union.

territories in order to increase trade and to promote jointly economic and social development.

Article 4

1. The tasks entrusted to the Community shall be carried out by the following institutions:

a EUROPEAN PARLIAMENT,
a COUNCIL,
a COMMISSION,
a COURT OF JUSTICE.

Each institution shall act within the limits of the powers conferred upon it by this Treaty.

2. Monetary policy shall be defined and pursued by a European System of Central Banks (hereinafter referred to as "Eurofed") acting within the limits of the powers conferred upon it by this Treaty and the Statute annexed hereto.

3. The Council and the Commission shall be assisted by an Economic and Social Committee acting in an advisory capacity.

4. The audit shall be carried out by a Court of Auditors acting within the limits of the powers conferred upon it by this Treaty.

Article 5

Member States shall take all appropriate measures, whether general or particular, to ensure fulfilment of the obligations arising out of this Treaty or resulting from action taken by the institutions of the Community. They shall facilitate the achievement of the Community's tasks. They shall abstain from any measure which could jeopardize the attainment of the objectives of this Treaty.

Article 6

(Coordination by Member States of their economic policies)

Repealed.

Articles 7 to 8c

Unchanged.

Part two: Foundations of the Community

TITLE I

Free movement of goods

Articles 9 to 37 unchanged.

TITLE II

Agriculture

Articles 38 to 47 unchanged.

TITLE III

Free movement of persons, services and capital

Chapter 1

Workers

Articles 48 to 51 unchanged.

Chapter 2

Right of establishment

Articles 52 to 58 unchanged.

Chapter 3

Services

Articles 59 to 66 unchanged.

Chapter 4[2]

Capital

Article 67

1. All restrictions on the movement of capital belonging to persons resident in Member States and any discrimination based on the nationality or on the place of residence of the parties or on the place where such capital is invested *shall be prohibited as between the Member States.*

2. Current payments connected with the movement of capital between Member States *shall be free.*

[The repeal of Articles 68 to 73 has still to be considered.]

TITLE IV

Transport

Articles 74 to 84 unchanged.

Part Three: Policy of the Community

TITLE I

Common rules

Articles 85 to 102 unchanged.

---

[2] This Chapter is to be brought into line with the content of Chapter 4 of the Title on economic and monetary union.

TITLE II

Economic and monetary union

Article 102a

Economic and monetary union shall be founded on close economic integration and a single monetary policy.

It shall be brought about gradually over a period divided into two stages preceding the final stage, with parallelism between economic policy and monetary policy being ensured.

Building on the developments which have taken place since Stage I began, on 1 July 1990, Stage II, or the transitional period, shall begin on 1 January 1994.

During this transitional period, Articles 109b to 109e shall apply. A finding that the conditions for transition to the final stage are met shall be made by the European Council in accordance with Article 109f.

Chapter 1

Economic policy

Article 102b

1. The economic policy of the Community shall aim to ensure growth, a high level of employment and equilibrium in the Community's balance of payments, in a context of price stability, generally balanced public finances, and economic and social cohesion.

It shall be based on an internal market which has been completed in accordance with the objectives of Article 8a and on the various policies of the Community, in particular competition policy, commercial policy, research policy and structural policies.

It shall also be based on the progress achieved with regard to convergence since the beginning of Stage 1 of economic and monetary union.

2. The Member States shall pursue their economic policies with a view to contributing to the realization of the objectives of economic and monetary union in the context of the measures adopted by the Community to that end.

Article 102c

1. The Commission shall submit multiannual guidelines to the European Council, which shall discuss them after consulting the European Parliament. The guidelines shall relate in particular to:

the development of Member States' budget balances;

the control of production costs, having due regard to the freedom of the two sides of industry to enter into contracts;

the level and promotion of saving and investment;

the adaptation of Community policies for achieving economic and social cohesion;

the development of structural policies in the Member States.

2. The Council, acting by a qualified majority and taking into account the deliberations of the European Council and the opinion of the European Parliament, shall adopt these guidelines.

3. On the basis of an annual report from the Commission, the Council shall each year decide, in accordance with the procedure provided for in paragraph 2, on the adjustments that need to be made to the multiannual guidelines.

Article 102d

1. Within the framework of the multiannual guidelines adopted pursuant to Article 102c, and without prejudice to Article 103, the Council, acting by a qualified majority on a proposal from the Commission and after consulting the European Parliament, which must issue an opinion within a maximum period of two months, may, where necessary, adopt recommendations specific to each Member State concerning the general thrust of its economic and budgetary policy.

2. The Commission shall see to it that these specific recommendations are implemented; it shall involve the relevant Committee of the European Parliament in the monitoring of their implementation.

3. Where it is observed that a Member State has failed to implement these recommendations, and notwithstanding Articles 169 to 171, the Commission shall, after alerting the Member State concerned, present to the Council a confidential proposal for a recommendation concerning the measures which must be taken to rectify the situation.

If the Council does not take a decision within one month, the Commission may make its proposal for a recommendation public.

Article 103

1. Member States shall regard their conjunctural policies as a matter of common concern. They shall consult each other and the Commission on the measures to be taken in the light of the prevailing circumstances.

In this connection, an overall evaluation shall be

carried out regularly at Community level of the short and medium-term economic developments in the Community and in each of its Member States.

Moreover, the guidelines and recommendations adopted in accordance with the procedure described in Articles 102c and 102d shall serve as a framework for the multilateral surveillance undertaken by the Council with a view to assessing the results of the coordination of Member States' economic policies.

2. Without prejudice to the other procedures provided for in this Treaty, the Council may, acting on a proposal from the Commission, decide unanimously on the measures appropriate to the situation.

3. The Council, acting by a qualified majority on a proposal from the Commission, shall, where necessary, issue the directives needed to give effect to the measures decided on under paragraph 2.

4. The procedures provided for in paragraphs 2 and 3 shall also apply if any difficulty should arise in the supply of certain products.

Article 104

1. Where a Member State is in difficulties or is seriously threatened with difficulties, the Commission may propose to the Council, which shall act by a qualified majority, that, subject to certain conditions, the Member State concerned be granted Community financial assistance which may take the form of a support programme accompanied by budgetary intervention or special loans.

2. The general conditions for such intervention by the Community shall be laid down by the Council, acting by a qualified majority on a proposal from the Commission and in cooperation with the European Parliament.

3. The Council may establish a system of borrowing in order to finance the special loans referred to in paragraph 1. It shall lay down the maximum volume of such borrowing. These measures shall be decided on in accordance with the procedure provided for in paragraph 2.

Article 104a

1. The following shall be recognized as incompatible with the economic and monetary union and shall accordingly be prohibited:

(a) the financing of budget deficits by means of direct assistance from Eurofed or through privileged access by the public authorities to the capital market;

(b) the granting by the Community or the Member States of an unconditional guarantee in respect of the public debt of a Member State.

2. Excessive budget deficits shall be avoided. The Council may, to this end, adopt appropriate measures pursuant to the provisions of this Chapter.

Article 105
(Coordination by Member States of their economic policies)

Paragraph 1 is repealed.

Paragraph 2 (Monetary Committee) is transferred, in an abridged form, to Article 109a.

Chapter 2

Monetary policy

Article 105
Monetary union shall entail the circulation of a single currency, the ecu, the pursuit of a single monetary policy and the establishment of Eurofed.

Article 106
1. Eurofed shall be made up of the European Central Bank and the central banks of the Member States.

2. The European Central Bank shall have legal personality.

3. The Statute of Eurofed and the European Central Bank is set out in a protocol annexed to this Treaty.

The Council may, acting by a qualified majority at the request of the European Central Bank, amend Articles [. . .] of the Statute after consulting the Commission and the European Parliament.

Article 106a
1. With a view to achieving the objective set out in Article 3(ga), the European Central Bank shall carry out its tasks on its own responsibility under the conditions laid down in this Treaty and in the Statute annexed hereto.

2. In performing their duties, the European Central Bank, a central bank of a Member State and members of their decision-making bodies shall neither seek nor take instructions from the institutions of the Community or its Member States or from any other body.

The Community and the Member States shall not seek to influence the European Central Bank, the central banks of the Member States and the members of their decision-making bodies in the performance of their tasks and shall respect their independence. To that end, the Member States shall amend, where necessary, legislation governing relations between their central banks and their national governments.

3. The European Central Bank may under no circumstances grant to the Community or to one of its Member States or to any public body a loan or other credit facility intended to make good a budget deficit.

Article 106b

1. For the purposes of the preceding Article, Eurofed's tasks shall be:

(i) to determine and conduct monetary policy:

(ii) to issue notes and coins denominated in ecus as the only legal tender throughout the Community, subject to the provisions of Article 109h(2);

(iii) to conduct foreign-exchange operations in accordance with the guidelines laid down by the Council;

(iv) to hold and manage foreign reserves;

(v) to participate in international monetary cooperation;

(vi) to monitor the smooth operation of the payments system;

(vii) to participate as necessary in the formulation, coordination and execution of policies relating to banking supervision and the stability of the financial system.

2. In order to carry out the tasks assigned to it, Eurofed shall:

(i) conduct credit operations and operate in the money and financial markets;

(ii) hold the foreign reserves of the Member States, ownership of which will have been transferred to the Community;

(iii) have its own decision-making powers, and in particular the power to require credit institutions to lodge reserves with it.

3. The European Central Bank shall be consulted by the Commission regarding any draft Community legislation or any proposed international agreement on monetary, prudential supervision, banking or financial matters.
It shall also be consulted by the authorities of the Member States regarding any draft legislation on such matters.

Article 107

1. Eurofed shall be administered by the decision-making bodies of the European Central Bank.

2. The European Central Bank shall be administered by a Council, hereinafter referred to as the "Council of the Bank" made up of the 12 governors of the national central banks and the six members of the Executive Board, one of whom, the President of the European Central Bank, shall chair meetings of the Council of the Bank.
The members of the Council and the Executive Board of the Bank shall carry out their tasks in a completely independent manner in the general interests of the Community.

3. After discussion by the European Council and after consulting the European Parliament, the President and the other members of the Executive Board of the Bank shall be appointed for a period of eight years by the Council, acting unanimously.

4. The Council of the Bank shall take the decisions necessary to ensure performance of the tasks entrusted to Eurofed under this Treaty. It shall determine the Community's monetary policy and shall adopt the guidelines necessary for its implementation.

5. The Council of the Bank shall adopt its decisions by a majority vote of its members.
The conditions governing the casting of votes by the members of the Executive Board are laid down in the Statute of Eurofed and the European Central Bank.

6. The Executive Board shall take the necessary administrative decisions in line with the guidelines and decisions adopted by the Council of the Bank.
In addition, the Executive Board may, subject to the conditions set out in the Statute, be delegated certain powers by decision of the Council of the Bank.

7. The President of the Bank shall chair the Executive Board, represent the European Central Bank externally, act in its name in judicial or other matters and exercise authority over all its departments.

8. The division of responsibilities between the Council of the Bank and the Executive Board is set out in the Statute.

Article 108

1. The Council, acting by a qualified majority on a proposal from the Commission and in close cooperation with the European Central Bank, shall lay down guidelines for the Community's exchange-rate policy.
In accordance with those guidelines, the Euro-

pean Central Bank shall conduct an appropriate intervention policy.

2. The Council shall adopt, in accordance with the same rules and, where necessary, by urgent procedure, the Community's position in international monetary or financial bodies.

3. Within those bodies, the Community shall be represented by the President of the Council, the President of the Bank and a Member of the Commission.

Chapter 3

Institutional provisions

Article 109
1. The President of the Bank shall attend meetings of the Council that deal with the coordination of economic policies and the examination of the specific recommendations referred to in Article 102d.
He may transmit to the Commission opinions of the Council of the Bank on developments in the economic and monetary situation in the Community or in certain Member States.

2. The President of the Council and a Member of the Commission may attend meetings of the Council of the Bank but shall not be entitled to vote.

3. The Commission may address to the President of the Council and to the President of the Bank observations which, in its view, have a bearing on the consistency between economic and monetary policy. Those observations may be published.

4. The European Central Bank shall, each year, transmit a report on Eurofed's activities and on monetary developments to the European Parliament, the European Council and the Commission.

5. The European Parliament shall hold a general debate once a year on the conduct of economic and monetary policy at Community level on the basis of a report from the Commission and the report from the European Central Bank.
The President of the Bank shall take part in that debate.

6. In addition, the President of the Bank may, at the request of the European Parliament or on its own initiative, be heard by the competent committee of the European Parliament.

Article 109a
(former Article 105(2))
A Monetary Committee with advisory status is hereby set up. It shall have the following tasks:

(i) to keep under review the monetary and financial situation of the Member States and of the Community and the general payments system of the Member States and to report regularly thereon to the Council and to the Commission;

(ii) to deliver opinions at the request of the Council or of the Commission or on its own initiative, for submission to these institutions.

The Member States and the Commission shall each appoint two members of the Monetary Committee.[3]

Chapter 4

(for information)

The contents and title of this chapter are to be determined in the light of the Treaty amendments relating to political union. This chapter could in particular group together all the other economic provisions relating to EMU in the Treaty (notably the provisions relating to the free movement of capital). (See Article 67 *et seq.* above).

Chapter 5

Transitional provisions

SECTION 1

Transitional period

Article 109b[4]
The transitional period[5] for achieving economic and monetary union shall begin on 1 January 1994.

2. By that date, the following shall have been achieved:

---

[3] The composition and functions of this Committee shall be amended in the light of the overall approach of economic and monetary union.
[4] The numbering is provisional and will have to be adjusted in line with the number of articles included in Chapter 4 above.
[5] *Corresponding to Stage II of the Delors Committee's plan.*

(i) the abolition, as between Member States, of all obstacles to the free movement of capital;

(ii) the participation of the largest possible number of Member States' currencies in the exchange-rate mechanism of the European Monetary System (EMS);

(iii) the existence of effective arrangements preventing, in each Member State, the monetary financing of public-sector budget deficits and ensuring that the Community or the Member States are not liable for the debts of another Member State.

3. [. . .]⁶, the Member States shall initiate the process for ensuring the independence of the members of Eurofed which is to be completed not later than the time of the transition to the final stage of economic and monetary union.

Article 109c

1. During the transitional period, the Community shall adopt appropriate measures to reinforce the convergence of economic and monetary developments in the various Member States and in particular price stability and the consolidation of public finances. It shall, in particular, ensure that the instruments and methods of the multilateral surveillance exercise are improved in the light of the experience gained during Stage 1.

2. The Council, acting unanimously on a proposal from the Commission and after consulting the European Parliament, may implement, in so far as necessary, some or all of the provisions set out in Articles 102d to 104 of the Treaty.

Article 109d

1. At the start of the transitional period, Eurofed shall be established pursuant to Article 106, in particular with a view to:

(i) reinforcing the coordination of monetary policies;

(ii) establishing the instruments and procedures necessary for the future conduct of the single monetary policy;

(iii) supervising the development of the ecu.

2. The Community and the Member States shall take all appropriate measures to set up the various bodies of the European Central Bank and to allow Eurofed to operate.

3. For the purposes referred to in paragraph 1, the Community shall adopt the acts provided for

in this Treaty and the Statute annexed hereto so as to enable Eurofed to perform its duties.

4. As soon as they are set up, the bodies of the European Central Bank shall perform the tasks and comply with the obligations provided for in Article 109.

Article 109e

1. As soon as it is set up, the European Bank, having due regard to the responsibilities incumbent upon the authorities of the Member States as regards the formulation and conduct of their monetary policies:

(i) shall perform the duties entrusted to the European Monetary Cooperation Fund (EMCF) and the Committee of Governors of the Central Banks and, in particular, shall ensure the smooth operation of the EMS;

(ii) shall be empowered to make recommendations, which it may publish, to the central banks of the Member States concerning the conduct of their monetary policy;

(iii) may hold and manage foreign-exchange reserves, assist in the definition and conduct of a Community exchange-rate policy and, in particular, intervene on the foreign exchange markets;

(iv) shall ensure the smooth operation of the ecu market and, in particular, shall assume responsibility for the ecu bank clearing system;

(v) shall participate in the harmonization of monetary and financial statistics and in the approximation of monetary policy instruments;

(vi) shall make preparations for linking up payments networks and money and financial markets;

(vii) shall supervise the devising and technical preparation of means of payment and notes and coins in ecus.

2. The European Central Bank shall be consulted by the Commission on any draft Community legislation or any proposed international agreements in the monetary, prudential supervision, banking or financial fields.
It shall also be consulted by the authorities of the Member States on any draft legislation on such matters.

3. Having due regard to the provisions of the Statute of Eurofed and of the European Central Bank, the Council, acting by a qualified

---

⁶ *Date of entry into force of the Treaty amending the EEC Treaty with a view to achieving economic and monetary union.*

majority on a proposal from the Commission, in cooperation with the European Parliament and after consulting the European Central Bank, shall adopt the measures required to allow the performance of the duties defined in paragraph 1.

Under the same procedure, the Council shall adopt the arrangements for transferring the assets and liabilities of the EMCF to Eurofed.

4. The Council, acting unanimously on a proposal from the Commission and after consulting the European Parliament and the European Central Bank, may entrust other functions to the European Central Bank within the limits provided for in Article 106b. It shall, in accordance with the same procedure and in so far as is necessary, adopt the measures required to allow the performance of such functions.

SECTION 2

Transition to the final stage

Article 109f

Within three years of the start of the transitional period, the Commission and the Council of the Bank shall report to the European Council on the results obtained and in particular on the progress achieved on convergence.

On the basis of such reports, and after consulting the European Parliament, the European Council shall establish that the conditions for moving from the transitional period to the final stage of economic and monetary union have been met.

It shall do so on the basis of an assessment of the results of market integration and of the convergence of economic and monetary developments in the Member States.

Article 109g

Having established the fact referred to in Article 109f, the Council, acting by a qualified majority in favour cast by at least eight members, shall immediately take the decisions required on a proposal from the Commission.

It may, in particular, decide on the principle of a temporary derogation for a Member State which, because of economic difficulties, is not yet in a position to participate fully in the monetary-policy mechanisms specified for the final stage of economic and monetary union.

On the basis of a report drawn up by the Commission and after consulting the European

Central Bank, it shall also lay down, in accordance with the same procedure, the duration and implementing arrangements for such derogation. The Council and the Commission shall immediately send the European Parliament a report on the decisions taken.

Article 109h

1. Immediately after establishing the fact referred to in Article 109f, the Council shall adopt the fixed exchange rates between Member States' currencies and the measures necessary for introducing the ecu as the single currency of the Community, acting in accordance with the procedure provided for in paragraph 3.

As from such time, Eurofed shall exercise fully its functions in the monetary policy field.

2. The Council, acting in accordance with the procedure provided for in paragraph 3, shall adopt, in so far as is necessary, the technical arrangements under which Member States' currencies may provisionally remain legal tender.

3. The measures provided for in paragraphs 1 and 2 shall be adopted by the Council, acting unanimously on a proposal from the Commission and in consultation with the European Central Bank.

Where, pursuant to Article 109g, the Council has decided on a derogation for one or more Member States, such measures shall be adopted unanimously by the Member States participating in the final stage.

4. Where, pursuant to Article 109g, the Council has decided on a derogation for one or more Member States, the Council, acting unanimously on a proposal from the Commission and in consultation with the European Central Bank, shall determine the conditions under which the qualified majority provided for in Article 108 are met.

Chapter 6[7]

Commercial policy

Articles 110 to 116: Unchanged (subject to amendments to be made to these Articles in the light of the work of the Intergovernmental Conference on political union).

TITLES III TO VII

Unchanged.

---

[7] Change in numbering: currently Chapter 4.

Part Four: Association of the overseas countries and territories

Unchanged.

Part Five: Institutions of the Community

TITLE I

Provisions governing the institutions

The provisions under this Title are unchanged *except* for Article 173 on legal review of acts of the institutions, which should read as follows:

Article 173

The Court of Justice shall review the legality of acts [of the European Parliament,][1] of the Council, the Commission *and the European Central Bank* other than recommendations or opinions. It shall for this purpose have jurisdiction in actions brought by [the European Parliament][8] a Member State, the Council or the Commission on grounds of lack of competence, infringement of an essential procedural requirement, infringement of this Treaty or of any rule of law relating to its application, or misuse of powers.

The European Central Bank may, in order to safeguard its prerogatives, bring an action based on grounds deriving from infringement of such prerogatives against acts of the Council and the Commission.

(Rest of Article unchanged).

TITLE II

Financial Provisions

Article 199

All items of revenue and expenditure of the Community, including those relating to the European Social Fund, shall be included in estimates to be drawn up for each financial year and shall be shown in the budget.

The revenue and expenditure shown in the budget shall be in balance.

Article 199a

The proceeds of borrowings contracted to finance the special loans referred to in Article 104(1) shall be shown as revenue in a special section of the budget. They may not be allocated by transfer or in any other way to the financing of the Community's normal operating expenditure.

[For information: The other budgetary provisions of the Treaty will have to be reviewed in the light of the work of the Intergovernmental Conference on political union.]

---

[8] Article to be completed in the light of the work of the Intergovernmental Conference on political union.

12. Spanish Government

Proposals Towards a European Citizenship, September 1990

I. Introduction

Since its creation, the Community has placed a priority on its efforts on creating a common area of an essentially economic order, which has been translated into concrete results at the level of activity of European economic operators, but into limited effects on the daily life of its citizens as such.

Over the last few years, all the initiatives and concrete measures were certainly taken for our fellow citizens to have a say in the matter and obtain more direct advantage from Community action. The objective conditions in which this occurred did not however allow clear progress to be achieved in the process which would make all Community citizens the centre of basic reference of the Community, its successes, and its progress. These initiatives and these measures, as commendable as they were, did not allow the notion of "privileged foreigners" to be overcome.

The transition to a political union, comprising a common foreign and security policy and an economic and monetary union, is radically changing the data which prevailed until now: it requires the creation of a common integrated area, where the European citizen will have a central and fundamental role.

On the road leading to political union, it is therefore important to define a citizenship of the European Political Union. This citizenship would be conceived as a "personal and inalienable status of citizens of Member States, which, by virtue of their membership in the Union, have special rights and tasks, inherent in the framework of the Union, which are exercised and protected specifically within the borders of the Community, without this prejudicing the possibility of taking advantage of this same quality of European citizen also outside the said borders."

As political union is a dynamic notion comprising the idea of a process of evolution towards a final objective, European citizenship is also a dynamic and evolving concept. The progress which will be made for the union to attain its final objective will be accompanied by a more precise and complete definition of the quality of European citizen. A real union should aim to overcome the inequalities which subsist between Community citizens because they live in different areas of the Community and through different means reinforce the economic and social cohesion in a concrete framework.

The notion, content and development of European citizenship should be an important part of all the institutional aspects to study during the intergovernmental conference for European union.

Depending on how important it is, the content of the notion of European citizenship will be closely related to the dimension itself of the union which should be achieved at the end of the conference. In all logic, a real union will require a European citizenship of great content. Nevertheless, whatever the content given to the union at the end of the conference, it appears clear to us that, in the present circumstances, it is important as of today to make a major qualitative step in defining the status of European citizen.

Taking account of the above, the conference should debate the necessity of changing or completing the treaties in such a way as to at least define and resolve the notion of citizenship, as well as the "status civitatis," designed as a set of rights, freedoms and obligations of citizens of the European Union.

It is clear that, given the flexible nature of the concept, the constituent aspects of European citizenship which could be retained during the conference do not all have to be translated into a modification of the treaties.

While this is a distinct and independent part of the quality of European citizen, the conference must also examine the necessity of uniformly guaranteeing human rights and basic freedoms of residents of the Community, independent of their nationalities.

II. Contents of European citizenship

The notion of European citizenship assumes a third set of rights and responsibilities, in addition to the two sets which existed until now: the set of national rights and responsibilities stemming from national citizenship at the level of Member States and which will subsist in any case, and the set of Community rights

156

and responsibilities stemming from the treaties for citizens of a Community Member State.

This third set, which results from the transformation of the Community into a Union, presupposes, as stated above, a major qualitative step, which, among others, makes the citizen of the Community, who is for the moment no more than a "privileged foreigner," a citizen of the European Union. Making this step will eliminate the negative effects presently accompanying the condition of foreigner for a citizen of a Member State living in another Member State.

For what are the contents of European citizenship, it is clear that a series of rights, freedoms and responsibilities can now be easily defined and that others progressively follow, as the process of building the Political Union progresses.

The reform to undertake could thus roughly be expressed around the following main points:

(a) Special basic rights of the European citizen

The set of rights of the European citizen would have as its principle core the three following rights: full and complete freedom of movement, free choice of place of residence and free participation in political life in the place of residence. Free movement, freedom of choice of place of residence and freedom of establishment are special rights stemming from the treaties: their development and their exercise must be extended and applied to all European citizens.

The participation of the European citizen in political life, which must begin with the full recognition of freedom of expression, association and assembly, must be progressively extended to electoral consultations organized in the country of residence.

As far as political participation in elections to the European Parliament are concerned, this right should be translated into two actions: on the one hand, adopting a uniform electoral procedure for the entire Community, as contained in article 138, paragraph 3 of the EEC treaty: on the other hand, progressively giving all citizens the right to be voters in their place of residence.

The difficulties currently existing in recognizing the right to be a voter in local elections in the place of residence and which appeared during negotiations on the adoption of a directive to this effect should nevertheless be able

to be progressively overcome and result in full participation when the own dynamics of the Community and the development of relations between Member States make it opportune. The ultimate goal of the right of participation in political life should be full voting participation by the European citizen in his place of residence.

These three basic rights are the starting point for a real human dimension of the Community and the future development which should include a necessarily dynamic concept like that of European citizenship.

(b) Rights stemming from the dynamic development of the Union

The full development of the contents of European citizenship, starting with the set of rights and responsibilities stemming from the treaties and the development of basic rights expressed below are made in parallel to the transfer to the Community of new policies: social relations, health, education, culture, environmental protection, consumers, etc.

All this is translated into the gradual acquisition by the European citizen, who must be the required reference of setting up the union, of specific rights in these areas.

The launching of new policies and benefits and resulting rights depend on the model of political union which is being moved towards.

(c) The European citizen outside the borders of the Community

A higher degree of assistance and diplomatic and consular protection by the Member State to other citizens of the Community will be proposed as concrete measures, so that a new relationship between European Union, as a whole, and the European citizen as a holder of rights derived from his "status civitatis" and, as such, holder of specific rights of the Union, gradually takes place.

This protection and this assistance require the negotiation of agreements with third countries to this effect, given that the Vienna conventions and the different bilateral conventions on this only cover protection of citizens of different states.

(d) Other possible developments of European citizenship

It could be proposed that the recognition and the validity of obligations such as military service or alternative service are in effect in any country of the Union.

(e) The protection of European citizens

It appears to be necessary that, in parallel with the development of the concept of European citizenship, mechanisms are envisaged allowing practical implementation. For this, it is necessary to envisage a certain form of protection, both at the national and the Union level.

The European citizen, who now already enjoys the right to petition the Petition Committee of the European Parliament and who also has access, in certain cases, to the Court of Justice, could benefit from the fact of setting up the Union, increased protection of his rights through the right which will be given him to present petitions or deliver complaints to a European "ombudsman", whose function would be to provide the protection of the specific rights of the European citizen, which would therefore be reinforced.

The ombudsman of European citizens could act through the intermediary of different ombudsmen or equivalent organisms existing in various Member States.

III. Conclusion

The transition of the European Community into Political Union and the objective conditions requires an effort either made to make a qualitative jump which allows an area of essentially economic character to be transformed into an integrated area which would be at the direct service of the citizen.

Along with Economic and Monetary Union and common foreign and security policy, European citizenship is one of the three main pillars of European Union. It is therefore one of the basic elements of the credibility of Political Union in the eyes of public opinion and an essential condition to guarantee the functioning and development of all the constituent elements of the Union, as the European citizen is the basis itself of democratic legitimacy.

13. Denmark

Danish Government Memorandum, approved by the Market Committee of the Folketing
4 October 1990

I. The European Community is embarking on a period of great significance for its future development. The deliberations due to take place in the near future could have a decisive effect on the Community's role in the future design of Europe.

The Danish Government considers that the main task must be to adapt and strengthen the Community so that it is in a position to play the leading role.

Developments in Central and Eastern Europe have highlighted the need to broaden the Community perspective. Cooperation must therefore be stepped up. Existing areas of cooperation must be further exploited and new ones introduced. At the same time the Community must remain open towards third countries, both via wider membership and through new cooperation structures. This must be accompanied by a reinforcement of democratic control over cooperation.

II. The Danish Government considers that discussions at the forthcoming intergovernmental conferences should go under the title of "The Community's role in the future design of Europe". The Community must be strengthened so that it provides a foundation for the political and economic unity of the whole of Europe.

It is very important for the credibility of cooperation that the Community should show itself capable of meeting the challenge and fulfilling third countries' natural expectations of closer ties. It has to be borne in mind that, by its structure and design, the Community is the best instrument for involving the other European countries in broadly-based and binding cooperation.

The forthcoming discussions must tackle the question of how the Community should adapt its working methods to the developments which are to be expected in the 1990s. The Community must of course welcome applications for membership from other countries, provided they fulfil the conditions for membership and are ready to take part in the further development of cooperation in accordance with the aims of the Treaty.

III. The main task at the forthcoming intergovernmental conferences must be to strengthen European cooperation on a broad front while maintaining the Community's role as an anchor point.

The elements of a stronger European cooperation are:

- Community cooperation
- Economic and Monetary Union
- Intergovernmental cooperation
- Cooperation on foreign policy.

In addition to strengthening cooperation in a whole series of specific areas the aim should also be to lay down certain guidelines or principles for further cooperation. This should be done with reference to the possibilities for a gradual deepening of cooperation and for a gradual widening of cooperation through greater involvement in policy areas where there are clear third-country aspects.

It is therefore necessary to lay down a method and certain principles for the gradual development of cooperation. The Danish Government considers that the principle of subsidiarity should be stated as a basic principle in the preamble and should be applied in each specific area.

On the basis of these considerations the Danish Government makes the following specific proposals.

A. Intergovernmental conference on political union

I. Environmental policy

1. The Danish Government considers it very important that environmental policy should occupy a much more central position in the Community's overall activities. The aim of ensuring environmentally sustainable development should therefore be one of the main principles of the Community.

2. The Treaty chapter on the environment should also be developed and reinforced. For example, solution of the fundamental problems of the environment should not be made secondary to other considerations.

3. Legal instruments in the field of environment policy should be adopted by qualified majority, while preserving the Member States' right to maintain or to introduce stricter protective measures.

II. *The social dimension*

1. The Danish Government considers it important to strengthen the social dimension as a means of distributing the benefits deriving from the internal market. The social dimension is part of the process of achieving the internal market. It should be included among the Community's basic tasks. It is important that solidarity in cooperation should also be shown in this area — by enshrining workers' basic labour social rights in the Treaty.

2. A firm legal basis should therefore be incorporated in the Treaty whereby the Commission, inter alia, is required to take the initiative in putting forward proposals. Where the area lends itself to such an arrangement, minimum provisions should be laid down. It should be made clear that one of the aims is to promote the improvement of workers' living and working conditions thereby permitting a gradual upward harmonization of those conditions.

The Danish Government considers that a series of fundamental principles should be enshrined in the Treaty. These include access to work and education, social security, protection against industrial accidents and diseases, co-determination, freedom of association and the right to collective bargaining. It should also be laid down that the principle of subsidiarity is essential in this area in order to ensure the right to negotiate freely in the labour market sector. In this connection reference should be made to the relevant passage in the Community Charter of the fundamental social rights of workers.

3. Legal instruments should as a rule be adopted by qualified majority.

III. *Tax policies*

1. The Danish Government considers it important that, not least in the light of the complete liberalization of capital movements and the impending establishment of EMU, there should be more effective rules for exchanging information necessary for tax control purposes and for mutual assistance in the tax sector.

2. The Danish Government is in favour of investigating the possibilities of introducing minimum rates for income tax, VAT and other taxes. This will prevent competition in the field of tax rebates, something which all Member States wish to avoid.

In the area of business taxation there are very special problems of tax undercutting, and these will increase in proportion to any reductions in general State support for businesses. This question should be looked into with a view to the submission of appropriate proposals for solving any problems.

IV. *Strengthening of the democratic basis for Community cooperation*

1. Greater Community integration calls for a strengthening of the democratic process.

With a view to achieving this aim, the Danish government proposes that the influence of both national parliaments and the European Parliament should be strengthened. It must be recognized that a considerable part of what is known as the democratic shortfall is attributable to the fact that apparently not all national parliaments have an adequate say in the decisions taken at Community level. In this connection the Danish government would point to the role played by the Folketing's Common Market Committee in Denmark.

2. As regards strengthening the European Parliament's role, the Danish government suggests extending the cooperation procedure to include all cases of internal policy decided on by qualified majority. It should not be necessary to amend the cooperation procedure itself. It should continue to be a written procedure.

The Treaty should also be revised with a view to creating appropriate guidelines for hearings of the European Parliament.

3. If the Commission fails to act the European Parliament should be able to compel it (for example by a majority of the elected members) to put forward proposals for legislation.

4. So that failures to comply with or implement legislation do not develop into a credibility problem for the Community, the Danish Government suggests that the European Parliament should be empowered to hold hearings at which Member States would be obliged to appear and explain their failure to comply. This procedure could be supplemented by an annual report from the Commission to the Council giving a clear account of cases of failure to comply by the individual Member States. A procedure should also be introduced whereby a Member State which has received a judgment from the Court of Justice must inform the European

Parliament of the way in which it has complied with the judgment within 6 months.

5. Democratic control should also be strengthened by the introduction of rules bringing greater openness to Community cooperation, and not least to the workings of the Community institutions. This would mean inter alia that certain Council meetings should be public and that citizens should be given the opportunity of obtaining direct knowledge of general administrative acts and also, where party interests are involved, of administrative acts which immediately concern them. Introduction of such principles would make a decisive contribution to greater understanding of cooperation and thereby help to remove numerous misconceptions.

6. An "ombudsman" system should be introduced under the aegis of the European Parliament.

7. The European Parliament's powers of control over the Commission should be strengthened in areas where the Council has given the Commission greater administrative powers.

8. To encourage greater solidarity between Community citizens, the Danish government would recommend introducing the right to vote in local elections in the Community for Community citizens who are resident in a Member State other than their own.

9. A common election date should be introduced for elections to the European Parliament.

10. So that the regions of the Member States have a greater interest in Community development in the longer term, it is suggested that a Committee should be set up under the auspices of the Council of Ministers (along the lines of the ESC) to enable the regions to be given a hearing before decisions are taken by the Council.

V. Effectiveness of the institutions

1. It should be acknowledged that the institutions have on the whole functioned satisfactorily under existing conditions. It is worth noting that they have proved capable of coping with the enormous number of proposals stemming from completion of the internal market. This strongly suggests that there is no need to consider any fundamental changes in the natural balance.

2. Voting by qualified majority should be introduced in areas such as the environment and the labour market with a view to ensuring the adoption of better minimum provisions.

3. Framework programmes for research and technology should be adopted by majority decision.

4. The number of Commissioners should be limited to one per Member State.

5. A permanent agreement should be reached on the seat of the Community institutions, giving guidelines for the future location of new institutions.

6. Means of enforcing obligations with which Member States fail to comply should be strengthened.

7. The role of the European Parliament should be strengthened with regard to effectively checking and supervising the Commission's management of the Community's financial resources.

8. Existing Community rules should be simplified with a view to avoiding fraudulent use of Community resources, and it may also be necessary to implement further measures.

9. In order to ensure that Community legal acts are easy to understand, there should be regular consolidation or simplification of legal acts when they have been the subject of major amendments.

VI. New policies

1. The Danish Government sees a great need to increase cooperation in new areas of policy. This would mean introducing a new basis into the Treaty in certain cases or considerably strengthening the existing basis.

2. The Danish Government considers that — in addition to environment policy, the social dimension and fiscal policy — it is necessary to aim at amending the rules in the following areas of policy:

- State aid — the provisions of the Treaty should be tightened up. The Commission's powers should be increased.

- Consumer protection — this should be a priority objective of Community cooperation and a basis should be introduced into the Treaty to safeguard consumers' fundamental rights — namely protection of health, safety and economic interests; compensation for injury; information and instruction; and representation.

- Community development aid policy — decisions on this should be taken by qualified majority.

- Health policy — a basis should be introduced into the Treaty where necessary, e.g. for aspects relating to the workplace and the external environment. Decisions in certain areas should be taken by qualified majority. The principle of subsidiarity should be applied in this sphere.

- Education policy — a specific section on this should be included in the Treaty. It should be noted that the principle of subsidiarity is fundamental in this area.

- Energy policy — the aim of Community energy policy must be to ensure Community self-sufficiency in this area, to ensure environmentally sound energy production and to promote the use of environment-friendly fuels, including renewable sources of energy.

- Telecommunications — consideration should be given to whether a basis is needed in the Treaty so that decisions in this sphere can be taken by qualified majority.

- Cultural policy — a chapter should be drawn up for the Treaty concerning cultural cooperation within the Community and with third countries. The primary aim should be to promote cross-border cultural exchanges. Such a process should be based on respect for the specific nature and potential of individual cultures and should allow for cultural aid resources to be managed along national cultural lines.

VII.   Unity and cohesion in the Community's international role

The Danish Government considers that the Community should step up its diplomatic and political efforts vis-à-vis third countries, in international organizations and in other multilateral fora.

This should be a gradual development, going hand in hand with the establishment of common positions.

The Danish Government is in favour of investigating the possibility of and scope for greater coordination of the economic, political and security aspects of external policy.

The Government rejects the idea that European Political Cooperation should come to include cooperation in defence policies, inter alia the setting-up of common military forces.

The Danish Government thinks that the consensus rule should continue to apply to matters affecting European Political Cooperation.

Denmark takes the view that it is necessary to augment those topics discussed within the framework of European Political Cooperation. For example, the Danish Government attaches considerable importance to greater coordination among the Twelve in CSCE matters. This would also make it possible for cooperation within the sphere of Community security policy to be pragmatically extended while at the same time taking account of cooperation on security policy in other fora.

The Danish Government would like a decision-taking structure to be set up in which the Council (General Affairs) would play a central role as a united forum for dealing with Community problems and matters covered by European Political Cooperation.

A consequence of such a united forum would be that prior preparation of dossiers would also have to be coordinated. The Danish Government remains open on the question of the forms which coordination of political and Community topics might take.

Greater coordination of Secretariat preparation is however expected in itself to make a major contribution to this process. It is therefore necessary to ensure that the EPC Secretariat and the Council Secretariat work together as smoothly as possible. The central role of the Council as a united forum might argue in favour of Secretariat functions for European Political Cooperation being transferred to a separate unit within the General Secretariat of the Council.

Furthermore a close relationship between the Commission and a strengthened Council Secretariat should be ensured. The Commission's current position as an equal partner in European Political Cooperation should be confirmed in the text of the Treaty.

Finally, the work of COREPER and the Political Committee should be coordinated.

B.   Intergovernmental Conference on Economic and Monetary Union

1. It is the view of the Danish Government that the introduction of EMU is a natural extension of the creation of the internal market and will be able to contribute to the furthering of growth and employment in all Member States.

The Danish Government accordingly considers it important that the conference on economic and monetary union result in a positive outcome so that the advantages deriving from such union may be achieved.

2. It is important to lay down the appropriate

objectives for EMU. The Danish Government feels that the goals in Articles 2 and 104 of the Treaty are a good basis, but that the objective of full employment should be expressly included among the higher principles of the Community. The existing balance between the principles in the two Articles should be maintained against this background.

It must be clearly stated in the Treaty that the coordination of economic and monetary policy in the EMU will endeavour to fulfil these objectives.

Experience since the drafting of the Treaty of Rome does, however, show that it is important for economic growth to respect environmental and energy use considerations. A further goal must thus be the requirement that developments be environmentally sustainable. The Danish Government proposes that this goal also be explicitly cited in the Treaty.

Monetary, financial and structural policies can all contribute to price stability, growth and employment. The Danish Government considers it natural for the European System of Central Banks (ESCB) to conduct monetary policy while the Council (Ministers of Finance and Economic Affairs) in setting economic policy, take care of the other objectives, including growth and high employment. It is accordingly the job of the ESCB to ensure price stability while supporting the general economic policy of the Community.

3. With a view to ensuring achievement of the Community's economic policy objectives the Council of Ministers of Finance and Economic Affairs (ECOFIN) should be strengthened. This would also ensure coordination vis-à-vis the ESCB.

4. On the question of democratic control (accountability) it is important that it balance the necessary independence of the ESCB. An important part of such control would be an obligation on the ESCB to make public regularly — and also when required — its monetary policy decisions and to explain them. Furthermore, the Chairman of the ESCB should have the duty to appear before the European Parliament when invited. The Danish Government considers that it should be for each Member State to decide whether its national governor can be called to appear before its national parliament. The same applies to national information procedures. This must be seen in continuation of the fact that the intention is to create a system of central banks.

5. Connected with the problem of democratic control and the independence of the ESCB is the question of voting rules in the ESCB Council. The Danish Government considers it of prime importance that the ESCB Council operate on the principle of one member, one vote. Decisions must be taken by simple majority except in special cases.

6. As regards the EMU's foreign exchange policy in respect of third countries it is the opinion of the Danish Government that the Council (ECOFIN) should take decisions concerning exchange rate arrangements and changes to any central rates or any fluctuation band in relation to third countries. It is evident that the ESCB must be responsible for the daily conduct of exchange rate policy.

Here too it is important to assure the Council of the necessary influence. This can be done through regular meetings between the leadership of ECOFIN and the ESCB. Changes in the exchange rates against the dollar and yen, etc. cannot be unilaterally determined by the Community but must take place in cooperation with the other major industrial countries. Discussions and decisions within the Council on the principal guidelines for exchange rate policy over the next six months could therefore take place at the half-yearly multilateral surveillance meetings in accordance with the model currently used in cooperation among the seven major industrial countries under the G-7 arrangements.

7. In the area of fiscal and budgetary policy of the individual Member States the Treaty must reflect the principle of subsidiarity. It must furthermore be clear that the Council will not be able to take legally binding decisions on any Member State's budget surplus or deficit or its revenue and expenditure, just as distribution policy must remain a national matter. Anything else would be unacceptable to the national parliaments. This approach also means that the Court cannot overturn national budget decisions.

This calls, on the other hand, for a high degree of responsibility regarding the national budgets. The Danish Government can therefore support the introduction of procedures to bring pressure to bear upon a Member State conducting an irresponsible fiscal and budgetary policy. As a component of this pressure the Council should be able to decide that a particular budget deficit is too high.

In a possible new Community policy towards Member States with major economic problems and a need for special adjustment measures it will be possible to make economic support conditional upon the observance of agreed requirements concerning budgetary policy.

The budgetary discipline requirement also applies to the Community budget, which by and large is of an appropriate magnitude in relation to the common policies currently adopted.

8. In the light of the general objectives of EMU it is in the common interest to assess whether the national budgets support the objectives, including those of growth and employment. It is thus natural that the Council should determine an appropriate budgetary stance for the Community as a whole, and it will be necessary for the Council to discuss the appropriate development of budget deficits as well as budget surpluses. In this way it will also be possible to bring political pressure to bear on Member States conducting a divergent policy in the form of an excessively restrictive or expansionist economic policy.

This process has already begun voluntarily in the EMU's first stage, and it is important that the Governments take this cooperation seriously. Experience with cooperation in the first stage will be a test of willingness to cooperate within EMU.

9. EMU does not in itself set the stage for extension of the structural funds beyond what has already been decided. The Danish Government is prepared to consider the advisability of replacing the present balance-of-payments facilities with a Community policy to support Member States with major economic problems and a need for special adjustment measures. This would be an instrument which would contribute to greater convergence.

The Danish Government is in favour of exploring the possibilities of creating new Community instruments (possibly in the form of a conjunctural fund) which can influence conjunctural development in the EC and thereby ensure a more active policy for strengthening employment.

10. Just as in the EMS there should be a possibility in EMU of linking currencies of European countries with particularly close economic and financial ties with the European Communities. This will strengthen trade relations and help to promote growth and employment together with price stability in those countries to the benefit both of the countries themselves and of the Community.

11. In order to reap the full economic benefits of EMU the Danish Government considers it most expedient to have a short second stage followed by a speedy transition to the final stage.

12. The basis of the Treaty must be that all EC countries are included in the EMU process. Certain countries may, however, still require transitional provisions.

14.   European Commission

Formal opinion pursuant to Article 236 of the EEC Treaty on the proposal for amendment of the Treaty establishing the European Economic Community with a view to political union, 21 October 1990

At its meeting of 28 April 1990, the European Council confirmed its commitment to political union and took the following decision:

"A detailed examination will be put in hand forthwith on the need for possible Treaty changes with the aim of strengthening the democratic legitimacy of the union, enabling the Community and its institutions to respond efficiently and effectively to the demands of the new situation, and assuring unity and coherence in the Community's international action."

It went on to issue the following instructions:

"Foreign Ministers will undertake this examination and analysis, and prepare proposals to be discussed at the European Council in June with a view to a decision on the holding of a second Intergovernmental Conference to work in parallel with the Conference on economic and monetary union with a view to ratification by Member States in the same timeframe."

Following a further in-depth discussion on the basis of an examination conducted by the Foreign Ministers, the European Council, at its meeting in Dublin on 25 and 26 June,

"noted the agreement to convene such a conference under Article 236 of the Treaty. The conference will open on 14 December 1990. It will adopt its own agenda and conclude its work rapidly with the objective of ratification by Member States before the end of 1992."

The European Council also agreed that:

"Foreign Ministers will prepare the conference. Preparatory work will be based on the results of the deliberations of Foreign Ministers (Annex I) and on contributions from national governments and the Commission, and will be conducted in such a way as to permit negotiations on a concrete basis to begin from the start of the conference.

Close dialogue will be maintained with the European Parliament both in the preparatory phase and in the conference phase on political union as well as on economic and monetary union.

The European Council considered that the necessary coherence in the work of the two conferences should be ensured by the General Affairs Council."

Before defining the main lines of the approach that the Commission will be defending at the Intergovernmental Conference on political union, it is appropriate to review the factors behind the growing awareness of the need to give the Community a genuine political dimension in the light of experience from the recent past. These factors are closely linked to recent or ongoing developments in Europe and the world.

(1) The 12 Member States have gradually come to accept the need for a higher profile on the international scene to enable them to give a collective response to a clear demand for Europe, to work together to defend their interests, and to contribute to the creation of a fairer, more efficient world order which respects the values they share, in particular human rights.

(2) The successes achieved through the impetus given by the 1992 deadline, the implementation of the common policies enshrined in the Single Act and the February 1988 agreement, raise the question of how the people of Europe can be genuinely involved in the shared adventure of European integration or, to put it another way, how the challenge of democratic legitimacy can be met.

(3) Despite general recognition and sometimes even envy of these successes there is still room for legitimate disappointment at the Community's overall progress, which falls short of the expectations for European integration over the last 40 years. Furthermore, the Community's decision-making process needs improvement given the rapidly changing world.

The convening of the Intergovernmental Conference on Political Union provides a golden opportunity to (a) broaden the Community's powers and (b) improve decision-making.

The basic conclusion lies at the heart of the Commission's reflections and its contribution to the proceedings of the Intergovernmental Conference. The Italian Presidency has asked it for its opinion on the basis of a proposal for amendment of the Treaty pursuant to Article 236 EEC.

The Commission clearly welcomes the convening of the Conference.

I —A single Community

In the first place the Commission will strenuously defend the thesis — as it did when the Single Act was being negotiated — that both the historic legacy of the founding fathers and the cumulative commitment to European integration argue in favour of concentrating the revision of the Treaty on the integration of new objectives into a single Community.

The osmosis between economic, social, financial and monetary policy on the one hand and foreign policy on the other is and should continue to be the underlying philosophy of a European Union, as affirmed in the preamble to the Single Act.

Only a single Community with a single institutional structure can bridge the gap that has opened up between progress on common policies on the one hand and advances on political cooperation on the other. Indeed, the challenges that the quickening pace of history has presented to the Community have highlighted the existence of a "grey area" where the role of the institutions is less than clear. For the Community this points to the need for consistency between the positions it adopts on the world stage and the conclusions it draws in the areas of external economic policy and relations with developing countries.

A single Community implies a single institutional structure flexible enough to take account of:

(a) the state of public opinion on the future of European integration, which varies considerably from country to country, and the way Member States perceive the joint exercise of pooled sovereignty;

(b) the need for caution, which militates against defining the final shape of European Union at this early stage in favour of keeping to the course charted by the Treaty of Rome, leading eventually to a federal-type organization;

(c) the likelihood of further institutional change to accommodate enlargement of the Community. Common sense dictates that in a much larger Community the institutions will have to be radically reformed to prevent Europe degenerating into a mere free trade area with loose arrangements for foreign policy consultation.

II —Ensuring unity and coherence in the Community's international action

The Commission is optimistic about the Community's ability to meet the historic challenge of ensuring unity and coherence in the Community's international action.

Three fundamental questions have to be answered in this context:

(1) Do the Member States consider that they share vital common interests and do they wish to act together to pursue them?

(2) What are the ambitions of the Community and its Member States and are they prepared to accept all the economic and financial consequences of their decisions?

(3) Should a common foreign policy also cover security matters, given that defence is an essential element of security?

The Commission's answer to all three questions is in the affirmative. And although it feels that the establishment of a common foreign and security policy will require a flexible and pragmatic approach, it nevertheless believes that the Treaty should outline the procedures and methods for a common policy leading towards European Union.

The term "common policy" has been chosen deliberately. In these matters it would be unrealistic to speak of political union when it is quite clear that, traditionally, Member States have special relations with certain parts of the world and geopolitical positions which are firmly anchored in their history. More importantly, the Twelve do not yet share the same assessment of their responsibilities or of their general and specific commitments in various parts of the world.

The same considerations have led the Commission to recommend a specific approach to security matters. The Treaty should include a reference to this subject and might incorporate the undertaking contained in Article 5 of the 1948 Brussels Treaty on the WEU which specifies that, in the event of an armed attack against one of the contracting parties, the others are obliged to provide aid and assistance.

More than that, the new Treaty should, in general terms, point the way towards a common security policy, including defence.

It is also in the common interest to bring defence equipment production and trade fully under the discipline of the common market, which would involve *inter alia* the removal of Article 223.

However, security is more than just a matter of military defence. It now covers all means of guaranteeing cohesion at national and Community level, from the preservation of a common model of society to the protection of citizens against terrorism, serious crime and the other scourges of the modern world.

The definition and implementation of a common foreign policy raises four questions:
(1) Who will prepare the decisions?
(2) Who will take the decisions?
(3) Who will implement the decisions?
(4) How can the expression of popular sovereignty, first and foremost the European Parliament, be involved in this process?

1. Preparation of decisions

The preparation of decisions should be based on the experience of the existing Community system whereby an *ad hoc* institution would act simultaneously as a focus for Community action and as the guarantor of consistency between the common foreign policy and the other common policies.

This observation, drawn from experience, does not mean that the Commission intends to lay claim to a monopoly of the right of initiative in this area. In fact, the very specific nature of foreign and security policy implies that the right of initiative must be shared between the Council Presidency, the Member States and the Commission, if only because of the close links between foreign policy on the one hand and external economic policy and development cooperation policy on the other.

For this reason, the body responsible for preparing decisions should include the present political secretariat — which will be strengthened — and representatives of the Commission, so that they can work together, with the necessary discretion, to draw up decisions on this new common policy. It would be attached to the General Secretariat of the Council.

At the same time, Coreper would be reorganized so that it could be apprised of foreign policy matters before the Council takes a decision.

2. The method of decision-making

The method of decision-making depends on the scope of foreign policy. This must be broadened gradually but it also needs to be consolidated quickly by joint action.

Should the scope of foreign policy be clearly defined in the Treaty? The Commission feels that this would not be the right approach. Any attempt to compile a list of areas considered to be of vital common interest would come up against insurmountable difficulties of interpretation. This being so, it would be preferable to leave it to the European Council to decide on the areas to be transferred from the scope of political cooperation to that of a common or Community policy.

Once these areas had been defined by the European Council, the Foreign Ministers, meeting within the Council, would take decisions by a qualified majority — except on matters directly related to security. However, this would be an augmented qualified majority requiring the votes of eight Member States.

In other areas, the consensus rule would apply as it already does for political cooperation.

3. Implementation

As regards implementation of the most important decisions, it would be for the Council to choose from a number of formulas depending on the circumstances, all of them involving Commission participation, as in the past.

The essential requirement is that once a common position has been decided on, the Community must speak with one voice.

4. Involvement of the European Parliament

Involvement of the European Parliament in foreign and security policy is less a matter of strict institutional rules than of general working practice. It would be up to those responsible for the common policy to consult Parliament on a regular basis and to keep it informed of the implications for the Community of the most important foreign policy developments either at a plenary session or in the relevant committees.

The revision of the Treaty should clarify the scope for application of the assent procedure to the most important agreements — in particular, association and cooperation agreements — whose purpose would be to define, within an overall framework, the political, economic, financial and cultural dimensions of the Community's relations with its main partners.

On the other hand, this procedure would not apply to ordinary trade agreements which involve implementation in strict compliance with Treaty provisions, notably Article 113, of broad principles of external economic policy defined by the Community's institutions.

III —Strengthening democratic legitimacy: Relations between the institutions and the people of Europe

Further democratization of the running of the Community must be seen from the twin standpoint of its institutions and its citizens.

1. The institutions

Without losing sight of the paramount need to reconcile democracy and efficiency, the objective as far as the institutions are concerned must be twofold:

(a) to strengthen the powers of the European Parliament;

(b) to increase the involvement of national parliaments.

(a) Aside from its involvement in foreign policy and joint security, the powers of the European Parliament must be strengthened *vis-à-vis* the Council and the Commission.

Notwithstanding the fears expressed in certain quarters, the cooperation procedure introduced by the Single Act has not led to disputes between Parliament and the Council or made decision-making more cumbersome. Parliament has shown that it is willing and able to play its full part as joint legislator. The Commission considers that a radical reform of the Treaty, such as that now under way, should involve an increase in Parliament's legislative powers. It therefore proposes:

(i) increasing the part played by Parliament in the cooperation procedure; one formula which would guarantee that a decision was taken would be a provision to the effect that, following Parliament's second reading, the Commission proposal incorporating Parliament's amendments would be deemed adopted unless the Council rejected it by a simple majority;

(ii) extending the cooperation procedure to all the new areas where qualified majority voting would apply;

(iii) strengthening the role of Parliament in the budget procedure and giving it joint responsibility for Community revenue.[1]

With regard to the appointment of the Commission, the only political body genuinely accountable to it, Parliament has consistently demanded the power to appoint, or at least to be involved in the appointment of, Members of the Commission. The formula which seems to have the most support would be a two-tier investiture: the first stage would involve investiture of the President of the Commission, who would be appointed by Parliament on a proposal from the European Council; and the second stage, following the appointment of the Members by agreement between the Member States after consultation of the President, would involve investiture of the Commission as a whole on the basis of its programme. In this way Parliament would be able to confirm the appointment of the entire Commission.

(b) A great deal of confusion still surrounds the request for more involvement of national parliaments in Community affairs. This needs to be dispelled.

In the case of decisions to transfer sovereignty by amending the Treaty, national parliaments are completely sovereign and, when a vote is taken on whether to ratify amendments to the Treaty, approve the principle and extent of such transfers in full knowledge of the facts. The use of mechanisms involving association in decision-making would conflict with the solemn, conclusive nature of ratification.

In the case of assessing the use made of powers transferred to the Community, it should not be forgotten that in the Community system it is national governments, sitting in the Council, that take the major decisions. Since national governments are accountable to national parliaments, it is for them to involve elected representatives in Community affairs in a manner which respects national traditions.

Having said this, the Commission nevertheless recognizes that a number of proposals have been made for improving relations between the European Parliament and national parliaments.

Should new arrangements prove to be essential, the Commission would favour the introduction of an information procedure, whereby a delegation from national parliaments would be given an opportunity to hear an explanation from the Council presidency and the Commission before major decisions are taken.

But the Commission believes that it is first and foremost for the European Parliament, in consultation with national parliaments, to consider what is the best way to improve relations between the elected representatives of the people.

Lastly, the Commission notes that on the evidence of experience over the last few years,

---

[1] See the section on public finances.

Parliament is still dissatisfied with the quality of its bilateral relations with the Council of Ministers.

2. Citizens' involvement

In the Commission's view, strengthening the institutions will not be enough of itself to ensure that citizens are genuinely involved in the Community's activities at every stage of the definition of policies in fields directly affecting them. That is why the Commission endorses the proposal put forward by the Spanish Prime Minister, Felipe González, for the introduction of the notion of European citizenship. This would take shape gradually, without encroaching in any way on national citizenship, which it would supplement rather than replace. In short, the object would be to encourage a feeling of involvement in European integration.

The basis for European citizenship along these lines could be a statement of rights and obligations focusing on:

(i) basic human rights, with a reference to the Strasbourg Convention;

(ii) the rights of European citizens to be written into the Treaty, including:

(a) the right of residence and movement, whether the individual is economically active or not,

(b) voting rights in European and local elections;

(iii) the setting of targets for the definition of the individual's civic, economic and social rights and obligations at a later stage.

It must not be forgotten that citizens are also involved in economic and social development. That is why, as far back as 1985, the Commission took the step of encouraging social dialogue at Community level between representatives of employers' organizations and trade unions. That process is now enshrined in the Single Act. But it should be given greater emphasis and its organization improved. This presupposes, *inter alia*, enhancing the status of the Economic and Social Committee and of its members.

Lastly, the Commission considers that the Intergovernmental Conference must take account of the demand for the creation of a body to represent the Community's regions. This is an important parameter of subsidiarity. The wide variety of regional structures in the Member States precludes — and will probably continue to do so — the involvement of such a body in the decision-making process. The Commission's suggestion therefore is that, pending fresh developments, it should hold regular consultations with a body representing all the regions of Europe.

IV —Improving the effectiveness of the institutions

Four questions arise when considering ways of improving the effectiveness of the institutions:

(1) the question of broadening the Community's powers;

(2) the question of subsidiarity;

(3) the question of improving the way the institutions operate while maintaining a general balance;

(4) the question of the status of the Community's public finances.

1. Powers

As in the case of the Single Act, the question of powers must not be seen in general terms but rather in terms of selecting the means of action the Community needs to ensure the balanced development of common policies.

As part of this selective approach, the Commission proposes that any increase in the Community's powers should concentrate on social affairs, major infrastructure networks and the free movement of persons, all three having a bearing on the optimum development of the single market. As far as the environment, research and taxation are concerned, it feels that the question is one of improving decision-making, in other words the use made of qualified majority voting, rather than redefining powers.

(a) For social affairs, the Commission's proposal is that the provisions of the Treaty be expanded and clarified, in the light of the principles laid down in the Community Charter of Fundamental Social Rights, to allow the Council to adopt directives by a qualified majority in areas such as:

(i) improvement of living and working conditions, in particular the duration and organization of working time, forms of employment other than open-ended contracts and other aspects of employment regulations which have a bearing on the protection of workers' fundamental rights, particularly in the case of cross-frontier operations;

(ii) basic and further vocational training;[2]

(iii) information and consultation for workers.

Finally, a legal basis should be provided to allow the Community to develop programmes to prevent and combat major threats to health such as cancer and AIDS, as it has already done at the request of the European Council.

(b) The development of major infrastructure networks to facilitate the movement of goods, services, persons, capital and information should be encouraged by making it possible for the Council to take appropriate action and adopt programmes.

(c) Although the Single Act introduced the concept of a frontier-free area, the Community's powers in relation to the free movement of persons raise difficulties which need to be resolved. The principle that freedom of movement, and the equality of treatment needed to exercise it, are rights enjoyed by Community nationals should be enshrined in the Treaty once and for all, as should the possibility of adopting the necessary measures by a qualified majority. This does not mean that all the rules would need to be standardized. Coordination or approximation should suffice.

Experience has shown that the provisions of the Single Act are less than satisfactory as far as non-Community nationals entering or residing in the Community are concerned. The Commission also notes that the intergovernmental method, which it supported, has failed to produce any meaningful results. The Commission suggests that this delicate issue, which undermines relations with non-Community countries, notably in the areas of immigration and the fight against drug abuse and serious crime, should be resolved by one or other of the following solutions:

(i) an explicit reference in the Treaty to a Community competence, which would require unanimity, at least initially, in relation to non-Community nationals to the extent needed for the free movement of persons and the creation of a frontier-free area;

(ii) recognition of the problems raised by the status of non-Community nationals, again to the extent to which these involve the free movement of persons, as one of the questions of vital common interest in foreign and common security policy.

(d) In the case of the environment and research and technology, the Treaty will have to be rewritten to increase the effectiveness of operations conducted at Community level and make it possible to create new financial instruments where appropriate. These could also be used for developing major infrastructure networks (see (b) above).

(e) In the area of taxation the aim must be to facilitate the adoption of measures linked to the completion and effective functioning of the single market.

(f) As far as energy is concerned, the treaties could be consolidated into a single chapter making it possible to implement a common energy policy or at least a common energy market.

(g) In line with the principle of subsidiarity, cultural affairs should continue to be a matter for the Member States and regions. It would be a good idea, however, to include an article on the cultural dimension of Community activities.[3]

2. Subsidiarity

The question of subsidiarity is closely linked to the redefinition of certain powers. The Commission considers that this common-sense principle should be written into the Treaty, as suggested by Parliament in its draft treaty on European Union. It should serve as a guideline for the institutions when, under a new Article 235 freed from its purely economic purpose, they have to take a unanimous decision of principle on new Community action in pursuit of general Treaty objectives. Compliance with the principle could be checked by a retrospective control of the institutions' activities to ensure that there is no abuse of powers.

3. Effectiveness

In the Commission's view, improving the effectiveness of the institutions largely depends on extending the use of qualified majority voting. In theory, this should apply to all areas of

[2] Among other things, this would make it possible to develop programmes similar to Erasmus, Comett and Yes for Europe.
[3] In particular, this would highlight the importance of the action taken to ensure the free movement of audiovisual works, to encourage creative artists in Europe, to promote high-definition television, and to expand the Media programme, to quote just a few examples.

Community competence except "constitutional" questions, and with possible restrictions in the areas of taxation, social security and the status of non-Community nationals.

Assuming that the cooperation procedure would be extended in line with the wider use of qualified majority voting, it would be important to define the time-limits within which the Council and the European Parliament would be required to act. This is a precondition for improving the way our democratic procedures operate.

In general terms, with a view to simplifying and clarifying Community legislation the Commission believes that the common policies can only develop satisfactorily if a clear distinction is made between legislative and regulatory measures.

As far as the delegation of power to the Commission is concerned, efficiency demands that both the letter and the spirit of the Single Act be fully applied in practice. Here a distinction has to be made between the implementation of decisions and the decisions themselves, whether they are legislative or regulatory.

The Commission takes the view that only two formulas should be allowed under the Treaty: the advisory committee and the management committee.

One disturbing fact remains: in the absence of sanctions, Court of Justice rulings are not always implemented. The Commission may consider proposing a system of sanctions to deal with this type of situation.

4. Status of the Community's public finances

This subject has to be considered in the light of the progress made since the adoption of the interinstitutional agreement proposed by the Commission in 1986, which has brought home a number of lessons:

(a) the need to reconsider the distinction between compulsory and non-compulsory expenditure, so as to combine the retention of certain guarantees with greater flexibility in budget management;

(b) the need to restore the institutional balance to allow the Commission to play its full part in the budgetary process;

(c) the possibility of Parliament being given some influence on a limited portion of revenue

to increase not only its powers but also its responsibility towards electors;

(d) incorporation of the principles of budgetary discipline into the Treaty.

. . .

The improvements put forward by the Commission are designed to maintain the current balance of the institutional triangle, since the most sensible course in making any substantial changes is to build on the existing model. In other words, we would base ourselves on the existing institutional structure, since its dynamic power is already proven.

The main advantage of the present system lies in its success in maintaining a balance between the institutions. It should therefore be preserved, but adapted to meet the needs of ever closer Community integration. And with the possibility of Parliament being given new legislative powers and the Council having wider decision-making powers in foreign and security policy,[4] it will be important to safeguard the Commission's right of initiative, which has proved to be one of the key factors in the Community's dynamism.[5]

At all events, the accountability of the executive to Parliament is a vital element in the equation, even if the executive does not have the right to dissolve it.

Alongside the traditional institutional triangle, the Community's new ambitions in terms of economic and monetary union as well as foreign and security policy highlight the need to formalize the "motor" role of the European Council, which has proved so invaluable in revitalizing the process of European integration over the past six years.

Building and expanding on the Treaty of Rome, political union would have the task of gradually creating the foundations of a future European Union through the process of economic and monetary integration, the furthering of social development, the implementation of economic and social cohesion and the pursuit of a common foreign and security policy.

Besides the amendments to Article 2 and 3 on the principles underlying the Treaty, the introduction of a title on economic and monetary union, the extension of certain powers and the strengthening of democratic legitimacy

---

[4] As in the area of economic and monetary union, which is discussed in SEC(90) 1659 final (21 August 1990).
[5] The same should apply to economic and monetary union (see reference above).

and efficiency, the revision of the Treaty will involve the inclusion of a new title on a common foreign and security policy — quite clearly the primary driving force behind the new revitalization.

This common policy will have to comprise three sets of provisions:

(i) a framework for decisions and action in the foreign policy field and provisions on security;

(ii) a new grouping of modified Treaty articles on the common commercial policy;

(iii) provisions strengthening the objectives and instruments of cooperation and development aid to make it more effective.

In this way the Community, given genuine political will, will be able to face up to its worldwide responsibilities, however varied the circumstances.

Set firmly on the foundations of economic, social and monetary union, its success and impact will be all the more assured, enabling it to satisfy the expectations placed in it.

Political union and economic, social and monetary union are thus inextricably linked.

15.   Dutch Government

Policy document on European Political Union presented to the Parliament,
26 October 1990

Introduction

Good progress was made in the discussions in Brussels during September in the Group of Personal Representatives of the Ministers of Foreign Affairs on the substance and form of European Political Union (EPU). These discussions are intended to prepare the ground for the Intergovernmental Conference on Political Union (IGC II) due to begin on 14 December 1990, which will run parallel to the Intergovernmental Conference on Economic and Monetary Union (EMU). On the basis of these discussions the Ministers of Foreign Affairs held informal talks, as part of the Gymnich meetings, on 6 and 7 October, and the General Council discussed this subject on 22 October. It was also considered on 27 and 28 October by the European Council in Rome. The European Council in Dublin in June this year identified four themes which were to be explored in these discussions:

- the overall objective of Political Union, including its scope and general principles;
- democratic legitimacy;
- efficiency and effectiveness of the Community and its institutions;
- unity and coherence of the Community's international action.

Preparations for the Intergovernmental Conference are still in the exploratory phase, but the outlines of what will be at issue are gradually emerging. Views are being formulated in European capitals on the basis of each government's ideas and analyses as well as contributions from other Member States and from various Community institutions. The Hague is far from having finalized its views, and this would not be opportune at this stage since there must be further consultation between the Twelve. So this document does no more than describe the situation at this point in time; it is a progress report on the policy document "Europe: the way forward II" and sets out the current position in the discussions within the Group of Personal Representatives. Specific choices will depend on concrete proposals submitted by us or by others. If necessary, further consultation will take place on such proposals. The Dutch Government intends to report regularly to Parliament, so that consultation will run parallel to the progress of negotiations.

On 22 October the European Commission published its recommendations under Article 236 of the EEC Treaty. These could not yet be taken into account in the preparation of this document.

1.   Political context, overall objectives and scope

1.2   The "why" of EPU

Before turning to the aims of EPU, we should consider the preliminary question of the reasons for now taking substantial measures to widen and deepen the process of integration so soon after the Single European Act of 1986. This Act set in motion a process of accelerated economic union by laying down the ultimate objective (abolishing internal borders), the date for achieving this objective (1 January 1993), the route to be followed (the White Paper) and the method (qualified majority decision and greater participation by the European Parliament). Various circumstances have led to the realization that it is necessary for the integration process to be deepened, broadened, streamlined and democratized. Recent developments on the world stage present the Community with many challenges. These include the fundamental changes in Europe, German unification, the Gulf crisis, changing economic relations between the major trade partners in the world, and the greater interest in the Community as either a partner (negotiations with the EFTA countries on the European Economic Area, the prospect of far-reaching association agreements with the countries of Central and Eastern Europe, a new relationship with the Mediterranean countries) or a haven (requests to join from Austria, Turkey, Malta and Cyprus). All these factors have led to the realization that the Community urgently needs further integration if it is to deal firmly with the challenges of the age. Democratization of the process of European integration is a central concern here. The present democratic vacuum between the European Parliament and the national parliaments should be ended. In addition, new transfers of competence to the Community should be accompanied by democratic controls at the European level.

1.3   EMU and EPU

As stated, two intergovernmental conferences will begin at the same time. It is also intended, as confirmed by the European Council in Dublin, that they should end at the same time. So they are clearly related in time, but that is not all. The progress made on institutional matters at the EPU conference will have its effect on the institutional shape of EMU. This is important not only for the methods of decision-making in EMU but also as regards the question of democratic control.

This is not to say that there are not also important differences between the two conferences. It could be said that EMU will complete the process of economic integration between the partners, which began with the European Coal and Steel Community, continued with the EEC, and was stimulated by the Single European Act and the Internal Market. As the rest of this document will show, EPU is exploring new territory beyond economic integration. So the two conferences face different challenges. It is important to bear this in mind, if only to prevent each conference — as a negotiating tactic — being held hostage by the other as regards their conclusions.

1.4   The current views of the other Member States

Recent ministerial meetings (Asolo 6/7 October, Luxembourg 22 October) made clear that, with one or two exceptions, the views of the other Member States have not yet been finalized.

Both as regards the definition of new areas to receive attention and the issues of democracy and decision-making, there is ample scope for views to be developed further. This is certain to become apparent in the course of the discussions up to the formal opening of the Intergovernmental Conference on 14 December. It is already clear that there is a general desire to broaden and deepen European integration. However, it is much less clear whether, in the case of new areas to be considered, the Member States are thinking in terms of Community integration — now or in the long term — or of intergovernmental cooperation.

There is also a tendency among some Member States to take a pragmatic approach: instead of taking a clear decision on institutional matters, the EC/EPU should get on with integration or cooperation in new fields and leave to the future the question of what results this will finally lead to. The Netherlands has repeatedly made it clear, both in the negotiations in Brussels and in bilateral contacts, that it is quite prepared to be pragmatic provided that the ultimate aim of a federal Europe remains intact. Particularly in the present circumstances, when not all the partners have finalized their views, it seems useful to draw their attention to the political and conceptual merits of the Netherlands perspective. This is also why this document puts the emphasis on presenting the views of the Netherlands.

1.5   Analysis of the problem

Of the four themes set out above, democratic legitimacy is given the most weight by the Netherlands. As more powers are transferred to the Community, it becomes increasingly important to ensure that democratic safeguards are built into Community decision-making. In the eyes of its own citizens and the rest of the world, the Community cannot allow itself to go on watering down democracy in the process of continuing integration. On the contrary, not only are new steps impossible without simultaneously extending the powers of the European Parliament, but consideration should again be given to the question of how democratic Community decision-making is at present. It is a matter, in other words, not only of strengthening the position of the European Parliament, but of combating those developments which may hinder democracy.

In direct relation to this, the question of the efficiency of Community decision-making should be considered. Both these themes are important in relation to the other two mentioned on page 1: widening the overall objective and field of activity of the Community, and interweaving European Political Cooperation (EPC) and the EC. Faced with having to weigh raising the level of democracy and improving decision-making on the one hand against wider objectives and interweaving on the other, the Netherlands lets the question of ways to achieve the latter depend on the progress made as regards democracy and institutions. After all, broader Community cooperation is not really possible unless the decision-making process meets the requirements which a democratic society is entitled to impose on it. Improving the efficiency of decision-making is, furthermore, of fundamental importance in relation to admitting new Member States in due course. Wider membership of the Community must not be allowed to weaken its strength, either internally or externally.

As regards the direction of integration, the Netherlands has chosen the federal option. The Government set out the reasons for this some months ago in its policy document "Europe: the way forward II" . Very recently, the Budget Debate showed that the Lower House of Parliament shared this view by a large majority. EPU ought to take us a step further in this direction. The length of this step is in principle less important than the direction. In itself this need not be a drawback. The whole process of integration is evolutive in character, and developments cannot be forced. However, it is important to ensure that possible intergovernmental elements in EPU can ultimately become subject to Community law. The acceptance of continuing exceptions to Community rules would undermine what has been achieved so far in the integration process.

This is why the Dutch Government has reservations about the proposals aired in the talks between the Personal Representatives, and subsequently in the press, to reserve a permanent place in the Union, under the motto of "common policy", for intergovernmental cooperation in a whole range of politically very important fields. The significance of this becomes all the greater when one considers the institutions proposed for the purposes of this "common policy". For example, it has been suggested that there should be a parliamentary "Congress" consisting of national delegates and a part of the European Parliament. The competence of the present European Parliament would extend solely to the existing Community, while the "Congress", without having any real powers, would be able to pronounce on matters affecting EPU and its future development. This would mean putting a stop to further development of the European Parliament and "renationalizing" parliamentary influence. It has also been proposed that the European Council, as the only body combining a Community and an intergovernmental position, should be responsible for the main lines of policy on the EC, EMU and EPU as a whole. This approach implies that EMU and EPU, at least as regards decision-making mechanisms and

democratic control, are separate from or above, rather than being part of, Community cooperation and law. In relation to both the further democratic development of the Community and improving its decision-making, the Dutch Government believes such proposals conflict with the ultimate aim of a federal Europe.

1.6   Overall objectives of the Community, scope and general principles

According to Article 2 of the EEC treaty, the authors had two particular aims in mind when the Community was founded:

- – promoting social and economic development and the concomitant raising of living standards;
- – promoting stability in relations between the Member States.

These emphases are entirely understandable given that the Treaty was written in the 1950s: it was a time of economic reconstruction and, as a common aim, joint economic development was intended to restore good relations between the members.

In the more than 30 years since the Community was founded, there have been so many changes in society and in the Community itself, both internally and externally, that we are justified in asking whether Article 2 should not be expanded. If the stated objectives are to be a fair reflection of the areas in which the Community is or ought to be active, there are good reasons for adding two new elements, namely concern for the quality of society and the Community's external responsibilities.

This raises the question of what powers should be transferred to the Community to enable it to fulfil these objectives, and this brings us to the debate on the subsidiarity principle.

In early October apparently contradictory views were expressed in the Lower House of the Netherlands Parliament. For example, it was rightly said that, "We do not by definition need to pass on to Brussels what we can well deal with at the national level." But another view put forward in the debate is also correct: "The Community institutions must be given the powers needed to realize the objectives of the Treaty of Rome."

The next question is how to reconcile these apparently contradictory views. "Apparently" because what has been said above implies a recognition that the transfer of powers is not an end in itself. It must always be justified by the absence in a particular situation of any possibility of taking adequate measures at the national level. This means that there will be a need for political judgements to be made case by case. It is not possible in the integration process to freeze the division of powers between the Community and the Member States. This is why in the discussions in Brussels the Netherlands has rejected the idea of so-called positive and negative lists respectively granting or not granting powers exclusively to the Community. The Netherlands would prefer to have a generally applicable provision, for example in the Preamble to the EEC Treaty.

In addition to issues of principle there are practical aspects. It is frequently said that efforts must be made to prevent excessive centralization of legislation and administration in Brussels. Consideration of the methods of integration thus raises the issue of centralization. The Government believes that unnecessary centralization should indeed be avoided. As was successfully done in the case of removing technical obstacles to trade, we should pursue integration through decentralized methods where possible.

The following review will be of value in the judgements to be made case by case as outlined above. During the Intergovernmental Conference the question will arise of whether, and if so to what extent, the Community powers should be extended in the areas mentioned. This review reflects the situation at present: it is quite possible that in the course of negotiations the list will be changed. For the record it should be said that not everything discussed below need necessarily lead to changes in the text of the Treaty. The text as it stands undoubtedly leaves ample scope for further development, certainly in the light of Article 235. In the event of a transfer of powers, care must be taken in defining the division of powers between the Community and the Member States.

It should again be stressed that in the Netherlands Government's view further improvements as regards democracy and institutions are a precondition for extending the activities of the Community.

(a) Free movement of persons
Bearing in mind that such matters as immigration, drugs, police and judicial cooperation come under this heading, it will be immediately apparent that the debate on free movement of persons, etc. raises fundamental aspects of law and order. It illustrates clearly that the realization of EPU — if the Union indeed strengthens the Community rather than the intergovernmental component in European integration — could be of fundamental, or in legal terms constitutional importance.

In the view of the Netherlands there need be no misunderstanding about the fact that, on the basis of the present Treaty, the Community already has the right to develop a Community policy covering the whole of this field. Reference is made to Article 235 in conjunction with Article 8 A EEC in particular. It is more a question of whether this would be politically opportune, and if so to what extent and in which fields. The limits of powers would have to be clearly defined, not least because room would have to be left for national policies on criminal justice in matters not directly related to free movement of persons.

On the question of what is politically opportune, it should be remembered that the Netherlands Government and a majority of the Lower House of Parliament are in favour of working towards a Community, rather than an intergovernmental, approach to this field. It is, however, a fact that at present many Member States prefer the intergovernmental approach. Moreover, in deciding a Community policy on free movement of persons, the Twelve as a whole are not yet prepared to go as far as what was agreed at Schengen. As a co-signatory of the Schengen Agreement, the Dutch Government would however be prepared to accept the Schengen acquis (with the exception, of course, of the intergovernmental decision-making procedures) as a basis for an EC agreement.

(b) Citizenship
The concept of "citizenship of the Community" is intended to express the direct involvement of the citizens of Europe in the process of integration. So this point brings us to the heart of the objective of according the quality of life a proper place in the integration process. The discussion of this point by the Personal Representatives is still at a very early stage. The ideas put forward, in addition to complete freedom of movement, include freedom of establishment and granting European citizens the right to vote in elections for local government and the European Parliament in their place of residence. It is important to note that the term now being used is "all Community citizens", not just economic agents. This could be taken further in the form of a gradual widening of the rights of residents

in the Community who are not citizens of one of the Member States, for example as regards the right to free movement of labour. Before determining a standpoint on this question, the effects on the labour market and the budgetary consequences, including as regards welfare benefits, must be considered.

To improve the protection of the EC citizen against arbitrary actions by Community institutions, consideration could be given to appointing a "Euro-ombudsman", in addition to a right of petition and the right of appeal to the EC Court of Justice (which already exists in certain cases).

(c) Social policy

Social policy is a field which belongs within both the original purely economic objectives of the EEC Treaty and the wider objectives in which the quality of life is accorded a proper place. From the start the EEC Treaty contained a social section, and the Community's social policy has in the past been given substance on the basis of this and other articles of the Treaty. One essential aspect of social policy, apart from the basic structural differences between societies, is the differences in the legal approach and traditions of policy in the various areas. An equally fundamental characteristic is the generally limited role of government in this field, certainly in recent years. Nevertheless, in the course of time Community legislation on social policy has been created. Apart from the social section mentioned above, Articles 100 and 235 played an important part in this.

The matters covered in this legislation include the free movement of labour, equal treatment of men and women in virtually all fields, the reporting of collective redundancies, the retention of the rights of employees when companies change hands, and many measures to do with working conditions. In the period ahead the Council will consider nearly 50 Commission proposals for the implementation of the Community Charter of Basic Social Rights for Workers which were approved by 11 of the 12 Member States at the European Council in Strasbourg. This clearly shows that attention will continue to be paid to social policy in the future. The present Treaty articles undoubtedly offer scope to make progress on this action programme. The fact that there is less EC legislation in this field than in others is not primarily due to the limitations of the Treaty as it stands. Nonetheless, the Netherlands will of course be prepared to give constructive consideration to a possible broadening of Title Three of the Treaty or the decision-making procedures laid down in it if future developments should make this necessary for the sake of the Community's stance on social matters.

(d) Culture

It can hardly be disputed that there is a perceptible tension between on the one hand the working of the Treaty (particularly as regards national support measures and competition) and on the other the widely felt need to protect or promote expressions of national culture. It must be recognized that the EC Court of Justice leaves some scope for national measures, but it may be doubted whether this will prove to be large enough or sufficiently safeguarded in the long term.

In principle there are two ways of working towards a solution:

1. the development at the Community level of a special Community policy which would guarantee room for national cultural policy and provide a basis for the Community itself to be active in the cultural field;

2. the formulation of an exception to existing Community law, which could take the form of redefining Articles 36 and 92 EEC.

A combination of both options could also be considered. In the light of the completion of the Internal Market and the effects of this on, for example, national restrictions on trade in cultural property, the European Commission is considering the second option. However, discussion of this problem as a whole is still at an early stage, so the choice of the most desirable form cannot yet be made.

(e) Education

The desirability of Community policy in the field of education is also increasingly evident. There are a number of reasons for this:

- the effects of the Internal Market make it necessary to have agreements on several points (such as admitting EC citizens to national education systems, and the comparability of qualifications and levels of education);

- the growing need for minimum qualifications for EC citizens with a view to social cohesion and realizing equal opportunities within the EC;

- increasing problems in the international recognition of qualifications.

This could produce a need to insert an education section into the Treaty which would open the way to an EC education policy which would be mainly concerned with coordination. National governments would of course retain their powers to conduct national education policy taking into account the different types of education systems and the economic, cultural and social realities in which they are rooted.

(f) Research

The EC programmes for research and technological development have played an important part in strengthening Europe's industrial competitiveness. Through the Single European Act this objective is incorporated in Article 130 F of the EEC Treaty.

Developments in the EC Framework Programme show that other Community tasks, for example in the environmental field, are not simply regarded as deriving from the need for industrial competitiveness but are given separate attention in the R & D programmes. There will be further studies of the desirability of adapting the Treaty provisions on research to the needs experienced in practice and the requirements for the coming years.

These studies will be concerned with the independent and not merely conditional power of the Community to finance research in fields involving issues that are evidently of international and common interest and where the Community is empowered to act. Another point to be examined will be the role the Community already plays, through the Framework Programme, in strengthening the scientific infrastructure. This includes programmes in the fields of mobility, training, networks of institutions and large-scale facilities.

Any changes must of course leave intact the principle of subsidiarity and the aim of research serving to support industrial competitiveness. Another point which will have to be considered is that the provisions dealing with research in the EC Treaty and the Euratom Treaty do not entirely correspond with each other.

(g) Health

A distinction should be made between on the one hand health protection (already the subject of EC policy), and on the other health care and questions of medical ethics (matters which can continue to be dealt with mainly at the national level). As regards health protection, the aim could be to achieve a recognizable EC policy (e.g. programmes such as "Europe against cancer") and to balance public health and economic considerations in decision-making. Of course the intention as such is not to legitimize breaches of the rules governing the operation of the Internal Market.

(h) Environment

Consideration could be given to adapting the Treaty so that a more decisive policy could be carried out, in particular by extending decision-making by qualified majority. There also seems to be a need to widen the Community's powers to monitor compliance with its environmental legislation.

(i) Energy

The Gulf crisis has again shown how vulnerable the world is when it comes to safeguarding energy supplies. It has made more pressing the question of whether the Community should have greater responsibility in the energy field. The Dutch Government answers this question in the affirmative. This means that in a new energy section to be added to the Treaty — which would leave intact the general principles on which the Community and in particular the Internal Market are founded — attention could be paid to a number of specific aspects. These could include safeguarding supplies as well as safeguarding and respecting the needs of the environment.

(j) Development cooperation

The definition of a Community competence in the field of development cooperation should take shape in parallel with and as an outcome of the need mentioned above to give shape to the external responsibility of the Community as an objective of policy, as is happening through the interweaving of EC and EPC (see 4 below). As an extension of the efforts of the Netherlands on this point when the Single European Act was drawn up, an attempt should be made to bring the text of the Treaty into line with modern reality and existing EC development policy (e.g. Lomé, the Mediterranean policy, the Central American programme, etc.). Attention should also be paid to the question of how to give substance to the relation between trade policy and development cooperation. There is a need to provide a structural basis for the existing instruments of EC development policy and to treat development cooperation in the Treaty in the same way as other EC policy areas. There would also seem to be a need to bring the EC development policy defined in this way into closer alignment with the policies of the Member States and to include coordinating powers in the Treaty for this purpose.

(k) Transport

The requirement for unanimity in Article 75, paragraph 3 could be deleted. The transport memorandum submitted by the Netherlands at the European Council in Dublin forms the basis of Dutch policy in the EC in this field. Partly in view of this memorandum, the Netherlands believes that Community transport policy should include policy on the transport infrastructure and road safety.

(l) Defence industry policy

Finally, aspects of defence industry policy should be considered. We must ask whether there is any justification for continuing to exempt the military sector from the Internal Market. Economically there seems to be no reason for this, and politically the defence industry should be seen as being of European, rather than national, strategic importance. In view of this, consideration should be given to deleting Article 223 or changing it to remove the distinction between the defence industry and civil industry.

2. Democratic legitimacy

2.1 The democratic deficit

The European Community still lacks adequate parliamentary democracy. As the process of integration proceeds, this democratic deficit is felt more strongly. The primary, but certainly not the only, objective of EPU must be to bring about a drastic improvement in this situation. The legitimacy of the Community, both as regards its own citizens and the outside world, is at stake.

The Netherlands' position on this point in negotiations at the Intergovernmental Conference will naturally be based on the preference expressed in the policy document "Europe: the way forward II" for a federal Europe. One starting point could be the rule that national parliamentary control should apply to national powers and European parliamentary control to the powers entrusted to the Community. Admittedly, this distinction would not provide a solution in all cases, for example in situations of shared competence — and, for example, in those fields where there are intergovernmental elements in decision-making, as has been the case so far in implementing free movement of persons in the EC. With these grey areas it should be realized that if the route of so-called "common policy" (*politique commune*) is followed rather than "community policy"

(*politique communautaire*), the problem of the democratic deficit will become all the more pressing. The loss of parliamentary powers at the national level would not then be automatically compensated for by an increase at the European level. In contrast, whenever the route of community policy is chosen, even in the initial phase when there may still be a grey area, there is at least the prospect of reducing the democratic deficit, since through proper decision-making it can subsequently be reduced.

In line with the starting point described above, it seems important that the Netherlands should oppose the suggestion that a place should be reserved at the European level for (representatives of) national parliaments. A question of an entirely different order is how national parliaments are to be more involved in European integration without abandoning the starting points given above. But perhaps this should be a task primarily for the national parliamentarians themselves.

The choice for a federal Europe would seem to lead to a second starting point for the Intergovernmental Conference: the positions of the European Parliament and the Commission should both be strengthened at the same time, with the proviso that strengthening the one should not have negative consequences for the other. It is understood that this aim does inevitably imply a weakening of the position of the Council.

2.2 Strengthening the role of the European Parliament in the legislative process

The role of the European Parliament in the legislative process can be strenghened by:

a. extending the use of the cooperation procedure to new policy areas;

b. strengthening the position of the European Parliament in the existing cooperation procedure.

Extending the use of the cooperation procedure seems an obvious step. There are many arguments for ending the situation created by the Single European Act of two parallel legislative procedures. It should be noted that the extent of the use of the cooperation procedure cannot be seen in isolation from the use of majority decision-making in the Council.

It should also be emphasized that the cooperation procedure applies to legislation in the

narrow sense. It would seem to be less applicable to matters of Community administration.
In the Brussels discussions the question was
raised of whether it was possible under the
existing Community system to introduce a distinction between legislative and administrative
measures. If it is decided to make such a
radical change, consideration could also be
given to the question of how the administrative
relationship between the Commission and the
Member States could be improved. Specifically,
the issue is how to implement the declaration
on comitology procedures appended to the Single European Act.

As regards the substance of the cooperation
procedure, the heart of the problem lies in
the second reading: at present decisions are
too often taken by the Council which ignore
changes made by the European Parliament in
the common position. Should the European
Parliament then make the final judgement?
Caution is required. While in the long term
the European Parliament is to develop into
the legislative body — as a bicameral system
in which the Council is part of the Parliament
— this does not seem to be the moment to
go as far as giving the Parliament the right to
decide independently to legislate at the end of
the cooperation procedure. What could now be
considered would be to give the Parliament the
power to definitively reject draft legislation, for
example in cases where at the second reading
the Council unanimously rejects amendments
made by the Parliament with the support of
the Commission. In connection with this, consideration could be given to granting the European Parliament the power of co-decision on
the content of EC legislation through some
form of conciliation procedure.

Alternative procedures for co-legislation can
also be discussed, provided they meet the chief
criterion already outlined: the granting to the
Parliament of powers of sanction, while taking
care not to erode the position of the Commission. In taking more detailed decisions, the
Netherlands could be guided by considerations
other than this chief criterion, such as the quality, speed and efficiency of decision-making.

In certain fields a parliamentary approval
procedure would seem more appropriate than
co-legislation. In principle this applies to all
cases in which decision-making by the Council
is by unanimous vote. As already stated, the
cooperation procedure applies only to majority
decisions. The European Parliament already
has this right of approval as regards accession

of new members (Article 237) and association
agreements (Article 238). It could be argued
that it should be extended to trade agreements
under Article 113 and decisions taken under
Articles 138, 201 and 236.

As regards the form of this procedure (positive decision by an absolute majority of the
members), an alternative would be approval
unless rejected by an absolute majority. The
choice made on this point could influence the
decision to be taken on the scope of this
procedure.

In the case of Article 235 it is less easy
to decide between the cooperation procedure
or the right of approval. While the requirement of unanimity in the Article suggests the
approval procedure, on the other hand it must
be remembered that by its nature the Article is in fact better suited to the cooperation
procedure.

In the specific field of EPC it is much more
a matter of policy actions than of legislation,
so here the need is for special consultative
structures, for example through European Parliament committees. One starting point could
be the granting to the Commission of the right
of co-initiative in the EPC field, as called for
elsewhere.

2.3 A parliamentary right of initiative?

In the light of the views of the Netherlands outlined above, the suggestion made by some that
the European Parliament should be granted
a formal right to initiate legislation needs to
be carefully weighed. In the present structure
of the EC the exclusive right to initiate legislation is deliberately granted to the Commission. At the present stage of European
integration (thus without prejudging the situation in which European Union has acquired its
final form, including the bicameral parliament
as the legislative body as described above),
there are reservations about giving the European Parliament a formal legislative right of
initiative (or co-initiative). Such a right would
undermine the present position of the Commission in the Community's decision-making
structure. As a matter of fact, as the position
of the European Parliament is strengthened
in relation to the Commission (investiture or
appointment, censure), and if the Parliament
is given a formal right to information from
other institutions, particularly the Commission,
there will be increasing opportunities for the
Parliament to give substance to a political right

of initiative. In that case real pressure could be put on the Commission to make use of its right to initiate legislation. The relationship between the European Parliament and the Commission would then gain more in openness and democracy than through giving both institutions all or part of the same right.

For these reasons the European Commission objects in principle to the granting of a legislative right of initiative. At the moment the discussion in Brussels is moving towards strengthening the European Parliament's political right of initiative. Incorporation of this right in the Treaty (in the form of a "formal right to request") is among the possibilities. It should, however, be noted that far from all Member States are prepared, like the Netherlands, to draw a link between such a "formal right to request" and the possibility of wider political sanctions.

Less far-reaching proposals have also been discussed in Brussels, such as the suggestion that the European Parliament should be granted a formal right to initiate legislation solely in cases where the Commission fails to act. It must, however, be remembered that the objections in principle mentioned above apply equally to such more limited proposals, while on the other hand the question arises of whether such a limited right would still meet a need when, as stated, the Parliament has a more substantial political right of initiative in relation to the Commission.

2.4 Strengthening the European Parliament's control function

It should be made possible for the European Parliament to exercise effective political control over the making and implementation of policy by the Commission. As the Commission's influence on Community decision-making grows, and as its tasks as the executive body increase, the European Parliament will be able to strengthen its control function. Apart from the power of collective investiture or appointment of the Commission, the Parliament should have the power of individual investiture or appointment and censure. Ways should also be found of ensuring that recommendations by the Court of Auditors and the European Parliament to correct abuses they uncover are actually carried out. The right of discharge, as regards the Parliament, should be of more than merely formal significance. It would be worth examining whether Article 206 iii should be

expanded so that the Commission would be obliged to implement decisions by the Parliament which are based on recommendations of the Court of Auditors. Other improvements, such as a right of inquiry and an obligation on institutions to provide information (corresponding to the Parliament's right to information), would be equally valuable.

2.5 Budgeting rights

It is clear that the European Parliament's democratic powers will not be complete until it has full rights of co-decision on both the expenditure and the income of the Community. The Netherlands is in favour of moving further in this direction. However, in order to move forward in a responsible way, it is desirable that this should be linked to two other aspects of the Community's financial structure which are to be recommended quite apart from the question of greater democracy.

- In the first place the expansion of the EC budget required for new policy should not too seriously affect the financial scope for national policy. This can be achieved by including in the Treaty a new norm for the annual maximum increase in all spending as a whole. This norm could be exceeded only after a major decision-taking procedure. As regards compliance with this norm, the principles set out in the Interinstitutional Agreement of 1988 could be added to the Treaty. In particular, consideration could be given to long-term differentiation by category of expenditure. In order to involve the European Parliament, a cooperation procedure could be adopted by which the institutions would draw up a long-term programme and a financial framework once every five years. The details of the expenditure categories and methods for adapting the ceilings could be worked out in the new Interinstitutional Agreement or the Financial Regulations. As part of this process, the possibilities for dropping the distinction between compulsory and non-compulsory expenditure could be examined. In addition, consideration could be given to shortening the budget procedure by having a single reading in the Council and the European Parliament, followed by a conciliation procedure.

- The EC must gradually move towards financial sovereignty. A Community tax is an indispensable component in this. Not until the EC levies its own taxes directly from the citizen will it be possible for the European Parliament to weigh costs against benefits properly, for which it will also be directly accountable to European voters. In view of this, the Commission could be asked during the coming Intergovernmental Conference to carry out a study of ways of instituting a Community tax. For the time being this would be no more than a limited partial replacement for or supplement to the EC's own resources at present. Many technical problems and issues of financial policy are involved in a Community tax, so a careful weighing of advantages and disadvantages will be required.

As a first step towards greater financial autonomy for the EC, the European Parliament could now be given increased responsibility for Community income by granting it a right of approval for the decision on the Community's own resources. This decision, which lays down both the methods of financing and the maximum amount of the Community's own resources, would thus in future require not only ratification by the Member States but also the assent of the European Parliament.

2.6 Right of petition; openness

At the European level the right of petition should be recognized. It would be desirable to establish a procedure whereby Community institutions would comply with the outcome of a parliamentary inquiry resulting from a petition. At the same time measures to increase the openness of administration at the European level should be examined.

3. The efficiency and effectiveness of the EC

At first sight it can seem as if increasing democratic legitimacy and increasing the effectiveness of decision-making are contradictory objectives, but the Netherlands rejects this view for two reasons. The first is that only a democracy can ensure that the Community can rely on broad-based support now and in the long term. Because of this, only a democratic decision-making process can provide the guarantees of effectiveness and continuity needed for the long term. The second reason is that both decision-making and democracy will be improved by wider application of the

cooperation procedure coupled with greater use of decisions by qualified majority.

The question of how to improve the efficiency and effectiveness of the EC must be considered not only in relation to the internal and external challenges it faces at present and the current problems in the functioning of EC institutions, but above all in relation to the inevitable expansion of the EC in the future and the consequences of that for its structure and decision-making processes.

3.1 The European Council

The Netherlands is far from being alone in having serious reservations about further strengthening the European Council and moving towards making it a policy-deciding body for the EC, EPU and EMU and in this way coordinating all three. These reservations are not inspired by dissatisfaction at the working of the European Council at present. It can be a major force in the work of the Community, as it has shown in the past. The Solemn Declaration on European Union adopted in Stuttgart in 1983 reflects this fact. Given the need to preserve and further develop the European, the Netherlands is not considering a formal upgrading of the position of the European Council. If the European Council wishes to exercise the right to function as the Council of the Community, the procedures laid down for this will have to be respected. At the same time we must beware of the danger that a strengthening of the position of the European Council may lead to a greater democratic deficit. The reader is referred to what has been said on this point in 1.5 (Analysis of the problem).

3.2 The Council

The central issue in this connection is undoubtedly to what extent and by what means the requirement for unanimity, as laid down in many provisions of the Treaty, can be abandoned. In answering this question it is of prime importance to distinguish between decision-making on new EC policy (where Article 235 applies) and on existing EC policy. In the latter case the essential criterion for assessing whether the unanimity requirement in a Treaty provision can be replaced by a decision by qualified majority would seem to be the need to ensure effectiveness and progress in decision-making. Whether this is required in a particular situation must be judged case by case. As stated in the policy document "Europe: the way forward" of last June, national interests naturally play a role in this judgement. But on this point the policy document concludes that the Netherlands will go on contributing constructively to identifying Treaty provisions judged suitable for majority decisions on the basis of these considerations.

In this connection it should be said that, where the Council takes a decision under Article 235, it should recognize that in the event of further measures in new policy fields the aim should be to have majority decisions (albeit possibly by an evolutionary path) for the reasons given above. The question of whether this last point should be incorporated in the Treaty in some way requires further study.

3.3 The Commission

The deficiencies in the present formula by which the number of commissioners is decided will become more of a problem as the number of Member States of the EC increases. The Netherlands believes it would be desirable to let the number of commissioners depend in principle on the requirements which arise from the policy fields covered by the EC. A good first step towards this would be for this Intergovernmental Conference to decide to appoint a maximum of one member of the Commission per Member State.

Investment is required if the Commission is to function properly. The Member States should realize when allocating new tasks to the Commission that they must accept the consequences in the form of quantitative and qualitative increases in the Commission's administration apparatus.

In some cases it may be possible to relieve the pressure of work on the Commission by establishing independent bodies which can take over some of its tasks. Further study of the advantages and disadvantages of this idea seems desirable. An important aspect here is democratic control: the question arises of whether a direct link to the European Parliament can be created. The reader is referred to what has been said about the issue of comitology in 2.2 above.

3.4 Implementation of EC law

The fact that Member States (and EC institutions) often do not fully comply with EC law is a matter of serious concern. This has a negative effect on the uniform application of EC law and threatens the credibility of the integration process.

The question of how to improve the implementation and enforcement of EC law is closely linked to whether the existing EC structure and division of tasks between the Community and the Member States are to form the starting point, or whether it is thought desirable to change the present structure or important parts of it. The present structure would seem to offer only limited scope for improving the implementation and enforcement of EC law.

The alternative would be to make the Community itself responsible for implementing the law. The feasibility and desirability of this are of course closely related to the federal structure of the future EPU and what form the subsidiarity principle takes within it.

For the time being there seem to be good reasons for a clear preference in favour of continuing the existing situation, in the sense that implementing EC law in national legal orders would remain within the competence of the Member States. Otherwise Community bodies could have an undesirable influence on the priorities set by national law enforcement agencies (the police and Public Prosecutions Department). The equally widely felt need for equality before the law and legal certainty in the EC should preferably be met in another way, namely by improving and strengthening the supervision by EC institutions of Member States and of the supervision which they in turn exercise ("control control"). This should be combined with certain Community norms for and harmonization of the way in which Member States carry out their responsibility for implementing and upholding EC law.

3.5 Court of Justice/compliance

What causes problems is compliance, and in particular enforcing the obligations on Member States which arise from judgements of the Court. To improve compliance by Member States with Court judgements, consideration could be given in certain cases to the imposition of financial sanctions, for example periodic penalty payments, punitive interest or retaliatory measures in the form of suspension of EC payments to the Member State. An important consideration in deciding whether it would be worthwhile to introduce such a system is the extent to which the measure can help to stimulate public interest in and increase political pressure on the Member State concerned.

It is important to ensure that the use of sanctions does not further undermine respect for EC law. Great caution is required. There is a real danger of escalation: the situation must be avoided in which a Member State that was unwilling to comply with EC law in the first instance goes on to resist implementation of the sanction in the second instance, or pays the financial penalty in order to go on avoiding complying with the original obligation.

The aim must be to mobilize political and public pressure on the authorities concerned. This applies particularly to the retaliation measures described. It is especially relevant for the perception of the at first sight unreasonable way in which people not directly involved (those receiving payments from regional or social funds, etc.) are affected by the suspension of EC payments to a Member State. In addition to political and public pressure, there remains the possibility of an appeal to the national or Community courts.

It goes without saying that great weight must be attached to the view taken by the Court itself, and it should be asked to express this.

3.6   The Court of Justice: Court of First Instance

The Netherlands is in favour of extending the tasks and powers of the Court of First Instance, among other things in relation to direct appeals by private individuals against trade measures taken by the Community.

3.7   The European Court of Auditors

The Netherlands is in favour of strengthening the powers of the Court of Auditors to obtain all the information relevant to its task of exercising financial control within the EC. Specifically, the Court of Auditors should be empowered to take legal steps to secure information required from Member States, local government and the other institutions. At the same time the obligation to provide this information should be made part of EC law. Once equipped with these powers, the Court of Auditors could be accorded the status of an Institution of the Community.

3.8   Local and regional governments

To enable them to put their specific points of view, local and regional governments should be involved in EC decision-making in good time. In recent years this has been done through the Consultative Council of Local and Regional Authorities set up by the Commission. How-

ever, the formal powers of this Council are limited. In accordance with the administrative agreement recently concluded with the municipalities and provinces, the Netherlands Government is seeking greater involvement of these authorities in European policy development. This will also be of benefit to the implementation of EC law. In view of this, it may be useful to look again at the tasks and powers of the Consultative Council.

4.   Unity and coherence of the Community's international action

The process of European integration will not be complete if it does not extend to foreign policy and security policy. External developments demand united and coherent international action from the Community. Thus, as European unity progresses, there is a growing need to interweave the EC and EPC. The ultimate aim is to realize a common foreign policy, including a defence component. In the view of a number of Member States, among them the Netherlands, this must ultimately entail communitarization of this field of policy.

In working towards this aim the Netherlands is in favour of an evolutional, step by step approach based on two conditions:

- the inclusion of foreign policy and security in EPU should not lead to an increase in the intergovernmental character of European integration; this is particularly important in connection with the decision-making procedures to be agreed;

- the decisions taken at the Intergovernmental Conference will have to be in line with cooperation within NATO and the discussions in the context of NATO on the future of the Atlantic Alliance. This is because of the central importance of the involvement of the United States in European security. This point is particularly important in connection with determining which policy areas are to be included in EPU.

As to decision-making procedures, the first concern of the Intergovernmental Conference will be to remove the procedural and institutional barriers between the EC and EPC. Provided it does not have a negative effect on Community decision-making, it seems advisable to allocate EPC decision-making to the General Council. This is the direction being taken in practice already. Other obvious steps are to merge the Council Secretariat and the EPC Secretariat and to have closer alignment between the Permanent Representatives Committee and the Political Committee.

The shape of an EC foreign policy will have to be determined through Community procedures, although the rules of decision-making need not be exactly the same as the EC prescribes for other policy areas. In practice this would mean among other things:

- decision-making by majority vote (not necessarily the same majority provisions as applied for Community matters in the strict sense);
- a right of co-initiative for the European Commission;
- a form of parliamentary control through the European Parliament.

The decision-making procedures will have to reflect the fact that, unlike many other EC policy areas, foreign policy consists almost entirely of policy development rather than regulation. There will always be a need for flexibility, adaptable procedures, and decisiveness in taking action. This is not to say that we should settle for intergovernmental decision-making when Community decision-making is possible. On the contrary, this would obstruct decisive action. But it does mean that the degree of interweaving between the EC and EPC may vary according to time and the policy area concerned. A Community approach cannot be achieved at a moment's notice.

In view of the above, an exclusive right of initiative for the Commission in this field cannot be regarded as realistic at present. But decision by majority vote as a rule must in principle be seen as a logical step towards a Community policy. Here especially, however, there will be a need for trust and familiarity to develop. The first policy areas suitable for decision by majority vote would seem to be those in which the policy objectives and national interests of the partners are already broadly similar, areas in which the interweaving of EPC and the EC is in fact already taking place: the political aspects of policy on Eastern Europe and of relations with the United States, Japan and the Mediterranean countries. There seems to be little point in laying down rules as to which aspects of foreign policy will be decided by which means. It is difficult to separate the different sectors, and there is a risk of disagreement or rigidification. Attempts to delimit the competences of the

EC and the Member States are also open to question. A (provisional) sharing of competence would seem to fit best with the flexibly functioning decision-making structure and the dynamic, gradual process of interweaving called for here.

Finally, as regards scrutiny by the European Parliament, structures will have to be found which are suited to the flexibility, adaptable procedures and decisive action described above. One possibility would be consultation, not only with the Parliament sitting as a whole but with Parliamentary committees.

What is to be EPU's field of activity in foreign and security policy in the near future? Two components have already been mentioned: everything at present covered by EPC, which includes the CSCE process, and foreign policy in those fields in which the interweaving of the EC and EPC is already taking place. At the same time membership of a body such as the UN Security Council should be made to serve the Community as a whole, or be replaced by membership of the Community. Communitarization is, after all, equally binding on all Member States. In addition, EPU will have to give more substance to EC cooperation in the field of security, including a defence component. It is difficult to separate the economic and political aspects of security from defence policy in the narrow sense. If only for this reason, decisions taken at the Intergovernmental Conference will have to take account of policy developments in NATO. Within the limits of the conditions set out above, there is reason and scope for close EC cooperation in various fields. The Netherlands argues in favour of making the maximum possible use of the opportunities for common agreements and activities. These could include:

- aspects of defence industry policy;
- policy on arms exports;
- aspects of arms control policy, e.g. non-proliferation;
- participation in UN peace-keeping forces;
- joint "out of area" operations.

In this approach European cooperation over defence policy in the narrow sense, which none of the Member States wants to bring into a Community framework in the near future, will continue to take place within the context of the WEU, complementing cooperation within NATO, as is the case at present.

Special attention should be given to the proposal by some Member States to incorporate the WEU in EPU. There is a risk that this will only lead to cooperation within EPU becoming more intergovernmental in character, without any real progress being made in cooperation over foreign and security policy. The limited membership of the WEU is another complication. Enlarging the WEU must not lead to new problems (e.g. the position of Turkey, Norway and Ireland). But attempts will have to be made to achieve greater coherence between the WEU and EPU.

The extent to which the Intergovernmental Conference will be able to give shape to a European security policy in the above sense largely depends on whether the political will is present among the EC partners. The debate on this subject is still at a very early stage. The Netherlands will make an active contribution to this important discussion.

16. United Kingdom Parliament

Extract from House of Lords select committee on the European Communities Twenty-Seventh Report: Economic and Monetary Union and Political Union, 30 October 1990

Part 8 General conclusions

178. The European Community has been remarkably successful in developing close cooperation between States which — whilst sharing common goals of economic and political freedom — have long histories and distinct traditions. The Community has built up an accepted way of making progress. Broad objectives are set, and then pragmatic means are agreed to move forward step-by-step. This has allowed the development of the Community to keep broadly in line with public opinion, and ensured that most Community action is well founded. The forthcoming Intergovernmental Conferences fit into this pattern; it has been agreed that progress is required towards economic and monetary union and political union, and the IGCs will sort out what this means in practice. The Treaty amendments agreed at these IGCs will be able to build on the experience of those made in the Single European Act. The Committee consider it likely that by the mid-1990s further IGCs will be called, when the time comes to develop the process further. The current round of Treaty amendment should not and cannot try to be the final word.

179. One compelling reason for this is that it is far too early to determine the final response of Western Europe to the liberalization of Central and Eastern Europe and to the end of the Cold War. The Gulf crisis has added an extra element of uncertainty. This does not mean that the Community should put its reforms on ice. On the contrary, further economic and political integration will be the best preparation for the challenges ahead. As long as the Community remains open to new applicants for membership, committed to global free trade, and aware that its responsibilities extend beyond its boundaries, a strong Community must be in the long-term interests of Europe as a whole.

180. In its Reports over many years, this Committee has held to the view that the interests of the United Kingdom and those of the Community as a whole, are the same: a strong Community progressing towards closer union in accordance with agreed aims would be to the benefit of both. The question has always been how, not whether, progress should be made. Such progress will not be in uncharted waters. The early Parts of this Report set out the political and legal commitments which the Community have unanimously accepted, and sought to define the terms in frequent use.

181. The Committee concluded that the goal of economic and monetary union, dating back to the years before United Kingdom membership, has long had a clear meaning to the majority of Member States. In contrast, political union has been defined as the process of seeking closer political unity, rather than a specific goal. These commitments naturally have a value of their own. But manifest acceptance of these commitments can also act as a barometer of confidence in the future of the Community. This means that the influence of Member States in the Community is weakened if they are suspected of reneging on such commitments.

182. For many years, there has been much public debate about whether the Community should seek to develop into a centralized State, a federal State, a confederation, or a union of sovereign States. The Committee consider that this can be a sterile debate. The constitution of the Community is unique, and will remain unique. Indeed, when the founding fathers chose the name "Community", they consciously avoided trapping the Community into a particular model of government. The IGC's task is to consider the wide range of practical proposals on the table, testing them against existing commitments and bearing the principles of sovereignty and subsidiarity in mind. All governments, parliaments and political parties are under an obligation to explain these proposals to the public. The public will not be properly informed if the debate on the current proposals is conducted in terms of rhetorical spectres such as "federalism" or fervently-expressed idealistic visions. Each time the Community takes a step forward, such steps must be judged on their own merits, and the key questions are how they will further the strength of the Community and the welfare and aspirations of its citizens.

183. Although the Member States of the Community have joined together to pursue a high standard of living and quality of life, and to maximize their influence on the international stage, they remain independent sovereign States. It is therefore right for them to consider the question of sovereignty. This Report discussed this issue in Part 2, and pointed to two particular areas where sovereignty is directly involved in the current debate.

184. In the United Kingdom, there is a strongly voiced political objection to economic and monetary union as defined by the majority in the Community. The control of monetary policy, it is said, is a central aspect of national and parliamentary sovereignty. The Committee concluded in Part 5 that the sovereignty question is not a fundamental objection to full monetary union. After all, in commending their "hard ecu" plan the Government have been happy to point out that it could lead to a single currency if people or governments so choose. This means that they do envisage that the people through Parliament could at some stage decide to pool United Kingdom power over monetary policy with other states, presumably without jeopardizing parliamentary sovereignty. The Committee therefore concentrated on the economic advantages and the economic problems of the various proposals. They hope that the IGC will do the same.

185. The importance of the closest cooperation on foreign policy between Member States is undeniable. But to include foreign policy as a whole within the competence of the Community would be inconsistent with Member States' international sovereignty. It would also be unnecessary, since great progress can still be made by extending the current system of European Political Cooperation, including the discussion of associated defence matters.

186. Such discussions about sovereignty often imply that the interests of the Community and the Member States are at variance. One of the reasons why this impression exists is that the current structure of the Community gives an inadequate role to national parliaments, exacerbated by their inadequate relations with the European Parliament. The Community must address the democratic deficiences in the current system. The democratic validity of the Commission and the Council is supposed to rest on their accountability to the European Parliament and to national parliaments. This partnership between the parliaments must be strengthened, and the other institutions must give parliaments enough information and enough time to do their job of scrutiny properly. A greater role for the European Parliament in decision-making will also produce more openness and better legislation.

187. As well as the democratic accountability of the Community, the effectiveness of legislation and of budgetary and financial control must be improved. While the Community continues to lose billions through fraud, and Member States adopt a selective attitude to the implementation of legislation they have agreed in Council, the public's response to the Community is likely to be tinged with cynicism. Ultimately the strength of the Community lies as much in the support of the peoples of Europe as it does in the quality of the decisions it makes.

188. The Committee believes that there is every reason why the United Kingdom should be at the forefront as the next stage in the Community's development takes shape. There can be no doubt that the United Kingdom's future lies in active membership of the Community. Throughout this Report, the Committee have stressed the importance of Europe moving forward together. Britain has much to give to the Community, as well as much to gain from it. The United Kingdom's long experience in developing democratic institutions to pass effective legislation and to scrutinize the executive, its respect for treaties and the rule of law, its record in international diplomacy and its long involvement in multilateral organizations enable ministers to bring sound and influential advice to the Council table. The process of negotiation must often involve differences of view. Persuasion will sometimes allow the British case to prevail, and sometimes will not. This Committee has consistently argued that the best way to maximize the influence of the United Kingdom is to show by word and deed that Britain in no way dissents from the Community's agreed objectives. They can best do this if public opinion is helped to understand the objectives of the Community as well as the disagreements of the moment. The arguments about accession in the early 1970s have no place in the 1990s. The current debate should be conducted in the language of progress, not the rhetoric of the battlefield.

Part 9 Summary of recommendations

Economic and Monetary Union

189. A single currency would bring substantial economic gains. The gains of a fixed exchange rate as an alternative would be far less. Eleven Member States are convinced of the benefits of monetary union (paragraphs 74, 76–77).

190. These benefits should outweigh fears about the loss of national control (paragraph 75).

191. The Government should accept the goal of a single currency (paragraph 78).

192. The hard ecu scheme is not viable as it stands. But elements of the scheme could be of benefit in the transitional stage (paragraphs 79–81).

193. The Intergovernmental Conference faces a formidable list of problems to resolve, laid out below, and the Government should play a constructive part in the negotiations (paragraphs 78, 82, 93).

194. A Community monetary authority should eventually be established with full control over a single Community monetary policy. Its goal should be price stability, but it will have to take the Community's other economic objectives into account. The IGC will have the difficult task of agreeing a sensible division of responsibility between the Community monetary authority and the national central banks (paragraphs 83–84).

195. A system of democratic scrutiny should be set up to ensure that the Community monetary authority's policies are explained to the European Parliament and to the national parliaments (paragraph 85).

196. Member States should retain control over budgetary policy. But to the extent that there is a danger that irresponsible budget deficits could threaten a monetary union, procedures to support national self-discipline and market pressures will be required (paragraph 86).

197. At least initially, the single currency could retain national names and symbols on one side of its notes and coins (paragraph 87).

198. The IGC should mandate the Commission to build on the 1992 programme and complete the Single Financial Area (paragraph 88).

199. Stage 2 will have a key role in preparing the Community for monetary union. It should begin in 1994 (paragraph 89).

200. The Committee do not believe that monetary union should be imposed before sufficient economic convergence is assured, or before full preparations are complete. It is therefore too early to fix the date for full monetary union, although it would be perverse to delay this unnecessarily. A date for simultaneous acceptance of a single currency should be fixed in due course, but if this does not prove possible, a timetable for entry will have to be agreed in the future (paragraphs 90–92).

201. It is of paramount importance to the United Kingdom economy to be at the forefront of steps towards monetary union. United Kingdom membership of a "second tier" would carry substantial economic cost (paragraph 93).

Political Union

202. The primary responsibility on negotiators at the IGC must be to seek consensus. The IGC will have to balance pursuit of the ideal of European Union with pragmatic action that addresses the Community's current needs (paragraphs 137–38).

203. The Community must take steps to meet the requirements of democratic principles. Community institutions must be, and must be seen to be, democratically accountable (paragraphs 140–42).

204. The IGC must address fears that too many decisions are being taken by the Community which could perfectly well be left to the Member States, and that the Community gives insufficient prominence to the place of the individual in the Community. The Community must hold fast to subsidiarity. Within these limits, Community action in the social, and particularly the environmental, sphere should be acceptable (paragraphs 143–44, 160).

205. Priority must be given to ensuring effective implementation of Community law. This requires more enforcement by Community institutions. Member States should make a written response to Commission reports on implementation. Those who consistently fail to apply Community law promptly and effectively should face penalties (paragraphs 145–48).

206. The Community is open to enlargement. A strong Community will be an attractive Community, so efforts at closer integration need not be delayed (paragraph 149).

207. The issue of the European Parliament's site must be resolved (paragraph 150).

208. The involvement of the European Parliament in Council legislation through the cooperation procedure should be extended. The Parliament should have the right to bring

other institutions before the Court of Justice. It should have greater powers over delegated legislation and international agreements. But it is not at present necessary to give the Parliament a right of initiation (paragraphs 151–55).

209. The Parliament should have enhanced powers to scrutinize Community activity, in particular over the efficiency of Community spending, and should devote more of its attention to this task (paragraph 156).

210. There must be a partnership between national parliaments and the European Parliament, based on mutual understanding and respect. But a senate of national parliamentarians is not the answer. National parliaments should make efforts to build up their own scrutiny procedures and to develop links with the European Parliament (paragraphs 144, 157–58).

211. The Council of Ministers is not yet ready to meet in public. But the Council, and individual governments, have a duty to be far more forthcoming about the intentions and the progress of legislation (paragraph 159).

212. Limited extensions should be made to the areas of legislation subject to qualified majority voting (paragraph 160).

213. The continued development of the role of the European Council is welcome (paragraph 161).

214. The European Parliament should hold confirmation hearings for European Commissioners. The number of Commissioners should be reduced, but a second rank of Commissioners, outside the college, should be established (paragraphs 162–63).

215. It is essential that the European Court of Justice is given sufficient resources and an adequate structure to enable it to meet new pressures quickly and effectively (paragraph 164).

216. The principle of subsidiarity should be written into the Treaty, but should not be justiciable before the Court. The balance between Community action and national action should remain a political responsibility (paragraph 165).

217. The powers and responsibilities of the Court of Auditors need revision, and its resources need strengthening. Corrective measures must be taken when the Court makes its reports (paragraph 166–67).

218. The IGC must consider what place the Economic and Social Committee now has in the Community (paragraph 168).

219. Member States must retain the right of independent action in foreign affairs. But the system of European Political Cooperation should continue to become more efficient and more effective. Coherent foreign policy discussion requires a relevant security dimension (paragraphs 169–77).

Recommendation

220. The Committee consider that economic and political union and monetary union raise important questions to which the attention of the House should be drawn, and they recommend their Report to the House for debate.

17. Italian Council Presidency

Institutional Conference on Political Union: report of 16 November 1990

The Community is engaged in a process of reforms with a view to expanding, in the framework of the existing institutions, the "acquis communautaire" and in particular to establishing an area without internal frontiers by 31 December 1992 to increase its economic and monetary integration and to develop a real political dimension.

These objectives are closely related and imply the dual requirements of greater efficiency and enhanced democratic legitimacy of the decision-making processes. The Community must transform itself into a Political Union, which implies changes in the institutions.

The pledge, reaffirmed at the Rome European Council, to develop the political dimension of the Community stems from various considerations:

(a) The events gathering force in Europe and abroad have induced the Member States of the Community to acknowledge the need for a higher profile on the international scene, the better to defend their interests collectively and to contribute to building an international order which is more just and has greater regard for human rights and other values they share. The effectiveness of their action in the world will depend on their capacity to adopt common positions, speak with a single voice and act together. The common foreign policy, which is partly foreshadowed by events, lies at the centre of Political Union.

(b) Foreign policy cannot be divorced from security. The need arises to pursue a common policy taking account of the changes under way in Europe, in order better to ensure their security in its broadest meaning. Questions relating to defence will also need to be taken into consideration in this context.

(c) The very success of Community policies, particularly in the wake of the Single Act, calls for the establishment of European citizenship and for greater participation by its citizens in the collective endeavour of building the Union, in particular in areas which have a direct bearing on their daily lives.

The Intergovernmental Conference to open in Rome on 14 December will provide an opportunity to meet these new challenges and to give the Community the necessary capacity to act.

The Rome European Council laid down guidelines in general but unequivocal terms regarding the major choices which will face the Conference on Political Union.

In line with the guidelines which emerged in Rome and the preparatory work carried out to date, the Presidency considers that the following approach should be adopted in the individual sectors, it being nevertheless borne in mind that one Member State expressed reservations on certain points of the conclusions of the Rome European Council.

1. Common foreign and security policy

The Rome European Council pronounced itself in favour of a common foreign and security policy. The ways and means must be specified as the Twelve identify their essential common objectives and interests. This implies a dynamic and forward-looking development of present-day political cooperation in order to achieve a qualitatively new level of common positions and actions. Consequently and in line with the conclusions of the European Council, which stated that no aspect of the Union's external relations would in principle be excluded from the common foreign and security policy, a basically all-encompassing approach is required.

An *a priori* definition of a list of sectors or areas considered to be of common interest would, however, raise difficulties of interpretation. Accordingly, the Community's priorities in foreign policy and on the actions most called for should be determined and carried out, by institutional procedures through a pragmatic evaluation (European Council and General Affairs Council), taking into account in particular the experience gained in political cooperation, shared values, the interests to be defended and the circumstances arising internationally.

The objectives pursued by the Union and the Member States should relate to consolidation of democracy, the peaceful settlement of disputes, arms reductions, the solution of crises which threaten international stability, monetary stability and economic growth, the expansion of international trade, the development of the least-favoured countries, the effectiveness of the action of international organizations, and in particular of the United Nations and the CSCE, on the basis of common positions.

A common policy does not imply a single policy. Insofar as the Member States have special relations or positions with deep historical roots, especially in certain areas of the world, or special obligations, specific fields could remain for the time being outside the common foreign and security policy. Nonetheless, individual actions of Member States should remain consistent with the Community policy through mutual information and consultation. Here too subsidiarity must play a part, to enhance the flexibility and effectiveness of Community action as a whole.

Development policy is a fundamental component of the Community's external action. It should be the subject of a separate treaty chapter. It should be conducted in such a way that consistency with the general objectives of foreign policy is ensured. Similar consistency should be achieved with the Community's foreign policy in the economic sphere.

As regards *security* in particular, the formulation and implementation of a common policy should, in accordance with the conclusions of the Rome European Council, "go beyond the present limits". Here again the idea will be to proceed "gradually in the light of the various aspects covered by this concept and without prejudice to the obligations arising out of the security arrangements to which Member States are party".

A way to make credible such a commitment could be to incorporate in the Treaty a pledge to afford mutual assistance automatically as provided for in Article 5 of the Brussels Treaty, stating that the Member States will endeavour to create the conditions necessary to make such assistance effective.

Over and beyond this, the Treaty should list certain subjects to be covered by the common security policy, specifying that security as a whole remains the responsibility of the Union and that such a list should accordingly not be deemed exhaustive. This would provide a feeling of a significant leap forward having being made in the foreign and security policy of the Union.

The subjects to be included should be:

- arms control, disarmament and confidence-building measures, in particular within the framework of the CSCE;
- participation in and coordination of military initiatives, for example in the context of actions carried out under a UN mandate;
- industrial and technological cooperation and export controls in the field of armaments.

By the same token, efforts to achieve a common policy at present under way in EPC in respect of UN security-related activities as well as of non-proliferation should be further developed.

Since it is clear that the development of the Union's role depends on the new security structure evolving in Europe, a pragmatic approach to increasing the responsibility of the Union for security matters should be sought. This objective could be achieved *inter alia* through the progressive reinforcement and extension to the Twelve of the WEU, through gradual coordination between the Community and the WEU and, in the longer term, through their merging. A suitable date in this respect could be the expiry of the Brussels Treaty in 1998. Defence Ministers and their representatives, who already take part in most WEU meetings, should be involved in the decision-making process as regards security and defence.

In the sectors thus identified, once again according to the guidelines of the Rome European Council, there would be "the need to review the procedures and mechanisms for preparing, adopting and implementing decisions" so as to increase the coherence, speed and effectiveness of the Community's international action.

The *preparation* of decisions should draw inspiration from experience both with the European Political Cooperation and the Community system. In this respect the present dichotomy of action of the Community and of political cooperation must be overcome by introducing a single Council and harmonizing the work of the collective bodies entrusted with preparation. In the same spirit the Commission must be given the right to take initiatives, even though it will obviously not have the sole right in this respect. The right of initiative would therefore be shared by the Presidency of the Council, the Member States and the Commission.

Suitably strengthened, the Political Cooperation General Secretariat will be incorporated in the General Secretariat of the Council while maintaining its specific profile. It will assist the Presidency and the Council in preparing and implementing the common foreign and security policy.

As to the *decision-making* procedures, it would appear advisable to maintain the present rule of consensus for decisions regarding the priorities and the basic lines of the common foreign and security policy, in particular those laid down by the European Council. However, the possibility of introducing the rule of qualified majority for decisions involving the practical application of lines of policy decided by consensus should be established. Provision could also be made for the possibility of abstention which does not prejudice the consensus or the non-participation of abstainees in the actions thus decided.

As regards the *implementation* of foreign policy, the objective should be the further development of the various instruments which represent the Union, namely the Presidency of the Council, the Presidency of the Council and the Commission, and the Troika. What is vital is that the Community should speak with a single voice.

2. Extension of Community competence

In confirming its determination to develop the Community's political dimension, the Rome European Council recommended that its powers be extended to "other supplementary sectors of economic integration which are essential for convergence and social cohesion".

In the social area, the relevant articles of the Treaty should be supplemented and its scope defined more closely, in the light of the Charter of Social Rights, also permitting directives and programmes relating to living and working conditions, vocational training, workers' information and consultation to be adopted by a qualified majority, with a view to the goal of increasing employment and improving dialogue with the social partners.

A legal basis should be provided in the field of health to combat today's major threats.

The extension of powers should also involve major infrastructures, through the adoption of appropriate programmes, in order to encourage the movement of goods, services, persons, capital and information.

As regards the environment, research and indirect taxation relating to the functioning of the common market, in addition to the redefinition of areas of competence, the decision-making procedure must be improved and the possibility of voting by a qualified majority accordingly extended.

For energy, a chapter should be incorporated to enable a common policy covering all the aspects of the sector, including external relations, to be laid down.

As regards culture, which in accordance with the principle of subsidiarity should be left to the responsibility of the Member States, an article should nevertheless be devoted to the cultural dimension of Community action.

The free movement of persons and the equality of treatment necessary to exercise such freedom should be definitively enshrined in the Treaty, if necessary by coordinating and approximating national provisions. As regards nationals of non-member countries, the Treaty could establish the competence of the Union to the extent necessary for the free movement of persons and the creation of an area without internal borders.

Certain sectors now falling within intergovernmental jurisdiction (e.g. drugs, police and judicial cooperation) could be given a basis in the Treaty to provide clearer guidelines for cooperation.

Thought could be given to devising a flexible instrument for the extension of Community competence to other sectors relating to the objectives of the new Treaty. Article 235 of the Treaty, dissociated from its economic aims, in particular through deletion of the words "in the functioning of the common market", could provide such an instrument for new areas of competence, possibly coupled with a provision on subsidiarity. The Council would decide unanimously, in conjunction with the European Parliament. Majority voting would subsequently apply for an area introduced under Community competence.

3. European citizenship

The definition of European citizenship should be enshrined in the Treaty. This would gradually supplement but not replace national citizenship and would include the existing rights as well as those which will be granted on the basis of the further development of the union. The content for such citizenship could be laid down in a declaration of rights and duties, to be annexed to the Treaty, covering:

- basic rights defined in the Strasbourg Convention;

- civic rights (the right to vote in elections for the European Parliament, according to a uniform procedure; the right to vote in local elections);
- economic and social rights (right of residence and movement irrespective of whether one engages in economic activity or not; equality of treatment within a Member State for residents, whether they are citizens of that Member State or not);
- rights of union citizens outside the Community frontiers (right to avail themselves of the protection of the diplomatic missions of any Member State).

As a further means of safeguarding the rights of citizens of the Union, in addition to the Court of Justice, consideration could be given to the appointment of an Ombudsman at Community level and in each Member State to facilitate and provide back-up for appeals by citizens before both the national administration and judicial bodies.

4. Enhancing democratic legitimacy and improving efficiency

As was pointed out at the Dublin European Council and endorsed in Rome, the achievement of such significant objectives and the setting up of the necessary instruments would not be possible without a review of the mechanisms of Community integration in terms of:

(a) democratic legitimacy;

(b) efficiency.

(a) Democratic legitimacy

The Rome European Council recommended "the development of the European Parliament's role in the legislative sphere with respect to the monitoring of the activities of the Union". The European Parliament will probably assess the appropriateness of its own role in the future Union on the basis of four criteria, i.e. its involvement in the appointment of the President and Members of the Commission, the extension of the use of the assent procedure, full participation in the Community's legislative process and greater powers regarding the budget.

As regards the Commission, the Parliament has consistently demanded the power to appoint the Members of the Commission or at least play a part in their appointment. The solution which springs to mind is double endorsement of the appointment, firstly of the President of the Commission, whose nomination on a proposal from the European Council would be endorsed by a vote of the European Parliament; subsequently, of the Members of the Commission as a whole. The latter, which would be nominated in agreement by the Member States after consultation of the President of the Commission, would be the subject of an overall endorsement by Parliament on the basis of the Commission's programme.

A fundamental reform of the Community framework must involve increasing the legislative powers of Parliament.

In particular:

- Parliament's role should be reinforced by extending the cooperation procedure to all legislative decisions to be taken by a qualified majority vote, including therefore all the new areas which the Conference will decide shall fall under qualified majority voting;
- Parliament's role in the cooperation procedure must be reinforced by recognizing a substantial power of co-decision for it in vital areas with the possibility of having the last word. Various formulae have been suggested. According to one, Parliament could reject by a two-thirds majority the text adopted by the Council at the end of the second reading. According to another, the proposal, once re-examined by the Commission and approved in agreement with Parliament, would be considered adopted if the Council was not able to approve it by a qualified majority, to reject it by a simple majority or to amend it unanimously. A third possibility would be to merge the two formulae set out above, combining them with a conciliation procedure in order to avoid responsibility for rejection falling on Parliament.

The extent of the role of co-legislator granted to Parliament would have to be defined by the Conference, also in the light of its decisions with regard to the type classification of Community acts, in particular bearing in mind the distinction between framework laws and measures of a rule-making nature, which would be adopted by the Council or the Commission. Framework laws should simply lay down the basic principles and the general outlines of measures to be adopted pursuant to the provisions of the Treaty.

Lastly, throughout this procedure, the Commission's right of initiative, in particular to amend its proposals and express a position on all amendments, should be maintained.

As regards legislative initiative, the European Parliament's possibility of calling on the Commission to act in cases where it deems that the Commission has failed to act on a particular point should also be formalized.

The extension of the assent procedure seems clearly required in the case of a uniform procedure for the election of the European Parliament but is more controversial as regards own resources and amendments to the Treaty.

In the area of foreign and security policy, Parliament should be consulted regularly and kept informed, in plenary session or in the relevant committees, of the basic decisions made. The assent procedure could be extended to the most important agreements, defining comprehensively the political, economic, financial and cultural dimensions of the Community's relations with its main partners. However, this procedure should not apply to merely commercial and technical agreements.

Provision should also be made to review the European Parliament's mechanisms for monitoring the application of Community policies (financial and budget control, right of inquiry, right to petition the Court of Justice), provided such powers are strictly limited to areas of Community competence and their limits are clearly defined.

As regards the national Parliaments, and their knowledge of and participation in the Community's activity, one should await the result of the November "Assizes" and their evaluation of the idea of a "Congress" comprising representatives of the national Parliaments and the European Parliament which, according to the proposal, could have tasks of a consultative nature or relating to the ratification of certain agreements, without prejudice to the prerogatives of the European Parliament.

Lastly, leaving aside the issue of the Community's overall budget and thus the revision of the Agreement of February 1988, consideration should be given to modification of the procedure for own resources and to reinforcing the role of the European Parliament in the light of the application of the Interinstitutional Agreement. In the last respect, the following could be contemplated:

- changing the current distinction between compulsory and non-compulsory expenditure;

- sanctioning the principles of budget discipline;

- providing for the European Parliament's possibility of taking decisions in respect of a limited proportion of revenue within the framework of own resources and the power of this raising a new resource to be devoted to a specific end.

(b)   Efficiency of the institutions

An improvement in the way the institutions operate should be sought first and foremost in the triangular relations between the Council, the Parliament and the Commission.

However, the role of the European Council should be sanctioned so that it may effectively exercise not only its special responsibilities in the sphere of foreign policy and security, including the expression of common positions, but also its role of providing impetus, laying down general orientations, ensuring the coherence of the Union's action.

As far as the Council is concerned, efficiency calls for the extension of majority voting. Majority voting should be applied in principle to all areas of Community competence, excepting constitutional matters and a very limited number of specific subjects which are particularly delicate, e.g. social security systems. One could also envisage that, in an initial transitional phase, decisions on certain particularly sensitive topics would continue for a time to be subject to unanimity and subsequently to a qualified majority.

The General Affairs Council's role as a body for general coordination should be strengthened to make it the only filter for the European Council. The number of specialized Councils could also be reduced by suitable groupings.

Especially if it entails a substantial element of co-decision, the extension of the cooperation procedure should be accompanied by the fixing of deadlines, binding on both the Council and the Parliament, by which they must state a position. Provision could also be made more systematically for interinstitutional consultations within such deadlines to forestall risks of conflict.

As for the Commission, its power of management should also be revised, in particular by introducing a clearer distinction between legislative, rule-making and executive functions. The committee procedures (comitology) should also be simplified. As regards foreign policy, its role together with that of the Presidency should be shaped in such a way that both may effectively represent the Community and its foreign policy.

The action of the Court of Justice and the Court of Auditors must be improved by enhancing the effectiveness of decisions of the former (which remain unenforced for lack of penalties) and the power of inquiry of the latter.

The role of the Economic and Social Committee must also be reinforced and thought given to new forms of participation of social partners in the definition of the outlines of Community policy as regards economic and social cohesion.

The revision of the Treaty must also take account of the requirement to establish a body representative of the Community's regions. The diversity of regional structures in the Member States must not be an obstacle to devising a mechanism giving a voice to the regions in the decision-making process affecting their interests.

. . .

The revision of the Treaty will have greater chances of success in promoting Community integration if it is based on preserving a set of balances:

Balance between the institutions, to prevent the strengthening of one institution from resulting in the weakening of the others. This should be possible if the allocation of new areas of competence enables each institution to develop its role within the Community system.

Balance in the breakdown of areas of competence between the States and the Community, to give real meaning to the principle of subsidiarity. The principle should be enshrined in the Treaty, without calling into question the "acquis communautaire" in the level of integration so far achieved. Subsidiarity should be a guiding criterion, although not so rigid as to hinder Community action. Respect for subsidiarity as regards the actual principle of a new policy should be a matter for political control by the Community institutions within the framework of their normal competences. However, subsidiarity should also be a guiding criterion for all the institutions in the exercise of their respective areas of competence, in order to prevent, *inter alia* by excessive regulations, abuse of power vis-à-vis citizens and undertakings. Accordingly, unlike the monitor-

ing of a new area of competence, which would continue to be mainly political, respect for subsidiarity involving post-control in the exercising of competence could be entrusted to the Court of Justice, especially from the viewpoint of correlation between means and goals.

Balance between the various models of integration, to take account of the fact that building Europe is a process and that an abstract argument on such an original creation, which cannot be reduced to a single model, must be avoided. That process must inevitably involve the concurrent existence of actions resulting from intergovernmental cooperation and logic of a confederal type, in the framework of a dynamic equilibrium, organized along lines which should be clearly federal in character.

Nevertheless, the incorporation of the new aims within the framework of a single Community must be considered the key factor in the revision of the Treaty. The convergence of the economic, social, financial and monetary aspects on the one hand and of foreign policy on the other will remain the armature of European Union.

A single Community implies a single constitutional structure, although the latter must be sufficiently flexible to take account of various factors at the same time:

- the different degrees of maturity in public opinion in the various countries and the way the Member States conceive of the joint exercise of their sovereignty;

- the difficulty of laying down, as of now, a definitive outline of the Union, without losing sight of the objective of an organization of a federal type;

- the likelihood of further institutional revisions connected with the extension of the Community.

In this connection, the Rome European Council reaffirmed that the European Community will remain "open to the world" and "will also strengthen its links with the other European countries for which ever-closer cooperation structures must be sought geared to their individual circumstances". Let us not forget we are discussing changes relating to the present Community but which may regulate our conduct for the next decade.

Hence the need to make the institutions fully responsive now and in the future to the requirements of a wider Community.

18. Italian Parliament

Resolution of Chamber of Deputies (Committee III) of 20 November 1990, accepted by the government

Committee III,

stressing the urgent need to transform the relations between the Member States of the Community into a Union on a federal basis in accordance with a precise timetable, modus operandi and guidelines, and on the basis of a draft constitution drawn up by the European Parliament (Colombo report) and whereas any immediate amendments to the Treaties must be adopted on the basis of the proposals put forward by the European Parliament (Martin and Herman reports);

(. . .)

expressing its support for the requests made by the European Parliament in its resolutions of 23 November 1989, 14 March, 11 July and 25 October 1990 and by the President of Parliament, Mr Baron Crespo, at the European Council meeting on 27 October 1990 regarding the European Parliament's role during the Intergovernmental Conferences;

Calls on the Government:

to make every effort at Community level to ensure that the European Parliament is asked to draw up a report on European Union (comprising precise proposals regarding the procedures for its establishment and the fundamental tasks to be assigned to it), to be submitted as a working document at the next European Council meeting,

to declare that in any event the Italian Government's position on the conclusions of the Intergovernmental Conferences must be absolutely consistent with the European Parliament's approval of them.

19. Conference of Parliaments of the European Community ("Assizes")

Final Declaration adopted on 30 November 1990

The Conference of the Parliaments of the European Community, meeting in Rome on 27 to 30 November 1990

- having regard to the decisions of the Presidents of the Parliaments of the Member States of the European Community and of the European Parliament meeting on 20 September 1990 in Rome and to the conclusions of the interparliamentary conferences of the national parliaments' committees responsible for Community affairs and the European Parliament's Committee on Institutional Affairs,

- having regard to the draft Treaty of 14 February 1984 establishing the European Union and the resolutions adopted by the European Parliament on the basis of the Colombo, D. Martin, Giscard d'Estaing, Duverger and Herman reports,

- having regard to the memoranda drawn up by the national parliaments in preparation for this Conference,

A. certain that Europe cannot be built merely on the basis of discussions at governmental and diplomatic level, but that the Parliaments of the European Community must be fully involved in laying down the general direction it is to take,

B. whereas once the single market is established in 1993, the Community must adopt social, economic, monetary and environmental policies which give practical expression to the need for both social justice and economic democracy,

C. welcoming what has already been achieved, while seeking to remodel the Community into a European Union on a federal basis and to provide it with the appropriate institutions,

D. espousing the principles of pluralist democracy and respect for fundamental human rights,

E. proposing that, in keeping with the subsidiarity principle, only those powers should be conferred on the common institutions that are necessary for the proper discharge of the Union's duties,

F. regretting that the powers devolved on the Community and exercised by its Institutions are not subject to a satisfactory degree of parliamentary scrutiny,

G. whereas the extension of the Community's sphere of activity should be accompanied by a substantial reinforcement of democratic control,

Calls on the Intergovernmental Conference to take into account the following opinions and proposals:

Towards European Union

1. Is convinced that the creation of a large market without internal frontiers implies the creation of a monetary union governed by an autonomous central banking system, which should arrive at the issuing of a single currency; this development requires an Economic Union with an increase in economic, social and regional cohesion together with an enhancing of the Community's democratic legitimacy;

2. Takes the view that EMU must be achieved on the basis of the timetable and conditions agreed by the European Council in Rome on 27/28 October 1990;

3. Takes the view that the Community must finance its policy activities from its own resources; considers that the decision concerning the Community's own resources should be taken in agreement with the European Parliament and the national parliaments and that the financial provisions contained in the Treaties must be thoroughly revised in order to ensure a more even balance between the two branches of the budgetary authority;

4. Takes the view that a Political Union comprising a foreign and security policy on matters of common interest must be established and that European Political Cooperation must be incorporated into the Treaty and into the Community structures;

5. Believes that the Community Treaties

must provide for a common social policy and include adequate provisions for economic and social cohesion; this requires not only stronger assertion of the objectives in the Treaties but also decision-taking in these areas by qualified majority voting; further believes that, in addition to the financial and economic aspects, the social dimension must be strengthened and that a European system of concerted action involving management and labour must be set up;

6. Calls on the Community to pursue active policies to promote the equality of men and women in the fields of work, social and civil rights, education, participation in public life and access to political office at all levels;

7. Takes the view that regional policy must aim gradually to eliminate the disparities between the regions and considers that the resources at the disposal of the Community, notably the structural funds, must be reinforced;

8. Calls for provision to be made for every means of cooperation between the Community institutions and the regions as they are defined in the constitution or in law in the Member States;

9. Takes the view that the Community should be given additional competences in the field of the environment and that decision-taking in this area should be by qualified majority voting and that the Community must pursue a policy to preserve the environmental balance in the Community and the world; calls for Article 2 of the Treaty to be amended to express this objective which requires a process of sustainable development;

10. Calls for the inclusion in the Treaties of provisions to establish the idea of European citizenship, including the right for Community citizens to vote in European elections in the Member State in which they reside; considers that respect for fundamental rights is the cornerstone of democracy; therefore requests the inclusion in the Treaties of the Declaration on Fundamental Rights and Freedoms adopted by the European Parliament on 12 April 1989 and the Community's accession to the European Convention on Human Rights;

11. Considers that a separate article on cultural policy should be inserted in the Treaty, stipulating that the cultural diversity and wealth of the Community nations must be respected and protected, particularly with regard to language;

Enhancing democratic legitimacy in the relationship between the Community and the Member States

12. Considers that the time is right to transform the entire complex of relations between the Member States into a European Union on the basis of a proposal for a constitution drawn up with the aid of procedures in which the European Parliament and the national parliaments will take part; takes the view that, in order to carry out the new tasks facing it at the monetary level and in external relations, the Community must transform itself into a European Union in order to meet the requirements of democracy, which entails adapting its Institutions and other bodies as follows:

– the Commission must progressively take on the role of the Union's executive;

– Parliament must play an equal part with the Council in the legislative and budgetary functions of the Union and its assent must be sought for all significant international agreements; it must be able to exercise democratic control, in the same way as the Council, over the executive bodies;

– the Council must be able to take its decisions by simple or qualified majority according to the circumstances; unanimity will only be required in the limited cases provided for by the Treaties.

13. Supports enhanced cooperation between the national parliaments and the European Parliament, through regular meetings of specialized committees, exchanges of information and by organizing Conferences of Parliaments of the European Community when the discussion of guidelines of vital importance to the Community justifies it, in particular when Intergovernmental Conferences are being held;

14. Takes the view that each national parliament must be able to bring its influence to bear on the shaping of its government's policy stances on the Community;

15. Takes the view that it is essential for the decisions taken by the Community to be implemented both by the Member States and the Community and calls on the Member States to take whatever legislative and executive

action is required to ensure that Community legislation is transposed into domestic law on schedule;

Enhancing democratic legitimacy within the Community Institutions

16. Takes the view that the process of amending the Treaties must involve the assent of the European Parliament before ratification by the national parliaments, given that the European Parliament must be closely involved in the proceedings of the Intergovernmental Conferences;

17. Calls for meetings of the Council, in its legislative role, to be open to the public and for it to act by majority voting except in connection with amendments to the Treaties, the accession of new member states and extension of powers;

18. Takes the view that the President of the Commission must be elected by the European Parliament, on a proposal from the European Council, by an absolute majority; that the President of the Commission, in agreement with Council, should appoint the members of the Commission, and that the incoming Commission as a whole should present itself and its programme to the European Parliament for a vote of confidence; believes that the Commission's term of office should start at the same time as that of the European Parliament; the same procedure should be followed if a new Commission has to be appointed during the parliamentary term;

19. Believes that, as regards the European Community's legislative powers, co-decision arrangements between the European Parliament and the Council must be devised and a right of initiative must be established in the event of the Commission failing to act;

20. Believes that the European Parliament's supervisory powers must be enhanced and formally enshrined in the Treaties, and that the position of the Court of Auditors should also be strengthened;

21. Takes the view that the Commission should enjoy executive powers and the right to verify the application of Community directives by the Member States; emphasizes as well the important role of national parliaments in transposing directives into national law; takes the view that the Commission must enjoy the power to implement Community legislation, this to be coordinated with national governments and scrutinized by the Council, the European Parliament and the national parliaments respectively;

22. Draws to the attention of Member States, as contributions to reducing the democratic deficit, the need to take measures systematically that give wide publicity to their citizens of the proposals for legislation put forward by Community Institutions, as well as the need for their parliaments to ensure that their national governments and Ministers remain fully accountable for their policy and actions within the European Community;

Subsidiarity

23. Takes the view that any allocation of new powers to the Union must be based on the subsidiarity principle, i.e. the Union will only act to discharge the duties conferred on it by the Treaties and to attain the objectives laid down therein; where powers have not been exclusively or completely assigned to the Union, it shall act to the extent that the attainment of these objectives requires its intervention because their scope or their implications transcend Member State frontiers or because they can be carried out more effectively by the Union than by the Member States acting alone;

24. Takes the view that the subsidiarity principle must be enshrined in the preamble to the Treaties, and that, as regards interpretation, there must be scope for *a priori* political evaluation, while enabling the Court of Justice to confirm *a posteriori* the extent of the powers of the Community; considers that the principle of subsidiarity must be consolidated in amending the Treaties, and its substance clearly defined;

25. Takes the view that in the context of Community law, the adoption of measures governing of economic, cultural and social conditions should remain the responsibility of the legally constituted regions of the Member States whose constitutions contain provisions to this effect;

Relations with other countries

26. Stresses that although Community preference is to be respected, it must not make a fortress of the Community;

27. Considers that strengthening the Community would make it receptive to all forms of cooperation with European countries, ranging

from free trade arrangements to accession for any democratic European state able and willing to accept the Community's objectives and responsibilities;

28. Believes, however, that the European Community must take account now of the welcome developments that have taken place in Central and Eastern Europe in recent months and that association agreements must be concluded with the new democracies, as well as with other European states wishing to strengthen their ties with the Community;

Relations with international organizations

29. Believes that efforts should be made with a view to collaboration with the EFTA institutions and that there should be ongoing cooperation with the Council of Europe;

30. Takes the view that the European Community has a role of its own to play within the UN, CSCE and the Atlantic Alliance, taking into account the particular situation of certain Member States, and that relations with the WEU should be redefined;

Relations with the developing nations

31. Takes the view that the European Community must continue to be permanently involved in the sustained development of all the world's nations, by giving absolute priority to measures to combat poverty and to aid for the least developed countries; in particular, it must strengthen its contribution to the development of the underdeveloped countries with which it has ties for historical or geographical reasons or by virtue of cooperation agreements;

32. Submits this text to the national parliaments, the European Parliament, the European Council and the Intergovernmental Conferences; calls on the European Council and the Intergovernmental Conferences to take this declaration into account and requests that it be considered as an official document and that its conclusions be endorsed by the two Intergovernmental Conferences.

20. Positions of the Party Political Federations

A. European People's Party (EPP) Dublin Congress Document: For a federal constitution of the European Union, 15–16 November 1990

Introduction: Background

1. The product of the bold, ambitious vision of its creators, headed by Christian Democrats Robert Schuman, Konrad Adenauer and Alcide De Gasperi, the European Community has made people's hopes a reality. Such an extended period of peace and prosperity is unique in European experience, and never before have the spirit of reconciliation and the willingness to work together had such a positive influence on the course of human history. By making the concept of a social and economic Community a reality, the people of Europe have made a decisive contribution to human achievement. This is a legacy which the Christian Democrats are proud to inherit and they are determined to continue the lengthy task of European integration despite the obstacles which still lie ahead.

2. The European Community is based on common institutions, strong and independent, on the joint exercise of sovereignty, on equality amongst its members and respect for national identity, on democratic relations amongst citizens and amongst nations and on respect for basic rights and freedoms. That these principles are sound and effective has been established beyond doubt. The EPP is committed to the Community institutions and wishes to see them extend throughout Europe.

3. European Union is the way ahead for our continent, for only as such can it meet the new challenges of the world and respond effectively to the upheavals of political geography. Western Europe's firm commitment to unity has enabled it to sustain hope, encourage democratic change in Eastern Europe and bring about the unification of Germany. This last achievement will contribute to the unity of Europe and therefore to its strength. Only a stronger more confident European Community will be able to offer the new democracies of Central and Eastern Europe the political support and the economic assistance which they need. The Christian Democrats of Europe wish to see close cooperation between the EC and the new democracies of Central and Eastern Europe in the form of association agreements,

possibly leading to accession which is in principle open to any European democracy.

4. The Christian Democrats are convinced that all the free peoples of Europe now share a common destiny. More than 400 million men and women will soon share the same values: freedom, respect for the individual, protection of creation, access to culture, wellbeing and social justice, human solidarity. The development of a cultural policy for the Community will strengthen European cohesion in the long term by developing the common European heritage.

5. The EPP firmly believes that a stronger, united Europe, with strong political institutions, a single currency and a common foreign, defence and security policy will be able to play a leading role in the world in the 21st century, contribute to international stability, Third World development, and a narrowing of the gap between rich and poor countries. It will establish relations with the United States and Japan as an equal partner, and will set up a security system guaranteeing its independence in its alliances with other organizations and enabling it to act effectively in the interest of the law and international legality.

Chapter I: Political Union

6. In line with its general political philosophy, the EPP considers that, for the European Community to become a European Union (i.e. a federal Europe), four objectives must be pursued:

- balanced, coherent progress on all fronts towards full political union;

- transfer of sovereignty from Member States to the Union and distribution of powers between the European Community (or Union) and the Member States on the basis of the subsidiarity principle, with due regard to local autonomy;

- improvement in the Community's ability to take decisions and act upon them, both within its boundaries and beyond;

- a guaranteed democratic basis for the Community with due regard to the principle of the separation of powers.

7. The fundamental rights and freedoms of the citizens have to be defined and guaranteed in the European constitution.

A. Balanced, coherent and comprehensive progress towards European Union

8. Our future lies in Europe, but for the EPP, the political future of Europe must be all-embracing and be based on a balanced society in which all sections work together towards European Union. The type of society we favour is based on the Christian-Democratic principles of social individuality, solidarity, respect for cultural differences, the social market economy and protection of the environment.

9. For the EPP, the ultimate aim of European integration is that first outlined in Robert Schuman's Declaration of 9 May 1950, in the preamble to the ECSC Treaty of 1951, then expressly stated in the preamble to the EEC Treaty in 1957: "to establish an ever-closer union among the peoples of Europe". The "sense of common purpose" regarding vital economic interests laid the foundations of this union. However, economic success is not an end in itself, but a means to creating a society based on the individual — on freedom and mutual support. European integration is therefore more than just economic integration.

10. In any case, the Community has, over the years, come to intervene in areas which are not strictly economic in nature, a development encouraged and supported by the EPP. Furthermore, the Single Act has explicitly confirmed or strengthened the Community's authority to intervene in social matters, scientific and technological development, consumer protection, the environment, and regional balance. It has also established and facilitated European political cooperation.

11. At present, economic and monetary union draw gradually closer, whilst renewed efforts are being made towards the federal form of political union.

With this in mind the EPP stresses the urgent need to:

– promote and achieve a model for social development in Europe;
– lay the foundations of a common foreign, defence and security policy which would be the basis of a combined European defence system;

– give the Community's two founding principles — political and cultural cooperation — a leading role in European integration;
– extend, improve and supplement the environmental policy contained in the Treaties.

B. Distribution of powers on the basis of the subsidiarity principle

12. The EPP considers that political union on federal lines must

– protect Europe's characteristic and historically derived "richness in diversity";
– ensure, when circumstances require it, a common approach to problem-solving.

13. These days, no crucial question can remain a purely national matter. To carry out their duties at home, the Member States will in future need European solutions more than ever before. For this reason, the EPP is strongly against frequent attempts to renationalize powers transferred to the Community.

14. The basis of European Union must be one of federation amongst its Member States, rather than one of subordination of those states to the Union. This federal structure will encompass the local, regional, national and European levels.

15. The subsidiarity principle must be the basis for distribution of powers amongst the Union, the Member States and the regions — i.e. action taken by the Union will be subsidiary. The Union should be granted those powers of which it can make best use or of which it will have sole use. In other words, the Union will have powers in those areas where it can act more effectively than the Member States working alone, particularly in cases where the scale or the effects of the action go beyond national frontiers.

16. The subsidiarity principle must be explicitly enshrined in the Union's constitution, and there must be political and legal guarantees that it will be observed. A political guarantee could be provided by turning the Council of Ministers into a chamber of Member States, whilst legal protection of the principle would be enhanced by making the Court of Justice a constitutional court.

17. Whilst it is important for the Member States and the regions to retain a sufficient degree of autonomy, it is equally important that the Union should be free from control by its individual members and by the regions

in areas where action on its part is essential to the good of all.

18. In the Union, as in any federal system, a distinction must be made between exclusive powers and concurrent powers — although the distinction is not absolute and concurrent powers may become exclusive powers (and vice-versa). And besides, powers are not fixed for all time.

19. Since powers must be clearly defined, the areas for which the Union must have sole responsibility include the following:

- the traditional "acquis communautaire": customs union, the common agricultural policy, (i.e. market organisation and the principles of the agricultural structural policy) trading policy, etc.;

- freedom of movement of persons, goods, services and capital;

- coordination of Member States' economic policies (establishment of guidelines; federal monitoring);

- monetary policy (regulating the amount of money in circulation and interest and exchange rates);

- the Union's own fiscal resources;

20. The main "intermediate" areas (i.e. under concurrent — even shared — responsibility) would be:

- strengthening of economic and social cohesion;

- general economic policy, including policy on prices, incomes and compulsory deductions;

- sectoral policies (agriculture, transport, telecommunications, research and development, industry, energy);

- the principles of the Charter of fundamental social rights and action related to social affairs (social policy, health, consumer protection, regional policy, the environment, education and research, cultural policy, access to information, young people and refugees);

- development cooperation;

- common foreign policy, and defence and security policy based on respect for the principles of solidarity and of the inviolability of the Community's external frontiers;

- harmonization of social provisions in the pursuit of progress.

21. In cultural matters, the Union may also play a role in representing Community interests. The cultural identities of the various peoples must be safeguarded constitutionally and respected in legislation. This also means that the various languages must be used on an equal basis in the work of the institutions.

22. The Union will have only those powers expressly allocated to it; all other areas will remain under national or regional control.

23. Lastly, the Union's constitution must include an effective procedure for allocating powers which were not foreseen when the constitution came into force. These new powers will be necessary to enable the Union to continue responding to new economic, social and technological challenges and to the demands imposed by developments in Europe and in the international political situation.

24. The EPP supports the institutional strategy followed by Parliament, which gave its Committee on Institutional Affairs the task of preparing a draft constitution in accordance with the guidelines adopted by the Colombo report and with due regard to the results of the Intergovernmental Conferences on Political Union and Economic and Monetary Union.

C. A more effective Community

25. The future of European integration will depend on the Community's ability to anticipate and solve problems. The current state of affairs in Europe as a whole makes it imperative for the Community to improve its ability to take decisions and act upon them both within its boundaries and beyond.

Ability to take decisions internally

26. The 1986 Single Act was a significant though limited step forward in the decision-making process: the adoption by a qualified majority of ten or so issues to do with 1992 increased the effectiveness of the Council of Ministers and gave it a greater sense of cooperation. As a result, the means now exist to liberalize capital movements, to monitor company mergers, to recognize qualifications and to open up public contracts.

27. However, progress on the most important measures is at a standstill:

- the move towards allowing the free movement of persons, which is under the sole control of the Member States, has been hindered;

- the achievement of other aims, such as the

harmonization of indirect taxation, which require a unanimous decision by the Council, has been postponed indefinitely.

It is clear that, in order to make the internal market a reality (an aim which has already been established and which lies at the heart of the Single Act) the vote by a qualified majority should apply to sectors which currently require a unanimous decision (taxation, free movement of persons, research, and the environment).

The same should apply even more to the objectives of implementing economic and monetary union, developing the Community as a social Union and developing a common foreign, defence and security policy.

28. Community law must be complied with, and decisions of the Court of Justice must be implemented. The Community (or Union) should be able to take direct action to implement the Court's decisions where the national authorities refuse to do so or have taken no action by the end of a reasonable period of time.

Ability to act beyond its boundaries

29. The Community must strengthen its ability and its common resolve to act beyond its boundaries in order to ensure — or acquire — credibility on the international political scene. Europe, although directly affected by world events (crises, conflicts, etc.), still does not play as full a part as she should in world politics.

30. In view of the uncertainty regarding the kind of order which will emerge following the collapse of the Communist regimes in Central and Eastern Europe, it is more important than ever to consolidate the Community as the sole existing source of strength. Since the Community has provided a model of reconciliation and prosperity for Europe as a whole for nearly 40 years, it is quite natural for it to be closely associated with the transformation of Central and Eastern Europe.

31. In general terms, the EPP believes that the Member States must speak with a single voice in their dealings with the outside world, and turn European Political Cooperation into a common foreign policy. In specific terms, the Union's international relations would encompass any matters in which the Member States have common interests.

32. The political restructuring in Central and Eastern Europe and the Soviet Union will require new European security arrangements, which must include, and respect the considerations of, all countries in order to contribute to peace and international security and to condemn the use of force (or threat to use force) by one country against another.

33. The Community's ability to act beyond its boundaries must now be strengthened in two directions:

- integration of European political cooperation into the Community system;

- extension of political cooperation to all aspects of security policy.

34. So as to strengthen the European pillar of the Atlantic Alliance the EPP proposes:

- For a period security policy will be defined by the European Council and executed by a Council of security Ministers, made up of Foreign and Defence Ministers, who could take decisions on a majority basis in a series of areas of common interest. The Council, in whose deliberations the Commission would participate, would account for its decisions before the Parliament. Council, Commission and Parliament would have rights of initiative. The secretariat of EPC would be integrated into the Council secretariat. The Defence Ministers would meet as a Defence Council with the power of decision, to execute policy decided by the Council of Security Ministers, so as to establish a common defence which would include notably common arms production, a common policy on the export of military material and strategic and military planning.

- As the institutions of political union take shape foreign and security policy would come within the purview of the Union. We want a European Security Union on the basis of a collective defence Treaty which would necessitate the integration of the organs of the WEU into the future European Union following the rules and principals of federal unity.

Decision making and implementation

35. The European Council, comprising the Heads of State and Government and the Commission President, has the strategic role of giving the Union political direction and impetus.

36. The Council of Ministers, drawn from the Member States, shares legislative power with the European Parliament. In a future Union it would act as the Second Chamber. In any

event, it is both essential and urgent to improve cooperation with the national parliaments.

37. The EPP proposes that the Council of Ministers should share with the European Parliament:

- the power to legislate on the basis of a qualified majority on all areas covered by the Treaties;
- the power to extend the Community's competence (Article 235) and to decide on constitutional provisions (revision of Treaties, accessions).

38. The EPP considers that the financial provisions contained in the Treaties should be fully revised to achieve a better balance between the two arms of the budgetary authority (Council and Parliament), particularly by eliminating the distinction between compulsory and non-compulsory expenditure.

39. The EPP calls for a stronger role for the Commission as the Community's executive body and, in particular, an increase in its independence from the Council:

- protection of the Commission's right and duty of initiative, without prejudice to any right granted to the European Parliament to initiate legislation;
- amendment of the EEC Treaty so that it states that powers of implementation are in certain cases to be granted to the Commission which, in such cases, could be assisted by a Consultative Committee;
- the Commission's right to represent the Community in international organizations and negotiations, where matters under Community jurisdiction are involved;
- the Commission would be responsible for ensuring that Community legislation was correctly implemented by the appropriate authorities;
- responsibility of the Commission to Parliament.

40. Regarding the composition of the Commission, the EPP advocates:

- election of the Commission President by an absolute majority of Parliament's members at the start of each parliamentary term, candidates being put forward by the European Council;
- the constitution of the Commission will coincide with the formation of the newly-elected European Parliament, and will

therefore also take place every five years;

- a reduction in the number of Commissioners;
- appointment of Commissioners by the Commission President from a list of three candidates put forward by each Member State;
- investiture by Parliament of the Commission.

41. The EPP calls for a Regional Consultative Council to be set up, through which the regional institutions of the Member States would be able to take part in the Community decision-making process.

D. Enhancing democratic legitimacy

42. Further efforts must be made to establish the Community once and for all on a sound basis of democratic legitimacy. The commitment to democratic principles, which is shared by all the Member States and which is required of countries wishing to join the Community, must become an integral part of the Community system in general, and of its decision-making process in particular.

43. Since the basis of European political integration is our common concept of the individual, it is imperative that the Union's constitution should affirm these basic values, starting with the rights of the individual. Furthermore, it must enshrine the terms of Community citizens' basic rights.

44. But the European Community (or Union) also requires active involvement on the part of its citizens. Europe is not — and cannot be — just a matter for governments; Europe must be the product of the thoughts and actions of its own citizens.

45. The EPP therefore calls for:

- the introduction of a uniform electoral law for European elections;
- the right for all citizens to take part in such elections, even if they live in another Member State or are temporarily resident there.

46. Furthermore, the national parliaments, which represent the citizens of Europe in the Member States, must be more closely involved in the Community decision-making process. In particular, they must have proper access to the information needed to enhance democratic control of the Council members representing their country.

47. Appropriate structures and institutions, such as a Community (or Union) Youth Council, should be set up to encourage young people to express their views. Joining associations should be encouraged, since it is a way of teaching young people to take part in the democratic process.

48. In any case, effective democratic checks on policy-making and the setting of standards in the Community would entail closer cooperation between national and regional parliaments and the European Parliament.

A more balanced and democratic institutional structure

49. The democratic deficit in the Treaties establishing the Community results from the fact that the power represented by some of the national parliaments' legislative power has been transferred to their respective governments without political representatives at European level being able to discharge their responsibilities properly. Since the European Parliament is the only directly elected Community institution, an adjustment in the balance between the various institutions would make its role in European integration an essential one.

50. The States which have sought closer union in the Community have done so with the intention of extending democracy, not restricting it, and the basis of democracy is the sovereignty of the people. In the Community as it stands at present, the sovereignty of the people exists in two different forms: as European sovereignty, expressed by a Parliament elected by universal, direct, free and secret suffrage throughout the Community; and as national sovereignty, expressed by the constitutions of the Member States.

51. Only the national sovereignty of individual States existed when the Community was first defined by the basic Treaties, and this was therefore possible only through diplomatic channels. This state of affairs could not be altered until the European Assembly came to be elected by universal suffrage, as a result of which it became a Parliament expressing European sovereignty in the areas for which the Community has responsibility. The principle of the sovereignty of the people implies that any amendment to the basic Treaties and the subsequent acts will in future be made by consultation and agreement between the institutions of the Member States (the representatives of national sovereignty) and those of the Union (the representatives of European sovereignty).

The Parliament's power of joint decision

52. The twin basis of the Community's legitimacy — the Council, composed of representatives of the Member States, and the European Parliament, composed of representatives of the people — necessarily implies a joint decision-making process, clearly indispensable if Parliament is to have the power to legislate, which is intrinsic to the very concept of Parliament.

53. In constitutional matters, no amendment to the Treaties would in future be valid without the joint approval of both the parliaments and governments of the Member States (the representatives of national sovereignty) and the European Parliament and the Council (the representatives of European sovereignty). This means, in particular, that the European Parliament, with the agreement of the Member States (or, exceptionally, of some of them), would be empowered to draw up a constitution which would be capable of encompassing and developing Community integration as a whole by eliminating any risk of worsening the democratic deficit and by guaranteeing the protection of rights and fundamental freedoms in any measures taken by the Union.

54. In legislative matters, Parliament's assent procedure should be extended to all matters within the Community's sphere of competence, whilst cooperation between Parliament and the Council should apply in all fields and be supplemented by the ability of Parliament itself to take decisions if the Council does not succeed in doing so within the time limits laid down in the Single Act. Furthermore, when the Treaties are next revised, it is essential that there should be set up, in the event of disagreement, a joint decision-making procedure ensuring equal participation by Parliament and the Council, as a result of the consultation procedure proposed by Parliament. The Council's legislative meetings would be held in public.

55. The Economic and Social Committee, whose statutes as a consultative institution must be ratified and be made obligatory, must be consulted on all social and economic matters.

Chapter II: Economic and Monetary Union, on the basis of a social market economy

56. The EPP considers that economic and monetary union and its institutional structures should be an integral part of the federal Union's constitution.

57. The EPP stresses the urgency of revising the EEC Treaty in order to bring about eco-

nomic and monetary union, complete the internal market, pursue the Community's objectives in social, regional and environmental policy, and supply the aid required by the countries of Eastern Europe and the South.

58. The specific aim of the basic Treaties was the setting up of a common market, accompanied by the introduction of various Community policies in particular sectors (agriculture, trade, competition, transport, iron and steel, regional policy, etc.). However, the EEC Treaty did not go into the details of macroeconomic policies (i.e. the means of directing the economy of the Community as a whole), which directly impinge on the sovereignty of the Member States. As a result, the only notable progress in 20 years has been the cooperation amongst a number of central banks in the European Monetary System.

59. The 1986 Single Act amending the EEC Treaty represented further, though limited, progress. The abolition of all restrictions on trade, planned for 1993, will have to be accompanied by Community measures to align Member States' economic and fiscal policies that go much further than the mere powers of recommendation currently in existence. It will gradually lead to the setting up of a central authority with economic and monetary powers. And the achievement of full economic integration necessarily involves the setting up of a central authority with political powers.

A. Economic Union

60. The main aims of economic union are an overall rise in Community living standards, reduced unemployment, a higher level of well-being for the citizens of Europe, and the improved international competitiveness of European economies within a social market economy.

61. The guiding principles of economic policy, regional cohesion and environmental protection (stability, growth and cohesion and social justice) which both the European institutions and the Member States should follow should be incorporated in the actual constitution of the Union.

62. The practical features of economic union are the following:

- a single internal market (freedom of movement for persons, goods, services and capital);
- the policies associated with the single market, and other measures to improve the workings of the market;

  • greater economic and social cohesion, especially by means of Community policies to reduce regional imbalances and to bring about structural reform, in order to ensure equal access to the opportunities of the market;

  • a social policy ensuring that competition does not lead to contraventions of minimum standards of health, safety, working practices and social benefits, worker participation and employee awareness, nor prevents the harmonization of these standards in the pursuit of progress.

  • an effective competition policy to prevent domination of the market by monopolies or cartels;

  • fiscal harmonization, particularly with regard to indirect taxation, insofar as this is necessary to prevent distortions of competition, whilst retaining desirable social rates;

  • common rules on consumer protection;

  • common rules on environmental protection which could be monitored by a European authority;

  • harmonization of certain aspects of company law and banking law;

  • common principles governing direct and indirect intervention by public authorities in specific sectors such as agriculture, energy, transport, research etc.;

- closer alignment of economic policies by means of coordinated conjunctural (especially budgetary) policies and increased Community budget resources for common policies, especially regional policy;

- the stabilization of prices in order to ensure balanced social and economic development in the Union;

- an end to the practice of financing budget deficits by printing more money, and the refusal by the Union to offer any kind of automatic or unconditional guarantee to Member States with budgetary problems;

- a Community policy to develop the major transport infrastructures throughout the Community, especially rail transport.

B. Monetary Union

63. In addition to price and currency stability, the aims of monetary union are to reduce the

cost of financial transactions (international ones in particular) and provide equal access to the Union's financial services and institutions.

64. The practical features of monetary union are the following:

- monetary stability first and foremost, in order to reduce and control inflation;
- the full and irreversible convertibility of all currencies;
- the complete liberalization of all capital movements, and the full integration of banking and other financial markets;
- the elimination of the margins within which exchange rates may fluctuate and the permanent fixing of those rates, in preparation for the introduction of a single currency, the ECU, in 1997;
- the move from coordinated monetary policies (monetary cooperation) to a single monetary policy operated by a (federal) European System of Central Banks (ESCB) involving:
  - setting up the ESCB as a fully independent Community institution, i.e. free from control by national governments, without prejudice to the economic policy guidelines laid down by the Council and the European Parliament on a proposal from the Commission;
  - in exchange for this freedom from political pressure, the possibility of making those responsible for running the Central Bank accountable to Parliament and the Council;
  - applying the subsidiarity principle to relations between the European Central Bank and the central banks of the Member States; the ESCB will make all decisions regarding money supply and price stability policy, whilst the central banks of the Member States, acting on behalf of the ESCB, will have responsibility for dealings on the international financial and monetary markets.

65. Progress towards economic and monetary union must be achieved in stages, in accordance with the following principles:

- maintaining the necessary balance (parallel development, coherence) between economic aspects and monetary aspects;
- applying the subsidiarity principle when distributing powers between the Member States and the Community (or Union),

the latter to be granted only those powers which it needs to ensure the successful operation of the Community as a whole;

- responding appropriately to specific circumstances, which must not undermine the obligation for each Member State to accept collective discipline and to make the efforts required for full convergence of the Member States economic performance.

C. The Social Market Economy

66. Aim of the social market economy should be to increase economical, monetary and social cooperation to guarantee the European citizens equal chances, more prosperity, a better protection of the environment and social progress.

67. The EPP considers that making financial and economic development the sole aim of European integration would put such strain on society as to destroy human bonds and cultures. For this reason, the Christian Democrats insist that the social and cultural aspects of European integration must be protected and developed.

68. To ensure balanced development, the Council must act by a majority vote on the social and environmental provisions of the Treaties.

69. Economic and monetary union must not be achieved at the expense of social justice and the general interest. The aim is to bring about the single market in a way that gives equal importance to social and economic considerations and to ensure the smooth development of the social aspect of economic and monetary union.

70. This involves broadening, upgrading and supplementing the social policy objectives laid down in the Treaties, which are to improve living and working conditions and raise them to the same standard throughout the Community. This is to be achieved by the following measures in particular:

- intervention by the Commission in cases where Community action produces economic or social distortion in certain Member States;
- the best possible allocation of resources and the maximum effectiveness of social policies;
- development of vocational training, with a view to enabling the unemployed to re-enter the job market;
- adopting a basic core of Community provisions concerning welfare and social secu-

rity, trade union rights and collective bargaining without forgetting the needs of citizens in extreme poverty and the necessity for them to be involved in the social and economic objectives of the Union;

– recognition of workers' rights to be informed and consulted and to participate in all decisions in their firms which concern them;

– improved equality of opportunity and of access to education and culture in particular by means of increased cooperation amongst universities and promotion of the audio-visual sector in Europe;

– the protection of children and adolescents, of the elderly and the handicapped;

– an increase in the resources of the Community's structural funds.

71. The EEC Treaty should also include the objective whereby the Community would contribute to international efforts to combat the risks to the ecological balance of the planet.

Conclusion

72. The need for balanced, coherent and comprehensive progress towards both economic and monetary union and a European social space is demonstrated by the fact that it will not be possible to achieve existing objectives without further political and institutional development of the Community.

73. The basic features of the social market economy are:

– improved living and working conditions through the recognition of the right to employment and to an adequate income;

the creation of new jobs and the fight against unemployment; recognition of the right to cooperation; and joint responsibility in the economy;

– promotion and development of vocational training and supplementary training measures, retraining and leave for vocational training, to enable the unemployed to re-enter the job market and those in work to meet the new challenges of modern employment.

74. The federal Europe for which the Christian Democrats have striven ever since the European Community was set up is now more than ever a political objective which is both necessary and realistic. Necessary, because the profound changes within Europe must be brought about within a structured, democratic and peaceful framework. Only institutions of a federal nature can satisfy the interests and aspirations of Europeans who wish to share a common destiny. Realistic, because the pace of progress is quickening, and the peoples of Europe are ready to accept a more rapid process of unification, based on some delegation of national sovereignty.

75. The EPP believes that, as a result of the two intergovernmental Conferences starting in December 1990, a degree of qualitative progress will be achieved in the form of substantial amendments to the existing Treaties. On the basis of this progress, to take effect from January 1993, the adoption of a federal constitution setting up a European government, a twin-chamber Parliament and a Supreme Court should be envisaged. This is the ambition which the Christian Democrats have set out to achieve.

B.   European Liberal, Democratic and Reform Parties: Declaration of the ELDR Summit in Berlin, 23 November 1990

THE LIBERAL LEADERS IN THE EUROPEAN COMMUNITY,

Welcoming the promising strides made in Eastern and Central Europe and in the USSR towards liberal democracy.

Stressing the urgent need to help and support these countries in their way to a free market economy.

Recognising that the end of the Cold War has

not eradicated the danger of military confrontation critical to the European Community.

Acknowledging that the EC incurs a special responsibility to eliminate its democratic deficit, build a common citizenship, finalize its economic and achieve its political integration.

Urge the Intergovernmental Conferences convened in December 1990 to take substantial steps towards transforming the Community into a genuine European Union based on a constitution of a federal type.

Shaping the European foreign, security and defence policy

The European Union shall have a common foreign and security policy, implying a common defence policy as a necessary complement to its non-military policy aspects.

The Common Foreign and Security Policy should actively pursue coordination and cooperation with NATO, which remains a cornerstone of the European security system.

The present European Political Cooperation should enter the formal EC framework. This implies the establishment of a Council of Ministers of Foreign Affairs, Security and Defence and the appointment of a Commissioner charged with security and defence matters. Democratic control by the European Parliament should be fully asserted.

The Council of Ministers of Foreign Affairs and Defence will be responsible for the shaping of a Common Foreign and Security Policy on the basis of general guidelines agreed by the European Council, thus integrating the policies of the Member States and gradually formulating a joint Community policy.

Multi-national forces should come into existence as a precursor of a genuine European defence force under a common military command, embracing operational units for peace keeping and verification functions.

Although the CSCE lacks the necessary integration to be the sole forum for a European security policy, it should already be used by its Member States to conclude disarmament agreements and to be the framework for ensuring their observance.

The present competences of WEU should be gradually absorbed by the EC Common Foreign and Security Policy.

Given that the non-military aspects of security are fundamental in achieving a stable and peaceful world order based on the rule of law and a decent living for all human beings, the EC should contribute to the economic take-off of Central and Eastern Europe, the Mediterranean Basin and the developing countries, insisting on further democratic reform in these countries and their respect of human rights and supporting their regional organisations.

Consolidating the 1992 objectives

To consolidate the Single Market, which must be completed by 31 December 1992, the Intergovernmental Conference should establish Economic and Monetary Union, in accordance with a mandatory timetable, including the necessary convergence of economic policies, leading to a single currency and an independent European Central Bank System.

The second phase of the EMU should start before 1 January 1994. The achievement of the EMU by January 1997 must be accompanied by policies which guarantee economic and social cohesion, full advantages of the Single Market to all regions and due respect for the environment.

These policies should be subject to subsidiarity, and advance decentralization and deregulation.

In order to make EMU a reality for the European citizens as well as in the market place, the private and public use of the Ecu should now be promoted.

As the financial arrangements laid down in the Treaties are no longer adequate, there is urgent need for an overall review of the EC's financial resources and allocations. Revenue should in future be determined by the Council of Ministers and the European Parliament, acting in common accord. In any case financial autonomy should not raise the overall tax-burden of the EC citizen.

Community spending should be better scrutinized by conferring greater powers to the Commission's own inspectors and the Court of Auditors.

Coping with the democratic deficit

The continuing democratic deficit within the EC resulting from the combined effects of the lack of grip on the EC of the national parliaments and the absence of true legislative powers of the European Parliament has to be finally tackled.

Democratic legitimacy should go together with growing efficiency of the decision-making process. Therefore all political institutions should be in the same city.

The Intergovernmental Conferences should make a qualitative leap forward to democracy by granting full co-decision powers to the directly elected European Parliament in all areas of Community legislation, with Council, when acting in its legislative capacity, deciding in public and by qualified majority. The assent procedure should be extended to all important international agreements of the EC. All decisions subject to ratification by the National

Parliaments should also be subject to ratification by the European Parliament.

The European Parliament must have the right to elect the President of the Commission on a proposal of the European Council and to submit the Commission to a vote of confidence. The Members of the Commission, the number of which should not be increased, are appointed by the President-elect on the basis of proposals by each of the Member States. Parliament and Council shall have the right of initiative if the Commission fails to respond to its requests for draft legislation. Parliament shall furthermore have the right of inquiry. Full executive powers should be granted to the Commission.

Compliance with EC legislation should be ensured by attaching financial penalties to the decisions of the Court of Justice.

Achieving European citizenship

A European citizenship paying tribute to our common democratic and cultural heritage should be the cornerstone of European Union.

European Parliament should be elected on the basis of a uniform electoral procedure based on proportionality with the right to vote for all EC citizens in their place of residence.

The Declaration on Fundamental Rights and Freedoms adopted by the European Parliament on 12 April 1989 should be enshrined in the Treaties, and the EC should adhere to the European Convention on Human Rights. Strict observance of these rights within the field of Community law shall be guaranteed by direct access to and scrutiny by the European Court of Justice.

. . .

By gradually accomplishing integration in the field of foreign and security policy, by achieving the Economic and Monetary Union and by giving the EC its much-needed democratic legitimacy, we will finally reach the goals set forward 40 years ago and be a lasting example for all peoples aiming at peace and human dignity.

The Liberal Leaders urge all Member States to engage fully in all aspects of Economic, Monetary and Political Union, ultimately leading to a union embracing all liberal democracies in Europe.

C.   Socialist Party Leaders' Declaration on the Intergovernmental Conferences, Madrid, 10 December 1990

1. The Intergovernmental Conferences on Economic and Monetary Union and Political Union which will open in Rome on 15th December 1990, present an exceptional opportunity to include the proposals of Socialists in the shaping of the future European Union.

2. The ever increasing internationalization of the economy and interdependence of our societies at every level means that it is increasingly difficult to respond on a national level to the new challenges which arise. Democratic control of the future remains possible, provided that those elements of sovereignty which can no longer be exercised in a purely national framework are pooled.

3. The two Intergovernmental Conferences are of necessity linked. They are characterized as one political process consisting of two interdependent negotiations which should lead to one single ratification process in order to revise the EC Treaties. Monetary integration and cooperation and enhanced convergence of economic policies must go hand in hand with an increase of the democratic legitimacy of the Community Institutions.

A strengthening of the Community would enable it to remain open to all forms of cooperation with other European countries ranging from free trade to full membership for any democratic European States which are capable and willing to accept the goals of the Community and to strive responsibly towards them.

Economic and Monetary Union

4. For democratic socialists, Economic and Monetary Union, if it is to have beneficial results for people across the European Community, should be much more than monetary policy on a European level: it reflects the economic-monetary integration of the European Community in an increasingly interde-

pendent world economy, it is an extension of the creation of the internal market which has to contribute to the furthering of sustainable growth and employment.

Economic and Monetary Union, like the internal market during the last decade, has become a focal point for a new step forward in the process of European integration. In this context the establishment of the operationally autonomous European Central Bank and therewith the transition to the final stage of EMU is conditional upon the fulfilment of certain economic and monetary criteria, including the implementation of accompanying economic policy at the European level. This requires economic convergence and policies for growth, regional development and social cohesion as well as accountability. Any monetary policy defined and implemented in isolation from other policies and objectives is unrealistic and undesirable.

5. *Political influence*: Apart from the direct economic and financial advantages, EMU should improve the political management of economic and monetary policies, where there has been a decline in national autonomy in recent years due to the increasing internationalization of the economy. The European Community has increasing weight on the world stage; it is hence the most important body in which to vest political influence over the international economy.

6. *Cohesion*: For Socialists, European integration must be far more than economic liberalization: steps forward in the field of Economic and Monetary Union must be designed to achieve a stronger socio-economic cohesion and be linked to policies ensuring social rights and environmental protection.

A strengthened cohesion policy has to be a core element of the implementation of EMU, since major inequalities and disequilibria between the Member States and regions present a major challenge to the capacity of EC economic and monetary policies to work for the benefit of the peoples of the European Community. There has to be parallelism between the implementation of EMU and policies aiming at the reduction of socio-economic disparities. In this context we call for the adjustment of the instruments for cohesion, such as regional policies and the EC Structural Funds, together with the adoption of complementary measures which, in parallel with the development of the Single Market and the implementation of EMU, will encourage the integration of the

least favoured regions in the EC as well as their economic growth.

Any extension of competence must include those elements necessary for the adoption of decisions in order to give the Community sufficient means for its own development.

7. *Monetary policy objectives and the Central Bank*: Only a monetary policy of which the first aim is stability can ensure the strength of a common European currency. The revised Treaty should make clear that the central objectives of monetary policy, ensuring price stability and maintaining the value of currencies, should be pursued taking due account of general economic policy goals, in particular the promotion of a high level of employment. The charter of the European System of Central Banks will have to be drafted accordingly: a European Central Banking System that decides autonomously how to implement the monetary policy objectives of price stability and maintaining the value of currencies, should pursue these objectives taking due account of general economic policy goals. Its board members should be appointed for a sufficiently long term of office.

This system should be democratically accountable. The overall aim should be to combine a clear and decisive level of accountability with the freedom of the bank in implementing monetary policy on an institutional and operational level.

The Council should have the overall responsibility for the external exchange rate policy of the Community.

8. *Budgetary responsibility*: In full EMU, with a single European currency (ECU), there will be a direct EC interest in budgetary responsibility at the national level. It is neither feasible nor desirable to introduce definite ceilings on national budget deficits. On the other hand national financial policies must not be allowed to undermine EC monetary stability. This could be achieved by laying down general rules for the financial basis of Member State budgets. Monetary financing of public budget deficits should be avoided: limits on the monetary financing of public deficits could be introduced. Furthermore, the EC and its Member States should be under no obligation to bail out a Member State which cannot meet its commitments.

9. *Economic policy*: The coordination of the economic policies of the different Member States should be reinforced by strengthened multilateral surveillance and the formulation of EC targets and guidelines. In this way it

will also be possible to bring political pressure to bear on Member States conducting a
divergent policy in the form of an excessively
restrictive or expansionist economic policy. The
Community should develop adequate instruments (if necessary implemented nationally in
a coordinated manner) in order to be able to
pursue an anti-cyclical economic and budgetary
policy and/or to react to sudden international
economic developments.

10. *Fiscal policy*: The relation between fiscal
policy, fiscal coordination and EMU has not
received adequate attention from the EC Institutions in the discussions so far.

Developments which could result in Member
States competing with one another to attract
capital flows on the basis of tax levels would
be highly undesirable and might result in an
erosion of the tax base of most Member States,
which in turn could endanger public policies
on e.g. social rights, regional development,
environmental protection and education.

In this context, taxation policy will have to
be a priority item on the agenda of the EMU
Intergovernmental Conference and should be
discussed on the basis of a comprehensive survey by the European Commission on the fiscal
aspects of EMU. The introduction of binding
minimum rates could be the most appropriate
form of coordination.

11. *The global financial system*: The creation of a central monetary system in Europe,
coupled with the strengthening of the ECU as
an international trading currency alongside the
US dollar and the Japanese yen, opens the way
for the re-establishment of an effective system
for international monetary cooperation. The
Community's strategy must be to encourage
the use of the ECU for investment and reserve
purposes.

Whether or not EFTA countries apply for
full EC membership, it should be possible for
them to link their currencies to the European
Monetary System. This should be done in such
a way as to avoid an inflationary impact. It is
essential to create the necessary conditions in
the Eastern and Central European countries
currently undergoing reform, for them to establish the convertibility of their currencies.

A stronger role of the Community in international monetary relations could lead to a more
stable context for the Third World economies.
A common position of the Community in monetary matters should also be used to promote a
more stable international monetary system and
a solution to the international debt crisis.

Political union

12. To create a framework in which sovereignty
can be shared on a European level, while safeguarding and respecting national identities, is
the raison d'être of the European Community.
Moreover it is necessary that we have Institutions which enable us to define and implement
the new common policies which we need. It is
also necessary to ensure that there is a guarantee of appropriate democratic control of these
Institutions. That is the reason why the European Community must today take the following
new steps towards genuine political unity:

13. *The development of European Citizenship*
as a sum total of the rights and duties of
European citizens which go beyond the freedoms of movement, residence and establishment which will be fully implemented as from
1st January 1993.

All Community policies must lead to the
improvement of the living standards of European citizens, who are the most fundamentally
affected and concerned by this integration. This
presupposes the development of certain measures relating to daily life. These should, subject to further consideration of constitutional
and citizenship arrangements in the Member
States, include political rights, like the right
to participate in local and European elections
in the state of residence and a common system of consular protection for Community citizens abroad, and possibly other things besides
the common passport and a common driving
licence.

As a consequence of free circulation arising
from the physical elimination of frontiers and
in view of maintaining a high level of security
for citizens, it is vital that common measures
are taken to combat major organized crime,
drug abuse and in particular the laundering
of money.

14. *A coherent approach to Social Policy*:
Socialists want the development of the Single
Market and the implementation of a concrete
social policy, which would meet the aspirations
of workers and citizens in general, to follow a
parallel course.

The Community Charter of Fundamental
Social Rights, approved in 1989 by the European Council in Strasbourg, following the mandate from the European Council in Madrid,
must be adopted as the basic document of
Social Europe, with mandatory effect.

The future treaty must make it possible to
make progress — which is so long overdue —

on such essential issues as establishing minimum rights for all workers with regard to contracts of employment, working hours and conditions, training, access to public employment services, collective bargaining and industrial democracy, and providing basic standards with regard to the employment of young people, and of people with disabilities as well as equality of treatment between men and women. The new treaty must clearly establish competences on these issues. Measures under new Community competence must be adopted by a qualified majority. However, decisions pertaining to the level of salaries and social benefits should be taken unanimously.

It is necessary that a common position is taken on the problem of immigration into the European Community from third countries.

15. *A much stronger emphasis on environmental protection*: The Intergovernmental Conferences must not fail to provide the Community with adequate instruments to play a leading role in combatting the enormous threats facing the global environment — the greenhouse effect, acid rain, desertification, local depletion of ozone levels, the over-exploitation of natural resources and the degradation of the tropical rain forests.

The principle of sustainable development must be included as one of the tasks of the Community: this will allow environmental policy objectives to be integrated throughout the EC's objectives. The cooperation procedure must be introduced for EC environmental legislation: this will accelerate the decision making process without jeopardizing the right of Member States to maintain and introduce more stringent protective legislation. The current approach of regulation and control must be complemented by economic and fiscal measures. The relationship between environmental and social development could be strengthened by introducing ecological elements in the Structural Funds.

In order to achieve these objectives, it will be necessary to implement the following reforms:

16. *An improvement of decision making* by extending the application of majority voting in the Council of Ministers: this extension must cover legislation defining certain fundamental social rights guaranteed to all within the Community, rules laying down minimum standards of environmental protection and, in general, decisions where the Community level is the most appropriate level at which decisions

should be taken. Unanimity must be retained, however, for all modifications of the Treaties, and in cases where the Council wishes to override the advice of the Commission.

17. *A strengthening of democratic control* by giving the European Parliament the right of co-decision with the Council in those fields where the Council takes majority decisions, the right of initiative over legislation vis-à-vis the Commission, and an increased control over the implementation of Community legislation. Co-decision could be achieved by, for instance, a procedure where the final approval of both Institutions is necessary. This strengthening of the role of the European Parliament ought to lead to closer relations with national Parliaments: their roles are not in competition with each other, but rather are complementary. National Parliaments will play their role in exercising effective scrutiny over their individual Ministers who are members of the Community's Council.

18. *A better definition of the executive* by the recognition of the role of the European Council and a strengthening of the legitimacy of the Commission. The role in providing overall guidance which belongs to the European Council ought to be incorporated in the Treaties. The Commission, which as the Community's executive plays an important role in carrying out its policies and initiating new proposals, must also be subject to stronger democratic accountability. The European Parliament, which already has the right to dismiss it, should be involved in its appointment by investing the President of the Commission on a proposal of the European Council and by taking a vote of confidence on the incoming Commission as a whole.

19. *The implementation of Common Foreign and Security Policies* to enable the Community and its Member States to maintain their roles on the world stage and contribute to the transition from confrontation to common and assured security by contributing through political action to the reduction of tension and the creation of areas of freedom, democracy and autonomy in the world.

Such policies must be based on agreed principles. Their implementation should have as objectives the maintenance of peace and security; the peaceful settlement of disputes through respect for international law and the prevention of aggression; mutual, balanced and verifiable reductions of armed forces and armaments; the promotion of social harmony and international order, based on respect for human rights and the improvement of living standards in the developing countries.

In the development of these policies, it will be necessary to integrate political cooperation in the work of the institutions; to consider an appropriate concept of European security and gradually to define priority subjects for joint action by common agreement on, for example, common relations with other European countries and with the U.S. and with Japan, participation in the CSCE and contribution to the strengthening of the United Nations.

20. Any new Treaty must guarantee the legitimate interests of every Member State. It must at the same time, however, allow us jointly to establish in the Community framework the necessary mechanisms to progress towards a society of democracy, of social justice and of peace.

DOCUMENTS DURING THE IGCs

1. Proposals during initial phase of the political union IGC (Selection)

A. European Commission proposal on common external policy

Draft text

TITLE Y

Common external policy

Article Y0

The common external policy shall cover common foreign and security policy, external economic policy and development cooperation policy as well as external relations in the other areas falling under Union responsibility. In the conduct of this policy, the Union shall seek to promote democracy, the rule of law and respect for human rights.

Chapter I

Common foreign and security policy

Article Y1

The Union shall pursue a common foreign and security policy aimed at maintaining peace and international stability, and developing friendly relations with all countries, without prejudice to the special relations of individual Member States.

This policy shall be governed both by general provisions and by specific provisions on security and defence.

Section 1

General provisions

Article Y2

Implementation of the common foreign and security policy shall rest on a distinction between matters that are deemed to be of vital interest for the Union and other matters in this sphere.

Article Y3

1. To ensure that common principles and objectives are formulated and that effective common action is taken by the Union under the common foreign policy, the European Council shall, without prejudice to powers conferred under the other provisions of the Treaties, decide what matters are of vital common interest, acting on the initiative of the Presidency, or of the Commission or of a simple majority of the Member States, after hearing the views of the European Parliament.

When deciding what matters are of vital common interest, the European Council shall specify the conditions under which a Member State may, at its request, be given dispensation from the obligations which common action entails. The Member State concerned shall refrain from taking any measures that may affect the implementation of Union decisions.

2. Except where this Treaty provides otherwise, in matters that have been declared to be of vital common interest, the Council, acting by the majority specified in the second indent of Article 148(2)[1] on the initiative of the Presidency or of the Commission or of a simple majority of the Member States, shall:

(i) formulate the principles of the common policy;

(ii) decide on action to be taken, whether it is to be implemented by the Union or by the Member States.

Article 149(1) shall not apply to Council Decisions under this Article.

Article Y4

1. In matters that have not been declared to be of vital common interest the Member States and the Commission shall coordinate their positions on any external policy issue of general interest within the Council to ensure that their combined influence is exercised as effectively as possible through concerted deliberation, con-

---

[1] Where the Treaty does not provide for a Commission proposal, this involves an augmented qualified majority which requires at least eight Member States to vote in favour.

vergence of positions, and the pursuit of common action. To this end the Member States shall consult each other and the Commission on all national foreign policy measures they intend to take.

2. To enhance their capacity for joint action, the Member States shall work to secure the formulation and progressive development of common principles and objectives.

3. The Member States shall refrain from hindering consensus and joint action that may flow from it.

4. In adopting positions and pursuing national action, each Member State shall take full account of the positions of its partners, shall give due consideration to the importance of adopting and implementing common positions and shall avoid any action that may impair the Union's effectiveness as a cohesive force in international relations and in international organizations. Decisions on common positions shall constitute a point of reference for national policies.

5. If a Member State deems it necessary to act in response to a particularly serious situation or exceptional circumstances, it shall, before taking action, refer the matter to the Council, which shall decide without delay under Article Y3(2) on whether action by the Union is called for.

Article Y5

The European Parliament shall be closely involved in the formulation and conduct of the common foreign and security policy. To this end the Council and the Commission shall keep the European Parliament regularly informed of the matters dealt with under the policy and shall make sure that the European Parliament's views are taken into consideration.

Each year the European Parliament shall hold a debate on the common foreign and security policy, during which statements shall be made to it by the Council and the Commission. The Council and the Commission may also appear before European Parliament committees, either at the European Parliament's request or on their own initiative.

Article Y6

The Council's deliberations and decisions shall be prepared and their implementation moni-

tored by the General Secretariat of the Council in structured cooperation with the Commission.

The Permanent Representatives Committee shall be responsible for preparing the deliberations of the Council under the common foreign and security policy and for carrying out the tasks assigned to it by the Council to this end.

Article Y7

1. In areas that come under the common foreign and security policy the Union shall be represented in relations with non-member countries and in international organizations and conferences by the Council Presidency and by the Commission, assisted where appropriate by the previous and next Member States to hold the Presidency.[2]

The Council, acting by the majority specified in the second indent of Article 148(2) on a proposal from the Commission or from one of the Member States, may entrust one or more Member States with the task of presenting the Union's position in specific instances, for example, before the United Nations Security Council or the organs of the Atlantic Alliance or Western European Union.

2. To ensure that the Union is represented as effectively as possible the Member States and the Commission shall furnish each other with assistance and information to strengthen cooperation between their missions accredited in non-member countries and to international organizations.

Article Y8

The foreign policies of the Member States and action by the Union under the other provisions of this Treaty shall be consistent with the common foreign and security policy.

Should the danger of inconsistency arise, the Commission or any Member State may call for the Council to be convened with a view to taking a decision in accordance with the procedure specified in Article Y3(2).

Article Y9

Wherever it considers it appropriate, the Union shall organize a political dialogue with non-member countries and regional groupings.

Article Y10

Articles 164 to 188 of the Treaty shall not apply to this Chapter.[3]

---

[2] Following the formula used for the troika, which here becomes a "quadriga", as the Commission is involved as well.

[3] This provision is designed to place the policy beyond the jurisdiction of the Court of Justice.

SECTION 2

Common security policy

Article Y11

The common security policy shall constitute an integral part of the Union's foreign policy. Its purpose shall be to strengthen security in Europe and to maintain peace in the world in accordance with the United Nations Charter. It shall rest on cooperation within the WEU. Its long-term objective shall be to establish a common European defence in full compliance with commitments entered into in the Atlantic Alliance.

Article Y12

If any of the Member States is the object of an armed attack in Europe, the other Member States shall, in accordance with Article 51 of the United Nations Charter, afford it all the military and other aid and assistance in their power.

Article Y13

1. Without prejudice to powers conferred under other provisions of this Treaty, in the areas of security and defence the Union shall treat as matters of vital common interest within the meaning of Article Y3 the control of armaments, disarmament and related questions, security questions related to the CSCE or debated in the United Nations, including peacekeeping operations, economic and technological cooperation in the field of armaments, and coordination of policy on arms exports and non-proliferation.[4]

Under the common security policy, the Union shall establish an arms research and production policy.

2. The European Council may identify other questions as being of vital common interest.

3. Where other provisions of the Treaty do not apply to questions declared to be of vital common interest, the Council shall:

(i) formulate unanimously[5] the principles of common policy and the procedures to be followed when deciding on action to be taken;

(ii) decide on action to be taken, whether it is to be implemented by the Union or by the Member States.

4. A Member State may be given dispensation under the decisions provided for in paragraphs 2 and 3 from some of the obligations flowing from them, if it so requests for compelling reasons. The Member State concerned shall nevertheless refrain from taking any measures that may affect the implementation of Union decisions.

The Council shall review such dispensations regularly in the light of common policy developments to assess whether they are still compatible with the common interest.

A Member State that has been given dispensation shall not participate in Council deliberations on the matter in question or on the formulation, extension or application of the obligations from which it has been dispensed.

Article Y14

The Ministers for Foreign Affairs and for Defence and the Commission shall hold a joint meeting at least twice each year to develop cooperation between the Member States in the field of defence. If necessary, they shall meet immediately, should a Member State so request.

Article Y15

1. When deciding on action to be taken pursuant to Article Y13(3), the Council shall also decide whether to refer implementation of the guidelines it has established to the WEU Council.

2. For the application of paragraph 1 the Union shall establish with the WEU such arrangements as may be necessary to enable Member States which are not members of the WEU and the Commission to attend meetings of the WEU bodies.

3. Member States which are members of the Atlantic Alliance shall express the Union position there when questions declared to be of vital common interest or questions dealt with by the WEU are discussed.

4. The Union shall endeavour to make use of the provisions of Article XII of the Treaty of Brussels of 17 March 1948 to promote the gradual integration of the WEU into the Union.

---

[4] As enumerated by the second Rome European Council.
[5] Abstentions shall not prevent the adoption of decisions.

Chapter II

External economic policy

Article Y16

External economic action by the Union shall contribute, in the common interest:

(i) to the harmonious development of the world economy and of world trade;

(ii) to the progressive strengthening of economic relations in Europe and in the world, notably by abolishing barriers to the liberalization of trade:

(iii) to the establishment of fair economic and social conditions in the world.

Article Y16a

External relations in the areas covered by economic and monetary union shall be governed by the specific provisions of Articles 106b(1) and (3), 108(2) and (3), and 105e(2), and by Article Y17.

Article Y17

1. The Union shall pursue a common policy on external economic relations covering:

(i) trade, including export credit and credit insurance schemes,

(ii) economic and commercial measures involving services, capital, intellectual property, investment, establishment and competition.

2. The Union shall have sole power to take measures, autonomous and conventional, in the field of economic and commercial policy as referred to in paragraph 1.

3. The Union may authorize the Member States to take some of the measures referred to in paragraph 2, within limits and subject to conditions which it shall lay down.

4. The autonomous measures referred to in paragraph 2 shall be adopted and the authorizations referred to in paragraph 3 shall be granted by the Commission on the basis of laws enacted under the co-decision procedure by the European Parliament and the Council on a proposal from the Commission.

5. The conventional commitments referred to in paragraph 2 shall be entered into in accordance with Article Y27.

6. In exercising the powers conferred upon it by this Article the Union shall be represented by the Commission in relations with non-member countries and in international organizations and conferences.

Article Y18

Where immediate action is needed to preserve Union interests, the Commission shall adopt the necessary measures. It shall inform the Council and the European Parliament accordingly without delay.

Article Y19

1. The Union shall have the power to take any economic measures in areas other than those referred to in Article Y17(1) with a view to achieving the objectives listed in Article Y16, notably in the context of financial and technical cooperation with one or more non-member countries not covered by Chapter III.

2. On any issues of general interest involving external economic relations the Union shall coordinate the positions of the Member States in relations with non-member countries and in international forums.

Chapter III

Development cooperation policy[6]

Article Y20

The aim of common policy on development cooperation shall be to promote the economic and social development of developing countries and their peoples and to help resolve the problems of structural poverty in those countries.

This policy shall seek to achieve a lasting balance between economic objectives, rational management of the environment, and optimum use of natural and human resources.

Article Y21

The common policy on development cooperation shall cover:

(i) action by the Union and joint action by the Union and the Member States;

(ii) coordination of other action by the Member States.

---

[6] Possibly insert an Article on what is to happen to the current arrangements for overseas countries and territories (Part Four of the EEC Treaty), which must in any event be aligned on — or incorporated in — the Chapter on development cooperation policy. One possibility would be a (sole) Article combining Articles 131 (principles) and 136 (procedures), redrafted accordingly.

Article Y22

1. Action by the Union shall include:

(i) the introduction of special arrangements and measures in the field of commercial policy, without prejudice to the action provided for in Chapter II;

(ii) measures designed to improve the operation of the international markets in commodities of export interest to developing countries[7] by increasing transparency and efficiency, taking market trends into account,[8] and secondly to contribute to the stabilization of export earnings from commodities originating in developing countries, in particular in the least-developed countries.

2. Action by the Union and joint action by the Union and the Member States shall cover:

(i) financial and technical cooperation;

(ii) food aid and humanitarian aid;

(iii) any other instrument likely to encourage development, notably involving establishment and services, movement of capital and movement of persons, and measures designed to encourage the promotion and protection of investments.

3. The instances in which joint action is to be taken by the Union and the Member States in the areas referred to in paragraph 2 shall be determined by the Council acting unanimously on a proposal from the Commission after receiving the assent of the European Parliament.

4. The European Investment Bank shall contribute through its operations to action by the Union and to joint action by the Union and the Member States.

Article Y23

1. The general guidelines and multiannual programmes specifying the action to be taken by the Union and the joint action by the Union and the Member States as determined in accordance with Article Y22(3) shall be adopted in the form of laws enacted under the co-decision procedure by the European Parliament and the Council on a proposal from the Commission. Such guidelines and programmes shall specify those implementing measures which are the responsibility of the Member States.

2. The Union, acting in accordance with Article Y27, shall have sole power to enter into any conventional commitments in the areas subject to action by the Union and to joint action by the Union and the Member States.

In such areas, the Union shall be represented by the Commission in relations with non-member countries and in international organizations and conferences.

Article Y24

1. In areas not subject to action by the Union or to joint action by the Union and the Member States as referred to in Article Y22, the Member States and the Commission shall liaise on all issues of general interest in the field of development cooperation policy.

2. To this end the Member States shall inform each other and the Commission in advance of all measures envisaged within the framework of national development cooperation, and in particular of national programmes and draft agreements to be concluded with non-member countries or international organizations.

3. The Member States shall refrain from any initiative likely to impair the consistency and effectiveness of action by the Union or joint action by the Union and the Member States as referred to in Article Y22. They shall, on the other hand, encourage such action as may usefully complement the above and enable the objectives defined in Article Y20 · to be achieved.

4. In the areas referred to in paragraph 1, the Commission shall coordinate the positions of the Member States in relations with non-member countries and in international forums.

5. For the purposes set out in paragraphs 1 to 4 the Commission shall forward recommendations to the Member States. Where necessary, coordinating measures shall be adopted on the basis of laws enacted in accordance with the procedure specified in Article Y23(1).

Chapter IV

General provisions

---

[7] Terminology used for the Unctad integrated programme, which covers 18 products (bananas, bauxite, cocoa, coffee, copper, cotton, hard fibres, jute, tea, etc.), oil and gold being, therefore, excluded.
[8] As in Article 74 of the fourth Lomé Convention.

SECTION 1

Agreements within the area of common foreign and security policy

Article Y25

1. Where an agreement with one or more States or with an international organization needs to be negotiated in areas in which Chapter 1 confers powers on the Union, the Council Presidency and the Commission shall jointly make recommendations to the Council, which, acting by the majority specified in Article Y3(2) or in accordance with Article Y13(3), as the case may be, shall authorize them to open the necessary negotiations.

The Presidency and the Commission[9] shall conduct these negotiations within the framework of such directives as the Council may issue to them, in consultation with a special committee appointed by the Council.

2. Agreements of the kind referred to in paragraph 1 shall be concluded by the Council, acting in accordance with the procedures referred to in that paragraph on the initiative of the Presidency or of the Commission, after consulting the European Parliament, whose opinion shall be given within the time-limit determined by the Council.

SECTION 2

Agreements falling within other areas of Union powers

Article Y26

1. In areas not covered by the common foreign and security policy[10] and in areas where the Union has exclusive powers in external relations expressly conferred on it by this Treaty,[11] the Union shall enjoy sole power to conclude, under Article Y27, agreements with one or more States or with international organizations provided it has already exercised those powers internally.

In areas where the Union has the sole power to conclude international agreements, it shall be represented by the Commission in relations with non-member countries and in international organizations and conferences.

2. The Union may also conclude international agreements in accordance with Article Y27 in areas where powers are conferred on it by Article 3 or by virtue of Article 235 but where it has not yet exercised them.

Where it has not made use of the option provided for in the first subparagraph, the Union shall coordinate the position of the Member States in relations with non-member countries and in international forums.

3. When concluding a multilateral international agreement the performance of which entails administrative and operating expenditure, the Union shall act with the same status and by the same procedure as the signatory States.

Article Y27

1. Where an agreement with one or more States or with an international organization needs to be negotiated, the Commission shall make recommendations to the Council, which, acting by a qualified majority, shall authorize the Commission to open the necessary negotiations.

The Commission shall conduct these negotiations within the framework of such directives as the Council may issue to it, after consulting a special committee appointed by the Council

2. The Council, acting by a qualified majority on a proposal from the Commission after receiving the assent of the European Parliament, which shall act by an absolute majority of its members, shall conclude, on behalf of the Union, agreements the content of which:

(i) involves amendment of a Union law;

(ii) involves amendment of the financial perspective;

(iii) establishes the basis for the Community's multilateral external relations in matters of trade or economic cooperation or the basis for development cooperation;

(iv) establishes an association between the Union and one or more non-member countries or a regional international organization involving durable links, reciprocal rights and obligations, common action and special procedures;[12]

(v) organizes, within a multilateral framework, the protection of human rights and the funda-

---

[9] Duopoly.

[10] Article Y25 regulates the conclusion of agreements in the field of common foreign and security policy; all other specific provisions governing that area are to be found in Chapter 1.

[11] This means external economic relations for areas covered by Article Y17(1), development cooperation policy for those covered by Article Y22(1) and EMU provisions where the Union has sole power.

[12] Criteria set out in Article 238 (which may possibly be modified).

mental rights of workers, or global protection of the atmosphere, water or natural resources,[13] or defines, within a multilateral framework, the fundamental principles of international law;

(vi) makes provision for accession by the Union to a universal or regional international organization other than an organization set up to administer a multilateral convention;

(vii) makes provision for participation by non-member countries or international organizations in bodies set up by Community law.[14]

However, the Council shall act unanimously where the agreement covers matters for which unanimity is required at internal level.

3. Other agreements shall be concluded by the Council acting by a qualified majority on a proposal from the Commission after consulting the European Parliament.

4. The Commission shall approve modifications to any agreement which provides for them to be adopted by a simplified procedure or by a body set up by the agreement.

In accordance with the procedure specified in the first subparagraph the Council may authorize the Commission to conclude, on behalf of the Union, certain other agreements or categories of agreement.

5. The provisions set out in paragraphs 1 and 3 shall apply subject to the powers conferred on the Commission by Article Y30.

6. The Commission shall administer the agreements concluded by the Union.

SECTION 3

Agreements in the field of foreign policy and other areas

Article Y28

1. Where agreements are to be negotiated which would lay durable and structured foundations for political relationships of cooperation or association between the Union and one or more States and which would also have an economic, financial and cultural dimension the procedure specified in Article Y25(1) shall apply;[15] however, the Commission shall conduct the negotiations in conjunction with the Council Presidency, after consulting a special committee appointed by the Council.

2. These agreements shall be concluded in accordance with the procedure specified in Article Y27(2).[16] However, the Presidency shall also have the right to take the initiative in requesting the Council to conclude an agreement.

3. The Commission shall administer these agreements in the areas referred to in Article Y26(1).

SECTION 4

Common provisions

Article Y29[17]

1. The European Parliament, the Council, the Commission or a Member State may seek the opinion of the Court of Justice as to whether an agreement envisaged is compatible with the provisions of this Treaty. Where the opinion of the Court of Justice is adverse, the agreement may enter into force only in accordance with Article 236.

2. Agreements concluded under these conditions shall be binding on the institutions of the Union and on the Member States.

Article Y30

The Commission shall maintain all appropriate forms of cooperation with international organizations.

It shall, *inter alia*, contribute to the development of regional integration organizations.

Article Y31

Articles 110 to 116, 130n, 130r(5), 223, 224,[18] 228 to 231 and 238 are repealed.

Article Y32

Title III of the Single Act is repealed.

---

[13] This may be expanded if the areas of Community competence are increased (health, culture, etc.) on condition obviously that the agreements in question are 'very important'; those not falling within this category will, irrespective of subject-matter, be covered by the procedure in paragraph 3.

[14] Agencies.

[15] Duopoly.

[16] Prior assent of Parliament.

[17] Text based on the second subparagraph of Article 228(1) and on Article 228(2).

[18] The question of 'serious internal disturbances' referred to in Article 224 is out of place in the Title on common foreign policy.

Explanatory memorandum

One of the foremost prerequisites for the European Union identified by the Commission in its opinion of 21 October 1990 was the emergence of a common foreign policy that would serve, through the osmosis between it and economic, social, and financial and monetary policy, to ensure unity and consistency in the Community's international action.

It concluded that such a policy would have to rest on a firm consensus among the Member States as to the extent of their common ambitions in broadening the international responsibilities of the Union, and should embrace their vital common interests and include security and defence.

The European Parliament, in its Resolution of 22 November 1990 on intergovernmental conferences in the framework of its strategy for European union, took a stand in favour of a common foreign and security policy.

On 14 and 15 December 1990 the European Council spoke of "the vocation of the Union to deal with aspects of foreign and security policy, in accordance with a sustained evolutive process and in a unitary manner . . ." It instructed the Intergovernmental Conference to "address the Union's objectives, the scope of its policies and the means of . . . ensuring their . . . implementation within an institutional framework".

The Commission, the European Council and the European Parliament agreed on the need for, *inter alia*, a single decision-making centre (namely the Council), the harmonization of preparatory work, a non-exclusive right of initiative for the Commission, procedures for informing and, as a rule, consulting Parliament — and obtaining its prior approval (in other words, assent) for the conclusion of major agreements — and procedures to ensure that the Union speaks with one voice in international organizations and *vis-à-vis* non-member countries.

Revision of the Treaty with a view to the creation of the European Union thus involves not only amendments to Articles 2 and 3 on the tasks and scope of the Treaty, the establishment of economic and monetary union, the extension of powers in specific areas and the strengthening of democratic legitimacy and the institutions' effectiveness, but also the incorporation of a new title on a common external policy.

A — The common external policy — general

The rules governing the common external policy comprise substantive provision in three broad areas:

common foreign and security policy (section B);

external economic policy (section C);

development cooperation (section D).

They also include procedural provisions for the conclusion by the Union of international agreements (section E) both in these areas and in any field where it already has powers internally (transport, environment and research, for instance), or might acquire them following revision of the Treaty, and within the limits of those powers. The new arrangements formally state that for every power conferred on the Union internally there is a corollary external power and that for any given area this power becomes exclusive once the Union exercises it internally. This constitutes the expression in the Treaty of the principle established by the Court in the AETR case, which is now an established part of the Community legal order.

The overall balance of the external policy provisions thus rests on an approach involving two indissociable elements.

In the areas of new powers (i.e. common foreign and security policy) specific decision-making procedures will apply, giving recognition to the European Council's fundamental role in setting the limits of the Union's powers and to the role of the Council (General Affairs) as the decision-maker on implementation.

Elsewhere, on the other hand, especially in the area of economic integration, the powers of the Union will be confirmed, resting on clear legal bases spelled out in the Treaty. The general use of qualified majority voting for decisions will also serve to secure efficiency and effectiveness.

B — Common foreign and security policy

1. Basic principles

The incorporation of rules on a common foreign and security policy serves a fundamental objective, namely to ensure unity and consistency in the Union's international action by giving it new powers in areas of foreign relations not covered by the present Treaty.

This common policy will centre on the idea of an evolutive process: it would be for the European Council to lay down and extend the Union's powers as the need arises. This

approach amounts to application of the principle of subsidiarity, leaving the Member States
with full power to act in areas where there is
felt to be no need for the Union to take responsibility, subject to intergovernmental cooperation on matters of general interest.

It is clear, then, that a common policy does
not mean a single policy. Where Member States
enjoy special relationships with certain parts of
the world or hold positions rooted in their
past history, the aim would be to coordinate
national action inside a common framework
rather than to replace it by a unitary approach.
Here, too, subsidiarity would have to play a
part. The essential point is that the Member
States fulfil their obligation to act.

The policy would be implemented using the
existing institutional framework so as to avoid
the emergence of dual structures in the Union
that is to take the place of the present Community, while making allowance for adjustments in the role of the institutions where
warranted by the subject areas in question
and the stage now reached in the process of
European integration.

Unlike European political cooperation, which
is no more than a form of intergovernmental
cooperation, the new common foreign and
security policy would involve the adoption and
implementation of decisions that are binding on
the Member States, taken unanimously or by
augmented qualified majority, as the case may
be, and with some scope for opting out.

2. Rules

Chapter 1 (Common foreign and security policy) encompasses general provisions covering
both foreign and security policy (Section 1) as
well as specific provisions relating to security,
including defence (Section 2).

(a) The implementation of foreign policy, the
objectives of which are defined in Article Y1,
rests on a distinction between:

(i) matters identified as being of "vital common
interest" by the European Council, where the
Council would decide what common action
should be pursued and how it should be implemented, acting by a qualified majority augmented by the requirement that at least eight
Member States must vote in favour; the European Council would lay down conditions under
which a Member State may, at its request,
be granted dispensation from the obligations
flowing from common action;

(ii) other matters, where joint action is a matter
for intergovernmental cooperation as at present, but with stricter provisions than Article
30 of the Single Act so that abstention by a
Member State would not prevent joint action
and consistency would be guaranteed between
national action and action by the Union.

A provision is also included whereby, in particularly serious or exceptional circumstances,
any Member State must refer a matter to the
Council to seek a swift decision on possible
common action.

(b) In matters of vital common interest, in other
words those falling within the scope of the common foreign and security policy, the right of
initiative for Council decisions would be shared
between the Member States and the Commission, while responsibility for preparatory
work and follow-up would rest on structured
cooperation, via Coreper, between the Council's General Secretariat and the Commission.
Democratic control would be ensured by the
close involvement of the European Parliament
in formulating and implementing the common
policy. Acts adopted would not be subject to
the jurisdiction of the Court of Justice.

In dealings with the outside world, especially
in international organizations, the Union would
be represented jointly by the Council Presidency and the Commission, the essential aim
being that the Union should speak with a single
voice.

(c) Common security policy, the objectives of
which are laid down in Article Y11, involves a
number of specific provisions (Section 2).

The scope of the policy would be defined in the
Treaty itself and would comprise:

(i) a guarantee of automatic assistance through
the incorporation of Article V of the Brussels Treaty establishing the Western European
Union, which would give substantive expression
to the will of the Member States to link their
destinies in the field of security and defence;
in the event of an armed attack on one of
the Member States of the Union, the others
would provide all the military and other aid
and assistance in their power;

(ii) a list of matters of vital common interest
in the field of security and defence, as defined
by the Rome European Council in December
1990, which the European Council could subsequently expand:

arms control and disarmament;

security matters covered by the CSCE and the UN;

cooperation on the production, export and non-proliferation of arms;

the Commission also proposes the establishment of an arms research and production policy, since the present Treaty makes no provision for this although aspects falling under the competition rules, for example, or the common commercial policy are already covered;

(iii) a mechanism for regular meetings of Foreign and Defence Ministers with a view to developing cooperation and making it possible to convene an immediate meeting if necessary, i.e. in the presence of a threat or danger to the Union.

In contrast to decision-making on matters falling under the common foreign policy, responsibility for defining the principles and deciding what action should be pursued under the common security policy would lie with the Council acting unanimously. However, the Council might be able to use other forms of decision-making for implementing certain measures.

A Member State may, if it so requests, be granted dispensation from some of the obligations flowing from such decision where there are compelling reasons — i.e. because of its own constitutional provisions or because of international commitments entered into previously; such dispensations would be re-examined periodically by the Council.

Some of these decisions, in particular those relating to defence cooperation, could be implemented, in compliance with NATO commitments, by means of specific arrangements with the WEU, which might act on behalf of the Union with a view to its gradual integration into the Union.

The introduction of a common security policy requires Articles 223 and 224 to be repealed, since their field of application now comes under the new policy.

The general provisions discussed in point (b) above would apply to both security and foreign policy, as would the possibility of dispensation for a Member State from certain obligations.

C — External economic policy

1. Chapter II on external economic policy, which will replace Articles 110 to 116 of the EEC Treaty, reiterates the Community's current objectives and powers under the common commercial policy, incorporates the external aspects of economic and monetary union, and maintains the applicability of the provisions specific to this area.

Setting as objectives the development of the economy and trade at world and European level means conferring a central role on the Union not only in promoting the prosperity of its Member States, businesses and citizens but also in contributing towards shaping the world economy and in generating momentum for the economic integration of Europe as a whole.

These objectives define the areas in which the Union can act explicitly and comprehensively enough to put an end to the constant controversy surrounding the scope of Article 113 and formally determine the position in accordance with the rulings of the Court of Justice. It should become possible for the Union, among other things, to work towards economic objectives such as reciprocal investment protection, access to production, and the reduction of disparities and imbalances between national legislation relating to capital.

The exclusive competence of the Union in such areas is confirmed, making the Commission, and the Commission alone, responsible for representing the Union on the external scene, notably in dealings with international organizations.

The Union should also be given power, though not necessarily sole power, to take the action needed to attain the objectives of external economic policy, in particular through bilateral and multilateral economic cooperation with non-developing countries: structural intervention (for example, in the G-24 context), participation in regional development banks (such as the EBRD), and debt relief.

2. The machinery for implementing this policy will be covered, in the case of measures other than international agreements,[19] by the general legislative pattern (law/regulation) to be incorporated in the new Treaty; with the law as the instrument providing the general

---

[19] The procedure governing the conclusion of international agreements is set out in Chapter IV of Title Y.

framework enabling the Commission to adopt the regulations and decisions needed for the day-to-day management of the common policy, the Commission must also be in a position to adopt urgent measures if necessary.

The specific possibility of authorizing Member States to act in this area, by *inter alia* concluding international agreements, should help reconcile exclusive Union competence — capable of encompassing national action if necessary — with the desire to leave a certain role for the Member States.

D — Development cooperation policy

1. Chapter III will at long last enshrine development cooperation policy in the Treaty; up until now, except in the case of certain forms of association, all action under this policy has had to be based on Article 235 given the absence of any other provision in the Treaty.

It will consequently be possible to state clearly the objectives of development cooperation, and in particular the importance and indeed the priority attached to the concept of poverty and the attention paid to the idea of balanced and durable development, taking account of environmental constraints. These are part of the general objectives of the common external policy, which explicitly refer to the promotion of democracy, the rule of law and respect for human rights.

Moreover, development cooperation policy can be made more consistent and effective, notably by stressing the fact that the powers of the Union complement rather than compete with those retained by the Member States in this area. For this reason both action specific to the Union and joint action by the Union and its Member States will be an integral part of common policy provided that the principle of such joint action has been approved by special procedure, with the Council acting unanimously after receiving the assent of Parliament.

2. The machinery for implementing the common policy will include all the instruments normally used in this area (financial and technical cooperation, humanitarian aid, commercial provisions, and so on) as well as action designed to encourage investment and debt relief measures for the developing countries.

In areas covered by the common policy the action to be undertaken by the Union and the joint action to be implemented by the Union and the Member States will be defined in general guidelines and multiannual programmes adopted in the form of laws enacted under the co-decision procedure by Parliament and the Council, acting on a proposal from the Commission.

The Union, which will have the sole power to conclude international agreements in areas where it acts either alone or jointly with the Member States, would also be so represented as to speak with a single voice in all international forums.

3. In areas not covered by Union action or by joint action by the Union and the Member States, provision will be made for close coordination, under the aegis of the Commission, in order to encourage potential complementarity, to avoid the risk of inconsistency and to demonstrate the specifically European nature of the action in question at international level.

E — General provisions

1. The general provisions in Chapter IV of the Treaty (common foreign policy) lay down rules applicable to international agreements concluded by the Union with non-member countries or international organizations.

2. As regards the common foreign and security policy, in accordance with the general scheme of things set out under A above, the Member State holding the Council Presidency and the Commission will have a joint right of initiative — the duopoly — at the various stages — requesting authorization to open negotiations, conducting negotiations and proposing conclusion of the agreement at the end of the negotiations.

Agreements would be concluded by the Council, acting by augmented qualified majority, or unanimously in security matters.

3. Outside the areas covered by the common foreign and security policy, in other words in external economic relations, development cooperation and all other areas where the Treaty confers powers on the Union, the principle of the single procedure would be confirmed and the broad outlines of the current Treaty would be preserved. Thus there would no longer be any need for specific provisions governing the conclusion of international agreements in those parts of the Treaty dealing with specific policies.

The Commission would have a monopoly of the right of initiative regarding the opening and conduct of negotiations and the conclusion of the agreement (after consulting a committee composed of representatives of the Member States); as a rule the Council would conclude the agreement by qualified majority after consulting the European Parliament.

However, the conclusion of important agreements, defined as such exhaustively by the Treaty itself, would require the assent of Parliament, currently required only for association agreements (Article 238 EEC).[20]

Lastly, in order to put an end to a situation which provokes controversy and hampers decision-making, it would be provided that the Commission could conclude certain agreements specified in the Treaty (adjustments to existing agreements) or covered by a Council decision empowering it to do so;[21] it would also be provided that the Commission would administer agreements.

4. A clear indication is also given that where accession to a multilateral convention has a financial impact, the Union will sign the convention on an equal footing with the signatory States.

F — Overall consistency

1. The fundamental question of ensuring consistency between the Union's common foreign and security policy and its other external policies is dealt with in a general fashion by a clause imposing an obligation to ensure such consistency and providing for a decision to be taken, on the initiative of the Commission or of a Member State, by the Council acting by the same procedure as applies generally to foreign policy questions.

The same procedure will be used to avert the risk of inconsistency between common foreign and security policy and national foreign policies, in addition to the rules governing the coordination of national policies.

There are also specific provisions relating to external economic relations and development policy to ensure that the Member States take a coordinated line on the international scene in matters which are not directly within the Union powers.

2. Provision is made for the case of international agreements with a content covered partly by foreign policy and partly by other external policies.

The procedure is a combination of those applicable to the two categories. Among other things, there is a diluted form of the duopoly of Commission and Council Presidency in the conduct of negotiations.

These agreements, which provide a general framework for relations with non-member countries in all their aspects, are of such a nature that the assent of Parliament should be required in the same way as for important agreements outside the foreign policy context.

The Commission would administer agreements in all areas other than foreign policy.

G — Conclusion

The changes that would flow from the guidelines set out above would make it possible to remedy the current difficult situation:

(i) first, the original Treaty was sketchy in its treatment of the external aspect of Community activities (being confined to commercial policy and association agreements); the gaps have had to be filled in by the Court of Justice and controversy and disagreement have always been the order of the day;

(ii) secondly, the Single Act went only part of the way towards solving this by adding specific references to external relations in a few areas (environment, research) while mixing up the two political contexts of intergovernmental political cooperation and decisions by the Community institutions.

---

[20] Most agreements currently concluded under Article 113, for example, would not be within this category, but association agreements under Article 238 and general agreements resulting from GATT rounds would inevitably be within it.

[21] The Commission's powers under Article 229 EEC are unchanged.

B. European Commission proposal on democratic legitimacy:[22] hierarchy of norms, executive powers, legislative procedure (co-decision)

Draft text

Hierarchy of norms — Executive powers

Deletion of Article 145, third indent.[23]

Deletion of Article 149.[24]

Article 155

In order to ensure the proper functioning and development of the union, the Commission shall:

(i) ensure that the provisions of this Treaty and the measures taken by the institutions pursuant thereto are applied;

(ii) formulate recommendations or deliver opinions on matters dealt with in this Treaty, if it expressly so provides or if the Commission considers it necessary;

(iii) have its own power of decision and participate in the shaping of measures taken by the Council and by the European Parliament in the manner provided for in this Treaty;

(iv) adopt, in the manner provided for in Article 189b, the regulations and take the decisions necessary to implement laws, without prejudice to the provisions of Article 189b(1) conferring a power of substitution on the European Parliament and the Council. It shall also adopt the administrative provisions necessary to implement the regulations.

Article 189

In order to carry out their task the institutions of the Union shall, in accordance with the provisions of this Treaty, adopt laws and regulations, take decisions, make recommendations or deliver opinions.

A law shall have general application. It shall be binding in its entirety; any provisions which do not call for implementing measures shall be directly applicable in all Member States.

Action to be taken to apply the provisions of this Treaty shall be defined by laws. Laws shall determine the fundamental principles, general guidelines and basic elements of the measures to be taken for their implementation.

Laws shall determine *inter alia* the rights and obligations of individuals and firms and the nature of the guarantees they should enjoy in every Member State. Implementation may be entrusted in whole or in part to the Member States, acting in accordance with their own constitutional requirements.

A regulation shall have general application. It shall be binding in its entirety and directly applicable in all Member States.

A decision shall be binding in its entirety upon those to whom it is addressed.

Recommendations and opinions shall have no binding force.

Article 189a (new)

(Legislative (co-decision) procedure as set out hereafter).

Article 189b (new)

1. Where a regulation implements a law, a power of substitution shall be reserved to the European Parliament and the Council in all cases where no provision is made for recourse to one of the procedures referred to in paragraph 2.

The following procedure shall apply:

(i) the Commission shall adopt the regulation in question and forward it to the European Parliament and the Council;

(ii) the Commission regulation shall enter into force on expiry of a period of two months reckoned from the date of transmission unless the European Parliament, by a majority of its members, or the Council, acting by a qualified majority, rejects the measure within that period;

(iii) in that event the Commission may either adopt a new regulation, which shall be subject to the substitution procedure, or submit a proposal for a regulation; in the latter case the procedure laid down in Article 189a shall apply.

2. A law may provide that, in the exercise of the powers referred to in the fourth indent of

---

[22] Parliamentary assent to international agreements is covered in the Chapter on common external policy.

[23] The delegation of executive powers to the Commission is determined in a general fashion; exceptions cannot be made to it by a law.

[24] Since the co-decision procedure takes over from the cooperation procedure this no longer appears in Article 149 (included in a second section, entitled "The Council" in Chapter 1 "The institutions") but in Chapter 2 "Provisions common to several institutions" of Title 1 of Part Five of the Treaty, Article 189a.

Article 155, the Commission shall be assisted by an advisory committee composed of representatives of the Member States, whose role shall be to deliver an opinion on the draft of the measures to be taken; where the measure to be taken is a regulation, a law may provide that the Commission shall be assisted by a management committee and that in the event of the Committee delivering a negative opinion by the majority provided for in the first indent of the second subparagraph of Article 148(2), the Council, acting by a qualified majority, may take a different decision within a given period.

For the record

NB: Consequential amendments (addition of "laws" and deletion of "directives") must be made to Articles 190 and 191.

Legislative procedure (Co-decision)

Article 189a

Where a law is enacted in pursuance of this Treaty, the following procedure shall apply:

1. (a) The Council, acting by a qualified majority under the conditions set out in paragraph 5, on a proposal from the Commission and after obtaining the opinion of the European Parliament, shall adopt a common position; the European Parliament shall have a period of four months from transmission of the proposals to give its opinion; if the European Parliament does not react within this period, it shall be deemed to have given a favourable opinion.

(b) If its common position is compatible with the European Parliament's opinion, the Council shall definitively enact the law. If not, the Council's common position shall be transmitted to the European Parliament within a period of four months following delivery of the European Parliament's opinion or, in the absence of an opinion, expiry of the period referred to in point (a). The Council and the Commission shall inform the European Parliament fully of the reasons which led the Council to adopt its common position and also of the Commission's position.

(c) If the Council fails to adopt a common position within the time allowed and if the European Parliament fails to deliver an express opinion, the procedure shall be closed.

If the Council fails to adopt a common position within the time allowed although the Euro-pean Parliament has delivered an express opinion, the procedure laid down in paragraph 2 shall apply.

2. Within one month of transmission as provided for in paragraph 1(b), the proposal shall be subject to a conciliation procedure within a committee composed of representatives of the European Parliament, the Council and the Commission.

If the conciliation procedure leads to agreement within two months on the drafting of a joint text, this text shall be deemed to be approved on expiry of a period of one month reckoned from the declaration that agreement has been reached unless the European Parliament, acting by an absolute majority of its members, or the Council, acting by a qualified majority, rejects it within that period.

3. If the conciliation procedure does not lead to agreement within a period of two months, the Commission shall re-examine its proposal within one month. The re-examined proposal shall be transmitted to the European Parliament, except where it incorporates Parliament's amendments, and to the Council.

If the European Parliament rejects a re-examined proposal within a period of two months by an absolute majority of its members, the procedure shall be closed.

If the European Parliament approves the re-examined proposal or fails to react within the time allowed, or if there is no need to refer it to the European Parliament pursuant to the first subparagraph, the Council may adopt the re-examined proposal by a qualified majority, amend it unanimously or reject it by a simple majority. If the Council has not acted on expiry of a period of two months reckoned from transmission of the European Parliament's approval or of the re-examined proposal incorporating the European Parliament's amendments, the re-examined proposal as approved by the European Parliament shall be deemed adopted. The declaration to that effect shall be made by the President of the European Parliament.

Where the Council amends the re-examined proposal, it shall be deemed adopted if, within a period of one month from transmission of the amended proposal to the European Parliament, the European Parliament has not rejected it by an absolute majority of its members. The declaration to that effect shall be made by the President of the Council.

4.[25] Unanimity shall be required for the Council to amend a proposal when adopting a common position or definitively enacting a law.

As long as a law has not been enacted, the Commission may alter its proposal at any time during the procedures provided for in paragraphs 1 to 3.

5. The periods referred to in this Article may be reduced by common accord between the European Parliament, the Council and the Commission. They shall be reduced by half where the European Parliament or the Council exercise their power of substitution in respect of an act adopted by the Commission, pursuant to Article 189b(1).

C. European Commission proposal on Union citizenship

Draft text

TITLE 0

Union citizenship

Article X1

1. Every person holding the nationality of a Member State[26] shall be a citizen of the Union.

2. Union citizens shall enjoy the rights conferred by this Treaty and be subject to the obligations imposed by it, which shall supplement the rights and obligations attaching to their status as citizens of a Member State.

Article X2

Every Union citizen shall be entitled to invoke the rights guaranteed by the European Convention for the Protection of Human Rights and Fundamental Freedoms, which the Union accepts.

Article X3

In the application of this Treaty, any discrimination on the basis of nationality, whether by a public authority or a private person, shall be prohibited. The Union and the Member States shall enforce this prohibition.

Article X4

1. Every Union citizen shall have the right to move and reside freely within Union territory, without limit as to duration, whether or not he pursues a gainful occupation.

2. Every Union citizen shall have the obligation to comply with the legislation of the Member State in which he resides.

He may not exercise his right to move and reside freely as a means of evading obligations incumbent upon him in relation to his State of origin or any other Member State.

Article X5

Every Union citizen shall have the right to be a member of a political association or group and shall have the right to vote and stand as a candidate at municipal and European elections held in the place in which he has habitually resided for at least [. . .] years(s) without prejudice to the option of exercising those rights, if he so wishes, in the Member State of which he is a national, providing he enjoys them under national law.

Article X6

Every Union citizen shall have the right to cultural expression and the obligation to respect cultural expression by others.

Article X7

Every Union citizen shall have the right to enjoy a healthy environment and the obligation to contribute to protecting it. To this end, he shall have the right to information and the right to consultation where appropriate.

Article X8

Every Union citizen shall, in the territory of a non-member country, be entitled to Union protection and to the protection of any Member State, on the same conditions as its nationals.

Article X9

Each Member State shall establish at least one national authority, possibly in the form of an office of ombudsman to which Union citizens may have recourse in defending the

---

[25] This paragraph takes over the substance of paragraphs 1 and 3 of Article 149, which is replaced in its entirety by the new Article 189a.

[26] Each Member State should make a declaration defining its concept of nationality.

rights conferred upon them by this Treaty, to assist them in dealings with the administrative authorities of the Union and the Member States and to defend those rights before courts and tribunals on behalf of those upon whom they are conferred.

These authorities shall also be responsible for giving Union citizens full and clear information on their rights and on the means available for the purpose of defending them.

Article X10

Measures to secure compliance with the prohibition laid down in Article X3, to facilitate the exercise of the rights conferred by Articles X4 and X8, to determine the conditions in which the rights conferred by Article X5 are to be exercised and to give effect to Articles X7 and X9, shall be adopted [. . .], acting on a proposal from the Commission after obtaining the opinion of the Economic and Social Committee.

Article X11

The objective of the Union shall be to ensure, by gradual stages, that acts adopted for the purpose of applying this Treaty:

(i) guarantee every Union citizen's right to equal treatment and equal opportunities and the enjoyment of social rights;

(ii) reflect every Union citizen's obligation to display solidarity with other Union citizens and with nationals of non-member countries resident in the Union; this obligation entails respect for each person's dignity and the rejection of any form of social marginalization;

(iii) guarantee every Union citizen's right to protection of his health and his obligation to safeguard the health of others, especially in his working environment.

Article X12

The Council, acting unanimously on a proposal from the Commission after receiving the assent of the European Parliament, may add rights to those conferred by this Title.

Explanatory memorandum

1.1. In its opinion of 21 October 1990 the Commission endorsed the proposal put forward by the Spanish Prime Minister, Mr González, for the introduction of the concept of European citizenship, which "would take shape gradually, without encroaching in any way on national citizenship, which it would supplement rather than replace". The object was that this "would encourage a feeling of involvement in European integration".

The Commission was also in favour of making a specific reference to the Convention for the Protection of Human Rights and Fundamental Freedoms and of writing into the Treaty rights linked specifically to the status of European citizens, including freedom of movement, freedom of residence, voting rights, and civic, economic and social rights and obligations to be decided at a later stage.

1.2. In its resolution of 22 November 1990 on the Intergovernmental Conferences, Parliament called for the inclusion in the new Treaty of a declaration of fundamental rights and freedoms designed for the protection of every individual who is subject to Community law. To some extent the catalogue of rights covered in the declaration is much the same as those dealt with in the European Convention for the Protection of Human Rights and Fundamental Freedoms and in the constitutions of the Member States. However, it also incorporates some rights specific to Union citizens, such as the right to move and reside freely within Union territory. Furthermore, it emphasizes the emergence of rights in connection with the exercise of certain Community powers: the promotion of health and safety at the workplace, for instance, or the protection and improvement of the environment.

2. The European Council meeting in Rome on 14 and 15 December 1990 also expressed support for the concept of European citizenship and made a specific reference to civic rights, social and economic rights based on the principle of equal treatment and opportunity for all Community citizens, and the protection of Community citizens outside the Community's borders. It also envisaged the possibility of setting up some form of ombudsman-type machinery for the defence of citizens' rights.

3.1. The attached draft Treaty Articles incorporate the ideas set out at 1 and 2 above.

3.2. The subject-matter involved is good reason for inserting the Articles on citizens' rights and obligations early on in the Treaty, and in any event before the Titles devoted to the four freedoms.

It is therefore proposed that the attached Articles be included as Title I of Part Two ("Foundations of the Union"), rather than in the preamble or in the introductory Articles setting out the objectives of the Union, thereby stressing that these are implementing measures and not just declaratory clauses.

3.3. Nevertheless, a distinction is made in those provisions between:

(i) rights which citizens derive directly from the Treaty (such as non-discrimination on grounds of nationality or freedom of movement), where it is simply a question of guaranteeing or facilitating the exercise of such rights, as the case may be, on the basis of the Court's case-law, and, possibly, by improving existing legal provisions;

(ii) rights which require to be put into effect by legislation, together with the necessary detailed rules and conditions (for example, the right to vote, which has already been the subject of a Commission proposal, or rights related to the environment, taken from existing or proposed texts);

(iii) the laying down of objectives for the granting of rights in the future and for defining obligations, especially in the social field.

4.1. In general terms, the concept of Union citizenship is based on two principles:

(i) it is a component factor in the move to strengthen democratic legitimacy in the Community, both supplementing and transcending national citizenship;

(ii) it reflects the aims of the Union, involving as it does an indivisible body of rights and obligations stemming from the gradual and coherent development of the Union's political, economic and social dimension.

4.2. The proposal includes:

(a) a definition of the concept of citizenship of the Union (Article X1);

(b) a reference, in the context of the protection of fundamental rights, to the European Convention on Human Rights, to which the Commission has now proposed the Community should accede (Article X2);

(c) a statement of the general principle prohibiting discrimination on the grounds of nationality, modelled on Article 7 (deleted) but extended to cover private persons (Article X3);[27]

(d) a list and definition of the rights and corresponding obligations of Union citizens in terms of:

(i) civic rights and obligations: freedom of movement and residence for all citizens, whether or not they pursue a gainful occupation, freedom of political association, right to vote and right to stand for election (Articles X4 and X5), along the lines of the Commission's proposal of June 1982;[28]

(ii) wider social rights and obligations: in the social field proper, as defined in the social provisions of the Treaty in the light of the Community Charter of the Fundamental Social Rights of Workers (Article X11), as well as in the fields of culture (Article X6) and the environment (Article X7); these rights and obligations are based in particular on the principles of equal treatment and opportunity, social solidarity and respect for the dignity and diversity of all individuals;

(e) the principle of equal protection for Union citizens in non-member countries (Article X8).

4.3. This list of rights and obligations is accompanied by a number of implementing provisions.

Firstly, an ombudsman-type function is created in the Member States, with the task of advising citizens of their rights and the courses of action open to them and of promoting the defence of those rights in dealings with the authorities and the courts (Article X9).

Secondly, provision is made for the adoption of measures to facilitate or, as appropriate, give effect to the rights and obligations of citizens (Article X10). This would cover measures designed solely to guarantee or facilitate the exercise of rights directly conferred by the Treaty (non-discrimination on the grounds of nationality or freedom of movement, for instance) or measures laying down detailed arrangements for giving effect to rights such as the right to vote and stand for election, possibly by gradual stages (Article X10). Obviously this in no way precludes the possibility of specific provisions in the Treaty laying down and guaranteeing the exercise of particular rights, as proposed in the case of social rights (Article X11).

Lastly, any subsequent extension of the rights of citizens of the Union would involve exacting procedural requirements similar or identical to those provided for in the new Article 235.

---

[27] This does not affect the exception provided for in Article 48(4), as interpreted by the Court, regarding posts involving the exercise of public authority.
[28] Detailed arrangements for the exercise of these rights will have to be laid down in an implementing regulation.

D. *European Commission proposal on the social dimension and the development of human resources*

Draft text

TITLE III

The social dimension and the development of human resources

Chapter 1

Social provisions

The provisions of Chapter 1 of Title III of Part Three of the Treaty are replaced by the following Articles.

Article 117

The Union's objectives shall be to improve living and working conditions, to guarantee fair social protection, to encourage the dialogue between management and labour, to develop human resources and to combat social marginalization.

These objectives shall be pursued through the completion of the internal market and economic and monetary union. They shall also be implemented through structural policies, the adoption of common rules and through agreements concluded between management and labour.

In pursuing these objectives, the Union shall have regard to the competitiveness of companies and the diversity of national practices, especially in the area of contractual relations.

Article 118

1. In order to attain the objectives set out in Article 117, the Union shall complement and support the action of the Member States in the following areas:

(i) the working environment and protection of the health and safety of workers;

(ii) living and working conditions, so as to ensure the protection of basic rights of workers;

(iii) basic and advanced vocational training;

(iv) levels of skills;

(v) information for and consultation and participation of workers;

(vi) the functioning of the labour market, in so far as this is made possible by economic convergence and the approximation of social practices in the Member States.

2. To this end the Council and the European Parliament, acting on a proposal from the Commission in accordance with the co-decision procedure and after consulting the Economic and Social Committee, shall adopt, by means of laws, minimum requirements applicable in each Member State.

3. Before presenting proposals in accordance with paragraph 2, the Commission shall consult . . . on the possibility of attaining the objectives set out in paragraph 1 through framework agreements in accordance with Article 118b. Where the Commission establishes that a framework agreement is possible, it shall take the initiative of initiating the procedure provided for in Article 118b.[29]

If such an agreement cannot be reached within a reasonable time, the procedure provided for in paragraph 2 shall apply.

4. Where a law is not to be implemented by the Member States, the Commission shall be assisted by a . . .[30] acting as a management committee within the meaning of Article 189b(2) in respect of such implementing regulations as it is to adopt.

A law may, however, in the first instance, leave the responsibility for implementation of all or some of its provisions to management and labour.

5. Provisions adopted pursuant to this Article shall not prevent any Member State from maintaining or introducing more stringent protective measures compatible with this Treaty.

6. This Article shall not apply to measures regarding the harmonization of social security systems, the right of association or the conditions governing the right to strike, nor to provisions regarding access to employment for nationals of non-member countries.

Measures in these areas shall be adopted in

---

[29] The Commission may adjust the proposed provisions of Articles 118(3) and 118b(2) in the light of:
(i) the outcome of discussions in the *ad hoc* Group on Social Dialogue;
(ii) the involvement in the procedure of a consultative body, the nature of which remains to be determined.
[30] A consultative organ of a type to be determined.

accordance with the procedure provided for in Article 235.

Article 118b[31]

1. The Commission shall endeavour to develop the dialogue between management and labour at European level which could, if the two sides consider it desirable, lead to relations based on agreements, including [framework] agreements applying throughout a trade or industry at European level.

2. At the request of the parties concerned, [framework] agreements may be the subject of a Commission recommendation or of a decision taken by the Council, acting by a qualified majority on a proposal from the Commission after consulting the European Parliament and the Economic and Social Committee, and addressed to the Member States so as to make them mandatory for the duration of their validity.

Article 119

1. Each Member State shall ensure equality of treatment between men and women at work. In particular, it shall ensure the application of the principle that men and women should receive equal pay for equal work and enjoy equal opportunities on the labour market.

2. For the purpose of this Article, "pay" means the ordinary basic or minimum wage and any other consideration, whether in cash or in kind, which the worker receives, directly or indirectly, in respect of his employment from his employer.

Equal pay without discrimination based on sex means:

(a) that pay for the same work at piece rates shall be calculated on the basis of the same unit of measurement,

(b) that pay for work at time rates shall be the same for the same job.

3. Measures to facilitate the implementation of the principles laid down in paragraph 1 shall be taken in the form of laws adopted in accordance with the co-decision procedure by the Council and the European Parliament, acting on a proposal from the Commission after consulting the Economic and Social Committee.

Article 120

A law adopted in accordance with the co-decision procedure by the Council and the European Parliament, acting on a proposal from the Commission after consulting the Economic and Social Committee, shall define the conditions in which actions to promote the attainment of the objectives set out in Article 117, (especially) through exchanges of information and experience, may be launched in the framework of multiannual programmes.

Article 121

The Commission shall each year make a report on the evolution of the social situation in the Union. It shall transmit this report to the European Parliament, the Council and the Economic and Social Committee.

The European Parliament may invite the Commission to draw up reports on specific problems concerning the social situation.

Explanatory memorandum

The objectives of social policy, which is inseparable from economic policy, are to ensure a high level of employment, to improve living and working conditions with a view to harmonizing them while maintaining the improvement, to develop human resources, to enhance solidarity and to combat all forms of social marginalization. These objectives are sacrosanct.

Object and methods of social regulation: changes and permanent features

However, in recent years the circumstances in which social policy is conducted have changed considerably and deep-set trends, common to all the Member States, have become apparent. In all likelihood, these trends will continue over the next few decades.

(a) In broad terms, the trends can be described as follows:

(i) The internationalization of economies, in some cases even their globalization, has intensified. In the Community, the removal of internal frontiers will lead to substantial transnational integration of firms and increased workforce mobility. Indeed, this is already well under way.

---

[31] The Commission may adjust the proposed provisions of Articles 118(3) and 118b(2) in the light of:
(i) the outcome of discussions in the *ad hoc* Group on Social Dialogue;
(ii) the involvement in the procedure of a consultative body, the nature of which remains to be determined.

(ii) In this context, improvement of the competitiveness of firms by keeping costs under control and seeking greater flexibility in working conditions and the organization of work is now a generally recognized imperative. This is to be perceived as the result of the acceptance of economic constraints by all those involved. The introduction of new technologies is of major significance here.

(iii) The quest for competitiveness is being pursued along specifically national lines. But it entails major changes in all the Member States, with considerable qualitative and quantitative effects on employment and labour relations.

Indeed, all the principal variables in the world of employment have altered as a result: the proportion of the labour force accounted for by the tertiary sector and by women has increased; forms of employment and methods of remuneration have become more diverse; the organization of work and working time has become more flexible; recognition has been given to the fundamental role of training, both initial and continuing; the mix of qualifications required is changing; geographical and occupational mobility is on the increase, and so on.

(iv) At the same time, the aspirations of workers — in fact, of the public at large — have also altered and diversified. In this way, the needs of firms and the aspirations of individuals have found new areas of convergence (e.g. new forms of employment).

(b) A basic feature of European patterns of change and of Europe's social model is that, in most cases, these developments have been kept under control and in balance by bargaining between the two sides of industry. Of course, this has caused adjustments to be made in the way in which developments are handled.

The main change has been a clear move to decentralize the handling of problems and in particular a shift towards negotiation at firm level. In some cases, direct relations (dialogue, participation) have been established between employers and workers.

In practice, decentralization takes the form of a new interplay between levels of negotiation: a wider range of issues is dealt with at firm level, though the higher levels are not abandoned. The role of the latter is developing: for example, framework or coordination agreements, which are essential for the development and harmonious application of company agreements, are tending to be worked out at interoccupational or industry level (e.g. the May 1990 agreement on working time in the German metal-working industry or the Italian labour costs agreement of January 1990).

At the same time, in several Member States central government has intervened, using a variety of methods, to change the rules and mechanisms of industrial relations (in France the Auroux Act of 1982; in Spain the Representation of Trade Unions and Employers Act of 1984; in the United Kingdom the 1984 Trade Union Act) or to regulate wage bargaining (indexation relaxed or dropped altogether in Belgium, Denmark, France, Italy and the Netherlands).

(c) Despite these developments and regardless of all the specifically national considerations, the fact remains that the autonomy of the two sides of industry — an autonomy conceded by the public authorities — has been maintained: negotiation at different levels has remained a basic component of regulation in all the Member States, which is something specific to the industrial relations field. The reasons why this is still the case are as much political as social or economic. As one of the recitals to the Charter states, "the social consensus contributes to the strengthening of the competitiveness of undertakings, of the economy as a whole and to the creation of employment; . . . in this respect it is an essential condition for ensuring sustained economic development".

Furthermore, in the attempt to keep change under control and to make structures and human resources more adaptable, the field covered by industrial agreements has been extended — to take in matters which had previously been dealt with separately (e.g. negotiations on flexibility) and to go beyond the limited context of the firm to encompass certain fundamental social values: for instance, anticipating social problems (particularly connected with employment) caused by decisions to invest or disinvest; the environment; lifestyles and family life; equal opportunities; solidarity and measures to combat social deprivation.

Over and above national initiatives and practices, the Community most certainly has a role to play in serving the purposes of social policy and in regulating certain changes.

But it has to adjust to developments, to changed circumstances, both in its own legislation and in encouraging regulation based on agreement. In other words, the Community's social policy has to provide the appropriate framework for the shared and balanced control of change while also helping to consolidate and improve the European social model.

The grounds for revision

With this in view, there are a number of arguments which plead in favour of modifying and extending the scope of the Community's social policy.

(a) First, there is the very nature of the process of European integration: the establishment of a single economic and social area in which economic and social advances are made in step. We need to keep up the momentum provided by the European Councils of Hanover (June 1988) and Madrid (June 1989: "the same importance must be given to social aspects as to economic aspects and they should consequently be developed in a balanced fashion").

(b) The Community Charter of the Fundamental Social Rights of Workers adopted by the Strasbourg European Council reflects the urge to establish and build upon a platform of fundamental rights shared by all the Member States. This solemn declaration voices two ambitions:

(i) it is a proclamation of European identity, reaffirming the plan to ensure the harmonious development of the Community on the basis of social progress, underlining the imperative need for increased solidarity and a refusal to allow changes to result in more and more people with outdated skills;

(ii) it is an expression of the determination to combat social dumping.

The enforcement of these rights — through the introduction of minimum provisions, for instance — is partly a matter for the Community, as far as its powers extend. The implementation of the social action programme to give effect to the Charter has shown how inconsistent and inappropriate (e.g. legal basis for the proposal for a Directive on non-standard forms of employment), how anachronistic (Articles 120 and 122) or how incomplete (Article 119) the Treaty is.

(c) Completion of the internal market and economic integration have clearly shown the need (given the transnational nature of the problems involved) for Community action in areas which have hitherto not been very sensitive or whose importance has been disputed, such as:

(i) the protection of workers' rights in the case of transfrontier operations (company mergers, takeover bids, bankruptcies, collective redundancies);

(ii) information/consultation, or even participation (industrial democracy and/or financial participation) of employees in transnational businesses;

(iii) new obstacles to mobility within the Community (supplementary pensions, etc.).

(d) In addition, steps must be taken to ensure that the economy of the internal market develops without any distortion of competition (examples of sensitive variables: health and safety, non-standard forms of employment, social security, equal treatment), and this calls for greater vigilance.

(e) More generally, at microeconomic level, consideration for the social dimension is increasingly becoming an integral part of management, and this contributes to added value and to competitiveness.

(f) The extension and/or redefinition of the Community's powers in the social field is/are not incompatible with the current trends towards decentralization of collective bargaining to be seen in the Member States (see above). The need to determine a Community framework for tackling the problems we have referred to remains.

Consequently, the wide gap between the powers available under the current legal bases and the ambitions set out in the Charter and the new constraints arising from completion of the internal market warrant a revision of the social provisions of the Treaty.

Assigning new powers to the Community in the social field is hardly an adventurous undertaking. Indeed it should be stressed that in those very fields in which new powers have been accorded by the Single Act, regulation at Community level has worked satisfactorily, has operated largely by consensus and has proceeded at a steady rate (e.g. application of Article 118a, health and safety for workers).

It is true, none the less, that the method and principles underlying any modification and extension of the Community's powers have to be clearly defined.

Principles and method

(a) There are three principles which should underpin the new Community social framework:

(i) Subsidiarity, with due regard for the specific nature of social matters.

First of all, the application of this principle lies not so much in choosing between social issues, distinguishing those for which Community jurisdiction is recognized, as in suggesting what, in the light of the needs identified and the potential value added by Community action, is the most appropriate in each case — harmonization, coordination, convergence, cooperation, etc.

It is true that the Community has means and resources other than regulation for pursuing social policy objectives. For example, completion of the internal market, backed up by the structural policies, is "the most effective means of creating employment and ensuring maximum well-being" (Charter).

Secondly, it has to be borne in mind that social issues are resolved not only by means of legislation but also on the basis of collective bargaining — through the autonomy of the two sides of industry, recognized by the public authorities. In social matters, then, there is a "dual subsidiarity", requiring a choice to be made:

between Community action and national (or infranational) action; and

between legislation and collective bargaining.

At Community level, then, the two sides of industry must be given the widest possible room for manoeuvre and precedence must be given to settlement by collective agreement.

(ii) Respect for the diversity of national systems, cultures and practices, provided this is constructive, i.e. consistent with the requirements of completing the single market and with the fundamental rights enshrined in the Charter. Constructive diversity is something to be exploited, making the various national models better known, tracing similarities between them and in some cases drawing inspiration from them.

(iii) Care to refrain from impairing the competitiveness for firms and to safeguard flexibility by reconciling economic and social considerations: whatever is done, there is a balance to be sought and found.

If then, it is to conform as closely as possible to the new realities which condition the approach to social matters, the Community will have to show great discernment in selecting from the whole range of functions and instruments available to it, whether they be mandatory or act as incentives, by choosing between Community level and national level on the one hand and between legislation and collective agreement on the other.

(b) The involvement of the two sides of industry in Community social regulation could take two forms:

one was already proposed by the Commission in 1990 in connection with the implementation of the action programme — for example, with the proposal for a Directive on non-standard forms of employment (based on Article 100a); this would allow Member States to entrust the task of achieving the objectives of a binding instrument adopted by the Council primarily to the two sides of industry;

the other would stipulate that certain objectives of the Treaty might be attained via framework agreements drawn up directly at European level.

(c) Lastly, qualified majority voting should be extended to certain fields, notably some of those covered by the Charter, with the proviso that other particularly sensitive areas — with too diverse an organization and with too varied national practices — will still be subject to unanimous voting (harmonization of social security systems, access to employment for nationals of non-member countries).

There are two main, connected reasons which militate in favour of qualified majority voting:

(i) a concern for effectiveness — to ensure that the economic and the social actually do move ahead in step;

(ii) the desire to secure consistency and balance within the Treaty itself by ensuring that a fundamental area such as the social field is not treated any differently from other fields.

The new articles

Modernizing the legal framework along the lines sketched out above entails substantial amendment of the Treaty Articles that already exist, the incorporation of new Articles and the removal of obsolete or inadequate Articles. This can be done within the basic structure of the existing Chapter, which will help to make matters clearer.

Inspiration has been drawn from three sources:

(i) certain provisions of the Community Charter of the Fundamental Social Rights of Workers;

(ii) the Commission opinion on Political union;

(iii) the results of the social dialogue, chiefly in the form of joint opinions on the introduction of new technology, the organization of work and the adaptability of the labour market.

The following basic structure is therefore proposed:

(a) The objectives set out in Article 117 would be updated in conformity with the far-reaching transformation of the social field

(b) A new version of Article 118 would expand the potential offered by the existing Article 118a, in accordance with the guidelines in the Commission opinion of 21 October 1990; this could provide a basis for most of the provisions needed to implement the Charter and control the process of economic and social change.[32]

This new legal basis has been drafted in such a way as to fully respect subsidiarity in relation to the Member States and the two sides of industry, and is confined to those areas which really are suitable for the co-decision procedure.

(c) Additional text in Article 118b provides a framework for collective bargaining at European level and for the approval of the resultant agreements, thus providing legal backing for the autonomy enjoyed by the two sides of industry in this respect.[32]

It is provided that, before submitting its proposals, the Commission would consult a consultative body, whose nature remains to be determined, on the prospect of attaining the objectives by means of a framework agreement between management and labour as provided in the new Article.

The Union would act by means of legislation only if it were not found possible to achieve results through collective bargaining.

(d) Article 119 is rewritten for two purposes:

to establish a legal basis for legislation to guarantee equal treatment for women and men;

to extend its scope to cover all aspects of equal opportunities on the labour market.

The new Article is largely inspired by the old one so as to preserve the practical benefits of the extensive body of Court of Justice case-law.

(e) A new Article 120 would provide a foundation and a framework for operational activities (multiannual programmes) as an alternative or a supplement to legislative measures.

(f) The existing Article 122 becomes Article 121. Its aim is to ensure broader dissemination of information on the social situation.

(g) The existing Articles 118, 120 and 121 would be repealed since they would have no purpose in the new context.

The Commission reserves the right to adjust the proposed provisions of Articles 118(3) and 118b(2) in the light of:

(i) the outcome of discussions in the *ad hoc* Group on Social Dialogue;

(ii) the involvement in the procedure of a consultative body, the nature of which remains to be determined.

E. Franco-German Proposals on Security Policy, 4 February 1991

Security policy cooperation in the framework of the common foreign and security policy of political Union

1. General aims and concepts

(a) Political Union and its Member States are to develop a Common Foreign and Security Policy (CFSP). The mission of the CFSP will be to extend to all areas of external relations.

(b) CFSP will have as its objective the defence of the fundamental interests and common values of political Union in its external relations. It should in particular reinforce the security of Member States, contribute to maintaining peace and international stability, develop friendly relations with other countries, and promote democracy, primacy of law and human rights as well as the economic development of all nations.

---

[32] The wording of this Article may have to be changed in the light of the outcome of discussions in the *ad hoc* Group on Social Dialogue.

(c) A common security policy implies the following:

(i) Within the framework of CFSP, political Union will implement a common security policy in the aim of setting up a common European defence system in due course without which the construction of European Union would remain incomplete.

(ii) This implies suppression of the restrictive indication "political and economic aspects of security" under Article 30, paragraph 6 (a) of the Single European Act.

(iii) The validity of the commitments that the partners undertake in the framework of the Atlantic Alliance and the objectives connected to them will not be questioned.

(iv) The Atlantic Alliance, and notably a permanent US military presence in Europe, remains indispensable for European security and stability.

(v) The possibilities given by the Western European Union should be put to use. WEU would become the cooperation channel between Political Union and NATO with a view to ensuring mutual reinforcement of European or trans-Atlantic security structures. As common European security policy develops, the formal link established between the WEU Treaty and the Alliance would be adapted in accordance.

(vi) WEU acquisitions should be preserved: WEU is founded on a treaty which includes a specific commitment for mutual defence and institutes an adequate organization which associates foreign affairs and defence representatives. The 1987 Platform underscores the fact that WEU activities, as a European defence organization, are carried out in the perspective of European Union.

(vii) The Atlantic Alliance as such will be strengthened by a more important role and greater responsibilities for Europeans as regards security and defence policies. In this perspective, a European identity for security and defence should be reflected in the development of a European pillar within the Alliance. It is hence necessary to take into account the interaction between the development of the security factor of the Union and the transformation that the Alliance undertakes further to political changes in Europe.

2. *Proposals*

(a) On these bases, the provisions relating to cooperation as regards security policy within political Union should be progressively established. To this end, the European Council should have the jurisdiction to decide what areas of security policy should be the subject of a common policy.

(b) As an example, the following elements can already be listed which should be tackled within the Union framework.

(i) Disarmament and control of armaments in Europe. Work in this field will take on particular importance after the CSCE Summit in 1992. Cooperation between the Twelve should make it possible for Europeans to put forward common positions as a contribution to the coordination taking place within NATO.

(ii) Security questions, including peace-keeping measures in the context of the United Nations. This will include the definition of common positions in the debates on disarmament and the control of arms within the United Nations.

(iii) Nuclear non-proliferation. The decision should be taken, on the base of results obtained in this field in the EPC context, to intensify efforts to implement a common non-proliferation policy dealing with all the aspects examined in the general debate on non-proliferation policy.

(iv) *Economic aspects of security*, namely *cooperation concerning armaments* (including questions relating to the arms market and competition) as well as the control of arms exports (notably for dual-purpose products, precursors of chemical and biological arms, installations and equipment, and ballistic technology) should, because of their link with external policy, be dealt with in the context of CFSP. The question of knowing to what extent these subjects should also come into the areas of Community policy in the framework of Community responsibilities, in relation to the achievement of the European Internal Market and Common Commercial Policy, should also be examined. Adequate coordination with the work of international bodies having jurisdiction in this field, and in particular the GEIP, should be studied.

(c) As regards the role of the WEU, it could be stipulated that the WEU makes up an integral part of the European unification process. The following points could be approved concerning this:

(i) *WEU will develop the common security policy on behalf of political Union*. The work of WEU should be organized in order to establish organizational relations between Political

Union and WEU, thus enabling the WEU, with a view to being part of Political Union in due course, to progressively develop the European common security policy on behalf of the Union.

(ii) *The obligation of aid and assistance in accordance with the Treaty of Brussels should be maintained* for as long as no other equivalent commitment exists between Political Union Member States.

(iii) The different forms of cooperation which exist within WEU on security and defence matters will be continued. After a certain period of time, and by 1996 at the latest — which is a period which will enable the link between the Union and WEU to be put to the test — it will be possible to examine, while taking into account the development of the European security structure, to what extent the pertinent stipulations of the Treaty should be revised.

(iv) Cooperation within the WEU will be made more operational in the politico-military area as well as in the purely military field, and the appropriate operational and institutional consequences will be drawn.

(d) In order to progressively bring WEU closer to Political Union, a cooperation in the sense of coordination of work and complementarity in the distribution of tasks between the Union (CFSP) and WEU should be sought by using the following methods:

(i) European Council decisions on the principles and guidelines of common foreign and security policy will serve as a guideline for cooperation in the framework of the Treaty of Brussels.

(ii) The order and duration of the terms of office for presidents of Political Union and Western European Union will be harmonized as far as possible (by adjusting the transitional provisions in the case of Denmark, Greece and Ireland).

(iii) The dates and places of Political Union Council and Western European Union meetings at ministerial level, as well as certain meetings of high-ranking officials will be harmonized.

(iv) The Secretariat General of the Council and the Secretariat General of the Western European Union should finalize appropriate provisions in order to ensure mutual information.

(v) Links should be established between the European Parliament and the WEU Assembly, taking the role of the "Congress" into account.

(e) Relations between WEU and NATO: the provisions of Article 4 of the modified Treaty of Brussels should be completely revised in order to establish new terms for cooperation between WEU and NATO.

(f) In order to promote cooperation between the various bodies of the Union and WEU, and given the links between WEU and NATO, it could be desirable to transfer WEU administrative divisions.

3.   Relations with the European states which are not WEU members.

(a) Relations between the WEU and the EC Member States which are not members of WEU will be progressively strengthened. WEU non-member States belonging to Political Union have the vocation of belonging to WEU should they so wish.

(b) Cooperation between WEU and the European members of the Alliance which are not EC members should also be increased. Specific contacts or specific forms of cooperation could also be approved with European members of the Alliance not belonging to Political Union.

F.   *Joint Declaration by Germany and Italy on strengthening the powers of the European Parliament 10 April 1991*

Considering the proposals on strengthening the role of the European Parliament, currently under examination by the Intergovernmental Conference on Political Union;

   Having noted a *common evaluation of the principles that should be followed* in the matter, the Foreign Ministers Mr. Hans-Dietrich Genscher and Mr. Gianni de Michelis declare:

1. The development in the process of political integration as well as the project of building European Union, forces us to face, in a clear and definitive manner, the strengthening of Community democratic legitimacy, notably concerning the powers of the European Parliament.

2. *It is no longer admissible that the Institu-*

tion, which is the direct expression of the will of the people, *be kept on the edge of the legislative process* of the Community and that the "last word" in this process be left to the Council alone. The European Parliament must fundamentally be able to participate in such a process on equal terms with the Council so that the two institutions which represent popular sovereignty sovereignty and governmental legitimacy, may determine, together and on equal terms, the drawing up of Community acts of a legislative nature ("co-decision"). The specific procedures to be established to arrive at the above goal can be manyfold. However, a stage of negotiations between the two Institutions seems indispensable, and which could be made easier by the creation of a conciliation procedure with the participation of the Commission. It is essential that in the co-decision procedure neither of the two Institutions may approve an act without the other having consented.

3. In the same context, *the European Parliament must enjoy*, as is the case for all national parliaments, *the right of own-initiative*, while still keeping the principle that the Commission retains that right. The EP's right of initiative could be conditional and subjected to certain guarantees so as to safeguard the Commission's specific role.

4. The European Parliament must also be able to participate effectively in the nomination of the Commission and its President. The current system leaves the Parliament a totally marginal role in such nominations. A proper relational structure between the Executive Power and the Legislative Power as well as respect for the principles of democracy demand a strengthening in ties of confidence between the Commission and the European Parliament. The latter must therefore fully participate in the nomination of the Commission within the formula of the double investiture which foresees, first of all, formal approval by the Parliament of the President appointed by the European Council and then confirmation (by the majority of MEPs) of the Commission as a college after presentation of the programme.

5. The role of the European Parliament must also be reinforced concerning the signing of international agreements by the Community. This could be achieved by a widening and improvement in Parliamentary consultation as well as by giving the latter the power of ratification of the more important international agreements.

6. The following points should further be taken into consideration:

- wider powers of control by the Parliament over the actions of the Commission, notably concerning the management of Community finances; a limited right to levy taxes, and restricted to the Community, in whose creation the EP could participate in a determining fashion.

- the principle of full participation by the EP, through general assent, in the revision procedure of the Treaties under article 236, in parallel to ratification by Member States with the participation of the national Parliaments;

- a power of investigation over breaches of provisions of Community law which could also be set in motion by a qualified majority of the EP;

- the rights of citizens of all Member States, alone or in association among themselves, to submit petitions to the EP.

The two delegations invite other delegations at the Intergovernmental Conference who share the principles listed above, to join in this declaration.

2.   Three visions of EMU

A.   Deutsche Bundesbank's statement on creating Economic and Monetary Union in Europe, 19 September 1990

I. The heads of state and government of the EC member states have decided to establish a European Economic and Monetary Union (EMU) in a multi-stage process. Stage one of EMU started in the middle of this year, and the further stages are to be laid down and the necessary contractual basis is to be created at the intergovernmental conference which is due to meet in December.

The Bundesbank considers it to be its duty to draw attention to the consequences associated with this process, and to point out which conditions must be met if monetary stability is to be assured in future, too.

II. The establishment of a Monetary Union signifies the irrevocable fixing of exchange rates between the currencies concerned (with the possibility of their subsequently giving way to a single currency), under conditions of complete, and durably guaranteed, freedom of capital movements. At the same time, this implies the necessity of relinquishing autonomous national domestic and external monetary policies, and of transferring the responsibility for such policies to Community institutions. In this way the participating economies will be inextricably linked to each other, come what may, in the monetary field. The implications of this — especially for the value of money — will depend crucially on economic and financial policy and on the behaviour of management and labour in *all* member states. They will have to satisfy in full the requirements of an Economic and Monetary Union. In the final analysis, a Monetary Union is thus an irrevocable sworn confraternity — "all for one and one for all" — which, if it is to prove durable, requires, judging from past experience, even closer links in the form of a comprehensive political union.

III. Economic and economic policy trends in the European Communities are still marked by great differences between the member states. It is true that among some member states — and owing in part to the European Monetary System (EMS) — substantial progress has been made since the beginning of the eighties towards greater convergence in the field of anti-inflation policy, with the Bundesbank having made a major contribution through its policy stance, consistently geared as it is to the stability of the Deutsche Mark. Throughout the EC, however, deep-seated divergences still remain, and in part are actually widening again — divergences which are reflected in particular in the movements of costs and prices, the huge deficits in the national budgets of individual countries, and massive external disequilibria. These divergences are especially pronounced in the case of the United Kingdom, Portugal and Greece (which are not as yet participating in the EMS exchange rate mechanism), and they are likewise unmistakable in the case of Italy and Spain. In the majority of instances, the reasons for this are to be sought not so much in temporary factors as in the considerable differences in institutional structures, economic fundamentals and the attitudes of management and labour.

IV. Given this economic and economic policy situation in the Community, an early irrevocable fixing of exchange rates and the transfer of monetary policy powers to Community institutions would involve considerable risks to monetary stability, especially for the Federal Republic of Germany. Furthermore, widespread additional calls for compensatory public financial adjustment would be very likely, especially from the countries of Southern Europe, since, in a Monetary Union, these countries would be faced with the unavoidable consequences of inadequate labour mobility and the continued existence of income and productivity differentials. Although the present situation in a number of member states cannot be compared to the conditions in the GDR, developments there do illustrate the consequences of a Monetary Union under conditions of markedly differing productivity levels.

Particularly at a time when the German economy is being confronted with substantial transitional problems as a result of the intra-German unification process, and when developments in eastern Europe are still unclear in many respects, there is much to be said for preserving such room for manoeuvre and for adjustment as still exists in the field of domestic and external monetary policy and budgetary policy until such time as the economic situation in Germany as a whole and in the European Communities can be regarded as sufficiently consolidated. By then, at all events, the risks inevitably associated with the transition to an Economic and Monetary Union in the EC will be more readily appraisable and presumably also easier to handle. In the meantime, it will be possible to press on resolutely with enhanced efforts to achieve greater convergence in the field of anti-inflation policy throughout the Community, which efforts were initiated upon the commencement of stage one.

V. In the concrete design of the further stages of EMU, and in determining the institutional structure for the final stage, the Bundesbank regards it as essential that due account should be taken of anti-inflation policy requirements. In particular, it must be ensured that the same stability record can in future be achieved at Community level as has hitherto been registered in the Federal Republic of Germany.

In the view of the Bundesbank, therefore, the contractual safeguarding of the following points is indispensable to the design of the *final stage*:

1. The basis of the Monetary Union must be an *economic union* comprising a common economic area without internal borders, which must also be as open as possible to third countries, as well as an adequate degree of lasting convergence of anti-inflation policy between the member states. An essential feature of the Single Market — besides the free movement of persons (including work permits), goods, services and capital — must be an efficient, market-orientated competitive system (including control of allowances) at Community level.

    As far as the Single Market programme is concerned, at present there are still some pronounced deficiencies as regards both decision-making and implementation and, unless these deficiencies are overcome, the elimination of border controls, which is envisaged for 1992, will be in jeopardy. This applies particularly to the harmonization of indirect taxes, which is regarded as an essential precondition for lifting the border controls.

    Another indispensable element of an economic union is an adequate commitment on the part of all member states to

gearing their financial policies to a lasting anti-inflationary stance. In the long run monetary stability can be achieved and maintained only if, in particular, government financial policy in all member states is likewise orientated towards fighting inflation. Since the financial policy decisions in EMU will largely remain in the hands of the member states, contractual arrangements (including binding rules and sanctions) to ensure effective budgetary discipline in all member states will have to be adopted at Community level.

2. In the final stage of the *Monetary Union*, monetary policy will have to be formulated uniformly and bindingly at Community level. This can only be done by a Community monetary authority in the form of a European Central Bank System (ECBS), which will have to satisfy the following requirements:

    (a) The ECBS must be able and obligated to give priority in its decisions to pursuing the objective of monetary stability.

    (b) The ECBS must be endowed with durably guaranteed independence in institutional, functional and personal terms. Its members, in the performance of their duties, may not be subject to any instructions or commitments given by other entities, and may not be restricted in their freedom to decide by overly far-reaching reporting requirements either. The principle of equal voting rights for all members is acceptable only if independence of this kind is assured vis-à-vis national influences as well.

    (c) The necessary uniformity of monetary policy-making requires that what have hitherto been national central banks should largely become integral parts of the ECBS, and thus should no longer be able to pursue policies of their own. This is possible only if the national central banks have previously been given the same degree of independence within their respective member states as the ECBS enjoys at Community level, and if the monetary policy instruments have been duly harmonized.

    (d) To guarantee the uniformity of monetary policy on the one hand and to take due account of the federative structure of the Community on the other, the ECBS should be given a management structure comprising two governing bodies: a Council and an Executive Board. The *Council* should be composed of the Governors of the national central banks and the members of the Executive Board. A sufficiently long term of office (without any possibility of dismissal) and an effectively independent status must be guaranteed for all members of the Council.

The *Executive Board* should be made up of five to seven members, who are appointed by the European Council by virtue of their experience and ability.

The duties should be divided up between the Council and the Executive Board in such a way that the Council is responsible for setting monetary policy targets and the Executive Board for the necessary decisions of detail and their implementation.

(e) The ECBS must be endowed with all the instruments necessary for conducting monetary policy. Administrative controls that distort market mechanisms should not be permissible.

(f) The internal monetary policy of the ECBS must not be hampered by decisions taken in the field of external monetary policy. Hence the ECBS must be given sole responsibility for exchange market intervention, too. In all other decisions affecting external monetary policy — and especially in the event of exchange-rate-policy decisions — the ECBS must be involved in good time and on a basis of co-responsibility.

(g) The ECBS must not be subject to any obligations to extend credit to public authorities in the Community or in member states.

3. Because of the far-reaching political implications, the by-laws of the ECBS and the rules on budgetary discipline should be specified in the Treaty, which is subject to ratification by national parliaments and may be amended only with their approval.

VI. In the Bundesbank's view, the economic and institutional conditions for the commencement of the final stage of the Monetary Union and thus for the establishment of the ECBS — which conditions must be met in all member states — can be fulfilled only in the course of a lengthy *transitional process*. During this process, no institutional changes which result in any curtailment of the freedom of action of national monetary policy may be made.

At the end of the transitional period, the following prerequisites for the commencement of the final stage must be satisfied in the Bundesbank's opinion:

1. The convergence of anti-inflation policy among all the member states participating in the Monetary Union must have progressed so far that

 – inflation has been very largely eliminated in all the countries, and price differences have been virtually stamped out,

 – the budget deficits in all participating countries have been reduced to a level which is tolerable over the longer term and unproblematic in terms of anti-inflation policy, and

 – the durability of the convergence achieved is reflected in the markets' verdict, too, i.e. in a virtual harmonization of capital market rates.

2. All the member states taking part in the Monetary Union must previously have participated, without any special arrangements, in the exchange rate mechanism of the EMS for a sufficiently long period, and must have finally dismantled all restrictions on capital movements.

3. Particularly with respect to their commitment to fight inflation and their independence, the by-laws of the national central banks must be harmonized to such an extent that these banks can become an integral part of the ECBS. Such harmonization also includes an adequate adjustment of their monetary policy instruments.

4. The contractual arrangements (including binding rules and sanctions) for ensuring effective budgetary discipline in all member states must be adopted at Community level.

5. The Single Market programme must have been realized in full, including the dismantling of fiscal border controls.

VII. In order to pave the way, as required, for the transition to the final stage, the following should be provided for in the Bundesbank's view:

1. The efforts already initiated to promote the coordination of monetary policy among the member states, with a view to combating inflation, should be continued and stepped up. At the same time, the monetary policy instruments should be harmonized increasingly. The Committee of EC Central Bank Governors could be transformed into a Council of Governors in due course.

2. In all member states, the by-laws of the central banks should safeguard those banks' independence of instructions from political entities, and of the influence of such entities, at an early date.

3. The fiscal policy divergences must be overcome as soon as possible by means of a marked reduction in the budget deficits of a number of member states. The EC Commission and the Ecofin Council should step up their efforts to ensure the observance of adequate budgetary discipline in all member states.

4. The convergence of anti-inflation policy within the Community could also be fostered by a hardening of the ECU through it being contractually stipulated that the ECU cannot be devalued against any Community currency. Such a hardening of the ECU calls neither for the development of a parallel currency nor for the creation of a new institution.

A particularly important point in the Bundesbank's eyes is that the transition to another stage (no matter whether this is a transitional stage or the final stage) should be made solely dependent of the fulfilment of previously defined economic and economic policy conditions, rather than on specific timetables. Hence the transition to another stage must not be linked to deadlines fixed in advance.

VIII. In the Bundesbank's opinion, the points listed above are indispensable, and not optional, requirements. The Bundesbank considers it necessary for the German delegation to advocate these points vigorously at the intergovernmental conference. The viability of the envisaged strategy for the Economic and Monetary Union must not be endangered in the above-mentioned key respects by the acceptance of compromises during the negotiations. Otherwise, in view of the substantial risks involved, the favourable expectations entertained of such a Union might well be disappointed.

B. French Government Proposal for a draft treaty on Economic and Monetary Union, January 1991

Note: The following draft treaty is submitted with its articles numbered in the order in which they appear. Its incorporation in the Treaty of Rome will merely require a change in the numbering and the deletion of those Articles of the Treaty of Rome that would be rendered obsolete.

Article 1

1. The objective of Economic and Monetary Union shall be to ensure sustained non-inflationary growth, a high level of employment and a high degree of convergence in the context of the internal market and of economic and social cohesion.

It shall be based on the following principles: stable prices, sound public finance and monetary conditions, sound global balances of payments and open, competitive markets.

It shall be supported by far-reaching economic integration, close coordination of the Members States' economic policies and the irrevocable fixing of parities leading to the introduction of a single currency.

2. Economic and monetary union shall develop gradually over a period comprising two stages before the final stage, ensuring the parallelism of economic and monetary policies.

Further to the developments that have occurred since the beginning of the first stage on 1 July 1990, the second stage or transitional period shall begin on 1 January 1994.

During that period, Articles 1–3(2), 1–4(2) and (3), 2–1, 2–3, 2–4, 3–1 and 4–5 shall not apply.

The European Council shall decide, in accordance with Article 5–9, on transition to the final stage.

Chapter 1: Economic Policy

Article 1–1

The Member States shall pursue their economic policies with a view to contributing to the realization of the objectives of Economic and Monetary Union in the context of the guidelines adopted by Union institutions to that end.

Article 1–2

The European Council shall, on the basis of a report by the Council, define the broad guidelines of Community economic policy.

Article 1–3

1. Within the framework of the guidelines referred to in Article 1–2, the Council shall coordinate the Member States' economic policies.

2. Each year it shall examine their economic situation and their economic policy objectives. If it appears that they do not comply with the guidelines set by the European Council and that they are likely to compromise the Union's monetary stability, the Council shall make recommendations to the Member State concerned, without prejudice to Article 4–3(3).

3. If a recommendation made to a Member State pursuant to paragraph 2 is not implemented the Council may make that recommendation public. It may also decide to reduce or suspend the commitments in the Community budget for the benefit of the State concerned after consultation of the European Parliament, in accordance with the procedures laid down in Article 203.

Article 1–4

1. The financing of budget deficits by means of direct assistance from the ESCB, set up pursuant to Article 2–2, or through privileged access by the public authorities to capital markets is incompatible with EMU and shall therefore be prohibited.

The Member States alone shall be responsible for their public debts and shall not benefit from any guarantee, under Economic and Monetary Union, from the Community or other Member States.

2. Excessive budget deficits must be avoided. To that end the Council and the Commission shall make the necessary recommendations, under Article 1–3, to the Member States concerned. Before transition to the final stage of Union, the Member States shall take all necessary steps to guarantee that the Council's recommendations concerning excessive deficits are implemented.

3. Where, however, a recommendation regarding the reduction of an excessive budget deficit is not implemented the Council may, over and above the measures provided for in Article 1–3(3), decide to:

- instruct the ESCB to restrict or suspend its transactions in the public debt securities of the State concerned;

- instruct the national authorities responsible for banking and financial supervision to take all necessary steps to safeguard the security of the Community's financial system.

Article 1–5

1. The Member States shall regard their conjunctural policies as a matter of common concern. They shall consult each other and the Commission on the measures to be taken in the light of the prevailing circumstances.

In this connection, an overall evaluation shall be carried out regularly at Community level of the short-term and medium-term economic developments in the Community and in each of its Member States.

Moreover, the guidelines and recommendations adopted in accordance with the procedure described in Articles 1–2 to 1–4 shall serve as a framework for the multilateral surveillance undertaken with a view to assessing the results of the coordination of Members States' economic policies.

2. Without prejudice to the other procedures provided for in this Treaty, the Council may, acting on a proposal from the Commission, decide unanimously on the measures appropriate to the situation.

3. The Council, acting by a qualified majority on a proposal from the Commission, shall, where necessary, issue the directives needed to give effect to the measures decided on under paragraph 2.

4. The procedures provided for in paragraphs 2 and 3 shall also apply if any difficulty should arise in the supply of certain products.

Chapter 2: Monetary policy

Article 2–1

Monetary union shall entail the irrevocable fixing of parities between the Member States' currencies, leading to the introduction of a single currency, the ecu, and the pursuit of a single monetary policy and the establishment of the European System of Central Banks (ESCB).

Article 2–2

1. The European System of Central Banks (ESCB) shall be made up of the European Central Bank and the Central Banks of the Member States.

2. The European Central Bank shall have legal personality.

3. The Statutes of the ESCB and the European Central Bank are set out in a protocol annexed to this Treaty. The Council may amend Articles . . . of the Statutes after consulting the Commission and the European Parliament.

The Council shall act by a qualified majority if the proposal for amendment obtains the agreement of the European Central Bank.

In other cases it shall act unanimously.

Article 2–3

1. The priority objective of the ESCB shall be to maintain the stability of prices.

Without prejudice to the objective of price stability, the ESCB shall support the Community's general economic policy.

The ESCB's actions shall be compatible with the principle of free, competitive markets.

2. In performing the tasks entrusted to it by this Treaty the ESCB shall neither seek nor take instructions from the Council, the Commission, the European Parliament or the Member States.

Article 2–4

1. The fundamental tasks of the ESCB shall be:

- to determine and implement the Community's monetary policy;
- to carry out foreign-exchange transactions and administer official foreign-exchange reserves in accordance with Chapter 3 below;

2. In order to carry out the tasks assigned to it the ESCB shall:

- regulate the issue of notes and coins denominated in ecus as the only legal tender throughout the Community;
- open accounts in the names of credit institutions, public bodies and other market operators;
- conduct credit transactions and operate on the money and financial markets;
- have the power to implement other monetary control methods under the conditions laid down in paragraph 3;
- have the power to establish relations with international and third-country banks and financial institutions and carry out exchange transactions;
- participate in the BIS and, subject to the Council's approval, in other international institutions;
- exercise any other power that might be delegated to it by the Council, acting unanimously.

3. The general rules concerning methods of monetary control and any sanctions shall be adopted by the Council, acting by a qualified majority, after consulting the Council of the Bank.

4. The ESCB shall be consulted on any draft Community legislation or any proposed international agreement having implications for the Community's monetary policy.

It shall also be consulted by the authorities of the Member States on any draft national legislation having such implications.

Article 2–5

1. The ESCB shall be administered by the decision-making bodies of the European Central Bank.

2. The European Central Bank shall be administered by a Council, hereinafter referred to as "the Council of the Bank", made up of the twelve Governors of the national central banks and the six members of the Executive Board, one of whom, the President of the European Central Bank, shall chair meetings of the Council of the Bank.

The members of the Council and the Executive Board of the Bank shall carry out their tasks in a completely independent manner in the general interests of the Community.

3. On a proposal by the Council and after consultation of the European Parliament, the President and the other members of the Execu-

tive Board of the Bank shall be appointed for a period of five years by the European Council.

4. The Council of the Bank shall take the decisions necessary to ensure performance of the tasks entrusted to the ESCB under this Treaty. It shall determine the Community's monetary policy and shall adopt the guidelines necessary for its implementation.

5. The Council of the Bank shall adopt its decisions by a majority vote of its members.

The conditions governing the casting of votes by members of the Executive Board shall be laid down in the Statutes of the ESCB and the European Central Bank.

6. The Executive Board shall take the necessary administrative decisions in line with the guidelines and decisions adopted by the Council of the Bank.

In addition, the Executive Board may, subject to the conditions set out in the Statutes, be delegated certain powers by decision of the Council of the Bank.

7. The President of the Bank shall chair the Executive Board, represent the European Central Bank externally, act in its name in judicial or other matters and exercise authority over all its departments.

8. The division of responsibilities between the Council of the Bank and the Executive Board shall be set out in the Statute.

Article 2–6

1. The capital of the European Central Bank shall be held by the Member States.

2. It shall be allocated to them in accordance with the table set out in annex to this Treaty; the allocation amongst the Member States must reflect their relative economic importances; it may be altered by decision of the Council, acting unanimously.

3. The capital of the Bank may be increased; detailed rules for such increases shall be adopted, by decision of the Assembly of the Member States, acting by a majority of two-thirds of the shares in the capital.

4. The consolidated profits made by the ESCB shall be allocated each year as follows:

 – x% of the profits shall be added to the reserves of the European Central Bank, up to a limit of y% of its capital;

 – the balance shall be distributed to the Member States in proportion to their shares of the capital.

Chapter 3: External monetary policy

Article 3–1

1. The Community shall conduct a single exchange-rate policy.

2. Acting by a qualified majority and after having consulted the Council of the Bank, the Council shall lay down guidelines for the Community's exchange-rate policy.

3. Transactions for the administration of foreign-exchange reserves and interventions on foreign-exchange markets shall be carried out by the European Central Bank within the guidelines laid down by the Council.

The European Central Bank shall keep the Council informed of its actions, of developments on the markets and any necessary interventions. The Monetary Committee referred to in Article 4–4 shall report to the Council on exchange-rate policy in accordance with detailed rules adopted by the Council.

Chapter 4: Institutional provisions

Article 4–1

1. On the basis of a report by the Council, the Commission and the ESCB, the European Council shall determine the broad guidelines for Economic and Monetary Union. It shall guarantee its satisfactory operation.

2. Whether Ministers for Finance participate in the European Council's discussions on matters relating to Economic and Monetary Union shall be decided by the President of the European Council.

Article 4–2

1. The Council's decisions on Economic and Monetary Union shall, in the absence of special provisions, be taken by a qualified majority.

2. In discussions governed by Articles 1–2 to 1–4 or concerning monetary policy, the organization or operation of the ESCB or exchange-rate policy, the Council shall take a decision on proposals submitted by the President, the Commission or the Member States.

On other matters relating to Economic and Monetary Union, Articles 148 and 149(1) shall apply as necessary.

Article 4–3

1. The President of the Council and a member of the Commission may attend meetings of the

Council of the Bank but shall not be entitled to vote.

The Council may submit motions for discussion by the Council of the Bank.

The President of the Council may ask the Council of the ESCB to postpone a decision for up to fifteen days.

2. The President of the Bank shall attend meetings of the Council that deal with the coordination of economic policies and the examination of the recommendations referred to in Articles 1–3 and 1–4.

He may transmit to the Council opinions of the Council of the Bank on developments in the economic and monetary situation in the Community or in certain Member States.

3. The Commission may address to the President of the Council and to the President of the Bank observations and recommendations on economic and monetary policy. Those observations and recommendations may be published.

4. The European Central Bank shall, each year, transmit a report on the activities of the European System of Central Banks and on monetary developments to the European Parliament, the European Council and the Commission.

5. Twice a year the Presidents of the Council and of the Commission shall report to the Congress on the state of Economic and Monetary Union.

6. The European Parliament shall be consulted regularly on the conduct of economic and monetary policy, on the basis of reports by the Presidents of the Council, the Commission and the ESCB. It shall be consulted before the Council finally adopts the economic guidelines referred to in Articles 1–2 and 4–1.

Article 4–4

1. A Monetary Committee with advisory status is hereby set up. It shall have the following tasks:

- to keep under review the monetary and financial situation of the Member States and of the Community and to report regularly thereon to the Council and to the Commission;
- to keep under review the development of foreign-exchange markets and the implementation of the Community's external monetary policy;
- to prepare the Council's discussions on Economic and Monetary Union.

2. The Monetary Committee shall consist of:

- the Deputy Minister for Economic and Financial Affairs and the governor of the national central bank or his representative, from each Member State;
- two members of the Commission;
- two members of the Executive Board of the ESCB.

Article 4–5

The European Council shall adopt arrangements enabling the Community to express its views in international bodies on matters governed by Chapters 1, 2 and 3 of this Title relating to Economic and Monetary Union, without reducing the Member States' participation, in accordance with the principle of subsidiarity.

Chapter 5: Transitional provisions

Section 1: Transitional period

Article 5–1

The transitional period for achieving Economic and Monetary Union shall begin on 1 January 1994.

Article 5–2

1. The Member States shall undertake to limit the relative fluctuations of their currencies within the framework of the exchange-rate mechanism of the European Monetary System.

2. The rules for the operation of the European Monetary System and its exchange-rate mechanism shall be the subject of an annex to this Treaty. Acting unanimously after consulting the Council of the Bank, the Council shall decide on any amendments to be made thereto and adopt the necessary decisions.

3. Acting unanimously, the Council may authorize a Member State which for serious reasons is unable to do so not to apply paragraph 1 immediately; under the same conditions it shall adopt the detailed provisions governing such derogations and their duration.

Article 5–3

1. During the transitional period the Community shall adopt appropriate measures to reinforce the convergence of economic and monetary developments in the various Member States and in particular price stability and the consolidation of public finances. It shall,

in particular, ensure that the instruments and methods of the multilateral surveillance exercise are improved in the light of the experience gained during stage 1.

2. Before the beginning of the transitional stage the Member States shall adopt the measures necessary for compliance with Article 1–4(1).

Article 5–4

1. At the start of the transitional period the ESCB shall be established pursuant to Article 2–2, in particular with a view to:

- reinforcing the coordination of monetary policies;
- establishing the instruments and procedures necessary for the future conduct of the single monetary policy;
- supervising the development of the ecu.

2. The Community and the Member States shall take all appropriate measures to set up the various bodies of the European Central Bank and to allow the ESCB to operate.

3. For the purposes referred to in paragraph 1, the Council shall unanimously adopt the acts provided for in this Treaty and the Statutes annexed hereto to enable the ESCB to perform its duties.

4. As soon as they are set up, the bodies of the European Central Bank shall perform the tasks and comply with the obligations laid down in Article 2–5.

Article 5–5

1. As soon as it is set up, the European Central Bank, having due regard to the responsibilities incumbent upon the authorities of the Member States as regards the formulation and conduct of their monetary policies:

- shall perform the duties entrusted to the European Monetary Co-operation Fund (EMCF) and the Committee of Governors of the Central Banks and, in particular, shall ensure the smooth operation of the EMS;
- shall be empowered to make recommendations, which it may publish, to national monetary authorities concerning the conduct of their monetary policy;
- may manage foreign-exchange reserves, assist in the implementation of a Community exchange-rate policy and, in

particular, intervene on the foreign-exchange markets within the guidelines laid down by the Council;
- shall implement the harmonization of monetary and financial statistics;
- shall participate in the approximation of monetary policy instruments;
- shall make preparations for linking up payments networks and money and financial markets.

2. The European Central Bank shall be consulted by the Council on any draft Community legislation or any proposed international agreements in the monetary field.

It shall also be consulted by the authorities of the Member States on any draft legislation on such matters.

Article 5–6

1. During the transitional stage the Community shall prepare for the introduction of the ecu as a single currency:

- by developing its role and extending its uses;
- by improving its characteristics so that the ecu becomes a strong and stable currency.

2. To that end the Council of the ESCB shall:

- ensure the smooth operation of the ecu market;
- take the measures necessary for the smooth operation of the ecu bank clearing system;
- supervise the technical preparation of means of payment and notes and coins in ecus.

Article 5–7

1. Having due regard to the provisions of the Statutes of the ESCB and the European Central Bank, the Council, acting by a qualified majority after consulting the European Central Bank, shall adopt the measures required to allow the performance of the duties outlined in Articles 5–5 and 5–6.

Under the same procedure, the Council shall adopt the arrangements for transferring the assets and liabilities of the EMCF to the European Central Bank.

2. The Council, acting unanimously after consulting the European Central Bank, may entrust other functions to the European Central Bank

within the limits laid down in Article 2–4. It shall, in accordance with the same procedure and insofar as is necessary, adopt the measures required to allow the performance of such functions.

Article 5–8

1. Before 1 January 1994 the Member States shall abolish all restrictions on movements of capital belonging to persons resident within the Member States and all discrimination in treatment based on the nationality or residence of persons or on the location of investments.

2. Current payments relating to movements of capital between Member States shall be freed of all restrictions no later than the end of the first stage.

Section 2: Transition to the final stage

Article 5–9

Within three years of the start of the transitional period the Commission and the Council of the ESCB shall report to the Council on the results obtained and in particular on the progress achieved on convergence.

On the basis of the Council's report and after consulting the Congress/European Parliament, the European Council shall verify that the conditions for moving from the transitional period to the final stage of Economic and Monetary Union have been met and shall lay down the period within which the decision to enter the final stage shall be taken.

It shall do so on the basis of an assessment of the results of market integration and of the convergence of economic and monetary developments in the Member States and the development of the role of the ecu.

Article 5–10

When the European Council has decided on transition to the final stage, the Council, acting by a qualified majority in favour cast by at least eight Member States, shall immediately take the decisions required.

It may, in particular, decide in principle on a temporary derogation for a Member State which is not yet in a position to participate fully in the monetary-policy mechanisms specified for the final stage of Economic and Monetary Union.

After consulting the Central Bank, it shall also lay down, in accordance with the same procedure, the duration and implementing arrangements for such derogation. The Council and the Commission shall immediately send the European Congress a report on the decisions taken.

Article 5–11

1. Immediately after the decision to enter the final stage, the Council shall adopt the fixed exchange rates between Member States' currencies and the measures necessary for introducing the ecu as the single currency of the Community, acting in accordance with the procedure provided for in paragraph 3. As from such time, the ESCB shall exercise fully its functions in the monetary policy field.

2. The Council, acting in accordance with the procedure provided for in paragraph 3, shall adopt, insofar as is necessary, the technical arrangements under which Member States' currencies may provisionally remain legal tender.

3. The measures provided for in paragraphs 1 and 2 shall be adopted by the Council, acting unanimously and in consultation with the European Central Bank.

Where, pursuant to Article 5–10, the Council has decided on a derogation for one or more Member States, such measures shall be adopted unanimously by the Member States participating in the final stage.

4. Where, pursuant to Article 5–10, the Council has decided on a derogation for one or more Member States, the Council, acting unanimously on a proposal from the Commission and in consultation with the European Central Bank, shall determine the conditions under which the qualified majority provided for in Article 4–2 is achieved.

C.   United Kingdom Proposal for the creation of a European Monetary Fund responsible for managing the hard Ecu, January 1991

Introduction

Last year the UK Government put forward proposals for the development of economic and monetary union beyond Stage 1. These involved the creation of a new Community monetary institution, the European Monetary Fund. Its main role would be the management of a common Community currency, tentatively called the hard ecu, designed to help strengthen anti-inflationary convergence throughout the Community.

The proposals were first outlined in the present Prime Minister's speech to the German Industry Forum on 20 June 1990. Further details were provided in subsequent speeches and papers, including an article in the Autumn 1990 Treasury Bulletin.

The recent European Council meeting and the inaugural sessions of the Inter-Governmental Conferences displayed the positive and cooperative approach of the Member States to the important questions now before the Community. It is in this positive spirit that the UK Government is now setting out detailed suggestions for the main legal texts designed to put the scheme it has proposed into effect. These texts are put forward now in order to facilitate early consideration in the Inter-Governmental Conference on Economic and Monetary Union.

In the United Kingdom's view, the first priority for the Inter-Governmental Conference should be to identify the next steps in the process of economic and monetary union and to reach agreement on arrangements which will permit practical progress towards that objective at an early stage. The texts attached provide the basis for such a discussion, by translating into legal form the policy proposal for the early introduction — as soon as possible after the ratification of the necessary provisions — of a new monetary institution and a common Community currency. The legal provisions are divided into proposals for Treaty amendments and a more detailed Statute (which could be annexed as a Protocol to the Treaty).

These proposals take account of the recent work of the Central Bank Governors on a European System of Central Banks and incorporate similar provisions into the European Monetary Fund where that is appropriate. For example a two-tier structure incorporating a Governing Board and an Executive Board is proposed. The membership structure of the two Boards would also be the same, with both chaired by a President serving an eight-year term.

Treaty Article III provides for the Council to confer additional tasks on the Fund. This could include possibilities identified at an earlier stage such as the management of the exchange rate mechanism. The UK Government is not able to accept the imposition of a single monetary policy and a single currency, and the text does not provide for this.

An important set of considerations for the European Monetary Fund concerns the issues of independence and accountability. The main provisions in these areas are set out in Treaty Articles V and IX. In relation to independence, the UK Government recognizes that there are different views within the Community, and Article V therefore puts forward two alternative approaches; the first broadly follows the proposals of the Central Bank Governors, while the second provides for the continuation of present arrangements in each Member State. Article IX sets out a range of provisions for the accountability of the Fund.

European Monetary Fund: treaty articles

Article I

A European Monetary Fund is hereby established with legal personality.

The members of the Fund shall be the central banks of the Member States.

The Fund shall be administered by a Governing Board and an Executive Board.

The Statute of the Fund is laid down in a Protocol annexed to this Treaty.

Commentary
This article establishes the European Monetary Fund ("the Fund"). Its members will be the central banks of Member States.

Article II

1. The overriding objective of the European Monetary Fund shall be to promote and maintain price stability in the Community as part of the progressive realization of Economic and Monetary Union.

2. Without prejudice to the objective of price stability, the Fund shall support the other economic policy objectives of the Community.

3. In exercising its functions the Fund shall at all times act consistently with free and competitive markets.

Commentary

This article sets out the objectives of the Fund.

Article III

1. For the purposes set out in Article II the European Monetary Fund shall have responsibility for the issue and management of a common currency which shall be called the [hard ECU].

2. The Fund shall undertake such additional tasks as the Council, acting unanimously and after consulting the Monetary Committee, may decide. The Commission may recommend to the Council additional tasks to be undertaken by the Fund.

3. Decisions of the Council under paragraph 2 shall lay down any measures necessary to give effect to, or facilitate the achievement of, additional tasks conferred on the Fund. Such measures may confer on the Fund powers for the implementation of rules laid down by the Council.

4. The provisions of this Article are without prejudice to the existing powers of the Member States to issue and manage their national currencies.

Commentary

This article sets out the tasks of the Fund. It focuses on the primary task of issuing and managing the common currency. Subsidiary tasks, such as managing the ERM and coordinating exchange rate intervention, would be left to subordinate legislation adopted by the Council.

"Hard ecu" is in square brackets in paragraph 1 because it is only one possible name for the common currency.

Article IV

Without prejudice to the powers of the Commission and the Council with regard to the negotiation and conclusion of agreements between the Community and third countries or international organizations, the European Monetary Fund shall be entitled to establish relations alongside the Member States with central banks and financial institutions in third countries and, where appropriate, with international organizations.

Commentary

This article confers on the Fund a limited measure of external competence. The Fund establishing "relations" with entities in third countries would not preclude Member States from doing the same.

Article V

ALTERNATIVE 1

1. In exercising the powers and performing the duties conferred on them by this Treaty the members of the Governing Board and Executive Board of the European Monetary Fund shall be completely independent and shall neither seek nor take instructions from any Community institution, national government or any other body or person.

2. Member States and the institutions of the Community shall respect the independence of the members of the Governing Board and Executive Board of the Fund and not seek to influence them in the performance of their duties.

ALTERNATIVE 2

The provisions of this Treaty are without prejudice to the existing relationships between national central banks and the governments of the Member States save to the extent that changes are necessary to ensure consistency with the provisions of the Treaty and the Protocol.

Commentary

Alternative texts, embodying different approaches, are offered.

Alternative 1 would explicitly establish the independence of the Fund. Alternative 2 would involve minimum change in the existing relationship between the national central bank and the government in each Member State

Article VI

1. The European Monetary Fund shall participate in the European Monetary System and the [hard ECU] shall be a participating currency in

the exchange rate mechanism of the System. Any alteration to the rules of operation of the exchange rate mechanism shall require the consent of the Fund.

2. Bilateral central rates for the [hard ECU] against the other currencies participating in the exchange rate mechanism shall be established by mutual agreement between the Fund and the Member States.

3. The Fund shall neither seek nor agree to a reduction in the bilateral central rate for the [hard ECU] against any of the other currencies participating in the exchange rate mechanism.

[4. The Fund shall not issue liabilities, by way of deposit or otherwise, except in exchange for national currencies of the Member States.]

5. The national monetary authorities of the Member States shall be obliged to repurchase excess quantities of their national currencies held by the Fund.

[6. The national monetary authority of each Member State shall guarantee the value, expressed in terms of the [hard ECU], of its national currency held by the Fund.]

7. The Council, acting unanimously after consulting the Monetary Committee and the Committee of Governors of the central banks of the Member States, shall adopt the measures necessary to give effect to this Article.

Commentary
This article sets out the Fund's obligations in relation to the common currency. Subordinate legislation adopted by the Council under paragraph 7 would:

— *enable the Fund to decline to accept excessive quantities of a particularly weak national currency*

— *provide rules for deciding what quantity of a national currency should be regarded as excess for the purposes of the repurchase obligation (including the possibility of a discretionary grey zone)*

— *amplify the nature and extent of the guarantee requirement (if included), and*

— *enable amendments to be made to existing EC legislation on the EMS (currently based on Article 235/EEC) to reflect the participation of the hard ECU in place of the basket ECU.*

The detailed arrangements under paragraph 4 are for further technical consideration; hence this paragraph is in square brackets. Paragraph 6 is treated in the same way to reflect its status as an option, not a requirement.

Article VII

1. If the Executive Board of the European Monetary Fund considers that a Member State or the central bank of a Member State has failed to fulfil an obligation under this Treaty or under the Statute of the Fund, it shall deliver a reasoned opinion on the matter after giving the Member State or the central bank concerned the opportunity to submit its observations.

If the Member State or the central bank concerned does not comply with the opinion within the period laid down by the Executive Board, the latter may bring the matter before the Court of Justice.

2. The Court of Justice shall, within the limits hereinafter laid down, have jurisdiction in disputes concerning:

(a) measures adopted by the Governing Board of the Fund. In this connection, any Member State, the Commission or the Executive Board of the Fund may institute proceedings under the conditions laid down in Article 173;

(b) measures adopted by the Executive Board of the Fund. Proceedings against such measures may be instituted only by Member States or the Commission under the conditions laid down in Article 173.

3. National central banks and the Fund shall be required to take the necessary measures to comply with judgments of the Court of Justice in proceedings instituted pursuant to this Article.

Commentary
This article provides for the Fund to be subject to judicial review, and adapts the approach adopted by Article 180/EEC in relation to the EIB. It gives a role, in enforcement matters, to the Governing Board or Executive Board of the Fund and makes national central banks liable to infraction proceedings. Failure on the part of a Member State or a national central bank to perform its obligations under the Treaty or the Statute of the Fund could be challenged by the Executive Board under paragraph 1. In addition, measures adopted by the Governing Board or the Executive Board which failed to comply with the provisions of Articles I to X (or other provisions of the Treaty or general principles of EC law) could be challenged under sub paragraphs (a) and (b) of paragraph 2.

Article VIII

Article 22 of the Protocol on the Privileges and Immunities of the European Communities shall apply to the European Monetary Fund as it applies to the European Investment Bank.

Commentary

This article deals with the privileges and immunities of the Fund and its staff by putting it on the same footing as the EIB.

Article IX

1. The President of the Governing Board of the European Monetary Fund shall be invited to participate in meetings of the European Council and the Council when matters relating to the objectives and tasks of the Fund are discussed.

2. The President of the Council and a member of the Commission may attend meetings of the Governing Board of the Fund. They may take part in the deliberations of the Board but shall not be entitled to vote.

3. The Fund shall draw up monthly reports on its activities for presentation to the Council, on which the Monetary Committee may express an opinion.

4. The Fund shall draw up an annual report on its activities. The President of the Governing Board shall present the annual report to the European Council, the Council and the European Parliament.

5. To assist in the implementation of Article II.2, the Council shall each year send to the Fund its annual economic report.

Commentary

This article sets out a framework for accountability. Paragraph 3 provides for a monthly reporting procedure to EcoFin, through the Monetary Committee. This would give the Council a regular opportunity to make its views clear to the head of the Fund. This would be in addition to the system of annual reporting set out in paragraph 4.

The Inter-Governmental Conference on Political Union may confer a role under the Treaty on national Parliaments. It may be appropriate to mirror any such development here.

Article X

[If any member of the Governing Board or the Executive Board of the Fund no longer fulfils the conditions required for the performance of his duties or if he has been guilty of serious misconduct, the Court of Justice may, on appli-cation by the Council or the Chairman of the Governing Board, compulsorily retire him.]

Commentary

The removal procedure in this article adapts for use in this context the procedure laid down in Article 160/EEC for removing individual members of the Commission.

This Article will need to be reviewed in the light of decisions on Article V.

European Monetary Fund: Statute

Chapter 1 — Constitution

Article 1

1.1 The European Monetary Fund established by Article I of this Treaty (hereinafter called "the Fund") is hereby constituted; it shall perform its functions and carry out its activities in accordance with the provisions of this Treaty and of this Statute.

1.2 The seat of the Fund shall be [ ] [determined by common accord of the Governments of the Member States].

Commentary

These three articles provide the principal link between the Treaty and the Statute (which would take the form of a Protocol annexed to the Treaty).

Article 2

The objectives of the Fund shall be those defined in Article II of this Treaty and its tasks shall be those defined in, or conferred on it by decision of the Council under, Article III of this Treaty.

Article 3

In accordance with Article I of this Treaty the following shall be members of the Fund:

[List of central banks and Institut Monétaire Luxembourgeois]

Chapter II — Organization

Article 4

The decision-making bodies of the Fund shall be the Governing Board and the Executive Board.

Commentary

This article sets out a two-tier structure for the Fund, with a Governing Board and an Executive Board.

Article 5 — The Governing Board

5.1 The Governing Board shall comprise the President, the Vice-President, the other members of the Executive Board and the Governors of the national central banks. The President of the Council of Ministers and a representative of the Commission may take part in the deliberations of the Governing Board but they may not vote.

5.2 Subject to Article 5.3 of this Statute, only members of the Governing Board present in person shall have the right to vote. Each member shall have one vote. Save as otherwise provided in the Statute, the Governing Board shall act by a simple majority. In the event of a tie, the President shall have the casting vote. In order for the Governing Board to vote, there shall be a quorum of two-thirds of the members.

5.3 Weighted voting shall apply in accordance with the provisions of Article 23 of this Statute. If a Governor is unable to be present, he may nominate an Alternate to cast his weighted vote.

5.4 The proceedings of the meetings shall be confidential. The Governing Board may decide to make the outcome of its deliberations public.

5.5 The Governing Board shall meet at least ten times a year.

Commentary

This Article prescribes the membership and main procedural rules of the Governing Board. Each member has one vote except that weighted voting (Article 5.3) would apply to decisions concerning capital and the allocation of profits and losses, for which members of the Executive Board would have no votes (see also Article 23 below). Since proxy voting is provided for in such matters, no quorum is set.

Article 6 — The Executive Board

6.1 The Executive Board shall comprise the President, the Vice-President, and 4 other members.

The members of the Executive Board shall be selected among persons of recognized standing and professional experience in monetary or banking matters.

No member shall, without approval of the Governing Board, receive a salary or other form of compensation from any source other than the Fund or occupy any other office or employment, whether remunerated or not, except as a nominee of the Fund.

6.2 The President shall be appointed for a period of 8 years by common accord of the Member States, after the Governing Board has given its opinion, and after consultation with the European Parliament.

6.3 The Vice-President and the other members of the Executive Board shall be appointed, for a period of eight years, by common accord of the Member States after consultation with the Governing Board.

6.4 [With the exception of the President,] no member of the Executive Board shall hold office beyond the age of 65.

6.5 All members of the Executive Board present in person shall have the right to vote and shall have, for that purpose, one vote. The Executive Board shall act by a simple majority of the votes cast. In the event of a tie, the President shall have the casting vote. The voting arrangements will be specified in the Rules of Procedure.

6.6 The Executive Board shall administer the Fund.

Commentary

This Article provides for the membership and main procedural rules of the Executive Board.

Articles 6.2 and 6.3 provide for the appointment of all members of the Executive Board by common accord of the Member States. The President (but not other Executive Board members) would be appointed only after consultation with the European Parliament.

The passage in square brackets in Article 6.4 would make provision for the President alone to hold office beyond the age of 65.

Article 7 — Responsibilities of the decision-making bodies

7.1 The Governing Board shall take the decisions necessary to ensure the performance of the tasks entrusted to the Fund under this Treaty and this Statute. The Governing Board shall formulate the policy of the Fund in respect of the [hard ECU] including, as appropriate, decisions relating to intermediate objectives, key interest rates and overall liquidity, and shall establish the necessary guidelines for their implementation.

7.2 The Executive Board shall implement the policy of the Fund in accordance with the decisions and guidelines established by the Governing Board.

7.3 The Executive Board shall, to the extent possible and appropriate, seek the assistance of the national central banks in the execution of the operations of the Fund.

7.4 The Executive Board shall have responsibility for the preparation of the meetings of the Governing Board.

7.5 The Governing Board shall adopt Rules of Procedure which determine the internal organization of the Fund and its decision-making bodies.

Commentary
This Article subordinates the Executive Board to the authority of the Governing Board.

Article 7.3 requires the Executive Board of the Fund to seek (as appropriate) the assistance of national central banks, thus reflecting the existence of national monetary policies side by side with the common currency.

Article 8 — The President

8.1 The President or, in his absence, the Vice-President shall chair the Governing Board and the Executive Board of the Fund.

8.2 The President or, if he is prevented, the Vice-President shall represent the Fund in judicial and other matters.

Commentary
Article 8.2 draws on Article 13.6 of the Protocol on the Statute of the EIB.

Article 9 — National central banks

9.1 At the request of the Executive Board, the national central banks shall assist the Fund in the execution of its tasks.

9.2 National central banks continue to carry out their responsibilities under national law provided that these do not interfere with their obligations under this Statute. In particular, the Member States shall ensure that the statutes of national central banks are compatible with this Statute and this Treaty.

Commentary
This Article recognizes the continuing responsibilities of national central banks for national monetary policies.

Chapter III — Monetary functions and operations of the system

Article 10 — Accounts with and held by the EMF

In order to carry out its tasks, the Fund may open accounts for, and hold accounts with, national central banks, other public entities, credit institutions and other market participants.

Commentary
This Article specifies the capacity to open accounts not only for but with national central banks and other market participants, which would be essential for the Fund to issue and manage the hard ECU.

Article 11 — Open market and credit operations

11.1 In order, and to the extent necessary, to carry out its tasks, the Fund may:

- operate in the financial markets by buying and selling outright (spot and forward) or under repurchase agreement, and at its discretion, claims and marketable instruments such as Treasury bills and other securities, denominated in [hard ECUs] and other Community currencies.
- conduct credit operations with credit institutions and other market participants.

11.2 The Fund shall establish general principles for open market and credit operations in [hard ECUs] carried out by itself or the national central banks on its behalf including the announcement of conditions under which it stands ready to enter into such transactions.

11.3 Open market and credit operations in [hard ECUs] carried out by the national monetary authorities on their own behalf shall be in accordance with principles agreed with the Fund.

Commentary
This Article provides for the Fund to carry out open market and credit operations. It might need to be reviewed in the light of decisions in relation to Article VI.4

Article 11.2 is intended to provide for the possibility that the Fund might carry out its operations through the agency of national central banks.

Article 11.3 has been added to govern market operations in hard ECUs by national monetary authorities on their own account.

Article 12 — Notes and coins

The Fund shall have the exclusive right to authorize the issue of notes and coins denominated in [hard ECUs] which shall have the status of legal tender in any particular Member State if the authorities in that Member State so decide.

Commentary

This Article gives the Fund the exclusive right to authorize the issue of hard ECU notes and coins. Actual issue would be made by national central banks or monetary authorities.

Article 13 — Other instruments

The Governing Board may decide [unanimously] upon such other methods or instruments for the implementation of monetary policy in relation to the [hard ECU], subject to the requirement of Article 11.3 of the Treaty, as it sees fit.

Commentary

This Article provides the means by which the Fund can adopt new methods and instruments of monetary policy.

Article 14 — Operations with public entities

14.1 The Fund shall not grant overdrafts or any other type of credit facilities to Community institutions, governments or other public entities of Member States or purchase debt instruments directly from them.

14.2 The provisions of this Article shall not apply to publicly-owned credit institutions.

Commentary

Article 14.1 prevents Community institutions and Member States from using the Fund's power to issue hard ECUs as a source of monetary financing.

The purpose of Article 14.2 is to enable the Fund to have dealings with publicly-owned commercial banks.

Article 15 — Clearing and payment systems

The Fund may provide facilities and establish provisions to ensure efficient and sound clearing and payment systems across the Community and with third countries.

Commentary

It is clear that some responsibility for hard ECU clearing and payment systems should reside with the Fund. This Article should also enable the Fund to play its part in such systems for Community currencies and between the Community and third countries.

[Article 16 — Operations with third countries]

[In order, and to the extent necessary, to carry out its tasks, the EMF shall be entitled to conduct all types of banking transactions [denominated in hard ECUs] in relation to third countries and international organizations, including borrowing and lending operations.]

Commentary

This Article provides the Fund with external operational powers should the hard ECU come to acquire an international role. It might need to be reviewed in the light of decisions taken in relation to Article V1.4.

Article 17 — Collection of statistical information

The Member States and the Community institutions shall cooperate with the Fund in providing, or collecting, on its behalf, such statistical or other information as may be necessary to enable it to perform its functions.

Article 18 — Other operations

In addition to operations arising from its tasks, the Fund may enter into operations that serve its administrative purposes or for its staff.

Article 19 — Reporting and financial statement

19.1 In addition to the reporting obligations laid down in Article IX of this Treaty, the Fund shall report on its activities at regular intervals. These reports are to be published and to be made available to interested parties free of charge.

19.2 A financial statement of the Fund shall be published each week. Copies shall be sent to the Council and to the European Parliament.

Commentary

Article IX of the Treaty obliges the Fund to present a monthly report to EcoFin and an annual report to the European Council, the Council and the European Parliament.

Chapter IV — Prudential supervision

Article 20 — Supervisory questions

20.1 The Fund shall be entitled to offer advice and to be consulted on the interpretation and implementation of Community legislation relating to the prudential supervision of credit and other financial institutions and financial markets insofar as such legislation may affect the management of the [hard ECU], for which the Fund has responsibility, or such other tasks as it may acquire, in accordance with Article III of this Treaty.

20.2 The Fund shall be entitled to offer advice to Community bodies and national authorities on measures relating to the [hard ECU] which it considers desirable for the purpose of maintaining the stability of the banking and financial systems.

Commentary
This Article provides the Fund with a locus in supervisory questions affecting the hard ECU.

Chapter V — Financial provisions

Article 21 — Financial accounts

21.1 The financial year of the Fund shall begin on the first day of January and end on the last day of December.

21.2 The annual accounts of the Fund shall be drawn up by the Executive Board in accordance with the principles established by the Governing Board. The accounts shall be approved by the Governing Board and shall thereafter be published.

Article 22 — Auditing

The accounts of the Fund shall be audited by independent external auditors recommended by the Governing Board and approved by the Council of Ministers. The auditors shall have full power to examine all books and accounts of the Fund and to require full information about its transactions.

Article 23 — Voting on financial matters

For the purposes of Articles 24 and 25 of this Statute decisions of the Governing Board shall be adopted by qualified majority, that is to say, the votes in the Governing Board shall be weighted according the the key attached to and forming part of this Statute and a decision shall be deemed to be approved if it carries [. . .] votes out of the total of [. . .].

Commentary
It is intended that the key, which would also be used for the provision of capital and the allocation of profits and losses, should correspond to the relative size of national GNP.

Because of the important financial implications, it is envisaged that modification of the key would entail a procedure requiring a Treaty amendment.

Article 24 — Capital of the Fund

24.1 The capital of the Fund shall, upon its establishment, be [hard ECU] [x] million. The capital may be increased from time to time by such amounts as may be decided by the Governing Board.

24.2 The national central banks shall be the sole subscribers to and holders of the capital of the Fund. The distribution of capital shall be according to the key attached to this Statute.

24.3 The Governing Board shall determine the extent to which and the form in which capital shall be paid-up.

24.4 The shares of the national central banks in the subscribed capital of the Fund may not be transferred, pledged or attached other than in accordance with a decision taken by the Governing Board.

Commentary
This Article sets out the rules relating to the capital of the Fund.

Article 25 — Allocation of income, losses and profits

25.1 The net profits of the Fund to be distributed shall be determined by the Governing Board on the basis of the balance sheet and the profit and loss account of the Fund. The Governing Board shall establish the accounting rules and procedures in this respect.

25.2 The Fund shall establish a General Reserve.

25.3 Following transfers to the General Reserve, the remaining net profits of the Fund shall be distributed to its shareholders according to the key which is attached to and forms part of this Statute.

25.4 In the event of a loss incurred by the Fund, the shortfall shall be offset, in order of priority:

- against the General Reserve;
- and, if necessary, following a decision by the Governing Board, by means of transfers of assets to the Fund by the national central banks according to the key which is attached to and forms part of this Statute.

Commentary
Profits and losses would be distributed or borne by national central banks in proportion to their capital subscriptions.

Chapter VI — General provisions

Article 26 — Staff

26.1 The Governing Board, on a proposal from the Executive Board, shall lay down the Staff Regulations of officials and the conditions of employment of other servants of the Fund.

26.2 The Court of Justice shall have jurisdiction in any dispute between the Fund and its servants within the limits and under the conditions laid down in the Staff Regulations and the Conditions of Employment.

Article 27 — Professional secrecy

Members of the Governing Board and of the Executive Board, officials and other servants of the Fund shall be required, even after their duties have ceased, not to disclose information of the kind covered by the obligation of professional secrecy.

Commentary

This Article is consistent with Article 214 of the Treaty.

Article 28 — Signatories

The Fund shall be legally committed vis-à-vis third parties either by the signature of the President or by the signatures of two members of the Executive Board or by two members of the staff of the Fund who have been duly authorized by the President to sign on behalf of the Fund.

3.   European Trade Union Confederation

Economic and Monetary Union: ETUC submission to Intergovernmental Conference (adopted by ETUC Executive Committee on 11–12 April 1991)

This Submission is in three parts:

- the first recalls the principal points made in the ETUC's April 1990 Statement;
- the second contains additional proposals in view of events since then;
- and the third comments accordingly on the Commission's proposed amendments to the Treaty.

The ETUC has made other submission to the IGC on political union and it is in those that the Confederation has developed in detail its views on the reforms to the Treaty which are required to give the Community a true social dimension. The two IGCs must in any event work in parallel. However, the social dimension must equally be an integral part of EMU — otherwise there must be doubts as to whether all the changes it involves will be accepted — and the ETUC will accordingly be judging the results of the two IGCs together.

1.   ETUC's April 1990 statement

1.1 The ETUC supports the creation of EMU provided it promotes unity within Europe, helps fight the scourge of mass unemployment and is compatible in general with the development of Europe's social dimension.

1.2 The fundamental objectives of EMU — and of both the **monetary and** economic policies which are introduced to achieve this — must be to promote sustainable development, full employment, and economic and social cohesion, as well as price stability.

1.3 The success of EMU requires the adoption by democratically-accountable bodies of overall macro-economic objectives: these can partly be achieved through the coordination of national policies, but a strengthening of the Community' own policies, resources and financial mechanisms is also required. In particular, there must be an effective coordination and management of regional policy at Community level, and the Structural Funds must be further enlarged so that they can better assume the task

of interregional redistribution and the achievement of greater economic and social cohesion.

1.4 As the body responsible for monetary policy, Eurofed must in addition to seeking price stability also take full account of the Community's overall economic policies; Eurofed must also be democratically accountable to the Community institutions and to the European Parliament in particular.

1.5 An advisory committee to Eurofed must be created to help to ensure the views of the social partners are not neglected.

1.6 The European institutions should assist the social partners in creating a European industrial relations area as part of the social dimension since without this the progressive creation of full EMU will neither be possible nor sustainable.

1.7 The timetable for completing the remaining two stages of EMU should be similar to that laid down for completing the Internal Market.

2.   Additional points

2.1 The ETUC has insisted that in order to meet economic and social goals EMU must be managed through a mixture of demand and supply-side policies and that competitive pressures should not be allowed to result in either social dumping or economic dumping (such as excessive subsidization). The ETUC rejects monetarist and neo-liberal doctrines and attempts to base EMU on them. The ETUC is therefore concerned that the official debate about the nature of economic union is currently centering on whether two new rules should be added to the Treaty — namely that there should be no monetary financing of public deficits and that no country should benefit from an unconditional guarantee concerning its public debt — and on how they should be enforced. Both relate essentially to the stability objective though pressures in this direction are already strong. The Community's real past weakness, however, has been related much more to its lack of ability to act together to increase, collectively, its margins for manoeuvre for growth and employment. To ensure a proper balance, the new Treaty must therefore give the Community the necessary powers not just to promote stability and to deal with an overheated economy but also to deal with one, as now, facing recession.

2.2 The scope for majority voting was substantially enlarged by Article 100 (a) of the Single European Act because it was recognized that the industrial aspects of the Internal Market could not be successfully completed by 1992 if any country was able to veto any part of the process. With regard to EMU, it is widely accepted that a single monetary policy is required, i.e. that no country would have a veto in this area either. Many economic issues will and should continue to be dealt with at the national and other levels in accordance with the principle of subsidiarity, but a Community role is required with regard to the coordination and management of macro-economic policy, and it should be accepted that this will not be effective if veto rights continue in this area as well. Once a course of action is decided upon, whether relating to monetary or economic policy, and by whatever procedure, then the ETUC regards it as natural that this should fully engage those concerned.

2.3 Taxes which directly affect, or are directly affected by, other member states' behaviour should be the subject of basic rules agreed at the Community level by majority voting. One such tax is that on income from capital, and the Commission's attempts to achieve harmonization in view of the liberalization of capital movements have failed because of lack of powers in the existing Treaty. As a result, there is now a risk that this kind of taxation could be destroyed. It would be totally unacceptable if one of the first effects of EMU would be that people who earn their incomes from work will pay tax while those who live on interest from capital will not.

2.4 With regard to the future size of the Community Budget, the Delors Committee itself recognized that in both Stages II and III of EMU the resources for supporting the structural policies of member states might have to be enlarged. The ETUC is convinced that this is so. The 1977 MacDougall Report considered that a Community Budget equal to 2–2.5% of EC GDP (compared to the current figure of 1.1%) could, through interregional transfers, significantly lessen the income disparities between rich and poor regions. The more recent Padoa-Schioppa Report (1987), which dealt with the economic implications

of completing the Internal Market, noted that the volume of intergovernmental grants in the federations of the industrialized world equalled at least 3% of GDP: the ETUC believes that this is the level which should be progressively introduced.

2.5 The ETUC has long recognized the necessity of reforming the CAP both for sound agricultural reasons and to prevent extra Community resources being diverted just to the problems of that sector. As the Budget is increased the Community's potential for promoting cohesion, particularly through giving the Structural Funds a wider remit, will be enhanced, though the ETUC also believes that other financial mechanisms, such as for R&D, the environment and infrastructure investment, should likewise be strengthened.

2.6 With regard to the raising of extra revenue for the Community Budget, the ETUC considers that both the proposal of the Padoa-Schioppa Report that the existing resource related to the size of each country's GDP should be made progressive, and the proposal that a new resource should be introduced, possibly related to an energy/environment tax, merit further study.

2.7 With regard to consultative arrangements, the social partners should be consulted on economic as well as monetary policies. Both the ETUC, UNICE, and CEEP have agreed that a macro-economic working party should be re-established in the framework of the Social Dialogue in order to make a positive input into the preparation of the Community's annual economic reports and their subsequent follow-up.

2.8 The ETUC endorses the timetable for introducing Stages II and III of EMU laid down by the Rome I European Council (October 1990). Accordingly, Stage II should begin on 1st January 1994 and Stage III should start probably three years' later following a report on the functioning of the second phase and particularly on progress made on real convergence. The ETUC agrees that it is not essential that all countries should have to introduce the single currency at the start of Stage III. Where there are economic or social difficulties, particularly related to a lack of sufficient convergence or cohesion, a member state should be entitled to temporary derogations.

2.9 With regard to the European industrial relations area, the ETUC has developed its thinking elsewhere. In summary, Article 118b in particular needs amending to ensure that

European framework collective agreements can be reached and enforced so that the social dimension can be built on the twin pillars of legislation and collective agreements.

3. The Commission's draft Treaty amendments

Article 2

3.1 The ETUC welcomes the addition of an employment objective to this Article, though reference should be to "full employment" rather than to "a high level". The ordering of the Article also needs improving: currently it almost reads as if the Community is based just on economic and monetary union which is based just on a single currency. It should be made clear that the Community must be based on "social union" just as much as economic and monetary union. The objective of economic and social development (which in fact is in the article) must therefore be brought out more. The objective of ensuring a form of development which promotes a healthy environment should also be added.

Article 3(g)

3.2 The ETUC welcomes the addition to the Community's existing common policies that of "a common economic policy". However, this common policy should also be based on a common budget (i.e. the coordination alone of national policies is not sufficient).

Article 3(ga)

3.3 The Article should be amended so that while a primary aim of monetary policy should be to promote price stability, it should not be the exclusive aim: monetary policy must also be framed taking into account investment and savings considerations and the overall effects on growth and employment.

Article 4.3

3.4 The Commission does not indicate that any change to this Article is being envisaged. The ETUC is proposing however to the IGC on Political Union that the Economic and Social Committee should be made into a full institution. Our arguments are developed elsewhere.

Articles 67–73

3.5 These articles should provide for the har-

monization by majority vote of the basic rules governing taxation on income from capital.

Articles 95–99

3.6 These articles should provide for majority voting on the basic rules governing those taxes which directly affect, or are directly affected by, other member states' behaviour.

Article 102b

3.7 The ETUC welcomes the reference to employment though the same points made in relation to Article 2 apply.

Articles 102c

3.8 Article 102c lays down a method of adopting the Community's common economic policy: however, this phrase is not used, but should be in accordance with Article 3(g). The role of the Commission, with which EcoFin will have to work closely, is rightly strengthened. However to ensure that the Parliament can play its proper role, the common economic policy should be subject to the cooperation procedure. The Economic and Social Committee should also be consulted.

3.9 The beginning of the second guideline, which is listed in Article 102c(1), should be amended to read "the evolution of competitive production costs . . .". The list is also unbalanced as it stands: the guidelines should also cover income and wealth distribution, and employment development. Certainly, the freedom of the social partners to enter contracts should be recognized — together therefore with the need for them to be fully involved in policy formulation, particularly through the social dialogue — but this should be a separate point.

Article 102d

3.10 This Article on the implementation of the common economic policy stops short of providing for sanctions as originally envisaged in the Delors Report if a member state fails to follow an agreed decision, preferring instead to rely on peer-group pressure and public exposure. If effective, the ETUC would not be opposed to such a procedure. If ineffective, the ETUC would be prepared to envisage "actions" or measures being provided for in the form, for example, of a withdrawal of Community financial and other benefits. However, the key issue is the need to ensure that effective procedures are also envisaged for use against countries which failed to pursue properly agreed growth and employment-related policies falling within the Community's competence, and not just against those failing to pursue agreed restrictive and stability-orientated policies.

Article 103

3.11 This Article, which is based substantially on the existing Treaty, lays down a somewhat different procedure to that of 102, i.e. it talks of evaluation exercises apparently independent of the guidelines exercise of Article 102 and, more damagingly, it provides for unanimous voting instead of majority voting as in Article 102. Article 103 therefore confuses the process and risks undermining Article 102: it should be deleted.

Article 104 (and Articles 130a–e)

3.12 Rather than just providing for the possibility of financial support for member states in difficulty, this Article, or the Economic and Social Cohesion Articles (i.e. 130a–e), should go further and provide for the Community Budget to be progressively enlarged, with new revenue resources, to make interregional transfers to ensure greater cohesion, particularly through the Structural Funds. (Currently, the Commission's draft Treaty just ends with an information note in brackets which says that the budgetary provisions of the Treaty will have to be reviewed in the light of the work of the IGC on Political Union.)

Article 104a

3.13 This is the Article which would add two new binding rules on budget deficits to the Treaty. In addition to the points made in para 2.1 above about the need for a proper balance between the stability objective and the growth and employment objectives, the ETUC also believes that the Article should attempt a more precise definition of what an "excessive" deficit is. This cannot be decided solely according to economic or monetary criteria: social ones have also to be taken into account. New restrictions on deficits have also to go hand in hand with greater tax harmonization.

Article 106a

3.14 This Article should spell out the mechanisms by which the democratic accountability of Eurofed will be ensured (e.g. by possibly moving to this Article some of the provisions of Article 109 relating to the European Parliament's role — which the ETUC supports).

Article 107 and Article 109

3.15 One or other of these Articles should provide for the establishment of a consultative committee to Eurofed made up of the social partners. This would be in line with the formal or informal practices of a majority of member states.

Article 109c

3.16 The first sub-paragraph envisages convergence essentially in a restrictive sense and applicable just to stability and public finances, though the Rome I European Council also insisted on the need for *real* convergence. Reference to this, and to the concept of cohesion, which does include convergence on economic performance, employment creation and living standards, is also required. Without real progress on these during the transitional period, and the promise of further progress thereafter, it must be doubtful whether political agreement on abandoning the possibility of parity changes will be possible.

3.17 Sub-paragraph 2 of Article 109c should be substantially amended in line with the comments made in relation to Article 104.

Article 109g

3.18 The ETUC accepts the provisions of this Article which could do a great deal to overcome the political differences which are otherwise threatening to disrupt progress towards EMU. This is not a question of institutionalizing a "two-speed Europe", anymore than are the current provisions within the EMS which allow some member states wider intervention margins, or which allow some states to belong to the System without belonging to its Exchange Rate Mechanisms.

4. Luxembourg Presidency "Non-paper"

Draft Treaty articles with a view to achieving political union, 12 April 1991

1. The annexed draft is intended to provide a general framework for further negotiations. It is based on the prevailing drift to emerge during the first reading of the contributions from Member States and the Commission and does not aim to reflect individual Member States' positions.

2. As a rule, the draft does not cover the question of amending voting procedures, or the scope of the cooperation procedure, issues which have been reserved for the final stage of the negotiations. As regards joint decision-making, the Presidency has at this stage merely indicated, by way of illustration, some areas where such a procedure could apply, without wishing to prejudice the final scope thereof.

For some topics, such as "the Congress", the Presidency has not proposed any wording because it takes the view that more detailed discussion is necessary before it can submit any texts.

3. In a number of areas, the text of the Treaty itself could be supplemented by declarations (i.e. on the role of the national parliaments, the revision of own resources to ensure adequate funds, the improvement of the quality of Community legislation and disclosure of information).

The Presidency has deleted a number of lapsed or obsolete Articles and reserves the right to continue to do so.[1]

Treaty on . . . . Union: Common provisions

Article A

By this Treaty, the High Contracting Parties establish among themselves a . . . . Union, hereinafter referred to as "the Union".

Article B

1. The Union shall be founded on the European Communities as established by the Treaties establishing the European Coal and Steel Community, the European Economic Community and the European Atomic Energy Community and on the subsequent Treaties and Acts modifying or supplementing them.

2. The Union shall also be founded on the provisions of this Treaty concerning foreign and security policy and cooperation on home affairs and judicial cooperation.

Article C

1. The Union shall have as its task to organize, according to principles of consistency and solidarity, the relations as a whole among its Member States and to achieve their gradual progress towards ever closer association.

2. The Union shall provide itself with the resources necessary to attain its objectives and carry through its policies.

Article D

1. The Union shall exercise its powers having due regard to the national identity of the Member States and their constitutional systems based on democratic principles.

2. The Union shall respect the fundamental rights and freedoms as recognized in the constitutions and laws of the Member States and in the European Convention for the Protection of Human Rights and Fundamental Freedoms.

Article E   (To be looked at again inter alia in the light of the work carried out on EMU. See also, in Annex A, the Stuttgart Declaration).

1. The European Council shall provide the necessary impetus for the Union in its various aspects and shall define the general political guidelines.

2. The European Council shall bring together the Heads of State or of Government of the Member States and the President of the Commission of the European Communities. They shall be assisted by the Ministers for Foreign Affairs of the Member States and by a Member of the Commission. The European Council shall meet at least twice a year under the Presidency of the Head of State or of Government of the Member State which holds the Presidency of the Council of the European Communities.

3. The European Council shall submit to the European Parliament a report after each of

---

[1] The existing Annexes, Protocols, Declarations, etc. will need to be similarly revised.

its meetings and yearly written report on the progress achieved by the Union.

* * *

Provisions amending the treaty establishing the European Economic Community with a view to establishing the European Community

(To facilitate reading of the draft Treaty, a number of Articles on Economic and Monetary Union have been included for reference, using the texts of the non-papers drawn up by the Presidency in the context of the Conference on EMU).

* * *

Part One: Principles

Article 1

By this Treaty, the High Contracting Parties establish among themselves a EUROPEAN COMMUNITY.

Article 2

The Community shall have as its task, by establishing a common market and economic and monetary union and by implementing the common policies or activities referred to in Article 3, to promote throughout the Community a harmonious development of economic activities, continuous growth which is non-inflationary and respects the environment, a high degree of convergence of economic performance, the increased competitiveness of European undertakings and industry, high employment, a high level of social protection, the raising of the standard of living, and economic and social cohesion and solidarity between Member States.

Article 3

For the purposes set out in Article 2, the activities of the Community shall include, as provided in this Treaty and in accordance with the timetable set out therein:

(a) the elimination, as between Member States, of customs duties and quantitative restrictions on the import and export of goods, and of all other measures having equivalent effect;

(b) an external economic policy;

(c) an internal market characterized by the abolition, as between Member States, of obstacles to freedom of movement of goods, persons, services and capital;

(d) a common policy in the sphere of agriculture;

(e) a common policy in the sphere of transport;

(f) a system ensuring that competition in the internal market is not distorted;

(g) the approximation of the laws of Member States to the extent required for the functioning of the common market;

(h) a social policy comprising a European Social Fund;

(i) the strengthening of its economic and social cohesion;

(j) an environmental policy;

(k) the strengthening of the competitiveness of industry;

(l) a technological research and development policy;

(m) an energy policy;

(n) encouragement for the establishment and development of trans-European networks;

(o) contribution to the attainment of a high level of health protection;

(p) contribution to education and training of high quality and to the flowering of European culture in all its forms;

(q) the establishment of a European Investment Bank;

(r) a development cooperation policy;

(s) the association of the overseas countries and territories in order to increase trade and promote jointly economic and social development;

(t) the strengthening of consumer protection;

(u) civil protection measures;

(v) measures in the sphere of tourism.

Article 3a

(for the record: EMU

1. For the purposes set out in Article 2, the activities of the Community shall include, as provided for in this Treaty and in accordance with the timetable set out therein, the adoption, within the framework of a system of markets which are competitive and open both internally and externally, of an economic policy based on the close coordination of Member States' economic policies, on the internal market, on the definition of common objectives and on the implementation of the policies and actions referred to in Article 3.

2. Concurrently with the foregoing, and as provided for in this Treaty and in accordance with the timetable set out therein, these activities shall include the irrevocable fixing of exchange rates between the currencies of the

Member States and the introduction of a single currency, the ecu, the definition and conduct of a single monetary and exchange policy the over-riding objective of which shall be to maintain price stability and, without prejudice to this objective, to support the general economic policy of the Community, in a manner compatible with free and competitive market principles.

3. These activities of the Community shall entail compliance with the following guiding principles: stable prices, sound public financing and monetary conditions and a healthy balance of payments.)

Article 3b

The Community shall act within the limits of the powers conferred upon it by this Treaty and of the objectives assigned to it therein. In the areas which do not fall within its exclusive jurisdiction, the Community shall take action, in accordance with the principle of subsidiarity, if and insofar as those objectives can be better achieved by the Community than by the Member States acting separately because of the scale or effects of the proposed action.

Article 4

for the record: — Economic and Social Committee

— Court of Auditoris

Article 4a

(for the record: EMU

A European System of Central Banks (ESCB) is hereby set up; it shall act within the limits of the powers conferred upon it by this Treaty and the Statutes annexed thereto.).

Article 5

unchanged

Article 6

(See EMU — to be examined later)

Articles 7 to 8c

unchanged

Part Two: Union citizenship

Article A

1. Every person holding the nationality of a Member State shall be a citizen of the Union.

2. Union citizens shall enjoy the rights conferred by this Treaty and be subject to the duties imposed by it.

Article B

1. Every Union citizen shall have the right to move and reside freely within the territory of the Member States of the Union, without limit as to duration.

2. The conditions for the exercise of this right, which shall be defined pursuant to Article F, shall lay down provisions to ensure fair distribution of the resulting burden on Member States, particularly in the area of social protection.

Article C

1. Every Union citizen shall have the right to vote at municipal and European Parliament elections in the Member State in which he resides, insofar as he has not been deprived of this right in the Member State of which he is a national and does not exercise it there.

2. The conditions for exercise of this right, which shall be defined pursuant to Article F, shall provide, inter alia, for a minimum residence period. Derogations warranted by specific problems peculiar to a Member State may be provided for.

Article D (This text may need to be reviewed in the light of discussions taking place in the context of political cooperation).

Every Union citizen shall, in the territory of a third country, be entitled to the protection of any Member State, on the same conditions as the nationals of that State. Before [31 December 1993], Member States shall establish the necessary rules between themselves and start the international negotiations required to secure this protection.

Article E

Every Union citizen shall have the right to petition the European Parliament in accordance with Article 137b(2). He may apply to the Ombudsman established in accordance with Article 137c.

Article F

The Council, acting unanimously on a proposal from the Commission and [role of the European Parliament] shall, before [31 December 1993], adopt the measures to be taken to give effect to the rights referred to in Articles B and C.

Article G

The Council, acting unanimously [role of the European Parliament] may adopt provisions amending or adding to the rights laid down in this Part, which it shall recommend to the Member States for adoption in accordance with their respective constitutional requirements.

Part Three: Policies of the Community

Title I —Free movement of goods

Articles 9–37

unchanged, except for

Article 28

deleted (substance incorporated in Article 113(2))

Title II — Agriculture

Articles 38–47

unchanged

Title III — Free movement of persons, services and capital

Articles 48–66

unchanged

Articles 67–73

(See EMU)

Title IV — Transport

Article 75

— replace present subparagraph (c) with the following text: "(c) measures to improve transport safety,",
— present subparagraph (c) will become subparagraph (d)

Articles 76–84

unchanged, except for

Article 82

deleted (division of Germany)

Title V — Common rules

Articles 85–102

unchanged, except for

Article 92

delete paragraph 2(c) = division of Germany
— new paragraph 3(d): "(d) aid to promote culture and heritage conservation." Present paragraph (d) shall become (e).

Articles 99, 100, 100a and 101

For the record: taxation (to be looked at in connection with the EMU discussions)

Articles 100a(2)

For the record: rights and interests of employed persons

Title VI — Economic and monetary policy

Chapters I–III = (Articles 102a–109)
(see EMU)

Chapter IV — External economic policy
(present title: "Commercial policy")

Article 110

Community action on external economic policy shall contribute, in the common interest, to the harmonious development of the economy and of world trade, the progressive abolition of restrictions on international trade, the lowering of customs barriers and the promotion internationally of the economic interests of the Community within the spheres of its competence.

Article 110a

External relations concerning monetary aspects of EMU shall be governed by the provisions of Article . . .

Articles 111 and 112 — for the record

Article 113

1. The Community shall conduct a common policy in respect of international trade in goods and services.

2. Where the implementation of this common policy requires unilateral measures to be adopted, such measures shall be adopted by the Council acting by a qualified majority on a proposal from the Commission.

3. Where the implementation of this common policy requires the conclusion of agreements with one or more States or international organizations, the provisions of Article 228 shall apply.

4. In matters covered by this Article and without prejudice to Article 228, the Community's position shall be set out by the Commission in its relations with third countries, within international organizations and at international conferences.

Article 114

deleted

Article 115

unchanged

Article 116

The first paragraph has been taken over in new Article 228a. — The second paragraph is repealed.

Title VII — Social policy

Article 117

The Community shall have as its objective to contribute towards the improvement of living and working conditions, to encourage the dialogue between both sides of industry, to develop human resources and to combat social exclusion.

These objectives shall be pursued by the

establishment of the internal market and the Economic and Monetary Union. They shall also be implemented by means of structural polices by the adoption of common rules, as well as by agreements concluded between both sides of industry.

In its pursuit of these objectives, the Community shall take into account the competitiveness of undertakings and the diverse forms of national practices, in particular in the field of relations based on agreement.

Article 118

Without prejudice to the other provisions of this Treaty, and in accordance with the general objectives thereof, the Commission shall have the task of encouraging close cooperation between the Member States in the social field.

To this end, the Commission shall act in close contact with the Member States, by means of studies and opinions and by organizing consultations, both for problems which arise at national level and for those which concern international organizations. Before delivering the opinions provided for in this Article, the Commission shall consult the Economic and Social Committee.

Article 118a

1. With a view to achieving the objectives of Article 117, the Community shall lend its support to Member States' activities in the following fields: — the working environment and, in particular, health and safety protection; — living and working conditions to ensure that workers' basic rights are protected; — the information and consultation of workers.

2. To this end, the Council, acting by a qualified majority on a proposal from the Commission, in cooperation with the European Parliament and after consulting the Economic and Social Committee, shall adopt, by means of directives, minimum requirements for gradual implementation, having regard to the conditions and technical rules obtaining in each of the Member States. Such directives shall avoid imposing administrative, financial and legal constraints in a way which would hold back the creation and development of small and medium-sized undertakings.

3. The provisions adopted pursuant to this Article shall not prevent any Member State from maintaining or introducing reinforced measures of protection of working conditions compatible with this Treaty.

4. The provisions of this Article shall not apply to the social security and social protection sector, the remunerations sector, the right of association sector, the conditions governing the exercise of the right to strike or the provisions relating to the access to employment for nationals of third countries.

Article 118b

The Commission shall have the task of promoting consultations between Community organizations representing workers and employers.

The consultations mentioned in the first paragraph may lead to collective agreements involving the whole of the Community and covering in particular the provisions for the implementation of the directives adopted pursuant to Article 118a.

Collective agreements shall be implemented in accordance with each Member State's own national procedures.

Article 118c

The Council, acting unanimously on a proposal from the Commission and after consulting the European Parliament, may adopt measures in the field of social security and social protection of workers insofar as this is necessary for the pursuit of the objectives referred to in Article 117.

Article 119

1. Each member State shall ensure that men and women are treated equally at work. In particular, it shall ensure that the principle of equal pay for equal work and that of equal opportunity on the employment market shall be applied.

2. For the purposes of this Article, "pay" shall mean the ordinary basic or minimum wage or salary and any other consideration, whether in cash or in kind, which the worker receives, directly or indirectly, in respect of his employment from his employer. Equal pay without discrimination based on sex shall mean: (a) that pay for the same work at piece rates shall be calculated on the basis of the same unit of measurement; (b) that pay for work at time rates shall be the same for the same job.

Articles 120 and 121

unchanged

Article 122

The Commission shall draw up a report each year on the development of the social situation in the Community. It shall forward the report to the European Parliament, the Council and the Economic and Social Committee.

The European Parliament may invite the

Commission to draw up reports on particular problems concerning the social situation.

Articles 123 to 127

unchanged

Article 128

The Council shall, acting by a qualified majority on a proposal from the Commission, in cooperation with the European Parliament and after consulting the Economic and Social Committee, adopt the general principles and necessary action for implementing a common vocational training policy capable of contributing to the harmonious development both of the national economies and of the common market.

Title VIII — The European Investment Bank

Article 129

unchanged

Article 130

Add at end: "In carrying out its task, the Bank shall facilitate the financing of programmes in conjunction with assistance from the structural Funds and other Community financial instruments."

p.m. The provisions concerning the EIB are to be looked at again in the light of the definition of the future role of the Bank in the field of external relations.

Title IX — Economic and social cohesion

Article 130a

In order to promote its overall harmonious development, the Community shall pursue and develop its actions leading to the strengthening of its economic and social cohesion.

In particular, the Community shall aim at reducing disparities between the various regions and the backwardnesss of the least-favoured regions.

Article 130aa

The European Regional Development Fund is intended to help redress the principal regional imbalances in the Community through participating in the development and structural adjustment of regions whose development is lagging behind and in the conversion of declining industrial regions.

Article 130b

Member States shall conduct their economic policies and shall coordinate them in such a way as, in addition, to attain the objectives set out in Article 130a. The implementation of the common policies, the internal market

and economic and monetary union shall take into account the objectives set out in Articles 130a, 130aa and 130c and shall contribute to their achievement. The Community shall support the achievement of these objectives by the action it takes through the structural Funds (European Agricultural Guidance and Guarantee Fund, Guidance Section, European Social Fund, European Regional Development Fund), the European Investment Bank and the other financial instruments.

The Community and the Member States shall endeavour to promote, in a concerted manner, a harmonious development of the territory, in particular by means of structural policies, relying on intervention by the Funds in the less favoured regions and zones, and by the constitution of trans-European networks and the implementation of joint action in the sectors covered by this Treaty.

The Commission shall submit a report to the European Parliament and the Council every five years on the progress made towards achieving economic and social cohesion, accompanied if necessary by appropriate proposals.

Article 130c

Within the context of Article 130a, the structural Funds shall pursue, without prejudicing the application of Article 130d and in the framework of their respective tasks, the following general objectives: **1.** the development and structural adjustment of regions which are lagging behind in development; **2.** the conversion of industrial regions and urban areas in decline; **3.** employment, the geographical and vocational mobility of workers, initial and on-going training and the integration of those excluded from the working environment; **4.** rural development.

Article 130d

1. Without prejudice to paragraph 2, a law shall define the tasks and prime objectives of the structural Funds. A law shall also define the general rules applicable to them and the provisions necessary to ensure their effectiveness and the coordination of the Funds with one another and with the other financial instruments.

A law may also be used to set up new structural Funds or regroup existing Funds.

2. With regard to the European Agricultural Guidance and Guarantee Fund, Guidance Section, and the European Social Fund, Articles 43, 126 and 127 shall continue to apply respectively.

Title X — Research and technological development

Article 130f

1. The Community's aim shall be to strengthen the scientific and technological bases of Community industry and to encourage it to become more competitive at international level, while promoting all the research activities necessary to pursue the objectives of this Treaty.

2. In order to achieve this, the Community shall encourage undertakings throughout the Community, including small and medium-sized undertakings, research centres and universities in their research and technological development activities; it shall support their efforts to cooperate with one another, aiming, notably, at enabling undertakings to exploit the internal market potential to the full.

3. Any research, technological development or demonstration activities necessary to achieve the objectives of this Treaty shall be decided on and implemented in accordance with the provisions of this Title.

Article 130g

In pursuing these objectives, the Community shall carry out the following activities, complementing the activities carried out in the Member States:

(a) implementation of research, technological development and demonstration programmes, by promoting cooperation with and between undertakings, research centres and universities;

(b) promotion of cooperation in the field of Community research, technological development, and demonstration with third countries and international organizations;

(c) dissemination and optimization of the results of activities in Community research, technological development, and demonstration;

(d) stimulation of the training and mobility of researchers;

Article 130h

1. The Community and the Member States shall work to coordinate their research and technological development activities so as to ensure that the policies of the Member States are consistent with one another and with Community policy, and with a view to developing common strategies. Member States shall also coordinate their rules on conducting experiments with animals.

2. In close contact with the Member States, the Commission may take any useful initiative to promote coordination. The Council may decide to involve third countries in such coordination by concluding agreements with them.

Article 130i

1. A multiannual framework programme shall be adopted by law, setting out all the activities of the Community. The framework programme shall comprise a limited number of specific programmes and shall lay down the necessary activities to promote, back up and monitor them. The framework programme shall: — fix the overall amount and the detailed rules for Community financial participation in the programme as a whole and the respective shares in each of the specific programmes; — establish the scientific and technological objectives to be attained by specific programmes; — fix the rules for the participation of undertakings, research centres and universities.

2. The framework programme may be adapted or supplemented, as the situation changes.

3. The Commission shall be empowered to define and carry out the specific programmes. The framework programme may make the exercise of such powers subject to the procedures established pursuant to Article 145.

Article 130j

In implementing the multiannual framework programme, supplementary programmes may be decided on involving the participation of certain Member States only, which shall finance them subject to possible Community participation.

The Council shall adopt the rules applicable to supplementary programmes, particularly as regards the dissemination of knowledge and the access of other Member States.

Article 130k

In implementing the multiannual framework programme, the Community may make provision, with the agreement of the Member States concerned, for participation in research and development programmes undertaken by several Member States, including participation in the structures created for the execution of those programmes.

Article 130l

In implementing the multiannual framework programme, the Community may make provision for cooperation in Community research, technological development and demonstration with third countries or international organizations.

The detailed arrangements for such cooperation may be the subject of agreements between the Community and the third parties concerned.

Article 130m

The Community may set up joint undertakings or any other structure necessary for the efficient execution of programmes of Community research, technological development and demonstration.

Article 130n

1. The multiannual framework programme shall be adopted by law.

2. The Council shall, acting [. . .] on a proposal from the Commission [. . . European Parliament] [Economic and Social Committee], adopt the provisions referred to in Articles 130j to m. Adoption of the supplementary programmes shall also require the agreement of the Member States concerned.

Article 130o

At the beginning of each year, the Commission shall send a report to the European Parliament and the Council. The report shall include information on research and technological development activities carried out during the previous year and on the work programme of the current year.

Title XI — Environment

Article 130r

1. The policy of the Community relating to the environment shall have the following objectives:

- to preserve, protect and improve the quality of the environment;
- to contribute towards protecting human health;
- to ensure a prudent and rational utilization of natural resources;
- to contribute to the taking of measures at international level in order to solve environmental problems and ensure the ecological balance of the planet.

2. The policy of the Community relating to the environment shall be based on the principles that preventive action should be taken, that environmental damage should as a priority be rectified at source and that the polluter should pay. Environmental protection requirements must be integrated into the definition and implementation of other policies.

3. In preparing its policy relating to the environment, the Community shall take account of:

- available scientific and technical data;
- environmental conditions in the various regions of the Community;
- the potential benefits and costs of action or lack of action;
- the economic and social development of the Community as a whole and the balanced development of its regions.

4. The Member States and the Community shall ensure the greatest possible access to information they possess relating to the environment.

5. Within their respective spheres of competence, the Community and the Member States shall cooperate with third countries and with the relevant international organizations. The arrangements for Community cooperation may be the subject of agreements between the Community and the third parties concerned.

This paragraph shall be without prejudice to the respective powers of the Community and the Member States to negotiate in international bodies and to conclude international agreements.

Article 130s

1. Without prejudice to paragraph 2, the Council, acting . . . on a proposal from the Commission and [role of the European Parliament] and after consulting the Economic and Social Committee, shall decide what action is to be taken by the Community in order to achieve the objectives referred to in Article 130r.

2. Environmental action programmes may be adopted by law.

Article 130t

The protective measures adopted pursuant to Article 103s shall not prevent any Member State from maintaining or introducing more stringent protective measures compatible with this Treaty.

Title XII — Energy

Article A

1. Without prejudice to the provisions of the Treaty establishing the European Coal and Steel Community and of the Treaty establishing the European Atomic Energy Community, action by the Community in the sphere of energy shall, in fields where the cross-border dimension so justifies, be complementary to that of Member States. It shall be aimed, inter alia, at: — guaranteeing security of supplies in the Community under satisfactory economic

conditions; — contributing to the stability of energy markets; — the establishment and functioning of the internal market in the energy sector; — defining the measures to be taken in respect of each of the energy sources in the event of a crisis; — promoting the rational use of energy and the development and use of new and renewable energy sources.

2. Action by the Community shall take account of the need to ensure a high level of protection of the environment, and the health and safety of persons.

3. Action by the Community shall be closely coordinated with the policies pursued in the framework of the Treaties establishing the European Coal and Steel Community and the European Atomic Energy Community.
It shall be consistent with the policies and programmes pursued by the Member States. The Commission shall take all appropriate steps to promote coordination between those policies and programmes and Community activities.

Article B

Within the framework of their respective powers, the Community and the Member States shall cooperate with third countries and the appropriate international organizations. The manner in which Community cooperation is to be implemented may be the subject of agreements between the Community and the third parties concerned. This Article shall not prejudice the respective powers of the Community and of the Member States to negotiate in international fora and to conclude international agreements.

Article C

1. The Council shall, acting by [. . .] on a proposal from the Commission [. . . European Parliament] [Economic and Social Committee], adopt the measures required to attain the objectives referred to in Article A(1).

2. Research, technological development and demonstration activities required to attain these objectives shall be adopted and implemented in accordance with the provisions of Title X.

Title XIII — Transeuropean networks

Article A

1. To help to attain the objectives referred to in Articles 8a and 130a of this Treaty and to enable citizens of the Union, economic operators and regional and local communities to derive full benefit from the setting up of an area without internal frontiers, the Community shall contribute to the establishment and development of transeuropean networks in the areas of transport, telecommunications and energy infrastructures.

2. Action by the Community shall aim in particular at promoting the interconnection and interoperability of national networks. It shall take account of the need to link landlocked and peripheral regions with central regions of the Community, and also of the demands of environmental protection, coordination with third countries, the economic viability of the projects in question and freedom of access to the networks.

Article B

1. In order to attain the objectives referred to in Article A, the Community: — shall establish blueprints for transeuropean networks laying down the objectives, priorities and broad lines of measures envisaged for each sector; these blueprints shall identify projects of common interest; — shall implement any measures that may prove necessary to ensure the interoperability of the networks, in particular in the field of technical standardization; — may provide additional financial support for projects of common interest identified in the framework of the blueprints.

2. Member States shall regard as a matter of common interest infrastructure programmes which may have a significant impact on the attainment of the objectives referred to in Article A. To this end they shall, in liaison with the Commission, coordinate among themselves the policies and programmes pursued at national level. The Commission may, in close collaboration with the Member States, take all appropriate steps to promote such cooperation.

Article C

The Council, acting by [ ] on a proposal from the Commission and, [role of the European Parliament], and after consulting the Economic and Social Committee, shall adopt the measures provided for in Article B.

Title XIV — Public health

Sole Article

1. The Community shall contribute towards ensuring a high level of human health protection by supplementing, and lending support to, action taken by Member States. Community action shall involve prevention and the promotion of healthy lifestyles, while paying particular attention to combating major health scourges.
Health protection demands shall form a con-

stituent part of the Community's other policies.

2. Member States shall, in liaison with the Commission, coordinate among themselves their policies and programmes in the areas referred to in paragraph 1. The Commission may, in close contact with the Member States, take all appropriate steps to promote such cooperation.

3. The Community and the Member States shall foster cooperation with third countries and the appropriate international organizations in the sphere of public health.

4. The Council shall, acting [by . . .] on a proposal from the Commission [role of the European Parliament] and after consulting the Economic and Social Committee, adopt the measures necessary to attain the objectives referred to in this Article.

5. Activities undertaken in the field of research shall be adopted and implemented in accordance with the provisions of Title X.

Title XV — Education

Sole Article

1. The Community shall contribute to the development of quality education and training by encouraging cooperation between Member States and, if necessary, by supporting and supplementing their action, while respecting the autonomy of education systems and cultural diversity.

2. Community action shall, in particular, be aimed at:

- promoting cooperation between educational establishments;
- encouraging mobility of students and teachers, including through the academic recognition of diplomas and periods of study;
- developing the European dimension of education, particularly through the teaching and dissemination of languages;
- organizing exchanges of experience and providing guidelines enabling a response to be made to problems shared by the education systems of the Member States.

3. The Community and the Member States shall foster cooperation with third countries and the appropriate international organizations in the sphere of education and training.

4. The Council, acting by . . . on a proposal from the Commission [role of the European

Parliament] shall adopt measures to contribute to the attainment of the objectives referred to in this Article.

Title XVI — Culture and heritage conservation

Sole Article

1. The Community shall contribute to the flowering of the cultures of each Member State, at the same time bringing European identity and the European cultural dimension to the fore.

2. Action by the Community, which shall respect the diversity of cultures in Europe, shall encourage cooperation between Member States and, if necessary, support and supplement their action in the following areas:

- improvement of the knowledge and dissemination of the culture and history of the European peoples;
- conservation and safeguarding of the cultural heritage;
- cultural exchanges;
- artistic and literary creation;
- training in the cultural field;
- development of the European audiovisual sector.

3. The Community and the Member States shall foster cooperation with third countries and the appropriate international organizations in the sphere of culture.

4. The Council, acting by . . . on a proposal from the Commission [role of the European Parliament], shall adopt measures to contribute to the attainment of the objectives referred to in this Article.

Title XVII — Consumer protection

Sole Article

1. The Community shall set itself the objective of contributing to the attainment of a high level of consumer protection. Its action, which supports and supplements that of Member States, shall relate to the protection of the health, security and legitimate economic interests of consumers and to providing information to consumers.

2. The Council, acting by a qualified majority on a proposal from the Commission [role of the European Parliament] [Economic and Social Committee] shall adopt the measures necessary to contribute to the attainment of the objectives referred to in this Article.

3. Measures adopted under this Article shall

not preclude the maintenance or establishment, by each of the Member States, of stronger protection measures compatible with this Treaty.

Title XVIII — Development cooperation

Article A

The Community shall act in the sphere of development cooperation in order to foster:

- the economic and social development of the developing countries, and most especially the most disadvantaged among them;
- the smooth integration of the developing countries into the world economy;
- the development and consolidation of democracy and the rule of law, and respect for human rights and democratic values.

Article B

The development policies pursued by the Community and the Member States shall be complementary. They shall be pursued in accordance with the commitments, obligations and objectives approved by the United Nations in respect of the developing countries.

Article C

The Community shall take account of the objectives referred to in Article A in the policies that it implements bilaterally and multilaterally which directly or indirectly affect developing countries.

Article D

1. Action by the Community in the sphere of development cooperation, which may form the subject of multiannual programmes, shall include:
   (a) food aid and humanitarian aid;
   (b) financial and technical cooperation;
   (c) action in the field of commercial policy;
   (d) specific actions to promote development.
2. General rules concerning the action referred to in 1(a) and 1(b) and multiannual programmes shall be laid down by law.
3. Without prejudice to Article 113, the Council, acting by . . . on a proposal from the Commission . . . [role of the European Parliament] shall adopt the measures necessary for the implementation of the action referred to in paragraph 1.

Article E

Member States shall, in close collaboration with the Commission, coordinate among themselves their policies in the area of development and shall agree on their aid programmes.

The Commission may, in close contact with the Member States, take all appropriate steps to promote such cooperation.

Article F

Within the framework of their respective powers, the Community and the Member States shall cooperate with third countries and the appropriate international organizations. The manner in which Community cooperation is to be implemented may be the subject of agreements between the Community and the third parties concerned.

This Article shall not prejudice the respective powers of the Community and of the Member States to negotiate in international fora and to conclude international agreements.

* * *

Part Four: Association of the overseas countries and territories

Articles 131 to 136a

unchanged

Part Five: Institutions

Title I — Provisions governing the institutions

Chapter 1 — The institutions

Section 1: The European Parliament

Article 137

The European Parliament, which shall consist of representatives of the peoples of the States brought together in the Community, shall exercise the legislative, consultative and supervisory powers which are conferred upon it by this Treaty.

Article 137a

Insofar as provided in this Treaty and in accordance with the powers conferred upon it for that purpose by the relevant provisions of this Treaty, the European Parliament shall participate in the process leading up to the adoption of Community acts by giving consultative Opinions or its assent and by exercising the functions assigned to it under the joint decision-making and cooperation procedures laid down in Articles 189a and 189b.

The European Parliament may, acting by a majority of its members, request the Commission to submit any appropriate proposal on matters on which it considers that Community acts are required.

Article 137b

1. In the course of its duties, the European Parliament may, at the request of a majority of its members, set up a temporary Committee of Enquiry to investigate, without prejudice to the powers conferred by the Treaty on other institutions or bodies, alleged contraventions or maladministration in the implementation of Community law, except where the alleged facts are being examined before a court and while the case is still subject to legal proceedings.

The temporary Committee of Enquiry shall cease to exist on the submission of its report.

The detailed provisions governing the exercise of the right of enquiry shall be determined by common agreement of the European Parliament, the Council and the Commission.

2. Any citizen of the Union and any natural or legal person residing or having its registered office in a Member State of the Community shall have the right to address, individually or in association with other citizens or persons, a petition to the European Parliament on a matter which comes within the Community's sphere of activity and which affects him, her or it directly and individually.

Article 137c

1. The European Parliament shall appoint an ombudsman empowered to receive complaints from natural or legal persons residing or having their headquarters in a Member State concerning shortcomings in the activities of the institutions. In accordance with his terms of reference, the ombudsman shall carry out enquiries for which he finds grounds on the basis of complaints submitted to him or shall conduct enquiries on his own initiative.

The ombudsman shall draw up an annual report to the European Parliament on the outcome of his enquiries.

2. The ombudsman shall be appointed after each election of the European Parliament for the duration of its term of office. The ombudsman shall be eligible for reappointment.

The ombudsman may be dismissed by the Court of Justice at the request of the European Parliament if he no longer fulfils the conditions required for the performance of his duties or if he has been guilty of serious misconduct.

3. The ombudsman shall be completely independent in the performance of his duties. In the performance of those duties he shall neither seek nor take instructions from anybody. The ombudsman may not, during his term of office, engage in any other occupation, whether gainful or not.

4. The European Parliament shall, after seeking an opinion from the Commission and with the approval of the Council, draw up the terms of reference of the ombudsman.

Article 138

Amend paragraph 3 to read as follows: The European Parliament shall draw up proposals for elections by direct universal suffrage in accordance with a uniform procedure in all Member States.

The Council shall, acting unanimously after obtaining the assent of the European Parliament, which shall act by an absolute majority of its members, lay down the appropriate provisions, which it shall recommend to Member States for adoption in accordance with their respective constitutional requirements.

Articles 139 to 144

unchanged

Section 2 — The Council

Article 145

– First indent (see EMU)
– second indent replaced by: — exercise the legislative power conferred upon it by this Treaty and have power to take decisions.
– third indent — unchanged

Articles 146 to 148

unchanged

Article 149

Where, in pursuance of this Treaty, the Council acts on a proposal from the Commission, and subject to the provisions of Article 189a:

(a) the Commission may amend its proposal as long as the Council has not finally adopted the act in question;

(b) the Council may adopt an act constituting an amendment to the proposal only by unanimity.

Articles 150 to 154

unchanged

Section 3 — The Commission

Article 155

unchanged

Article 156

unchanged

Article 157
(Article 10 of the Merger Treaty)
1. The Commission shall consist of a number of members equal to that of the Member States, who shall be chosen on the grounds of their general competence and whose independence is beyond doubt.
(For reference: Question of Deputy Commissioners.)
Only nationals of Member States may be members of the Commission; the Commission shall include one national of each Member State.
2. (unchanged)

Article 158
(Article 11 of the Merger Treaty)
1. The Members of the Commission shall be appointed, for a period of four years, in accordance with the procedure referred to in paragraph 2. Their term of office shall be renewable.
2. The Governments of the Member States shall nominate by common accord, after consulting the European Parliament, the person they intend to appoint as President of the Commission.
The Governments of the Member States shall, in consultation with the nominee for President, nominate the other members of the Commission.
The President and the other members of the Commission thus nominated shall be subject as a body to a vote of approval by the European Parliament.
The President and the other members of the Commission shall be appointed by common accord of the Governments of the Member States, after approval by the European Parliament.

Article 159
(Article 12 of the Merger Treaty)
Apart from normal replacement, or death, the duties of a member of the Commission shall end when he resigns or is compulsorily retired. The vacancy thus caused shall be filled for the remainder of the member's term of office by a new member appointed by common accord of the Governments of the Member States. The Council may, acting unanimously, decide that such a vacancy need not be filled. The procedure laid down in Article 158(2) shall be applicable for the replacement of the President.

Article 160 — (Article 13 of the Merger Treaty)
unchanged

Article 161 — (Article 14 of the Merger Treaty)
The President may appoint a Vice-President or two Vice-Presidents from among the members of the Commission.

Articles 162 to 163
(Articles 15, 16 and 17 of the Merger Treaty)
unchanged

Section 4 — The Court of Justice

Article 164
unchanged

Article 165
The third paragraph shall be deleted.

Article 166
unchanged

Article 167
The final paragraph should be amended to read as follows: "The Judges and Advocates-General shall elect the President of the Court from among the Judges for a term of three years. He may be re-elected."

Articles 168 to 170
unchanged

Article 171
Add the following two paragraphs: "If a Member State fails to adopt such measures within a reasonable time, any Member State or the Commission may refer the matter to the Council, which may, acting by a qualified majority, make recommendations.
Should the Court of Justice, on having the matter referred to it by the Commission, find in a second judgment that a Member State has not taken the necessary measures to comply with a previous judgment, the Commission shall refer the matter to the Council, which shall, acting by a qualified majority and after consulting the European Parliament, take any relevant measures."

Article 172
unchanged

Article 173
Add the following at the beginning: "The Court of Justice shall review the legality of laws and of acts . . . (remainder unchanged)".
In the third line of the second paragraph, add "a law", before "a regulation".

Article 174
Second paragraph, first line, add "a law" before "a regulation", and in the second line "of the law" before "of the regulation".

Articles 175 to 183

unchanged

Article 184

In the second line add "a law" before "a regulation" and add "of that law" before "of that regulation" at the end of the Article.

Article 185 to 188

unchanged

Chapter 2: Provisions common to several institutions

Article 189

Add the following as paragraph 1: 1. In the cases provided for in this Treaty, the European Parliament and the Council shall adopt Community laws, hereinafter referred to as "laws", according to the joint decision-making procedure.

A law shall define the fundamental principles or general rules applicable to a given matter. It shall be of general application.

A law shall have greater legal status than any other Community act.

A law shall empower the Council or the Commission to adopt the texts necessary for its implementation.

(The present wording of Article 189 shall become paragraph 2).

Article 189a

A law shall be adopted in accordance with the following procedure:

1. The Commission shall submit a proposal for a law to the European Parliament and the Council.

The Council, acting by a qualified majority, except in the case referred to in Article 149b and after obtaining the Opinion of the European Parliament and of the Economic and Social Committee shall adopt a common position. That common position shall be communicated to the European Parliament. The Council shall inform the European Parliament fully of the reasons which led it to adopt its common position.

The Commission shall inform the European Parliament fully of its position.

If, within three months of such communication, the European Parliament

(a) approves the common position, the Council shall definitively adopt the law in accordance with that common position;

(b) has not taken a decision, the Council shall adopt the law in accordance with its common position;

(c) rejects the common position by a majority of its members, the proposal for a law shall be deemed not to have been adopted;

(d) proposes amendments to the common position, the amended text shall be forwarded to the Council and to the Commission, which shall deliver an opinion on those amendments.

3. If within three months of the matter being referred to it, the Council approves, by a qualified majority, all the amendments of the European Parliament, it shall adopt the law. If, within the same period, the Council adopts, by a qualified majority, a text which departs from that of the European Parliament or if it does not take a decision, the President of the Council, in agreement with the President of the European Parliament, shall forthwith convene a meeting of the Conciliation Committee.

4. The Conciliation Committee, which shall be composed of the members of the Council and an equal number of representatives of the European Parliament, shall have the task of reaching agreement on a joint text, by a qualified majority of the members of the Council and by a majority of the representatives of the European Parliament. The Commission shall take part in the Conciliation Committee's proceedings and shall take all the necessary initiatives with a view to reconciling the positions of the European Parliament and the Council.

5. If, within six weeks of its being convened, the Conciliation Committee approves a joint text, the European Parliament, acting by a majority, and the Council, acting by a qualified majority, shall have a period of six weeks from that approval in which to adopt the law in accordance with the joint text. If one of the two institutions fails to give its approval, the proposal for a law shall be deemed not to have been adopted.

6. Where the Conciliation Committee does not approve a joint text, the proposal for a law shall be deemed not to have been adopted unless the Council, acting by a qualified majority within six weeks of expiry of the period granted to the Conciliation Committee, confirms the text to which it agreed before the conciliation procedure was initiated, possibly with amendments proposed by the European Parliament. In this case, the law shall be finally adopted unless the European Parliament, within six weeks of the date of confirmation by the Council, rejects the text by a majority of its members, in which case the proposal for a law shall be deemed not to have been adopted.

7. The periods of three months and six weeks

referred to in this Article may be extended by a maximum of one month and two weeks respectively by common accord between the European Parliament and the Council.

Article 189b
Reproduce present Article 149 with the following amendments:

- Deletion of paragraphs 1 and 3.
- The present text of paragraph 2 describing the cooperation procedure will therefore need to be adapted; certain points of the text which have given rise to differing interpretations could be clarified.

Article 190
The beginning should be amended as follows: "Laws, regulations . . ." (remainder unchanged).

Article 191
1. Laws shall be signed by the President of the European Parliament and by the President of the Council and published in the Official Journal of the Community. They shall enter into force on the date specified in them or, in the absence thereof, on the twentieth day following their publication.

2. Regulations and directives which are addressed to all Member States shall be published in the Official Journal of the Community. They shall enter into force on the date specified in them or, in the absence thereof, on the twentieth day following their publication.

3. Other directives, and decisions, shall be notified to those to whom they are addressed and shall take effect upon such notification.

Article 192
unchanged

Chapter III — Economic and Social Committee

Articles 193 to 198
unchanged

TITLE II — Financial provisions

Article 199
unchanged

Article 200
deleted

Article 201
Without prejudice to other revenue, the Communities' budget shall be financed wholly from the Communities' own resources.

The Council, acting unanimously on a proposal from the Commission and after consulting the European Parliament, shall lay down provisions relating to the system of own resources of the Communities, which it shall recommend to the Member States for adoption in accordance with their respective constitutional requirements.

Articles 202 to 204
unchanged

Article 205
The first paragraph should be replaced by the following:
"The Commission shall implement the budget, in accordance with provisions of the regulations made pursuant to Article 209, on its own responsibility and within the limits of the appropriations, having regard to the principles of sound financial management."

Articles 205a and 206
unchanged

Article 206a
Add to paragraph 1:
"The Court of Auditors shall provide the Council and the European Parliament with a statement of assurance as to the reliability of the accounts and the legality and regularity of the underlying transactions."
The second subparagraph of paragraph 4 shall read:
"The Court of Auditors may also, at any time, submit observations, particularly in the form of special reports, on specific questions and deliver opinions at the request of one of the institutions of the Community."

Article 206b
1. The European Parliament, acting on a recommendation from the Council which shall act by a qualified majority, shall give a discharge to the Commission in respect of the implementation of the budget. To this end, the Council and the European Parliament in turn shall examine the accounts and the financial statement referred to in Article 205a, the annual report and any relevant special reports by the Court of Auditors together with the replies of the institutions under audit to the observations of the Court of Auditors.

2. Before giving a discharge to the Commission, or for any other purpose in connection with the exercise of its powers over the implementation of the budget, the European Parliament may ask to hear the Commission

give evidence with regard to the execution of expenditure or the maintenance of financial control systems. The Commission shall submit any necessary information to the European Parliament at the latter's request.

3. The Commission shall take all appropriate steps to act on the comments in the decisions giving discharge and on other observations by the European Parliament relating to the execution of expenditure.

At the request of the European Parliament or the Council, the Commission shall report on the measures taken in the light of these comments. These reports shall also be forwarded to the Court of Auditors.

Articles 207 to 209

unchanged

Article 209a

Acting individually or in concert, Member States shall take all appropriate measures to counter fraud affecting the financial interests of the Community (An alternative or additional solution might be to add the following to the areas covered by Article A of the chapter on Cooperation on Home Affairs and Judicial Cooperation: — prevention and investigation of infringements of Community financial interests, including fraud).

* * *

Part Six: General and final provisions

Articles 210 to 226

unchanged

Article 227

Paragraph 2 — delete the words "Algeria and".

Paragraph 5(a) — add the word "Greenland" after "Faroe Islands" and delete the rest of the text of this point.

Article 228

1. Where agreements with one or more States or with an international organization in fields covered by this Treaty need to be negotiated, the Commission shall make recommendations to the Council, which, acting by a qualified majority, except in the cases laid down in paragraph 4, for which it shall act unanimously, shall authorize the Commission to open the necessary negotiations.

The Commission shall conduct these negotiations in consultation with a special committee appointed by the Council to assist it in this task, and within the framework of such directives as the Council may issue to it.

2. Agreements shall be concluded by the Council acting by a qualified majority on a proposal from the Commission.

3. The Council shall act after consulting the European Parliament, including when the agreement covers a field for which the cooperation procedure is required internally. The European Parliament shall deliver its Opinion within a time limit which the Council may lay down according to the urgency of the matter. On expiry of the time limit, the failure to deliver an Opinion may be ignored.

4. By way of derogation from the provisions of paragraph 2, the Council shall act unanimously when the agreement covers a field for which unanimity is required internally, and for agreements establishing an association involving reciprocal rights and obligations, common action and special procedures.

5. By way of derogation from the provisions of paragraph 3, when an agreement calls for amendment of a Community law, has important financial implications for the Community, establishes an association as defined in paragraph 4 or establishes a specific institutional framework by organizing cooperation procedures, the Council shall act after receiving the assent of the European Parliament.

6. When concluding an agreement, the Council may, by way of derogation from the provisions of paragraph 2, authorize the Commission to approve modifications on behalf of the Community where the agreement provides for them to be adopted by a simplified procedure or by a body set up by the agreement; it may attach specific conditions to this authorization.

7. When the Council concludes agreements which call for amendments to this Treaty, the amendments must first be adopted in accordance with the procedure laid down in Article 236.

The Council, the Commission or a Member State may obtain beforehand the opinion of the Court of Justice as to whether the agreement envisaged is compatible with the provisions of this Treaty. An agreement on which the Court of Justice has delivered an adverse opinion may enter into force only in accordance with the conditions set out in Article 236.

8. Agreements concluded under the conditions set out in this Article shall be binding on the Community and on Member States.

Article 228a

For all questions which are of particular interest for the common market, Member States shall act jointly in international organizations of an economic nature. To this end, the Commission shall submit to the Council, which shall act by a qualified majority, proposals concerning the scope and implementation of such joint action.

Article 229 to 230

unchanged

Article 231

The words "Organization for European Economic Cooperation" shall be replaced by "Organization for Economic Cooperation and Development".

Articles 232 to 234 — unchanged

Article 235

1. Should it prove that attainment of one of the objectives of the Community calls for action by the Community in one of the fields covered by Articles 3, 3a and 3b and this Treaty has not provided the necessary powers, the Council shall, acting unanimously on a proposal from the Commission and after receiving the assent of the European Parliament, adopt the appropriate measures while taking into account the principle of subsidiarity as defined in Article 3c.

2. The Council shall determine, under the conditions laid down in paragraph 1, what shall be covered by decisions to be taken by a qualified majority.

Article 236[2]

[for the record — European Parliament assent?]

Article 237[3]

unchanged

Article 238

deleted

Articles 239 to 240[1]

unchanged

* * *

Provisions amending the Treaty establishing the European Coal and Steel Community

(for the record)

Provisions amending the Treaty establishing the European Atomic Energy Community

(for the record)

Common foreign and security policy

Objectives and means

Article A

1. The Union and its Member States shall define and implement a common foreign and security policy with the aim of reinforcing the identity and role of the Union as a political entity on the international scene. The policy of the Union may extend to all areas of foreign and security policy.

2. The objectives of the common foreign and security policy shall be:

- to defend the common values, fundamental interests and independence of the Union;
- to strengthen the security of the Union and its Member States in all ways, [including the eventual framing of a common defence policy];
- to preserve peace and strengthen international security, in accordance with the principles of the United Nations Charter;
- to promote international cooperation;
- to develop and consolidate democracy and the rule of law, and respect for human rights and fundamental freedoms.

Article B

1. The Union shall pursue its common foreign and security policy objectives within a single institutional framework by establishing systematic cooperation between Member States in the conduct of policy and by gradually introducing joint action in all areas where the Member States have essential interests in common.

2. The consistency of measures carried out under the common foreign and security policy with measures carried out by the Community in the context of external economic relations and development cooperation policy and in all other areas of the Community's external relations shall be ensured by the Council and the Commission. Any Member State or the Commission may refer matters relating to the observance of such consistency to the Council.

[2, 3] Position to be revised; may perhaps be made a common factor for all the general and final provisions of the Union Treaty.

Institutional framework

Article C

1. The European Council shall define the principles of, and general guidelines for, the common foreign and security policy, in accordance with the objectives of Article A.

2. The Council shall be responsible for the conduct of common foreign and security policy on the basis of the general guidelines adopted by the European Council. It shall ensure the unity, consistency and effectiveness of action taken by the Union.

3. Any Member State or the Commission may refer to the Council any question relating to the common foreign and security policy and may submit proposals to the Council. In all matters covered by this Treaty, the Council shall act unanimously save in the case referred to in the second subparagraph of Article J(2) [and in Article N].

4. In cases requiring a rapid decision, the Presidency, of its own motion or at the request of the Commission or a Member State, shall convene an extraordinary Council meeting within 48 hours or, in an emergency, within a shorter period.

Article D

1. The Permanent Representatives Committee shall be responsible for preparing Council meetings and shall carry out the instructions given to it by the Council.

2. The Political Committee, composed of the heads of the political departments of the Member States, shall have as its tasks: — to monitor the situation in the area covered by the Union's foreign and security policy; — to formulate opinions, either at the request of the Council or on its own initiative for the attention of the Council.

3. The Council and the Presidency shall be assisted by the General Secretariat of the Council in the preparation and implementation of the Union's common foreign and security policy.

4. The Commission shall act in full association with the work carried out in the common foreign and security policy field.

5. A crisis mechanism shall be set up to deal with emergencies.

Article E

The European Parliament shall be regularly informed by the Presidency and the Commission of the basic choices made in the context of the Union's foreign and security policy. The Presidency shall consult the European Parliament on the main lines of the common foreign and security policy and shall ensure that the views of the European Parliament are duly taken into consideration.

Without prejudice to its other powers, the European Parliament may put questions to the Council on any matter of common interest relating to foreign and security policy and may make recommendations.

Article F

In matters covered by the common foreign and security policy, the Presidency shall be responsible for the external representation of the Union, assisted where appropriate by the previous and next Member State to hold the Presidency. The Commission shall assist the Presidency in this task.

Cooperation

Article G

Without prejudice to Articles J, K and N, Member States shall inform and consult one another within the Council on any matter of foreign and security policy of general interest in order to ensure that their combined influence is exerted as effectively as possible by means of concerted and convergent action.

The Council shall define a common position of the Union wherever necessary and the Member States shall base their policies and action on that position.

Article H

Member States shall support the Union's foreign and security policy actively and unreservedly in a spirit of loyalty and mutual solidarity. They shall ensure that their national policies are in line with the common positions agreed on. They shall refrain from any action which is contrary to the interests of the Union or likely to impair its effectiveness as a cohesive force in international relations.

The Council shall ensure that these principles are complied with.

Article I

1. Member States shall coordinate their action and, where necessary, define common positions in international organizations and at international conferences.

2. In international organizations and at international conferences where not all the Member States participate, those which do take part shall comply with the common positions agreed on and shall keep the other Member States informed of any matter of general interest.

Joint action

Article J

1. On the basis of general guidelines from the European Council, the Council may decide that an area or matter covered by the foreign and security policy should be the subject of joint action.

2. Whenever the Council decides on the principle of joint action, it shall lay down the Union's general and specific objectives in carrying out such action and the conditions, means and procedures for its implementation.

It may stipulate that the detailed arrangements for carrying out joint action shall be adopted [by a qualified majority] [by a majority to be defined].

The Council shall adapt joint action to changes in the situation.

Article K

1. Once the objectives and means of a joint line of action have been defined, each Member State shall be bound by the joint line of action in the conduct of its international activity. At international conferences and in international organizations, the Union's position shall, as a rule, be put by the Presidency.

2. Whenever there is any plan to adopt a national position or take national action pursuant to a joint line of action, information shall be provided in time to enable the other Member States and the Commission, if necessary, to be consulted in advance. The obligation to provide prior information shall not apply to measures which are merely a national transposition of Union decisions.

3. In cases of urgent need arising from changes in the situation, and failing a Council decision, Member States may take the necessary measures, because of their urgent nature, in accordance with the objectives of the joint line of action. They shall inform the Council immediately of any such decisions.

4. Should there by any major difficulties in implementing a joint line of action, a Member State shall refer them to the Council which shall discuss them and seek appropriate solutions. Such solutions shall not run counter to the objectives of the joint line of action nor impair its effectiveness.

Security

Article L

1. Decisions by the Union on security matters which have defence implications may be wholly or partly implemented in the framework of the Western European Union, insofar as they also fall within that organization's sphere of competence.

2. Decisions taken pursuant to paragraph 1 shall not affect the obligations arising for certain Member States from the Treaties establishing the Atlantic Alliance and the Western European Union and the situation of each Member State in that connection.

3. [With a view to the eventual implementation of a common defence policy, the provisions of paragraph 1 may be reviewed on the basis of a report to be submitted to the European Council in 1996 at the latest. On the basis of general guidelines from the European Council, the Council shall adopt the necessary provisions and shall recommend their adoption by the Member States in accordance with their respective constitutional requirements.]

General provisions

Article M

The Council shall adopt the necessary measures for implementing the provisions of this Title, particularly Articles D, F, K(2) and L(1).

Article N

Should action by the Union prove necessary, either in order to honour commitments enterd into by the Community or the Member States for the purpose of maintaining peace and international security or in order to safeguard important Union interests, the Council, acting [by a qualified majority] [unanimously] on a proposal from a Member State or the Commission, shall, as a matter of urgency and in derogation from the provisions relating to the European Communities, take appropriate measures to break off, partially or entirely, economic relations with one or more third countries.

Article O

1. The provisions of this Title shall not affect the powers of the European Communities.

2. The provisions of the Treaties establishing the European Communities which concern the jurisdiction of the Court of Justice of the European Communities and the exercise of that jurisdiction shall not apply to the provisions of this Title, with the exception of those of Article N.

3. The institutional and financial provisions of the Treaties establishing the European Communities shall apply to the provisions of this Title insofar as the latter do not derogate from them.

Article P

On the occasion of any review of the security provisions under Article L(3), the Council shall examine, by the same procedure, whether any other amendments need to be made to this Title.

****

Annex I: Declaration by the Member States

The Member States agree that the following topics can be a joint action priority as soon as this Treaty enters into force:

- industrial and technological cooperation in the armaments field;
- the transfer of military technology to third countries and the control of arms exports (Possibly to be supplemented by the inclusion of an Article in the EC Treaty reading as follows: "To the extent necessary, Member States shall align their laws, regulations and administrative provisions relating to the export of arms. The Commission shall make all appropriate recommendations to the Member States for this purpose");
- non-proliferation issues;
- arms control, negotiations on arms reduction and confidence-building measures, particularly in the CSCE context;
- involvement in peace-keeping operations in the United Nations context;
- involvement in humanitarian intervention measures;
- [CSCE, USSR, transatlantic relations].

******

Annex II: Declaration by the Member States which are members of the WEU on cooperation between the WEU and the Union

Declaration of political intent
    Practical arrangements (e.g. Secretariat, Presidency, scheduling etc.).

Annex III

Organizational arrangements
[in particular: — secretariat
                — collaboration between diplomatic missions
                — crisis mechanism]

Provisions on cooperation on home affairs and judicial cooperation

Article A

1. For the purpose of achieving the objectives of the Union, as a result of the free movement of persons and the establishing of Union citizenship, and without prejudice to the powers of the European Communities, Member States shall regard the following areas as matters of common interest: (a) controlling the crossing of the external borders of the Member States; (b) authorized entry, movement and residence on the territory of the Member States by nationals of third countries (in particular conditions of access, visa policies, asylum policies); (c) combating unauthorized immigration and residence on the territory of the Member States by nationals of third countries; (d) combating illegal trafficking, in particular illegal drug trafficking; (e) customs cooperation in fields not falling within the powers of the European Communities; (f) judicial cooperation in civil and criminal matters, with particular reference to the recognition and enforcement of judgments; (g) prevention and prosecution of all forms of delinquency. (See also Article 209a of the EC Treaty).

2. Without prejudice to the powers of the European Communities, the matters of common interest set out in paragraph 1 may be the subject of action by the Union under the conditions and in accordance with the procedures laid down in Articles B to J.

Article B

In the areas referred to in Article A(f) and (g), Member States shall inform and consult one another and may, using the appropriate form and procedures, jointly take any measures contributing to the pursuit of the objectives of the Union.

Article C

1. In the areas referred to in Article A(a) to (e), Member States shall inform and consult one another and the Commission within the Council, with a view to coordinating their action and, if necessary, adopting a common position. To that end, they shall establish collaboration between the relevant departments of their administrations.

2. Member States meeting within the Council may, on the initiative of any Member State or the Commission: (a) unanimously adopt joint action to the extent to which the objectives of the Union can be attained better by joint action

than by the Member States acting individually; they may decide that measures implementing joint action will be adopted by [a qualified majority] [a majority to be defined]; (b) unanimously adopt draft conventions and recommend adoption thereof in accordance with their respective constitutional rules; unless otherwise provided by the agreements: — measures implementing such conventions shall be adopted within the Council by a majority [of two thirds] of the High Contracting Parties; — the Court of Justice shall ensure compliance with the law in the interpretation and application of such conventions.

3. If action by the Community seems necessary in order to achieve the objectives of the Union in one of the areas referred to in paragraph 1, the Council, acting unanimously on a proposal from the Commission, [role of the European Parliament], shall take any appropriate measures.

Article D

1. The Member States meeting within the Council, on the basis of general guidelines from the European Council, may adopt provisions extending the scope of Article A to other areas of activity related to the objectives of the Union and recommend adoption thereof in accordance with their respective constitutional rules.

2. Following the same procedure, Member States may decide to transfer an area of activity from Article B to Article C.

Article E

The Union shall allow for the responsibilities incumbent upon national authorities with regard to the maintaining of law and order and the safeguarding of internal State security.

Article F

Within international organizations and at international conferences in which they take part, Member States shall defend the positions adopted jointly under the provisions of this Title.

Article G

The Presidency and the Commission shall regularly inform the European Parliament of discussions in the areas covered by this Title. They shall ensure that the European Parliament's views are duly taken into account.

The European Parliament may draw the attention of the Council and the Commission to any question relating to the areas referred to in Article A.

Article H

1. The Permanent Representatives Committee of the Member States shall be responsible for preparing the Council's discussions and shall carry out any tasks entrusted to it by the Council.

2. A Coordinating Committee shall be set up consisting of senior officials of the Member States, with the task of, in the areas referred to in Article C:

- monitoring the situation,
- giving opinions, either at the request of the Council or on its own initiative, for the attention of the Council.

3. The Council and the Presidency of the Council shall be assisted by the General Secretariat of the Council in preparing and implementing the policy of the Union in these areas.

4. The Commission shall be fully associated in the work on cooperation in the field of home affairs and judicial affairs.

Article I

The provisions of this Title shall not prevent the establishing or developing of closer cooperation between two or more Member States to the extent to which such cooperation does not conflict with, or impede, that provided for in this Title.

Article J

1. The provisions of this Title shall not affect the powers of the European Communities.

2. The provisions of the Treaties establishing the European Communities concerning the power of the Court of Justice of the European Communities and the exercise of that power shall not apply to the provisions of Articles A to I, with the exception of those of Article C(2)(b) and Article C(3).

3. The provisions of an institutional and financial nature in the Treaties establishing the European Communities shall apply to the provisions of this Title to the extent to which the latter do not derogate therefrom.

General and final provisions

for the record
(Possibly a repeat of Articles 236–240 of the EEC Treaty)

****

Annex A: Stuttgart Declaration

2.1. The European Council

2.1.1. The European Council brings together the Heads of State or Government and the President of the Commission assisted by the Foreign Ministers of the Member States and a member of the Commission.

2.1.2. In the perspective of European Union, the European Council:

- provides a general political impetus to the construction of Europe;

- defines approaches to further the construction of Europe and issues general political guidelines for the European Communities and European Political Cooperation;

- deliberates upon matters concerning European Union in its different aspects with due regard to consistency among them;

- initiates cooperation in new areas of activity;

- solemnly expresses the common position in questions of external relations.

2.1.3. When the European Council acts in matters within the scope of the European Communities, it does so in its capacity as the Council within the meaning of the Treaties.

2.1.4. The European Council will address a report to the European Parliament after each of its meetings. This report will be presented at least once during each Presidency by the President of the European Council.

The European Council will also address a written annual report to the European Parliament on progress towards European Union.

In the debates to which these reports give rise, the European Council will normally be represented by its President or one of its members."

5. European Commission Amendments

Amendments to Luxembourg Presidency "Non-Paper" concerning the structure of the draft treaty on the Union

Draft Text

CONTENTS

Treaty on . . . union
Principles
Union citizenship
Union policies

- External policy[1]
- [Union policy on home affairs and judicial cooperation]

The institutions of the Union
General and final provisions
Provisions amending the ECSC Treaty
Provisions amending the Euratom Treaty

PRINCIPLES

Article A

unchanged

Article B

The Union shall take the place of the European Communities as established by the Treaties establishing the European Coal and Steel Community, the European Economic Community and the European Atomic Energy Community and subsequent treaties and acts modifying or supplementing them; *they constitute the original nucleus of the Community edifice and their federal vocation is thus confirmed.*

Article C

1. The Union shall have as its task to organize, according to principles of consistency and solidarity, relations as a whole among its Member States and their peoples and to achieve their gradual progress towards ever closer association.
2. (Set out Union objectives based on Article 2 of the EEC Treaty, as updated by the SEA, together with those of EMU and common foreign and security policy. (Article A(2) on p. 76 of the Presidency draft)
3. *The Union shall have the resources needed to attain the objectives it has set itself and to carry through the policies to that end.* (Rome II)
4. *Moreover, the Member States of the Union shall provide mutual assistance in all circumstances where the interests of any of them are threatened.*

Article D

1. Unchanged
2. [See Presidency text but spell out its scope]
3. [Possibility of a provision on subsidiarity (see Article B on p. 14 of the Presidency draft), subject to the outcome of negotiations, particularly on Article 235]

Article Da

[List Union activities, taken over from Article 3 of the EEC Treaty, as updated by the SEA, together with those of EMU and common foreign and security policy]

Article E

[Article 4 of the EEC Treaty, listing the institutions and other bodies but adding the European Council and the Central Bank]

Article F

Article 5 of the EEC Treaty
NB: Articles 6, 8a, 8b and 8c of the EEC Treaty to be reviewed.

UNION CITIZENSHIP

Presidency text, subject to points under discussion at the Conference, in conjunction with Article 7 of the EEC Treaty.

UNION POLICIES

TITLE X

THE EXTERNAL POLICY OF THE UNION

Article

1. *The purpose of the external policy of the Union is to secure the coherence of the whole of the Community's external activities in the*

---

[1] Common foreign and security policy, commercial and economic policy, and development cooperation policy (including association of OCTs).

framework of its foreign, security, economic and development policies. (Rome II)

2. [Article B(2) on p. 77 of the Presidency draft unchanged, except for replacing "Community" by "Union"]

Chapter I

Common foreign and security policy

Article A

1. The Union shall define and implement a common foreign and security policy . . . (rest unchanged).

2. Moved to Article C2, above.

Article B

1. Unchanged
2. Moved to new Article above.

Article C

unchanged

Article D

1. Unchanged

2. The Political Committee, composed of the heads of the political departments of the Member States and of the Commission shall have as its tasks: . . . (rest unchanged).

3. *Council proceedings and decisions shall be prepared and their implementation monitored by the General Secretariat of the Council, cooperating in organized fashion with the Commission.*

The Commission shall participate fully in the work carried out in the common foreign and security policy field.

4. Unchanged

Articles E, F, G, H and I

Unchanged, subject to current negotiations.

Articles J and K

Replace "joint action" by "Union action".

Article L

Unchanged, subject to current negotiations.

Articles M to P (general provisions)

The Commission considers that Article N should be reviewed in the light of changes made to other articles.

Article 228a applies to the conclusion of international agreements under the common foreign and security policy.

Chapter II

Commercial policy and external economic policy

The Commission reminds the Conference that it has proposed an amended version of the existing Treaty articles for insertion in this Chapter.

Article 228 applies to the conclusion of international agreements in areas covered by this Chapter.

Chapter III

Development cooperation policy

The Commission reminds the Conference that it has proposed a set of provisions to govern this policy and give it an explicit legal basis in the Treaty.

Article 228 applies to the conclusion of international agreements in areas covered by this Chapter.

Chapter IV

"Multidimensional" agreements

Article 228b applies to the conclusion of agreements in areas covered both by the common foreign and security policy and by other Union policies.

GENERAL AND FINAL PROVISIONS

Article 223

The Commission reminds the Conference that it has proposed that this Article be deleted.

Article 228

Presidency draft, pp. 69 and 70.

Article 228a

[Provisions derogating from the Article 228 procedure as regards the conclusion of agreements relating to common foreign and security policy]

Article 228b

[Provisions derogating from the Article 228 procedure as regards the conclusion of agreements relating to common foreign and security policy and to areas covered by other Union policies ("multidimensional" agreements)]

Article 228c

1. In areas to which the procedure of Article 228 applies, the Union shall be represented by the Commission in relations with non-member countries and in international organizations and conferences.

2. For all questions of specific interest to the Union, without prejudice to the provisions of Chapter I, the Member States shall act jointly in international organizations and conferences. To this end, the Commission shall present proposals relating to the scope and implementation of such joint action to the Council, which shall act by a qualified majority.

Explanatory memorandum

1. The Dublin and Rome European Councils, responding among other things to initiatives by Mr Kohl and Mr Mitterrand, declared the intention of transforming the Community into a European Union, and of developing its political dimension notably on the international scene. The Commission considers that the Intergovernmental Conference should be guided by the basic thinking which has been behind the construction of Europe for 40 years now, namely that all progress made towards economic, monetary, social or political integration should gradually be brought together in a single Community as the precursor of a European Union.

This being so, it is somewhat paradoxical that the current trend in the Intergovernmental Conference favours a kind of revision of the Treaty of Rome that would depart from this general unification process and keep the Community no longer as the focal point but simply as one entity among others in a political union with ill-defined objectives and a variety of institutional schemes.

True enough, the Intergovernmental Conference is faced with the difficult task of generating a consensus on a common foreign and security policy at a time when the 12 Member States are faced with a series of challenges on the world scene.

It is equally true that the foreign and security policy will undoubtedly involve adjustments to the way in which common decisions are prepared and implemented and confer an eminent role on the European Council.

But in this area, as with EMU, where a new institution is also to be established, this adjustment to the Community approach cannot be allowed to go so far as to break up its existing model, which has demonstrated its dynamism and efficiency.

2. In its instructions to the Intergovernmental Conference, the Rome European Council laid emphasis on "the vocation of the Union to deal with aspects of foreign and security policy, in accordance with a sustained evolutive process and in a unitary manner, on the basis of general objectives laid down in the Treaty" as a fundamental principle. It was on this basis that the Commission supported a single Treaty. Yet the structure of the draft Articles presented by the Luxembourg Presidency on 15 April highlights the risk that the Conference will depart from this basic orientation.

In that draft foreign and security policy is conceived and defined as standing alone as a separate pillar of the general structure. It is fully separated from all other policies, described as Community policies. A third pillar, also to be set up alongside the Community, is also envisaged as consisting of "home affairs and judicial cooperation". These new entities are attached to the Community only artificially and only under the heading of a political union which, in Article B(2), gives equal but separate status to the Community, foreign and security policy and cooperation. This jeopardizes the Rome European Council's avowed objective of securing "coherence of the overall external action of the Community in the framework of its foreign, security, economic and development policies".

3. Following the guidelines set by the European Council, the Commission stands by the view set out in its opinion of 21 October 1990 that the main, indeed the central, objective of transforming the Community into a European Union should be to ensure the unity, the consistency and, as a result, the efficiency of its international activities. It is, of course, clear that a common foreign and security policy is a *sui generis* policy that can be implemented only gradually; but it is not possible to affirm the identity of the Union and the consistency of its international personality simply be adding a foreign and security policy to existing policies. The reality of international life makes clear how closely political relations, extending from external security to compliance with human rights, are related to economic policies. This consistency can be guaranteed in full only if the construction of the Community is conceived on a unitary base. Consequently, there can be no question of grafting the Union concept onto the existing Treaty; the Union must absorb the Community and all that it has achieved.

4. The Commission accordingly proposes that the Presidency draft be amended on a number of points which are essential if objectives defined by the European Council are to be achieved. In particular:

(a) the external policy of the Union can be made efficient and coherent by:

(i) the existence of institutional machinery for the preparation and implementation of Union decisions in the common foreign and security policy area;

(ii) strengthening the existing external policies — a redefined common commercial policy; cooperation with European countries to be written into the Treaties; likewise for developing countries;

(iii) a clear statement of the Union's international identity in terms of its treaty-making power in areas within its general jurisdiction, particularly, of course, in relation to its common foreign and security policy and its presence on the international scene;

(b) the unitary character of the European construction should be reflected in the structure of the Treaty:

(i) by combining in the introductory articles all the foundations and objectives of the Union, both those already covered by the existing Community, including the single market, and those of economic and monetary union and of the new foreign and security policy;

(ii) placing in this first part of the Treaty both the provisions for the Union institutions and the concept of Union citizenship, with the rights and obligations pertaining to it.

The few proposed amendments to the Presidency draft annexed to this paper chiefly concern the structure of certain parts of the Treaty and affect the texts of the relevant articles only in so far as is strictly necessary.

6. Luxembourg Presidency "Draft Treaty on the Union"

18 June 1991

Conference of the Representatives of the Governments of the Member States

Political Union

Economic and Monetary Union

Common Provisions

Article A

By this Treaty, the High Contracting Parties establish among themselves a Union. The Union shall be founded on the European Communities supplemented by the policies and cooperations established by this Treaty. It shall have as its task to organize, according to the principles of consistency and solidarity, the relations among the Member States and among their peoples. This Treaty marks a new stage in a process leading gradually to a Union with a federal goal.

Article B

The Union's aims shall be from the starting point of the acquis communautaire which is called upon to develop:

- to promote economic and social progress which is balanced and sustainable in particular through the creation of an area without internal frontiers, through the reinforcement of economic and social cohesion and the establishment of economic and monetary union including, finally, a single currency,

- to assert its identity on the international scene, in particular through the implementation of a common foreign and security policy which shall include the eventual framing of a defence policy,

- to reinforce the protection of the rights and interests of its Member States' nationals, through the introduction of a citizenship of the Union,

- to promote a close cooperation on home affairs and in the judicial field.

Article C

The Union shall be served by a single institutional framework which shall ensure the consistency and the continuity of the actions carried out in order to reach its objectives while respecting and developing the acquis communautaire. The Union shall in particular ensure the consistency of its external actions as a whole in the implementation of its external relations, defence, economic and development policies.

Article D

The European Council shall provide the Union with the necessary impetus for its development and shall define the general political guidelines. The European Council shall bring together the Heads of State or of Government and the President of the Commission. They shall be assisted by the Ministers for Foreign Affairs of the Member States and by a Member of the Commission.[1]

The European Council shall meet at least twice a year under the Presidency of the Head of State or of Government of the Member state which holds the Presidency of the Council. The European Council shall submit to the European Parliament a report after each of its meetings and a yearly written report on the progress achieved by the Union.

Article E

The Council, the Commission and the Court of Justice shall exercise their powers under the conditions and for the purposes provided for by the provisions of the Treaties establishing the European Communities, the subsequent Treaties and Acts modifying and supplementing them and by the provisions of this Treaty.

Article F

p.m. Conference of Parliaments

Article G

1. The Union shall have due regard to the national identity of its Member States whose

---

[1] A declaration of the Conference will state that the President of the European Council shall invite Economic and Finance Ministers to assist in work on Economic and Monetary Union.

systems of government are founded on the principles of democracy.

2. The Union shall respect the rights and freedoms as recognized in the European Convention for the Protection of Human Rights and Fundamental Freedoms.

3. The Union shall provide itself with the resources necessary to attain its objectives and carry through its policies.

Provisions amending the Treaty establishing the European Economic Community with a view to establishing the European Community

Part One: Principles

Article 1

By this Treaty, the High Contracting Parties establish among themselves a EUROPEAN COMMUNITY.

Article 2

The Community shall have as its task, by establishing a common market and economic and monetary union and by implementing the common policies or activities referred to in Article 3, to promote throughout the Community a harmonious and balanced development of economic activities, sustainable and non-inflationary growth respecting the environment, a high degree of convergence of economic performance, a high level of employment, and of social protection, the raising of the standard and quality of living, and economic and social cohesion and solidarity between Member States.

Article 3

For the purposes set out in Article 2, the activities of the Community shall include, as provided in this Treaty and in accordance with the timetable set out therein:

(a) the elimination, as between Member States, of customs duties and quantitative restrictions on the import and export of goods, and of all other measures having equivalent effect;

(b) a common commercial policy;

(c) an internal market characterized by the abolition, as between Member States, of obstacles to freedom of movement of goods, persons, services and capital;

(d) a common policy in the sphere of agriculture and fisheries;

(e) a common policy in the sphere of transport;

(f) a system ensuring that competition in the internal market is not distorted;

(g) the approximation of the laws of Member States to the extent required for the functioning of the common market;

(h) a policy in the social sphere comprising a European Social Fund;

(i) the strengthening of its economic and social cohesion;

(j) a policy in the sphere of the environment;

(k) the strengthening of the competitiveness of the Community's industry;

(l) a policy in the sphere of research and technological development;

(m) a policy in the area of energy;

(n) encouragement for the establishment and development of trans-European networks;

(o) contribution to the attainment of a high level of health protection;

(p) contribution to education and training of high quality and to the flowering of the cultures in Europe in all their forms;

(q) a policy in the sphere of development cooperation;

(r) the association of the overseas countries and territories in order to increase trade and promote jointly economic and social development;

(s) contribution to the strengthening of consumer protection;

(t) civil protection measures;

(u) measures in the sphere of tourism.

Articles 3a, 3b, 4, 4a and 4b

(No change of substance from text of "Non-paper".)

Article 5[2]

Add the following third paragraph: On the basis of a periodic report prepared by the Commission, the Member States and the Commission shall establish close cooperation between their administrative departments in order to ensure full compliance with Community law.

Article 6

deleted

Articles 7 to 8c

unchanged

---

[2] Declaration concerning the non-contractual responsibility of Member States to redress damages caused by any failure to fulfil their obligations under Community law.

Part Two: Union citizenship

Article A

1. Union citizenship is hereby introduced. Every person holding the nationality of a Member State shall be a citizen of the Union.

2. Union citizens shall enjoy the rights conferred by this Treaty and shall be subject to the duties imposed by it.

Article B

1. Every Union citizen shall have the right to move and reside freely within the territory of the Member States, under the conditions laid down in this Treaty and by the measures adopted to give it effect.

2. The Council may, adopt provisions with a view to facilitating the exercise of the rights referred to in the preceding paragraph; it shall act unanimously on a proposal from the Commission and after receiving assent from the European Parliament unless the present treaty stipulates otherwise.

Article C

1. Every Union citizen shall have the right to vote and to stand as a candidate at municipal elections in the Member State in which he resides, under the same conditions as nationals of that State, subject to detailed arrangements to be adopted before 31.12.1993 by the Council, acting unanimously on a proposal from the Commission and after consulting the European Parliament; these arrangement may provide for derogations where warranted by problems specific to a Member State.

2. Without prejudice to the provisions of Article 138(3) and of the provisions adopted for its implementation, every Union citizen shall have the right to vote and to stand as a candidate in elections to the European Parliament in the Member State in which he resides, under the same conditions as nationals of that State, subject to detailed arrangements to be adopted before 31.12.1993 by the Council, acting unanimously on a proposal from the Commission and after consulting the European Parliament; these arrangements, may provide for derogations where warranted by problems specific to a Member State.

Article D

Every Union citizen shall, in the territory of a third country in which the Member State of which he is a national is not represented, be entitled to protection by diplomatic or consular authorities of any Member State, on the same conditions as the nationals of that State. Before 31.12.1993, Member States shall establish the necessary rules among themselves and start the international negotiations required to secure this protection.

Article E

Every Union citizen shall have the right to petition the European Parliament in accordance with Article 137bb. Every Union citizen may apply to the Ombudsman established in accordance with Article 137c.

Article F

The Commission shall report to the Council and to the European Parliament before 31.12.1993 and then every 3 years on the implementation of the provisions of this Part. This report shall take account of the development of the Union. On this basis, and without prejudice to the other provisions of this Treaty, the Council acting unanimously on a proposal from the Commission, and after obtaining the assent of the European Parliament, may adopt provisions to strengthen or to add to the rights laid down in this Part, which it shall recommend to the Member States for adoption in accordance with their respective constitutional rules.

Part Three: Policies of the Community

Title I — Free movement of goods

Articles 9–37

unchanged

Title II — Agriculture

Articles 38–47

unchanged

Title III — Free movement of persons, services and capital

Articles 48–50

unchanged

Article 51

First paragraph, replace "acting by unanimity on a proposal from the Commission" by "acting by a qualified majority on a proposal from the Commission in cooperation with the European Parliament and after consulting the Economic and Social Committee".

Articles 52–73

unchanged

Article 73 A

From 1 January 1994, Articles 67 to 73 shall be replaced by Articles 73 B, C, D, and E.

Article 73 B

All restrictions on the Movement of capital belonging to persons resident in Member States and any discrimination based on the nationality or on the place of residence of the parties or on the place where such capital is invested shall be prohibited, without prejudice to other provisions of this Treaty. Current payments connected with the movement of capital shall be free.

Article 73 C

The provisions of Article 73 B shall be without prejudice to the right of Member States to take all requisite measures to prevent infringements of their national law, in particular in the field of taxation and the prudential supervision of financial institutions, or to lay down procedures for the declaration of capital movements for purposes of administrative or statistical information.

These measures and procedures shall not, however, constitute a means of arbitrary discrimination or a disguised restriction on the free movement of capital as defined in Article 73 B.

Article 73 D

By way of derogation from Article 73 B, the Council, acting by a qualified majority on a proposal from the Commission and following consultation with the Committee provided for in Article 109 B, may authorize those Member States which, on 31.12.1993, enjoy derogations or safeguard measures on the basis of Community law, to maintain, until 31.12.1995 at the latest, restrictions on movements of capital covered by such measures.

Article 73 E

Where, in exceptional circumstances, movements of capital to or from third countries cause, or threaten to cause, serious difficulties for the operation of economic and monetary union, the Council, acting by a qualified majority on a proposal from the Commission and following consultation with the Committee provided for in Article 109B, may take those safeguard measures which are strictly necessary and of limited duration.

Title IV — Transport

Article 74

unchanged

Article 75

1. For the purpose of implementing Article 74, and taking into account the distinctive fea-tures of transport, the Council shall, acting by a qualified majority on a proposal from the Commission in cooperation with the European Parliament, lay down: (a) and (b) unchanged; (c) measures to improve transport safety; (d) any other appropriate provisions.

2. and 3. — unchanged

Articles 76–84

unchanged

Title V — Common rules

(competition, fiscality, approximation of legislation)

Articles 85–91

unchanged

Article 92

delete paragraph 2(c) = division of Germany
    new paragraph 3(d):
"(d) aid to promote culture and heritage conservation where such aid does not adversely affect trading conditions and competition in the Community. Present paragraph (d) shall become (e).

Articles 93–98

unchanged

Article 99

Without prejudice to Article 101, the Council shall, acting unanimously on a proposal from the Commission and after consulting the European Parliament and the Economic and Social Committee, adopt provisions for the harmonization of legislation concerning turnover taxes, excise duties and other forms of indirect taxation to the extent that such harmonization is necessary to ensure the establishment and the functioning of the internal market within the time limit laid down in Article 8a.

Article 100

The Council shall, acting unanimously on a proposal from the Commission and after consulting the European Parliament and the Economic and Social Committee, issue directives for the approximation of such provisions laid down by law, regulation or administrative action in Member States as directly affect the establishment or functioning of the Common Market.

Articles 100A–102 unchanged

Title VI — Economic and monetary policy

Chapter 1: Economic policy

Article 102 A

Member States shall conduct their economic

policy with a view to contributing to the achievement of the objectives of economic and monetary union, as defined in Article 2, within the framework of the guidelines and measures adopted by the competent Community institutions.

The Member States and the institutions shall act in accordance with a free and competitive market economy system, favouring an efficient allocation of resources, and in compliance with the principles set out in Article 3 A.

Article 103

1. Member States shall regard their economic policies as a matter of common concern and shall coordinate them within the Council.[3]

2. After discussion in the European Council, the Council, acting by qualified majority on a proposal from the Commission, shall define the broad outlines of the economic policy of the Community and of its Member States.

3. The Council shall regularly carry out an overall assessment to monitor the economic developments of the Community and of each of its Member States as well as compliance of economic policies with the guidelines referred to in the preceding paragraph. This monitoring shall include the forwarding of details by Member States of any important measure to be taken in the field of their economic policy.

[Without prejudice to any other procedures provided for in this Treaty, the Council may, acting unanimously on a proposal from the Commission, decide upon the measures appropriate to the situation.]

[Where a Member State is in difficulties or is seriously threatened with difficulties, due to events beyond its control, the Commission may propose to the Council, which shall act by a qualified majority, the granting under certain conditions of Community financial assistance to the Member State concerned, which may take the form of a support programme accompanied by budget intervention or special loans.]

4. The Council, acting by a qualified majority on a proposal from the Commission, shall establish the detailed rules of application necessary to implement the provisions of paragraphs 1 and 3 of this Article.

5. By way of derogation from Article 151, the Committee referred to in Article 109 B shall be responsible for preparing the work of the Council referred to in this Article and for carrying out the tasks assigned to it by the Council.

Article 103 A

1. Where it is established under the procedure referred to in Article 103(3), that the economic policy of a Member State proves to be incompatible with the broad guidelines laid down in Article 103(2) or that it risks jeopardizing the achievement of the objectives of economic and monetary union, the Council, acting by a qualified majority on a proposal from the Commission, may make the necessary recommendations to that State. Subject to the provisions of paragraph 2 of this Article, these recommendations shall not be made public.

2. Where it is established that there has been no effective follow-up to the recommendations provided for in paragraph 1 within any period that may have been laid down by the Council or within a reasonable period, the Council, acting by a qualified majority on a proposal from the Commission, may make public its recommendations, having first adapted them, if necessary, to developments in the situation.

Article 104

1.(a) The granting of overdrafts or any other type of credit facility by the European Central Bank or by the central banks of the Member States to Community institutions or bodies, Member States, public authorities or other bodies governed by public law of Member States and the obligatory purchase from them of debt instruments shall be recognized as incompatible with economic and monetary union and shall accordingly be prohibited. This prohibition also includes any measure determining a privileged access by the aforementioned authorities to the financial institutions.

(b) The Community shall not be liable for the commitments of governments, local authorities or other public agencies of Member States, without prejudice to mutual financial guarantees for the joint execution of a specific economic project. The Member States shall not be liable for the commitments of governments, local authorities or other public agencies of another Member State, without prejudice to mutual financial guarantees for the joint execution of a specific economic project.

---

[3] The Conference considers that the necessary provisions should be laid down to ensure that the Ministers for Economic Affairs and Finance play their role within the Economic and Monetary Union.

(c) The Council, acting by a qualified majority on a proposal from the Commission, may stipulate, after consulting the Committee provided for in Article 109 B, the prohibitions laid down in this paragraph.

2. Excessive public budgetary deficits must be avoided. The Council shall, acting by a qualified majority on a proposal from the Commission, adopt the necessary provisions for the application of that principle. These provisions shall take account of all the relevant factors and in particular the development of the relationship between public debt and the gross domestic product, the relationship between the public deficit and the gross domestic product, and also of the development of the relationship between the said deficit and public investment expenditure. The provisions thus adopted shall apply as from 1 January 1994 at the latest.

3. The Commission shall follow the development of budgetary situations in the Member States and shall inform the Council of the risk of an excessive deficit in a Member State. The Council shall establish, by a qualified majority, whether an excessive budget deficit exists.

Article 104 A

1. Where it establishes the existence of an excessive budgetary deficit, the Council, acting by a qualified majority on a proposal from the Commission, shall make recommendations to the Member State concerned with a view to bringing that situation to an end within a given time limit. Subject to the provisions of paragraph 2, these recommendations shall not be made public.

2. Where it establishes that there has been no effective follow-up to its recommendations within the time limits laid down, the Council shall make them public.

3. In cases where a Member State persists, in a continuous and repeated manner, in failing to put into practice the Council's recommendations, the Council, acting by a qualified majority on a proposal from the Commission, may decide to give notice to the competent authorities of the Member State concerned to take, within a given time limit, the specific measures judged necessary by the Council in order to remedy the situation.

4. Where it establishes a failure to fulfil a decision it has taken in accordance with paragraph 3, the Council, acting by a qualified majority on a proposal from the Commission, may decide on appropriate penalties.[4] The rights to bring actions provided for in Article 169 and 170 may not be exercised within the framework of application of this Article.

5. The Council, acting unanimously on a proposal from the Commission, may stipulate the detailed rules for implementing the provisions of paragraph 4.

6. By way of derogation from Article 151, the Committee referred to in Article 109 B shall be responsible for preparing the work of the Council referred to in this Article and for carrying out the tasks assigned to it by the Council.

Chapter 2: Monetary Policy

Article 105

1. The ESCB shall define and implement the monetary policy of the Community with a view to contributing to the realization of the objectives of economic and monetary union, as laid down in Article 2, in accordance with the principles set out in Article 3 A. The ESCB shall conduct the exchange transactions and shall hold and manage official exchange reserves[5] in accordance with the provisions of Article 109. It shall ensure the smooth operation of the systems of payment. It shall take part, as required, in the definition, coordination and execution of policies relating to the prudential control and stability of the financial system.

2. The ESCB shall regulate the issue and circulation of notes and coins, which alone shall be legal tender.

3. The ESCB shall carry out the duties, and avail itself of the instruments, provided for in the Statutes referred to in Article 106 (4).

Article 106

1. The ESCB shall be composed of the European Central Bank and of the central banks of the Member States.

2. The European Central Bank shall have legal personality.

3. The decision-making bodies of the Euro-

---

[4] Possibly to be clarified in future discussions.
[5] Still under discussion at this stage is the question whether the ESCB holds and manages "the" (i.e. all) exchange reserves or simply "exchange reserves" (i.e. some of them) and the way in which these reserves are to be held and managed.

pean Central Bank are the Council of the European Central Bank and the Executive Board.

4. The statutes of the ESCB and the European Central Bank shall be the subject of a protocol which is annexed to this Treaty and of which it forms an integral part. Without prejudice to the provisions concerning revision of the present Treaty[6] Articles 5, 17, 18[19], 21.2, 21.3, 21.4, 21.5, 22, 23, 24, 26, 32.2, 32.3, 32.4, 32.6 and 36 of the Statutes may be amended at the request of the European Central Bank, and following consultation of the Commission and the European Parliament, by the Council acting by a qualified majority.

5. In the performance of the tasks entrusted to the ESCB and within the conditions provided for in the Statutes, the European Central Bank shall adopt regulations, take decisions and issue recommendations or opinions.

Article 107

When exercising the powers and carrying out the tasks and duties conferred upon them, neither the European Central Bank, nor a central bank of a Member State, nor any member of their decision-making bodies shall seek or take instructions from Community institutions or bodies, from any governments of a Member State or from any other body. The Community institutions and bodies and the Governments of the Member States undertake to respect this principle and not to seek to influence the members of the decision-making bodies of the European Central Bank and of the central banks of the Member States in the performance of their tasks.

Article 108

1. The Council of the European Central Bank, hereinafter referred to as the "Council of the Bank" shall consist of the Governors of the central banks of the Member States and the [6] members of the Executive Board, one of whom, the President or, in his absence, the Vice-President, of the European Central Bank shall hold the office of President of the Council of the Bank.

2. The President, the Vice-President and the other members of the Executive Board shall be appointed by common accord by the governments of the Member States after consultation of the European Parliament and the Council of the Bank, from among persons of good repute with professional experience in the monetary or

banking sectors. Their term of office shall be 8 years. It shall not be renewable.

3. The Council of the Bank, acting in accordance with the procedures laid down in the Statute, shall adopt whatever guidelines and take whatever decisions are necessary for the ESCB to be able to carry out the tasks assigned to it.

4. The Executive Board shall implement monetary policy in accordance with the guidelines and decisions adopted by the Council of the Bank; this shall include giving the necessary instructions to the central banks of the Member States. In addition, the Executive Board may, under the conditions laid down by the Statutes, have certain powers delegated to it where the Council of the Bank so decides.

5. To the extent deemed possible and appropriate, and without prejudice to the provisions of paragraph 4, the European Central Bank shall have recourse to the central banks of the Member States to carry out operations which form part of the system's tasks.

Article 109

1. The Council, acting [by a qualified majority/unanimously] on a proposal from the Commission, from a Member State or from the European Central Bank, and after consultation by the Council of the Bank in an endeavour to reach a consensus with the Council of the Bank with the objective of price stability, shall determine [guidelines for the Community's exchange policy,] the exchange rate system of the Community, including, in particular, the adoption, adjustment and abandoning of central rates vis-à-vis third currencies.

2. The Council shall decide by a qualified majority on the position of the Community and its representation on the international stage in compliance with the allocation of powers laid down in Articles 103, 105 and in the first paragraph of this Article as regards the issue of particular relevance to economic and monetary union.

Chapter 3: Provisions governing the institutions

Article 109 A

1. The President of the Council and a member of the Commission may participate, without having the right to vote, in meetings of the Council of the Bank. The President of the

---

[6] cf. Article W (former Article 236).

Council may in this context submit a motion for deliberation by the Council of the Bank.

2. The President of the European Central Bank shall be invited to participate in Council meetings when the Council is discussing matters relating to the objectives and tasks of the ESCB.

3. The European Central Bank shall address an annual report on the activities of the ESCB and on the monetary policy of both the previous and current year to the European Parliament, the European Council, the Council and the Commission. The President of the European Central Bank shall present this report to the Council and to the European Parliament; the latter may open a general debate on that basis. Furthermore, the President of the European Central Bank and the other members of the Executive Board may, at the request of the European Parliament or on their own initiative, be heard by the competent committees of the European Parliament.

Article 109 B

1. In order to promote coordination of the policies of Member States in the monetary field to the full extent needed for the functioning of the common market, a Monetary Committee with advisory status is hereby set up. It shall have the following tasks:

- to keep under review the monetary and financial situation of the Member States and of the Community and the general payments system of the Member States and to report regularly thereon to the Council and to the Commission;

- to deliver opinions at the request of the Council or of the Commission or on its own initiative, for submission to these institutions. The Member States and the Commission shall each appoint two members of the Monetary Committee.

2. As from the date on which the ESCB begins to assume its duties in accordance with Article 109 E(1), an economic and financial Committee shall take the place of the Monetary Committee; it shall have the following tasks:

- to draw up opinions, at the request of the Council, the Commission or the European Central Bank, or on its own initiative, for submission to them,

- to keep under review the economic and financial situation of the Member States and of the Community and to report

regularly to the Council and the Commission, in particular on financial relations with third countries and international institutions,

- to accomplish the other tasks provided for by this treaty.

3. The Committee shall be composed of representatives from the Member States, from the Commission and from the ESCB. The Council, acting by a qualified majority on an opinion of the Commission, the ESCB and the Monetary Committee, shall determine the composition of the Committee and approve its rules of procedure.

Chapter 4: Transitional provisions

Article 109 C

1. The transitional period for achieving economic and monetary union shall begin on 1 January 1994.

2. Before that date, Member States shall : — adopt the measures necessary to comply with Articles 73 B and 104(1), — start the process with a view to the independence of their central bank under the provisions of Article 107 and Article 14.2 of the Statute being achieved not later than at the date of transition to the final stage of economic and monetary union, — adopt, if necessary and as soon as possible, with a view to permitting the assessment provided for in paragraph 3, within the framework of the procedure laid down in Article 103(3), multiannual programmes intended to ensure the lasting convergence necessary for the achievement of economic and monetary union, in particular with regard to price stability and balanced public finances.

3. Before the beginning of the transitional period, the Council shall, on the basis of a report from the Commission, assess the progress made with regard to economic and monetary convergence and shall adopt the provisions to be taken by virtue of the application of Articles 103 to 104 A according to the procedure provided for therein.

Article 109 D

1. On the entry into force of these provisions, a Board of Governors of the Central Banks of the Member States, here in after referred to as the "Board of Governors", shall be set up. The Board of Governors shall substitute itself for the European Monetary Cooperation Fund and shall assume the powers entrusted to the Committee of the Governors of the Central Banks of the Member States.

2. The Board of Governors, which shall enjoy the autonomy necessary for the exercise of its powers, shall: — see to it that the European Monetary System operates smoothly, — strengthen the cooperation between the central banks of the Member States, — step up coordination of the monetary policies of the Member States with the aim of ensuring price stability, and — promote the development of the ecu.

3. The Board of Governors may formulate opinions on the general line to be taken by monetary policy and the exchange policy of the Member States and may address, to the latter and to the Council, opinions on policies likely to have an effect on the Community's internal and external monetary situation.

4. The Council, acting by a qualified majority, on a proposal from the Committee of Governors of the Central Banks of the Member States and following an opinion from the Commission, shall adopt the statutes and measures necessary for the exercise of the powers of the Board of Governors.

Article 109 D bis

1. All Member States shall take the measures necessary to enable them to take part in the exchange-rate mechanism of the European Monetary System as from the beginning of the transitional period.

2. As from the beginning of the transitional period, the Council, acting by a qualified majority, and the Board of Governors shall take the measures necessary to enable the ecu to become a strong and stable currency.

Article 109 E

1. The European System of Central Banks (ESCB) shall be set up at the beginning of the transitional period. It shall begin to operate on 1 January 1996, unless the Council, acting unanimously following an opinion from the Board of Governors, decides on an earlier date. It shall substitute itself for the Board of Governors, whose duties it shall assume. At the latest on whichever of these dates applies, the Member States shall respect the normal fluctuation margins provided for by the exchange-rate mechanism of the European Monetary System. The Council, acting by a qualified majority on a proposal from the Commission and after consulting the European Parliament and the Board of Governors, may decide on the principle of a temporary derogation in favour of a Member State which, because of its economic situation, is not yet capable of taking a full part in the mechanisms provided for in the first two subparagraphs and may define the duration of such derogation and the ways in which it is to be implemented.

2. As from the date on which the ESCB begins to operate, and in compliance with the responsibilities which, during the transitional period, devolve upon the authorities of the Member States as regards the definition and carrying out of their monetary policy, the European Central Bank shall:

- encourage the promotion of the ecu, in particular by developing its role and extending its uses, and shall assume responsibility for the system of bank compensation in ecus;

- prepare instruments which are in conformity with the mechanisms of the market and the procedures necessary for carrying out the single monetary policy in the future;

- prepare the interconnection of payments networks and monetary and financial markets, and

- take part in the harmonization of monetary and financial statistics.

3. Once the date for transition to the final stage has been fixed, the European Central Bank: — shall contribute towards creating the conditions necessary for transition to the final stage and supervise, in particular, the technical preparation of notes and coins in ecus; — may make recommendations to the central banks of Member States concerning the way in which their monetary policy is to be carried out; it may make such recommendations public; — shall be empowered to hold and manage exchange reserves on behalf of one or more Member States.

4. The European Central Bank shall be consulted by the Council on each proposal for a Community act dealing with monetary matters. It shall also be consulted by the authorities of the Member States on any draft legislative provision relating to such matters.

5. The Council, acting by a qualified majority on a proposal from the European Central Bank and following an Opinion by the European Parliament and the Commission, shall adopt the measures necessary to enable the ESCB to exercise its powers.

6. The Council, acting unanimously on a proposal from the Commission and following consultation with the European Parliament and the European Central Bank, may confer upon

the European Central Bank other powers for preparation of the final stage. According to the same procedure, it shall adopt, as required, the measures necessary to enable these powers to be carried out.

Article 109 F[7]

The Commission and the European Central Bank shall report to the Council no later than 31 December 1996, on progress made in the fulfilment, by Member States, of their obligations regarding the achievement of economic and monetary union, in particular of those enshrined in Articles 104 and 107, and on progress made in matters of convergence. On the basis of a report from the Council, drawn up following consultation with the European Parliament, the European Council, once it has ascertained that the conditions for transition to the final stage of economic and monetary union are united, shall set the date for the beginning of this stage. In so doing, the European Council shall assess the results of the integration of the markets and satisfy itself that the required degree of convergence in the field of price stability, balancing of the budget and interest rates has been attained. It shall also take account of the development of the role of the ecu.

Article 109 G[8]

1. Once the European Council has set the date for the beginning of the final stage, the Council, acting by a qualified majority which expresses a vote in favour cast by at least eight members, shall take the necessary decisions, on a proposal from the Commission. The Council and the Commission shall forthwith send a report on these decisions to the European Parliament.

2. The Council may, in particular, according to this procedure and after consulting the European Central Bank, where the conditions required for full participation in the final stage are not yet fulfilled by a Member State, adopt the appropriate measures, in the form of derogations, and decide on the duration of the measures and the way in which they are to be implemented. The Council shall take a decision on the consequences at institutional a level, which entail in particular the suspension of voting rights in the field of monetary policy.

3. Acting on a proposal from the Commission and in close cooperation with the European Central Bank, the Council, acting with the unanimity of the Member States taking part in the final stage, shall adopt the fixed exchange rates between the currencies of the said Member States and the measures necessary for the introduction of the ecu as the single currency of the Community. The ESCB shall thereafter have full exercise of its powers as regards monetary policy.

Chapter 4: Commercial Policy

Article 110

1. By establishing a customs union between themselves Member States aim to contribute, in the common interest, to the harmonious development of world trade, the progressive abolition of restrictions on international trade and the lowering of customs barriers.

2. The Community shall conduct a common commercial policy covering international trade in goods and the services directly related to such trade. The common commercial policy shall also cover other services if and insofar as the Community has the powers to adopt internal rules in the field concerned.

3. The common commercial policy shall be based on uniform principles, particularly in regard to changes in tariff rates, the conclusion of tariff and trade agreements, the achievement of uniformity in measures of liberalization, export policy and measures to protect trade such as those to be taken in case of dumping or subsidies.

Articles 111

deleted

Article 112

unchanged

Article 113

1. The Council, acting by a qualified majority on a proposal from the Commission, shall adopt the measures necessary for the implementation of the common commercial policy. However, if those measures concern services not directly related to trade in goods, the Council shall act unanimously where unanimity is required for the adoption of internal rules.

2. Where agreements with one of more States or international organizations need to be negotiated, the Commission shall, in accordance with Article 228, make recommendations to the Council, which shall authorize the Commission to open the necessary negotiations. The Commission shall conduct these negotiations in

---

7, 8 Drafting to be reviewed in the light of the debate on the transition to the final stage.

consultation with a special committee appointed by the Council to assist it in its task, and within the framework of such directives as the Council may issue to it.

3. In matters covered by this Article and without prejudice to Article 228, the Community's position shall be set out by the Commission in its relations with third countries, within international organizations and at international conferences.

Article 114

deleted

Article 115

for the record

Article 116

delete second paragraph

Title VII: Social policy, education, vocational training and youth

Article 117

The Community and its Member States shall have as their objectives the promotion of improved living and working conditions, proper social protection, the promotion of dialogue between management and labour, the development of human resources with a view to lasting high employment and the combatting of exclusion. To this end the Community and its Member States shall implement measures which take account of the diverse forms of national practices, in particular in the field of relations based on agreement, and the need to maintain the competitiveness of the EC economy.

Article 118

1. With a view to achieving the objectives of Article 117, the Community shall support and complement Member States' activities in the following fields: — the working environment and in particular the protection of workers' health and safety; — working conditions; — the information and consultation of workers; — equal opportunity on the employment market, and equal treatment; — the vocational integration of persons excluded from the labour market.

2. To this end, the Council, acting by a qualified majority on a proposal from the Commission, in cooperation with the European Parliament and after consulting the Economic and Social Committee, may adopt, by means of directives, minimum requirements for gradual implementation, having regard to the conditions and technical rules obtained in each of the Member States. Such directives shall avoid imposing administrative, financial and legal constraints in a way which would hold back the creation and development of small and medium-sized undertakings.

3. The Council, acting unanimously on a proposal from the Commission and after consulting the European Parliament and the Economic and Social Committee, may adopt provisions in the field of social security and social protection of workers and of conditions of access to employment for third-country nationals, insofar as is necessary for the pursuit of the objectives referred to in Article 117.

4. A Member State may entrust management and labour with the implementation of all or part of the measures which it has laid down in order to implement the directives adopted in accordance with paragraphs 2 and 3.

5. The provisions adopted pursuant to this Article shall not prevent any Member State from maintaining or introducing more stringent measures for the protection of living and working conditions compatible with this Treaty.

6. The provisions of this Article shall not apply to pay, the right of association or the right to strike.

Article 118a

Before submitting proposals in the social policy field, the Commission shall consult management and labour on the advisability of Community action.

Article 118b

1. Should management and labour so desire, the dialogue between them at Community level may lead to relations based on agreement including agreement which shall be implemented in accordance with the procedures and practices peculiar to each Member State.

2. In the field referred to in Article 118, where management and labour so desire, the Commission may submit proposals to translate the agreement referred to in paragraph 1 into Community legislation. The Council shall act as laid down in Article 118.

Article 118c

With a view to achieving the objectives of Article 117 and without prejudice to the other provisions of this Treaty, the Commission shall encourage cooperation between the Member States and facilitate the coordination of their action in all social policy fields under this Title.

Article 119

1. Each Member State shall ensure that the

principle of equal pay for male and female workers for equal work is applied.

2. For the purpose of this Article, "pay" means the ordinary basic or minimum wage or salary and any other consideration, whether in cash or in kind, which the worker receives directly or indirectly, in respect of his employment from his employer.

Equal pay without discrimination based on sex means: (a) that pay for the same work at piece rates shall be calculated on the basis of the same unit of measurement; (b) that pay for work at time rates shall be the same for the same job.

3. This Article shall not prevent any Member State from maintaining or adopting specific advantages in order to make it easier for women to pursue a vocational activity.

Articles 120 and 121

deleted

Article 122

The Commission shall draw up a report each year on the development of the social situation in the Community. It shall forward the report to the European Parliament, the Council and the Economic and Social Committee. The European Parliament may invite the Commission to discuss the situation.

Chapter 2: the European Social Fund

Articles 123–127

NB: Technical modifications will be necessary in order to codify the present legal situation, according to which the missions of the Social Fund are determined in the global framework regulation on the Structural Funds (cf. Article 130 D where the Presidency proposes the co-decision procedure). This codification will, inter alia, imply the deletion of Article 126 b).

Article 128

deleted

Chapter 3: Education, vocational training and youth

Article A

1. The Community shall contribute to the development of quality education by encouraging cooperation between Member States and, if necessary, by supporting and complementing their action, while respecting the autonomy of education systems and linguistic and cultural diversity.

2. Community action shall, in particular, be aimed at: — developing the European dimension of education, particularly through the teaching and dissemination of the languages of the Member States; — encouraging mobility of students and teachers, inter alia by encouraging the academic recognition of diplomas and periods of study; — promoting cooperation between educational establishments; — organizing exchanges of information and experience on issues common to the education systems of the Member States; — encouraging the development of youth exchanges; — encouraging the development of distance education.

3. The Community and the Member States shall foster cooperation with third countries and the appropriate international organizations in the sphere of education, particularly with the Council of Europe.

4. The Council, acting by a qualified majority on a proposal from the Commission in cooperation with the European Parliament and after consulting the Economic and Social Committee, shall adopt action programmes with a view to giving incentive to the attainment of the objectives referred to in this Article.

Article B

1. The Community shall implement a vocational training policy which shall reinforce and supplement the action of the Member States, while respecting the autonomy and diversity of training systems.

2. Community action shall aim to: — improve social and vocational integration and reintegration into the labour market and vocational training: — facilitate access to vocational training and encourage mobility of instructors and trainees and particularly young people; — develop exchanges of information and experience on issues common to the training systems of the Member States.

For the purpose of implementing this action, with reference to workers, Article 118b shall apply.

3. The Community and the Member States shall foster cooperation with third countries and the appropriate international organizations in the sphere of vocational training.

4. The Council, acting by a qualified majority on a proposal from the Commission in cooperation with the European Parliament and after consulting the Economic and Social Committee, shall adopt measures to contribute to the attainment of the objectives referred to in this Article.

Title VIII: The European Investment Bank

Article 129

The European Investment Bank shall have legal personality. The members of the European Investment Bank established under Article 4B shall be the Member States. The Statute of the European Investment Bank is laid down in a Protocol annexed to this Treaty.

Article 130

Add at end: "In carrying out its task, the Bank shall facilitate the financing of programmes in conjuction with assistance from the structural Funds and other Community financial instruments."

Title IX: Economic and social cohesion

Article 130a

In order to promote its overall harmonious development, the Community shall pursue and develop its actions leading to the strengthening of its economic and social cohesion. In particular, the Community shall aim at reducing disparities between the levels of development of the various regions and the backwardness of the least-favoured regions.

Article 130b

Member States shall conduct their economic policies and shall coordinate them in such a way as in addition to attain the objectives set out in Article 130a. The formation and implementation of the Community's policies and actions and the implementation of the internal market shall take into account the objectives set out in Article 130a and shall contribute to their achievement. The Community shall also support the achievement of these objectives by the action it takes through the Structural Funds (European Agricultural Guidance and Guarantee Fund, Guidance Section, European Social Fund, European Regional Development Fund), the European Investment Bank and the other existing financial instruments.

The Commission shall submit a report to the European Parliament and the Council every three years on the progress made towards achieving economic and social cohesion, accompanied if necessary by appropriate proposals. If specific actions prove necessary outside the Funds and without prejudice to the measures decided upon within the framework of the other Community policies, such actions may be adopted by the Council acting unanimously on a proposal from the Commission and after consulting the European Parliament, the Economic and Social Committee and the Committee of the Regions.

Article 130c

The European Regional Development Fund is intended to help to correct the main regional imbalances in the Community.

Article 130d

Without prejudice to Article 130e, a Community law shall define the tasks, prime objectives and the organization of the Structural Funds, which may involve regrouping the Funds. A Community law shall also define the general rules applicable to them and the provisions necessary to ensure their effectiveness and the coordination of the Funds with one another and with the other existing financial instruments. The Council, acting unanimously on a proposal from the Commission and after obtaining the assent of the European Parliament, may set up new structural Funds.

Article 130e[9]

Implementing decisions relating to the European Regional Development Fund shall be taken by the Council, acting by a qualified majority on a proposal from the Commission and in cooperation with the European Parliament. With regard to the European Agricultural Guidance and Guarantee Fund, Guidance Section, and the European Social fund, Articles 43, 126 and 127 shall continue to apply respectively.

Title X: Research and technological development

Article 130f

1. The Community's aim shall be to strengthen the scientific and technological bases of Community industry and to encourage it to become more competitive at international level, while promoting all the research activities deemed necessary by virtue of other chapters of this Treaty.

2. In order to achieve this, the Community shall encourage undertakings throughout the Community, including small and medium-sized undertakings, research centres and universities in their research and technological development activities; it shall support their efforts to

---

[9] cf. observations to Articles 123 to 127.

cooperate with one another, aiming, notably, at enabling undertakings to exploit the internal market potential to the full, by such means as opening up national public contracts, defining common standards and eliminating legal and fiscal obstacles to such cooperation.

3. All Community activities in the area of research and technological development shall be decided on and implemented in accordance with the provisions of this Title.

Article 130g
(No change from "Non-paper".)

Article 130h
1. The Community and the Member States shall work to coordinate their research and technological development activities so as to ensure that national policies and Community policy are mutually consistent.

2. In close contact with the Member States, the Commission may take any useful initiative to promote coordination.

Article 130i
1. A multiannual framework programme shall be adopted by law, setting out all the activities of the Community.

The framework programme shall:

- define the specific programmes necessary to implement it and establish priorities for them;
- fix the maximum overall amount and the detailed rules for Community financial participation in the programme as a whole and the respective shares in each of the specific programmes;
- establish the scientific and technological objectives to be attained by specific programmes and, where applicable, the activities defined in Articles 130j and 130k;
- fix the rules for the participation of undertakings, research centres and universities.
- fix the rules for disseminating the results of research.

2. The framework programme may be adapted or supplemented by Community law, as the situation changes.

3. Without prejudice to the application of Articles 130j and 130k, the Commission shall adopt and carry out the specific programmes. In exercising these powers the Commission shall be assisted by a committee appointed by the Council.

Article 130j–130m
(no change from "Non-paper")

Article 130n
The Council, acting by unanimity on a proposal from the Commission and after consulting the European Parliament, shall adopt the provisions referred to in Article 130m. The Council, acting by a qualified majority on a proposal from the Commission and in cooperation with the European Parliament after consulting the Economic and Social Committee, shall adopt the provisions referred to in Articles 130j to l. Adoption of the supplementary programmes shall also require the agreement of the Member States concerned.

Article 130o
(no change from "Non-paper")

Title XI: Environment

Article 130r
1. The policy of the Community relating to the environment shall contribute towards pursuing the following objectives:

- preserving, protecting and improving the quality of the environment;
- protecting human health;
- prudent and rational utilization of natural resources;
- promoting of measures on the international level to deal with regional or world-wide environmental problems.

2. The policy of the Community relating to the environment shall target a high level of protection. It shall be based on the precautionary principle and on the principles that preventive action should be taken, that environmental damage should as a priority be rectified at source and that the polluter should pay. Environmental protection requirements must be integrated into the definition and implementation of other Community policies.

3. In preparing its policy relating to the environment, the Community shall take account of:

- available scientific and technical data:
- environmental conditions in the various regions of the Community;
- the potential benefits and costs of action or lack of action;
- the economic and social development of the Community as a whole and the balanced development of its regions.

4. Within their respective spheres of competence, the Community and the Member States shall cooperate with third countries and with the relevant international organizations. The arrangements for Community cooperation may be the subject of agreements between the Community and the third parties concerned.

Article 130s

1. The Council, acting by a qualified majority on a proposal from the Commission in cooperation with the European Parliament and after consulting the Economic and Social Committee, shall decide what action is to be taken by the Community in order to achieve the objectives referred to in Article 130r.

2. Multiannual action programmes setting out priority objectives to be achieved shall be adopted by Community law in specific areas. The Council, acting under the terms of paragraph 1, shall adopt the measures necessary for the implementation of these programmes.

Article 130t

The protective measures adopted pursuant to Article 130s shall not prevent any Member State from maintaining or introducing more stringent protective measures. Such measures must be compatible with this Treaty. The Commission shall be notified of them.

Title XII — Energy[10]

Article A

1. Action by the Community in the sphere of energy, which shall support and complement that of the Member States, shall be aimed at the following objectives within the framework of a market economy:

- guaranteeing security of supplies in the Community under satisfactory economic conditions;
- the establishment and functioning of the internal market in the energy sector;
- ensuring a suitable reaction in the event of a crisis, particularly in the oil sector;

- promoting the rational use of energy and the development and use of new and renewable energy sources.

2. Action by the Community shall take account of the need to ensure a high level of protection of the environment, and the health and safety of persons.

3. Action by the Community shall be closely coordinated with the policies pursued in the framework of the Treaties establishing the European Coal and Steel Community and European Atomic Energy Community.

4. The Commission, in close liaison with the Member States, shall take all appropriate steps to promote consistency between Member States' activities and those of the EEC.

Article B

Within the framework of their respective powers, the Community and the Member States shall cooperate with third countries and the appropriate international organizations. The manner in which Community cooperation is to be implemented may be the subject of agreements between the Community and the third parties concerned.

Article C

The Council, acting by a qualified majority on a proposal from the Commission in cooperation with the European Parliament and after consulting the Economic and Social Committee, shall adopt the measures required to attain the objectives referred to in Article A(1).

Title XIII — Trans-European networks

Article A

1. To help to attain the objectives referred to in Articles 8a and 130a and to enable citizens of the Union, economic operators and regional and local communities to derive full benefit from the setting up of an area without internal frontiers, the Community shall contribute to the establishment and development of trans-European networks in the areas of transport, telecommunications and energy infrastructures.

---

[10] Commission statement "The provisions of Article 85(1) may be declared inapplicable to any agreement in the energy sector which contributes to guaranteeing security of supplies in the Community, where the restrictions which such an agreement may contain are essential for the attainment of this objective and do not afford the undertakings concerned the opportunity of eliminating competition with respect to substantial part of the products in question. The aid referred to in Article 92(1), where, in actual fact, it contributes to guaranteeing security of supplies in the Community and does not harm the functioning of the internal market in energy to an extent which runs counter to the common interest, may be regarded as compatible with the common market."

2. Within the framework of a system of open and competitive markets, action by the Community shall aim in particular at promoting the interconnection and inter-operability of national networks as well as access to such networks. It shall take account in particular of the need to link island, landlocked and peripheral regions with the central regions of the Community. It shall meet the demands of environmental protection and economic viability of the projects.

Article B

1. In order to attain the objectives referred to in Article A, the Community:

- shall establish blueprints for trans-European networks laying down the objectives, priorities and broad lines of measures envisaged for each sector; these blueprints shall identify projects of common interest;
- shall implement any measures that may prove necessary to ensure the interoperability of the networks, in particular in the field of technical standardization;
- may support the financial efforts made by the Member States for projects of common interest identified in the framework of the blueprints, particularly through feasibility studies or loan guarantees.

2. Member States shall, in liaison with the Commission, coordinate among themselves the policies pursued at national level which may have a significant impact on the attainment of the objectives referred to in Article A. The Commission may, in close collaboration with the Member States, take all appropriate steps to promote such cooperation.

3. The Community may decide to involve third countries in its activity in certain areas by concluding agreements with them.

Article C

The blueprints referred to in Article B(1) shall be adopted by Community law. The Council shall consult the Committee of the Regions before adopting its common position. The Council, acting by a qualified majority on a proposal from the Commission in cooperation with the European Parliament and after consulting the Economic and Social Committee and the Committee of the Regions, shall adopt the other measures provided for in Article B(1).

Title XIV — Industry

1. The Community and the Member States shall ensure that the conditions necessary for the competitiveness of the Community's industry exist. For that purpose, in accordance with a system of open, competitive markets their action shall be aimed at:

- speeding up the adjustment of industry to structural changes;
- ensuring a favourable environment for initiative and the development of undertakings throughout the Community, particularly SMEs;
- encouraging cooperation between undertakings;
- fostering better exploitation of the industrial potential of policies of innovation, research and technological development.

2. The Member States shall consult each other in liaison with the Commission and, where necessary, shall coordinate action they take. The Commission may take all appropriate steps to promote such coordination.

3. The Community shall contribute to the achievement of the objectives set out in paragraph 1 through the policies and activities it pursues, particularly in connection with the internal market and research and technological development policy. In addition to the action taken by the Community under other provisions of this Treaty, the Council, acting by a qualified majority on a proposal from the Commission in cooperation with the European Parliament after consulting the Economic and Social Committee, may decide on specific measures, in particular on behalf of the industries of the future in support of action taken in the Member States to achieve the objectives set out in paragraph 1.

Title XV — Tourism

1. The Community shall encourage cooperation between the Member States with a view to contributing to the development of their activities in the field of tourism. To this end the Commission shall act in particular by carrying out studies, producing opinions and organizing consultations in the following areas: — collection and distribution of data on tourist flows and related information; — exchange of information and experience; — coordination of Member States' action with a view to implementing common projects; — promotion of Community tourism in third countries.

2. Without prejudice to the other provisions of this Treaty the Council, acting by a qualified majority on a proposal from the Commission in cooperation with the European parliament and after consulting the Economic and Social Committee and the Committee of the Regions, may adopt measures to encourage action in the fields referred to in paragraph 1.

Title XVI — Consumer protection

1. The Community shall contribute to the attainment of a high level of consumer protection through:

(a) measures adopted pursuant to Article 100a in the context of the completion of the internal market;
(b) specific action which supports and supplements the policy pursued by the Member States to protect the health, safety and economic interests of consumers and to providing adequate information for consumers.

2. The Council, acting by a qualified majority on a proposal from the Commission in cooperation with the European Parliament and after consulting the Economic and Social Committee, shall adopt the specific action referred to in paragraph 1(b).

3. Action adopted pursuant to paragraph 2 shall not prevent any Member State from maintaining or introducing more stringent protective measures. Such measures must be compatible with this Treaty. The Commission shall be notified of them.

Title XVII — Public Health

Sole Article

1. The Community shall contribute towards ensuring a high level of human health protections by encouraging cooperation between the Member States and, if necessary, lending support to their action. Community action shall be directed towards the prevention of diseases, while paying particular attention to combatting major health scourges. Health protection demands shall form a constituent part of the Community's other policies.

2. Member States shall, in liaison with the Commission, coordinate among themselves their policies and programmes in the areas referred to in paragraph 1. The Commission may, in close contact with the Member States, take all appropriate steps to promote such coordination.

3. The Community and the Member States shall foster cooperation with third countries and the appropriate international organizations in the sphere of public health.

4. The Council, acting by a qualified majority on a proposal from the Commission in cooperation with the European Parliament and after consulting the Economic and Social Committee, shall adopt the action programmes necessary to attain the objectives referred to in this Article.

Title XVIII — Civil protection

1. The Community shall encourage and support the development of cooperation between the Member States in the area of civil protection, which is considered a matter of common interest; it shall also encourage cooperation between the Member States and third countries, and the competent international bodies.

2. In order to achieve the objectives set out in paragraph 1:
(a) the Commission shall, in close cooperation with the Member States, organize the exchange of information and experience on issues relating to civil protection, and hold appropriate consultations;
(b) the Council, acting by a qualified majority on a proposal from the Commission and in cooperation with the European Parliament, shall adopt the measures deemed necessary to encourage action in this area.

Title XIX — Culture

Sole Article

1. The Community shall contribute to the flowering of the cultures of the Member States, while respecting their national and regional diversity, and at the same time bringing the common cultural heritage to the fore.

2. Action by the Community shall encourage cooperation between Member States and, if necessary, support and complement their action in the following areas: — improvement of the knowledge and dissemination of the culture and history of the European peoples; — restoration of the cultural heritage; — cooperation and exchanges in the sphere of culture; — artistic and literary creation; — the European audio-visual sector.

3. The Community and the Member States shall foster cooperation with third countries and the appropriate international organizations in the sphere of culture, particularly with the Council of Europe.

4. The Council, acting by a qualified majority on a proposal from the Commission in cooperation with the European Parliament, shall adopt

measures of encouragement in order to contribute to the attainment of the objectives referred to in this Article.

Title XX — Development cooperation

Article A

The policy of the Community in the sphere of development cooperation, which shall be complementary to the polices pursued by the Member States, shall foster: — the lasting economic and social development of the developing countries, and most especially the most disadvantaged among them; — the gradual smooth integration of the developing countries into the world economy; — the campaign against poverty.

Community policy in this area shall contribute to the general objective of developing and consolidating democracy and the rule of law, and to that of respecting human rights and basic freedoms. The Community and the Member States shall comply with the commitments and take account of the objectives they approved in the context of the United Nations and other appropriate international organizations.

Article B

The Community shall take account of the objectives referred to in Article A in the policies that it implements which are likely to affect developing countries. The Community and its Member States shall ensure that their development policies are consistent with the common foreign and security policy.

Article C

1. Action by the Community in the sphere of development cooperation shall include, in addition to action in the field of trade:

(a) financial and technical cooperation;

(b) food aid and humanitarian aid;

(c) any other specific action to promote development.

2. Community action may be the subject of multiannual programmes adopted by Community law.

3. General rules concerning the action referred to in 1(a) and 1(b) shall be adopted by Community law. The Commission shall adopt the necessary implementing measures in consultation with a committee appointed by the Council.

4. The action referred to in paragraph 1(c) shall be adopted by the Council, acting by a qualified majority on a proposal from the Commission in cooperation with the European Parliament.

5. The European Investment Bank shall contribute, under the terms laid down in its Statute, to the implementation of the action referred to in paragraph 1.

6. The provisions of this Article shall not affect cooperation with the ACP countries in the framework of the ACP-EEC Convention.

Article D

1. The Community and the Member States shall coordinate their policies on development cooperation and shall consult each other on their aid programmes. They may adopt joint actions. In this context, Member States contribute to the implementation of the Community's aid programmes.

2. The Commission may take all appropriate steps to promote the coordination referred to in paragraph 1.

Article E

Within the framework of their respective powers, the Community and the Member States shall cooperate with third countries and the appropriate international organizations.

The manner in which Community cooperation is to be implemented may be the subject of agreements between the Community and the third parties concerned.

Part Four: Association of the overseas countries and territories

Articles 131 to 136a

unchanged

Part Five: Institutions

Title 1

Provisions governing the institutions

Chapter 1: The Institutions

Section 1: the European Parliament

Article 137

The European Parliament, which shall consist of representatives of the peoples of the States brought together in the Community shall exercise the powers conferred upon it by this Treaty.

Article 137a

Insofar as provided in this Treaty, the European Parliament shall participate in the process leading up to the adoption of Community legislative acts by exercising the functions assigned to it under the co-decision and cooperation procedures laid down in Articles 189a and 189b and by giving its assent or delivering consultative Opinions. The European Parliament may, acting by a majority of its members, request the Commission to submit any appropriate proposal on matters on which it considers that a Community legislative act is required for the purpose of implementing this Treaty.

Article 137b
(unchanged from text of Article 137b, paragraph 1 of "Non-paper")

Article 137 bb
Any citizen of the Union and any natural or legal person residing or having a registered office in a Member State of the Community shall have the right to address, individually or in association with other citizens or persons, a petition to the European Parliament on a matter which comes within the Community's sphere of activity and which affects him, her or it directly.

Article 137c
1. The European Parliament shall appoint an ombudsman empowered to receive complaints from any citizen of the Union or any natural or legal person residing or having its registered office in a Member State concerning instances of maladministration in the activities of the Community institutions or bodies with the exception of the Court of Justice and the Court of First Instance acting in their judicial role.

In accordance with his duties, the ombudsman shall conduct enquiries for which he finds grounds, either on his own initiative on the basis of complaints submitted to him directly or through a member of the European Parliament, except where the alleged facts are or have been the subject of legal proceedings.

Where the ombudsman establishes an instance of maladministration, he shall inform the institution concerned, which shall have a period of three months in which to inform him of its views. The ombudsman shall then forward a report to the European Parliament and the institution concerned. The person lodging the complaint shall be informed of the outcome of such enquiries. The ombudsman shall draw up an annual report to the European Parliament on the outcome of his enquiries.

(Paragraphs 2 and 3 unchanged from "Non-paper")

4. The European Parliament shall, after seeking an opinion from the Commission and with the approval of the Council acting by a qualified majority, lay down the regulations and general conditions governing the performance of the ombudsman's duties.

Articles 138–144
(unchanged from "Non-paper".)

Section 2: the Council

Article 145
unchanged

Article 146
Replace the first paragraph by the following paragraph: "The Council shall consist of a representative of each Member State at ministerial level, authorized to take binding decisions for the government of that Member State." (rest of the article unchanged)

Articles 147 and 148
unchanged

Article 149
deleted (see Article 189b)

Articles 150 to 154
unchanged

Section 3: the Commission

Articles 155 to 160
(unchanged in substance from "Non-paper".)

Article 161
(Article 14 of the Merger Treaty) The Commission may appoint a Vice-President or two Vice-Presidents from among its members.

Articles 162 to 163
(Articles 15, 16 and 17 of the Merger Treaty) unchanged.

Section 4: The Court of Justice

Article 164
unchanged

Article 165
The third paragraph is deleted; it is replaced by a paragraph worded as follows: "The Court of Justice shall sit in plenary session when a Member State or a Community institution that is a party to the body so requests."

Article 166
unchanged

Article 167
(unchanged from "Non-paper")

Article 168
unchanged

Article 168a

1. A Court shall be attached to the Court of Justice with jurisdiction to hear and determine at first instance, subject to a right of appeal to the Court of Justice on points of law only and in accordance with the conditions laid down by the Statute, certain classes of action or proceeding defined in accordance with the conditions laid down in paragraph 2. The Court of First Instance shall not be competent to hear and determine questions referred for a preliminary ruling under Article 177.

2. At the request of the Court of Justice and after consulting the Commission and the European Parliament, the Council, acting unanimously, shall determine the classes of action or proceeding referred to in the first paragraph and the composition of the Court of First Instance and shall adopt the necessary adjustments and additional provisions of the Statute of the Court of Justice. Unless the Council decides otherwise, the provisions of this Treaty relating to the Court of Justice, in particular the provisions of the Protocol on the Statute of the Court of Justice, shall apply to the Court of First Instance.

3. The Members of the Court of First Instance shall be chosen from persons whose independence is beyond doubt and who possess the ability required for appointment to judicial office; they shall be appointed by common accord of the Governments of the Member States for a term of six years. The membership shall be partially renewed every three years. Retiring members shall be eligible for re-appointment.

4. The Court of First Instance shall establish its rules of procedure in agreement with the Court of Justice. Those rules shall require the unanimous approval of the Council.

Articles 169 and 170

unchanged

Article 171

1. Text of the present Article 171

2. (new) If the Commission considers that the State concerned has not taken such measures it shall, after giving that State the opportunity to submit its comments, issue a reasoned opinion specifying the points on which the State has not complied within a reasonable period of time with the judgment of the Court of Justice. If the State concerned fails to take the necessary measures to comply with the Court's judgment within the time-limit laid down by the Commission, the latter may bring the case before the Court of Justice. In so doing it shall specify the amount of the lump sum or penalty payment to be paid by the Member State concerned which it considers appropriate in the circumstances. If the Court of Justice finds that the State concerned has not complied with its judgment it may impose a lump sum or penalty payment on it.

Article 172

unchanged, except for the addition of "Community law"

Article 173

The Court of Justice shall review the conformity with the law of Community laws and of acts of the Council, the Commission and the European Central Bank other than recommendations and opinions as well as the legality of acts of the European Parliament intended to produce legal effects vis-à-vis third parties. It shall for this purpose have jurisdiction in actions brought by a Member State, the Council or the Commission on grounds of lack of competence, infringement of an essential procedural requirement, infringement of this Treaty or of any rule of law relating to its application, or misuse of powers.

The Court shall have jurisdiction under the same conditions in actions brought by the European Parliament and by the European Central Bank for the purpose of protecting their prerogatives.

Second and third paragraphs: present text of the Treaty unchanged, except for the addition of "Community law" in the second paragraph.

Article 174

Second paragraph, first line, add "a Community law" before "a regulation", and in the second line "of the Community law" before "of the regulation".

Article 175

Add a new fourth paragraph: "The Court of Justice shall have jurisdiction, under the same conditions, in actions or proceedings brought by the European Central Bank in the areas falling within the latter's competence and in actions or proceedings brought against the latter."

Article 176

unchanged

Article 177

Read little b) as follows (the rest is unchanged: "b) the validity and interpretation of acts of the institutions of the Community and of the European Central Bank;"

Article 178 and 179

unchanged

Article 180

Add a fourth sub-paragraph reading as follows: "d) the fulfilment by national central banks of obligations under the Treaty and the ESCB. In that respect the powers of the Council of the Bank vis à vis national central banks shall be the same as those granted to the Commission in respect of Member States under Article 169."

Articles 181 to 183

unchanged

Article 184

Notwithstanding the expiry of the period laid down in the third paragraph of Article 173, any party may, in proceedings in which a Community law or a regulation of the Council, the Commission, or of the European Central Bank is in issue, plead the grounds specified in the first paragraph of Article 173, in order to invoke before the Court of Justice, the inapplicability of that Community law or of that regulation.

Articles 185 to 188

unchanged

Chapter 2: Provisions common to several institutions

Article 189

1. In order to carry out their task and in accordance with the provisions of this Treaty:

   - the European Parliament and the Council shall adopt Community laws in the cases provided for in this Treaty in accordance with the procedure laid down in Article 189a;
   - the Council and the Commission shall make regulations, issue directives, take decisions, make recommendations or deliver opinions.

2. A Community law shall have general application. Its provisions may either be binding in their entirety and directly applicable in all Member States or may be binding, as to the result to be achieved, upon the Member States, but shall leave to the national authorities the choice of form and methods.

3. A regulation shall have general application. It shall be binding in its entirety and directly applicable in all Member States. A directive shall be binding, as to the result to be achieved, upon each Member State to which it is addressed, but shall leave to the national authorities the choice of form and methods. A decision shall be binding in its entirety upon those to whom it is addressed. Recommendations and opinions shall have no binding force.

4. The scope of the Community law shall be reviewed in 1996 in accordance with the provisions of Article W.

Article 189a

A Community law shall be adopted in accordance with the following procedure:

1. The Commission shall submit a proposal for a Community law to the European Parliament and the Council. The Council, acting by a qualified majority after obtaining the Opinion of the European Parliament and of the Economic and Social Committee, shall adopt a common position. Rest of Article 189a unchanged in substance from the "Non-Paper".

Article 189b

Reproduce the present Article 149 of the Treaty, amending paragraph 1 to read: "1. Where, in pursuance of this Treaty, the Council acts on a proposal from the Commission, unanimity shall be required for an act constituting an amendment to that proposal, subject to the provisions of Article 189a, paragraphs 3 and 4."

Article 190

The beginning should be amended as follows: "Community laws, regulations . . ." (remainder unchanged).

Articles 191 and 192

(unchanged from "Non-paper".)

Chapter 3: The Economic and Social Committee[11]

Article 193

unchanged

Article 194

First and second paragraphs — unchanged.

The members of the Committee may not be bound by any mandatory instructions. They shall be completely independent in the perfor-

---

[11] For the record: statement according to which the Committee will have the same independence as the Court of Auditors with regard to its budget and staff matters.

mance of their duties, in the general interest of the Community. The Council, acting by a qualified majority, shall determine the allowances of members of the Committee.

Article 195

unchanged

Article 196

The Committee shall elect its chairman and officers from among its members for a term of two years. It shall adopt its rules of procedure. The Committee shall be convened by its chairman at the request of the Council or of the Commission. It may also meet on its own initiative.

Article 197

unchanged

Article 198

The Committee must be consulted by the Council or by the Commission where this Treaty so provides. The Committee may be consulted by these institutions in all cases in which they consider it appropriate. It may take the initiative of issuing an opinion in cases in which it considers such action appropriate. The Council or the Commission shall, if it considers it necessary, set the Committee for the submission of its opinion, a time limit which may not be less than one month from the date which the Chairman receives notification to this effect. Upon expiry of the time limit, the absence of an opinion shall not prevent further action.
Third paragraph — unchanged.

Chapter 4: The Committee of the Regions

Article 198a

A Committee consisting of representatives of regional and local authorities, hereinafter referred to as the "Committee of the Regions", is hereby established, attached to the Economic and Social Committee, with advisory status. The number of members of the Regional Committee shall be as follows: Belgium 12; Denmark 9; Germany 24; Greece 12; Spain 21; France 24; Ireland 9; Italy 24; Luxembourg 6; Netherlands 12; Portugal 12; United Kingdom 24.

The members of the Committee shall be appointed by the Council acting unanimously, for four years. Their appointments shall be renewable. The members of the Committee may not be bound by any mandatory instructions. They shall be completely independent in the performance of their duties, in the general interest of the Community. For the appoint-

ment of the members of the Committee, each Member State shall provide the Council with a list containing twice as many candidates as there are seats allotted to its nationals.

Article 198b

The Committee of the Regions shall elect its chairman and officers from among its members for a term of two years. It shall adopt its rules of procedure. The Committee shall be convened by its chairman at the request of the Council or of the Commission. It may also meet on its own initiative.

Article 198c

The Committee of the Regions shall be consulted by the Council or by the Commission where this Treaty so provides. The Committee may be consulted by these institutions in all cases in which they consider it appropriate. The Council or the Commission shall, if it considers it necessary, set the Committee, for the submission of its opinion, a time-limit which may not be less than one month from the date on which the chairman receives notification to this effect. Upon expiry of the time-limit, the absence of an opinion shall not prevent further action.

The opinion of the Committee, together with a record of the proceedings, shall be forwarded to the Council and to the Commission. Where the Economic and Social Committee is consulted pursuant to Article 198, the Committee of the Regions shall be informed by the General Secretariat of the Economic and Social Committee of the request for an opinion. Where it considers that specific regional interests are involved, the Committee of the Regions may submit an opinion on the matter to the Economic and Social Committee. In that event, the opinion of the Committee of the Regions shall be forwarded to the Council and the Commission together with the opinion of the Economic and Social Committee.

TITLE II — Financial provisions

Articles 199 to 201
(unchanged from "Non-paper".)

Article 201A

With a view to maintaining budgetary discipline, the Commission shall not make any proposal for a Community act, nor alter or accept any amendment to that act, nor adopt any implementing measure which is likely to have appreciable implications for the budget of the European Communities unless it is sure that that proposal or that measure is capable of being financed within the limit of the Community's own resources arising under provisions laid down by the Council pursuant to Article 201 of the Treaty establishing the European Economic Community.

Articles 202 to 206
(unchanged from "Non-paper".)

Article 206a
1. The Court of Auditors shall examine the accounts of all revenue and expenditure of the Community. It shall also examine the accounts of all revenue and expenditure of all bodies set up by the Community insofar as the relevant constituent instruments do not preclude such examination. The Court of Auditors shall provide the Council and the European Parliament with a statement of assurance as to the reliability of the accounts and the legality and regularity of the underlying transactions.
2nd and 3rd — unchanged.
4. The Court of Auditors shall draw up an annual report after the close of each financial year. It shall be forwarded to the institutions of the Community and shall be published, together with the replies of these institutions to the observations of the Court of Auditors, in the Official Journal of the European Communities. The Court of Auditors may also, at any time, submit observations, particularly in the form of special reports, on specific questions and deliver opinions at the request of one of the institutions of the Community. It shall adopt its annual reports, special reports or opinions by a majority of its members. It shall assist the European Parliament and the Council in exercising their powers of control over the implementation of the budget.

Article 206b
Paragraphs 1 and 2 unchanged from "Non-Paper".
3. The Commission shall take all appropriate steps to act on the observations in the decisions giving discharge and on other observations by the European Parliament relating to the execution of expenditure, as well as on comments accompanying the recommendations on discharge adopted by the Council.
At the request of the European Parliament or the Council, the Commission shall report on the measures taken in the light of these observations and comments and in particular on the instructions given to the departments which are responsible for the implementation of the budget. These reports shall also be forwarded to the Court of Auditors.

Articles 207 and 208
unchanged

Article 209
The Council, acting unanimously on a proposal from the Commission and after consulting the European Parliament and obtaining the opinion of the Court of Auditors, shall: paragraph a) and b) — present text of the treaty unchanged. c) lay down rules for the responsibility of financial controllers, authorizing officers and accounting officers, and concerning appropriate arrangements for inspection.

Article 209a
Member States shall take the same measures to counter fraud affecting the financial interests of the Community as they take to counter fraud affecting their own financial interests. Without prejudice to other provisions of the Treaty Member States shall coordinate their actions aiming at protecting the financial interests of the Community against fraud. To this end they shall organize, with the help of the Commission, close and regular cooperation between the competent services of their administrations.

Part Six: General provisions

Articles 210 to 214
unchanged

Article 215
Add a new third paragraph which reads as follows: "The preceding paragraph shall apply under the same conditions to the European Central Bank and its servants". Present paragraph 3 becomes new paragraph 4.

Articles 216 to 226
unchanged

Articles 227
Paragraph 2 — delete the words "Algeria and".
Paragraph 5(a) — read as follows: "This Treaty shall not apply to the Faroe Islands." (rest of text deleted).

Article 228
1. Where agreements with one or more States or international organizations in fields covered by this Treaty need to be negotiated, the Commission shall make recommendations to the Council, which, acting by a qualified majority, except in the cases laid down in the second subparagraph of paragraph 2 for which it shall act unanimously, shall authorize the Commission to open the necessary negotiations. The Commission shall conduct these negotiations in consultation with special committees appointed

by the Council to assist it in this task, and within the framework of such directives as the Council may issue to it.

2. Agreements shall be concluded by the Council acting by a qualified majority on a proposal from the Commission. The Council shall act unanimously when the agreement covers a field for which unanimity is required for the adoption of internal rules, and for the agreements referred to in Article 238.

3. The Council shall conclude agreements after consulting the European Parliament, including when the agreement covers a field for which the cooperation procedure is required for the adoption of internal rules. The European Parliament shall deliver its Opinion within a time limit which the Council may lay down according to the urgency of the matter. On expiry of the time limit, the Council may act. By way of derogation from the provisions of the previous subparagraph, agreements calling for amendment of a Community law, agreements having important financial implications for the Community, association agreements as referred to in Article 238 and other agreements establishing a specific institutional framework by organizing cooperation procedures shall be concluded after the assent of the European Parliament has been obtained.

4. When concluding an agreement, the Council may, by way of derogation from the provisions of paragraph 2, authorize the Commission to approve modifications on behalf of the Community where the agreement provides for them to be adopted by a simplified procedure or by a body set up by the agreement; it may attach specific conditions to this authorization.

5. When the Council envisages concluding an agreement which calls for amendments to this Treaty, the amendments must first be adopted in accordance with the procedure laid down for modifying this Treaty. The Council, the Commission or a Member State may obtain beforehand the opinion of the Court of Justice as to whether the agreement envisaged is compatible with the provisions of this Treaty. An agreement on which the Court of Justice has delivered an adverse opinion may enter into force only in accordance with the conditions set out in the article concerning the procedure for modifying this Treaty.

6. Agreements concluded under the conditions set out in this Article shall be binding on the institutions of the Community and on Member States.

Article 228a

If an action by the Community should prove necessary to interrupt or to reduce, in part or completely, economic relations with one or more Third countries, the Council shall, on the basis of a common position or a joint action adopted according to the provisions of the Treaty on the Union relating to the Common Foreign and Security Policy, take the necessary measures as a matter of urgency. The Council shall act by a qualified majority on a proposal from the Commission.

Articles 229 to 230

unchanged

Article 231

The words "Organization for European Economic Cooperation" shall be replaced by "Organization for Economic Cooperation and Development".

Articles 232 to 234

unchanged

Article 235

1. Should it prove that attainment of one of the objectives of the Community calls for action by the Community in one of the fields covered by Articles 3 [and 3a][12] and this Treaty has not provided the necessary powers, the Council shall, acting unanimously on a proposal from the Commission and after receiving the assent of the European Parliament, adopt the appropriate measures while taking into account the principle of subsidiarity as defined in Article 3b.

2. The Council shall determine, under the conditions laid down in paragraph 1, what shall be covered by decisions to be taken by a qualified majority.

Article 235A

The Community shall support the objectives referred to in Article A of the provisions of the Treaty on the Union dealing with home affairs and judicial affairs.

Without prejudice to other provisions of this Treaty the Council may, on the basis of a decision taken pursuant to Article C, paragraph 3 of the provisions of the Treaty on the Union dealing with home affairs and judicial affairs, adopt the necessary measures acting unani-

---

[12] If the reference to which 3a is included, consultation of the ESCB should be introduced.

mously on a proposal from the Commission and after consulting the European Parliament.

Articles 236 and 237

deleted

Article 238

The European Community may conclude with one or more States or international organizations agreements establishing an association involving reciprocal rights and obligations, common action and special procedures.

Articles 239 and 240

unchanged

Articles 241 to 246

deleted

Provisions amending the Treaty establishing the European Coal and Steel Community (for the record)

* * *

Provisions amending the Treaty establishing the European Atomic Energy Committee (for the record)

* * *

Provisions on common foreign and security policy

Objectives and means

Article A

1. The Union and its Member States shall define and implement a common foreign and security policy with the aim of reinforcing the identity and role of the Union as a political entity on the international scene. The policy of the Union may extend to all areas of foreign and security policy.

2. The objectives of the common foreign and security policy shall be:

- to safeguard the common values, fundamental interests and independence of the Union;

- to strengthen the security of the Union and its Member States in all ways, including, eventually, the framing of a defence policy;

- to preserve peace and strengthen international security, in accordance with

the principles of the United Nations Charter;

- to promote international cooperation;

- to develop and consolidate democracy and the rule of law, and respect for human rights and fundamental freedoms.

Articles B to K

(unchanged from text of "Non-paper", except for deletion of cross-references to former Article N and choice of "qualified majority" in Article J, paragraph 2)

Security

Article L

1. The common foreign and security policy includes all questions related to the security of the Union.

2. Decisions by the Union on security matters which have defence implications may be wholly or partly implemented in the framework of the Western European Union, insofar as they also fall within that organization's sphere of competence.

3. Decisions taken pursuant to paragraph 2 shall not affect the obligations arising for certain Member States from the Treaties establishing the Atlantic Alliance and the Western European Union and the situation of each Member State in that connection.

4. The provisions of the present article shall not prevent the establishment of the development of closer cooperation between two or more Member States, to the extent to which such cooperation does not conflict with, or impede, that provided for in this title.

5. With a view to the eventual framing of a defence policy, the provisions of this article may be reviewed as provided for in article W.2, on the basis of a report to be submitted by the Council to the European Council in 1996 at the latest.

General provisions

Article M

The Council shall adopt the necessary measures for implementing the provisions of this Title, particularly Articles D, F, K(2) as well as for the provisions which are necessary in order to apply article L(2). The Council shall adopt the necessary provisions to ensure the confidentiality of the work.

Article N

On the occasion of any review of the security

provisions under Article L(5), the Conference which is convened to that effect shall also examine whether any other amendments need to be made to the provisions relating to the common foreign and security policy.

Article O

1. The provisions relating to the common foreign and security policy shall not affect the powers of the European Communities.

2. The provisions of the Treaties establishing the European Communities which concern the jurisdiction of the Court of Justice of the European Communities and the exercise of that jurisdiction shall not apply to the provisions of Articles A to N.

3. The institutional and financial provisions of the Treaties establishing the European Communities shall apply to the provisions relating to the common foreign and security policy insofar as the latter do not derogate from them.

Provisions on cooperation on home affairs and judicial cooperation

Article A

1. For the purpose of achieving the objectives of the Union, in particular the free movement of persons and without prejudice to the powers of the European Community, Member States shall regard the following areas as matters of common interest:

(a) controlling the crossing of the external borders of the Member States;

(b) authorized entry, movement and residence on the territory of the Member States by nationals of third countries (in particular conditions of access, visa policies, asylum policies);

(c) combating unauthorized immigration and residence on the territory of the Member States by nationals of third countries;

(d) fight against drugs;

(e) customs cooperation in fields not falling within the powers of the European Communities;

(f) judicial cooperation in civil and criminal matters, with particular reference to the recognition and enforcement of judgments;

(g) fight against terrorism, large scale crime and international criminality.

2. Without prejudice to the powers of the European Communities, the matters of common interest set out in paragraph 1 may be the subject of action by the Union under the conditions and in accordance with the procedures laid down in Articles B to J.

Article B
(unchanged from "Non-paper")

Article C

1. In the areas referred to in Article A(a) to (e), Member States shall inform and consult one another and the Commission within the Council, with a view to coordinating their action and, if necessary, adopting a common position. To that end, they shall establish collaboration between the relevant departments of their administrations.

2. The Council may, acting by unanimity on the initiative of any Member State or the Commission:

(a) adopt joint action to the extent to which the objectives of the Union can be attained better by joint action than by the Member States acting individually; it may decide that measures implementing joint action will be adopted by a qualified majority;

(b) without prejudice to the provisions of Article 220 of the Treaty establishing the European Communities adopt draft conventions which it shall recommend to the Member States for adoption in accordance with their respective constitutional requirements; unless otherwise provided by the agreements: — measures implementing such conventions shall be adopted within the Council by a majority of two thirds of the High Contracting Parties; — the Court of Justice shall ensure compliance with the law in the interpretation and application of such conventions.

3. If the Council, acting unanimously at the initiative of the Commission or a Member State decides that an action of the Community is necessary in order to achieve the objectives of the Union in the areas referred to in paragraph 1, Article 235A of the Treaty establishing the European Communities shall apply.

Article D

1. The Council acting unanimously, on the basis of general guidelines from the European Council, may adopt provisions extending the scope of Article A to other areas of activity related to the objectives of the Union and recommend adoption thereof to the Member States in accordance with their respective constitutional rules.

2. Following the same procedure, it may decide to transfer an area of activity from Article B to Article C.

Articles E, F and G
(unchanged from "Non-paper")

Article H

1. The Permanent Representative Committee of the Member States shall be responsible for preparing the Council's discussions and shall carry out any tasks entrusted to it by the Council.

2. A Coordinating Committee shall be set up consisting of senior officials of the Member States, with the task to coordinate work in the areas referred to in Article C and to give opinions, either at the request of the Council or on its own initiative, for the attention of the Council.

3. The Council and the Presidency of the Council shall be assisted by the General Secretariat of the Council in preparing and implementing the policy of the Union in these areas.

4. The Commission shall be fully associated in the work on cooperation in the field of home affairs and judicial affairs.

5. The Council, acting by unanimity shall adopt the provisions necessary to ensure the confidentiality of the work.

Article I
(unchanged from "Non-paper")

Article J

The provisions relating to cooperation in the field of home affairs and judicial cooperation shall be reviewed in 1996, as provided for in Article W(2).

Article K

1. The provisions relating to cooperation in the field of home affairs and judicial cooperation shall not affect the powers of the European Communities.

2. The provisions of the Treaties establishing the European Communities concerning the power of the Court of Justice of the European Communities and the exercise of that power shall not apply to the provisions of Articles A to I, with the exception of those of paragraph 2(b) of Article C and the first paragraph of this Article.

3. The provisions of an institutional and financial nature in the Treaties establishing the European Communities shall apply to the provisions relating to cooperation in the field of home affairs and judicial cooperation to the extent to which the latter do not derogate therefrom.

Final provisions

Article W[13]

1. The Government of any Member State or the Commission may submit to the Council proposals for the amendment of the Treaties on which the Union is founded.

If the Council, after consulting the European Parliament and, where appropriate, the Commission, delivers an opinion in favour of calling a conference of representatives of the governments of the Member States, the conference shall be convened by the President of the Council for the purpose of determining by common accord the amendments to be made to those treaties. The Council of the European Central Bank shall also be consulted in the case of institutional modifications in the monetary field.

2. A conference of representatives of the governments of the Member States shall be convened in 1996 in the perspective of strengthening the federal character of the Union to examine those provisions of this Treaty which provide for such a revision.

Article X[14]

Any European State may apply to become a Member of the Union. It shall address its application to the Council, which shall act unanimously after consulting the Commission and after receiving the assent of the European Parliament which shall act by an absolute majority of its component members.

The conditions of admission and the adjustments to the Treaties on which the Union is founded necessitated thereby shall be the subject of an agreement between the Member States and the applicant State.

This agreement shall be submitted for ratification by all the Contracting States in accordance with their respective constitutional requirements.

[13] Articles 236 EEC, 96 ECSC and 204 EAEC are repealed.
[14] Articles 237 EEC, 98 ECSC and 205 EAEC are repealed.

Article Y[15]

This Treaty is concluded for an unlimited period.

Article Z

1. This Treaty will be ratified by the High Contracting Parties in accordance with their respective constitutional requirements. The instruments of ratification will be deposited with the Government of the Italian Republic.

2. This Treaty will enter into force on the first day of the month following the deposit of the instrument of ratification by the last signatory State to take this step.

Article Z bis

This Treaty, drawn up in a single original in the Danish, Dutch, English, French, German, Greek, Irish, Italian, Portuguese and Spanish languages, the texts in each of these languages being equally authentic, will be deposited in the archives of the Government of the Italian Republic, which will remit a certified copy to each of the Governments of the other Signatory States.

Annex I: Declaration by the Member States

The Member States agree that the following topics can be a joint action priority as soon as this Treaty enters into force:

- industrial and technological cooperation in the armaments field;
- the transfer of military technology to third countries and the control of arms exports;
- non-proliferation issues;
- arms control, negotiations on arms reduction and confidence-building measures, particularly in the CSCE context;
- involvement in peace-keeping operations in the United Nations context;
- involvement in humanitarian intervention measures;
- questions relating to the CSCE;
- relations with the USSR;
- transatlantic relations.
- ......

The Member States agree that the following subjects shall fall under Article C(3) as soon as this Treaty enters into force:

- visa policy
- asylum policy
- imigration.
- ......

Annex II: Declaration by the Member States which are members of the WEU on cooperation between the WEU and the Union

- Declaration of political intent
- Practical arrangements (e.g. Secretariat, Presidency, scheduling etc.).

[15] Articles 240 EEC Treaty (unlimited), 97 ECSC Treaty (50 years) and 208 EACA Treaty (unlimited) are retained.

7. Belgian Chamber of Representatives

Resolution on the Intergovernmental Conferences on European Political Union and Economic and Monetary Union, 27 June 1991

Having regard to the report of its advisory committee on European affairs (Chamber Document No. 1668/1–90/91).

Having regard to the memorandum of the Belgian Parliament in preparation for the Conference of Parliaments of the European Community, adopted on 22 November 1990.

Having regard to the final declaration of the Conference of Parliaments of the European Community held in Rome, adopted on 30 November 1990.

Having regard to the conclusions of the European Council of 14 and 15 December 1990.

Having regard to the resolutions of the European Parliament, notably the resolution on Economic and Monetary Union of 10 October 1990; the resolution on the Intergovernmental Conferences in the context of European Parliament strategy for European Union, of 22 November 1990; and the resolution on strengthening democratic legitimacy in the context of the Intergovernmental Conference on Political Union, of 18 April 1991.

Having regard to the statements made before the Advisory Committee on European Affairs by the Minister of Foreign Affairs, the Minister of Finance, the Minister of Employment and Labour and the State Secretary for Europe 1992, on the state of progress of the Intergovernmental Conferences on Political Union and Economic and Monetary Union.

The Chamber of Representatives.

As regards European unification

1. — notes with satisfaction that the Belgian Government is giving its full support at the intergovernmental conferences for the federal development of the EC;

2. — recalls that European integration must lead to a union with a democratic system and a federal structure;

— rejects the tripartite structure proposed by the Presidency of the EC Council of Ministers in April 1991 and calls on the Government to ensure that the intermediate intergovenmental stages do not mortgage the final aim (a single unified European structure);

— accepts cooperation on an intergovernmental basis in certain fields for a provisional period only and urges that the decision-making process of the Union be organized on a Community-wide basis as soon as possible;

— considers that the time has come to transform relations between the Member States into a European Union, in accordance with the draft constitution to be drawn up through procedures in which the European Parliament and the national parliaments will take part.

As regards democratic legitimacy

3. welcomes the support given by several governments for the principle of co-decision-making powers for the European Parliament and the Council, but notes that the proposals by the Presidency of the EC Council of Ministers in April 1991 merely make provision only for limited co-decision in a limited number of fields;

4. considers that the democratic legitimacy of the results of the intergovernmental conferences must be examined in the light of the following principles;

   - future adjustments to the EC Treaties should be subject to approval by the European Parliament, as Parliament should be closely involved in their revision;

   - the principle of subsidiarity must form the basis for each extension of Community powers and of intergovernmental cooperation; at the same time, effective parliamentary control at an appropriate level should be guaranteed;

   - all legislative acts should be drawn up in co-decision between the European Parliament and the Council, in accordance with a procedure requiring the approval of both branches of the legislative power;

   - the European Parliament must have a right of initiative to be used in the event of default by the Commission;

   - the new legislative hierarchy must not

lead to any erosion of the European Parliament's right of co-decision;

- the Commission should be appointed in a democratic manner at the start of each electoral period of the European Parliament, which means that the Commission President must be elected by Parliament, and the Commission must submit a policy programme to Parliament, to be followed by a vote of confidence;
- the Commission should carry out its executive function under European Parliament supervision and subject to the right of the Council and Parliament to summon it;

5. urges the Belgian Government to oppose any proposals contrary to the above principles;

As regards common foreign, security and defence policy

6. considers that too little thought was given to democratic parliamentary control in the course of discussion on the establishment of common foreign and security policy;

7. hopes that a Community decision-making process will be adopted as soon as possible for foreign and security policy and that the foundations will be laid for the gradual integration of defence policy;

8. considers that a common foreign, security and defence policy must be developed parallel to the movement of the European Institutions towards a political union organized on democratic principles in which the European Parliament must play a full role;

9. urges that development cooperation policy, the main aim of which should be to promote the self-reliance and economic resilience of the Third World, be organized on Community lines;

As regards the elimination of the social deficit

10. is concerned at the difficulties which arose during discussion on the elimination of the social deficit;

11. considers that the EC Treaties must make provision for a common social policy and must lay down appropriate provisions on economic and social cohesion; this implies that the Treaties must affirm these aims more strongly and that decisions in this field must be taken by a qualified majority;

As regards fiscal harmonization and Economic and Monetary Union

12. gives its full support to the proposal to replace the requirement of unanimity in decision-making on fiscal harmonization by the requirement of a qualified majority;

13. insists that progress on fiscal harmonization must be backed up by stringent budgetary control by the Community;

14. considers that the monetary policy of the Union should be pursued in conjunction with general economic policy aims taking account of social and ecological priorities;

15. considers that steps must be taken to guarantee the democratic responsibility of the European central banks system;

As regards Community industrial policy

16. takes the view that the aim of a European industrial policy must be to promote European competitiveness;

As regards regional policy

17. expresses its hope that sufficient resources will be provided for cooperation between the Community institutions and the regions established by constitution or law in the Member States, particularly in the context of structural funds policy;

As regards environmental policy

18. believes that the Community must be endowed with additional powers in environmental matters; that decisions in this field must be taken by a qualified majority and that Community policy must be aimed at protecting the ecological balance in the Community and on our planet as a whole; and proposes that Article 2 of the Treaty be amended so as to include the above aim, which implies a process of long-term development;

As regards European citizenship

19. stresses the importance of a European regulation on the free movement of individuals, including a European policy on immigration, founded on respect for the rights of the citizen;

20. calls for the incorporation in the Treaties of provisions aimed at the establishment of European citizenship, notably by giving all citizens of the Community the right to vote in the European elections in the Member State where

they are resident; calls for the incorporation in the Treaties of the Declaration of fundamental rights and liberties adopted by the European Parliament on 12 April 1989, and the accession of the Community to the European Convention on Human Rights;

As regards cultural policy

21. considers that a section pertaining specifically to culture must be inserted in the European Treaties, in order to support the cultural influence of Europe, and notes in this context that the cultural diversity and languages of the peoples of the Community must be respected and protected;

In conclusion

22. announces that it will take the initiative of convening a new Conference of the Parliaments of the European Community before the work of the Intergovernmental Conferences is wound up, in order to determine a common stance on the proposed amendments to the Treaties;

23. announces that it will under no circumstances approve the amendments to the Treaties if the results of the intergovernmental conferences do not comply with the final declaration of the Conference of Parliaments of the European Community in Rome, adopted on 30 November 1990;

24. resolves not to approve the results of the two Intergovernmental Conferences on Political Union and Economic and Monetary Union if the European Parliament refuses to give its assent on account of the absence of the necessary democratic legitimacy;

25. takes the view that, given the close links between European Political Union and Economic and Monetary Union, the results of the two Intergovernmental Conferences must be submitted for approval at the same time;

26. resolves to forward this resolution to the Senate, the Councils of the Communities and the Regions; the European Parliament and the national parliaments of the European Community, the European Council, the Council of Ministers and the Commission of the European Communities.

8. European Council

Extracts from the conclusions of the meeting held in Luxembourg 28–29 June 1991

Conclusions of the Presidency

Intergovernmental Conferences

The European Council heard a statement by Mr Barón, President of the European Parliament, devoted mainly to outlining Parliament's position on current discussions in the Intergovernmental Conference on Political Union and that on Economic and Monetary Union.

The European Council took note of the draft Treaty prepared by the Luxembourg Presidency in the light of proceedings at the two Conferences. It welcomed the considerable progress that had been made since the two European Councils held in Rome.

The European Council confirms that the proceedings of these two Conferences should continue in parallel. The final decision on the text of the Treaty on Political Union and on Economic and Monetary Union will be taken by the Maastricht European Council so that the results of the two Conferences can be submitted for ratification simultaneously during 1992 and the new Treaty can enter into force on 1 January 1993.

The European Council considers that the Presidency's draft forms the basis for the continuation of negotiations, both as regards most of the principal points contained in it and the state of play at the two Conferences, on the understanding that final agreement by the Member States will only be given to the Treaty as a whole.

Political union

The European Council's discussions have gone into greater detail on some issues for which a solution is crucial to the success of the negotiations. It has established the following general guidelines:

Principles

The European Council considers that the Union should be based on the following principles, as decided at the European Council in Rome on 14 and 15 December 1990: full maintenance of the *acquis communautaire* and development thereof, a single institutional framework with procedures appropriate to the requirements of the various spheres of action, the evolving nature of the process of integration or union, the principle of subsidiarity and the principle of economic and social cohesion.

The European Council also stresses the importance of establishing Union citizenship as a fundamental element in the construction of Europe.

Common foreign and security policy

The Presidency's draft reflects the unanimous desire to reinforce the identity and role of the Union as a political entity on the international scene, as well as the concern to ensure the consistency of all its external activities. The decision-making process for implementation of the common foreign and security policy has still to be examined. Common foreign and security policy will extend to all questions relating to the security of the Union.

The European Council has agreed that the question of strengthening the defence identity of the Union will be decided at the final stage of the Conference. That identity will take account of the traditional positions of certain Member States.

The role of the WEU, which is an essential part of the process of European integration, will be clarified. The Community Member States which are party to the Treaty on the Atlantic Alliance, in accordance with the guidelines established at the recent meeting of NATO Foreign Ministers in Copenhagen, regard the ultimate reinforcement of a European defence identity as an important contribution to the strengthening of the Atlantic Alliance. In the immediate future, they will endeavour to work out common guidelines with a view to the forthcoming NATO Summit in Rome.

Democratic legitimacy

The European Council considers the Presidency's draft to contain significant proposals strengthening the European Parliament's political, legislative and monitoring role, which must go hand in hand with development of the Union. The European Council has also noted that achieving a consensus on the principle of a co-decision procedure will be an important political part of the final agreement. In the

Presidency's view, this procedure will initially be applied to a number of suitable areas, with the possibility of extending it further as the Union progresses.

For some Member States, acceptance of the co-decision principle is linked to overall progress in the development of Community policies, particularly in the social and environmental fields, in accordance with the proposals contained in the Presidency's draft.

Social policy
The European Council emphasized the need to strengthen the Community's social dimension in the context of political union and economic and monetary union. It thinks that the Community's role in this area should be stepped up and its action made more effective, with due regard for the principle of subsidiarity and the respective roles of the Member States and the social partners, in accordance with national practices and traditions. This general approach must not call into question or in any way affect national social security and social protections schemes.

Economic and social cohesion
The European Council believes that ever closer economic and social cohesion is an integral part of the general development of the Union, and it considers that this aspect should be embodied in the Treaty in an appropriate way.

It heard a statement from the President of the Commission on the effects of the policies currently being pursued by the Community from the point of view of economic and social cohesion, and on the outlook in this area. It asked the Commission to clarify the various ideas put forward in the statement in time for the next European Council.

The European Council has already stressed the particular importance in this context of establishing major infrastructure networks at European level.

Implementation of Community law
The European Council agreed in principle to the approach in the Presidency's draft, designed to improve the implementation of Community law.

Home affairs and judicial cooperation
The European Council noted with interest the practical proposals submitted by the German delegation, which supplement the work already carried out in this area (see Annex I).

The European Council agreed on the objectives underlying these proposals and instructed the Conference to examine them further with a view to revision of the Union Treaty.

Economic and monetary union
The Intergovernmental Conference has revealed, with its draft Treaty and the draft statute of the ESCB annexed thereto, that there are broad areas of agreement on the basic components of EMU. At the next European Council these draft texts should be finalized according to the guidelines worked out there and in keeping with the European Council's conclusions of 27 and 28 October 1990, recalling the United Kingdom reserve attached thereto.

The European Council emphasizes the need to make satisfactory and lasting progress with economic and monetary convergence as of now, and as part of the first stage of economic and monetary union, with particular reference to price stability and sound public finance.

In this context, the European Council notes that, in the near future, several governments intend to submit specific multiannual programmes designed to secure the requisite progress on convergence, which will quantify the objectives and the means of securing them. The European Council would encourage other governments to submit such programmes and calls upon the Commission and the Council (economic and financial affairs) to report regularly on the implementation of these programmes and on progress with convergence.

9.   European Parliament

Resolution on the European Council meeting in Luxembourg on 28 and 29 June 1991, 10 July 1991

The European Parliament,

- having regard to its proposals and pronouncements on Political Union and Economic and Monetary Union, and in particular its resolutions of 18 April and 14 June 1991
- having regard to the conclusions of the European Council meeting in Luxembourg on 28 and 29 June 1991,

A.   having regard to the role which the European Council should have played in providing political momentum and direction,

B.   deeply regretting that the national interests of certain countries prevented any improvements being made to the proposals drawn up by the Luxembourg Presidency, which must be congratulated on its efforts,

C.   deploring the fact that the European Council has not provided the necessary political momentum for the work of the IGCs and that on the contrary it has merely postponed all the crucial decisions to the European Council meeting in Maastricht in December 1991, and fearing that this jeopardizes both the timetable and the objectives of the Intergovernmental Conferences; welcoming, however, the confirmation of the dates for the two IGCs, the fact that they will be concurrent and the confirmation of the mandates given by the two European Councils in Rome in 1990,

D.   taking the view that the basis for the future work of the IGCs can only be the Community patrimony and its development towards a federal-type European Union.

I.   As regards the Conference on Political Union

1. Considers that Political Union must be based on a single institutional framework, on full retention of the Community's past gains, on the principles of subsidiarity and economic and social cohesion and on European citizenship;

2. Points out that the democratic deficit has been undermining European integration since the Community's inception and has not therefore been brought about by the subsequent course taken by Community policies, and insists that its elimination should be the key political feature of the final agreement, in accordance with the final declaration issued by the Conference of Parliaments of the European Community;

3. Regrets that no satisfactory answer was given to the question of the unity of the Treaties and considers from this point of view that the draft Treaty of the Luxembourg Presidency constitutes a poor basis for the future work of the IGCs, and that progress would have been possible on the basis of the Commission's proposals in Dresden;

4. Reaffirms its rejection of the approach prevailing in the governments of the Member States, giving preference to integration based on intergovernmental cooperation.

5. Confirms the crucial importance of the co-decision procedure, which must end with an explicit vote by the two branches of the legislative authority approving an identical text; notes that the unity and transparency of the institutional system can be guaranteed only if this procedure is applied to all legislative decisions;

6. Takes the view, with regard to the co-decision procedure, that the Commission's right to accept or reject, at its discretion, amendments adopted by the elected Parliament, irrespective of the majority by which they are adopted, would be incompatible with the principle of equality between the two branches of the legislative authority;

7. Recalls that it is imperative that Parliament should give its assent to any decision of a constitutional nature, in particular those covered by Article 236 of the EEC Treaty, and stresses that the term of office of the Commission should coincide with each parliamentary term, so as to prevent serious institutional instability;

8. Draws attention to its proposals concerning the hierarchy of legislative acts and considers that the introduction of the term "Community law" to designate multiannual programmes, whilst keeping the terms "direc-

tive" and "regulation" for other legislative acts, is unsatisfactory;

9. Notes the absence of any agreement as regards the fundamental elements of the common foreign and security policy; regrets that the questions of decision-making procedures and the role of the WEU have still to be resolved and that the question of European defence was held over to the final stage of the proceedings and points out that the achievement of a common foreign and security policy must be based on a fixed timetable laying down effective and democratically controlled Community procedures;

10. Notes the objectives laid down for establishing joint action in the area of internal and legal affairs and asks that such action be incorporated in the creation of a European legal area and conform to the fundamental principles and components of European citizenship; calls, however, for more information on the role to be assigned to the Commission, the Court of Justice and the European Parliament;

11.Deplores the fact that the Council has merely issued vague declarations of intent with regard to social policy, demonstrating its inability to provide the impetus needed to achieve progress in this area;

12. Deplores the absence of any explicit decision on the essential aspects to be included in the Treaty in the field of environmental policy, notably the principle of ecologically sustainable development and responsibility for a "common policy" on the environment;

13. Notes the willingness shown by the European Council to strengthen economic and social cohesion, a vital aspect of the EMU's credibility, which will be embodied in the Treaties;

14. Recalls its proposals for the revision of the Euratom and ECSC Treaties and considers that these treaties should conform to the new Treaty's decision-making procedures;

15. Reiterates that the development of the Community's democratic legitimacy requires the adjustment of budgetary procedures and Parliament's role in these procedures as well as the adoption of the necessary financial resources;

16. Agrees with the statement by the Commission that the process of implementing the Single Market cannot be dissociated from implementation of the five other objectives in the Single Act, which are economic and social cohesion, social policy, the environment, research policy and the enhancement of economic and monetary cooperation;

17. Draws emphatic attention to the fact that, in the context of establishing Economic and Monetary Union, convergence between countries and regions must cover the whole range of economic and social aspects, and considers that the means employed to bring about such convergence in all its dimensions remain inadequate;

II. As regards the Conference on Economic and Monetary Union

18. Considers that the Treaty on Economic and Monetary Union should respect the prerogatives of the Community Institutions and, in particular, those of the European Parliament and Commission in the drafting of the legislative framework and the definition of general economic and monetary policies; draws attention, in this connection, to its resolution of 14 June 1991[1] and 10 October 1990[2] on Parliament's role in appointing Members of the Board of Directors and the need for parallel coordination of economic policy, economic, social and regional cohesion and monetary integration;

19. Considers that the Treaty on EMU must be finalized in line with the conclusions of the European Council of 27 and 28 October 1990 on the basis of the following points:

- a precise and binding timetable for the beginning of the second stage and for the procedures for the beginning of the third stage;

- the creation at the beginning of the second stage of a European system of central banks enjoying the powers necessary to attain the objectives laid down in the Treaty;

- the creation at the beginning of the third stage of a single currency, i.e. a strong and stable ECU;

- the attainment, starting now and byway of the first stage, of satisfactory and lasting progress on economic and monetary convergence with particular reference to price stability and the restoration of sound public finances;

[1] Part II, item 3 of that day's minutes.
[2] OJ No C 284, 12.11.1990, p. 62.

III. As regards the approval of the new treaty

20. Recalls that its approval of the new treaty will depend on the following minimum objectives being met:

    - introduction of the co-decision procedure involving Parliament and the Council for the adoption of Community legislation;
    - enshrinement in the treaty of Parliament's involvement in the appointment of the Commission (vote of confidence) and its President;
    - extension of majority voting in the Council, particularly to all social and environmental matters:

and welcomes the fact that the Belgian Chamber of Representatives has joined the Italian Parliament in declaring that it will not approve ratification of the new treaty unless it is approved by the European Parliament;

IV. As regards federalism

21. Recalls that the federal objective has been present right from the creation of the Community when, in the Schuman Declaration, the French Government proposed the establishment of a Coal and Steel Community as the first step towards a European Federation, and is still supported by an overwhelming majority of Europe's major political parties which, in the European Parliament, have called on the IGCs to establish a "union of federal type";

22. Points out that the Community already possesses a number of federal characteristics, but does not yet have the full range of powers which should, under the subsidiarity principle, be allocated to it, and exercises its responsibilities in a manner which is neither sufficiently efficient nor sufficiently democratic;

23. Confirms its endorsement of a federal structure for Europe, stresses that federalism does not imply the creation of a unitary super-state, but rather the establishment of a federation of states and nations, each retaining its own identity and with powers distributed in accordance with the principle of subsidiarity,

and recalls its undertaking to draw up a draft Constitution;

V. As regards external relations

24. Welcomes the declarations made at the Summit on human rights, improved arrangements for providing emergency aid via the United Nations, the non-proliferation of weapons and arms exports;

25. Notes the increasing number of statements concerning external relations with reference to the USSR, the European Economic Area, Central and Eastern Europe, the Baltic states, the Middle East, the Western Sahara, Algeria, the United States, Canada, Japan and Southern Africa, which demonstrate that the European Community is increasingly coming to play a genuine role in international relations, but deplores the lack of proposals on Ethiopia and Cyprus;

VI. As regards the Dutch Presidency

26. Urges the Dutch Presidency of the Council to do its utmost to ensure that the impetus provided at Rome in December 1990 is amplified at Maastricht at the end of the year by taking greater account of the legitimate demands of the European Parliament, which represents the interest of the Community's citizens, and to achieve a proper balance in Community legislation between the liberalizing measures needed to complete the single market and the social measures needed to ensure that that market operates to the benefit of all European citizens; without the latter, the former will be jeopardized;

27. Supports the request of the President of the Commission for the European Environment Agency to be taken out of global negotiations on the seats of the Community Institutions because of the urgent need to make this body operational;

28. Calls on the Presidency to take steps to ensure that the conditions for reaching an agreement within GATT are finally met at the summit of industrialized countries in London;

29. Instructs its President to forward this resolution to the Commission, the Council and the heads of State or Government of the Member States.

10. Dutch Presidency Draft Treaty "Towards European Union"

24 September 1991

Part One: Principles

Article 1

By this Treaty, which marks a new stage in a process leading gradually to a European Union with a federal goal, the High Contracting Parties establish among themselves a EUROPEAN COMMUNITY.

Article 2

The Community shall have as its task, by establishing a common market, an internal market as defined in Article 8a, an economic and monetary union and by implementing the common policies or activities referred to in Article 3, the promotion, throughout the Community, of a harmonious and balanced development of economic activities, which is also sustainable, and non-inflationary growth respecting the environment, a high degree of convergence of economic performance, a high level of employment and of social protection, the raising of the standard and quality of living, and economic and social cohesion and solidarity between Member States.

The Community and its Member States, each in accordance with its own powers, shall set itself the following tasks, starting from the "acquis communautaire", on which it is to build, to assert its identity on the international scene, in particular through the implementation of a common foreign and security policy which shall include the eventual framing of a defence policy, to strengthen the protection of the rights and interests of its Member States' nationals, through the introduction of a citizenship of the Community, and to develop a close cooperation in the field of home and judicial affairs.

These tasks shall be carried out in accordance with this Treaty.

Article 2a

The Community shall act within the limits of the powers conferred upon it by this Treaty and of the objectives assigned to it therein.

In the areas which do not fall within its exclusive jurisdiction, the Community shall take action, in accordance with the principle of subsidiarity, only if, and insofar as, these objectives can be better achieved by the Community than by the Member States acting separately, by reason of the scale or effects of the proposed action.

Article 3

(to be definitively reviewed after decisions are taken on new powers)

For the purposes set out in Article 2, the activities of the Community shall include, as provided in this Treaty and in accordance with the timetable set out therein:

(a) the elimination, as between Member States, of customs duties and quantitative restrictions on the import and export of goods, and of all other measures having equivalent effect;

(b) a common commercial policy;

(c) an internal market characterized by the abolition, as between Member States, of obstacles to freedom of movement of goods, persons, services and capital;

(d) a common foreign and security policy

(e) a common monetary policy,

(f) the coordination of the economic policies of the Member States,

(g) a common policy in the sphere of agriculture and fisheries;

(h) a common policy in the sphere of transport;

(i) a system ensuring that competition in the internal market is not distorted;

(j) the approximation of the laws of Member States to the extent required for the functioning of the common market, taking into account consumer interests;

(k) a policy in the social sphere comprising a European Social Fund;

(l) the strengthening of economic and social cohesion;

(m) a policy in the sphere of the environment;

(n) the strengthening of the competitiveness of the Community's industry;

(o) a policy in the sphere of research and technological development;

(p) coordination in the sphere of energy;

(q) encouragement for the establishment and development of trans-European networks;

(r) contribution to the attainment of a high level of health protection;

(s) contribution to education and training of high quality;

(t) contribution to the flowering of the cultures in Europe in all their forms;

(u) a policy in the sphere of development cooperation;

(v) the association of the overseas countries and territories in order to increase trade and promote jointly economic and social development.

Article 4

1. The Community shall be served by a single institutional framework which shall ensure the consistency and the continuity of the actions carried out in order to attain its objectives while observing and building upon the "acquis communautaire".

The Community shall in particular ensure the consistency of its external actions as a whole in the context of its external relations, security, economic and development policies.

2. The tasks entrusted to the Community shall be carried out by the following institutions:

- a European Parliament
- a Council
- a Commission
- a Court of Justice.

Each institution shall act within the limits of the powers conferred upon it by this Treaty.

3. The Council and the Commission shall be assisted by an Economic and Social Committee acting in an advisory capacity.

4. The audit shall be carried out by a Court of Auditors acting within the limits of the powers conferred upon it by this Treaty.

Article 4a

The European Council shall provide the Community with the necessary impetus for its development and shall define the general political guidelines thereof, whilst observing the institutional balance defined by this Treaty.

The European Council shall bring together the Heads of State or of Government of the Member States and the President of the Commission. They shall be assisted by the Ministers for Foreign Affairs of the Member States and by a Member of the Commission.

The European Council shall meet at least twice a year under the Presidency of the Head of State or of Government of the Member State which holds the Presidency of the Council.

The European Council shall submit to the European Parliament a report after each of its meetings and a yearly written report on the progress achieved by the Union referred to in Article 1.

Article 4b

A European System of Central Banks (ESCB) is hereby set up in accordance with the procedures laid down by this Treaty, which shall act within the limits of the powers conferred upon it by this Treaty and the Statutes annexed thereto.

Article 4c

A European Investment Bank is hereby established, which shall act within the limits of the powers conferred upon it by this Treaty and the Statutes annexed thereto.

Article 5[1]

Add the following third paragraph:

On the basis of a periodic report prepared by the Commission, the Member States and the Commission shall establish close cooperation between their administrative departments in order to ensure full compliance with Community law.

Article 6

Replace by:

1. The Community shall have due regard to the national identity of its Member States, whose systems of government are founded on the principles of democracy.

2. The Community shall respect the rights and freedoms as recognized in the Convention for the Protection of Human Rights and Fundamental Freedoms.

3. The Community shall provide itself with the resources necessary to attain its objectives and carry through its policies.

Article 7–8c

Unchanged

---

[1] Declaration concerning the non-contractual liability of Member States to redress damages caused by any failure to fulfil their obligations under Community law.

Part Two: Community citizenship

Article A

1. Community citizenship is hereby established. Every person holding the nationality of a Member State shall be a citizen of the Community.

2. Community citizens shall enjoy the rights conferred by this Treaty and shall be subject to the duties imposed thereby.

Article B

1. Every Community citizen shall have the right to move and reside freely within the territory of the Member States, under the conditions laid down in this Treaty and by the measures adopted to give it effect.

2. The Council may adopt provisions with a view to facilitating the exercise of the rights referred to in the preceding paragraph; unless this Treaty stipulates otherwise, the Council shall act unanimously on a proposal from the Commission and after consulting the European Parliament. Provisions thus adopted shall be subject to the assent of the European Parliament which shall decide by an absolute majority of its component members.

Article C

1. Every Community citizen shall have the right to vote and to stand as a candidate at municipal elections in the Member State in which he resides, under the same conditions as nationals of that State, subject to detailed arrangements to be adopted before 31 December 1993 by the Council, acting unanimously on a proposal from the Commission and after consulting the European Parliament; these arrangements which shall be subject to the assent of the European Parliament, which shall decide by an absolute majority of its component members, may provide for derogations where warranted by problems specific to a Member State.

2. Without prejudice to the provisions of Article 138(3) and of the provisions adopted for its implementation, every Community citizen shall have the right to vote and to stand as a candidate in elections to the European Parliament in the Member State in which he resides, under the same conditions as nationals of that State, subject to detailed arrangements to be adopted before 31 December 1993 by the Council, acting unanimously on a proposal from the Commission and after consulting the European Parliament; decisions thus taken shall be subject to the assent of the European Parliament acting by an absolute majority of its component members; these arrangements, may provide for derogations where warranted by problems specific to a Member State.

Article D

Every Community citizen shall, in the territory of a third country in which the Member State of which he is a national is not represented, be entitled to protection by diplomatic or consular authorities of any Member State, on the same conditions as the nationals of that State. Before 31 December 1993, Member States shall establish the necessary rules among themselves and start the international negotiations required to secure this protection.

Article E

Every Community citizen shall have the right to petition the European Parliament in accordance with Article 137bb.

Every Community citizen may apply to the Ombudsman established in accordance with Article 137c.

Article F

The Commission shall report to the Council and to the European Parliament before 31 December 1993 and then every three years on the implementation of the provisions of this Part. This report shall take account of the development of the Community.

On this basis, and without prejudice to the other provisions of this Treaty, the Council, acting unanimously on a proposal from the Commission, and after obtaining the assent of the European Parliament, may adopt provisions to strengthen or to add to the rights laid down in this Part, which it shall recommend, after having obtained the assent of the European Parliament, which shall decide by an absolute majority of its component members, to the Member States for adoption in accordance with their respective constitutional rules.

Part Three: Policies of the Community

Title I — Free movement of goods

Articles 9–37

unchanged

Title II — Agriculture

Article 38–47

unchanged

Title III — Free movement of persons, services and capital

Articles 48–56
(unchanged from previous draft of Luxembourg Presidency)

Title IV — Transport

Article 74–86
(unchanged from previous draft of Luxembourg Presidency)

Title V — Common rules

(Competition, taxation, approximation of laws)

Article 87
Paragraph 1, second subparagraph
"and after consulting the European Parliament" shall be replaced by "and in cooperation with the European Parliament"".

Article 88–91
unchanged

Article 92
{Conference Declaration leading to the possibility of granting financial aid for cultural purposes being governed subsequently by way of a decision taken pursuant to Article 92(3)(d)}

Article 93
unchanged

Article 94
Add after "from the Commission":
"and in cooperation with the European Parliament."

Article 95–98
unchanged

Article 99
unchanged

Article 100
The Council shall, acting unanimously on a proposal from the Commission and after consulting the European Parliament and the Economic and Social Committee, issue directives for the approximation of such provisions laid down by law, regulation or administrative action in Member States as directly affect the establishment or functioning of the Common Market.

Articles 100a
unchanged

Article 100a bis
"For the purposes of achieving the internal market, the Council shall, acting unanimously on a proposal from the Commission and after consulting the European Parliament and the Economic and Social Committee, adopt the necessary measures concerning the entry into and movement on the territory of the Member States of nationals from third countries"[2]

Title VI — Economic and monetary policy

Article 101
unchanged

Articles 102 to 101
{To be reviewed in the light of the Intergovernmental Conference on EMU}

Article 110–113
See Title II of Part Four, except for Article III which will be deleted

Article 114
deleted

Article 115
deleted

Article 116
See Article B of Title IV of Part Four

Title VII — Social policy, education, vocational training and youth

(virtually no changes from previous Luxembourg Presidency text)

Title VIII — The European Investment Bank

(no changes from previous Luxembourg Presidency text)

Title IX — Economic and Social Cohesion[3]

(no changes of substance from previous Luxembourg Presidency text)

Title X — Research and technological development

Articles 130f, 130g and 130h
(no change from previous Luxembourg Presidency text)

---

[2] Declaration: The measures referred to in Article 100a shall be taken before 31 December . . .
[3] For the sake of good order, the Presidency refers to the introductory note where it is stated that it proposes drawing up new proposals on the subject, in the light of discussions to be carried out within the Intergovernmental Conference.

Article 130i

1. The Council, acting by a qualified majority on a proposal from the Commission under the procedure for co-decision with the European Parliament, shall adopt a multiannual framework programme setting out all the activities of the Community.

The framework programme shall

- define the specific programmes necessary to implement it and establish priorities for them;

- fix the maximum overall amount and the detailed rules for Community financial participation in the programme as a whole and the respective shares in each of the specific programmes;

- establish the scientific and technological objectives to be achieved by specific programmes and, where applicable, the activities defined in Articles 130j and 130k;

- fix the rules for the participation of undertakings, research centres and universities;

- fix the rules for disseminating the results of research.

2. The framework programme may be adapted or supplemented, as the situation changes.

3. The Council, acting by a qualified majority on a proposal from the Commission and after consulting the European Parliament, shall adopt the specific programmes.

4. Without prejudice to the application of Articles 130j and 130k, the Commission shall carry out the specific programmes.

In exercising these powers the Commission shall be assisted for each specific programme by a committee appointed by the Council.

Article 130j, 130k, 130l, 130m and 130o
(no change from Luxembourg Presidency draft)

Article 130n

The Council, acting unanimously on a proposal from the Commission and after consulting the European Parliament, shall adopt the provisions referred to in Article 130m. These provisions shall be subject to the assent of the European Parliament which shall decide by an absolute majority of its component members.

The Council, acting by a qualified majority on a proposal from the Commission and in cooperation with the European Parliament after consulting the Economic and Social Committee, shall adopt the provisions referred to in Articles 130j to l. Adoption of the supplementary programmes shall also require the agreement of the Member States concerned.

Title XI — Environment[4]

(no changes of substance from Luxembourg Presidency draft)

Title XII — Energy

Article A

Member States agree on the necessity of promoting coordination between them in the energy sphere, with the aim of:

- promoting security of supplies in the Community under satisfactory economic conditions;

- contributing to a high level of protection of the environment;

- promoting the rational use of energy and the development and use of new and renewable energy sources.

Article B

The Commission may take all appropriate steps to promote the coordination referred to in Article A.

Title XIII — Transeuropean networks

(no change of substance from Luxembourg Presidency draft)

Title XIV — Industry

Sole Article

1. Member States consider their actions aimed at creating conditions for industry to benefit from the establishment of the Internal Market, and achievement of Economic and Monetary Union and from the research and technological development policy as a matter of common interest.

2. Without prejudice to Articles 85 to 94 and in accordance with a system of open and competitive markets, the Council voting by

---

[4] For the sake of good order, the Presidency refers to the introductory note where it is stated that it proposes drawing up new proposals on the subject concerning the financing of expenditure in the context of environment policy, in the light of discussions to be carried out within the Intergovernmental Conference.

a qualified majority on a proposal from the Commission, in cooperation with the European Parliament and after consulting the Economic and Social Committee, may adopt specific programmes particularly in favour of key industries aimed at:

- speeding up the adjustment of industry to structural changes;
- ensuring a favourable environment for initiatives and the development of undertakings throughout the Community, particularly small and medium-sized undertakings;
- creating a climate favourable to cooperation between undertakings;
- fostering better exploitation of the industrial potential of policies of innovation, research and technological development.

Title XV — Public health

Title XVI — Culture

(no change from Luxembourg Presidency draft)

Part Four: External relations of the Community

Title I — Common foreign and security policy

Article A

1. The Community and its Member States shall define and implement a common foreign and security policy with the aim of reinforcing the identity and role of the Community as a political entity on the international scene. The policy of the Community may extend to all areas of foreign and security policy.

2. The objectives of the common foreign and security policy shall be:

- to safeguard the common values, fundamental interests and independence of the Community;
- to strengthen the security of the Community and its Member States in all ways, including, eventually, the framing of a defence policy;
- to preserve peace and strengthen international security, in accordance with the principles of the United Nations Charter;

- to promote international cooperation;
- to develop and consolidate democracy and the rule of law, and respect for human rights and fundamental freedoms.

Article B

1. The Community shall pursue its common foreign and security objectives by gradually introducing joint action in all areas where the Member States have essential interests in common. For the areas of political cooperation and security which are not covered by this Treaty, the provisions of Title III (Article 30 of the Single Act) shall continue to apply.

2. Each Member State or the Commission may submit proposals to the Council with the object of initiating a joint action for an area or a question falling under foreign and security policy. The Council[5] acting unanimously shall set the general and specific objectives that the Community attributes to itself in the pursuit of such action.

3. The Council, acting (unanimously) (by a qualified majority), shall set the conditions, means and procedures applicable to the implementation of the joint action. The Council shall adapt the joint action to the evolving nature of the situation.

Former Article K, paragraph 2 of the Luxembourg Presidency proposal:

4. Whenever there is any plan to adopt a national position or take national action pursuant to a joint line of action, information shall be provided in time to enable the other Member States and the Commission, if necessary, to be consulted in advance. The obligation to provide prior information shall not apply to measures which are merely a national transposition of Community decisions.

Former Article K, paragraph 4 of the Luxembourg Presidency proposal:

4. Should there be any major difficulties in implementing a joint action, a Member State shall refer them to the Council which shall discuss them and seek appropriate solutions. Such solutions shall not run counter to the objectives of the joint line of action nor impair its effectiveness.[6]

---

[5] Conference Declaration, in which reference is made to Article 4a.
[6] The question arises of whether this "opting out" provision should be retained.

Article C

Security[7]

1. The common foreign and security policy shall include all questions relating to security.

2. Common security policy shall complement the security policy resulting from the obligations flowing for certain Member States from the Treaties establishing the North Atlantic Treaty Organization and the Western European Union, which continue to contribute in a significant fashion to security and stability.

3. The Council shall ensure that cohesion is promoted between the Community security policy and the policy followed by a certain number of Member States within the framework of the Western European Union and the North Atlantic Treaty Organization, whilst observing the powers peculiar to each of those organizations.

4. The provisions of this Article shall not prevent the establishment of the development of closer cooperation between two or more Member States, to the extent to which such cooperation does not conflict with, or impede, that provided for in this Title.

5. With a view to the eventual framing of a defence policy, further measures to be undertaken in this respect must be examined by 1996 at the latest, in the light of intervening developments.

Article D

A continued dialogue shall be instituted between the European Parliament and the Council as well as the Commission in order to keep the European Parliament regularly informed of the fundamental choices of the Community foreign and security policy. The European Parliament shall be consulted on the broad guidelines of the common foreign and security policy.

Without prejudice to its other powers, the European Parliament may put questions to the Council on any matter of common interest relating to foreign and security policy and frame recommendations. Where the implementation of the joint action takes place in the form of an act of legislation the European Parliament shall be involved in accordance with the relevant Articles of the Treaty.

Article E

The jurisdiction of the Court of Justice of the European Communities shall only extend to the review of the legality of the application of the procedures for deciding upon the joint action referred to in this Title of the Treaty.

Title II — Commercial policy

Article A

Former Article 110
unchanged

Article B

Former Article 112
unchanged

Article C

Former Article 113

1. Unchanged

2. The Council, acting by a qualified majority on a proposal from the Commission and after consulting the European Parliament, shall adopt the measures necessary to implement the common commercial policy.

3. Negotiations on agreements with one or more States or international organizations shall be carried out by the Commission in consultation with a Special Committee appointed by the Council under the procedure provided for in Article C of Title IV of this Part.

Title III — Development cooperation

(no changes of substance from Luxembourg Presidency draft)

The provisions of Title IV of this Part shall apply.
{Conference Declaration: the European Development Fund shall continue to be financed by national contributions in accordance with existing provisions.}

Title IV — Representation of the Community in external relations

Article A

(See Article 113 (3) proposal from the Luxembourg Presidency).

Without prejudice to Articles C, G, H and I, in areas where the Community enjoys exclusive powers, the position of the Community in relations with third countries, within international organizations and at international conferences shall be put by the Commission.

---

[7] Annex: See Annex I of the text of the Luxembourg Presidency, to be reviewed in the negotiations.

Article B

(Article 116(1))

In respect of all other matters for which the Community is competent, the Member States shall proceed within the framework of international organizations only by common action. To this end, the Commission shall submit to the Council, which shall act by a qualified majority, proposals concerning the scope and implementation of such common action.

Article C

1. Where agreements with one or more States or international organizations in fields for which the Community is competent need to be negotiated, the Commission shall make recommendations to the Council, which, acting by a qualified majority, except in the cases laid down in the second subparagraph of paragraph 2, for which it shall act unanimously, shall authorize the Commission to open the necessary negotiations.

The Commission shall conduct these negotiations in consultation with committee referred to in Article C of Title II to assist it in this task, and within the framework of such directives as the Council may issue to it. The composition of the Committee shall be determined by the object of the negotiations.

(Rest of Article C and Articles D, E and F unchanged from Luxembourg Presidency's draft)

Article G

(See Article F: Proposal from the Luxembourg Presidency.) Without prejudice to the provisions of Article C, for joint action covered by Title I of this Part the external representation of the Community shall be the responsibility of the Presidency, assisted where appropriate by the Member State which held the preceding Presidency and by the Member State that will hold the ensuing Presidency. The Commission shall be associated with this task.

Article H

(EMU)

Article I

Without prejudice to Article C, with respect to cooperation in the field of home and judicial affairs, Member States shall coordinate their action and adopt where appropriate common positions within international organizations and at international conferences in which they participate.

Part Five: Association of the overseas countries and territories

Articles 131 to 136a

unchanged

Part Six: Institutions

Title I — Provisions governing the institutions

Chapter 1 — The Institutions[8]

Section 1 — The European Parliament

Article 137

The European Parliament, which shall consist of representatives of the peoples of the States brought together in the Community shall exercise the powers conferred upon it by this Treaty.

Article 137a

Insofar as provided in this Treaty, the European Parliament shall participate in the process leading up to the adoption of Community legislative acts by exercising its powers under the cooperation procedure laid down in Article 149 and by giving its assent or delivering consultative Opinions.

The European Parliament may, acting by a majority of its members, request the Commission to submit any appropriate proposal on matters on which it considers that a Community legislative act is required for the purpose of implementing this Treaty.

Articles 137b, 137bb and 137c

(no changes of substance from Luxembourg Presidency draft)

Article 138

Amend paragraph 3 to read as follows:

The European Parliament shall draw up proposals for elections by direct universal suffrage in accordance with a uniform procedure in all Member States.

The Council shall, acting unanimously lay down the appropriate provisions, which it shall recommend to Member States for adoption in

---

[8] For the sake of good order, the Presidency refers to the introductory note where it is stated that it proposes submitting concrete suggestions concerning political and institutional aspects of EMU, including, where appropriate, Article 149.

accordance with their respective constitutional requirements after obtaining the assent of the European Parliament, which shall act by an absolute majority of its component members.

Articles 139 to 144
unchanged

Section 2 — The Council

Article 145
unchanged

Article 146
Replace the first paragraph by the following paragraph:
"The Council shall consist of a representative of each Member State at ministerial level, authorized to take binding decisions for the government of that Member State." (remainder of the Article unchanged)

Articles 147 and 148
unchanged

Article 149
1. Where, in pursuance of this Treaty, the Council acts on a proposal from the Commission, unanimity shall be required for an act constituting an amendment to that proposal, subject to the provisions of Article 149a(3) and (4).

Add:

(f) The decision referred to in point (e) shall be forwarded to the European Parliament, which within a period of two months, may reject it by an absolute majority of its component members.

(Points (f) and (g) become (g) and (h).)

Article 149b
Where, by virtue of this Treaty, a Council act is taken under the procedure for co-decision with the European Parliament, the following procedure shall apply:
(procedure identical to that of Article 189a in draft of Luxembourg Presidency)

Article 149c
(See Article 228a of the Luxembourg Presidency)
Where exceptional circumstances require immediate action from the Community, the Council acting by a qualified majority on a proposal from the Commission shall provisionally adopt

the necessary measures and shall inform the European Parliament without delay.

On the expiry of a period of . . . months, these measures shall be confirmed pursuant to the procedures and provisions of this Treaty.

Note: It is suggested that the possibility should be studied in consultation with the European Parliament of drawing up a procedure which permits the European Parliament or its representatives to be rapidly consulted in cases of emergency.

Articles 150 to 154
unchanged

Section 3 — The Commission

Articles 155 to 160
(unchanged from Luxembourg Presidency Draft Treaty)

Article 161
(Article 14 of the Merger Treaty)
The Commission may appoint two Vice-Presidents from among its members.

Articles 162 to 163
(Articles, 15, 16 and 17 of the Merger Treaty) (unchanged)

Section 4 — The Court of Justice

Articles 164–188
(no changes of substance from Luxembourg Presidency Draft Treaty)

Chapter 2: Provisions common to several Institutions

Article 189
unchanged

Article 190
unchanged

Article 191
unchanged

Article 192
unchanged

Chapter 3: The Economic and Social Committee[9]

Chapter 4: The Committee of the Regions

(no changes of substance from Luxembourg Presidency Draft Treaty)

[9] For the record: Statement according to which the Committee will have the same independence as the Court of Auditors with regard to its budget and staff matters.

Articles 199 – 208
(unchanged from Luxembourg Presidency Draft Treaty)

Article 209

The Council, acting by a qualified majority on a proposal from the Commission and in cooperation with the European Parliament and after obtaining the opinion of the Court of Auditors, shall:

paragraph (a) and (b) unchanged

(c) lay down rules concerning the responsibility of financial controllers, authorising officers and accounting officers, and concerning appropriate arrangements for inspection.

Article 209a

unchanged

Part Seven: General provisions

Articles 210 to 214

unchanged

Article 215

unchanged

Articles 216 to 219

unchanged

Article 220

unchanged

Chapter X: Home and judicial affairs

Article 220a

1. Without prejudice to the other provisions of this Treaty, and in accordance with the general objectives thereof, the Member States shall introduce cooperation in the following fields:

(a) harmonization of the formal and substantive aspects of the residence of third country nationals on the territory of the Member States;

(b) harmonization of the formal and substantive aspects of asylum policy;

(c) combating unauthorized immigration and residence on the territory of the Member States by third country nationals;

(d) fight against drugs in fields not falling within the powers of the European Communities;

(e) combating fraud in fields not falling within the powers of the European Communities;

(f) customs cooperation in fields not falling within the powers of the European Communities;

(g) judicial cooperation;

(h) police cooperation with a view to the prevention of and fight against terrorism and other forms of serious international crime, including the organization of a system of exchange of information on investigations at European level. The Commission shall be fully associated in this cooperation.

2. Measures in the fields referred to in paragraph 1(a) to (c) shall be taken on the initiative of a Member State or the Commission.

3. Measures in the fields referred to in paragraph 1(d) to (h) shall be taken on the initiative of a Member State. Member States may decide that those measures could also be taken on the initiative of the Commission.

4. When those measures are adopted, Member States may specify that the Court of Justice shall have jurisdiction to interpret the law and, if necessary, to decide on disputes.

5. Decisions under this Article shall be taken by common accord, including decisions setting the conditions, means and procedures applicable to the implementation of the measures laid down.

{Option: add a second paragraph:
"In this context Member States may decide that the implementing measures shall be adopted by a qualified majority expressing votes in favour by at least eight Member States".}

6. Without prejudice to Article 4 of the Merger Treaty a Co-ordination Committee shall be set up composed of senior officials whose task it shall be to coordinate work in the field of home and judicial affairs and to formulate opinions, either at the request of Member States or on its own initiative.

The Member States shall be assisted by the General Secretariat of the Council of the European Communities in the preparation and implementation of policy in these fields.

7. The Member State that holds the Presidency of the Council and the Commission, each in accordance with its own powers, shall regularly inform the European Parliament of work carried out in the fields referred to in this Article.

They shall ensure that the views of the European Parliament are duly taken into consideration. The European Parliament may draw the attention of the Member States and the Commission to any question relating to the fields referred to in the first paragraph.

8. The provisions on cooperation referred to in this Article shall not prevent the introduction or development of closer cooperation between two or more Member States, to the extent that such cooperation does not contravene that provided for in this Treaty nor hinder it.

Articles 221 to 226

unchanged

Article 227

unchanged

Articles 228 to 230

See Title IV of Part Four.

Articles 232 to 234

unchanged

Article 235

Add at the end:

"These provisions shall be subject to the assent of the European Parliament which shall decide by an absolute majority of its component members.

Paragraph 2 shall be added reading as follows:

The Council shall determine, under the conditions laid down in paragraph 1, what shall be covered by decisions to be taken by a qualified majority.

Articles 236 and 237

unchanged

Article 238

The Community may conclude with one or more States or international organizations, agreements establishing an association involving reciprocal rights and obligations, common action and special procedures.

Articles 239 and 240

unchanged

Articles 241 to 246

deleted

****

Draft conference declaration

A Conference of the Representatives of the Governments of the Member States will be convened in 1996 to examine what provisions of this Treaty will be liable to amendment.

In particular the Conference agrees that the procedures for taking decisions laid down in Articles 149 and 149a shall be the object of amendment in 1996 by an Inter-governmental Conference, on the basis of experience gained,

with a view to introducing a uniform procedure for taking decisions in order to guarantee parliamentary democracy in the legislative field within the Community.

The participation of the European Parliament in the decision-making process on the basis of Articles 43, 99 and 113 will be strengthened on that occasion.

The Conference also agrees that the above-named Intergovernmental Conference will examine to what extent it is possible to introduce a hierarchy of norms in the system of acts whereby the Community can take decisions laid down in Article 189.

******

Proposal from the Presidency to amend Article 30 of the Single Act

Article 30 of the Single Act

Article 30(1)

unchanged

Article 30(2)(a)

Add a second subparagraph reading as follows: "They shall define, whenever necessary, a common position, on which the policies or actions adopted by the Member States shall be based".

Article 30(2)(b)

unchanged

Article 30(2)(c)

Replace first subparagraph by the following: "Member States shall support the common foreign and security policy actively and unreservedly in a spirit of loyalty and mutual solidarity. They shall ensure that their national policies are in line with the common positions agreed on. They shall refrain from any action which is contrary to the interests of the Community or likely to impair its effectiveness as a cohesive force in international relations."

Second subparagraph unchanged

Third subparagraph deleted

Article 30(2)(d)

deleted

Article 30(3)(a)

The paragraph shall be replaced by a new paragraph reading as follows:

"Matters of common foreign and security policy shall be discussed on the occasion of meetings of the Council of the European Communities."

Article 30(3)(b)

unchanged

Article 30(3)(c)

unchanged

Article (30)(4)

unchanged

Article 30(5)

unchanged

Article 30(6)

unchanged

Article 30(7)(a)

To be changed as follows:

"In international organizations and at international conferences which they attend, the High Contracting Parties shall adopt common positions on the subjects covered by this Title."

Article 30(7)(b)

The paragraph is deleted and replaced by the following:

"In international organizations and at international conferences in which not all the High Contracting Parties participate, those who do participate shall put the common positions agreed on and shall keep the other Member States informed of any matter of general interest."

Article 30(8)

unchanged

Article 30(9)

unchanged

Article 30(10)(a) and (b)

unchanged

Article 30(10)(c) to (g)

deleted

Article 30(11)

unchanged

Article 30(12)

To be changed as follows:

"In 1996 the High Contracting Parties shall examine whether any amendment of Title III is required."

Draft conference declaration

Position of the Political Committee

Declaration to be added to Article 4 of the Treaty establishing a Single Council and a Single Commission of the European Communities of 1965.

The Permanent Representatives Committee meets in three parts, the first two of which discuss matters that do not fall within the common foreign and security policy, and the third part will be responsible for the common foreign and security policy. The third part of the Permanent Representatives Committee will be composed of Political Directors or their representatives.

11.   Italy and United Kingdom

Declaration on European security and defence in the context of the Intergovernmental Conference on Political Union, 5 October 1991

1. Italy and United Kingdom are fully aware of the challenge that Europe will have to face in the new political and strategic environment of the 90s. For this reason, they wish to contribute – in close association with other partners – to the definition of the framework in which Europe will be able to play a fuller role on the international scene by establishing a political Union.

I.   The European identity in the field of security and defence

2. Political Union implies the gradual elaboration and implementation of a common foreign and security policy and a stronger European defence identity with the longer term perspective of a common defence policy compatible with the common defence policy we already have with all our allies in NATO.

3. The development of a European identity in the field of security and defence shall be pursued through an evolutionary process involving successive phases.

4. The special relationship between Western Europe and North America, resting on shared values and interests and expressed through the Alliance, is a key element of the European identity. Our mutual defence commitment in the Alliance and the presence of North American forces in Europe as part of a collective structure, are therefore essential to the common defence of Europe.

5. The revision of the Alliance's tasks and strategy and the development of a common foreign and security policy in the context of the political union are complementary. They must proceed in parallel and reach mutually satisfactory results. NATO's reform should imply a reinforced European contribution as part of a changed and rebalanced relationship between North America and a more cohesive Europe.

6. The transatlantic relationship is an integral part of the broader idea of Europe which is reflected in the CSCE process. A reformed NATO embodying the transatlantic relationship will therefore be the key component in the development of a system of security including the whole of Europe.

II.   The European defence identity and the Alliance

7. The development of a European identity in the field of defence should be construed in such a way as to reinforce the Atlantic Alliance. Such a process will not be contradictory but compatible with a strengthened and reformed NATO.

8. WEU should be entrusted with the task of developing the European dimension in the field of defence, it will develop its role in two complementary directions: as the defence component of the Union and as the means to strengthen the European pillar of the Alliance.

9. In order to perform these functions better, WEU ministerial organs should be transferred to Brussels. The role of WEU and its relationship with the Alliance and the Union should be reviewed by 1998 in the context of article XII of the Brussels Treaty. In order to ensure a better coordination of the activities of WEU, meetings should be synchronized: links appropriate to the different institutions should be established between Secretariats as well as between Presidencies and Parliamentary Assemblies.

10. Consistant with the above, the WEU will take into account in its activities the decisions of the European Council in the context of the common foreign and security policy and positions adopted in the context of the Alliance, bearing in mind the different nature of its relations with each body.

11. In order to achieve complementarity between the European defence identity and the Alliance two principles should apply:

(a) Intensified coordination among Europeans on security and defence issues will respect the principle of openness in consultations, in accordance with the Rome Declaration of 1984 on the contribution of all European allies to NATO and The Hague platform of 1987 on the need to keep all Allies informed of WEU activities.

(b) Complementarity to the decisional process. The Alliance remains the essential forum for agreements on policies which refer to the commitments of their Members in matters of security and defence according to the Washington Treaty. Members of WEU will consult with the allies in a spirit of openness based on concerted positions. On other questions related to the European security identity (for instance collective actions to defend the European interests outside of the NATO area) decisions will be made by WEU in close consultation with the other allies.

12. A special relationship of association should be envisaged for other European partners and Allies. Liaison arrangements will be made for other European partners and allies. Liaison arrangements will be made for other European countries where appropriate.

III.   The European defence identity: operational role

13. In order to give a first practical content to the European defence identity, members of WEU should develop a European reaction force. This would be capable of responding flexibly in a range of possible circumstances outside the NATO area, for example in response to threats to the interests of WEU members or in peacekeeping operations. It would thereby make a new contribution to the Common defence.

14. Such a force would be autonomous, separate from the NATO structure, and would have its own peacetime planning cell to develop contingency plans and organize exercises. Political control would be exercised by WEU Ministers.

15. There should be coordination with other members of the Alliance, so that such a force could deploy alongside forces of other allies.

12. French, German and Spanish Foreign Ministers

Joint communiqué, Paris, October 1991

"Mr Genscher, Mr Ordonez and Mr Dumas met on 11 October. The main subject on the menu was the preparation for the coming bilateral summits and the European Council in Maastricht.

The three ministers reaffirmed their will to help the Presidency make a success of the coming European Council.

To succeed in Maastricht and thus move towards a European Union with a federal vocation, the three ministers recall that:

- Economic and Monetary Union and Political Union form a whole
- The setting up of a foreign and security policy is a necessary component in Political Union; it has to include all the questions relating to security and defence, with the long term prospect of a common defence; we plead for qualified majority voting over the modalities in setting up the common foreign and security policy;
- The WEU, which is an integral part of the process leading to European Union, could be given the responsibility of setting up the defence and security policy.

These are some of the essential principles on which the new Treaty must be based. France, the FRG and Spain will act along the lines of this reinforcement of European identity in the fields of security and defence."

13. France and Germany

Joint initiative on foreign, security and defence policy (Letter to Dutch Prime Minister Ruud Lubbers, published 16 October 1991)

Mr President:

A few weeks from now, the Maastricht European Council will be held, which will be called upon to conclude the negotiations on Political Union and on Economic and Monetary Union. All of the members of the European Council are aware of how extremely important the success of this summit is for the Community, but also for Europe as a whole. We know how hard you and the members of your government have worked to this end.

Since the opening of the inter-governmental conferences on 14 December 1990, the work carried out by the Luxembourg and then the Dutch Presidency have led to significant progress. The negotiations are now in a decisive phase. One of the central questions for the future Treaty of Political Union is a common foreign and security policy, as we wrote in our message of 6 December 1990. In the course of the year, the discussions have advanced considerably thanks to various contributions, including the recent joint Anglo–Italian text.

At this point in time, we would like to give these debates new impetus: it is important in our opinion that the Europeans show clearly, by means of specific decisions and institutional measures, that they want to take on greater responsibility in the areas of security and defence.

Below you will find our initiative in the form of draft texts: they contain an article on the general objectives of the Treaty, an article on security and defence, along with a statement on the priority areas of the common foreign and security policy and a statement by the WEU Member States on cooperation between the WEU, the Union, and the Atlantic Alliance. We also want to make you aware of our intentions regarding the evolution of Franco–German military cooperation with a European perspective.

We would be grateful if you would convey this message to the other members of the European Council.

Very sincerely yours,

Helmut Kohl

François Mitterrand

Treaty on Political Union: Common foreign and security policy

I. Article . . . of the draft Treaty on Political Union on basic objectives:

"The objectives of the Union are . . .:

    –   . . .

    – to affirm its identity on the international scene, particularly with regard to the implementation of a common foreign and security policy which, in the long term, would include a common defence."

II. Article . . . of the draft Treaty on Political Union on security and defence

1. The common foreign and security policy will include questions relative to the security and defence of the Union.

2. The decision and measures taken by the Union in this area may be developed and implemented entirely or in part by the WEU, which is an integral part of the process of European Union, in the context of the areas of competence of this organization and in conformity with the orientations established by the Union.

3. The Council shall oversee relations between the Union and the WEU in agreement with the institutions of the WEU, and shall ensure the progressive development of the Union's common security policy.

4. For some Member States of the Union, the obligations arising from the Treaties bearing upon the creation of the WEU and the Atlantic Alliance are not affected by the provisions of this present chapter, nor are the specific points of the defence policy of some of the Member States.

In addition, the provisions of this present chapter shall present no obstacle to closer bilateral cooperation between two or several Member States of the Union, within the WEU and the Atlantic Alliance.

5. The provisions of this present article will be revised on the basis of a report presented

by the Council to the European Council in 1996 at the latest, in cooperation with the competent institutions of the WEU and in light of progress and experience up to that point.

In conformity with the orientations established by the European Council, the Council shall establish all provisions necessary for the subsequent development of the process.

III. Statement of the Member States on the priority areas of a common foreign and security policy.

The Member States agree that the following topics in particular are likely to be the subject of joint action, in conformity with Article . . .

- political and economic relations and cooperation with the Soviet Union,
- political and economic relations and cooperation with the countries of Central and Eastern Europe,
- the CSCE process, including the implementation of the results of the Paris CSCE summit of November 1990,
- relations with the United States of America and Canada on the basis of joint declarations of November 1990,
- political and economic relations with the Mediterranean region and with the Middle East,
- policy and cooperation within the United Nations and other international organizations,
- participation in humanitarian measures.

With regard to Article . . . , the following areas are taken into consideration:

- disarmament policy and arms control in Europe, including confidence-building measures,
- participation in peace-keeping measures, especially within the framework of the United Nations,
- nuclear non-proliferation,
- the economic aspects of security, i.e., cooperation regarding arms exports and the control of arms exports.

IV. Essential points of the statement by the WEU Member States on Article . . . regarding the foundations for cooperation between the WEU and the Union, and between the WEU and the Atlantic Alliance

1. The WEU's objectives:
- In conformity with the WEU Treaty, the Hague "Platform" of 1986, and the Vianden communique of 27 June 1991:
  - strengthening the role of the WEU, which is a full partner in the process of European unification and whose goal is union,
  - the necessity to develop a genuine European defence and security identity and to assume increasing responsibility in the area of defence,
  - the subsequent step-by-step building up of the WEU as a component of the Union's defence.
- an invitation to the members of the Community which also belong to the Alliance to become part of the WEU, and for those which do not belong to the Alliance, the granting of observer status within the WEU,
- consultation of the Commission: in accordance with its competencies, the Commission will be kept informed by the Presidency of the WEU.

2. Creation of an organic link between the WEU and the Union:
- Development of a clear organic relationship between the WEU and the Union, and the operational organization of the WEU, which shall act in conformity with the Directives of the Union, and to this end:
  - harmonization of the sequence and length of Presidencies,
  - synchronization of sessions and working methods,
  - closer cooperation between the General Secretariat of the WEU and the Council of Ministers, on the one hand, and between the General Secretariat of the Council and the Council of Ministers of the Union on the other hand, and between the WEU Parliamentary Assembly and the European Parliament,
  - creation of a military planning and coordination group within the WEU which will be in charge of the following tasks:
- planning of joint actions, including in cases of crisis,

- operational planning for cooperation in the case of natural disasters,
- coordination of needs studies in all areas of cooperation,
- organization of joint manoeuvres.
  - closer military cooperation with the Alliance, especially in the areas of logistics, transport, training and information,
  - increased cooperation in the area of armaments, with a view to creating a European armaments agency,
  - regular meetings between Joint Chiefs of Staff,
  - transformation of the WEU Institute into a European security and defence academy.
- As a consequence of the above measures to strengthen the WEU, transfer of the WEU's General Secretariat to Brussels,
- The setting up of military units under the WEU.

3. WEU–NATO cooperation:

- This is a matter of strengthening the Atlantic Alliance as a whole "by increasing the role and responsibility of Europe and by establishing a European pillar." (joint letter of 6 December 1990).
- in conformity with NATO's Copenhagen communique and the WEU's Vianden communique, the establishment of practical provisions ensuring transparency and complementarity between the WEU and NATO,
- development of cooperation between the WEU General Secretariat and that of NATO
- regulation coordination of the WEU Member States with a view to developing common positions on all essential questions within the Alliance,
- for representation to the WEU, the development of a "two-hat" formula to include representatives to the Alliance and to the Community,
- association with the countries of the Alliance which are not part of the Community through consultations when the interests of these countries are affected.

4. *Relations with the other States of Europe, in particular those in Central, Eastern, and Southeastern Europe*

(developments corresponding to the Copenhagen communique for the Alliance and to the Vianden communique for the WEU).

For the record: Franco–German military cooperation will be strengthened beyond the present Brigade.

Thus, the reinforced Franco–German units could serve as the core of a European corps, including the forces of other WEU Member States. This new structure could also become the model for closer military cooperation between the WEU Member States.

14. European Trade Union and Employers' Organizations (ETUC and UNICE)

Joint proposal on Social Chapter

New Proposals for the drafting of Articles 118.4–118 A–118 B

Article 118.4

On a joint request by the social partners, a Member State may entrust them with the implementation of the directives prepared on the basis of paragraphs 2 and 3.

In this case, it shall ensure that, by the date of entry into force of a directive at the latest, the social partners have set up the necessary provisions by agreement, the Member State concerned being required to take any necessary provisions enabling it to guarantee the results imposed by the directive.

Article 118A

118A.1

The Commission has the task of promoting the consultation of the social partners at the Community level and shall take any useful measure to facilitate their dialogue, ensuring balanced support of the parties.

118A.2

To this end, before presenting proposals in the field of social policy, the Commission shall consult the social partners on the possible direction of Community action.

118A.3

If, following this consultation, the Commission should consider Community action advisable, it shall consult the social partners on the content of the proposal under consideration. The social partners shall submit an opinion to the Commission, or where appropriate, a recommendation.

118A.4

During this consultation, the social partners may inform the Commission of their wish to initiate the process provided pursuant to article 118B, para. 1 and 2. The procedure may not last more than nine months, save when an extension is decided by common agreement by the social partners concerned.

118 B

118B.1

If the social partners so desire, their dialogue at Community level may lead to contractual relations, including agreements.

118B.2

Agreements concluded at the Community level may be implemented either according to the procedures and practices specific to the social partners and the Member States or, in matters falling within Article 118, by joint request of the signatories, on the basis of a Council decision on a proposal for the Commission concerning the agreements as they have been concluded.

15. Dutch Presidency Draft Union Treaty

Working document, 8 November 1991

Common provisions

Article A

By this Treaty, the High Contracting Parties establish among themselves a Union.

The Union shall be founded on the European Communities, supplemented by the policies and cooperation established by this Treaty. Its task shall be to organize, in a manner demonstrating consistency and solidarity, relations between the Member States and between their peoples.

This Treaty marks a new stage in a process leading gradually to a Union with a federal goal.

Article B

The Union shall set itself the following objectives, starting from the "acquis communautaire", on which it is to build:

— to promote economic and social progress which is balanced and sustainable in particular through the creation of an area without internal frontiers, through the strengthening of economic and social cohesion and the establishment of economic and monetary union including, finally, a single currency,

— to assert its identity on the international scene, in particular through the implementation of a common foreign and security policy which shall include the eventual framing of a defence policy,

— to strengthen the protection of the rights and interests of its Member States' nationals, through the introduction of a citizenship of the Union,

— to develop a close cooperation on home affairs and in the judicial field.

Article C

The Union shall be served a single institutional framework which shall ensure the consistency and the continuity of the actions carried out in order to attain its objectives while observing and building upon the "acquis communautaire".

The Union shall in particular ensure the consistency of its external actions as a whole in the context of its external relations, security, economic and development policies.

Article D

The European Council shall provide the Union with the necessary impetus for its development and shall define the general political guidelines thereof.

The European Council shall bring together the Heads of State or of Government of the Member States and the President of the Commission. They shall be assisted by the Ministers for Foreign Affairs of the Member States and by a Member of the Commission.[1]

The European Council shall meet at least twice a year under the Presidency of the Head of State or of Government of the Member State which holds the Presidency of the Council.

The European Council shall submit to the European Parliament a report after each of its meetings and a yearly written report on the progress achieved by the Union.

Article E

The European Parliament, the Council, the Commission and the Court of Justice shall exercise their powers under the conditions and for the purposes provided for by the provisions of the Treaties establishing the European Communities, the subsequent Treaties and Acts modifying and supplementing them and by the provisions of this Treaty.

Article F

for the record: Conference of Parliaments

Article G

1. The Union shall have due regard to the national identity of its Member States, whose systems of government are founded on the principles of democracy.

2. The Union shall respect the rights and freedoms as recognized in the European Convention for the Protection of Human Rights and Fundamental Freedoms.

3. The Union shall provide itself with the resources necessary to attain its objectives and carry through its policies.

---

[1] A declaration of the Conference will state that the President of the European Council will invite Economic and Finance Ministers to participate in work on Economic and Monetary Union.

Provisions amending the Treaty establishing the European Economic Community with a view to establishing the European Community

Part One: Principles

Article 1

By this Treaty, the High Contracting Parties establish among themselves a EUROPEAN COMMUNITY.

Article 2

The Community shall have as its task, by establishing a common market, an economic and monetary union and by implementing the common policies or activities referred to in Article 3, the promotion, throughout the Community, of a harmonious and balanced development of economic activities, sustainable and non-inflationary growth respecting the environment, a high degree of convergence of economic performance, a high level of employment and of social protection, the raising of the standard and quality of living, and economic and social cohesion and solidarity between Member States.

Article 3

For the purposes set out in Article 2, the activities of the Community shall include, as provided in this Treaty and in accordance with the timetable set out therein:

(a) the elimination, as between Member States, of customs duties and quantitative restrictions on the import and export of goods, and of all other measures having equivalent effect;

(b) a common commercial policy;

(c) an internal market characterized by the abolition, as between Member States, of obstacles to freedom of movement of goods, persons, services and capital;

(d) measures concerning the entry and movement of persons in the internal market;

(e) a common policy in the sphere of agriculture and fisheries;

(f) a common policy in the sphere of transport;

(g) a system ensuring that competition in the internal market is not distorted;

(h) the approximation of the laws of Member States to the extent required for the functioning of the common market;

(i) a policy in the social sphere comprising a European Social Fund;

(j) the strengthening of economic and social cohesion;

(k) a policy in the sphere of the environment;

(l) the strengthening of the competitiveness of the Community's industry;

(m) the promotion of research and technological development;

(n) measures in the sphere of energy;

(o) encouragement for the establishment and development of trans-European networks;

(p) contribution to the attainment of a high level of health protection;

(q) contribution to education and training of high quality and to the flowering of the cultures of the Member States;

(r) a policy in the sphere of development cooperation;

(s) the association of the overseas countries and territories in order to increase trade and promote jointly economic and social development;

(t) contribution to the strengthening of consumer protection;

(u) civil protection measures;

(v) measures in the sphere of tourism.

Article 3a

[Economic and Monetary Union]

Article 3b

The Community shall act within the limits of the powers conferred upon it by this Treaty and of the objectives assigned to it therein. In the areas which do not fall within its exclusive jurisdiction, the Community shall take action, in accordance with the principle of subsidiarity, only if, and insofar as, these objectives can be better achieved by the Community than by the Member States acting separately, by reason of the scale or effects of the proposed action.

Action by the Community shall not go beyond what is necessary to achieve the objectives of the Treaty.

Article 4

Paragraph 2 should read:

"The Council and the Commission shall be assisted by an Economic and Social Committee and a Committee of the Regions acting in an advisory capacity.".

Article 4a

[EMU]

Article 4b

A European Investment Bank is hereby established, which shall act within the limits of the powers conferred upon it by this Treaty and the Statutes annexed thereto.

Article 5[2]

Unchanged

Article 6

(deleted)

Article 7

The second paragraph should read:

"The Council, acting in accordance with the procedure referred to in Article 189 . . .".

Articles 8 to 8c

Unchanged

Part Two: Union citizenship

Article A[3]

1. Union citizenship is hereby established.

Every person holding the nationality of a Member State shall be a citizen of the Union.

2. Union citizens shall enjoy the rights conferred by this Treaty and shall be subject to the duties imposed thereby.

Article B

1. Every Union citizen shall have the rights to move and reside freely within the territory of the Member States, subject to the limitations and under the conditions laid down in this Treaty and by the measures adopted to give it effect.

2. The Council may adopt provisions with a view to facilitating the exercise of the rights referred to in the preceding paragraph; unless this Treaty stipulates otherwise, the Council shall act unanimously on a proposal from the Commission and after obtaining the assent of the European Parliament.

Article C

1. Every Union citizen residing in a Member State of which he is not a national shall have the right to vote and to stand as a candidate at municipal elections in the Member State in which he resides, under the same conditions as nationals of that State. This right shall be exercised subject to detailed arrangements to be adopted before 31 December 1993 by the Council, acting unanimously on a proposal from the Commission and after consulting the European Parliament; these arrangements may provide for derogations where warranted by problems specific to a Member State.

2. Without prejudice to the provisions of Article 138(3) and of the provisions adopted for its implementation, every Union citizen residing in a Member State of which he is not a national shall have the right to vote and to stand as a candidate in elections to the European Parliament in the Member State in which he resides, under the same conditions as nationals of that State. This right shall be exercised subject to detailed arrangements to be adopted before 31 December 1993 by the Council, acting unanimously on a proposal from the Commission and after consulting the European Parliament; these arrangements, may provide for derogations where warranted by problems specific to a Member State.

Article D

Every Union citizen shall, in the territory of a third country in which the Member State of which he is a national is not represented, be entitled to protection by diplomatic or consular authorities of any Member State, on the same conditions as the nationals of that State. Before 31 December 1993, Member States shall establish the necessary rules among themselves and start the international negotiations required to secure this protection.

Article E

Every Union citizen shall have the right to petition the European Parliament in accordance with Article 137bb.

Every Union citizen may apply to the Ombudsman established in accordance with Article 137c.

Article F

The Commission shall report to the Council, to

---

[2] Declaration concerning the non-contractual liability of Member States to redress damages caused by any failure to fulfil their obligations under Community law.

[3] Declaration in the Final Act of the Conference "The Conference declares that wherever in this Treaty reference is made to nationals of the Member States, the question whether an individual possesses that nationality shall be settled solely by reference to the national law of the Member State concerned. Member States may declare for information who are to be considered their nationals for Community purposes by way of a declaration lodged with the Presidency and may amend any such declaration when necessary."

the European Parliament and to the Economic and Social Committee before 31 December 1993 and then every three years on the implementation of the provisions of this Part. This report shall take account of the development of the Union.

On this basis, and without prejudice to the other provisions of this Treaty, the Council, acting unanimously on a proposal from the Commission, and after consulting the European Parliament, may adopt provisions to strengthen or to add to the rights laid down in this Part, which it shall recommend to the Member States for adoption in accordance with their respective constitutional rules.

Protocol

Laying down certain provisions on the acquisition of property in Denmark

The High Contracting Parties,
Desiring to settle certain particular problems relating to Denmark, Have agreed upon the following provisions, which shall be annexed to this Treaty:
Notwithstanding the provisions of the Treaty, Denmark may maintain the existing legislation on the acquisition of properties which are not permanent residences.

Part Three: Policies of the Community

Title I — Free movement of goods

Articles 9–37
Unchanged

Title II — Agriculture

Articles 38–47
Unchanged

Title III — Free movement of persons, services and capital

Article 48
Unchanged

Article 49
This should read:
". . . the Council, acting in accordance with the procedure referred to in Article 189b and after consulting the Economic and Social Committee . . .".

Article 50
Unchanged

Article 51
This should read:
". . . the Council, acting in accordance with the procedure referred to in Article 189c and after consulting the Economic and Social Committee".

Articles 52 and 53
Unchanged

Article 54
Paragraph 2 should read:
". . . the Council, acting in accordance with the procedure referred to in Article 189b and after consulting the Economic and Social Committee . . ."

Article 55
Unchanged

Article 56
In the second sentence of paragraph 2, read:
". . . the Council, acting in accordance with the procedure referred to in Article 189b . . .".

Article 57
In paragraph 1, read:
". . . the Council, acting in accordance with the procedure referred to in Article 189b . . .".
The last sentence of paragraph 2, should read:
"In other cases the Council shall act in accordance with the procedure referred to in Article 189b".

Articles 58–66
Unchanged

Articles 67–73e
[For the record: Economic and Monetary Union]

Title IV — Transport

Articles 74–84
(No change of substance from Luxembourg Presidency Draft Treaty)

Title V — Common rules

(competition, taxation, approximation of laws)

Articles 85–86
Unchanged

Article 87
In the second subparagraph of paragraph 1, read:
". . . the Council, acting in accordance with the procedure referred to in Article 189c.".

Articles 88–91
Unchanged

Article 92

delete paragraph 2(c) = division of Germany
   new paragraph 3(d):
   "(d) aid to promote culture and heritage
conservation where such aid does not adversely
affect trading conditions and competition in the
Community."
   Present paragraph (d) shall become (e).

Article 93

Unchanged

Article 94

To read:
   "The Council, acting in accordance with the
procedure referred to in Article 189c . . ."

Articles 95–98

Unchanged

Article 99

To read as follows:
   "Without prejudice to Article 101, the Council shall, acting unanimously on a proposal
from the Commission and after consulting the
European Parliament and the Economic and
Social Committee, adopt provisions for the harmonization of legislation concerning turnover
taxes, excise duties and other forms of indirect
taxation to the extent that such harmonization
is necessary to ensure the establishment and
the functioning of the internal market within
the time limit laid down in Article 8a".

Article 100

The Council shall, acting unanimously on a proposal from the Commission and after consulting
the European Parliament and the Economic
and Social Committee, issue directives for the
approximation of such provisions laid down
by law, regulation or administrative action in
Member States as directly affect the establishment or functioning of the Common Market.

Article 100a

First paragraph, second sentence, should read:
   "The Council, acting in accordance with the
procedure referred to in Article 189b, and
after consulting the Economic and Social Committee . . ."

Article 100b

Unchanged

Article 100c

1. The Council, acting unanimously on a proposal from the Commission or on the initiative
of any Member State, and after consulting the
European Parliament, shall adopt the directives relating to the approximation of the laws,
regulations and administrative provisions of the
Member States which concern the following
areas, to the extent that such approximation
is necessary to ensure the free movement of
persons within the internal market:
   (a) the rules governing the crossing by persons of the external borders of the Member
States and the exercise of controls thereon;
   (b) the general conditions governing authorized entry to and movement within the territory
of the Member States as a whole by nationals
of third countries for short stays, including the
determination of the travel documents required
for crossing the external borders of the Member
States.
   The Council shall, in the manner laid down
in the previous paragraph, decide which of
the decisions are to be taken by a qualified
majority.

2. The Council, acting by a qualified majority, on a proposal from the Commission or on
the initiative of any Member State, and after
consulting the European Parliament, shall:

   – determine the third countries whose
      nationals must be in possession of a
      visa when crossing the external borders
      of the Member States;

   – adopt the measures relating to the intro-
      duction of a uniform visa.

3. This Article shall be without prejudice to
the exercise of the responsibilities incumbent
upon the Member States with regard to the
maintaining law and order and the safeguarding
of internal State security.

4. The provisions of this Article shall apply
to other subjects on which a decision has been
taken pursuant to Article K of the provisions
in the Treaty on Union which relates to Cooperation in the field of Home Affairs and
Judicial Co-operation.

5. The provisions of the Conventions in force
between the Member States governing issues
covered by this Article shall remain in force
until their content is replaced by directives or
measures adopted pursuant thereto.

Article 100d

The Co-ordinating Committee consisting of
Senior Officials set up by Article D of the
provisions of the Treaty on Union on Cooperation in the Field of Home Affairs and
Judicial Co-operation shall contribute, without
prejudice to the provisions of Article 151, to the
preparation of the proceedings of the Council in
the fields referred to in Article 100c.

Articles 101 and 102

Unchanged

Title VI — Economic and Monetary Policy

For the record [see EMU IGC documents]

Common commercial policy

Article 110

Unchanged

Article 111

Deleted

Article 112

Unchanged

Article 113

1. The common commercial policy shall be based on uniform principles, particularly in regard to changes in tariff rates, the conclusion of tariff and trade agreements, the achievement of uniformity in measures of liberalization, export policy and measures to protect trade such as those to be taken in case of dumping or subsidies.

2. The Commission shall submit proposals to the Council for implementing the common commercial policy.

3. Where agreements with one or more States or international organizations need to be negotiated, the Commission shall make recommendations to the Council, which shall authorize the Commission to open the necessary negotiations.

The Commission shall conduct these negotiations in consultation with a special committee appointed by the Council to assist the Commission in this task and within the framework of such directives as the Council may issue to it.

The relevant provisions of Article 228 shall apply.

4. In exercising the powers conferred upon it by this Article, the Council shall act by a qualified majority.

5. In matters covered by this Article and without prejudice to Article 228, the Community's position shall be set out by the Commission in its relations with third countries, within international organizations and at international conferences[4]

Article 114

Deleted

Article 115

In order to ensure that the execution of measures of commercial policy taken in accordance with this Treaty by any Member State is not obstructed by deflection of trade, or where differences between such measures lead to economic difficulties in one or more of the Member States, the Commission shall recommend the methods for the requisite cooperation between Member States. Failing this, the Commission may authorize Member States to take the necessary protective measures, the conditions and details of which it shall determine.

In case of urgency, Member States shall request authorization to take the necessary measures themselves from the Commission which shall take a decision as soon as possible; they shall then notify the measures to the other Member States. The Commission may decide at any time that the Member States concerned shall amend or abolish the measures in question.

In selection of such measures, priority shall be given to those which cause the least disturbance to the functioning of the common market.

Article 116

Deleted

Title VII — Social policy, education, vocational training and youth

Chapter 1: Social provisions

Article 117

The Community and its Member States shall have as their objectives the promotion of employment, improved living and working conditions, proper social protection, dialogue between management and labour, the development of human resources with a view to lasting high employment and the combating of exclusion. To this end the Community and its Member States shall implement measures which take account of the diverse forms of national practices, in particular in the field of relations based on agreement, and the need to maintain the competitiveness of the Community economy.

---

[4] Declaration by the Commission and the Member States in the Final Act of the Conference "Article 113(5) does not preclude the possibility of Member States speaking within international fora provided they abide by the position adopted by the Community".

Article 118

1. With a view to achieving the objectives of Article 117, the Community shall support and complement Member States' activities in the following fields:

- improvement in particular of the working environment to protect workers' health and safety;
- working conditions;
- the information and consultation of workers;
- equality between men and women with regard to labour market opportunities and treatment at work;
- the integration of persons excluded from the labour market, without prejudice to the provisions of Article . . . [vocational training].

2. To this end, the Council may adopt, by means of Directives, minimum requirements for gradual implementation, having regard to the conditions and technical rules obtaining in each of the Member States. Such Directives shall avoid imposing administrative, financial and legal constraints in a way which would hold back the creation and development of small and medium-sized undertakings.

The Council shall act in accordance with the procedure referred to in Article 189c after consulting the Economic and Social Committee. However, the Council shall act unanimously on a proposal from the Commission, after consulting the European Parliament and the Economic and Social Committee, in the following areas:

- social security and social protection of workers;
- protection of workers where their employment contract is terminated;
- representation and collective defence of the interests of workers and employers, including co-determination, subject to paragraph 5;
- conditions of employment for third-country nationals legally present in Community territory;
- financial contributions for promotion of employment and job-creation.

3. A Member State may entrust management and labour, at their joint request, with the implementation of directives adopted pursuant to paragraph 2.

In this case, it shall ensure that, not later than the date of entry into force of a directive, management and labour have introduced the necessary measures by agreement, the Member State concerned being required to take any necessary measure enabling it at any time to be in a position to guarantee the results imposed by the Directive.

4. The provisions adopted pursuant to this Article shall not prevent any Member State from maintaining or introducing more stringent preventive measures compatible with this Treaty.

5. The provisions of this Article shall not apply to pay, the right of association, the right to strike or the right to impose lock-outs.

Article 118a

1. The Commission shall have the task of promoting the consultation of management and labour at Community level and shall take any relevant measures to facilitate their dialogue by ensuring balanced support for the parties.

2. To this end, before submitting proposals in the social policy field, the Commission shall consult management and labour on the possible direction of Community action.

3. If, after such consultation, the Commission considers Community action advisable, it shall consult management and labour on the envisaged proposal. Management and labour shall forward to the Commission an opinion, and, where appropriate, a recommendation.

4. On the occasion of such consultation, management and labour may inform the Commission of their wish to initiate the procedure provided for in Article 118b(1) and (2). The duration of the procedure shall not exceed nine months, unless the management and labour concerned and the Commission decide jointly to extend it.

Article 118b

1. Should management and labour so desire, the dialogue between them at Community level may lead to contractual relations including agreements.

2. Agreements concluded at Community level shall be implemented either in accordance with the procedures and practices specific to management and labour and the Member States or, in matters covered by Article 118, at the joint request of the signatory parties, by a Council decision on a proposal from the Commission.

This decision will be taken according to the voting procedures laid down in Article 118.

Article 118c

With a view to achieving the objectives of Article 117 and without prejudice to the other provisions of this Treaty, the Commission shall encourage cooperation between the Member States and facilitate the coordination of their action in all social policy fields under this Title.

Article 119

1. Each Member State shall ensure that the principle of equal pay for male and female workers for equal work is applied.

2. For the purpose of this Article, "pay" means the ordinary basic or minimum wage or salary and any other consideration, whether in cash or in kind, which the worker receives directly or indirectly, in respect of his employment, from his employer. Equal pay without discrimination based on sex means:

(a) that pay for the same work at piece rates shall be calculated on the basis of the same unit of measurement;

(b) that pay for work at time rates shall be the same for the same job.

3. This Article shall not prevent any Member State from maintaining or adopting measures providing for specific advantages in order to make it easier to women to pursue a vocational activity.

Articles 120 and 121

Deleted

Article 122

The Commission shall draw up a report each year on progress in achieving the objectives of Article 117, including the demographic situation in the Community. It shall forward the report to the European Parliament, the Council and the Economic and Social Committee.

The European Parliament may invite the Commission to draw up reports on particular problems concerning the social situation.

Chapter 2: The European Social Fund[5]

Article 123

In order to improve employment opportunities for workers in the internal market and to contribute thereby to raising the standard of living, a European Social Fund is hereby established in accordance with the provisions set out below; it shall aim to render the employment of workers easier and to increase their geographical and occupational mobility within the Community.

Article 124

Unchanged

Articles 125 and 126

Deleted

Article 127

The Council, acting in accordance with the procedure referred to in Article 189c, and after consulting the Economic and Social Committee, shall adopt the regulatory provisions necessary for the application of Article 130e.

Article 128

Deleted

Chapter 3: Education, vocational training and youth

Article A

1. The Community shall contribute to the development of quality education by encouraging cooperation between Member States and, if necessary, by supporting and supplementing their action, while fully respecting the responsibility of the Member States for the content of teaching and the organization of education systems.

2. Community action shall be aimed at:

 – developing the European dimension in education, particularly through the teaching and dissemination of the languages of the Member States;

 – encouraging mobility of students and teachers, inter alia by encouraging the academic recognition of diplomas and periods of study;

 – promoting cooperation between educational establishments;

 – organizing exchanges of information and experience on issues common to the education systems of the Member States;

 – encouraging the development of youth exchanges and of exchanges of socio-educational instructors;

 – encouraging the development of distance education.

3. The Community and the Member States shall foster cooperation with third countries and the competent international organizations

---

[5] These provisions have still to be examined by the Personnel Representatives

in the sphere of education, and in particular with the Council of Europe.

4. The Council, acting in accordance with the procedure referred to in Article 189c and after consulting the Economic and Social Committee and the Committee of the Regions, shall, in order to contribute to the achievement of the objectives referred to in this Article, adopt recommendations and incentive measures, to the exclusion of any harmonization of the legislative and regulatory provisions of the Member States.

Article B

1. The Community shall implement a vocational training policy which shall support and supplement the action of the Member States, while fully respecting the responsibility of the Member States for the content and organization of vocational training.

2. Community action shall aim to:

- improve initial vocational training and continuous training in order to facilitate vocation integration and reintegration into the labour market;
- facilitate access to vocational training and encourage mobility of instructors and trainees and particularly young people;
- stimulate cooperation on training between training establishments and firms;
- develop exchanges of information and experience on issues common to the training systems of the Member States.

For the purposes of implementing this action, with reference to workers, Article 118b shall apply.

3. The Community and the Member States shall foster cooperation with third countries and the competent international organizations in the sphere of vocational training.

4. The Council, acting in accordance with the procedure referred to in Article 189c and after consulting the Economic and Social Committee, shall adopt measures to contribute to the achievement of the objectives referred to in this Article.

Title VIII — The European Investment Bank

Article 129–130

(No change of substance from Luxembourg Presidency Draft Treaty)

Title IX — Economic and social cohesion

Articles 130a–130b

(No change from Luxembourg draft other than to enhance reporting duty of Commission)

Article 130c

The European Regional Development Fund is intended to help to redress the main regional imbalances in the Community through participating in the development and structural adjustment of regions whose development is lagging behind and in the conversion of declining industrial regions.

Article 130d

Without prejudice to Article 130e, the Council, acting unanimously on a proposal from the Commission and after obtaining the assent of the European Parliament and consulting the Economic and Social Committee and the Committee of the Regions, shall define the tasks, prime objectives and the organization of the structural Funds, which may involve regrouping the Funds. The Council, acting by the same procedure, shall also define the general rules applicable to them and the provisions necessary to ensure their effectiveness and the coordination of the Funds with one another and with the other existing financial instruments.

The Council, acting in accordance with the same procedure, may set up new structural Funds.

Article 130e

Implementing decisions relating to the European Regional Development Fund shall be taken by the Council, acting by a qualified majority on a proposal from the Commission and in accordance with the procedure referred to in Article 189c and after consulting the Economic and Social Committee and the Committee of the Regions.

With regard to the European Agricultural Guidance and Guarantee Fund, Guidance Section, and the European Social Fund, Articles 43 and 127 shall continue to apply respectively.

Title X — Research and technological development

Articles 130f, 130g and 130h

(No change from Luxembourg Presidency Draft Treaty).

Article 130i

1. A multiannual framework programme, setting out all the activities of the Community,

shall be adopted by the Council acting in accordance with the procedure referred to in Article 189b, after consultation of the Economic and Social Committee. The Council shall act unanimously throughout the procedures referred to in this Article.

The framework programme shall:

- establish the scientific and technological objectives to be achieved by the activities provided for in Article 130g and fix the relevant priorities;
- indicate the broad lines of such activities;
- fix the maximum overall amount and the detailed rules for Community financial participation in the framework programme and the respective shares in each of the actions provided for.

2. The framework programme may be adapted or supplemented, as the situation changes.

3. The framework programme shall be implemented through specific programmes developed within each activity. Each specific programme shall define the detailed rules for implementing it, fix its duration and provide for the means deemed necessary. The sum of the amounts deemed necessary may not exceed the overall maximum amount fixed for the framework programme.

4. The Council, acting by a qualified majority on a proposal from the Commission, and after consulting the European Parliament, shall adopt the specific programmes.

Article 130j
For the implementation of the multiannual framework programme, the Council shall;

- determine the rules for the participation of undertakings, research centres and universities;
- lay down the rules governing the dissemination of research results.

Articles 130k, 130l and 130m
(Unchanged from 130j, k and l respectively in Luxembourg Presidency draft)

Article 130n
The Community may set up joint undertakings or any other structure necessary for the effi-

cient execution of Community research, technological development and demonstration programmes.

Article 130o
The Council, acting unanimously on a proposal from the Commission and after consulting the European Parliament and the Economic and Social Committee, shall adopt the provisions referred to in Article 130n.

The Council, acting in accordance with the procedure referred to in Article 189c, and after consulting the Economic and Social Committee, shall adopt the provisions referred to in Articles 130j to m. Adoption of the supplementary programmes shall also require the agreement of the Member States concerned.

Article 130p
At the beginning of each year, the Commission shall send a report to the European Parliament and the Council. The report shall include information on research and technological development activities and dissemination of the results carried out during the previous year and on the work programme of the current year.

Title XI — Environment

Article 130r
(Paragraph 1, 2 and 3 unchanged from Luxembourg Presidency Draft Treaty)

4. Within their respective spheres of competence, the Community and the Member States shall cooperate with third countries and with the relevant international organizations. The arrangements for Community cooperation may be the subject of agreements between the Community and the third parties concerned, which shall be negotiated and concluded in accordance with Article 228.

The previous paragraph shall be without prejudice to Member States' competence to negotiate in international bodies and to conclude international agreements.[6]

Article 130s
1. The Council, acting in accordance with the procedure referred to in Article 189c and after consulting the Economic and Social Committee, shall decide what action is to be taken by the Community in order to achieve the objectives referred to in Article 130r.

[6] Declaration in the Final Act of the Conference "The Conference considers that the second subparagraph of Article 130r(4) does not affect the principles resulting from the judgment of the Court of Justice in the AETR case".

2. By way of derogation from the previous paragraph, the Council, acting unanimously on a proposal from the Commission and after consulting the European Parliament, shall adopt

- provisions of a fiscal nature;
- measures concerning town and country planning and land use relating to the achievement of the objectives of this Title.

3. Multiannual action programmes setting out priority objectives to be attained in specific areas shall be adopted by the Council, acting in accordance with the procedure referred to in Article 189b.

The Council, acting under the terms of paragraph 1, shall adopt the measures necessary for the implementation of these programmes.

4. Without prejudice to certain measures of a Community nature, the Member States shall finance and implement the environment policy.

5. If a measure adopted pursuant to paragraph 1 involves disproportionate costs for the public authorities of a Member State, the Council may, when adopting the said measure, provide for

- temporary derogation and/or
- financial support [from an environmental Fund]

Article 130t

The protective measures adopted pursuant to Article 130s shall not prevent any Member State from maintaining or introducing more stringent protective measures. Such measures must be compatible with this Treaty. The Commission shall be notified of them.

Title XII — Energy[7]

Article A

1. Action by the Community in the sphere of energy, which shall support and supplement that of the Member States, shall be aimed at the following objectives within the framework of a market economy:

- promoting security and regularity of supplies in the Community under satisfactory economic conditions;
- ensuring the establishment and functioning of the internal market in this sphere;
- ensuring a suitable reaction in the event of a crisis, particularly in the oil sector;
- promoting the rational use of energy and the development and use of potentially profitable new and renewable energy sources.

2. Action by the Community shall be closely coordinated with the policies pursued in the framework of the Treaties establishing the European Coal and Steel Community and the European Atomic Energy Community.

3. The Commission, in close liaison with the Member States, shall take all appropriate steps to promote consistency between Member States' activities and those of the Community.

Article B

Within the framework of their respective powers, the Community and the Member States shall cooperate with third countries and the competent international organizations. The manner in which Community cooperation is to be implemented may be the subject of agreements between the Community and the third parties concerned[8] which shall be negotiated and concluded in accordance with Article 228.

The previous paragraph shall be without prejudice to Member States' competence to negotiate in international bodies and to conclude international agreements.[9]

---

[7] Commission declaration
"The provisions of Article 85(1) may be declared inapplicable to any agreement in the energy sector which contributes to guaranteeing security of supplies in the Community, where the restrictions which such an agreement may contain are essential for the attainment of this objective and do not afford the undertakings concerned the opportunity of eliminating competition with respect to a substantial part of the products in question.
The aid referred to in Article 92(1), where, in actual fact, it contributes to guaranteeing security of supplies in the Community and does not harm the functioning of the internal market in energy to an extent which runs counter to the common interest, may be regarded as compatible with the common market."
[8] See cover note, point . . .
[9] Declaration in the Final Act of the Conference "The Conference considers that the second subparagraph of Article 130r(4) does not affect the principles resulting from the judgment of the Court of Justice in the AETR case".

Article C

The Council, acting in accordance with the procedure referred to in Article 189c and after consulting the Economic and Social Committee, shall adopt the measures required to achieve the objectives referred to in Article A(1).

Title XIII — Transeuropean networks

Article A

1. To help achieve the objectives referred to in Articles 8a and 130a and to enable citizens of the Union, economic operators and regional and local communities to derive full benefit from the setting up of an area without internal frontiers, the Community shall contribute to the establishment and development of transeuropean networks in the areas of transport, telecommunications and energy infrastructures.

2. Within the framework of a system of open and competitive markets, action by the Community shall aim in particular at promoting the interconnection and inter-operability of national networks as well as access to such networks. It shall take account in particular of the need to link island, landlocked and peripheral regions with the central regions of the Community.

Article B

1. In order to achieve the objectives referred to in Article A, the Community:

- shall establish a series of guidelines covering the objectives, priorities and broad lines of measures envisaged in the sphere of transeuropean networks; these guidelines shall identify projects of common interest;
- shall implement any measures that may prove necessary to ensure the interoperability of the networks, in particular in the field of technical standardization;
- may support the financial efforts made by the Member States for projects of common interest identified in the framework of the guidelines referred to in the first indent, particularly through feasibility studies, loan guarantees or interest rate subsidies.

The Community's activities shall take into account the potential economic viability of the projects.

2. Member States shall, in liaison with the Commission, coordinate among themselves the policies pursued at national level which may have a significant impact on the achievement of the objectives referred to in Article A. The Commission may, in close cooperation with the Member States, take all appropriate steps to promote such coordination.

3. The Community may decide to cooperate with third countries to promote projects of mutual interest and to ensure the interoperability of the networks.

Article C

The guidelines referred to in Article B(1) shall be adopted by the Council, acting in accordance with the procedure referred to in Article 189b and after consulting the Economic and Social Committee and the Committee of the Regions.

The Council, acting in accordance with the procedure referred to in Article 189c and after consulting the Economic and Social Committee and the Committee of the Regions, shall adopt the other measures provided for in Article B(1).

Title XIV — Industry

1. The Community and the Member States shall ensure that the conditions necessary for the competitiveness of the Community's industry exist.

For that purpose, in accordance with a system of open, competitive markets, their action shall be aimed at:

- speeding up the adjustment of industry to structural changes;
- encouraging a favourable environment for initiative and the development of undertakings throughout the Community, particularly small and medium-sized undertakings;
- encouraging a favourable environment for cooperation between undertakings;
- fostering better exploitation of the industrial potential of policies of innovation, research and technological development.

2. The Member States shall consult each other in liaison with the Commission and, where necessary, shall coordinate action they take. The Commission may take all appropriate steps to promote such coordination.

3. The Community shall contribute to the achievement of the objectives set out in paragraph 1 through the policies and activities it

pursues under other provisions of this Treaty. The Council, acting in accordance with the procedure referred to in Article 189c and after consulting the Economic and Social Committee, may decide on specific measures, in particular in favour of the industries of the future, in support of action taken in the Member States to achieve the objectives set out in paragraph 1.

Title XV — Tourism

1. The Community shall encourage cooperation between the Member States with a view to contributing to the development of their activities in the field of tourism. To this end the Commission shall act in particular by carrying out studies, producing opinions and organizing consultations in the following areas:

– collection and distribution of data on tourist flows and related information;

– exchange of information and experience;

– coordination of Member States' action with a view to implementing common projects;

– promotion, in third countries, of the Community as a destination for tourism.

2. Without prejudice to the other provisions of this Treaty, the Council, acting in accordance with the procedure referred to in Article 189c and after consulting the Economic and Social Committee and the Committee of the Regions, shall, in order to contribute to the achievement of the objectives referred to in this Article, adopt recommendations and incentive measures, to the exclusion of any harmonization of the legislative and regulatory provisions of the Member States.

Title XVI — Consumer protection

1. The Community shall contribute to the achievement of a high level of consumer protection through:

(a) measures adopted pursuant to Article 100a in the context of the completion of the internal market;

(b) specific action which supports the policy pursued by the Member States with a view to protecting the health, safety and economic interests of consumers and to providing adequate information for consumers.

2. The Council, acting in accordance with the procedure referred to in Article 189b and after consulting the Economic and Social Committee, shall adopt the specific action referred to in paragraph 1(b).

3. Action adopted pursuant to paragraph 2 shall not prevent any Member State from maintaining or introducing more stringent protective measures. Such measures must be compatible with this Treaty. The Commission shall be notified of them.

Title XVII — Public health

Sole Article

1. The Community shall contribute towards ensuring a high level of human health protection by encouraging cooperation between the Member States and, if necessary, lending support to their action. Community action shall be directed towards the prevention of diseases, in particular the major health scourges, especially by promoting research into their causes and their transmission, as well as health information and education.

Health protection demands shall form a constituent part of the Community's other policies.

2. Member States shall, in liaison with the Commission, coordinate among themselves their policies and programmes in the areas referred to in paragraph 1. The Commission may, in close contact with the Member States, take all appropriate steps to promote such coordination.

3. The Community and the Member States shall foster cooperation with third countries and the competent international organizations in the sphere of public health.

4. Without prejudice to the other provisions of this Treaty, the Council, acting in accordance with the procedure referred to in Article 189c and after consulting the Economic and Social Committee and the Committee of Regions, shall, in order to contribute to the achievement of the objectives referred to in this Article, adopt recommendations and incentive measures, to the exclusion of any harmonization of the legislative and regulatory provisions of the Member States.

Title XVIII — Civil protection

1. The Community shall encourage and support the development of cooperation between the Member States in the area of civil protection; it shall also encourage cooperation between the

Member States and third countries, and the competent international organizations.

2. In order to achieve the objectives set out in paragraph 1:

(a) the Commission shall facilitate the exchange of information and experience between Member States on issues relating to civil protection and shall hold appropriate consultations;

(b) the Council, acting unanimously on a proposal from the Commission and after consulting the European Parliament, shall adopt recommendations and incentive measures, to the exclusion of any harmonization of the legislative and regulatory provisions of the Member States.

Title XIX — Culture

Sole Article

1. The Community shall contribute to the flowering of the cultures of the Member States, while respecting their national and regional diversity, and at the same time bringing the common cultural heritage to the fore.

2. Action by the Community shall encourage cooperation between Member States and, if necessary, support and supplement their action in the following areas:

- improvement of the knowledge and dissemination of the culture and history of the European peoples;
- conservation and safeguarding of the cultural heritage of European significance;
- cultural exchanges;
- artistic and literary creation, including in the audiovisual sector.

3. The Community and the Member States shall foster cooperation with third countries and the competent international organizations in the sphere of culture and in particular with the Council of Europe.

4. The Community shall take cultural aspects into account in its action under other provisions of this Treaty.

5. The Council, acting in accordance with the procedure referred to in Article 189c and after consulting the Committee of the Regions, shall, in order to contribute to the achievement of the objectives referred to in this Article,

adopt recommendations and incentive measures, to the exclusion of any harmonization of the legislative and regulatory provisions of the Member States.

Title XX — Development cooperation

Article A
(Unchanged in substance from Luxembourg Presidency Draft Treaty)

Article B
The Community shall take account of the objectives referred to in Article A in the policies that it implements which are likely to affect developing countries.

Article C
1. Without prejudice to the other provisions of this Treaty, the Council, acting in accordance with the procedure referred to in Article 189c, shall adopt the measures necessary to further the objectives referred to in Article A. Such action may take the form of multiannual programmes.

2. The European Investment Bank shall contribute, under the terms laid down in its Statute, to the implementation of the action referred to in paragraph 1.

3. The provisions of this Article shall not affect cooperation with the African, Caribbean and Pacific countries in the framework of the ACP–EEC Convention[10]

Article D
1. The Community and the Member States shall coordinate their policies on development cooperation and shall consult each other on their aid programmes.

They may undertake joint actions.
Member States shall contribute if necessary to the implementation of the Community's aid programmes.

2. The Commission may take all appropriate steps to promote the coordination referred to in paragraph 1.

Article E
Within their respective spheres of competence, the Community and the Member States shall cooperate with third countries and with the relevant international organizations.

The arrangements for Community coopera-

[10] Declaration by the Conference "The European Development Fund will continue to be financed by national contributions in accordance with the present provisions."

tion may be the subject of agreements between the Community and the third parties concerned, which shall be negotiated and concluded in accordance with Article 228.

The previous paragraph shall be without prejudice to Member States' competence to negotiate in international bodies and to conclude international agreements.[11]

Part Four: Association of the overseas countries and territories

Articles 131 to 136a

Unchanged

Part Five: Institutions

Title I — Provisions governing the institutions

Chapter I — The Institutions

Section 1 — The European Parliament

Articles 137–144
(No changes of substance from previous Dutch draft)

Section 2 — The Council

Articles 145 to 148
(Unchanged from previous Dutch draft)

Article 149
Deleted (see Articles 189a and 189c)

Article 150
Unchanged

Article 151
A committee consisting of the Permanent Representatives of the Member States shall be responsible for preparing the work of the Council and for carrying out the tasks assigned to it by the Council.

Article 151a
1. The Council shall be assisted by a General Secretariat, under the direction of a Secretary–General. The Secretary–General shall be appointed by the Council acting unanimously.

The Council shall decide on the organization of the General Secretariat.

2. The Council shall adopt its rules of procedure.

Articles 152 to 154
Unchanged

Section 3 — The Commission

Articles 155 to 163
(Unchanged from previous Dutch draft)

Section 4 — The Court of Justice

Articles 164 to 174
(No changes of substance from previous Dutch draft)

Article 165
The third paragraph is deleted; it is replaced by a paragraph worded as follows:
"The Court of Justice shall sit in plenary session when a Member State or a Community institution that is a party to the proceedings so requests."

Article 175
Read first paragraph as follows:
"Should the European Parliament and the Council, the Council and the Commission, in infringement of this Treaty, fail to act . . .".

- Read the first, second and third lines of the second paragraph as follows:
  ". . . the institution or institutions concerned have first . . . the institution or institutions concerned have not . . .".
- Add a new fourth paragraph:
  "The Court of Justice shall have jurisdiction, under the same conditions, in actions or proceedings brought by the European Central Bank in the areas falling within the latter's competence and in actions or proceedings brought against the latter."

Article 176
Read the first paragraph as follows:
"The institution or institutions whose acts . . .".

Article 177
Read (b) as follows (remainder unchanged):
"(b) the validity and interpretation of acts of the institutions of the Community and of the European Central Bank;"

Articles 178 and 179
Unchanged

---

[11] Declaration in the Final Act of the Conference "The Conference considers that the provisions of Title XX, Article E, do not affect the principles resulting from the judgment of the Court of Justice in the AETR case".

Article 180

Add a fourth subparagraph reading as follows:

"(d) the fulfilment by national central banks of obligations under the Treaty and the Statute of the ESCB. In this connection the powers of the Council of the European Central Bank vis-à-vis national central banks shall be the same as those conferred upon the Commission in respect of Member States by Article 169."

Articles 181 to 183

Unchanged

Article 184

Notwithstanding the expiry of the period laid down in the third paragraph of Article 173, any party may, in proceedings in which a regulation of the European Parliament and of the Council, or a regulation of the Council, of the Commission, or of the European Central Bank is in issue, plead the grounds specified in the first paragraph of Article 173, in order to invoke before the Court of Justice the inapplicability of that regulation.

Articles 185 to 188

Unchanged

Chapter 2: Provisions common to several institutions

Article 189[12]

First paragraph to read:

"In order to carry out their task and in accordance with the provisions of this Treaty:

- the European Parliament and the Council shall make regulations and issue directives;
- the Council and the Commission shall make regulations, issue directives, take decisions, make recommendations or deliver opinions."

Article 189a

1. Where, in pursuance of this Treaty, the Council acts on a proposal from the Commission, unanimity shall be required for an act constituting an amendment to that proposal, subject to the provisions of Article 189b(4) and (5).

2. As long as the Council has not acted, the Commission may alter its proposal at any time during the procedures leading to the adoption of a Community act. The Commission may not withdraw its proposal once it has been the subject of a common position of the Council within the meaning of Articles 189b and 189c.

Article 189b

1. Where reference is made in this Treaty to this Article for the adoption of an act, the following procedure shall apply.

2. The Commission shall submit a proposal to the European Parliament and the Council.

The Council, acting by a qualified majority after obtaining the Opinion of the European Parliament, shall adopt a common position. The common position shall be communicated to the European Parliament. The Council shall inform the European Parliament fully of the reasons which led it to adopt its common position. The Commission shall inform the European Parliament fully of its position.

If, within three months of such communication, the European Parliament:

(a) approves the common position, the Council shall definitively adopt the act in question in accordance with that common position;

(b) has not taken a decision, the Council shall adopt the act in question in accordance with its common position:

(c) indicates, by an absolute majority of its component members, that it intends to reject the common position, it shall immediately inform the Council. The Council may convene a meeting of the Conciliation Committee referred to in paragraph 3 to explain further its position. The European Parliament shall thereafter either confirm, by an absolute majority of its component members, its rejection of the common position, in which event the proposed act shall be deemed not to have been adopted, or propose amendments in accordance with the provisions of point (d) of this paragraph;

(d) proposes amendments to the common position by an absolute majority of its component members, the amended text shall be forwarded to the Council and to the Commission, which shall deliver an opinion on those amendments.

3. If, within three months of the matter being referred to it, the Council, acting by a qualified majority, approves all the amend-

[12] Declaration in the Final Act of the Conference "The High Contracting Parties agree that the Intergovernmental Conference to be convened in 1996 will examine to what extent it might be possible to review the classification of Community acts with a view to establishing an appropriate relativity between the different categories of act."

ments of the European Parliament, it shall amend its common position accordingly, and adopt the act in question; however, the Council shall act unanimously on the amendments on which the Commission has delivered a negative opinion. If the Council does not approve the act in question, the President of the Council, in agreement with the President of the European Parliament, shall forthwith convene a meeting of the Conciliation Committee.

4. The Conciliation Committee, which shall be composed of the members of the Council or their representatives and an equal number of representatives of the European Parliament, shall have the task of reaching agreement on a joint text, by a qualified majority of the members of the Council or their representatives and by a majority of the representatives of the European Parliament. The Commission shall take part in the Conciliation Committee's proceedings and shall take all the necessary initiatives with a view to reconciling the positions of the European Parliament and the Council.

5. If, within six weeks of its being convened, the Conciliation Committee approves a joint text, the European Parliament, acting by an absolute majority of the votes cast, and the Council, acting by a qualified majority, shall have a period of six weeks from that approval in which to adopt the act in question in accordance with the joint text. If one of the two institutions fails to adopt the proposed act, it shall be deemed not to have been adopted.

6. Where the Conciliation Committee does not approve a joint text, the proposed act shall be deemed not to have been adopted unless the Council, acting by a qualified majority within six weeks of expiry of the period granted to the Conciliation Committee, confirms the common position to which it agreed before the conciliation procedure was initiated, possibly with amendments proposed by the European Parliament. In this case, the act in question shall be finally adopted unless the European Parliament, within six weeks of the date of confirmation by the Council, rejects the text by an absolute majority of its component members, in which case the proposed act shall be deemed not to have been adopted.

7. The periods of three months and six weeks referred to in this Article may be extended by a maximum of one month and two weeks respectively by common accord between the European Parliament and the Council. The period of three months referred to in paragraph 2 shall be automatically extended by two months in the event of the provisions of point (c) applying.

Article 189c

1. Where reference is made in this Treaty to this Article for the adoption of an act, the following procedure shall apply:

The present text of subparagraphs (a) to (g) of Article 149(2) is incorporated as it stands, subject to the re-numbering of paragraphs and to the fact that the phrase "under the conditions of paragraph 1" in subparagraph (a) is deleted.

Article 190

The beginning should be amended as follows: "Regulations and directives of the European Parliament and the Council and regulations, directives and decisions of the Council and the Commission . . .".

Article 191

1. Acts adopted in accordance with the procedure referred to in Article 189b shall be signed by the President of the European Parliament and by the President of the Council and published in the Official Journal of the Community. They shall enter into force on the date specified in them or, in the absence thereof, on the twentieth day following their publication.

2. Regulations, as well as directives which are addressed to all Member States, shall be published in the Official Journal of the Community. They shall enter into force on the date specified in them or, in the absence thereof, on the twentieth day following their publication.

3. Other directives, and decisions, shall be notified to those to whom they are addressed and shall take effect upon such notification.

Article 192

Unchanged

Chapter 3: The Economic and Social Committee[13, 14]

Articles 193 to 198

(No change of substance from previous Dutch draft)

---

[13] For the record: Declaration stating that the Committee will have the same independence as the Court of Auditors with regard to its budget and staff matters.
[14] Protocol annexed to the Treaty.

Chapter 4: The Committee of the Regions[15]

Article 198a

A Committee consisting of representatives of regional and local authorities, hereinafter referred to as the "Committee of the Regions", is hereby established with advisory status.

The number of members of the Committee of the Regions shall be as follows: Belgium 12; Denmark 9; Germany 24; Greece 12; Spain 21; France 24; Ireland 9; Italy 24; Luxembourg 6; Netherlands 12; Portugal 12; United Kingdom 24.

The members of the Committee and an equal number of alternate members, shall be appointed by the Council acting unanimously on proposals from the respective Member States for four years. Their appointments shall be renewable.

The members of the Committee may not be bound by any mandatory instructions. They shall be completely independent in the performance of their duties, in the general interest of the Community.

Article 198b

The Committee of the Regions shall elect its chairman and officers from among its members for a term of two years.

It shall adopt its rules of procedure and shall submit them for approval to the Council, acting unanimously.

The Committee shall be convened by its chairman at the request of the Council or of the Commission. It may also meet on its own initiative.

Article 198c

The Committee of the Regions shall be consulted by the Council or by the Commission where this Treaty so provides and in all other cases in which one of these two Institutions considers it appropriate. The Council or the Commission shall, if it considers it necessary, set the Committee for the submission of its opinion, a time-limit which may not be less than one month from the date on which the chairman receives notification to this effect. Upon expiry of the time-limit, the absence of an opinion shall not prevent further action.

Where the Economic and Social Committee is consulted pursuant to Article 198, the Committee of the Regions shall be informed by the Council or the Commission of the request for an opinion.

Where it considers that specific regional interests are involved, the Committee of the Regions may submit an opinion on the matter. The opinion of the Committee, together with a record of the proceedings, shall be forwarded to the Council and to the Commission.

Title II — Financial provisions

Article 199

Insert a second paragraph reading as follows:

"The administrative expenditure occasioned for the Institutions by the provisions of the Treaty on Union relating to common foreign and security policy shall be charged to the budget. The operational expenditure occasioned by the implementation of the said provisions may, under the conditions referred to therein, be charged to the budget."

Article 200

Deleted

Article 201 to 206a

(No changes of substance from previous Dutch draft)

Article 206b

1. The European Parliament, acting on a recommendation from the Council which shall act by a qualified majority, shall give a discharge to the Commission in respect of the implementation of the budget. To this end, the Council and the European Parliament in turn shall examine the accounts and the financial statement referred to in Article 205a, the annual report and any relevant special reports by the Court of Auditors together with the replies of the institutions under audit to the observations of the Court of Auditors.

2. Before giving a discharge to the Commission, or for any other purpose in connection with the exercise of its powers over the implementation of the budget, the European Parliament may ask to hear the Commission give evidence with regard to the execution of expenditure or the maintenance of financial control systems. The Commission shall submit any necessary information to the European Parliament at the latter's request.

3. The Commission shall take all appropriate steps to act on the observations in the

---

[15] Protocol annexed to the Treaty: The Economic and Social Committee and the Committee of the Regions shall have a common organizational structure.

decisions giving discharge and on other observations by the European Parliament relating to the execution of expenditure, as well as on comments accompanying the recommendations on discharge adopted by the Council.

At the request of the European Parliament or the Council, the Commission shall report on the measures taken in the light of these observations and comments and in particular on the instructions given to the departments which are responsible for the implementation of the budget. These reports shall also be forwarded to the Court of Auditors.

Articles 207 and 208

Unchanged

Article 209

The Council, acting unanimously on a proposal from the Commission and after consulting the European Parliament and obtaining the opinion of the Court of Auditors, shall:

Subparagraphs (a) and (b) – unchanged.

(c) lay down rules concerning the responsibility of financial controllers, authorizing officers and accounting officers, and concerning appropriate arrangements for inspection.

Article 209a

Member States shall take the same measures to counter fraud affecting the financial interests of the Community as they take to counter fraud affecting their own financial interests.

Without prejudice to other provisions of the Treaty, Member States shall coordinate their actions aimed at protecting the financial interests of the Community against fraud.

To this end they shall organize, with the help of the Commission, close and regular cooperation between the competent services of their administrations.

Part Six: General provisions

Articles 210 to 214

Unchanged

Article 215

Add a new third paragraph which reads as follows:

"The preceding paragraph shall apply under the same conditions to damage caused by the European Central Bank or by its servants in the performance of their duties."

The present paragraph 3 becomes a new paragraph 4.

Articles 216 to 226

Unchanged

Article 227

Paragraph 2 – delete the words "Algeria and".

Paragraph 5(a) – read as follows:

"This Treaty shall not apply to the Faroe Islands."

(Remainder of the text deleted).

Article 228

1. Where this Treaty provides for the conclusion of agreements between the Community and one or more States or international organizations, the Commission shall make recommendations to the Council, which shall authorize the Commission to open the necessary negotiations. The Commission shall conduct these negotiations in consultation with special committees appointed by the Council to assist it in this task and within the framework of such directives as the Council may issue to it. In exercising the powers bestowed upon it by this paragraph, the Council shall act by a qualified majority, except in the cases provided for in the second sentence of paragraph 2, for which it shall act unanimously.

2. Subject to the powers vested in the Commission in this field, the agreements shall be concluded by the Council, acting by a qualified majority on a proposal from the Commission. The Council shall act unanimously when the agreement covers a field for which unanimity is required for the adoption of internal rules, and for the agreements referred to in Article 238.

3. The Council shall conclude agreements after consulting the European Parliament, except for the agreements referred to in Article 113(3), including cases when the agreement covers a field for which the cooperation procedure is required for the adoption of internal rules. The European Parliament shall deliver its Opinion within a time limit which the Council may lay down according to the urgency of the matter. In the absence of an Opinion within that time limit, the Council may act.

By way of derogation from the provisions of the previous subparagraph, agreements referred to in Article 238, other agreements establishing a specific institutional framework by organizing cooperation procedures, agreements having important budgetary implications for the Community and agreements entailing amendment of an act adopted under the procedure referred to in Article 189b shall be concluded after the assent of the European Parliament has been obtained.

The Council and the European Parliament

may, in an urgent situation, agree upon a time limit for the assent.

4. When concluding an agreement, the Council may, by way of derogation from the provisions of paragraph 2, empower the Commission to approve modifications on behalf of the Community where the agreement provides for them to be adopted by a simplified procedure or by a body set up by the agreement; it may attach specific conditions to such entitlement.

5. When the Council envisages concluding an agreement which calls for amendments to this Treaty, the amendments must first be adopted in accordance with the procedure laid down for modifying this Treaty.

The Council, the Commission or a Member State may obtain beforehand the opinion of the Court of Justice as to whether the agreement envisaged is compatible with the provisions of this Treaty. An agreement on which the Court of Justice has delivered an adverse opinion may enter into force only in accordance with the conditions set out in the Article concerning the procedure for modifying this Treaty.

6. Agreements concluded under the conditions set out in this Article shall be binding on the institutions of the Community and on Member States.

Article 228a

If on the basis of a common position or a joint action adopted according to the provisions of the Treaty on the Union relating to the common foreign and security policy, an action by the Community should prove necessary to interrupt or to reduce, in part or completely, economic relations with one or more third countries, the Council shall take the necessary measures as a matter of urgency. The Council shall act by a qualified majority on a proposal from the Commission.

Articles 229 to 230

Unchanged

Article 231

The words "Organization for European Economic Co-operation" shall be replaced by "Organization for Economic Co-operation and Development".

Articles 232 to 234

Unchanged

Article 235

Should it prove that attainment of one of the tasks of the Community referred to in Article 2 makes it necessary for the Community to act in one of the fields covered by Articles 3 [and 3a][16] and this Treaty has not provided the necessary powers, the Council shall, acting unanimously on a proposal from the Commission and after consulting the European Parliament, adopt the appropriate measures while taking into account the principle of subsidiarity as defined in Article 3b.

Articles 236 and 237

Deleted

Article 238

The Community may conclude with one or more States or international organizations agreements establishing an association involving reciprocal rights and obligations, common action and special procedures.

Articles 239 and 240

Unchanged

Articles 241 to 246

Deleted

Articles 247 and 248

Unchanged

Provisions amending the Treaty establishing the European Coal and Steel Community (for the record)

Provisions amending the Treaty establishing the European Atomic Energy Community (for the record)

Provisions on a common foreign and security policy

[External policy of the union][17]

Common foreign and security policy

Article A

1. The Union and its Member States shall define and implement a common foreign and

---

[16] If the reference to Article 3a is included, consultation of the ESCB should be introduced.
[17] The Treaty will comprise provisions aimed at ensuring consistency between foreign and security policy and the activities carried out by the Community in the framework of external economic relations and development policy. The content of these provisions and their place will be examined in the light of the presentation of the various sections of the Treaty.

security policy, governed by the provisions of this Title and covering all areas of foreign and security policy [including, in the longer term, the formulation of a common defence policy].

2. The objectives of the common foreign and security policy shall be:

- to safeguard the common values, fundamental interests and independence of the Union;
- to strengthen the security of the Union and its Member States in all ways;
- to preserve peace and strengthen international security, in accordance with the principles of the United Nations Charter as well as the principles of the Helsinki Act and the objectives of the Paris Charter;
- to promote international cooperation;
- to develop and consolidate democracy and the rule of law, and respect for human rights and fundamental freedoms.

3. The Union shall pursue these objectives:

- by establishing systematic cooperation between Member States in the conduct of policy, in accordance with Article B;
- by gradually introducing, in accordance with Article C, joint action in the areas in which the Member States have essential interests in common.

4. The Member States shall support the Union's external and security policy actively and unreservedly in a spirit of loyalty and mutual solidarity. They shall refrain from any action which is contrary to the interests of the Union or likely to impair its effectiveness as a cohesive force in international relations.

The Council shall ensure that these principles are complied with.

Article B

1. Member States shall inform and consult one another within the Council on any matter of foreign and security policy of general interest in order to ensure that their combined influence is exerted as effectively as possible by means of concerted and convergent action. Whenever it deems it necessary, the Council shall define a common position.

Member States shall ensure that their national policies conform to the common positions.

3. Member States shall coordinate their action in international organizations[18] and at international conferences.

They shall uphold the common positions in such fora.

In international organizations[19] and at international conferences where not all the Member States participate, those which do take part shall uphold the common positions.

Article C

1. On the basis of general guidelines from the European Council, the Council shall decide that an area or matter covered by the foreign and security policy should be the subject of joint action.

Whenever the Council decides on the principle of joint action, it shall lay down the Union's general and specific objectives in carrying out such action and the conditions, means and procedures for and, if necessary, the duration of its implementation.

The Council shall stipulate as a general rule that the detailed arrangements for carrying out joint action shall be adopted by a qualified majority.

Where the Council is required to act by a qualified majority pursuant to the preceding paragraph, the votes of its members shall be weighted in accordance with Article 148(2) of the Treaty establishing the European Community, and for their adoption, acts of the Council shall require at least fifty-four votes in favour, cast by at least eight members.

2. Joint actions shall be binding upon the Member States in the positions they adopt and in the conduct of their activity.

3. Whenever there is any plan to adopt a national position or take national action pursuant to a joint line of action, information shall be provided in time to allow, if necessary, for prior consultations within Council. The obligation to provide prior information shall not apply to measures which are merely a national transposition of Council decisions.

4. In cases of imperative need arising from changes in the situation, and failing a Council

---

18. 19 Declaration in the Final Act of the Conference "The term "in international organizations" covers all the bodies of such organizations".

decision. Member States may take the necessary measures as a matter of urgency, in accordance with the objectives of the joint action. They shall inform the Council immediately of any such decisions.

5. Should there be any major difficulties in implementing a joint action, a Member State shall refer them to the Council which shall discuss them and seek appropriate solutions. Such solutions shall not run counter to the objectives of the joint line of action nor impair its effectiveness.

Article D

1. The common foreign and security policy shall include all questions related to the security of the Union.

2. Decisions by the Union on security matters which have defence implications may be wholly or partly implemented in the framework of the Western European Union, insofar as they also fall within that organization's sphere of competence.

3. Decisions taken pursuant to paragraph 2 shall not affect the obligations arising for certain Member States from the Treaties establishing the Atlantic Alliance and the Western European Union and the situation of each Member State in that connection.

4. The provisions of this Article shall not prevent the establishment or development of closer cooperation between two or more Member States, provided such cooperation does not run counter to or impede that provided for in this Title.

5. With a view to the definition, at a later stage, of a defence policy, the provisions of this Article may be revised, as provided for in Article W(2), on the basis of a report to be submitted by the Council to the European Council in 1996 at the latest.]

Article E

1. The Presidency shall represent the Union for matters coming within the common foreign and security policy.

2. The Presidency shall be responsible for the implementation of common measures; in that capacity it shall in principle express the position of the Union in international organizations and international conferences.

3. In the tasks referred to in the preceding paragraphs, the Presidency shall be assisted if need be by the previous and next Member State to hold the Presidency. The Commision shall be fully associated in these tasks.

4. Without prejudice to the provisions of Article B(3) and Article C(2), Member States represented in international organizations or international conferences[20] where not all the Member States participate shall keep the latter informed of any matter of common interest.

Article E

The diplomatic and consular missions of the Member States and the Commission Delegations in third countries and international conferences, and their representations to international organizations, shall cooperate in ensuring that the common positions and common measures adopted by the Council are complied with and implemented. They shall step up cooperation by exchanging information, carrying out joint assessments and contributing to the implementation of the provisions referred to in Article D on Citizenship of the Union.

Article G

The European Parliament shall be kept regularly informed by the Presidency and the Commission of the basic choices made in the Union's foreign and security policy. The Presidency shall consult the European Parliament on the main aspects of the common foreign and security policy and shall ensure that the views of the European Parliament are duly taken into consideration.

The European Parliament may put questions or make recommendations to the Council. It shall hold an annual debate on progress in implementing the common foreign and security policy.

Article H[21]

1. The European Council shall define the principles of and general guidelines for the common foreign and security policy.

[20] Declaration in the Final Act of the Conference "The expression "in international organizations" covers all the subsidiary bodies of such organizations".

[21] To guarantee the secrecy of proceedings, the following provision will be introduced into Article 18 of the Rules of Procedure of the Council:
"The Council shall adopt the measures necessary to guarantee the secrecy of all work done by the Council pursuant to the provisions of the Treaty on the Union concerning co-operation in the spheres of justice and home affairs."

2. The Council shall take the decisions necessary for defining and implementing common foreign and security policy on the basis of the general guidelines adopted by the European Council. It shall ensure the unity, consistency and effectiveness of action by the Union.

The Council shall act unanimously, except for procedural questions [and in the case referred to in Article C(1), third subparagraph].

3. Any Member State or the Commission may refer to the Council any question relating to the common foreign and security policy and may submit proposals to the Council.

4. In cases requiring a rapid decision, the Presidency, of its own motion, or at the request of the Commission or a Member State, shall convene an extraordinary Council meeting within forty-eight hours or, in an emergency, within a shorter period.

Article I

The Commission shall act in full association with the work carried out in the common foreign and security policy field.

Article J

For the record: developments clause.

Article K

1. The provisions mentioned in Articles 137, 138 to 142, 146, 147, 150 to 153, 157 to 163 of the Treaty establishing the European Community shall apply to provisions relating to common foreign and security policy.

2. The administrative expenditure incurred by the Institutions through the provisions concerning the common foreign and security policy shall be charged to the budget of the European Community.

The Council may also:

- either decide unanimously that the operational expenditure involved in the implementation of the said provisions is to be charged to the budget of the European Community; in this case, the budgetary procedures provided for in the Treaty establishing the European Community shall apply;
- or find that such expenditure should be charged to the Member States, possibly in accordance with a scale to be determined.

Article L[22]

The provisions of the Treaties establishing the European Communities concerning the powers of the Court of Justice and the exercise of those powers shall not apply to any of the provisions of this Title other than those in Article M.

Article M

The provisions concerning common foreign and security policy shall not affect the powers of the European Communities.

For the record: The breakdown of proceedings between the Political Committee and the Permanent Representatives Committee will be examined at a later stage as will the practical arrangements for cooperation between the General Secretariat and the Commission.

Annex I: Declaration by the Member States

The Member States agree that the following topics may be the subject of a joint action as soon as this Treaty enters into force:

- industrial and technological cooperation in the armaments field;
- the transfer of military technology to third countries and the control of arms exports;
- non-proliferation issues;
- arms control, negotiations on arms reduction and confidence-building measures, particularly in the CSCE context;
- involvement in peace-keeping operations in the United Nations context;
- involvement in humanitarian intervention measures;
- questions relating to the CSCE;
- relations with the USSR;
- transatlantic relations;
- . . .

Annex II: Declaration by the Member States which are members of the WEU on cooperation between the WEU and the Union

Declaration of political intent
Practical arrangements (e.g. Secretariat, Presidency, scheduling etc.).

---

[22] It has been proposed that this provision, together with those contained in Articles K and M, should be placed in the final provisions of the Treaty on the Union. The Presidency reserves the right to take this idea into account as part of the overall proposal which it is to prepare.

Provisions on cooperation in judicial and home affairs

Article A

For the purposes of achieving the objectives of the Union, in particular the free movement of persons, and without prejudice to the powers of the European Community, Member States shall regard the following areas as matters of common interest:

1. asylum policy;

2. immigration policy and policy regarding nationals of third countries:

(a) conditions of entry and movement by nationals of third countries on the territory of Member States for long periods of residence;

(b) conditions of residence by nationals of third countries on the territory of Member States, including family reunion and access to employment;

(c) combating unauthorized immigration, residence and work by nationals of third countries on the territory of Member States;

3. combating drug addiction insofar as this is not covered by 6 to 8 below;

4. combating fraud on an international scale insofar as this is not covered by 6 to 8 below;

5. judicial cooperation in civil matters;

6. judicial cooperation in criminal matters;

7. customs cooperation;

8. police cooperation for the purposes of preventing and combating terrorism, unlawful drug trafficking and other serious forms of international crime, including the organization of a Union-wide system for exchanging information within a European Police Office (Europol).

Article B

1. The matters referred to in Article A shall be dealt with in compliance with the European Convention for the Protection of Human Rights and Fundamental Freedoms of 4 November 1950 and the Convention relating to the Status of Refugees of 28 July 1951 and having regard to the protection afforded by Member States to persons persecuted on political grounds.

2. This Title shall not affect the exercise of the responsibilities incumbent upon Member States with regard to the maintaining of law and order and the safeguarding of internal security.

Article C

1. In the areas referred to in Article A, Member States shall inform and consult one another within the Council with a view to coordinating their action.

To that end, they shall establish collaboration between the relevant departments of their administrations.

2. The Council may:

– on the initiative of any Member State or of the Commission as regards Article A(1) to (5);

– on the initiative of any Member State as regards Article A(6) to (8):

(a) adopt joint positions and promote, using the appropriate form and procedures, any cooperation contributing to the pursuit of the objectives of the Union;

(b) adopt joint action in the extent to which the objectives of the Union can be attained better by joint action than by the Member States acting individually on account of the scale or effects of the action envisaged; it may decide that measures implementing joint action are to be adopted by a qualified majority;

(c) without prejudice to the provisions of Article 220 of the Treaty establishing the European Community, draw up conventions which it shall recommend to the Member States for adoption in accordance with their respective constitutional rules.

Unless otherwise provided by such conventions, measures implementing them shall be adopted within the Council by a majority of two-thirds of the High Contracting Parties.

Such conventions may stipulate that the Court of Justice shall have jurisdiction to interpret their provisions and to rule on any disputes regarding their application, in accordance with such arrangements as they may lay down.

Article D[23]

1. A Co-ordinating Committee shall be set up consisting of Senior Officials. In addition to its

[23] In order to guarantee the secrecy of the discussions, the following provision should be inserted in Article 18 of the Council's Rules of Procedure:

"The Council shall adopt the necessary measures to ensure the secrecy of all the work carried out by the Council in implementation of the provisions relating to co-operation in judicial and home affairs in the Treaty on the Union."

coordinating role, it shall be the task of the Committee to

- give opinions for the attention of the Council, either at the Council's request or on its own initiative;
- contribute to the preparation of the Council's discussions in the areas referred to in Article A and, in accordance with the conditions laid down in Article 100d of the Treaty establishing the European Community, in the area referred to in Article 100c of that Treaty.

2. The Commission shall be fully associated with the work in the areas referred to in this Title.

3. The Council shall act unanimously, except on matters of procedure and in cases where Article C expressly provides for other voting rules.

Where the Council is required to act by a qualified majority, the votes of its members shall be weighted as laid down in Article 148(2) of the Treaty establishing the European Community, and for their adoption, acts of Council shall require at least fifty-four votes in favour, cast by at least eight members.

Article E
Within international organizations and at international conferences in which they take part, Member States shall defend the common positions adopted under the provisions of this Title.

Article F
The Presidency and the Commission shall regularly inform the European Parliament of discussions in the areas covered by this Title.

The Presidency shall consult the European Parliament on the principal aspects of activities in the areas referred to in this Title and shall ensure that the views of the European Parliament are duly taken into consideration.

The European Parliament may ask questions of the Council or make recommendations to it. Each year, it shall hold a debate on the progress made in implementation in the areas referred to in this Title.

Article G
The provisions of this Title shall not prevent the establishing or developing of closer cooperation

between two or more Member States to the extent to which such cooperation does not conflict with, or impede, that provided for in this Title.

Article H
1. The provisions referred to in Articles 137, 138 to 142, 146, 147, 150 to 153, and 157 to 163 of the Treaty establishing the European Community shall apply to the provisions relating to the areas referred to in this Title.

2. Administrative expenditure which the provisions relating to the areas referred to in this Title entail for the Institutions shall be charged to the budget of the European Community. The Council may also

- either decide unanimously that operating expenditure to which the implementation of those provisions gives rise is to be charged to the budget of the European Community; in that event, the budgetary procedure laid down in the Treaty establishing the European Community shall be applicable;
- or determine that such expenditure shall be charged to the Member States, where appropriate in accordance with a system of allocation to be decided.

Article I[24]
The provisions of the Treaty establishing the European Community which concern the jurisdiction of the Court of Justice and the exercise of that jurisdiction shall not apply to any of the provisions of this Title, with the exception of Article J and the eventuality of jurisdiction being conferred on the Court by conventions adopted pursuant to Article C(2)(c).

Article J
The provisions referred to in this Title shall not affect the powers of the European Communities.

Article K
The Council, acting unanimously on the initiative of the Commission or a Member State, may decide to apply Article 100c of the EEC Treaty to action in areas referred to in Article(A(1) to (5), and at the same time determining the relevant voting conditions relating to it.

It shall recommend the Member States to adopt that decision in accordance with their respective constitutional rules.

---

[24] It was proposed that this provision and those set out in Articles H and J should be included in the final provisions of the Treaty on the Union. The Presidency reserved the right to take this idea into account as part of the overall proposal which it was going to draft.

Annex

Statement re Article A(1)

1. Member States agree that, in the context of the proceedings provided for in Articles A and C of the provisions on cooperation in judicial and home affairs, the Council will consider as a matter of priority questions concerning Member States' asylum policies, with the aim of adopting, by the end of 1993, common action to harmonize aspects of them, in the light of the work programme and timetable contained in the report on asylum drawn up at the European Council's request.

2. In this connection, the Council will also consider, by the end of 1994, on the basis of a report, the possibility of applying Article K to such matters.

Declaration of the Conference re Article A(8) [Police cooperation]

Member States confirm agreement on the objectives underlying the German delegation's proposals at the European Council meeting in Luxembourg on 28 and 29 June 1991.

For the present, the Member States agree to examine as a matter of priority the drafts submitted to them, on the basis of the work programme and timetable agreed upon in the report drawn up at the request of the Luxembourg European Council, and they are willing to envisage the adoption of practical measures in areas such as those suggested by the German delegation, relating to the following functions in the exchange of information and experience:

- support for national criminal investigation and security authorities, in particular in the coordination of investigations and search operations;
- compilation of data files;
- central analysis and assessment of information in order to take stock of the situation and identify investigative approaches;
- collection and analysis of national prevention programmes for forwarding to Member States and for drawing up Europe-wide prevention strategies;

- measures relating to further training, research, forensic matters and criminal records departments. Member States agree to consider on the basis of a report, during 1995 at the latest, whether the scope of such cooperation should be extended.

Final provisions

Article W[25]

1. The Government of any Member State or the Commission may submit to the Council proposals for the amendment of the Treaties on which the Union is founded.

If the Council, after consulting the European Parliament and, where appropriate, the Commission, delivers an opinion in favour of calling a conference of representatives of the governments of the Member States, the conference shall be convened by the President of the Council for the purpose of determining by common accord the amendments to be made to those treaties. The Council of the European Central Bank shall also be consulted in the case of institutional modifications in the monetary field.

The amendments shall enter into force after being ratified by all the Member States in accordance with their respective constitutional requirements.

2. A conference of representatives of the governments of the Member States shall be convened in 1996 in the perspective of strengthening the federal character of the Union to examine those provisions of this Treaty which provide for such an amendment.

Article X[26]

Any European State may apply to become a Member of the Union. It shall address its application to the Council, which shall act unanimously after consulting the Commission and after receiving the assent of the European Parliament which shall act by an absolute majority of its component members.

The conditions of admission and the adjustment to the Treaties on which the Union is founded necessitated thereby shall be the subject of an agreement between the Member States and the applicant State. This agreement

---

[25] Articles 236 EEC, 96 ECSC and 204 EAEC are repealed.
[26] Articles 237 EEC, 98 ECSC and 205 EAEC are repealed.

shall be submitted for ratification by all the Contracting States in accordance with their respective constitutional requirements.

Article Y[27]

This Treaty is concluded for an unlimited period.

Article Z

1. This Treaty shall be ratified by the High Contracting Parties in accordance with their respective constitutional requirements. The instruments of ratification shall be deposited with the Government of the Italian Republic.

2. This Treaty shall enter into force on the first day of the month following the deposit of the instrument of ratification by the last signatory State to take this step.

Article Za

This Treaty, drawn up in a single original in the Danish, Dutch, English, French, German, Greek, Irish, Italian, Portuguese and Spanish languages, the texts in each of these languages being equally authentic, shall be deposited in the archives of the Government of the Italian Republic, which will transmit a certified copy to each of the Governments of the other Signatory States.

Texts to be annexed to the Treaty

I.   Protocols

1. Protocol laying down certain provisions on the acquisition of property in Denmark
2. Protocol on the common organizational structure of the Economic and Social Committee and the Committee of the Regions

II.   Declarations to be annexed to the Final Act of the Conference

NB: The following declarations have not yet been examined by the personal representatives.

1. Declaration on the role of national parliaments in the European Union (CONF-UP 1762/91)
2. Declaration on the right of access to information (see draft Articles in CONF-UP 1709/91)
3. Declaration on improving the quality of Community legislation (CONF-UP 1765/91)
4. Declaration on the review of the Decision on own resources and related measures
5. Declaration on the implementation of Community law (CONF-UP 1721/91 Annex 1 Annex B)
6. Declaration on the enforcement of Community law (CONF-UP 1721/91 Annex I Annex C)
7. Declaration on appraisal of the environmental aspects of Community measures (CONF-UP 1763/91 Annex B)
8. Declaration on the Court of Auditors
9. Declaration on the attestation of compatibility with the budget procedure
10. Declaration on the protection of animals (CONF-UP 1841/91)
11. Declaration on cooperation with charitable associations
12. Declaration on the overseas territories to which the Treaty establishing the European Community does not apply.

---

[27] Articles 240 EEC Treaty (unlimited), 97 ECSC Treaty (50 years) and 208 EAEC Treaty (unlimited) are retained.

16. Noordwijk "Conclave" of Foreign Ministers

Dutch Presidency Note in the light of discussions at the Noordwijk "conclave" of Foreign Ministers 12–13 November 1991 proposing modifications to its working document

I. Institutional provisions

1. Representation in the Council (Article 146)
The footnote to this article is deleted.

2. Creation and number of Deputy Commissioners Article 161 shall read as follows:
"The Commission may appoint a Vice-President or two vice-Presidents from among its members.
The Commission may also nominate up to five Deputy Commissioners. They shall be appointed by the Council acting by qualified majority."
N.B: The provisions of Article 157(2) shall apply by analogy to the Deputy Commissioners.

3. Number of MEP's (Article 138)

Paragraph 2 is amended as follows (sole change):
"Germany . . . 99"
Paragraph 3: unchanged.

4. Legislative procedure (Article 189 a)
The last sentence of paragraph 2 is deleted.

5. Co-decision procedure (Article 189 b)
The Presidency suggests the following scope:

- Article 49: free movement of workers
- Article 54(2), 56(2) and 57: right of establishment
- Articles 100a and 100b: internal market
- Article 130i: research and technological development, framework-programme

(Note: adoption by qualified majority)

- Article 130s(3): environment, multi-annual action programmes
- Title XIII, Article C: transeuropean networks, guidelines
- Title XVI: consumer protection
- Title XVII: public health
= measures of encouragement
   (the co-decision procedure shall not apply to the adoption of recommendations)
- Title XIX: culture
= measures of encouragement
   (the co-decision procedure shall not apply to the adoption of recommendations)

The Presidency also notes that the great majority of the delegations wishes to see education and social chapter (provisions adopted by a qualified majority) added to this list.
Revision clause (as a new paragraph 8 to Article 189b):
"The procedure under this Article may be extended to further areas, in accordance with the procedure provided for under Article W(2), on the basis of a report to be submitted to the Council by the Commission."
(Note – Date: 1996: ratification by Member States)

6. Co-operation procedure (Article 189c)
Scope: unchanged, except as regards Article 94 (state aids), where the European Parliament should be consulted.

7. Assent procedure
Unchanged

II. Competencies

1. Subsidiarity

(a) Article 3b of the EEC Treaty shall read as follows:
"The Community shall act within the limits of the powers conferred upon it by this Treaty and of the objectives assigned to it therein.
In the areas which do not fall within its exclusive jurisdiction, the Community shall take action, in accordance with the principle of subsidiarity, only if and to the extent that these objectives can be better achieved by the Community than by Member States acting separately by reason of the scale or effects of the proposed action.
Action by the Community shall not go beyond what is necessary to achieve the objectives of this Treaty."

(b) Article B of the common provisions of the Treaty on the Union shall begin:
"The Union shall, while respecting the principle of subsidiarity as defined in Article 3b of the EC Treaty, set itself the following objectives . . . (the rest unchanged).

2. Article 235
Reproduce the text of Article 235 of the EEC Treaty.

The question of the application of this Article in the area of EMU will be examined by the Conference on EMU.

3. Citzenship
Article C(1)
Read: "31 December 1994"

4. Article 100c
Replace the initiative of the Member States by the Euratom Treaty formula (Article 32) whereby "the Commission shall examine any request made by a Member State"

5. Social policy
The Presidency maintains the text set out, with the inclusion of the following two declarations in the final act of the Conference;

(a) The Conference declares that the first of the arrangements for application of the agreements between management and labour Community-wide – referred to in Article 118b(2) – will consist in developing, by collective bargaining according to the rules of each Member State, the content of the agreements, and that consequently this arrangement implies no obligation on the Member States to apply the agreements directly or to work out rules for their transposition, nor any obligation to amend national legislation in force to facilitate their implementation.

(b) The Conference declares that when the rules on the Structural Funds are reviewed in 1992, the Council will consider whether to adapt the provisions relating to the tasks of the European Social Funds in order to allow it to facilitate adaptation to industrial changes, in particular through training and vocational retraining.

(N.B. the location of this declaration will be determined subsequently)

In addition, the Presidency is continuing its bilateral contracts and reserves the right to submit a new proposal on social provisions.

6. Vocational training
Article B(4) shall read as follows:
"The Council, acting in accordance with the procedure referred to in Article 189c and after consulting the Economic and Social Committee, shall adopt measures to contribute to the achievement of the objectives referred to in this Article, with the exclusion of any harmonization of the legislative and regulatory provisions of the Member States."

7. Research and technological development.
Article 130i(1)
For the record: framework programme: qualified majority (co-decision).

8. Environment
(a) Article 130r(2), to reads as follows:
The policy of the Community relating to the environmental shall target a high level of protection, taking into account the diversity of situations in the various regions of the Community. It shall be based on the precautionary principle and on the principles that preventive action should be taken, that environmental damage should as a priority be rectified at source and that the polluter should pay. Environmental protection requirements must be integrated into the definition and implementation of other Community policies.

In this context, harmonization measures answering these requirements shall include, where appropriate, a safeguard clause allowing Member States to take provisional measures, for non-economic environmental reasons, subject to Community inspection procedure".

(b) Article 130s
(i) paragraph 2, read:
". . . shall adopt
– measures including provisions of a fiscal nature,
– measures concerning town and country planning and land use, including management of water resources".

(ii) the second subparagraph of paragraph 3 to read:
"The Council, acting under the terms of paragraph 1 or paragraph 2 as appropriate, shall adopt the measures necessary for the implementation of these programmes".

The Presidency is continuing its bilateral contacts on certain problems specific to the chapter on the environment.

9. Transeuropean networks
unchanged

10. Industry
Deletion in paragraph 3 of the phrase "in particular in favour of the industries of the future"

11. Public Health
(a) paragraph 1, second subparagraph: delete the words "in particular"
(b) paragraph 4: (for the record) co-decision

12. Culture
(a) Paragraph 2, third indent, to read: "non commercial cultural exchanges"

(b) Paragraph 5: (for the record) co-decision

13. Development cooperation

(a) Article D(1), first sentence, to read:

"The Community and the Member States shall coordinate their policies on development cooperation and shall consult each other on their aid programmes, including in international organizations and during international conferences".

(b) Footnote to read:

"Conference declaration:

"The European Development Fund will continue to be financed by national contributions".

14. As part of an overall compromise based on the Presidency proposals on other points, in particular on voting by a qualified majority, the Presidency proposes deleting the Titles concerning energy, tourism, consumer protection and civil protection on the understanding that:

- these subjects will be included on the list in Article 3;
- the matter of the insertion of these Titles in the Treaty will be examined during the revision referred to in Article W(2);

- the Commission states that Community action in these areas will be continued on the basis of the current provisions of the Treaty.

III. Miscellaneous

1. Article 51

The text of the Treaty of Rome is retained.

2. Article 92

(i) Paragraph 2(c) of the EC Treaty (aid to certain areas of the Federal Republic of Germany) is unchanged in relation to the Treaty of Rome.

(ii) New paragraph 3(d):

Aid to promote culture and heritage conservation where such aid does not adversely affect trading conditions and competition in the Community to an extent which is contrary to the common interests".

3. Article 113

Delete paragraph 5 and the related declaration.

4. Protocol on the right to life in Ireland (to be drafted).

17. European Commission

Declaration on the two Intergovernmental Conferences published on 27 November 1991

On 23, 24 and 27 November the Commission discussed the draft Treaties for Political Union and Economic and Monetary Union, as they stand at the current stage of progress in the Intergovernmental Conferences. The Commission has contributed all that it can in the preparation of these drafts and in the search for a dynamic compromise. It is, after all, keenly aware of their importance and of the promise they hold out for the construction of a United Europe.

The Commission conceives this unity in a perspective which would guarantee the effectiveness of the Community, its democratization and a clear distinction between the powers enjoyed by the Community, its Member States and their regions, in full respect of the principles of subsidiarity and diversity. To qualify this perspective as a federal one reflects the present construction of the Community as well as the conception of future developments.

In this spirit the Commission expresses its concern about the concept of Union, as defined in the current version of the draft Political Union Treaty. As matters stand the Union is to develop alongside the Community without there being an explicit restatement, as there was in the Single Act, of the determination to bring together in a single entity all the powers which the Member States plan to exercise jointly in political and economic matters. Moreover, the Union is not expressly given a legal personality in international law. This raises serious difficulties about the Union's representation and about the coherence between foreign policy as such and external economic relations or development cooperation.

The Commission believes that these difficulties could be overcome by spelling out the fact that all the activities provided for by the Treaties are part of a process leading progressively towards attaining Union or a political Community.

To go to the root of the problem, the new Political Union Treaty must make a qualitative leap forward towards a common foreign and security policy, greater democracy in decision-making and a coherent, balanced economic and social area. The planned provisions should also put the 12 Member States in a position to step up the quality and effectiveness of their cooperation in matters of law enforcement and the protection of the individual as this common area is established.

Regarding foreign policy, the proposed new framework of "common actions" will have little meaning unless the Union has the capacity to take quicker decisions and act more effectively in those areas where the Twelve unanimously decide that they share a common interest which they must defend and promote. Within this framework and taking account of the guidelines decided by the European Council, the Council of Ministers of Foreign Affairs should be able to decide by qualified majority, possibly reinforced.

Injecting greater democracy into Community life should be achieved primarily by giving the European Parliament greater powers. Parliament should be able to confirm the Commission by a vote of investiture. Its ultimate role is to become fully a co-legislator through the establishment of a co-decision procedure which, while respecting the rules governing efficiency, should apply generally in respect of competences where the Council acts by qualified majority. The number of areas where Parliament's assent is required should be extended.

The Commission regards the Community as an area where the spirit of competition, the will to cooperate and a sense of solidarity reign. Its powers need to be extended and strengthened on the basis of these three principles. Hence the importance attached by the Commission to improving Treaty provisions on research and technology, energy, industry, the environment, consumer protection and the social dimension. Hence, also, its proposal that the effectiveness of the internal market be boosted by the full application of competition policy and buttressed by infrastructure programmes designed to contribute to improved competitiveness and greater cohesion.

The point is that this economic monetary and social area will be unsatisfactory if each and every region and each and every Member State does not enjoy truly equal opportunities under the Treaty. The Single Act expressed this requirement by introducing economic and social cohesion, which is now one of the pillars of the Community. By adopting the Commission's proposal, the February 1988 European Council made it possible to develop policies designed to promote that cohesion. A new set of proposals will be made next year in the context of the new financial perspective for 1993–97. It will contain measures affecting both the structure of expenditure, in particular the reinforcement of structural policies, and the structure of resources. Its political basis would be strengthened if the new Treaty contained a provision for the establishment of a progressive resource.

Stronger economic and social cohesion would make a vital contribution to the success of economic and monetary union, to the benefit of all Member States. The discussions at the IGC have confirmed that there is absolute opposition to the idea of a two-speed Europe. But some countries might be allowed derogations, if need be, to give them a few extra years to catch up with those which have already reached the final stage of economic and monetary union – the single currency and an independent central bank ranking among its salient features.

As the present stage of development of European construction, it is vital that all the Member States confirm their full acceptance of the objective of economic and monetary union. The Commission therefore alerts the Member States to the risks of a general opting-out clause. There was no question of any such clause, for example, when the Twelve adopted the 1992 programme. That programme has hence attained full credibility and the Community institutions are correspondingly stronger. The Community's dynamism has been strengthened and this is precisely what makes it possible to take new decisive steps towards a stronger economic and social area, towards economic and monetary union.

The Commission obviously understands the problems that this or that Member State might have in accepting the full twofold package. But there are compromise solutions which, while meeting the sensibilities of certain Member States, will avoid the risk referred to above and guarantee the political credibility of the European venture. The Commission will do all it can to help the necessary consensus emerge and make the forthcoming European Council a complete success.

The Community has too many international responsibilities to allow itself the luxury of failing to clear the hurdle that so many convinced Europeans want it to clear.

TREATY ON EUROPEAN UNION
(THE TREATY OF MAASTRICHT)

TREATY
ON EUROPEAN UNION

HIS MAJESTY THE KING OF THE BELGIANS,

HER MAJESTY THE QUEEN OF DENMARK,

THE PRESIDENT OF THE FEDERAL REPUBLIC OF GERMANY,

THE PRESIDENT OF THE HELLENIC REPUBLIC,

HIS MAJESTY THE KING OF SPAIN,

THE PRESIDENT OF THE FRENCH REPUBLIC,

THE PRESIDENT OF IRELAND,

THE PRESIDENT OF THE ITALIAN REPUBLIC,

HIS ROYAL HIGHNESS THE GRAND DUKE OF LUXEMBOURG,

HER MAJESTY THE QUEEN OF THE NETHERLANDS,

THE PRESIDENT OF THE PORTUGUESE REPUBLIC,

HER MAJESTY THE QUEEN OF THE UNITED KINGDOM OF GREAT BRITAIN AND NORTHERN IRELAND,

RESOLVED to mark a new stage in the process of European integration undertaken with the establishment of the European Communities,

RECALLING the historic importance of the ending of the division of the European continent and the need to create firm bases for the construction of the future Europe,

CONFIRMING their attachment to the principles of liberty, democracy and respect for human rights and fundamental freedoms and of the rule of law,

DESIRING to deepen the solidarity between their peoples while respecting their history, their culture and their traditions,

DESIRING to enhance further the democratic and efficient functioning of the institutions so as to enable them better to carry out, within a single institutional framework, the tasks entrusted to them,

RESOLVED to achieve the strengthening and the convergence of their economies and to establish an economic and monetary union including, in accordance with the provisions of this Treaty, a single and stable currency,

DETERMINED to promote economic and social progress for their peoples, within the context of the accomplishment of the internal market and of reinforced cohesion and environmental protection, and to implement policies ensuring that advances in economic integration are accompanied by parallel progress in other fields,

RESOLVED to establish a citizenship common to the nationals of their countries,

RESOLVED to implement a common foreign and security policy including the eventual framing of a common defence policy, which might in time lead to a common defence, thereby reinforcing the European identity and its independence in order to promote peace, security and progress in Europe and in the world,

REAFFIRMING their objective to facilitate the free movement of persons while ensuring the safety and security of their peoples, by including provisions on justice and home affairs in this Treaty,

RESOLVED to continue the process of creating an ever closer union among the peoples of Europe, in which decisions are taken as closely as possible to the citizen in accordance with the principle of subsidiarity,

IN VIEW of further steps to be taken in order to advance European integration,

HAVE DECIDED to establish a European Union and to this end have designated as their plenipotentiaries:

HIS MAJESTY THE KING OF THE BELGIANS:

Mark EYSKENS,
Minister for Foreign Affairs;

Philippe MAYSTADT,
Minister for Finance;

HER MAJESTY THE QUEEN OF DENMARK:

Uffe ELLEMANN-JENSEN,
Minister for Foreign Affairs;

Anders FOGH RASMUSSEN,
Minister for Economic Affairs;

THE PRESIDENT OF THE FEDERAL REPUBLIC OF GERMANY:

Hans-Dietrich GENSCHER,
Federal Minister for Foreign Affairs;

Theodor WAIGEL,
Federal Minister for Finance;

THE PRESIDENT OF THE HELLENIC REPUBLIC:

Antonios SAMARAS,
Minister for Foreign Affairs;

Efthymios CHRISTODOULOU,
Minister for Economic Affairs;

HIS MAJESTY THE KING OF SPAIN:

Francisco FERNÁNDEZ ORDÓÑEZ,
Minister for Foreign Affairs;

Carlos SOLCHAGA CATALÁN,
Minister for Economic Affairs and Finance;

THE PRESIDENT OF THE FRENCH REPUBLIC:

Roland DUMAS,
Minister for Foreign Affairs;

Pierre BEREGOVOY,
Minister for Economic and Financial Affairs and the Budget;

THE PRESIDENT OF IRELAND:

Gerard COLLINS,
Minister for Foreign Affairs;

Bertie AHERN,
Minister for Finance;

THE PRESIDENT OF THE ITALIAN REPUBLIC:

Gianni DE MICHELIS,
Minister for Foreign Affairs;

Guido CARLI,
Minister for the Treasury;

HIS ROYAL HIGHNESS THE GRAND DUKE OF LUXEMBOURG:

Jacques F. POOS,
Deputy Prime Minister,
Minister for Foreign Affairs;

Jean-Claude JUNCKER,
Minister for Finance;

HER MAJESTY THE QUEEN OF THE NETHERLANDS:

Hans van den BROEK,
Minister for Foreign Affairs;

Willem KOK,
Minister for Finance;

THE PRESIDENT OF THE PORTUGUESE REPUBLIC:

João de Deus PINHEIRO,
Minister for Foreign Affairs;

Jorge BRAGA de MACEDO,
Minister for Finance;

HER MAJESTY THE QUEEN OF THE UNITED KINGDOM OF GREAT BRITAIN AND
NORTHERN IRELAND:

The Rt. Hon. Douglas HURD,
Secretary of State for Foreign and Commonwealth Affairs;

The Hon. Francis MAUDE,
Financial Secretary to the Treasury;

WHO, having exchanged their full powers, found in good and due form, have agreed as follows:

TITLE I
COMMON PROVISIONS

Article A

By this Treaty, the High Contracting Parties establish among themselves a European Union, hereinafter called "the Union".

This Treaty marks a new stage in the process of creating an ever closer union among the peoples of Europe, in which decisions are taken as closely as possible to the citizen. The Union shall be founded on the European Communities, supplemented by the policies and forms of cooperation established by this Treaty. Its task shall be to organize, in a manner demonstrating consistency and solidarity, relations between the Member States and between their peoples.

Article B

The Union shall set itself the following objectives:

– to promote economic and social progress which is balanced and sustainable, in particular through the creation of an area without internal frontiers, through the strengthening of economic and social cohesion and through the establishment of economic and monetary union, ultimately including a single currency in accordance with the provisions of this Treaty;

– to assert its identity on the international scene, in particular through the implementation of a common foreign and security policy including the eventual framing of a common defence policy, which might in time lead to a common defence;

- to strengthen the protection of the rights and interests of the nationals of its Member States through the introduction of a citizenship of the Union;

- to develop close cooperation on justice and home affairs;

- to maintain in full the *acquis communautaire* and build on it with a view to considering, through the procedure referred to in Article N(2), to what extent the policies and forms of cooperation introduced by this Treaty may need to be revised with the aim of ensuring the effectiveness of the mechanisms and the institutions of the Community.

The objectives of the Union shall be achieved as provided in this Treaty and in accordance with the conditions and the timetable set out therein while respecting the principle of subsidiarity as defined in Article 3b of the Treaty establishing the European Community.

Article C

The Union shall be served by a single institutional framework which shall ensure the consistency and the continuity of the activities carried out in order to attain its objectives while respecting and building upon the *acquis communautaire*.

The Union shall in particular ensure the consistency of its external activities as a whole in the context of its external relations, security, economic and development policies. The Council and the Commission shall be responsible for ensuring such consistency. They shall ensure the implementation of these policies, each in accordance with its respective powers.

Article D

The European Council shall provide the Union with the necessary impetus for its development and shall define the general political guidelines thereof.

The European Council shall bring together the Heads of State or of Government of the Member States and the President of the Commission. They shall be assisted by the Ministers for Foreign Affairs of the Member States and by a Member of the Commission. The European Council shall meet at least twice a year, under the chairmanship of the Head of State or of Government of the Member State which holds the Presidency of the Council.

The European Council shall submit to the European Parliament a report after each of its meetings and a yearly written report on the progress achieved by the Union.

Article E

The European Parliament, the Council, the Commission and the Court of Justice shall exercise their powers under the conditions and for the purposes provided for, on the one hand, by the provisions of the Treaties establishing the European Communities and of the subsequent Treaties and Acts modifying and supplementing them and, on the other hand, by the other provisions of this Treaty.

Article F

1. The Union shall respect the national identities of its Member States, whose systems of government are founded on the principles of democracy.   2. The Union shall respect fundamental rights, as guaranteed by the European Convention for the Protection of Human Rights and Fundamental Freedoms signed in Rome on 4 November 1950 and as they result from the constitutional traditions common to the Member States, as general principles of Community law.   3. The Union shall provide itself with the means necessary to attain its objectives and carry through its policies.

TITLE II
PROVISIONS AMENDING THE TREATY ESTABLISHING THE EUROPEAN ECONOMIC COMMUNITY WITH A VIEW TO ESTABLISHING THE EUROPEAN COMMUNITY

Article G

The Treaty establishing the European Economic Community shall be amended in accordance with the provisions of this Article, in order to establish a European Community.

A — Throughout the Treaty:

(1) The term "European Economic Community" shall be replaced by the term "European Community".

B — In Part One "Principles":

(2) Article 2 shall be replaced by the following:

"Article 2

The Community shall have as its task, by establishing a common market and an economic and monetary union and by implementing the common policies or activities referred to in Articles 3 and 3a, to promote throughout the Community a harmonious and balanced development of economic activities, sustainable and non-inflationary growth respecting the environment, a high degree of convergence of economic performance, a high level of employment and of social protection, the raising of the standard of living and quality of life, and economic and social cohesion and solidarity among Member States."

(3) Article 3 shall be replaced by the following:

"Article 3

For the purposes set out in Article 2, the activities of the Community shall include, as provided in this Treaty and in accordance with the timetable set out therein:

(a) the elimination, as between Member States, of customs duties and quantitative restrictions on the import and export of goods,

and of all other measures having equivalent effect;

(b) a common commercial policy;

(c) an internal market characterized by the abolition, as between Member States of obstacles to the free movement of goods, persons, services and capital;

(d) measures concerning the entry and movement of persons in the internal market as provided for in Article 100c;

(e) a common policy in the sphere of agriculture and fisheries;

(f) a common policy in the sphere of transport;

(g) a system ensuring that competition in the internal market is not distorted;

(h) the approximation of the laws of Member States to the extent required for the functioning of the common market;

(i) a policy in the social sphere comprising a European Social Fund;

(j) the strengthening of economic and social cohesion;

(k) a policy in the sphere of the environment;

(l) the strengthening of the competitiveness of Community industry;

(m) the promotion of research and technological development;

(n) encouragement for the establishment and development of trans-European networks;

(o) a contribution to the attainment of a high level of health protection;

(p) a contribution to education and training of quality and to the flowering of the cultures of the Member States;

(q) a policy in the sphere of development cooperation;

(r) the association of the overseas countries and territories in order to increase trade and promote jointly economic and social development;

(s) a contribution to the strengthening of consumer protection;

(t) measures in the spheres of energy, civil protection and tourism."

(4) The following Article shall be inserted:

"Article 3a

1. For the purposes set out in Article 2, the activities of the Member States and the Community shall include, as provided in this Treaty and in accordance with the timetable set out therein, the adoption of an economic policy which is based on the close coordination of Member States' economic policies, on the internal market and on the definition of common objectives, and conducted in accordance with the principle of an open market economy with free competition.

2. Concurrently with the foregoing, and as provided in this Treaty and in accordance with the timetable and the procedures set out therein, these activities shall include the irrevocable fixing of exchange rates leading to the introduction of a single currency, the ECU, and the definition and conduct of a single monetary policy and exchange rate policy the primary objective of both of which shall be to maintain price stability and, without prejudice to this objective, to support the general economic policies in the Community, in accordance with the principle of an open market economy with free competition.

3. These activities of the Member States and the Community shall entail compliance with the following guiding principles: stable prices, sound public finances and monetary conditions and a sustainable balance of payments."

(5) The following Article shall be inserted:

"Article 3b

The Community shall act within the limits of the powers conferred upon it by this Treaty and of the objectives assigned to it therein.

In areas which do not fall within its exclusive competence, the Community shall take action, in accordance with the principle of subsidiarity, only if and in so far as the objectives of the proposed action cannot be sufficiently achieved by the Member States and can therefore, by reason of the scale or effects of the proposed action, be better achieved by the Community.

Any action by the Community shall not go beyond what is necessary to achieve the objectives of this Treaty."

(6) Article 4 shall be replaced by the following:

"Article 4

1. The tasks entrusted to the Community shall be carried out by the following institutions:

– a EUROPEAN PARLIAMENT,

– a COUNCIL,

– a COMMISSION,

– a COURT OF JUSTICE,

– a COURT OF AUDITORS.

Each institution shall act within the limits of the powers conferred upon it by this Treaty.

2. The Council and the Commission shall be assisted by an Economic and Social Committee and a Committee of the Regions acting in an advisory capacity."

(7) The following Articles shall be inserted:

"Article 4a

A European System of Central Banks (hereinafter referred to as "ESCB") and a European Central Bank (hereinafter referred to as "ECB") shall be established in accordance with the procedures laid down in this Treaty; they shall act within the limits of the powers conferred upon them by this Treaty and by the Statute of the ESCB and of the ECB (hereinafter referred to as "Statute of the ESCB") annexed thereto.

"Article 4b

A European Investment Bank is hereby established, which shall act within the limit of the powers conferred upon it by this Treaty and the Statute annexed thereto."

(8) Article 6 shall be deleted and Article 7 shall become Article 6. Its second paragraph shall be replaced by the following:

"The Council, acting in accordance with the procedure referred to in Article 189c,

may adopt rules designed to prohibit such discrimination."

(9)   Articles 8, 8a, 8b and 8c shall become respectively Article 7, 7a, 7b and 7c.

C — The following Part shall be inserted:

"PART TWO

CITIZENSHIP OF THE UNION

Article 8

1.   Citizenship of the Union is hereby established.

Every person holding the nationality of a Member State shall be a citizen of the Union.

2.   Citizens of the Union shall enjoy the rights conferred by this Treaty and shall be subject to the duties imposed thereby.

Article 8a

1.   Every citizen of the Union shall have the right to move and reside freely within the territory of the Member States, subject to the limitations and conditions laid down in this Treaty and by the measures adopted to give it effect.

2.   The Council may adopt provisions with a view to facilitating the exercise of the rights referred to in paragraph 1; save as otherwise provided in this Treaty, the Council shall act unanimously on a proposal from the Commission after obtaining the assent of the European Parliament.

Article 8b

1.   Every citizen of the Union residing in a Member State of which he is not a national shall have the right to vote and to stand as a candidate at municipal elections in the Member State in which he resides, under the same conditions as nationals of that State. This right shall be exercised subject to detailed arrangements to be adopted before 31 December 1994 by the Council, acting unanimously, on a proposal from the Commission and after consulting the European Parliament; these arrangements may

provide for derogations where warranted by problems specific to a Member State.

2.   Without prejudice to Article 138(3) and to the provisions adopted for its implementation, every citizen of the Union residing in a Member State of which he is not a national shall have the right to vote and to stand as a candidate in elections to the European Parliament in the Member State in which he resides, under the same conditions as nationals of that State. This right shall be exercised subject to detailed arrangements to be adopted before 31 December 1993 by the Council, acting unanimously on a proposal from the Commission and after consulting the European Parliament; these arrangements may provide for derogations where warranted by problems specific to a Member State.

Article 8c

Every citizen of the Union shall, in the territory of a third country in which the Member State of which he is a national is not represented, be entitled to protection by the diplomatic or consular authorities of any Member State, on the same conditions as the nationals of that State. Before 31 December 1993, Member States shall establish the necessary rules among themselves and start the international negotiations required to secure this protection.

Article 8d

Every citizen of the Union shall have the right to petition the European Parliament in accordance with Article 138d.

Every citizen of the Union may apply to the Ombudsman established in accordance with Article 138e.

Article 8e

The Commission shall report to the European Parliament, to the Council and to the Economic and Social Committee before 31 December 1993 and then every three years on the application of the provisions of this Part. This report shall take account of the development of the Union.

On this basis, and without prejudice to the other provisions of this Treaty, the Council, acting unanimously on a proposal from the Commission and after consulting the European Parliament, may adopt provisions to strengthen or to add to the rights laid down in this Part, which it shall recommend to the Member States for adoption in accordance with their respective constitutional requirements."

D — Parts Two and Three shall be grouped under the following Title:

"PART THREE

COMMUNITY POLICIES"

and in this Part:

(10)　The first sentence of Article 49 shall be replaced by the following:

"As soon as this Treaty enters into force, the Council shall, acting in accordance with the procedure referred to in Article 189b and after consulting the Economic and Social Committee, issue directives or make regulations setting out the measures required to bring about, by progressive stages, freedom of movement for workers, as defined in Article 48, in particular."

(11)　Article 54(2) shall be replaced by the following:

"2. In order to implement this general programme or, in the absence of such programme, in order to achieve a stage in attaining freedom of establishment as regards a particular activity, the Council, acting in accordance with the Procedure referred to in Article 189b and after consulting the Economic and Social Committee, shall act by means of directives."

(12)　Article 56(2) shall be replaced by the following:

"2. Before the end of the transitional period, the Council shall, acting unanimously on a proposal from the Commission and after consulting the European Parliament, issue directives for the coordination of the above mentioned provisions laid down by law, regulation or administrative action. After the end of the second stage, however, the Council shall, acting in accordance with the procedure referred to in Article 189b, issue directives for the coordination of such provisions as, in each Member State, are a matter for regulation or administrative action."

(13)　Article 57 shall be replaced by the following:

"Article 57

1. In order to make it easier for persons to take up and pursue activities as self-employed persons, the Council shall, acting in accordance with the procedure referred to in Article 189b, issue directives for the mutual recognition of diplomas, certificates and other evidence of formal qualifications.

2. For the same purpose, the Council shall, before the end of the transitional period, issue directives for the coordination of the provisions laid down by law, regulation or administrative action in Member States concerning the taking up and pursuit of activities as self-employed persons. The Council, acting unanimously on a proposal from the Commission and after consulting the European Parliament, shall decide on directives the implementation of which involves in at least one Member State amendment of the existing principles laid down by law governing the professions with respect to training and conditions of access for natural persons. In other cases the Council shall act in accordance with the procedure referred to in Article 189b.

3. In the case of the medical and allied and pharmaceutical professions, the progressive abolition of restrictions shall be dependent upon coordination of the conditions for their exercise in the various Member States."

(14)　The title of Chapter 4 shall be replaced by the following:

"CHAPTER 4

Capital and payments"

(15)　The following Articles shall be inserted:

"Article 73a

As from 1 January 1994, Articles 67 to 73 shall be replaced by Articles 73b, c, d, e, f and g.

Article 73b

1. Within the framework of the provisions set out in this Chapter, all restrictions on the movement of capital between Member States and between Member States and third countries shall be prohibited.

2. Within the framework of the provisions set out in this Chapter, all restrictions on payments between Member States and between Member States and third countries shall be prohibited.

Article 73c

1. The provisions of Article 73b shall be without prejudice to the application to third countries, of any restrictions which exist on 31 December 1993 under national or Community law adopted in respect of the movement of capital to or from third countries involving direct investment — including investment in real estate — establishment, the provision of financial services or the admission of securities to capital markets.

2. Whilst endeavouring to achieve the objective of free movement of capital between Member States and third countries to the greatest extent possible and without prejudice to the other Chapters of this Treaty, the Council may, acting by a qualified majority on a proposal from the Commission, adopt measures on the movement of capital to or from third countries involving direct investment — including investment in real estate — establishment, the provision of financial services or the admission of securities to capital markets. Unanimity shall be required for measures under this paragraph which constitute a step back in Community law as regards the liberalization of the movement of capital to or from third countries.

Article 73d

1. The provisions of Article 73b shall be without prejudice to the right of Member States:

(a) to apply the relevant provision of their tax law which distinguish between tax-payers who are not in the same situation with regard to their place of residence or with regard to the place where their capital is invested;

(b) to take all requisite measures to prevent infringements of national law and regulations, in particular in the field taxation and the prudential supervision of financial institutions, or to lay down procedures for the declaration of capital movements for purposes of administrative or statistical information, or to take measures which are justified on grounds of public policy or public security.

2. The provisions of this Chapter shall be without prejudice to the applicability of restrictions on the right of establishment which are compatible with this Treaty.

3. The measures and procedures referred to in paragraphs 1 and 2 shall not constitute a means of arbitrary discrimination or a disguised restriction on the free movement of capital and payments as defined in Article 73b.

Article 73e

By way of derogation from Article 73b, Member States which, on 31 December 1993, enjoy a derogation on the basis of existing Community law, shall be entitled to maintain, until 31 December 1995 at the latest, restrictions on movements of capital authorized by such derogations as exist on that date.

Article 73f

Where, in exceptional circumstances, movements of capital to or from third countries cause, or threaten to cause, serious difficulties for the operation of economic and monetary union, the Council, acting by a qualified majority on a proposal from the Commission and after consulting the ECB, may take safeguard measures with regard to third countries for a period not exceeding six months if such measures are strictly necessary.

Article 73g

1. If, in the cases envisaged in Article 228a, action by the Community is deemed necessary, the Council may, in accordance with the procedure provided for in Article 228a, take the necessary urgent measures on the movement of capital and on payments as regards the third countries concerned.

2. Without prejudice to Article 224 and as long as the Council has not taken measures pursuant to paragraph 1, a Member State may, for serious political reasons and on grounds of urgency, take unilateral measures against a third country with regard to capital movements and payments. The Commission and the other Member States shall be informed of such measures by the date of their entry into force at the latest.

The Council may, acting by a qualified majority on a proposal from the Commission, decide that the Member State concerned shall amend or abolish such measures. The President of the Council shall inform the European Parliament of any such decision taken by the Council.

Article 73h

Until 1 January 1994, the following provisions shall be applicable:

(1) *Each Member State undertakes to authorize, in the currency of the Member State in which the creditor or the beneficiary resides, any payment connected with the movement of goods, services or capital, and any transfers of capital and earnings, to the extent that the movement of goods, services, capital and persons between Member States has been liberalized pursuant to this Treaty.*

The Member States declare their readiness to undertake the liberalization of payments beyond the extent provided in the preceding subparagraph, in so far as their economic situation in general and the state of their balance of payment in particular so permit.

(2) *In so far as movement of goods, services and capital are limited only by restrictions on payments connected therewith, these restrictions shall be progressively abolished by applying, mutatis mutandis, the provisions of this Chapter and the Chapters relating to the abolition of qualitative restrictions and to the liberalization of services.*

(3) *Member States undertake not to introduce between themselves any new restrictions on transfers connected with the invisible transactions listed in Annex III to this Treaty.*

The progressive abolition of existing restrictions shall be effected in accordance with the provisions of Articles 63 to 65, in so far as such abolition is not governed by the provisions contained in paragraphs 1 and 2 or by the other provisions of this Chapter.

(4) *If need be, Member States shall consult each other on the measures to be taken to enable the payment and transfers mentioned in this Article to be effected; such measures shall not prejudice the attainment of the objectives set out in this Treaty."*

(16) Article 75 shall be replaced by the following:

"Article 75

1. For the purpose of implementing Article 74, and taking into account the distinctive features of transport, the Council shall, acting in accordance with the procedure referred to in Article

189c and after consulting the Economic and Social Committee, lay down:

(a) *common rules applicable to international transport to or from the territory of a Member State or passing across the territory of one or more Member States;*

(b) *the conditions under which non-resident carriers may operate transport services within a Member State;*

(c) *measures to improve transport safety;*

(d) *any other appropriate provisions.*

2. The Provisions referred to in (a) and (b) of paragraph 1 shall be laid down during the transitional period.

3. By way of derogation from the procedure provided for in paragraph 1, where the application of provisions concerning the principles of the regulatory system for transport would be liable to have a serious effect on the standard of living and on employment in certain areas and on the operation of transport facilities, they shall be laid down by the Council acting unanimously on a proposal from the Commission, after consulting the European Parliament and the Economic and Social Committee. In so doing, the Council shall take into account the need for adaptation to the economic development which will result from establishing the common market."

(17) The title of Title I in Part Three shall be replaced by the following:

"TITLE V

COMMON RULES ON COMPETITION, TAXATION AND APPROXIMATION OF LAWS"

(18) In Article 92(3):

– the following point shall be inserted:

"(d) aid to promote culture and heritage conservation where such aid does not affect trading conditions and competition in the Community to an extent that is contrary to the common interest."

– the present point (d) shall become (e).

(19) Article 94 shall be replaced by the following:

"Article 94

The Council, acting by a qualified majority on a proposal from the Commission and after consulting the European Parliament, may make any appropriate regulations for the application of Articles 92 and 93 and may in particular determine the conditions in which Article 93(3) shall apply and the categories of aid exempted from this procedure."

(20) Article 99 shall be replaced by the following:

"Article 99

The Council shall, acting unanimously on a proposal from the Commission and after consulting the European Parliament and the Economic and Social Committee, adopt provisions for the harmonization of legislation concerning turnover taxes, excise duties and other forms of indirect taxation to the extent that such harmonization is necessary to ensure the establishment and the functioning of the internal market within the time limit laid down in Article 7a."

(21) Article 100 shall be replaced by the following:

"Article 100

The Council shall, acting unanimously on a proposal from the Commission and after consulting the European Parliament and the Economic and Social Committee, issue directives for the approximation of such laws, regulations or administrative provisions of the Member States as directly affects the establishment or functioning of the common market."

(22) Article 100a(1) shall be replaced by the following:

*"1. By way of derogation from Article 100 and save where otherwise provided in this Treaty, the following provisions shall apply for the achievement of the objectives set out in Article 7a. The Council shall, acting in accordance with the procedure referred to in Article 189b and after consulting the Economic and Social Committee, adopt the measures for the approximation of the provisions laid down by law, regulation or administrative action in Member States which have as their object the establishment and functioning of the internal market."

(23) The following Article shall be inserted:

"Article 100c

1. The Council, acting unanimously on a proposal from the Commission and after consulting the European Parliament, shall determine the third countries whose nationals must be in possession of a visa when crossing the external borders of the Member States.

2. However, in the event of an emergency situation in a third country posing a threat of a sudden inflow of nationals from that country into the Community, the Council, acting by a qualified majority on a recommendation from the Commission, may introduce, for a period not exceeding six months, a visa requirement for nationals from the country in question. The visa requirement established under this paragraph may be extended in accordance with the procedure referred to in paragraph 1.

3. From 1 January 1996, the Council shall adopt the decisions referred to in paragraph 1 by a qualified majority. The Council shall, before that date, acting by a qualified majority on a proposal from the Commission and after consulting the European Parliament, adopt measures relating to a uniform format for visas.

4. In the areas referred to in this Article, the Commission shall examine any request made by a Member State that it submit a proposal to the Council.

5. This Article shall be without prejudice to the exercise of the responsibilities incumbent upon the Member States with regard to the maintenance of law and order and the safeguarding of internal security.

6. This Article shall apply to other areas if so decided pursuant to Article K.9 of the provisions of the Treaty on European Union which relate to cooperation in the fields of justice and home affairs, subject to the voting conditions determined at the same time.

7. The provisions of the conventions in force between the Member States governing areas covered by this Article shall remain in force until their content has been replaced by directives or measures adopted pursuant to this Article."

(24) The following Article shall be inserted:

"Article 100d

The Coordinating Committee consisting of senior officials set up by Article K.4 of the Treaty on European Union shall contribute, without prejudice to the provisions of Article 151, to the preparation of the proceedings of the Council in the fields referred to in Article l00c."

(25)   Title II, Chapters 1, 2 and 3 in Part Three shall be replaced by the following:

"TITLE VI

ECONOMIC AND MONETARY POLICY

CHAPTER 1

Economic Policy

Article 102a

Member States shall conduct their economic policies with a view to contributing to the achievement of the objectives of the Community, as defined in Article 2, and in the context of the broad guidelines referred to in Article 103(2). The Member States and the Community shall act in accordance with the principle of an open market economy with free competition, favouring an efficient allocation of resources, and in compliance with the principle set out in Article 3a.

Article 103

1.   Member States shall regard their economic policies as a matter of common concern and shall coordinate them within the Council, in accordance with the provisions of Article 102a.

2.   The Council shall, acting by a qualified majority on a recommendation from the Commission, formulate a draft for the broad guidelines of the economic policies of the Member States and of the Community, and shall report its findings to the European Council.

The European Council shall, acting on the basis of the report from the Council, discuss a conclusion on the broad guidelines of the economic policies of the Member States and of the Community.

On the basis of this conclusion, the Council shall, acting by a qualified majority, adopt a recommendation setting out these broad guidelines. The Council shall inform the European Parliament of its recommendation.

3.   In order to ensure closer coordination of economic policies and sustained convergence of the economic performances of the Member States, the Council shall, on the basis of reports submitted by the Commission, monitor economic development in each of the Member States and in the Community as well as the consistency of economic policies with the broad guidelines referred to in paragraph 2, and regularly carry out an overall assessment.

For the purpose of this multilateral surveillance, Member States shall forward information to the Commission about important measures taken by them in the field of their economic policy and other information as they deem necessary.

4.   Where it is established, under the procedure referred in paragraph 3, that the economic policies of a Member State are not consistent with the broad guidelines referred to in paragraph 2 or that they risk jeopardizing the proper functioning of economic and monetary union, the Council may, acting by a qualified majority on a recommendation from the Commission, make the necessary recommendations to the Member State concerned. The Council may, acting by a qualified majority on a proposal from the Commission, decide to make its recommendations public.

The President of the Council and the Commission shall report to the European Parliament on the result of multilateral surveillance. The President of the Council may be invited to appear before the competent Committee of the European Parliament if the Council has made its recommendations public.

5.   The Council, acting in accordance with the procedure referred to in Article 189c, may adopt detailed rules for the multilateral surveillance procedure referred to in paragraphs 3 and 4 of this Article.

Article 103a

1.   Without prejudice to any other procedures provided for in this Treaty, the Council may, acting unanimously on a proposal from the Commission, decide upon the measures appropriate to the economic situation, in particular if severe difficulties arise in the supply of certain products.

2.   Where a Member State is in difficulties or is seriously threatened with severe difficulties caused by exceptional occurrences beyond its control, the Council may, acting unanimously on a proposal from the Commission, grant,

under certain conditions, Community financial assistance to the Member State concerned. Where the severe difficulties are caused by natural disasters, the Council shall act by qualified majority. The President of the Council shall inform the European Parliament of the decision taken.

Article 104

1. Overdraft facilities or any other type of credit facility with the ECB or with the central banks of the Member States (hereinafter referred to as "national central banks") in favour of Community institutions or bodies, central governments, regional, local or other public authorities, other bodies governed by public law, or public undertakings of Member States shall be prohibited, as shall the purchase directly from them by the ECB or national central banks of debt instruments.

2. Paragraph 1 shall not apply to publicly-owned credit institutions which, in the context of the supply of reserves by central banks, shall be given the same treatment by national central banks and the ECB as private credit institutions.

Article 104a

1. Any measure, not based on prudential considerations, establishing privileged access by Community institutions or bodies, central governments, regional, local or other public authorities, other bodies governed by public law, or public undertakings of Member States to financial institutions shall be prohibited.

2. The Council, acting in accordance with the procedure referred to in Article 189c, shall, before 1 January 1994, specify definitions for the application of the prohibition referred to in paragraph 1.

Article 104b

1. The Community shall not be liable for or assume the commitments of central governments, regional, local or other public authorities, other bodies governed by public law, or public undertakings of any Member State, without prejudice to mutual financial guarantees for the joint execution of a specific project. A Member State shall not be liable for or assume the commitments of central governments, regional, local or other public authorities, other bodies governed by public law or public undertakings

of another Member State, without prejudice to mutual financial guarantees for the joint execution of a specific project.

2. If necessary, the Council, acting in accordance with the procedure referred to in Article 189c, may specify definitions for the application of the prohibitions referred to in Article 104 and in this Article.

Article 104c

1. Member States shall avoid excessive governmental deficits.

2. The Commission shall monitor the development of the budgetary situation and of the stock of government debt in the Member States with a view to identifying gross errors. In particular it shall examine compliance with budgetary discipline on the basis of the following two criteria:

(a) whether the ratio of the planned or actual government deficit to gross domestic product exceeds a reference value, unless

  – either the ratio has declined substantially and continuously and reached a level that comes close to the reference value;

  – or, alternatively, the excess over the reference value is only exceptional and temporary and the ratio remains close to the reference value;

(b) whether the ratio of government debt to gross domestic product exceeds a reference value, unless the ratio is sufficiently diminishing and approaching the reference value at a satisfactory pace.

The reference values are specified in the Protocol on the excessive deficit procedure annexed to this Treaty.

3. If a Member State does not fulfil the requirements under one or both of these criteria, the Commission shall prepare a report. The report of the Commission shall also take into account whether the government deficit exceeds government investment expenditure and take into account all other relevant factors, including the medium term economic and budgetary position of the Member State.

The Commission may also prepare a report if, notwithstanding the fulfilment of the requirement under the criteria, it is of the opinion that there is a risk of an excessive deficit in a Member State.

4.   *The Committee provided for in Article 109c shall formulate an opinion on the report of the Commission.*

5.   *If the Commission considers that an excessive deficit in a Member State exists or may occur, the Commission shall address an opinion to the Council.*

6.   *The Council shall, acting by a qualified majority on a recommendation from the Commission, and having considered any observations which the Member State concerned may wish to make, decide after an overall assessment whether an excessive deficit exists.*

7.   *Where the existence of an excessive deficit is decided according to paragraph 6, the Council shall make recommendations to the Member State concerned with a view to bringing that situation to an end within a given period. Subject to the provisions of paragraph 8, these recommendations shall not be made public.*

8.   *Where it establishes that there has been no effective action in response to its recommendations within the period laid down, the Council may make its recommendations public.*

9.   *If a Member State persists in failing to put into practice the recommendations of the Council, the Council may decide to give notice to the Member State to take, within a specified time limit, measures for the deficit reduction which is judged necessary by the Council in order to remedy the situation.*

In such a case, the Council may request the Member State concerned to submit reports in accordance with a specific timetable in order to examine the adjustment efforts of that Member State.

10.   *The right to bring actions provided for in Articles 169 and 170 may not be exercised within the framework of paragraphs 1 to 9 of this Article.*

11.   *As long as a Member State fails to comply with a decision taken in accordance with paragraph 9, the Council may decide to apply the following measures:*

– *to require the Member State concerned to publish additional information, to be specified by the Council, before issuing bonds and securities;*

– *to invite the European Investment Bank to reconsider its lending policy towards the Member State concerned;*

– *to require the Member State concerned to make a non-interest-bearing deposit of an appropriate size with the Community until the excessive deficit has, in the view of the Council, been corrected;*

– *to impose fines of an appropriate size.*

The President of the Council shall inform the European Parliament of the decisions taken.

12.   *The Council shall abrogate some or all of its decisions referred to in paragraphs 6 to 9 and 11 to the extent that the excessive deficit in the Member State concerned has, in the view of the Council, been corrected. If the Council has previously made public recommendations, it shall, as soon as the decision under paragraph 8 has been abrogated, make a public statement that an excessive deficit in the Member State concerned no longer exists.*

13.   *When taking the decisions referred to in paragraphs 7 to 9, 11 and 12, the Council shall act on a recommendation from the Commission by a majority of two thirds of the votes of its members weighted in accordance with Article 148(2), excluding the votes of the representative of the Member State concerned.*

14.   *Further provisions relating to the implementation of the procedure described in this Article are set out in the Protocol on the excessive deficit procedure annexed to this Treaty.*

The Council shall, acting unanimously on a proposal from the Commission and after consulting the European Parliament and the ECB, adopt the appropriate provisions which shall then replace the said Protocol.

Subject to the other provisions of this paragraph the Council shall, before 1 January 1994, acting by a qualified majority on a proposal from the Commission and after consulting the European Parliament, lay down detailed rules and definitions for the application of the provisions of the said Protocol.

CHAPTER 2

Monetary policy

Article 105

1.   *The primary objective of the ESCB shall be to maintain price stability. Without prejudice to the objective of price stabilty, the ESCB shall*

support the general economic policies in the Community with a view to contributing to the achievement of the objectives of the Community as laid down in Article 2. The ESCB shall act in accordance with the principle of an open market economy with free competition, favouring an efficient allocation of resources, and in compliance with the principles set out in Article 3a.

2.   The basic tasks to be carried out through the ESCB shall be:

−   to define and implement the monetary policy of the Community;

−   to conduct foreign-exchange operations consistent with the provisions of Article 109;

−   to hold and manage the official foreign reserves of the Member States;

−   to promote the smooth operation of payment systems.

3.   The third indent of paragraph 2 shall be without prejudice to the holding and management by the governments of Member States of foreign-exchange working balances.

4.   The ECB shall be consulted:

−   on any proposed Community act in its fields of competence;

−   by national authorities regarding any draft legislative provision in its fields of competence, but within the limits and under the conditions set out by the Council in accordance with the procedure laid down in Article 106(6).

The ECB may submit opinions to the appropriate Community institutions or bodies or to national authorities on matters in its fields of competence.

5.   The ESCB shall contribute to the smooth conduct of policies pursued by the competent authorities relating to the prudential supervision of credit institutions and the stability of the financial system.

6.   The Council may, acting unanimously on a proposal from the Commission and after consulting the ECB and after receiving the assent of the European Parliament, confer upon the ECB specific tasks concerning policies relating to the prudential supervision of credit institutions and other financial institutions with the exception of insurance undertakings.

Article 105a

1.   The ECB shall have the exclusive right to authorize the issue of banknotes within the Community. The ECB and the national central banks may issue such notes. The banknotes issued by the ECB and the national central banks shall be the only such notes to have the status of legal tender within the Community.

2.   The Member States may issue coins subject to approval by the ECB of the volume of the issue. The Council may, acting in accordance with the procedure referred to in Article 189c and after consulting the ECB, adopt measures to harmonize the denominations and technical specifications of all coins intended for circulation to the extent necessary to permit their smooth circulation within the Community.

Article 106

1.   The ESCB shall be composed of the ECB and of the national central banks.

2.   The ECB shall have legal personality.

3.   The ESCB shall be governed by the decision-making bodies of the ECB which shall be the Governing Council and the Executive Board.

4.   The Statute of the ESCB is laid down in a Protocol annexed to this Treaty.

5.   Articles 5.1, 5.2, 5.3, 17, 18, 19.1, 22, 23, 24, 26, 32.2, 32.3., 32.4, 32.6, 33.1(a) and 36 of the Statute of the ESCB may be amended by the Council, acting either by a qualified majority on a recommendation from the ECB and after consulting the Commission or unanimously on a proposal from the Commission and after consulting the ECB. In either case, the assent of the European Parliament shall be required.

6.   The Council, acting by a qualified majority either on a proposal from the Commission and after consulting the European Parliament and the ECB or on a recommendation from the ECB and after consulting the European Parliament and the Commission, shall adopt the provisions referred to in Articles 4, 5.4, 19.2, 20, 28.1, 29.2, 30.4 and 34.3 of the Statute of the ESCB.

Article 107

When exercising the powers and carrying out the tasks and duties conferred upon them by this Treaty and the Statute of the ESCB, neither the ECB, nor a national central bank, nor any member of their decision-making bodies shall seek or take instructions from Community institutions or bodies, from any government of a Member State or from any other body. The Community institutions and bodies and the governments of the Member States undertake to respect this principle and not to seek to influence the members of the decision-making bodies of the ECB or of the national central banks in the performance of their tasks.

Article 108

Each Member State shall ensure, at the latest at the date of the establishment of the ESCB, that its national legislation including the statutes of its national central bank is compatible with this Treaty and the Statute of the ESCB.

Article 108a

1. In order to carry out the tasks entrusted to the ESCB, the ECB shall, in accordance with the provisions of this Treaty and under the conditions laid down in the Statute of the ESCB:

– make regulations to the extent necessary to implement the tasks defined in Article 3.1, first indent, Articles 19.1, 22 and 25.2 of the Statute of the ESCB and in cases which shall be laid down in the acts of the Council referred to in Article 106(6);

– take decisions necessary for carrying out the tasks entrusted to the ESCB under this Treaty and the Statute of the ESCB;

– make recommendations and deliver opinions.

2. A regulation shall have general application. It shall be binding in its entirety and directly applicable in all Member States.

Recommendations and opinions shall have no binding force.

A decision shall be binding in its entirety upon those to whom it is addressed.

Articles 190 to 192 shall apply to regulations and decisions adopted by the ECB.

The ECB may decide to publish its decisions, recommendations and opinions.

3. Within the limits and under the conditions adopted by the Council under the procedure laid down in Article 106(6), the ECB shall be entitled to impose fines or periodic penalty payments on undertakings for failure to comply with obligations under its regulations and decisions.

Article 109

1. By way of derogation from Article 228, the Council may, acting unanimously on a recommendation from the ECB or from the Commission, and after consulting the ECB in an endeavour to reach a consensus consistent with the objective of price stability, after consulting the European Parliament, in accordance with the procedure in paragraph 3 for determining the arrangements, conclude formal agreements on an exchange-rate system for the ECU in relation to non-Community currencies. The Council may, acting by a qualified majority on a recommendation from the ECB or from the Commission, and after consulting the ECB in an endeavour to reach a consensus consistent with the objective of price stability, adopt, adjust or abandon the central rates of the ECU within the exchange-rate system. The President of the Council shall inform the European Parliament of the adoption, adjustment or abandonment of the ECU central rates.

2. In the absence of an exchange rate system in relation to one or more non-Community currencies as referred to in paragraph 1, the Council, acting by a qualified majority either on a recommendation from the Commission and after consulting the ECB or on a recommendation from the ECB, may formulate general orientations for exchange-rate policy in relation to these currencies. These general orientations shall be without prejudice to the primary objective of the ESCB to maintain price stability.

3. By way of derogation from Article 228, where agreements concerning monetary or foreign exchange regime matters need to be negotiated by the Community with one or more States or international organizations, the Council, acting by a qualified majority on a recommendation from the Commission and after consulting the ECB, shall decide the arrangements for the negotiation and for the conclusion of such agreements. These arrangements shall ensure that the Community expresses a single position. The Commission shall be fully associated with the negotiations.

Agreements concluded in accordance with this paragraph shall be binding on the institutions of the Community, on the ECB and on Member States.

4.   *Subject to paragraph 1, the Council shall, on a proposal from the Commission and after consulting the ECB, acting by a qualified majority decide on the position of the Community at international level as regards issues of particular relevance to economic and monetary union and, acting unanimously, decide its representation in compliance with the allocation of powers laid down in Articles 103 and 105.*

5.   *Without prejudice to Community competence and Community agreements as regards economic and monetary union, Member States may negotiate in international bodies and conclude international agreements.*

CHAPTER 3

Institutional provisions

Article 109a

1.   *The Governing Council of the ECB shall comprise the members of the Executive Board of the ECB and the Governors of the national central banks.*

2   (a) *The Executive Board shall comprise the President, the Vice-President and four other members.*

(b) *The President, the Vice-President and the other members of the Executive Board shall be appointed from among the persons of recognized standing and professional experience in monetary or banking matters by common accord of the Governments of the Member States at the level of Heads of State or of Government, on a recommendation from the Council, after it has consulted the European Parliament and the Governing Council of the ECB.*

Their term of office shall be eight years and shall not be renewable.

Only nationals of Member States may be members of the Executive Board.

Article 109b

1.   *The President of the Council and a member of the Commission may participate, without having the right to vote, in meetings of the Governing Council of the ECB.*

The President of the Council may submit a motion for deliberation to the Governing Council of the ECB.

2.   *The President of the ECB shall be invited to participate in Council meetings when the Council is discussing matters relating to the objectives and tasks of the ESCB.*

3.   *The ECB shall address an annual report on the activities of the ESCB and on the monetary policy of both the previous and current year to the European Parliament, the Council and the Commission, and also to the European Council. The President of the ECB shall present this report to the Council and to the European Parliament, which may hold a general debate on that basis.*

The President of the ECB and the other members of the Executive Board may, at the request of the European Parliament or on their own initiative, be heard by the competent Committees of the European Parliament.

Article 109c

1.   *In order to promote coordination of the policies of Member States to the full extent needed for the functioning of the internal market, a Monetary Committee with advisory status is hereby set up.*

It shall have the following tasks:

–   *to keep under review the monetary and financial situation of the Member States and of the Community and the general payments system of the Member States and to report regularly thereon to the Council and to the Commission;*

–   *to deliver opinions at the request of the Council or of the Commission, or on its own initiative for submission to those institutions;*

–   *without prejudice to Article 151, to contribute to the preparation of the work of the Council referred to in Articles 73f, 73g, 103(2), (3), (4) and (5), 103a, 104a, 104b, 104c, 109e(2), 109f(6), 109h, 109i, 109j(2) and 109k(1);*

–   *to examine, at least once a year, the situation regarding the movement of capital and the freedom of payments, as they result from the application of this Treaty and of measures adopted by the Council; the examination shall cover all measures relat-*

ing to capital movements and payments; the Committee shall report to the Commission and to the Council on the outcome of this examination.

The Member States and the Commission shall each appoint two members of the Monetary Committee.

2. At the start of the third stage, an Economic and Financial Committee shall be set up. The Monetary Committee provided for in paragraph 1 shall be dissolved.

The Economic and Financial Committee shall have the following tasks:

— to deliver opinions at the request of the Council or of the Commission, or on its own initiative for submission to those institutions;

— to keep under review the economic and financial situation of the Member States and of the Community and to report regularly thereon to the Council and to the Commission, in particular on financial relations with third countries and international institutions;

— without prejudice to Article 151, to contribute to the preparation of the work of the Council referred to in Article 73f, 73g, 103(2), (3),(4) and (5), 103a, 104a, 104b, 104c, 105(6), 105a(2), 106(5) and (6), 109, 109h, 109i(2) and (3), 109k(2), 109l(4) and (5), and to carry out other advisory and preparatory tasks assigned to it by the Council;

— to examine, at least once a year, the situation regarding the movement of capital and the freedom of payments, as they result from the application of this Treaty and of measures adopted by the Council; the examination shall cover all measures relating to capital movements and payments; the Committee shall report to the Commission and to the Council on the outcome of this examination.

The Member States, the Commission and the ECB shall each appoint no more than two members of the Committee.

3. The Council shall, acting by qualified majority on a proposal from the Commission and after consulting the ECB and the Committee referred to in the Article, lay down detailed provisions concerning the composition of the Economic and Financial Committee. The President of the

Council shall inform the European Parliament of such a decision.

4. In addition to the tasks set in paragraph 2, if and as long as there are Member States with a derogation as referred to in Articles 109k and 109l, the Committee shall keep under review the monetary and financial situation and the general payments system of those Member States and report regularly thereon to the Council and to the Commission.

Article 109d

For matters within the scope of Articles 103(4), 104c with the exception of paragraphs 14, 109, 109j, 109k and 109l(4) and (5), the Council or a Member State may request the Commission to make a recommendation or a proposal, as appropriate. The Commission shall examine this request and submit its conclusions to the Council without delay.

CHAPTER 4

Transitional provisions

Article 109e

1. The second stage for achieving economic and monetary union shall begin on 1 January 1994.

2. Before that date

(a) each Member State shall:

— adopt, where necessary, appropriate measures to comply with the prohibitions laid down in article 73b, without prejudice to Article 73e, and in Articles 104 and 104a(1);

— adopt, if necessary, with a view to permitting the assessment provided for in subparagraph (b), multiannual programmes intended to ensure the lasting convergence necessary for the achievement of economic and monetary union, in particular with regard to price stability and sound public finances;

(b) the Council shall, on the basis of a report from the Commission, assess the progress made with regard to economic and monetary convergence, in particular with regard to price stability and sound public finances, and the progress made with the implemen-

tation of Community law concerning the internal market.

3.   The provision of Articles 104, 104a(1), 104b(1), and 104c with the exception of paragraphs 1,9,11 and 14 shall apply from the beginning of the second stage.

The provision of Articles 103a(2), 104c(1), (9) and (11), 105, 105a, 107, 109, 109a, 109b and 109c(2) and (4) shall apply from the beginning of the third stage.

4.   In the second stage, Member States shall endeavour to avoid excessive government deficits.

5.   During the second stage, each Member State shall, as appropriate, start the process leading to the independence of its central bank, in accordance with Article 108.

Article 109f

1.   At the start of the second stage, a European Monetary Institute (hereinafter referred to as "EMI") shall be established and take up its duties; it shall have legal personality and be directed and managed by a Council, consisting of a President and the Governors of the national central banks, one of whom shall be Vice-President.

The President shall be appointed by common accord of the Governments of the Member States at the level of Heads of State or of Government, on a recommendation from, as the case may be, the Committee of Governors of the central banks of the Member States (hereinafter referred to as "Committee of Governors") or the Council of the EMI, and after consulting the European Parliament and the Council. The President shall be selected from among persons of recognized standing and professional experience in monetary or banking matters. Only nationals of Member States may be President of the EMI. The Council of the EMI shall appoint the Vice-President.

The Statute of the EMI is laid down in a Protocol annexed to this Treaty.

The Committee of Governors shall be dissolved at the start of the second stage.

2.   The EMI shall:

- *strengthen cooperation between the national central banks;*

- *strengthen the coordination of monetary*

policies of the Member States, with the aim of ensuring price stability;

- *monitor the functioning of the European Monetary System;*

- *hold consultations concerning issues falling within the competence of the national central banks and affecting the stability of financial institutions and markets;*

- *take over the tasks of the European Monetary Cooperation Fund, which shall be dissolved; the modalities of dissolution are laid down in the Statute of the EMI;*

- *facilitate the use of the ECU and oversee its development, including the smooth functioning of the ECU clearing system.*

3.   For the preparation of the third stage, the EMI shall:

- *prepare the instruments and procedures necessary for carrying out a single monetary policy in the third stage;*

- *promote the harmonization, where necessary, of rules and practices governing the collection, compilation and distribution of statistics in the areas within its field of competence;*

- *prepare the rules for operations to be undertaken by the national central banks within the framework of the ESCB;*

- *promote the efficiency of cross-border payments;*

- *supervise the technical preparation of ECU banknotes.*

At the latest by 31 December 1996, the EMI shall specify the regulatory, organizational and logistical framework necessary for the ESCB to perform its tasks in the third stage. This framework shall be submitted for decision to the ECB at the date of its establishment.

4.   The EMI, acting by a majority of two thirds of the members of its Council, may:

- *formulate opinions or recommendations on the overall orientation of monetary policy and exchange rate policy as well as on related measures introduced in each Member State;*

- *submit opinions or recommendations to Governments and to the Council on policies which might affect the internal or external monetary situation in the Community and,* in particular, the functioning of the European Monetary System;

– make recommendations to the monetary authorities of the Member States concerning the conduct of their monetary policy.

5.   The EMI, acting unanimously, may decided to publish its opinions and its recommendations.

6.   The EMI shall be consulted by the Council regarding any proposed Community act within its field of competence.

Within the limits and under the conditions set out by the Council, acting by a qualified majority on a proposal from the Commission and after consulting the European Parliament and the EMI, the EMI shall be consulted by the authorities of the Member States on any draft legislative provision within its field of competence.

7.   The Council may, acting unanimously on a proposal from the Commission and after consulting the European Parliament and the EMI, confer upon the EMI other tasks for the preparation of the third stage.

8.   Where this Treaty provides for a consultative role for the ECB, reference to the ECB shall be read as referring to the EMI before the establishment of the ECB.

Where this Treaty provides for a consultative role for the EMI, references to the EMI shall be read, before 1 January 1994, as referring to the Committee of Governors.

9.   During the second stage, the term "ECB" used in Articles 173, 175, 176, 177, 180 and 215 shall be read as referring to the EMI.

Article 109g

The currency composition of the ECU basket shall not be changed.

From the start of the third stage, the value of the ECU shall be irrevocably fixed in accordance with Article 109l(4).

Article 109h

1.   Where a Member State is in difficulties or is seriously threatened with difficulties as regards its balance of payments either as a result of an overall disequilibrium in its balance of payments, or as a result of the type of currency at its disposal, and where such difficulties are liable in particular to jeopardize the functioning of the common market or the progressive implementation of the common commercial policy, the Commission shall immediately investigate the position of the State in question and the action which, making use of all means at its disposal, that State has taken or may take in accordance with the provisions of this Treaty. The Commission shall state what measures it recommends the State concerned to take.

If the action taken by a Member State and the measures suggested by the Commission do not prove sufficient to overcome the difficulties which have arisen or which threaten, the Commission shall, after consulting the Committee referred to in Article 109c, recommend to the Council the granting of mutual assistance and appropriate methods therefor.

The Commission shall keep the Council regularly informed of the situation and of how it is developing.

2.   The Council, acting by a qualified majority, shall grant such mutual assistance; it shall adopt directives or decisions laying down the conditions and details of such assistance, which may take such forms as:

(a) a concerted approach to or within any other international organizations to which Member States may have recourse;

(b) measures needed to avoid deflection of trade where the State which is in difficulties maintains or reintroduces quantitative restrictions against third countries;

(c) the granting of limited credits by other Member States, subject to their agreement.

3.   If the mutual assistance recommended by the Commission is not granted by the Council or if the mutual assistance granted and the measures taken are insufficient, the Commission shall authorize the State which is in difficulties to take protective measures, the conditions and details of which the Commission shall determine.

Such authorization may be revoked and such conditions and details may be changed by the Council acting by a qualified majority.

4.   Subject to Article 109k(6), this Article shall cease to apply from the beginning of the third stage.

Article 109i

1.   Where a sudden crisis in the balance of payments occurs and a decision within the meaning

of Article 109h(2) is not immediately taken, the Member State concerned may, as a precaution, take the necessary protective measures. Such measures must cause the least possible disturbance in the functioning of the common market and must not be wider in scope than is strictly necessary to remedy the sudden difficulties which have arisen.

2. The Commission and the other Member State shall be informed of such protective measures not later than when they enter into force. The Commission may recommend to the Council the granting of mutual assistance under Article 109h.

3. After the Commission has delivered an opinion and the Committee referred to in Article 109c has been consulted, the Council may, acting by a qualified majority, decide that the State concerned shall amend, suspend or abolish the protective measures referred to above.

4. Subject to Article 109k(6), this Article shall cease to apply from the beginning of the third stage.

Article 109j

1. The Commission and the EMI shall report to the Council on the progress made in the fulfilment by the Member States of their obligations regarding the achievement of economic and monetary union. These reports shall include an examination of the compatibility between each Member State's national legislation, including the statutes of its national central bank, and Articles 107 and 108 of this Treaty and the Statute of the ESCB. The report shall also examine the achievement of a high degree of sustainable convergence by reference to the fulfilment by each Member State of the following criteria:

- the achievement of a high degree of price stability; this will be apparent from rate of inflation which is close to that of, at most, the three best performing Member States in terms of price stability;

- the sustainability of the government financial position; this will be apparent from having achieved a government budgetary position without a deficit that is excessive as determined in accordance with Article 104c(6);

- the observance of the normal fluctuation margins provided for by the Exchange Rate Mechanism of the European Monetary System, for at least two years, without devaluing against the currency of any other Member State;

- the durability of convergence achieved by the Member State and of its participation in the Exchange Rate Mechanism of the European Monetary System being reflected in the long-term interest rate levels.

The four criteria mentioned in this paragraph and the relevant periods over which they are to be respected are developed further in a Protocol annexed to this Treaty. The reports of the Commission and the EMI shall also take account of the development of the ECU, the results of the integration of markets, the situation and development of the balances of payments on current account and an examination of the development of unit labour costs and other price indices.

2. On the basis of these reports, the Council, acting by a qualified majority on a recommendation from the Commission, shall assess:

- for each Member State, whether it fulfils the necessary conditions for the adoption of a single currency;

- where a majority of the Member States fulfil the necessary conditions for the adoption of a single currency,

and recommend its findings to the Council, meeting in the composition of the Heads of State or Government. The European Parliament shall be consulted and forward its opinion to the Council, meeting in the composition of the Heads of State or Government.

3. Taking due account of the reports referred to in paragraph 1 and the opinion of the European Parliament referred to in paragraph 2, the Council, meeting in the composition of Heads of State or of Government, shall, acting by a qualified majority, not later than 31 December 1996:

- decide, on the basis of the recommendations of the Council referred to in paragraph 2, whether a majority of the Member States fulfil the necessary conditions for the adoption of a single currency;

- decide whether it is appropriate for the Community to enter the third stage, and if so

- set the date for the beginning of the third stage.

4. *If by the end of 1997 the date for the beginning of the third stage has not been set, the third stage shall start on 1 January 1999.*

Before 1 July 1998, the Council, meeting in the composition of Heads of State or of Government, after a repetition of the procedure provided for in paragraphs 1 and 2, with the exception of the second indent of paragraph 2, taking into account the reports referred to in paragraph 1 and the opinion of the European Parliament, shall, acting by a qualified majority and on the basis of the recommendations of the Council referred to in paragraph 2, confirm which Member States fulfil the necessary conditions for the adoption of a single currency.

Article 109k

1. *If the decision has been taken to set the date in accordance with Article 109j(3), the Council shall, on the basis of its recommendations referred to in Article 109j(2), acting by a qualified majority on a recommendation from the Commission, decide whether any, and if so which, Member States shall have a derogation as defined in paragraph 3 of this Article. Such Member States shall in this Treaty be referred to as 'Member States with a derogation'.*

If the Council has confirmed which Member States fulfil the necessary conditions for the adoption of a single currency, in accordance with Article 109j(4), those Member States which do not fulfil the conditions shall have a derogation as defined in paragraph 3 of this Article. Such Member States shall in this Treaty be referred to as 'Member States with a derogation'.

2. *At least once every two years, or at the request of a Member State with a derogation, the Commission and the ECB shall report to the Council in accordance with the procedure laid down in Article 109j(1). After consulting the European Parliament and after discussion in the Council, meeting in the composition of the Heads of State or of Government, the Council shall, acting by a qualified majority on a proposal from the Commission, decide which Member States with a derogation fulfil the necessary conditions on the basis of the criteria set out in Article 109j(1), and abrogate the derogations of the Member States concerned.*

3. *A derogation referred to in paragraph 1 shall entail that the following Articles do not*

apply to the Member State concerned: Articles 104c(9) and (11), 105(1),(2), (3) and (5), 105a, 108a, 109, 109a(2)(b). The exclusion of such a Member State and its national central bank from rights and obligations within the ESCB is laid down in Chapter IX of the Statute of the ESCB.

4. *In Articles 105(1), (2) ,and (3), 105a, 108a, 109 and 109a(2)(b), 'Member States' shall be read as 'Member States without a derogation'.*

5. *The voting rights of Member States with a derogation shall be suspended for the Council decisions referred to in the Articles of this Treaty mentioned in paragraph 3. In that case, by way of derogation from Articles 148 and 189a(1), a qualified majority shall be defined as two thirds of the votes of the representatives of the Member States without derogation weighted in accordance with Article 148(2), and unanimity of those Member States shall be required for an act requiring unanimity.*

6. *Articles 109h and 109i shall continue to apply to a Member State with a derogation.*

Article 109l

1. *Immediately after the decision on the date for the beginning of the third stage has been taken in accordance with Article 109j(3), or, as the case may be, immediately after 1 July 1998:*

– *the Council shall adopt the provisions referred to in Article 106(6);*

– *the governments of the Member States without a derogation shall appoint, in accordance with the procedure set out in Article 50 of the Statute of the ESCB, the President, the Vice-President and the other members of the Executive Board of the ECB. If there are Member States with a derogation, the number of members of the Executive Board may be smaller than provided for in Article 11.1 of the Statute of the ESCB, but in no circumstances shall it be less than four.*

As soon as the Executive Board is appointed, the ESCB and the ECB shall be established and shall prepare for their full operation as described in this Treaty and the Statute of the ESCB. The full exercise of their powers shall start from the first day of the third stage.

2. *As soon as the ECB is established, it shall, if necessary, take over tasks of the EMI. The EMI shall go into liquidation upon the establishment*

of the ECB; the modalities of liquidation are laid down in the Statute of the EMI.

3. If and as long as there are Member States with a derogation, and without prejudice to Article 106(3) of this Treaty, the general Council of the ECB referred to in Article 45 of the Statute of the ESCB shall be constituted as a third decision-making body of the ECB.

4. At the starting date of the third stage, the Council shall, acting with the unanimity of the Member States without derogation, on a proposal from the Commission and after consulting the ECB, adopt the conversion rates at which their currencies shall be irrevocably fixed and at which irrevocably fixed rate the ECU shall be substituted for these currencies, and the ECU will become a currency in its own right. This measure shall by itself not modify the external value of the ECU. The Council shall, acting according to the same procedure, also take the other measures necessary for the rapid introduction of the ECU as the single currency of those Member States.

5. If it is decided, according to the procedure set out in Article 109k(2), to abrogate a derogation, the Council shall, acting with the unanimity of the Member States without a derogation and the Member State concerned, on a proposal from the Commission and after consulting the ECB, adopt the rate at which the ECU shall be substituted for the currency of the Member State concerned, and take the other measures necessary for the introduction of the ECU as the single currency in the Member State concerned.

Article 109m

1. Until the beginning of the third stage, each Member State shall treat its exchange rate policy as a matter of common interest. In doing so, Member States shall take account of the experience acquired in cooperation within the framework of the European Monetary System (EMS) and in developing the ECU, and shall respect existing powers in this field.

2. From the beginning of the third stage and for as long as a Member State has a derogation, paragraph 1 shall apply by analogy to the exchange rate policy of that Member State."

(26) In Title II of Part Three, the title of Chapter 4 shall be replaced by the following:

"TITLE VII

COMMON COMMERCIAL POLICY"

(27) Article 111 shall be repealed.

(28) Article 113 shall be replaced with the following:

"Article 113

1. The common commercial policy shall be based on uniform principles, particularly in regard to changes in tariff rates, the conclusion of tariff and trade agreements, the achievement of uniformity in measures of liberalization, export policy and measures to protect trade such as those to be taken in the event of dumping or subsidies.

2. The Commission shall submit proposals to the Council for implementing the common commercial policy.

3. Where agreements with one or more States or international organizations need to be negotiated, the Commission shall make recommendations to the Council, which shall authorize the Commission to open the necessary negotiations.

The Commission shall conduct these negotiations in consultation with a special committee appointed by the Council to assist the Commission in this task and within the framework of such directives as the Council may issue to it.

The relevant provision of Article 228 shall apply.

4. In exercising the powers conferred upon it by this Article, the Council shall act by a qualified majority."

(29) Article 114 shall be repealed.

(30) Article 115 shall be replaced by the following:

"Article 115

In order to ensure that the execution of measures of commercial policy taken in accordance with this Treaty by any Member State is not obstructed by deflection of trade, or where differences between such measures lead to economic difficulties in one or more Member States, the Commission shall recommend the methods for the requisite cooperation between Member States. Failing this, the Commission *may authorise Member States to take the necessary protective measures, the conditions and details of which it shall determine.*

In case of urgency, Member States shall request authorization to take the necessary measures themselves from the Commission, which shall take a decision as soon as possible; the Member States concerned shall then notify the measures to the other Member States. The Commission may decide at any time that the Member States concerned shall amend or abolish the measures in question.

In the selection of such measures, priority shall be given to those which cause the least disturbance to the functioning of the common market."

(31)   Article 116 shall be repealed.

(32)   In Part Three, the title of Title III shall be replaced by the following:

"TITLE VIII

SOCIAL POLICY, EDUCATION, VOCATIONAL TRAINING AND YOUTH"

(33)   The first subparagraph of Article 118a(2) shall be replaced by the following:

"2. In order to help achieve the objective laid down in the first paragraph, the Council, acting in accordance with the procedure referred to in Article 189c and after consulting the Economic and Social Committee, shall adopt by means of directives, minimum requirements for gradual implementation, having regard to the conditions and technical rules obtaining in each of the Member States."

(34)   Article 123 shall be replaced by the following:

"Article 123

In order to improve employment opportunities for workers in the internal market and to contribute thereby to raising the standard of living, a European Social Fund is hereby established in accordance with the provisions set out below; it shall aim to render the employment of workers easier and to increase their geographical and

occupational mobility within the Community, and to facilitate their adaptation to industrial changes and to changes in production systems, in particular through vocational training and retraining".

(35)   Article 125 shall be replaced by the following:

"Article 125

The Council, acting in accordance with the procedure referred to in Article 189c and after consulting the Economic and Social Committee, shall adopt implementing decisions relating to the European Social Fund."

(36)   Articles 126, 127 and 128 shall be replaced by the following:

"CHAPTER 3
Education, vocational training and youth

Article 126

1.   The Community shall contribute to the development of quality education by encouraging cooperation between Member States and, if necessary, by supporting and supplementing their action, while fully respecting the responsibility of the Member States for the content of teaching and the organization of education systems and their cultural and linguistic diversity.

2.   Community action shall be aimed at:

– *developing the European dimension in education, particularly through the teaching and dissemination of the languages of the Member States;*

– *encouraging mobility of students and teachers, inter alia by encouraging the academic recognition of diplomas and periods of study;*

– *promoting cooperation between educational establishments;*

– *developing exchanges of information and experience on issues common to the education systems of the Member States;*

– *encouraging the development of youth exchanges and of exchanges of socio-educational instructors;*

– *encouraging the development of distance education.*

3. The Community and the Member States shall foster co-operation with third countries and the competent international organizations in the field of education, in particular the Council of Europe.

4. In order to contribute to the achievement of the objectives referred to in this Article, the Council:

- acting in accordance with the procedure referred to in Article 189b, after consulting the Economic and Social Committee and the Committee of the Regions, shall adopt incentive measures, excluding any harmonization of the laws and regulations of the Member States;

- acting by a qualified majority on a proposal from the Commission, shall adopt recommendations.

Article 127

1. The Community shall implement a vocational training policy which shall support and supplement the action of the Member States, while fully respecting the responsibility of the Member States for the content and organization of vocational training.

2. Community action shall aim to:

- facilitate adaptation to industrial changes, in particular through vocational training and retraining;

- improve initial and continuing vocational training in order to facilitate vocational integration and reintegration into the labour market;

- facilitate access to vocational training and encourage mobility of instructors and trainees and particularly young people;

- stimulate cooperation on training between educational or training establishments and firms;

- develop exchanges of information and experience on issues common to the training systems of the Member States.

3. The Community and the Member States shall foster cooperation with third countries and the competent international organizations in the sphere of vocational training.

4. The Council, acting in accordance with the procedure referred to in Article 189c and after

consulting the Economic and Social Committee, shall adopt measures to contribute to the achievement of the objectives referred to in this Article, excluding any harmonization of the laws and regulations of the Member States."

(37)   The following shall be inserted:

"TITLE IX

CULTURE

Article 128

1.   The Community shall contribute to the flowering of the cultures of the Member States, while respecting their national and regional diversity and at the same time bringing the common cultural heritage to the fore.

2.   Action by the Community shall be aimed at encouraging cooperation between Member States and, if necessary, supporting and supplementing their action in the following areas:

- improvement of the knowledge and dissemination of the culture and history of the European peoples;

- conservation and safeguarding of cultural heritage of European significance;

- non-commercial cultural exchanges;

- artistic and literary creation, including in the audiovisual sector.

3.   The Community and the Member States shall foster cooperation with third countries and the competent international organizations in the sphere of culture, in particular the Council of Europe.

4.   The Community shall take cultural aspects into account in its action under other provisions of this Treaty.

5.   In order to contribute to the achievement of the objectives referred to in this Article, the Council:

- acting in accordance with the procedure referred to in Article 189b and after consulting the Committee of the Regions, shall adopt incentive measures, excluding any harmonization of the laws and regulations of the Member States. The Council shall act unanimously throughout the procedures referred to in Article 189b;

– *acting unanimously on a proposal from the Commission, shall adopt recommendations.*"

(38) Titles IV, V, VI and VII shall be replaced by the following:

"TITLE X

PUBLIC HEALTH

Article 129

1. The Community shall contribute towards ensuring a high level of human health protection by encouraging cooperation between the Member States and, if necessary, lending support to their action.

Community action shall be directed towards the prevention of diseases, in particular the major health scourges, including drug dependence, by promoting research into their causes and their transmission, as well as health information and education.

Health protection requirements shall form a constituent part of the Community's other policies.

2. Member States shall, in liaison with the Commission, coordinate among themselves their policies and programmes in the areas referred to in paragraph 1. The Commission may, in close contact with the Member States, take any useful initiative to promote such coordination.

3. The Community and the Member States shall foster cooperation with third countries and the competent international organizations in the sphere of public health.

4. In order to contribute to the achievement of the objectives referred to in this Article, the Council:

– *acting in accordance with the procedure referred to in Article 189b, after consulting the Economic and Social Committee and the Committee of the Regions, shall adopt incentive measures, excluding any harmonization of the laws and regulations of the Member States;*

– *acting by a qualified majority on a proposal from the Commission, shall adopt recommendations.*

TITLE XI

CONSUMER PROTECTION

Article 129a

1. The Community shall contribute to the attainment of a high level of consumer protection through:

(a) measures adopted pursuant to Article 100a in the context of the completion of the internal market;

(b) specific action which supports and supplements the policy pursued by the Member States to protect the health, safety and economic interests of consumers and to provide adequate information to consumers.

2. The Council, acting in accordance with the procedure referred to in Article 189b and after consulting the Economic and Social Committee, shall adopt the specific action referred to in paragraph 1(b).

3. Action adopted pursuant to paragraph 2 shall not prevent any Member State from maintaining or introducing more stringent protective measures. Such measures must be compatible with this Treaty. The Commission shall be notified of them.

TITLE XII

TRANS-EUROPEAN NETWORKS

Article 129b

1. To help achieve the objectives referred to in Articles 7a and 130a and to enable citizens of the Union, economic operators and regional and local communities to derive the full benefit from the setting up of an area without internal frontiers, the Community shall contribute to the establishment and development of trans-European networks in the areas of transport, telecommunications and energy infrastructures.

2. Within the framework of a system of open and competitive markets, action by the Community shall aim at promoting the interconnection and inter-operability of national networks as well as access to such networks. It shall take account in particular of the need to link island, land-

locked and peripheral regions with the central regions of the Community.

Article 129c

1. In order to achieve the objectives referred to in Article 129b, the Community:

-   shall establish a series of guidelines covering the objectives, priorities and broad lines of measures envisaged in the sphere of trans-European networks; these guidelines shall identify projects of common interest;

-   shall implement any measures that may prove necessary to ensure the inter-operability of the networks, in particular in the field of technical standardization;

-   may support the financial efforts made by the Member States for projects of common interest financed by Member States, which are identified in the framework of the guidelines referred to in the first indent, particularly through feasibility studies, loan guarantees or interest rate subsidies; the Community may also contribute, through the Cohesion Fund to be set up no later than 31 December 1993 pursuant to Article 130d, to the financing of specific projects in Member States in the area of transport infrastructure.

The Community's activities shall take into account the potential economic viability of the projects.

2. Member States shall, in liaison with the Commission, coordinate among themselves the policies pursued at national level which may have a significant impact on the achievement of the objectives referred to in Article 129b. The Commission may, in close cooperation with the Member States, take any useful initiative to promote such coordination.

3. The Community may decide to cooperate with third countries to promote projects of mutual interest and to ensure the inter-operability of networks.

Article 129d

The guidelines referred to in Article 129c(1) shall be adopted by the Council, acting in accordance with the procedure referred to in Article 189b and after consulting the Economic and Social Committee and the Committee of the Regions.

Guidelines and projects of common interest which relate to the territory of a Member State shall require the approval of the Member State concerned.

The Council, acting in accordance with the procedure referred to in Article 189c and after consulting the Economic and Social Committee and the Committee of the Regions, shall adopt the other measures provided for in Article 129c(1).

TITLE XIII

INDUSTRY

Article 130

1. The Community and the Member States shall ensure that the conditions necessary for the competitiveness of the Community's industry exist. For that purpose, in accordance with a system of open andcompetitive markets, their action shall be aimed at:

-   speeding up the adjustment of industry to structural changes;

-   encouraging an environment favourable to initiative and to the development of under-takings throughout the Community, particularly small and medium-sized under-takings;

-   encouraging an environment favourable to cooperation between undertakings;

-   fostering better exploitation of the industrial potential of policies of innovation, research and technological development.

2. The Member States shall consult each other in liaison with the Commission and, where necessary, shall coordinate their action. The Commission may undertake any useful initiative to promote such coordination.

3. The Community shall contribute to the achievement of the objectives set out in paragraph 1 through the policies and activities it pursues under other provisions of this Treaty. The Council, acting unanimously on a proposal from the Commission, after consulting the European Parliament and the Economic and Social Committee, may decide on specific measures in support of action taken in the Member States to achieve the objectives set out in paragraph 1.

This Title shall not provide a basis for the introduction by the Community of any measure which could lead to a distortion of competition.

TITLE XIV

ECONOMIC AND SOCIAL COHESION

Article 130a

In order to promote its overall harmonious development, the Community shall develop and pursue its actions in leading to the strengthening of its economic and social cohesion.

In particular, the Community shall aim at reducing the disparities between the levels of development of the various regions and the backwardness of the least-favoured regions, including rural areas.

Article 130b

Member States shall conduct their economic policies and shall coordinate them is such a way as, in addition, to attain the objectives set out in Article 130a. The formulation and implementation of the Community's policies and actions and the implementation of the internal market shall take into account the objectives set out in Article 130a and shall contribute to their achievement. The Community shall also support the achievement of these objectives by the action it takes through the Structural Funds (European Agricultural Guidance and Guarantee Fund, Guidance Section; European Social Fund; European Regional Development Fund), the European Investment Bank and other existing financial instruments.

The Commission shall submit a report to the European Parliament, the Council, the Economic and Social Committee and the Committee of the Regions every three years on the progress made towards achieving economic and social cohesion and on the manner in which the various means provided for in this Article have contributed to it. This report shall, if necessary, be accompanied by appropriate proposals.

If specific actions prove necessary outside the Funds and without prejudice to the measures decided upon within the framework of the other Community policies, such actions may be adopted by the Council acting unanimously on a proposal from the Commission and after consulting the European Parliament, the Economic and Social Committee and the Committee of the Regions.

Article 130c

The European Regional Development Fund is intended to help redress the main regional imbalances in the Community through participation in the development and structural adjustments of regions whose development is lagging behind and in the conversion of declining industrial regions.

Article 130d

Without prejudice to Article 130e, the Council, acting unanimously on a proposal from the Commission and after obtaining the assent of the European Parliament and consulting the Economic and Social Committee and the Committee of the Regions, shall define the tasks, priority objectives and the organization of the Structural Funds, which may involve grouping the Funds. The Council, acting by the same procedure, shall also define the general rules applicable to them and the provisions necessary to ensure their effectiveness and the coordination of the Funds with one another and with the other existing financial instruments.

The Council, acting in accordance with the same procedure, shall before 31 December 1993 set up a Cohesion Fund to provide a financial contribution to projects in the fields of environment and trans-European networks in the area of transport infrastructure.

Article 130e

Implementing decisions relating to the European Regional Development Fund shall be taken by the Council, acting in accordance with the procedure referred to in Article 189c and after consulting the Economic and Social Committee and the Committee of the Regions.

With regard to the European Agricultural Guidance and Guarantee Fund — Guidance Section, and the European Social Fund, articles 43 and 125 respectively shall continue to apply.

TITLE XV

RESEARCH AND TECHNOLOGICAL DEVELOPMENT

Article 130f

1.   The Community shall have the objective of strengthening the scientific and technological bases of Community industry and encouraging it to become more competitive at international level, while promoting all the research activities deemed necessary by virtue of other chapters of this Treaty.

2.   For this purpose the Community shall, throughout the Community, encourage undertakings, research centres and universities in their research and technological development activities of high quality; it shall support their efforts to cooperate with one another, aiming, notably, at enabling undertakings to exploit the internal market potential to the full, in particular through the opening up of national public contracts, the definition of common standards and the removal of legal and fiscal obstacles to that cooperation.

3.   All Community activities under this Treaty in the area of research and technological development, including demonstration projects, shall be decided on and implemented in accordance with the provisions of this Title.

Article 130g

In pursuing these objectives, the Community shall carry out the following activities, complementing the objectives carried out in the Member States:

(a) implementation of research, technological development and demonstration programmes, by promoting cooperation with and between undertakings, research centres and universities;

(b) promotion of cooperation in the field of Community research, technological development and demonstration with third countries and international organizations;

(c) dissemination and optimization of the results of activities in Community research, technological development and demonstration;

(d) stimulation of the training and mobility of researchers in the Community.

Article 130h

1.   The Community and the Member States shall coordinate their research and technological development activities so as to ensure that national policies and Community policy are mutually consistent.

2.   In close cooperation with the Member States, the Commission may take any useful initiative to promote the coordination referred to in paragraph 1.

Article 130i

1.   A multiannual framework programme, setting out all activities of the Community, shall be adopted by the Council, acting in accordance with the procedure referred to in Article 189b after consulting the Economic and Social Committee. The Council shall act unanimously throughout the procedures referred to in Article 189b.

The framework programme shall:

–   establish the scientific and technological objectives to be achieved by the activities provided for in Article 130g and fix the relevant priorities;

–   indicate the broad lines of such activities;

–   fix the maximum overall amount and the detailed rules for Community financial participation in the framework programme and the respective shares in each of the activities provided for.

2.   The framework programme shall be adapted or supplemented as the situation changes.

3.   The framework programme shall be implemented through specific programmes developed within each activity. Each specific programme shall define the detailed rules for implementing it, fix its duration and provide for the means deemed necessary. The sum of the amounts deemed necessary, fixed in the specific programmes, may not exceed the overall maximum amount fixed for the framework programme and each activity.

4.   The Council, acting by a qualified majority on a proposal from the Commission and after consulting the European Parliament and the Economic and Social Committee, shall adopt the specific programmes.

Article 130j

For the implementation of the multiannual framework programme the Council shall:

- determine the rules for the participation of undertakings, research centres and universities;

- lay down the rules governing the dissemination of research results.

Article 130k

In implementing the multiannual framework programmes, supplementary programmes may be decided on involving the participation of certain Member States only, which shall finance them subject to possible Community participation.

The Council shall adopt the rules applicable to supplementary programmes, particularly as regards the dissemination of knowledge and access by other Member States.

Article 130l

In implementing the multiannual framework programme the Community may make provision, in agreement with the Member States concerned, for participation in research and development programmes undertaken by several Member States, including participation in the structures created for the execution of those programmes.

Article 130m

In implementing the multiannual framework programme the Community may make provision for cooperation in Community research, technological development and demonstration with third countries or international organizations.

The detailed arrangements for such cooperation may be the subject of agreements between the Community and the third parties concerned, which shall be negotiated and concluded in accordance with Article 228.

Article 130n

The Community may set up joint undertakings or any other structure necessary for the efficient execution of Community research, technological development and demonstration programmes.

Article 130o

The Council, acting unanimously on a proposal from the Commission and after consulting the European Parliament and the Economic and Social Committee, shall adopt the provisions referred to in Article 130n.

The Council, acting in accordance with the procedure referred to in Article 189c and after consulting the Economic and Social Committee, shall adopt the provisions referred to in Articles 130j to l. Adoption of the supplementary programmes shall require the agreement of the Member States concerned.

Article 130p

At the beginning of each year the Commission shall send a report to the European Parliament and the Council. The report shall include information on research and technological development activities and the dissemination of results during the previous year, and the work programme for the current year.

TITLE XVI

ENVIRONMENT

Article 130r

1. Community policy on the environment shall contribute to pursuit of the following objectives:

- preserving, protecting and improving the quality of the environment;

- protecting human health;

- prudent and rational utilization of natural resources;

- promoting measures at international level to deal with regional or worldwide environmental problems.

2. Community policy on the environment shall aim at a high level of protection taking into account the diversity of situations in the various regions of the Community. It shall be based on the precautionary principle and on the principles that preventative action should be taken, that environmental damage should as a priority be rectified at source and that the polluter should pay. Environmental protection require-

ments must be integrated into the definition and implementation of other Community policies.

In this context, harmonization measures answering these requirements shall include, where appropriate, a safeguard clause allowing Member States to take provisional measures, for non-economic environmental reasons, subject to a Community inspection procedure.

3. In preparing its policy on the environment, the Community shall take account of:

– available scientific and technical data;

– environmental conditions in the various regions of the Community;

– the potential benefits and costs of action or lack of action;

– the economic and social development of the Community as a whole and the balanced development of its regions.

4. Within their respective spheres of competence, the Community and the Member States shall cooperate with third countries and with the competent international organizations. The arrangements for Community cooperation may be the subject of agreements between the Community and the third parties concerned, which shall be negotiated and concluded in accordance with Article 228.

The previous subparagraph shall be without prejudice to Member States' competence to negotiate in international bodies and to conclude international agreements.

Article 130s

1. The Council, acting in accordance with the procedure referred to in Article 189c and after consulting the Economic and Social Committee, shall decide what action is to be taken by the Community in order to achieve the objectives referred to in Article 130r.

2. By way of derogation from the decision-making procedure provided for in paragraph 1 and without prejudice to Article 100a, the Council, acting unanimously on a proposal from the Commission and after consulting the European Parliament and the Economic and Social Committee, shall adopt:

– provisions primarily of a fiscal nature;

– measures concerning town and country planning, land use with the exception of

waste management and measures of a general nature, and management of water resources;

– measures significantly affecting a Member State's choice between different energy sources and the general structure of its energy supply.

The Council may, under the conditions laid down in the preceding subparagraph, define those matters referred to in this paragraph on which decisions are to be taken by a qualified majority.

3. In other areas, general action programmes setting out priority objectives to be attained shall be adopted by the Council, acting in accordance with the procedure referred to in Article 189b and after consulting the Economic and Social Committee. The Council, acting under the terms of paragraph 1 or paragraph 2 according to the case, shall adopt the measures necessary for the implementation of these programmes.

4. Without prejudice to certain measures of a Community nature, the Member States shall finance and implement the environment policy.

5. Without prejudice to the principle that the polluter should pay, if a measure based on the provisions of paragraph 1 involves costs deemed disproportionate for the public authorities of a Member State, the Council shall, in the act adopting that measure, lay down appropriate provisions in the form of:

– temporary derogations and/or

– financial support from the Cohesion Fund to be set up no later than 31 December 1993 pursuant to Article 130d.

Article 130t

The protective measures adopted pursuant to Article 130s shall not prevent any Member State from maintaining or introducing more stringent protective measures. Such measures must be compatible with this Treaty. They shall be notified to the Commission.

TITLE XVII

DEVELOPMENT COOPERATION

Article 130u

1. Community policy in the sphere of development cooperation, which shall be complemen-

tary to the policies pursued by the Member States, shall foster:

- the sustainable economic and social development of the developing countries, and more particularly the most disadvantaged among them;

- the smooth and gradual integration of the developing countries into the world economy;

- the campaign against poverty in the developing countries.

2. Community policy in this area shall contribute to the general objective of developing and consolidating democracy and the rule of law, and to that of respecting human rights and fundamental freedoms.

3. The Community and the Member State shall comply with the commitments and take account of the objectives they have approved in the context of the United Nations and other competent international organizations.

Article 130v

The Community shall take account of the objectives referred to in Article 130u in the policies that it implements which are likely to affect developing countries.

Article 130w

1. Without prejudice to the other provisions in this Treaty the Council, acting in accordance with the procedure referred to in Article 189c, shall adopt the measures necessary to further the objectives referred to in Article 130u. Such measures may take the form of multiannual programmes.

2. The European Investment Bank shall contribute, under the terms laid down in its Statute, to the implementation of the measures referred to in paragraph 1.

3. The provisions of this Article shall not affect cooperation with the African, Caribbean and Pacific countries in the framework of the ACP-EEC Convention.

Article 130x

1. The Community and the Member States shall coordinate their policies on development cooperation and shall consult each other on their aid programmes, including in international organizations and during international conferences. They may undertake joint action. Member States shall contribute if necessary to the implementation of Community aid programmes.

2. The Commission may take any useful initiative to promote the coordination referred to in paragraph 1.

Article 130y

Within their respective spheres of competence, the Community and the Member States shall cooperate with third countries and with the competent international organizations. The arrangements for Community cooperation may be the subject of arrangements between the Community and the third parties concerned, which shall be negotiated and concluded in accordance with Article 228.

The previous paragraph shall be without prejudice to Members States' competence to negotiate in international bodies and to conclude international agreements."

E — In Part Five "Institutions of the Community"

(39)   Article 137 shall be replaced by the following:

"Article 137

The European Parliament, which shall consist of representatives of the peoples of the States brought together in the Community, shall exercise the powers conferred upon it by this Treaty."

(40)   Paragraph 3 of Article 138 shall be replaced by the following:

"3. The European Parliament shall draw up proposals for elections by direct universal suffrage in accordance with a uniform procedure in all Member States.

The Council shall, acting unanimously after obtaining the assent of the European Parliament, which shall act by a majority of its component members, lay down the appropriate provisions, which it shall recommend to Member States for adoption in accordance with their respective constitutional requirements."

(41)   The following Articles shall be inserted:

"Article 138a

Political parties at European level are important as a factor for integration within the Union. They contribute to forming a European awareness and to expressing the political will of the citizens of the Union.

Article 138b

In so far as provided in this Treaty, the European Parliament shall participate in the process leading up to the adoption of Community acts by exercising its powers under the procedures laid down in Articles 189b and 189c and by giving its assent or delivering advisory opinions.

The European Parliament may, acting by a majority of its members, request the Commission to submit any appropriate proposal on matters on which it considers that a Community act is required for the purpose of implementing this Treaty.

Article 138c

In the course of its duties, the European Parliament may, at the request of a quarter of its members, set up a temporary Committee of Inquiry to investigate, without prejudice to the powers conferred by this Treaty on other institutions or bodies, alleged contraventions or maladministration in the implementation of Community law, except where the alleged facts are being examined before a court and while the case is still subject to legal proceedings.

The temporary Committee of Inquiry shall cease to exist on the submission of its report.

The detailed provisions governing the exercise of the right of inquiry shall be determined by common accord of the European Parliament, the Council and the Commission.

Article 138d

Any citizen of the Union, and any natural or legal person residing or having his registered office in a Member State, shall have the right to address, individually or in association with other citizens or persons, a petition to the European Parliament on a matter which comes within the Community's fields of activity and which affects him directly.

[Editor's note: in the EEC publication of the Treaty ISBN 92-824-0959-7 the above phrase has been replaced by "which affects him directly".]

Article 138e

1. The European Parliament shall appoint an Ombudsman empowered to receive complaints from any citizen of the Union or any natural or legal person residing its or having his registered office in a Member State concerning instances of maladministration in the activities of the Community institutions or bodies, with the exception of the Court of Justice and the Court of First Instance acting in their judicial role.

In accordance with his duties, the Ombudsman shall conduct inquiries for which he finds grounds, either on his own initiative or on the basis of complaints submitted to him direct or through a member of the European Parliament, except where the alleged facts are or have been the subject of legal proceedings. Where the Ombudsman establishes an instance of maladministration, he shall refer the matter to the institution concerned, which shall have a period of three months in which to inform him of its views. The Ombudsman shall then forward a report to the European Parliament and the institution concerned. The person lodging the complaint shall be informed of the outcome of such inquiries.

The Ombudsman shall submit an annual report to the European Parliament on the outcome of his inquiries.

2.   The Ombudsman shall be appointed after each election of the European Parliament for the duration of its term of office. The Ombudsman shall be eligible for reappointment.

The Ombudsman may be dismissed by the Court of Justice at the request of the European Parliament if he no longer fulfils the conditions required for the performance of his duties or if he is guilty of serious misconduct.

3.   The Ombudsman shall be completely independent in the performance of his duties. In the performance of those duties he shall seek nor take instructions from any body. The Ombudsman may not, during his term of office, engage in any other occupation, whether gainful or not.

4.   The European Parliament shall, after seeking an opinion from the Commission and with the approval of the Council acting by a qualified majority, lay down the regulations and general conditions governing the Ombudsman's duties."

(42)   The second subparagraph of Article 144 shall be supplemented by the following sentence:

"In this case, the term of office of the members of the Commission appointed to replace them shall expire on the date which the term of office of the members of the Commission obliged to resign as a body would have expired."

(43) The following Article shall be inserted:

"Article 146

The Council shall consist of a representative of each Member State at ministerial level, authorized to commit the government of that Member State.

The office of President shall be held in turn by each Member State in the Council for a term of six months, in the following order of Member States:

– *for a first cycle of six years: Belgium, Denmark, Germany, Greece, Spain, France, Ireland, Italy, Luxembourg, Netherlands, Portugal, United Kingdom;*

– *for the following cycle of six years: Denmark, Belgium, Greece, Germany, France, Spain, Italy, Ireland, Netherlands, Luxembourg, United Kingdom, Portugal."*

(44) The following Article shall be inserted:

"Article 147

The Council shall meet when convened by its President on his initiative or at the request of one of its members or of the Commission."

(45) Article 149 shall be repealed.

(46) The following Article shall be inserted:

"Article 151

1. A committee consisting of the Permanent Representatives of the Member States shall be responsible for preparing the work of the Council and for carrying out the tasks assigned to it by the Council.

2. The Council shall be assisted by a General Secretariat, under the direction of a Secretary-General. The Secretary-General shall be appointed by the Council acting unanimously.

The Council shall decide on the organization of the General Secretariat.

3. The Council shall adopt its rules of procedure."

(47) The following Article shall be inserted:

"Article 154

The Council shall, acting by a qualified majority, determine the salaries, allowances and pensions of the President and members of the Commission, and of the president, Judges, Advocates-General and Registrar of the Court of Justice. It shall also, again by a qualified majority, determine any payment to be made instead of remuneration."

(48) The following Articles shall be inserted:

"Article 156

The Commission shall publish annually, not later than one month before the opening of the session of the European Parliament, a general report on the activities of the Community.

Article 157

1. The Commission shall consist of seventeen members, who shall be chosen on the grounds of their general competence and whose independence is beyond doubt.

The number of members of the Commission may be altered by the Council, acting unanimously.

Only nationals of Member States may be members of the Commission.

The Commission must include at least one national of each of the Member States, but may not include more than two members having the nationality of the same State.

2. The members of the Commission shall, in the general interest of the Community, be completely independent in the performance of their duties.

In the performance of these duties, they shall neither seek nor take instructions from any government or from any other body. They shall refrain from any action incompatible with their duties. Each Member State undertakes to respect this principle and not to seek to influence the members of the Commission in the performance of their tasks.

The members of the Commission may not, during their term of office, engage in any other occupation, whether gainful or not. When entering upon their duties they shall give a solemn undertaking that, both during and after their term of office, they will respect the obligations arising therefrom and in particular their duty to behave with integrity and discretion as regards the acceptance, after they have ceased to hold office, of certain appointments or benefits. In the event of any breach of these obligations, the Court of Justice may, on application by the Council or the Commission, rule that the member concerned be, according to the circumstances, either compulsorily retired in accordance with Article 160 or deprived of his rights to a pension or benefits in its stead.

Article 158

1. The members of the Commission shall be appointed, in accordance with the procedure referred to in paragraph 2, for a period of five years, subject, if need be, to Article 144.

Their term of office shall be renewable.

2. The governments of the Member States shall nominate by common accord, after consulting the European Parliament, the person they intend to appoint as President of the Commission.

The governments of the Member States shall, in consultation with the nominee for President, nominate the other persons whom they intend to appoint as members of the Commission.

The President and the other members of the Commission thus nominated shall be subject as a body to a vote of approval by the European Parliament. After approval by the European parliament, the President and the other members of the Commission shall be appointed by common accord of the governments of the Member States.

3. Paragraphs 1 and 2 shall be applied for the first time to the President and the other members of the Commission whose term of office begins on 7 January 1995.

The President and the other members of the Commission whose term of office begins on 7 January 1993 shall be appointed by common accord of the governments of the Member States. Their term of office shall expire on 6 January 1995.

Article 159

Apart from normal replacement, or death, the duties of a member of the Commission shall end when he resigns or is compulsorily retired.

The vacancy thus caused shall be filled for the remainder of the member's term of office by a new member appointed by common accord of the governments of the Member States. The

Council may, acting unanimously, decide that such a vacancy need not be filled.

In the event of resignation, compulsory retirement or death, the President shall be replaced for the remainder of his term of office. The procedure laid down in Article 158(2) shall be applicable for the replacement of the President.

Save in the case of compulsory retirement under Article 160, members of the Commission shall remain in office until they have been replaced.

Article 160

If any member of the Commission no longer fulfills the conditions required for the performance of his duties or if he has been guilty of serious misconduct, the Court of Justice may, on application by the Council or the Commission, compulsorily retire him.

Article 161

The Commission may appoint a Vice-President or two Vice-Presidents from among its members.

Article 162

1. The Council and the Commission shall consult each other and shall settle by common accord their methods of cooperation.

2. The Commission shall adopt its rules of procedure so as to ensure that both it and its departments operate in accordance with the provisions of this Treaty. It shall ensure that these rules are published.

Article 163

The Commission shall act by a majority of the number of members provided for in Article 157.

A meeting of the Commission shall be valid only if the number of members laid down in its rules of procedure is present."

(49) Article 165 shall be replaced by the following:

"Article 165

The Court of Justice shall consist of thirteen judges.

The Court of Justice shall sit in plenary session. It may, however, form chambers each consisting of three of five judges, either to undertake certain preparatory inquiries or to adjudicate on particular categories of cases in accordance with rules laid down for these purposes.

The Court of Justice shall sit in plenary session when a Member State or a Community institution that is a party to the proceedings so requests.

Should the Court of Justice so request, the Council may, acting unanimously, increase the number of judges and make necessary adjustments to the second and third paragraphs of this Article and to the second of Article 167."

(50) Article 168a shall be replaced by the following:

"Article 168a

1. *The Court of First Instance shall be attached to the Court of Justice with jurisdiction to hear and determine at first instance, subject to a right of appeal to the Court of Justice on points of law only and in accordance with the conditions laid down by the Statute, certain classes of action or proceeding defined in accordance with the conditions laid down in paragraph 2. The Court of First Instance shall not be competent to hear and determine questions referred for a preliminary ruling under Article 177.*

2. *At the request of the Court of Justice and after consulting the European Parliament and the Commission, the Council, acting unanimously, shall determine the classes of action or proceeding referred to in paragraph 1 and the composition of the Court of First Instance and shall adopt the necessary adjustments and additional provisions to the Statute of the the Court of Justice. Unless the Council decides otherwise, the provisions of this Treaty relating to the Court of Justice, in particular the provisions of the Protocol on the Statute of the Court of Justice, shall apply to the Court of First Instance.*

3. *The members of the Court of First Instance shall be chosen from persons whose independence is beyond doubt and who possess the ability required for appointment to judicial office; they shall be appointed by common accord of the governments of the Member States for a term of six years. The membership shall be partially renewed every three years. Retiring members shall be eligible for re-appointment.*

4. *The Court of First Instance shall establish its rules of procedure in agreement with the Court of Justice. Those rules shall require the unanimous approval of the Council."*

(51) Article 171 shall be replaced by the following:

"Article 171

1. *If the Court of Justice finds that a Member State has failed to fulfil an obligation under this Treaty, the State shall be required to take the necessary measures to comply with the judgment of the Court of Justice.*

2. *If the Commission considers that the Member State concerned has not taken such measures it shall, after giving that State the opportunity to submit its observations, issue a reasoned opinion specifying the points on which the Member State concerned has not complied with the judgment of the Court of Justice.*

If the Member State concerned fails to take the necessary measures to comply with the Court's judgment within the time-limit laid down by the Commission, the latter may bring the case before the Court of Justice. In so doing it shall specify the amount of lump sum or penalty payment to be paid by the Member State concerned which it considers appropriate in the circumstances.

If the Court of Justice finds that the Member State concerned has not complied with its judgment it may impose a lump sum or penalty payment on it.

This procedure shall be without prejudice to Article 170."

(52) Article 172 shall be replaced by the following:

"Article 172

Regulations adopted jointly by the European Parliament and the Council, and by the Council, pursuant to the provisions of this Treaty, may give the Court of Justice unlimited jurisdiction with regard to the penalties provided for in such regulations."

(53) Article 173 shall be replaced by the following:

"Article 173

The Court of Justice shall review the legality of acts adopted jointly by the European Parliament and the Council, of acts of the Council, of the Commission and of the ECB, other than recommendations and opinions, and of acts of the European Parliament intended to produce legal effects vis-à-vis third parties.

It shall for this purpose have jurisdiction in actions brought by a Member State, the Council or the Commission on grounds of lack of competence, infringement of an essential procedural requirement, infringement of this Treaty or of any rule of law relating to its application, or misuse of powers.

The Court shall have jurisdiction under the same conditions in actions brought by the European Parliament and by the ECB for the purpose of protecting their prerogatives.

Any natural or legal person may, under the same conditions, institute proceedings against a decision addressed to that person or against a decision which, although in the form of a regulation or a decision addressed to another person, is of direct and individual concern to the former.

The proceedings provided for in this Article shall be instituted within two months of the publication of the measure, or of its notification to the plaintiff, or, in the absence thereof, of the day on which it came to the knowledge of the latter, as the case may be."

(54) Article 175 shall be replaced by the following:

"Article 175

Should the European Parliament, the Council or the Commission, in infringement of this Treaty, fail to act, The Member States and the other institutions of the Community may bring an action before the Court of Justice to have the infringement established.

The action shall be admissible only if the institution concerned has first been called upon to act. If, within two months of being so called upon, the institution concerned has not defined its position, the action may be brought within a further period of two months.

Any natural or legal person may, under the conditions laid down in the preceding paragraphs, complain to the Court of Justice that an institution of the Community has failed to address to that person any act other than a recommendation or an opinion.

The Court of Justice shall have jurisdiction, under the same conditions, in actions or proceedings brought by the ECB in the areas falling within the latter's field of competence and in actions or proceedings brought against the latter."

(55) Article 176 shall be replaced by the following:

"Article 176

The institution or institutions whose act has been declared void or whose failure to act has been declared contrary to this Treaty shall be required to take the necessary measures to comply with the judgment of the Court of Justice.

This obligation shall not affect any obligation which may result from the application of the second paragraph of Article 215.

This Article shall also apply to the ECB."

(56) Article 177 shall be replaced by the following:

"Article 177

The Court of Justice shall have jurisdiction to give preliminary rulings concerning:

(a) the interpretation of this Treaty;

(b) the validity and interpretation of acts of the institutions of the Community and of the ECB;

(c) the interpretation of the statutes of bodies established by an act of the Council, where those statutes so provide.

Where such a question is raised before any court or tribunal of a Member State, that court of tribunal may, if it considers that a decision on the question is necessary to enable it to give judgment, request the Court of Justice to give a ruling thereon.

Where any such question is raised in a case pending before a court or tribunal of a Member State against whose decisions there is no judicial remedy under national law, the court or tribunal shall bring the matter before the Court of Justice."

(57) Article 180 shall be replaced by the following:

"Article 180

The Court of Justice shall, within the limits hereinafter laid down, have jurisdiction in disputes concerning:

(a) the fulfilment by Member States of obligations under the Statute of the European Investment Bank. In this connection, the Board of Directors of the Bank shall enjoy the powers conferred upon the Commission by Article 169;

(b) measures adopted by the Board of Governors of the European Investment Bank. In this connection, any Member State, the Commission or the Board of Directors of the Bank may institute proceedings under the conditions laid down in Article 173;

(c) measures adopted by the Board of Directors of the European Investment Bank. Proceedings against such measures may be instituted only by Member States or by the Commission, under the conditions laid down in Article 173, and solely on the grounds of non-compliance with the procedure provided for in Article 21(2), (5), (6) and (7) of the Statute of the Bank;

(d) the fulfilment by the national central banks of obligations under this Treaty and the Statute of the ESCB. In this connection the powers of the Council of the ECB in respect of national central banks shall be the same as those conferred upon the Commission in respect of Member States by Article 169. If the Court of Justice finds that a national central bank has failed to fulfill an obligation under this Treaty, that bank shall be required to take the necessary measures to comply with the judgment of the Court of Justice."

(58) Article 184 shall be replaced by the following:

"Article 184

Notwithstanding the expiry of the period laid down in the fifth paragraph of Article 173, any party may, in proceedings in which a regulation adopted jointly by the European Parliament and the Council, or a regulation of the Council, of the Commission, or of the ECB is at issue, plead the grounds specified in the second paragraph of Article 173 in order to invoke before the Court of Justice the inapplicability of that regulation."

(59) The following section shall be inserted:

"SECTION 5

The Court of Auditors

Article 188a

The Court of Auditors shall carry out the audit.

Article 188b

1.   The Court of Auditors shall consist of twelve members.

2.   The members of the Court of Auditors shall be chosen from among persons who belong or have belonged in their respective countries to external audit bodies or who are especially qualified for this office. Their independence must be beyond doubt.

3.   The members of the Court of Auditors shall be appointed for a term of six years by the Council, acting unanimously after consulting the European Parliament.

However, when the first appointments are made, four members of the Court of Auditors, chosen by lot, shall be appointed for a term of office of four years only.

The members of the Court of Auditors shall be eligible for reappointment.

They shall elect the President of the Court of Auditors from among their number for a term of three years. The President may be re-elected.

4.   The members of the Court of Auditors shall, in the general interest of the Community, be completely independent in the performance of their duties.

In the performance of these duties, they shall neither seek nor take instructions from any government or from any other body. They shall refrain from any action incompatible with their duties.

5.   The members of the Court of Auditors may not, during their term of office, engage in any other occupation, whether gainful or not. When entering upon their duties they shall give a solemn undertaking that, both during and after their term of office, they will respect the obligations arising therefrom and in particular their duty to behave with integrity and discretion as regards the acceptance, after they have ceased to hold office, of certain appointments or benefits.

6. *Apart from normal replacement, or death, the duties of a member of the Court of Auditors shall end when he resigns, or is compulsorily retired by a ruling of the Court of Justice pursuant to paragraph 7.*

The vacancy thus caused shall be filled for the remainder of the member's term of office.

Save in the case of compulsory retirement, members of the Court of Auditors shall remain in office until they have been replaced.

7. *A member of the Court of Auditors may be deprived of his office or of his right to a pension or other benefits in its stead only if the Court of Justice, at the request of the Court of Auditors, finds that he no longer fulfills the requisite conditions or meets the obligations arising from his office.*

8. *The Council, acting by a qualified majority, shall determine the conditions of employment of the President and the members of the Court of Auditors and in particular their salaries, allowances and pensions. It shall also, by the same majority, determine any payment to be made instead of remuneration.*

9. *The provisions of the Protocol on the Privileges and Immunities of the European Communities applicable to the Judges of the Court of Justice shall also apply to the members of the Court of Auditors.*

Article 188c

1. *The Court of Auditors shall examine the accounts of all revenue and expenditure of the Community. It shall also examine the accounts of all revenue and expenditure of all bodies set up by the Community in so far as the relevant constituent instrument does not preclude such examination.*

The Court of Auditors shall provide the European Parliament and the Council with a statement of assurance as to the reliability of the accounts and the legality and regularity of the underlying transactions.

2. *The Court of Auditors shall examine whether all revenue has been received and all expenditure incurred in a lawful and regular manner and whether the financial arrangement has been sound.*

The audit of revenue shall be carried out on the basis both of the amounts established as due and the amounts actually paid to the Community.

The audit of expenditure shall be carried out on the basis both of commitments undertaken and payments made.

These audits may be carried out before the closure of accounts for the financial year in question.

3. *The audit shall be based on records and, if necessary, performed on the spot in other institutions of the Community and Member States. In the Member States the audit shall be carried out in liaison with the national audit bodies or, if these do not have the necessary powers, with the competent national departments. These bodies or departments shall inform the Court of Auditors whether they intend to take part in the audit.*

The other institutions of the Community and the national audit bodies or, if these do not have the necessary powers, the competent national departments, shall forward to the Court of Auditors, at its request, any document or information necessary to carry out its task.

4. *The Court of Auditors shall draw up an annual report after the close of each financial year. It shall be forwarded to the other institutions of the Community and shall be published, together with the replies of these institutions to the observations of the Court of Auditors, in the Official Journal of the European Communities.*

The Court of Auditors may also, at any time, submit observations, particularly in the form of special reports, on specific questions and deliver opinions at the request of one of the other institutions of the Community.

It shall adopt its annual reports, special reports or opinions by a majority of its members.

It shall assist the European Parliament and the Council in exercising their powers of control over the implementation of the budget."

(60)   Article 189 shall be replaced by the following:

"Article 189

In order to carry out their task and in accordance with the provisions of the Treaty, the European Parliament acting jointly with the Council, the Council and the Commission shall make regulations and issue directives, take decision, make recommendations or deliver opinions.

A regulation shall have general application. It

shall be binding in its entirety and directly applicable in all Member States.

A directive shall be binding, as to the result to be achieved, upon each Member State to which it is addressed, but shall leave to the national authorities the choice of form and methods.

A decision shall be binding in its entirety upon those to whom it is addressed.

Recommendations and opinions shall have no binding force."

(61) The following Articles shall be inserted:

"Article 189a

1. Where, in pursuance of the Treaty, the Council acts on a proposal from the Commission, unanimity shall be required for an act constituting an amendment to that proposal, subject to Article 189b(4) and (5).

2. As long as the Council has not acted, the Commission may alter its proposal at any time during the procedures leading to the adoption of a Community act.

Article 189b

1. Where reference is made in the Treaty to this Article for the adoption of an act, the following procedures shall apply.

2. The Commission shall submit a proposal to the European Parliament and the Council.

The Council, acting by a qualified majority after obtaining the opinion of the European Parliament, shall adopt a common position. The common position shall be communicated to the European Parliament. The Council shall inform the European Parliament fully of the reasons which led it to adopt its common position. The Commission shall inform the European Parliament fully of its position.

If, within three months of such communication, the European Parliament:

(a) approves the common position, the Council shall definitively adopt the act in question in accordance with that common position;

(b) has not taken a decision, the Council shall adopt the act in question in accordance with its common position;

(c) indicates, by an absolute majority of its component members, that it intends to reject the common position, it shall immediately inform the Council. The Council may convene a meeting of the Conciliation Committee referred to in paragraph 4 to explain further its position. The European Parliament shall thereafter either confirm, by an absolute majority of its component members, its rejection of the common position, in which event the proposed act shall be deemed not to have been adopted, or propose amendments in accordance with subparagraph (d) of this paragraph;

(d) proposes amendments to the common position by an absolute majority of its component members, the amended text shall be forwarded to the Council and to the Commission which shall deliver an opinion on those amendments.

3. If, within three months of the matter being referred to it, the Council acting by a qualified majority, approves all the amendments of the European Parliament, it shall amend its common position accordingly and adopt the act in question; however, the Council shall act unanimously on the amendments on which the Commission has delivered a negative opinion. If the Council does not approve the act in question, the President of the Council, in agreement with the President of the European Parliament, shall forthwith convene a meeting of the Conciliation Committee.

4. The Conciliation Committee, which shall be composed of the members of the Council or their representatives and an equal number of representatives of the European Parliament, shall have the task of reaching agreement on a joint text, by a qualified majority of the members of the Council or their representatives and by a majority of the representatives of the European Parliament. The Commission shall take part in the Conciliation Committee's proceedings and shall take all the necessary initiatives with a view to reconciling the positions of the European Parliament and the Council.

5. If within six weeks of its being convened, the Conciliation Committee approves a joint text, the European Parliament, acting by an absolute majority of the votes cast, and the Council, acting by a qualified majority, shall have a period of six weeks from that approval in which to adopt the act in question in accordance with the joint text. If one of the two institutions fails to approve the proposed act, it shall be deemed not to have been adopted.

6.   *Where the Conciliation Committee does not approve a joint text, the proposed act shall be deemed not to have been adopted unless the Council, acting by a qualified majority within six weeks of expiry of the period granted to the Conciliation Committee, confirms the common position to which it agreed before the conciliation procedure was initiated, possibly with the amendments proposed by the European Parliament. In this case, the act in question shall be finally adopted unless the European Parliament, within six weeks of the date of confirmation by the Council, rejects the text by an absolute majority of its component members, in which case the proposed act shall be deemed not to have been adopted.*

7.   *The periods of three months and six weeks referred to in this Article may be extended by a maximum of one month and two weeks respectively by common accord of the European Parliament and the Council. The period of three months referred to in paragraph 2 shall be automatically extended by two months where paragraph 2(c) applies.*

8.   *The scope of the procedure under this Article may be widened, in accordance with the procedure provided for in Article N(2) of the Treaty on European Union, on the basis of a report to be submitted to the Council by the Commission by 1996 at the latest.*

Article 189c

Where reference is made in this Treaty to this Article for the adoption of an act, the following procedure shall apply:

(a) *The Council, acting by a qualified majority on a proposal from the Commission and after obtaining the opinion of the European Parliament, shall adopt a common position.*

(b) *The Council's common position shall be communicated to the European Parliament. The Council and the Commission shall inform the European Parliament fully of the reasons which led the Council to adopt its common position and also of the Commission's position.*

If, within three months of such communication, the European Parliament approves this common position or has not taken a decision within that period, the Council shall definitively adopt the act in question in accordance with the common position.

(c) *The European Parliament may, within the period of three months referred to in point (b), by an absolute majority of its component members, propose amendments to the Council's common position. The European Parliament may also, by the same majority, reject the Council's common position. The result of the proceedings shall be transmitted to the Council and the Commission. If the European Parliament has rejected the Council's common position, unanimity shall be required for the Council to act on a second reading.*

(d) *The Commission shall, within a period of one month, re-examine the proposal on the basis of which the Council adopted its common position, by taking into account the amendments proposed by the European Parliament.*

The Commission shall forward to the Council, at the same time as its re-examined proposal, the amendments of the European Parliament which it has not accepted, and shall express its opinion on them. The Council may adopt these amendments unanimously.

(e) *The Council, acting by a qualified majority, shall adopt the proposal as re-examined by the Commission. Unanimity shall be required for the Council to amend the proposal as re-examined by the Commission.*

(f) *In the cases referred to in points (c),(d) and (e), the Council shall be required to act within a period of three months. If no decision is taken within this period, the Commission proposal shall be deemed not to have been adopted.*

(g) *The periods referred to in points (b) and (f) may be extended by a maximum of one month by common accord between the Council and the European Parliament."*

(62)   Article 190 shall be replaced by the following:

"Article 190

Regulations, directives and decisions adopted jointly by the European Parliament and the Council, and such acts adopted by the Council or the Commission, shall state the reasons on which they are based and shall refer to any proposals or opinions which were required to be obtained pursuant to this Treaty."

(63)   Article 191 shall be replaced by the following:

"Article 191

*1. Regulations, directives and decisions adopted
in accordance with the procedures referred to in
Article 189b shall be signed by the President of
the European Parliament and by the President of
the Council and published in the Official Journal
of the European Communities. They shall enter
into force on the date specified in them or, in the
absence thereof, on the twentieth day following
that of their publication.*

*2. Regulations of the Council and of the Com-
mission, as well as directives of those institutions
which are addressed to all Member States, shall
be published in the Official Journal of the
European Communities. They shall enter into
force on the date specified in them or, in the
absence thereof, on the twentieth day following
that of their publication.*

*3. Other directives, and decisions, shall be
notified to those to whom they are addressed
and shall take effect upon such notification."*

(64)   Article 194 shall be replaced by the following:

"Article 194

*The number of members of the Economic and
Social Committee shall be as follows:*

Belgium	*12*
Denmark	*9*
Germany	*24*
Greece	*12*
Spain	*21*
France	*24*
Ireland	*9*
Italy	*24*
Luxembourg	*6*
Netherlands	*12*
Portugal	*12*
United Kingdom	*24*

*The members of the Committee shall be ap-
pointed by the Council, acting unanimously,
for four years. Their appointments shall be
renewable.*

*The members of the Committee may not be
bound by any mandatory instructions. They
shall be completely independent in the performance of their duties, in the general interest of
the Community.*

*The Council, acting by a qualified majority,
shall determine the allowances of members of
the Committee."*

(65)   Article 196 shall be replaced by the following:

"Article 196

*The Committee shall elect its chairman and
officers from among its members for a term of
two years.*

It shall adopt its rules of procedure.

*The Committee shall be convened by its chair-
man at the request of the Council or of the Commission. It may also meet on its own initiative."*

(66)   Article 198 shall be replaced by the following:

"Article 198

*The Committee must be consulted by the Coun-
cil or the Commission where this Treaty so provides. The Committee may be consulted by these
institutions in all cases in which they consider
it appropriate. It may issue an opinion on its
own initiative in cases in which it considers such
action appropriate.*

*The Council or the Commission shall, if it
considers it necessary, set the Committee, for
the submission of its opinion, a time limit which
may not be less than one month from the date on
which the chairman receives notification to this
effect. Upon expiry of the time limit, the absence
of an opinion shall not prevent further action.*

*The opinion of the Committee and that of the
specialized section, together with a record of the
proceedings, shall be forwarded to the Council
and to the Commission."*

(67)   The following Chapter shall be inserted:

"CHAPTER 4

The Committee of the Regions

Article 198a

*A Committee consisting of representatives of
regional and local bodies, hereinafter referred
to as "the Committee of the Regions", is hereby
established with advisory status.*

The number of members of the Committee of the Regions shall be as follows:

Belgium	12
Denmark	9
Germany	24
Greece	12
Spain	21
France	24
Ireland	9
Italy	24
Luxembourg	6
Netherlands	12
Portugal	12
United Kingdom	24

The members of the Committee and an equal number of alternate members shall be appointed for four years by the Council acting unanimously on proposals from the respective Member States. Their term of office shall be renewable.

The members of the Committee may not be bound by any mandatory instructions. They shall be completely independent in the performance of their duties, in the general interest of the Community.

Article 198b

The Committee of the Regions shall elect its chairman and officers from among its members for a term of two years.

It shall adopt its rules of procedure and shall submit them for approval to the Council, acting unanimously.

The Committee shall be convened by its chairman at the request of the Council or of the Commission. It may also meet on its own initiative.

Article 198c

The Committee of the Regions shall be consulted by the Council or by the Commission where this Treaty so provides and in all other cases in which one of these two institutions considers it appropriate.

The Council or the Commission shall, if it considers it necessary, set the Committee, for the submission of its opinion, a time-limit which may not be less than one month from the date on which the chairman receives notification to this effect. Upon expiry of the time-limit the absence of an opinion shall not prevent further action.

Where the Economic and Social Committee is consulted pursuant to Article 198, the Committee of the Regions shall be informed by the Council or the Commission of the request for an opinion. Where it considers that specific regional interests are involved, the Committee of the Regions may issue an opinion on the matter.

It may issue an opinion on its own initiative in cases in which it considers such action appropriate.

The opinion of the Committee, together with a record of the proceedings, shall be forwarded to the Council and to the Commission."

(68)   The following chapter shall be inserted:

"CHAPTER 5

European Investment Bank

Article 198d

The European Investment Bank shall have legal personality. The members of the European Investment Bank shall be the Member States.

The Statute of the European Investment Bank is laid down in a Protocol annexed to this Treaty.

Article 198e

The task of the European Investment Bank shall be to contribute, by having recourse to the capital market and utilizing its own resources, to the balanced and steady development of the common market in the interest of the Community. For this purpose the Bank shall, operating on a non-profit-making basis, grant loans and give guarantees which facilitate the financing of the following projects in all sectors of the economy:

(a) projects for developing less-developed regions;

(b) projects for modernizing or converting undertakings or for developing fresh activities called for by the progressive establishment of the common market, where these projects are of such a size or nature that they cannot be entirely financed by the various means available in the individual Member States;

(c) projects of common interest to several Member States which are of such a size or nature *that they cannot be entirely financed by the various means available in the individual Member States.*

In carrying out its task, the Bank shall facilitate the financing of investment programmes in conjunction with assistance from the structural Funds and other Community financial instruments."

(69) Article 199 shall be replaced by the following:

"Article 199

All items of revenue and expenditure of the Community, including those relating to the European Social Fund, shall be included in estimates to be drawn up for each financial year and shall be shown in the budget.

Administrative expenditure occasioned for the institutions by the provisions of the Treaty on European Union relating to common foreign and security policy and to cooperation in the fields of justice and home affairs shall be charged to the budget. The operational expenditure occasioned by the implementation of the said provisions may, under the conditions referred to therein, be charged to the budget.

The revenue and expenditure shown in the budget shall be in balance."

(70) Article 200 shall be repealed.

(71) Article 201 shall be replaced by the following:

"Article 201

Without prejudice to other revenue, the budget shall be financed wholly from own resources.

The Council, acting unanimously on a proposal from the Commission and after consulting the European Parliament, shall lay down provisions relating to the system of own resources of the Community, which it shall recommend to the Member States for adoption in accordance with their respective constitutional requirements."

(72) The following Article shall be inserted:

"Article 201a

With a view to maintaining budgetary discipline, the Commission shall not make any proposal for a Community act, or alter its proposals, or adopt any implementing measure which is likely to have appreciable implications

for the budget without providing the assurance that the proposal or that measure is capable of being financed within the limit of the Community's own resources arising under provisions laid down by the Council pursuant to Article 201."

(73) Article 205 shall be replaced by the following:

"Article 205

The Commission shall implement the budget, in accordance with the provisions of the regulations made pursuant to Article 209, on its own responsibility and within the limits of the appropriations, having regard to the principles of sound financial management.

The regulations shall lay down detailed rules for each institution concerning its part in effecting its own expenditure.

Within the budget, the Commission may, subject to the limits and conditions laid down in the regulations made pursuant to Article 209, transfer appropriations from one chapter to another or from one subdivision to another."

(74) Article 206 shall be replaced by the following:

"Article 206

1.   The European Parliament, acting on a recommendation from the Council which shall act by qualified majority, shall give a discharge to the Commission in respect of the implementation of the budget. To this end, the Council and the European Parliament in turn shall examine the accounts and the financial statement referred to in Article 205a, the annual report by the Court of Auditors together with the replies of the institutions under audit to the observations of the Court of Auditors and any relevant special reports by the Court of Auditors.

2.   Before giving a discharge to the Commission, or for any other purpose in connection with the exercise of its power over the implementation of the budget, the European Parliament may ask to hear the Commission give evidence with regard to the execution of expenditure or the operation of financial control systems. The Commission shall submit any necessary information to the European Parliament at the latter's request.

3.   The Commission shall take all appropriate steps to act on the observations in the deci-

sions giving discharge and on other observations by the European Parliament relating to the execution of expenditure, as well as on comments accompanying the recommendations on discharge adopted by the Council.

At the request of the European Parliament or the Council, the Commission shall report on the measures taken in the light of these observations and comments and in particular on the instructions given to the departments which are responsible for the implementation of the budget. These reports shall also be forwarded to the Court of Auditors."

(75) Articles 206a and 206b shall be repealed.

(76) Article 209 shall be replaced by the following:

"Article 209

The Council, acting unanimously on a proposal from the Commission and after consulting the European Parliament and obtaining the opinion of the Court of Auditors, shall:

(a) make Financial Regulations specifying in particular the procedure to be adopted for establishing and implementing the budget and for presenting and auditing accounts;

(b) determine the methods and procedure whereby the budget revenue provided under the arrangements relating to the Community's own resources shall be made available to the Commission, and determine the measures to be applied, if need be, to meet cash requirements;

(c) lay down rules concerning the responsibility of financial controllers, authorizing officers and accounting officers, and concerning appropriate arrangements for inspection."

(77) The following article shall be inserted:

"Article 209a

Member States shall take the same measures to counter fraud affecting the financial interests of the Community as they take to counter fraud affecting their own financial interests.

Without prejudice to the other provisions of the Treaty, Member States shall coordinate their action aimed at protecting the financial interests of the Community against fraud. To this end they shall organize, with the help of the Commission, close and regular cooperation between the competent departments of their administrations."

(78) Article 215 shall be replaced by the following:

"Article 215

The contractual liability of the Community shall be governed by the law applicable to the contract in question.

In the case of non-contractual liability, the Community shall, in accordance with the general principles common to the law of the Member States, make good any damage caused by its institutions or by its servants in the performance of their duties.

The preceding paragraph shall apply under the same conditions to damage caused by the ECB or by its servants in the performance of their duties.

The personal liability of its servants towards the Community shall be governed by the provisions laid down in their Staff Regulations or in the Conditions of Employment applicable to them."

(79) Article 227 shall be amended as follows:

(a) paragraph 2 shall be replaced by the following:

"2. With regard to the French overseas departments, the general and particular provisions of this Treaty relating to:

– the free movement of goods;

– agriculture, save for Article 40 (4);

– the liberalization of services;

– the rules on competition;

– the protective measures provided for in Articles 109h, 109i and 226;

– the institutions,

shall apply as soon as this Treaty enters into force.

The conditions under which the other provisions of this Treaty are to apply shall be determined, within two years of entry into force of this Treaty, by decisions of the Council, acting unanimously on a proposal from the Commission.

The institutions of the Community will, within the framework of the procedures provided for in this Treaty, in particular Article 226, take *care that the economic and social developments of these areas is made possible."*

(b) in paragraph 5, subparagraph (a) shall be replaced by the following:

"(a) this treaty shall not apply to the Faeroe Islands."

(80)   Article 228 shall be replaced by the following:

"Article 228

1.   Where this Treaty provides for the conclusion of agreements between the Community and one or more States or international organizations, the Commission shall make recommendations to the Council, which shall authorize the Commission to open the necessary negotiations. The Commission shall conduct these negotiations in consultation with special committees appointed by the Council to assist it in this task and within the framework of such directives as the Council may issue to it.

In exercising the powers conferred upon it by this paragraph, the Council shall act by a qualified majority, except in the cases provided for in the second sentence of paragraph 2, for which it shall act unanimously.

2.   Subject to the powers vested in the Commission in this field, the agreements shall be concluded by the Council, acting by a qualified majority on a proposal from the Commission. The Council shall act unanimously when the agreement covers a field for which unanimity is required for the adoption of internal rules, and for the agreements referred to in Article 238.

3.   The Council shall conclude agreements after consulting the European Parliament, except for the agreements referred to in Article 113(3), including cases where the agreement covers a field for which the procedure referred to in Article 189b or that referred to in Article 189c is required for the adoption of internal rules. The European Parliament shall deliver its opinion within a time limit which the Council may lay down according to the urgency of the matter. In the absence of an opinion within that time limit, the Council may act.

By way of derogation from the previous subparagraph, agreements referred to in Article 238, other agreements establishing a specific institutional framework by organizing cooperation procedures, agreements having important budgetary implications for the Community and

agreements entailing amendment of an act adopted under the procedure referred to in Article 189b shall be concluded after the assent of the European Parliament has been obtained.

The Council and the European Parliament may, in an urgent situation, agree upon a time limit for the assent.

4.   When concluding an agreement , the Council may, by way of derogation from paragraph 2, authorize the Commission to approve modifications on behalf of the Community where the agreement provides for them to be adopted by a simplified procedure or by a body set up by the agreement; it may attach specific conditions to such authorization.

5.   When the Council envisages concluding an agreement which calls for amendments to the Treaty, the amendments must first be adopted in accordance with the procedure laid down in Article N of the Treaty on European Union.

6.   The Council, the Commission or a Member State may obtain the opinion of the Court of Justice as to whether an agreement envisaged is compatible with the provisions of this Treaty. Where the opinion of the Court of Justice is adverse, the agreement may enter into force only in accordance with Article N of the Treaty on European Union.

7.   Agreements concluded under the conditions set out in this Article shall be binding on the institutions of the Community and on Member States."

(81)   The following Article shall be inserted:

"Article 228a

Where it is provided, in a common position or in a joint action adopted according to the provisions of the Treaty on European Union relating to the common foreign and security policy, for an action by the Community to interrupt or to reduce, in part or completely, economic relations with one or more third countries, the Council shall take the necessary urgent measures. The Council shall act by a qualified majority on a proposal from the Commission."

(82)   Article 231 shall be replaced by the following:

"Article 231

The Community shall establish close cooperation with the Organization for Economic Coopera-

tion and Development, the details of which shall be determined by common accord."

(83) Article 236 and 237 shall be repealed.

(84) Article 328 shall be replaced by the following:

"Article 238

The Community may conclude with one or more states or international organizations agreements establishing an association involving reciprocal rights and obligations, common action and special procedures."

F — In Annex III:

(85) The title shall be replaced by the following:

"List of invisible transactions referred to in Article 73h of this Treaty".

G — In the Protocol on the Statue of the European Investment Bank:

(86) The reference to Articles 129 and 130 shall be replaced by a reference to Articles 198d and 198e.

TITLE III
PROVISIONS AMENDING THE TREATY ESTABLISHING THE EUROPEAN COAL AND STEEL COMMUNITY

(Identical amendments to the equivalent articles of the EEC Treaty were agreed and are not reprinted here)

TITLE IV
PROVISIONS AMENDING THE TREATY ESTABLISHING THE EUROPEAN ATOMIC ENERGY COMMUNITY

(Identical amendments to the equivalent articles of the EEC Treaty were agreed and are not reprinted here)

TITLE V
PROVISIONS ON A COMMON FOREIGN AND SECURITY POLICY

Article J

A common foreign and security policy is hereby established which shall be governed by the following provisions.

Article J.1

1. The Union and its Member States shall define and implement a common foreign and security policy, governed by the provisions of this Title and covering all areas of foreign and security policy.

2. The objectives of the common foreign and security policy shall be:

- to safeguard the common values, fundamental interests and independence of the Union;

- to strengthen the security of the Union and its Member States in all ways;

- to preserve peace and strengthen international security, in accordance with the principles of the United Nations Charter as well as the principles of the Helsinki Final Act and the objectives of the Paris Charter;

- to promote international cooperation;

- to develop and consolidate democracy and the rule of law, and respect for human rights and fundamental freedoms.

3. The Union shall pursue these objectives;

- by establishing systematic cooperation between Member States in the conduct of policy, in accordance with Article J.2;

- by gradually implementing, in accordance with Article J.3, joint action in the areas in which the Member States have important interests in common.

4. The Member States shall support the Union's external and security policy actively and unreservedly in a spirit of loyalty and mutual solidarity. They shall refrain from any action which is contrary to the interests of the Union or likely to impair its effectiveness as a cohesive force in international relations. The Council shall ensure that these principles are complied with.

Article J.2

1. Member States shall inform and consult one another within the Council on any matter of foreign and security policy of general interest in order to ensure that their combined influence is exerted as effectively as possible by means of concerted and convergent action.

2. Whenever it deems it necessary, the Council shall define a common position.

Member States shall ensure that their national policies conform to the common positions.

3. Member States shall coordinate their action in international organizations and at international conferences. They shall uphold the common positions in such forums.

In international organizations and at international conferences where not all the Member States participate, those which do take part shall uphold the common positions.

Article J.3

The procedure for adopting joint action in matters covered by foreign and security policy shall be the following:

1. The Council shall decide, on the basis of general guidelines from the European Council, that a matter should be the subject of joint action.

Whenever the Council decides on the principle of joint action, it shall lay down the specific scope, the Union's general and specific objectives in carrying out such action, if necessary its duration, and the means, procedures and conditions for its implementation.

2. The Council shall, when adopting the joint action and at any stage during its development, define those matters on which decisions are to be taken by a qualified majority.

Where the Council is required to act by a qualified majority pursuant to the preceding subparagraph, the votes of its members shall be weighted in accordance with Article 148(2) of the Treaty establishing the European Community, and for their adoption, acts of the Council shall require at least fifty-four votes in favour, cast by at least eight members.

3. If there is a change in circumstances having a substantial effect on a question subject to joint action, the Council shall review the principles and objectives of that action and take the necessary decisions. As long as the Council has not acted, the joint action shall stand.

4. Joint actions shall commit the Member States in the positions they adopt and in the conduct of their activity.

5. Whenever there is any plan to adopt a national position or take national action

pursuant to a joint action, information shall be provided in time to allow, if necessary, for prior consultations within the Council. The obligation to provide prior information shall not apply to measures which are merely a national transposition of Council decisions.

6. In cases of imperative need arising from changes in the situation and failing a Council decision, Member States may take the necessary measures as a matter of urgency having regard to the general objectives of the joint action. The Member State concerned shall inform the Council immediately of any such measures.

7. Should there be any major difficulties in implementing a joint action, a Member State shall refer them to the Council which shall discuss them and seek appropriate solutions. Such solutions shall not run counter to the objectives of the joint action or impair its effectiveness.

Article J.4

1. The common foreign and security policy shall include all questions related to the security of the Union, including the eventual framing of a common defence policy, which might in time lead to a common defence.

2. The Union requests the Western European Union (WEU), which is an integral part of the development of the Union, to elaborate and implement decisions and actions of the Union which have defence implications. The Council shall, in agreement with the institutions of the WEU, adopt the necessary practical arrangements.

3. Issues having defence implications dealt with under this Article shall not be subject to the procedures set out in Article J.3.

4. The policy of the Union in accordance with this Article shall not prejudice the specific character of the security and defence policy of certain Member States and shall respect the obligations of certain Member States under the North Atlantic Treaty and be compatible with the common security and defence policy established within that framework.

5. The provisions of this Article shall not prevent the development of closer cooperation between two or more Member States on a bilateral level, in the framework of the WEU and the Atlantic Alliance, provided such cooperation does not run counter to or impede that provided for in this Title.

6. With a view to furthering the objective of this Treaty, and having in view the date of 1998 in the context of Article XII of the Brussels Treaty, the provisions of this Article may be revised as provided for in Article N(2) on the basis of a report to be presented in 1996 by the Council to the European Council, which shall include an evaluation of the progress made and the experience gained until then.

Article J.5

1. The Presidency shall represent the Union in matters coming within the common foreign and security policy.

2. The Presidency shall be responsible for the implementation of common measures; in that capacity it shall in principle express the position of the Union in international organizations and international conferences.

3. In the tasks referred to in paragraphs 1 and 2, the presidency shall be assisted if needs be by the previous and next Member States to hold the Presidency. The Commission shall be fully associated in these tasks.

4. Without prejudice to Article J.2(3) and Article J.3(4), Member States represented in international organizations or international conferences where not all the Member States participate shall keep the latter informed of any matter of common interest.

Member States which are also members of the United Nations Security Council will concert and keep the other Member States fully informed. Member States which are permanent members of the Security Council will, in the execution of their functions, ensure the defence of the positions and the interests of the Union, without prejudice to their responsibilities under the provisions of the United Nations Charter.

Article J.6

The diplomatic and consular missions of the Member States and the Commission Delegations in third countries and international conferences, and their representations to international organizations, shall cooperate in ensuring that the common positions and common measures adopted by the Council are complied with and implemented.

They shall step up cooperation by exchanging information, carrying out joint assessments and contributing to the implementation of the provisions referred to in Article 8c of the Treaty establishing the European Community.

Article J.7

The Presidency shall consult the European Parliament on the main aspects and the basic choices of the common foreign and security policy and shall ensure that the views of the European Parliament are duly taken into consideration. The European Parliament shall be kept regularly informed by the Presidency and the Commission of the development of the Union's foreign and security policy.

The European Parliament may ask questions of the Council or make recommendations to it. It shall hold an annual debate on progress in implementing the common foreign and security policy.

Article J.8

1. The European Council shall define the principles of and general guidelines for the common foreign and security policy.

2. The Council shall take the decisions necessary for defining and implementing the common foreign and security policy on the basis of the general guidelines adopted by the European Council. It shall ensure the unity, consistency and effectiveness of action by the Union.

The Council shall act unanimously, except for procedural questions and in the case referred to in Article J.3(2).

3. Any Member State or the Commission may refer to the Council any question relating to the common foreign policy and may submit proposals to the Council.

4. In cases requiring a rapid decision, the Presidency, of its own motion, or at the request of the Commission or a Member State, shall convene an extraordinary Council meeting within forty-eight hours or, in an emergency, within a shorter period.

5. Without prejudice to Article 151 of the Treaty establishing the European Community, a Political Committee consisting of Political Directors shall monitor the international situation in the areas covered by common foreign and security policy and contribute to the definition of policies by delivering opinions to the Council at the request of the Council or on its own initiative. It shall also monitor the implementation of agreed policies, without prejudice to the responsibility of the Presidency and the Commission.

Article J.9

The Commission shall be fully associated with the work carried out in the common foreign and security policy field.

Article J.10

On the occasion of any review of the security provisions under Article J.4, the Conference which is convened to that effect shall also examine whether any other amendments need to be made to provisions relating to the common foreign and security policy.

Article J.11

1. The provisions referred to in Articles 137, 138, 139 to 142, 146, 147, 150 to 153, 157 to 163 and 217 of the Treaty establishing the European Community shall apply to the provisions relating to the areas referred to in this Title.

2. Administrative expenditure which the provisions relating to the areas referred to in this Title entail for the institutions shall be charged to the budget of the European Communities. The Council may also:

– either decide unanimously that operational expenditure to which the implementation of those provisions gives rise is to be charged to the budget of the European Communities; in that event, the budgetary procedure laid down in the Treaty establishing the European Community shall be applicable;

– or determine that such expenditure shall be charged to the Member States, where appropriate in accordance with a scale to be decided.

TITLE VI
PROVISIONS ON COOPERATION IN THE FIELDS OF JUSTICE AND HOME AFFAIRS

Article K

Cooperation in the fields of justice and home affairs shall be governed by the following provisions.

Article K.1

For the purposes of achieving the objectives of the Union, in particular the free movement of persons, and without prejudice to the powers of the European Community, Member States shall regard the following areas as matters of common interest:

(1) asylum policy;

(2) rules governing the crossing by persons of the external borders of the Member States and the exercise of controls thereon;

(3) immigration policy and policy regarding nationals of third countries;

    (a) conditions of entry and movement by nationals of third countries on the territory of Member States;

    (b) conditions of residence by nationals of third countries on the territory of Member States, including family reunion and access to employment;

    (c) combatting unauthorized immigration, residence and work by nationals of third countries on the territory of Member States;

(4) combating drug addiction in so far as this is not covered by 7 to 9;

(5) combating fraud on an international scale in so far as this is not covered by 7 to 9;

(6) judicial cooperation in civil matters;

(7) judicial cooperation in criminal matters;

(8) customs cooperation;

(9) police cooperation for the purposes of preventing and combating terrorism, unlawful drug trafficking and other serious forms of international crime, including if necessary certain aspects of customs cooperation, in connection with the organization of a Union-wide system for exchanging information within a European Police Office (Europol).

Article K.2

1. The matters referred to in Article K.1 shall be dealt with in compliance with the European Convention for the Protection of Human Rights and Fundamental Freedoms of 4 November 1950 and the Convention relating to the Status of Refugees of 28 July 1951 and having regard to the protection afforded by Member States to persons persecuted on political grounds.

2. This Title shall not affect the exercise of the responsibilities incumbent upon Member States with regard to the maintenance of law and order and the safeguarding of internal security.

Article K.3

1. In the areas referred to in Article K.1, Member States shall inform and consult one another within the Council with a view to coordinating their action. To that end, they shall establish collaboration between the relevant departments of their administrations.

2. The Council may:

– on the initiative of any Member State of the Commission, in the areas referred to in Article K.1(1) to (6);

– on the initiative of any Member State, in the areas referred to Article K1(7) to (9):

    (a) adopt joint positions and promote, using the appropriate form and procedures, any cooperation contributing to the pursuit of the objectives of the Union;

(b) adopt joint action in so far as the objectives of the Union can be attained better by joint action than by the Member States acting individually on account of the scale or effects of the action envisaged; it may decide that measures implementing joint action are to be adopted by a qualified majority;

(c) without prejudice to Article 220 of the Treaty establishing the European Community, draw up conventions which it shall recommend to the Member States for adoption in accordance with their respective constitutional requirements.

Unless otherwise provided by such conventions, measures implementing them shall be adopted within the Council by a majority of two-thirds of the High Contracting Parties.

Such conventions may stipulate that the Court of Justice shall have jurisdiction to interpret their provisions and to rule on any disputes regarding their application, in accordance with such arrangements as they may lay down.

Article K.4

1. A Coordinating Committee shall be set up consisting of senior officials. In addition to its coordinating role, it shall be the task of the Committee to;

– give opinions for the attention of the Council, either at the Council's request or on its own initiative.

– contribute, without prejudice to Article 151 of the Treaty establishing the European Community, to the preparation of the Council's discussions in the areas referred to in Article K.1 and, in accordance with the conditions laid down in Article 100d of the Treaty establishing the European Community, in the areas referred to in Article 100c of that Treaty.

2. The Commission shall be fully associated with the work in the areas referred to in this Title.

3. The Council shall act unanimously, except on matters of procedure and in cases where Article K.3 expressly provides for other voting rules.

Where the Council is required to act by a qualified majority, the votes of its members shall be weighted as laid down in Article 148(2) of the Treaty establishing the European Community, and for their adoption, acts of the Council shall require at least fifty-four votes in favour, cast by at least eight members.

Article K.5

Within international organizations and at international conferences in which they take part, Member States shall defend the common positions adopted under the provisions of this Title.

Article K.6

The Presidency and the Commission shall regularly inform the European Parliament of discussions in the areas covered by this Title.

The Presidency shall consult the European Parliament on the principal aspects of activities in the areas referred to in this Title and shall ensure that the views of the European Parliament are duly taken into consideration.

The European Parliament may ask questions of the Council or make recommendations to it. Each year, it shall hold a debate on the progress made in implementation of the areas referred to in this Title.

Article K.7

The provisions of this Title shall not prevent the establishment or development of closer cooperation between two or more Member States in so far as such cooperation does not conflict with, or impede, that provided for in this Title.

Article K.8

1. The provisions referred to in Article 137, 138, 139 to 142, 146, 147, 150 to 153, 157 to 163 and 217 of the Treaty establishing the European Community shall apply to the provisions relating to the areas referred to in this Title.

2. Administrative expenditure which the provisions relating to the areas referred to in this Title entail for the institutions shall be charged to the budget of European Communities.

The Council may also:

- either decide unanimously that operational expenditure to which the implementation of those provisions gives rise is to be charged to the budget of the European Communities; in that event, the budgetary procedure laid down in the Treaty establishing the European Community shall be applicable;

- or determine that such expenditure shall be charged to the Member States, where

appropriate in accordance with a scale to be decided.

Article K.9

The Council, acting unanimously on the initiative of the Commission or a Member State, may decide to apply Article 100c of the Treaty establishing the European Community to action in areas referred to in Article K.1(1) to (6), and at the same time determine the relevant voting conditions relating to it. It shall recommend the Member States to adopt that decision in accordance with their respective constitutional requirements.

TITLE VII
FINAL PROVISIONS

Article L

The provisions of the Treaty establishing the European Community, the Treaty establishing the European Coal and Steel Community and the Treaty establishing the European Atomic Energy Community concerning the powers of the Court of Justice of the European Communities and the exercise of those powers shall apply only to the following provisions of this Treaty:

(a) provisions amending the Treaty establishing the European Economic Community, the Treaty establishing the European Coal and Steel Community and the Treaty establishing the European Atomic Energy Community;

(b) the third subparagraph of Article K.3(2)(c);

(c) Articles L to S.

Article M

Subject to the provisions amending the Treaty establishing the European Economic Community with a view to establishing the European

Community, the Treaty establishing the European Coal and Steel Community and the Treaty establishing the European Atomic Energy Community, and to these final provisions, nothing in this Treaty shall effect the Treaties establishing the European Communities or the subsequent Treaties and Acts modifying or supplementing them.

Article N

1. The government of any Member State or the Commission may submit to the Council proposals for the amendment of the Treaties on which the Union is founded.

If the Council, after consulting the European Parliament and, where appropriate, the Commission, delivers an opinion in favour of calling a conference of representatives of the governments of the Member States, the conference shall be convened by the President of the Council for the purpose of determining by common accord the amendments to be made to those Treaties. The European Central Bank shall also be consulted in the case of institutional changes in the monetary area.

The amendments shall enter into force after being ratified by all the Member States in accordance with their respective constitutional requirements.

2. A conference of representatives of the governments of the Member States shall be convened in 1996 to examine those provisions of this Treaty for which revision is provided, in accordance with the objectives set out in Articles A and B.

Article O

Any European State may apply to become a Member of the Union. It shall address its application to the Council, which shall act unanimously after consulting the Commission and after receiving the assent of the European Parliament, which shall act by an absolute majority of its component members.

The conditions of admission and the adjustments to the Treaties on which the Union is founded which such admission entails shall be the subject of an agreement between the Member States and the applicant State. This agreement shall be submitted for ratification by all the contracting States in accordance with their respective constitutional requirements.

Article P

1. Articles 2 to 7 and 10 to 19 of the Treaty establishing a Single Council and a Single Commission of the European Communities, signed in Brussels on 8 April 1965, are hereby repealed.

2. Article 2, Article 3(2) and Title III of the Single European Act signed in Luxembourg on 17 February 1986 and in the Hague on 28 February 1986 are hereby repealed.

Article Q

This Treaty is concluded for an unlimited period.

Article R

1. This Treaty shall be ratified by the High Contracting Parties in accordance with their respective constitutional requirements. The instruments of ratification shall be deposited with the government of the Italian Republic.

2. This Treaty shall enter into force on 1 January 1993, provided that all the instruments of ratification have been deposited, or, failing that, on the first day of the month following the deposit of the instrument of ratification by the last signatory State to take this step.

Article S

This Treaty, drawn up in a single original in the Danish, Dutch, English, French, German, Greek, Irish, Italian, Portuguese and Spanish languages, the texts in each of these languages being equally authentic, shall be deposited in the archives of the government of the Italian Republic, which will transmit a certified copy to each of the governments of the other signatory States.

IN WITNESS WHEREOF, the undersigned Plenipotentiaries have signed this Treaty.

Done at Maastricht on the seventh day of February one thousand nine hundred and ninety two

[Editor's note: the above sentence appears in all 10 languages, the signatures follow.]

PROTOCOLS

PROTOCOL
ON THE ACQUISITION OF PROPERTY IN DENMARK

THE HIGH CONTRACTING PARTIES,

DESIRING to settle certain particular problems relating to Denmark,

HAVING AGREED UPON the following provision, which shall be annexed to the Treaty establishing the European Community:

Notwithstanding the provisions of this Treaty, Denmark may maintain the existing legislation on the acquisition of second homes.

PROTOCOL
CONCERNING ARTICLE 119 OF THE TREATY
ESTABLISHING THE EUROPEAN COMMUNITY

THE HIGH CONTRACTING PARTIES,

HAVE AGREED UPON the following provision, which shall be annexed to the treaty establishing the European Community:

For the purposes of Article 119 of this Treaty, benefits under occupational social security schemes shall not be considered as remuneration if an in so far as they are attributable to periods of employment prior to 17 May 1990, except in the case of workers or those claiming under them who have before that date initiated legal proceedings or introduced an equivalent claim under the applicable national law.

PROTOCOL
ON THE STATUTE OF THE EUROPEAN SYSTEM OF CENTRAL
BANKS AND OF THE EUROPEAN CENTRAL BANK

THE HIGH CONTRACTING PARTIES,

DESIRING to lay down the Statute of the European System of Central Banks and of the European Central Bank provided for in Article 4a of the Treaty establishing the European Community,

HAVE AGREED upon the following provisions, which shall be annexed to the Treaty establishing the European Community:

CHAPTER I

CONSTITUTION OF THE ESCB

Article 1

The European System of Central Banks

1.1.   The European System of Central Banks (ESCB) and the European Central Bank (ECB) shall be established in accordance with Article 4a of this Treaty; they shall perform their tasks and carry on their activities in accordance with the provisions of this Treaty and of this Statute.

1.2.   In accordance with Article 106(1) on this Treaty, the ESCB shall be composed of the ECB and of the central banks of the Member States ("national central banks"). The Institut monétaire luxembourgeois will be the central bank of Luxembourg.

CHAPTER II

OBJECTIVES AND TASKS OF ESCB

Article 2

Objectives

In accordance with Article 105(1) of this Treaty, the primary objective of the ESCB shall be to maintain price stability. Without prejudice to the objective of price stability, it shall support the general economic policies in the Community with a view to contributing to the achievement of the objectives of the Community as laid down in Article 2 of this Treaty. The ESCB shall act in accordance with the principle of an open market economy with free competition, favouring an efficient allocation of resources, and in compliance with the principles set out in Article 3a of this Treaty.

Article 3

Tasks

3.1.   In accordance with Article 105(2) of this Treaty, the basic tasks to be carried out through the ESCB shall be:

– to define and implement the monetary policy of the Community;

– to conduct foreign-exchange operations consistent with the provisions of Article 109 of this Treaty;

– to hold and manage the official foreign reserves of the Member States;

– to promote the smooth operation of payment systems.

3.2.   In accordance with Article 105(3) of this Treaty, the third indent of Article 3.1 shall be without prejudice to the holding and management by the governments of Member States of foreign exchange working balances.

3.3.   In accordance with Article 105(5) of this Treaty, the ESCB shall contribute to the smooth conduct of policies pursued by the competent authorities relating to the prudential supervision of credit institutions and the stability of the financial system.

Article 4

Advisory functions

In accordance with Article 105(4) of this Treaty:

(a) the ECB shall be consulted:

– on any proposed Community act in its fields of competence;

– by national authorities regarding any draft legislative provision in its fields of competence, but within the limits and under the conditions set out by the Council in accordance with the procedure laid down in Article 42;

(b) the ECB may submit opinions to the appropriate Community institutions or bodies or to national authorities on matters in its fields of competence.

Article 5

Collection of statistical information

5.1. In order to undertake the tasks of the ESCB, the ECB, assisted by the national central banks, shall collect the necessary statistical information either from the competent national authorities or directly from economic agents. For these purposes it shall cooperate with the Community institutions or bodies and with the competent authorities of the Member States or third countries and with international organizations.

5.2. The national central banks shall carry out, to the extent possible, the tasks described in Article 5.1.

5.3. The ECB shall contribute to the harmonization, where necessary, of the rules and practices governing the collection, compilation and distribution of statistics in the areas within its fields of competence.

5.4. The Council, in accordance with the procedure laid down in Article 42, shall define the natural and legal persons subject to reporting requirements, the confidentiality regime and the appropriate provisions for enforcement.

Article 6

International cooperation

6.1. In the field of international cooperation involving the tasks entrusted to the ESCB, the ECB shall decide how the ESCB shall be represented.

6.2. The ECB and, subject to its approval, the national central banks may participate in international monetary institutions.

6.3. Articles 6.1 and 6.2 shall be without prejudice to Article 109(4) of this Treaty.

CHAPTER III

ORGANIZATION OF THE ESCB

Article 7

Independence

In accordance with Article 107 of this Treaty, when exercising the powers and carrying out the tasks and duties conferred upon them by this Treaty and this Statute, neither the ECB, nor a national central bank, nor any member of their decision-making bodies shall seek or take instructions from Community institutions or bodies, from any government of a Member State or from any other body. The Community institutions and bodies and the governments of the Member States undertake to respect this principle and not to seek to influence the members of the decision-making bodies of the ECB or of the national central banks in the performance of their tasks.

Article 8

General principle

The ESCB shall be governed by the decision-making bodies of the ECB.

Article 9

The European Central Bank

9.1. The ECB which, in accordance with Article 106(2) of this Treaty, shall have legal personality, shall enjoy in each of the Member States the most extensive legal capacity accorded to legal persons under its law; it may, in particular, acquire or dispose of movable and immovable property and may be a party to legal proceedings.

9.2. The ECB shall ensure that the tasks conferred upon the ESCB under Article 105(2), (3) and (5) of this Treaty are implemented either by its own activities pursuant to this Statute or through the national central bank pursuant to Articles 12.1 and 14.

9.3 In accordance with Article 106(3) of this Treaty, the decision-making bodies of the ECB shall be the Governing Council and the Executive Board.

10.4. The proceedings of the meetings shall be confidential. The Governing Council may decide to make the outcome of its deliberations public.

10.5. The Governing Council shall meet at least ten times a year.

Article 10

The Governing Council

10.1. In accordance with Article 109a(1) of this Treaty, the Governing Council shall comprise the members of the Executive Board of the ECB and the Governors of the national central banks.

10.2. Subject to Article 10.3, only members of the Governing Council present in person shall have the right to vote. By way of derogation from this rule, the Rules of Procedure referred to in Article 12.3 may lay down that members of the Governing Council may cast their vote by means of teleconferencing. These rules shall also provide that a member of the Governing Council who is prevented from voting for a prolonged period may appoint an alternate as a member of the Governing Council.

Subject to Articles 10.3 and 11.3, each member of the Governing Council shall have one vote. Save as otherwise provided for in this Statue, the Governing Council shall act by a simple majority. In the event of a tie the President shall have the casting vote.

In order for the Governing Council to vote, there shall be quorum of two-thirds of the members. If the quorum is not met, the President may convene and extraordinary meeting at which decisions may be taken without regard to the quorum.

10.3. For any decisions to be taken under Articles 28, 29, 30, 32, 33 and 51, the votes in the Governing Council shall be weighted according to the national central banks' shares in the subscribed capital of the ECB. The weight of the votes of the members of the Executive Board shall be zero. A decision requiring a qualified majority shall be adopted if the votes cast in favour represent at least two thirds of the subscribed capital of the ECB and represent at least half of the shareholders. If a Governor in unable to be present, he may nominate an alternate to cast his weighted vote.

Article 11

The Executive Board

11.1. In accordance with Article 109a(2)(a) of this Treaty, the Executive Board shall comprise the President, the Vice-President and four other members.

The members shall perform their duties on a full-time basis. No member shall engage in any occupation, whether gainful or not, unless exemption is exceptionally granted by the Governing Council.

11.2. In accordance with Article 109a(2)(b) of this Treaty, the President, the Vice-President and the other Members of the Executive Board shall be appointed from among persons of recognized standing and professional experience in monetary or banking matters by common accord of the governments of the Member States at the level of the Heads of State or government, on a recommendation from the Council after it has consulted the European Parliament and the Governing Council.

Their term of office shall be eight years and shall not be renewable. Only nationals of Member States may be members of the Executive Board.

11.3. The terms and conditions of employment of the members of the Executive Board, in particular their salaries, pensions and other social security benefits shall be the subject of contracts with the ECB and shall be fixed by the Governing Council on a proposal from a Committee comprising three members appointed by the Governing Council and three members appointed by the Council. The members of the Executive Board shall not have the right to vote on matters referred to in this paragraph.

11.4. If a member of the Executive Board no longer fulfils the conditions required for the performance of his duties or if he has been guilty of serious misconduct, the Court of Justice may, on application by the Governing

Council or the Executive Board, compulsorily retire him.

11.5. Each member of the Executive Board present in person shall have the right to vote and shall have, for that purpose, one vote. Save as otherwise provided, the Executive Board shall act by a simple majority of the votes cast. In the event of a tie, the President shall have the casting vote. The voting arrangements shall be specified in the Rules of Procedure referred to in Article 12.3.

11.6. The Executive Board shall be responsible for the current business of the ECB.

11.7. Any vacancy on the Executive Board shall be filled by the appointment of a new member in accordance with Article 11.2.

Article 12

Responsibilities of the decision-making bodies

12.1. The Governing Council shall adopt the guidelines and take the decisions necessary to ensure the performance of the tasks entrusted to the ESCB under this Treaty and this Statute. The Governing Council shall formulate the monetary policy of the Community including, as appropriate, decisions relating to intermediate monetary objectives, key interest rates and the supply of reserves in the ESCB and shall establish the necessary guidelines for their implementation.

The Executive Board shall implement monetary policy in accordance with the guidelines and decisions laid down by the Governing Council. In doing so the Executive Board shall give the necessary instructions to national central banks. In addition the Executive Board may have certain powers delegated to it where the Governing Council so decides.

To the extent deemed possible and appropriate and without prejudice to the provisions of this Article, the ECB shall have recourse to the national central banks to carry out operations which form part of the tasks of the ESCB.

12.2. The Executive Board shall have the responsibility for the preparation of meetings of the Governing Council.

12.3. The Governing Council shall adopt Rules of Procedure which determine the inter-

nal organization of the ECB and its decision-making bodies.

12.4. The Governing Council shall exercise the advisory functions referred to Article 4.

12.5. The Governing Council shall take the decisions referred to Article 6.

Article 13

The President

13.1. The President or, in his absence, the Vice-President shall chair the governing Council and the Executive Board of the ECB.

13.2. Without prejudice to Article 39, the President or his nominee shall represent the ECB externally.

Article 14

National Central Banks

14.1. In accordance with Article 108 of this Treaty, each Member State shall ensure, at the latest at the date of the establishment of the ESCB, that its national legislation, including the statues of its national central bank, is compatible with this Treaty and this Statute.

14.2. The statutes of the national central banks shall, in particular, provide that the term of office of a Governor of a national central bank shall be no less than five years.

A Governor may be relieved from office only if he no longer fulfils the conditions required for the performance of his duties or if he has been guilty of serious misconduct. A decision to this effect may be referred to the Court of Justice by the Governor concerned or the Governing Council on grounds of infringement of this Treaty or of any rule of law relating to its application. Such proceedings shall be instituted within two months of the publication of the decision or of its notification to the plaintiff or, in the absence thereof, of the day on which it came to knowledge of the latter, as the case may be.

14.3. The national central banks are an integral part of the ESCB and shall act in accordance with the guidelines and instructions of ECB. The Governing Council shall take the necessary steps to ensure compliance with the guidelines and instructions of the ECB, and shall require that any necessary information be given to it.

14.4. National central banks may perform functions other than those specified in this Statute unless the Governing Council finds, by a majority of two thirds of the votes cast, that these interfere with the objectives and tasks of the ESCB. Such functions shall be performed on the responsibility and liability of national central banks and shall not be regarded as being part of the functions of the ESCB.

Article 15

Reporting commitments

15.1. The ECB shall draw up and publish reports on the activities of the ESCB at least quarterly.

15.2. A consolidated financial statement of the ESCB shall be published each week.

15.3. In accordance with Article 109b(3) of this Treaty, the ECB shall address an annual report on the activities of the ESCB and on the monetary policy of both the previous and the current year to the European Parliament, the Council and the Commission, and also to the European Council.

15.4. The reports and statements referred to in this Article shall be made available to interested parties free of charge.

Article 16

Bank notes

In accordance with Article 105a(1) of this Treaty, the Governing Council shall have the exclusive right to authorize the issue of bank notes within the Community. The ECB and the national central banks may issue such notes. The bank notes issued by the ECB and the national central banks shall be the only such notes to have the status of legal tender within the Community.

The ECB shall respect as far as possible existing practices regarding the issue and design of bank notes.

CHAPTER IV

MONETARY FUNCTIONS AND OPERATIONS OF THE ESCB

Article 17

Accounts with the ECB and the national central banks

In order to conduct their operations, the ECB and the national central banks may open accounts for credit institutions, public entities and other market participants and accept assets, including book-entry securities, as collateral.

Article 18

Open market and credit operations

18.1. In order to achieve the objectives of the ESCB and to carry out its tasks, the ECB and the national central banks may:

– operate in the financial markets by buying and selling outright (spot and forward) or under repurchase agreement and by lending or borrowing claims and marketable instruments, whether in Community or in non-Community currencies, as well as precious metals;

– conduct credit operations with credit institutions and other market participants, with lending being based on adequate collateral.

18.2. The ECB shall establish general principles for open market and credit operations carried out by itself or the national central banks, including for the announcement of conditions under which they stand ready to enter into such transactions.

Article 19

Minimum reserves

19.1. Subject to Article 2, the ECB may require credit institutions established in Member States to hold minimum reserves on accounts with the ECB and national central banks in pursuance of monetary policy objectives. Regulations concerning the calculation and determination of the required minimum reserves may be established by the Governing Council. In cases of non-compliance the ECB shall be entitled to levy penalty interest and to impose other sanctions with comparable effect.

19.2. For the application of this Article, the Council shall, in accordance with the procedure laid down in Article 42, define the basis for minimum reserves and the maximum reserves and the maximum permissible ratios between those reserves and their basis, as well as the appropriate sanctions in cases of non-compliance.

Article 20

Other instruments of monetary control

The Governing Council may, by a majority of two thirds of the votes cast, decide upon the use of such other operational methods of monetary control as it sees fit, respecting Article 2.

The Council shall, in accordance with the procedure laid down in Article 42, define the scope of such methods if they impose obligations on third parties.

Article 21

Operations with public entities

21.1. In accordance with Article 104 of the Treaty, overdrafts or any other type of credit facility with the ECB or with the national central banks in favour of Community institutions or bodies, central governments, regional, local or other public authorities, other bodies governed by public law, or public undertakings of Member States shall be prohibited, as shall the purchase directly from them by the ECB or national central banks of debt instruments.

21.2. The ECB and national central banks may act as fiscal agents for the entities referred to in 21.1.

21.3. The provisions of this Article shall not apply to publicly-owned credit institutions which, in the context of the supply of reserves by central banks, shall be given the same treatment by national central banks and the ECB as private credit institutions.

Article 22

Clearing and payment systems

The ECB and national central banks may provide facilities, and the ECB may make regulations, to ensure efficient and sound clearing and payment systems within the Community and with other countries.

Article 23

External operations

The ECB and national central banks may:

– establish relations with central banks and financial institutions in other countries and, where appropriate, with international organizations;

– acquire and sell spot and forward all types of foreign exchange assets and precious metals; the term "foreign exchange asset" shall include securities and all other assets in the currency of any country or units of account in whatever form held;

– hold and manage the assets referred to in this Article;

– conduct all types of banking transactions in relations with third countries and international organizations, including borrowing and lending operations.

Article 24

Other operations

In addition to operations arising from their tasks, the ECB and national central banks may enter into operations for their administrative purposes or for their staff.

CHAPTER V

PRUDENTIAL SUPERVISION

Article 25

Prudential supervision

25.1.   The ECB may offer advice to and be consulted by the Council, the Commission and the competent authorities of the Member States on the scope and implementation of Community legislation relating to the prudential supervision of credit institutions and to the stability of the financial system.

25.2.   In accordance with any decision of the Council under Article 105(6) of this Treaty, the ECB may perform specific tasks concerning policies relating to the prudential supervision of credit institutions and other financial institutions with the exception of insurance undertakings.

CHAPTER VI

FINANCIAL PROVISIONS OF THE ESCB

Article 26

Financial accounts

26.1.   The financial year of the ECB and national central banks shall begin on the first day of January and end on the last day of December.

26.2.   The annual accounts of the ECB shall be drawn up the Executive Board, in accordance with the principles established by the Governing Council. The accounts shall be approved by the Governing Council and shall thereafter be published.

26.3.   For analytic and operational purposes, the Executive Board shall draw up a consolidated balance sheet of the ESCB, comprising those assets and liabilities of the national central banks that fall within the ESCB.

26.4.   For the application of this Article, the Governing Council shall establish the necessary rules for standardizing the accounting and reporting of operations undertaken by the national central banks.

Article 27

Auditing

27.1.   The account of the ECB and national central banks shall be audited by independent external auditors recommended by the Governing Council and approved by the Council. The auditors shall have full power to examine all books and accounts of the ECB and national central banks and obtain full information about their transactions.

27.2.   The provisions of Article 188c of this Treaty shall only apply to an examination of the operational efficiency of the management of the ECB.

Article 28

Capital of the ECB

28.1.   The capital of the ECB, which shall become operational upon its establishment, shall be ECU 5 000 million. The capital may be increased by such amounts as may be decided by the Governing Council acting by the qualified majority provided for in Article 10.3, within the limits and under the conditions set by the Council under the procedure laid down in Article 42.

28.2.   The national central banks shall be the sole subscribers to and holders of the capital of the ECB. The subscription of capital shall be according to the key established in accordance with Article 29.

28.3.   The Governing Council, acting by the qualified majority provided for in Article 10.3, shall determine the extent to which and the form in which the capital shall be paid up.

28.4.   Subject to Article 28.5, the shares of the national central banks in the subscribed capital of the ECB may not be transferred, pledged or attached.

28.5.   If the key referred to in Article 29 is adjusted, the national central banks shall transfer among themselves capital shares to the extent necessary to ensure that the distribution of capital shares corresponds to the adjusted key. The Governing Council shall determine the terms and conditions of such transfers.

Article 29

Key for capital subscription

29.1.　When in accordance with the procedure referred to in Article 109l(1) of this Treaty the ESCB and the ECB have been established, the key for subscription of the ECB's capital shall be established. Each national central bank shall be assigned a weighting in this key which shall be equal to the sum of:

– 50% of the share of its respective Member State in the population of the Community in the penultimate year preceding the establishment of the ESCB;

– 50% of the share of its respective Member State in the gross domestic product at market prices of the Community as recorded in the last five years preceding the penultimate year before the establishment of the ESCB;

The percentages shall be rounded up to the nearest multiple 0.05 percentage points.

29.2.　The statistical data to be used for the application of this Article shall be provided by the Commission in accordance with the rules adopted by the Council under the procedure provided for in Article 42.

29.3.　The weighting assigned to the national central banks shall be adjusted every five years after the establishment of the ESCB by analogy with the provisions laid down in Article 29.1. The adjusted key shall apply with effect from the first day of the following year.

29.4.　The Governing Council shall take all other measures necessary for the application of this Article.

Article 30

Transfer of foreign reserve assets to the ECB

30.1.　Without prejudice to Article 28, the ECB shall be provided by the national central banks with foreign reserve assets, other than Member States' currencies, ECUs, IMF reserve positions andSDRs, up to an amount equivalent to ECU 50 000 million. The Governing Council shall decide upon the proportion to be called up by the ECB following its establishment and the amounts called up at later dates. The ECB shall have the full right to hold and manage the foreign reserves that are transferred to it and to use them for the purposes set out in this Statute.

30.2.　The contributions of each national central bank shall be fixed in proportion to its share in the subscribed capital of the ECB.

30.3.　Each national central bank shall be credited by the ECB with a claim equivalent to its contribution. The Governing Council shall determine the denomination and remuneration of such claims.

30.4.　Further calls of foreign reserve assets beyond the limit set in Article 30.1 may be effected by the ECB, in accordance with Article 30.2, within the limits and under the conditions set by the Council in accordance with the procedure laid down in Article 42.

30.5.　The ECB may hold and manage IMF reserve positions and SDRs and provide for the pooling of such assets.

30.6.　The Governing Council shall take all other measures necessary for the application of this Article.

Article 31

Foreign reserve assets held by national central banks

31.1.　The national central banks shall be allowed to perform transactions in fulfilment of their obligations towards international organizations in accordance with Article 23.

31.2.　All other operations in foreign reserve assets remaining with the national central banks after the transfers referred to in Article 30, and Member States' transactions with their foreign exchange working balances shall, above a certain limit to be established within the framework of Article 31.3, be subject to approval by the ECB in order to ensure consistency with the exchange rate and monetary policies of the Community.

31.3.   The Governing Council shall issue guidelines with a view to facilitating such operations.

Article 32

Allocation of monetary income of national central banks

32.1.   The income accruing to the national central banks in the performance of the ESCB's monetary policy function (hereinafter referred to as "monetary income") shall be allocated at the end of each financial year in accordance with the provisions of this Article.

32.2.   Subject to Article 32.3, the amount of each national central bank's monetary income shall be equal to its annual income derived from its assets held against notes in circulation and deposit liabilities to credit institutions. These assets shall be earmarked by national central banks in accordance with guidelines to be established by the Governing Council.

32.3.   If, after the start of the third stage, the balance sheet structures of the national central banks do not, in the judgment of the Governing Council, permit the application of Article 32.2, the Governing Council, acting by a qualified majority, may decide that, by way of derogation form Article 32.2, monetary income shall be measured according to an alternative method for a period of not more than five years.

32.4.   The amount of each national central bank's monetary income shall be reduced by an amount equivalent to any interest paid by that central bank on its deposit liabilities to credit institutions in accordance with Article 19.

The Governing Council may decide that national central banks shall be indemnified against costs incurred in connection with the issue of bank notes or in exceptional circumstances for specific losses arising from monetary policy operations undertaken for the ESCB.Indemnification shall be in a form deemed appropriate in the judgment of the Governing Council; these amounts may be offset against the national central banks' monetary income.

32.5.   The sum of the national central banks' monetary income shall be allocated to the national central banks in proportion to their paid-up shares in the capital of the ECB,

subject to any decision taken by the Governing Council pursuant to Article 33.2.

32.6.   The clearing and settlement of the balances arising from the allocation of monetary income shall be carried out by the ECB in accordance with guidelines established by the Governing Council.

32.7.   The Governing Council shall take all other measures necessary for the application of this Article.

Article 33

Allocation of net profits and losses of the ECB

33.1.   The net profit of the ECB shall be transferred in the following order:

(a) an amount to be determined by the Governing Council, which may not exceed 20% of the net profit, shall be transferred to the general reserve fund subject to a limit equal to a 100% of the capital;

(b) the remaining net profit shall be distributed to the shareholders of the ECB in proportion to their paid-up shares.

33.2.   In the event of a loss incurred by the ECB, the shortfall may be offset against the general reserve fund of the ECB and, if necessary, following a decision by the Governing Council, against the monetary income of the relevant financial year in proportion and up to the amounts allocated to the national central banks in accordance with Article 32.5.

CHAPTER VII

GENERAL PROVISIONS

Article 34

Legal acts

34.1.   In accordance with Article 108a of this Treaty, the ECB shall:

– make regulations to the extent necessary to implement the tasks defined in Article 3.1., first indent, Articles 19.1, 22 or 25.2 and in cases which shall be laid down in the acts of the Council referred to in Article 42;

- take decisions necessary for carrying out the tasks entrusted to the ESCB under this Treaty and this Statute;

- make recommendations and deliver opinions.

34.2.   A regulation shall have general application. It shall be binding in its entirety and directly applicable in all Member States. Recommendations and opinions shall have no binding force.

A decision shall be binding in its entirety upon those to whom it is addressed.

Articles 190 to 192 of this Treaty shall apply to regulations and decisions adopted by the ECB.

The ECB may decide to publish its decisions, recommendations and opinions.

34.3.   Within the limits and under the conditions adopted by the Council under the procedure laid down in Article 42, the ECB shall be entitled to impose fines or periodic penalty payments on undertakings for failure to comply with obligations under its regulations and decisions.

Article 35

Judicial control and related matters

35.1.   The acts or omissions of the ECB shall be open to review or interpretation by the Court of Justice in the cases and under the conditions laid down in this Treaty. The ECB may institute proceedings in the cases and under the conditions laid down in this Treaty.

35.2.   Disputes between the ECB, on the one hand, and its creditors, debtors or any other person, on the other, shall be decided by the competent national courts, save where jurisdiction has been conferred upon the Court of Justice.

35.3.   The ECB shall be subject to the liability regime provided for in Article 215 of this Treaty. The national central banks shall be liable according to their respective national laws.

35.4.   The Court of Justice shall have jurisdiction to give judgment pursuant to any arbitration clause contained in a contract concluded by or on behalf of the ECB, whether that contract be governed by public or private law.

35.5.   A decision of the ECB to bring an action before the Court of Justice shall be taken by the Governing Council.

35.6.   The Court of Justice shall have jurisdiction in disputes concerning the fulfilment by a national central bank of obligations under this Statute. If the ECB considers that a national central bank has failed to fulfil an obligation under this Statute, it shall deliver a reasoned opinion on the matter after giving the national central bank concerned the opportunity to submit its observations. If the national central bank concerned does not comply with the opinion within the period laid down by the ECB, the latter may bring the matter before the Court of Justice.

Article 36

Staff

36.1.   The Governing Council, on a proposal from the Executive Board, shall lay down the conditions of employment of the staff of the ECB.

36.2.   The Court of Justice shall have jurisdiction in any dispute between the ECB and its servants within the limits and under the conditions laid down in the conditions of employment.

Article 37

Seat

Before the end of 1992, the decision as to where the seat of the ECB will be established shall be taken by common accord of the governments of the Member States at the level of Heads of State or Government.

Article 38

Professional secrecy

38.1.   Members of the governing bodies and the staff of the ECB and the national central banks shall be required, even after their duties have ceased, not to disclose information of the kind covered by the obligation of professional secrecy.

38.2.   Persons having access to data covered by Community legislation imposing an obligation of secrecy shall be subject to such legislation.

Article 39

Signatories

The ECB shall be legally committed to third parties by the President or by two members of the Executive Board or by the signatures of two members of the staff of the ECB who have been duly authorized by the President to sign on behalf of the ECB.

Article 40

Privileges and immunities

The ECB shall enjoy in the territories of the Member States such privileges and immunities as are necessary for the performance of its tasks, under the conditions laid down in the Protocol on the Privileges and Immunities of the European Communities annexed to the Treaty establishing a Single Council and a Single Commission of the European Communities.

CHAPTER VIII

AMENDMENT OF THE STATUTE AND COMPLEMENTARY LEGISLATION

Article 41

Simplified amendment procedure

41.1.   In accordance with Article 106(5) of this Treaty, Articles 5.1, 5.2, 5.3, 17, 18, 19.1, 22, 23, 24, 26, 32.2, 32.3, 32.4, 32.6, 33.1(a) and 36 of this Statute may be amended by the Council, acting either by a qualified majority

on a recommendation from the ECB and after consulting the Commission, or unanimously on a proposal from the Commission and after consulting the ECB. In either case the assent of the European Parliament shall be required.

41.2.   A recommendation made by the ECB under this Article shall require a unanimous decision by the Governing Council.

Article 42

Complementary legislation

In accordance with Article 106(6) of this Treaty, immediately after the decision on the date for the beginning of the third stage, the Council, acting by a qualified majority either on a proposal from the Commission and after consulting the European Parliament and the ECB or on a recommendation from the ECB and after consulting the European Parliament and the Commission, shall adopt the provisions referred to in Articles 4, 5.4, 19.2, 20, 28.1, 29.2, 30.4 and 34.3 of this Statute.

CHAPTER IX

TRANSITIONAL AND OTHER PROVISIONS FOR THE ESCB

Article 43

General provisions

43.1.   A derogation as referred to in Article 109k(1) of this Treaty shall entail that the following Articles of this Statute shall not confer any rights or impose any obligations on the Member State concerned: 3, 6, 9.2, 12.1, 14.3, 16, 18, 19, 20, 22, 23, 26.2, 27, 30, 31, 32, 33, 34, 50 and 52.

43.2.   The central banks of Member States with a derogation as specified in Article 109k(1) of this Treaty shall retain their powers in the field of monetary policy according to national law.

43.3.   In accordance with Article 109k(4) of this Treaty, "Member States" shall be read as

"Member States without a derogation" in the following Articles of this Statute: 3, 11.2, 19, 34.2 and 50.

43.4. "National central banks" shall be read as "central banks of Member States without a derogation" in the following Articles of this Statute: 9.2, 10.1, 10.3, 12.1, 16, 17, 18, 22, 23, 27, 30, 31, 32, 33.2 and 52.

43.5. "Shareholders" shall be read as "central banks of Member States without a derogation" in Articles 10.3 and 33.1.

43.6. "Subscribed capital of the ECB" shall be read as "capital of the ECB subscribed by the central banks of Member States without a derogation" in Articles 10.3 and 30.2.

Article 44

Transitional tasks of the ECB

The ECB shall take over those tasks of the EMI which, because of the derogations of one or more Member States, will have to be performed in the third stage.

The ECB shall give advice in the preparations for the abrogation of the derogations specified in Article 109k of this Treaty.

Article 45

The General Council of the ECB

45.1. Without prejudice to Article 106(3) of this Treaty, the General Council shall be constituted as third decision-making body of the ECB.

45.2. The General Council shall comprise the President and Vice-President of the ECB and the Governors of the national central banks. The other members of the Executive Board may participate, without having the right to vote, in meetings of the General Council.

45.3. The responsibilities of the General Council are listed in full in Article 47 of this Statute.

Article 46

Rules of procedure of the General Council

46.1. The President or, in his absence, the Vice-President of the ECB shall chair the General Council of the ECB.

46.2. The President of the Council and a member of the Commission may participate, without having the right to vote, in meetings of the General Council.

46.3. The President shall prepare the meetings of the General Council.

46.4. By way of derogation from Article 12.3, the General Council shall adopt its Rules of Procedure.

46.5. The Secretariat of the General Council shall be provided by the ECB.

Article 47

Responsibilities of the General Council

47.1. The General Council shall:

- perform the tasks referred to in Article 44;

- contribute to the advisory functions referred to in Articles 4 and 25.1.

47.2. The General Council shall contribute to:

- the collection of statistical information as referred to in Article 5;

- the reporting activities of the ECB as referred to in Article 15;

- the establishment of the necessary rules for the application of Article 26 as referred to in Article 26.4;

- the taking of all other measures necessary for the application of Article 29 as referred to in Article 29.4;

- the laying down of the conditions of employment of the staff of the ECB as referred to in Article 36.

47.3. The General Council shall contribute to the necessary preparations for irrevocably fixing the exchange rates of the currencies of Member States with a derogation against the currencies, or the single currency, of the Member States without a derogation, as referred to in Article 109*l*(5) of this Treaty.

47.4. The General Council shall be informed by the President of the ECB of decisions of the Governing Council.

Article 48

Transitional provisions for the capital of the ECB

In accordance with Article 29.1 each national central bank shall be assigned a weighting in the key for subscription of the ECB's capital. By way of derogation from Article 28.3, central banks of Member States with a derogation shall not pay up their subscribed capital unless the General Council, acting by a majority representing at least two-thirds of the subscribed capital of the ECB and at least half of the shareholders, decides that a minimal percentage has to be paid up as a contribution to the operational costs of the ECB.

Article 49

Deferred payment of capital, reserves and provisions of the ECB

49.1. The central bank of a Member State whose derogation has been abrogated shall pay up its subscribed share of the capital of the ECB to the same extent as the central banks of other Member States without a derogation, and shall transfer to the ECB foreign reserve assets in accordance with Article 30.1. The sum to be transferred shall be determined by multiplying the ecu value at current exchange rates of the foreign reserve assets which have already been transferred to the ECB in accordance with Article 30.1, by the ratio between the number of shares subscribed by the national central bank concerned and the number of shares already paid up by the other national central banks.

49.2. In addition to the payment to be made in accordance with Article 49.1, the central bank concerned shall contribute to the reserves of the ECB, to those provisions equivalent to reserves, and to the amount still to be appropriated to the reserves and provisions corresponding to the balance of the profit and loss account as at 31 December of the year prior to the abrogation of the derogation. The sum to be contributed shall be determined by multiplying the amount of the reserves, as defined above and as stated in the approved balance sheet of the ECB, by the ratio between the number of shares subscribed by the central bank concerned and the number of shares already paid up by the other central banks.

Article 50

Initial appointment of the members of the Executive Board

When the Executive Board of the ECB is being established, the President, the Vice-President and the other members of the Executive Board shall be appointed by common accord of the governments of the Member States at the level of Heads of State or Government, on a recommendation from the Council and after consulting the European Parliament and the Council of the EMI. The President of the Executive Board shall be appointed for eight years. By way of derogation from Article 11.2, the Vice-President shall be appointed for four years and the other members of the Executive Board for terms of office of between five and eight years. No term of office shall be renewable. The number of members of the Executive Board may be smaller than provided for in Article 11.1, but in no circumstance shall it be less than four.

Article 51

Derogation from Article 32

51.1. If, after the start of the third stage, the Governing Council decides that the application of Article 32 results in significant changes in national central banks' relative income positions, the amount of income to be allocated pursuant to Article 32 shall be reduced by a uniform percentage which shall not exceed 60% in the first financial year after the start of the third stage and which shall decrease by at least 12 percentage points in each subsequent financial year.

51.2.   Article 51.1 shall be applicable for not more than five financial years after the start of the third stage.

necessary measures to ensure that banknotes denominated in currencies with irrevocably fixed exchange rates are exchanged by the national central banks at their respective par values.

Article 52

Exchange of banknotes in Community currencies

Following the irrevocable fixing of exchange rates, the Governing Council shall take the

Article 53

Applicability of the transitional provisions

If and as long as there are Member States with a derogation Articles 43 to 48 shall be applicable.

PROTOCOL
ON THE STATUTE OF THE EUROPEAN MONETARY INSTITUTE

THE HIGH CONTRACTING PARTIES,

DESIRING to lay down the Statute of the European Monetary Institute,

HAVE AGREED upon the following provisions, which shall be annexed to the Treaty establishing the European Community:

Article 1

Constitution and name

1.1.   The European Monetary Institute (EMI) shall be established in accordance with Article 109f of this Treaty; it shall perform its functions and carry out its activities in accordance with the provisions of this Treaty and of this Statute.

1.2.   The members of the EMI shall be the central banks of the Member States ("national central banks"). For the purposes of this Statute, the Institut monétaire luxembourgeois shall be regarded as the central bank of Luxembourg.

1.3.   Pursuant to Article 109f of this Treaty, both the Committee of Governors and the European Monetary Cooperation Fund (EMCF) shall be dissolved. All assets and liabilities of the EMCF shall pass automatically to the EMI.

Article 2

Objectives

The EMI shall contribute to the realization of the conditions necessary for the transition to the third stage of economic and monetary union, in particular by:

- strengthening the coordination of monetary policies with a view to ensuring price stability;

- making the preparations required for the establishment of the European System of Central Banks (ESCB), and for the conduct of a single monetary policy and the creation of a single currency in the third stage;

- overseeing the development of the ECU.

Article 3

General principles

3.1.   The EMI shall carry out the tasks and functions conferred upon it by this Treaty and this Statute without prejudice to the responsibility of the competent authorities for the conduct of the monetary policy within the respective Member States.

3.2.   The EMI shall act in accordance with the objectives and principles stated in Article 2 of the Statute of the ESCB.

Article 4
Primary tasks

4.1.   In accordance with Article 109f(2) of this Treaty, the EMI shall:

- strengthen cooperation between the national central banks;

- strengthen the coordination of the monetary policies of the Member States with the aim of ensuring price stability;

- monitor the functioning of the European Monetary System (EMS);

- hold consultations concerning issues falling within the competence of the national central banks and affecting the stability of financial institutions and markets;

- take over the tasks of the EMCF; in particular it shall perform the functions referred to in Articles 6.1, 6.2 and 6.3;

- facilitate the use of the ECU and oversee its development, including the smooth functioning of the ECU clearing system.

The EMI shall also:

- hold regular consultations concerning the course of monetary policies and the use of monetary policy instruments;

- normally be consulted by the national monetary authorities before they take decisions on the course of monetary policy in the context of the common framework for *ex ante* coordination.

4.2.   At the latest by 31 December 1996, the EMI shall specify the regulatory, organizational and logistical framework necessary for the ESCB to perform its tasks in the third stage, in accordance with the principle of an open market economy with free competition. This framework shall be submitted by the Council of the EMI for decision to the ECB at the date of its establishment.

In accordance with Article 109f(3) of this Treaty, the EMI shall in particular:

- prepare the instruments and the procedures necessary for carrying out a single monetary policy in the third stage;

- promote the harmonization, where necessary, of the rules and practices governing the collection, compilation and distribution of statistics in the areas within its field of competence;

- prepare the rules for operations to be undertaken by the national central banks in the framework of the ESCB;

- promote the efficiency of cross-border payments;

- supervise the technical preparation of ECU banknotes.

Article 5
Advisory functions

5.1.   In accordance with Article 109f(4) of this Treaty, the Council of the EMI may formulate opinions or recommendations on the overall orientation of monetary policy and exchange-rate policy as well as on related measures introduced in each Member State. The EMI may submit opinions or recommendations to governments and to the Council on policies which might affect the internal or external monetary situation in the Community and, in particular, the functioning of the EMS.

5.2.   The Council of the EMI may also make recommendations to the monetary authorities of the Member States concerning the conduct of their monetary policy.

5.3.   In accordance with Article 109f(6) of this Treaty, the EMI shall be consulted by the Council regarding any proposed Community act within its field of competence.

Within the limits and under the conditions set out by the Council acting by a qualified majority on a proposal from the Commission and after consulting the European Parliament and the EMI, the EMI shall be consulted by the authorities of the Member States on any draft legislative provision within its field of competence, in particular with regard to Article 4.2.

5.4.   In accordance with Article 109f(5) of this Treaty, the EMI may decide to publish its opinions and its recommendations.

Article 6

Operational and technical functions

6.1.   The EMI shall:

– provide for the multilateralization of positions resulting from interventions by the national central banks in Community currencies and the multilateralization of intra-Community settlements;

– administer the very short-term financing mechanism provided for by the Agreement of 13 March 1979 between the central banks of the Member States of the European Economic Community laying down the operating procedures for the European Monetary System (hereinafter referred to as "EMS Agreement") and the short-term monetary support mechanism provided for in the Agreement between the central banks of the Member States of the European Economic Community of 9 February 1970, as amended;

– perform the functions referred to in Article 11 of Council Regulation (EEC) No 1969/88 of 24 June 1988 establishing a single facility providing medium-term financial assistance for Member States' balances of payments.

6.2.   The EMI may receive monetary reserves from the national central banks and issue ECUs against such assets for the purpose of implementing the EMS Agreement. These ECUs may be used by the EMI and the national central banks as a means of settlement and for transactions between them and the EMI. The EMI shall take the necessary administrative measures for the implementation of this paragraph.

6.3.   The EMI may grant to the monetary authorities of third countries and to international monetary institutions the status of "other holders" of ECUs and fix the terms and conditions under which such ECUs may be acquired, held or used by other holders.

6.4.   The EMI shall be entitled to hold and manage foreign exchange reserves as an agent for and at the request of national central banks. Profits and losses regarding these reserves shall be for the account of the national central bank depositing the reserves. The EMI shall perform this function on the basis of bilateral contracts in accordance with rules laid down in a decision of the EMI. These rules shall ensure that transactions with these reserves shall not interfere with the monetary policy and exchange-rate policy of the competent monetary authority of any Member State and shall be consistent with the objectives of the EMI and the proper functioning of the exchange-rate mechanism of the EMS.

Article 7

Other tasks

7.1.   Once a year the EMI shall address a report to the Council on the state of the preparations for the third stage. These reports shall include an assessment of the progress towards convergence in the Community, and cover in particular the adaptation of monetary policy instruments and the preparation of the procedures necessary for carrying out a single monetary policy in the third stage, as well as the statutory requirements to be fulfilled for national central banks to become an integral part of the ESCB.

7.2.   In accordance with the Council decisions referred to in Article 109f(7) of this Treaty, the EMI may perform other tasks for the preparation of the third stage.

Article 8

Independence

The members of the Council of the EMI who are the representatives of their institutions shall, with respect to their activities, act according to their own responsibilities. In exercising the powers and performing the tasks and duties conferred upon them by this Treaty and this Statute, the Council of the EMI may not seek or take any instructions from Community institutions or bodies or governments of Member States. The Community institutions and bodies as well as the governments of the Member States undertake to respect this principle and not to seek to influence the Council of the EMI in the performance of its tasks.

Article 9

Administration

9.1.   In accordance with Article 109f(1) of this Treaty, the EMI shall be directed and managed by the Council of the EMI.

9.2.   The Council of the EMI shall consist of a President and the Governors of the national central banks, one of whom shall be Vice-President. If a Governor is prevented from attending a meeting, he may nominate another representative of his institution.

9.3.   The President shall be appointed by common accord of the governments of the Member States at the level of Heads of State or Government, on a recommendation from, as the case may be, the Committee of Governors or the Council of the EMI, and after consulting the European Parliament and the Council. The President shall be selected from among persons of recognized standing and professional experience in monetary or banking matters. Only nationals of Member States may be President of the EMI. The Council of the EMI shall appoint the Vice-President. The President and Vice-President shall be appointed for a period of three years.

9.4.   The President shall perform his duties on a full-time basis. He shall not engage in any occupation, whether gainful or not, unless exemption is exceptionally granted by the Council of the EMI.

9.5.   The President shall:

– prepare and chair the meetings of the Council of the EMI;

– without prejudice to Article 22, present the views of the EMI externally;

– be responsible for the day-to-day management of the EMI.

In the absence of the President, his duties shall be performed by the Vice-President.

9.6.   The terms and conditions of employment of the President, in particular his salary, pension and other social security benefits, shall be the subject of a contract with the EMI and shall be fixed by the Council of the EMI on a proposal from a Committee comprising three members appointed by the Committee of Governors or the Council of the EMI, as the case may be, and three members appointed by the Council. The President shall not have the right to vote on matters referred to in this paragraph.

9.7.   If the President no longer fulfils the conditions required for the performance of his duties or if he has been guilty of serious misconduct, the Court of Justice may, on application by the Council of the EMI, compulsorily retire him.

9.8.   The Rules of Procedure of the EMI shall be adopted by the Council of the EMI.

Article 10

Meetings of the Council of the EMI and voting procedures

10.1.   The Council of the EMI shall meet at least 10 times a year. The proceedings of Council meetings shall be confidential. The Council of the EMI may, acting unanimously, decide to make the outcome of its deliberations public.

10.2.   Each member of the Council of the EMI or his nominee shall have one vote.

10.3.   Save as otherwise provided for in this Statute, the Council of the EMI shall act by a simple majority of its members.

10.4.   Decisions to be taken in the context of Articles 4.2, 5.4, 6.2 and 6.3 shall require unanimity of the members of the Council of the EMI.

The adoption of opinions and recommendations under Articles 5.1 and 5.2, the adoption of decisions under Articles 6.4, 16 and 23.6 and the adoption of guidelines under Article 15.3 shall require a qualified majority of two thirds of the members of the Council of the EMI.

Article 11

Interinstitutional cooperation and reporting requirements

11.1.   The President of the Council and a member of the Commission may participate, without having the right to vote, in meetings of the Council of the EMI.

11.2.   The President of the EMI shall be invited to participate in Council meetings when the Council is discussing matters relating to the objectives and tasks of the EMI.

11.3.   At a date to be established in the Rules of Procedure, the EMI shall prepare an annual report on its activities and on monetary and financial conditions in the Community. The annual report, together with the annual accounts of the EMI, shall be addressed to the European Parliament, the Council and the Commission and also to the European Council.

The President of the EMI may, at the request of the European Parliament or on his own initiative, be heard by the competent Committees of the European Parliament.

11.4.   Reports published by the EMI shall be made available to interested parties free of charge.

Article 12

Currency denomination

The operations of the EMI shall be expressed in ECUs.

Article 13

Seat

Before the end of 1992, the decision as to where the seat of the EMI will be established shall be taken by common accord of the governments of the Member States at the level of Heads of State or Government.

Article 14

Legal capacity

The EMI, which in accordance with Article 109f(1) of this Treaty shall have legal personality, shall enjoy in each of the Member States the most extensive legal capacity accorded to legal persons under their law; it may, in particular, acquire or dispose of movable or immovable property and may be a party to legal proceedings.

Article 15

Legal acts

15.1.   In the performance of its tasks, and under the conditions laid down in this Statute, the EMI shall:

– deliver opinions;

– make recommendations;

– adopt guidelines, and take decisions, which shall be addressed to the national central banks.

15.2.   Opinions and recommendations of the EMI shall have no binding force.

15.3.   The Council of the EMI may adopt guidelines laying down the methods for the implementation of the conditions necessary for the ESCB to perform its functions in the third stage. EMI guidelines shall have no binding force; they shall be submitted for decision to the ECB.

15.4.   Without prejudice to Article 3.1, a decision of the EMI shall be binding in its entirety upon those to whom it is addressed. Articles 190 and 191 of this Treaty shall apply to these decisions.

Article 16

Financial resources

16.1.   The EMI shall be endowed with its own resources. The size of the resources of the EMI shall be determined by the Council of the EMI with a view to ensuring the income deemed necessary to cover the administrative expenditure incurred in the performance of the tasks and functions of the EMI.

16.2.   The resources of the EMI determined in accordance with Article 16.1 shall be provided out of contributions by the national central banks in accordance with the key referred to in Article 29.1 of the Statute of the ESCB and be paid up at the establishment of the EMI. For this purpose, the statistical data to be used for the determination of the key shall be provided by the Commission, in accordance with the rules adopted by the Council, acting by a qualified majority on a proposal from the Commission and after consulting the European

Parliament, the Committee of Governors and the Committee referred to in Article 109c of this Treaty.

16.3.   The Council of the EMI shall determine the form in which contributions shall be paid up.

Article 17

Annual accounts and auditing

17.1.   The financial year of the EMI shall begin on the first day of January and end on the last day of December.

17.2.   The Council of the EMI shall adopt an annual budget before the beginning of each financial year.

17.3.   The annual accounts shall be drawn up in accordance with the principles established by the Council of the EMI. The annual accounts shall be approved by the Council of the EMI and shall thereafter be published.

17.4.   The annual accounts shall be audited by independent external auditors approved by the Council of the EMI. The auditors shall have full power to examine all books and accounts of the EMI and to obtain full information about its transactions.

The provisions of Article 188c of this Treaty shall only apply to an examination of the operational efficiency of the management of the EMI.

17.5.   Any surplus of the EMI shall be transferred in the following order:

(a)   an amount to be determined by the Council of the EMI shall be transferred to the general reserve fund of the EMI;

(b)   any remaining surplus shall be distributed to the national central banks in accordance with the key referred to in Article 16.2.

17.6.   In the event of a loss incurred by the EMI, the shortfall shall be offset against the general reserve fund of the EMI. Any remaining shortfall shall be made good by contributions from the national central banks, in accordance with the key as referred to in Article 16.2.

Article 18

Staff

18.1.   The Council of the EMI shall lay down the conditions of employment of the staff of the EMI.

18.2.   The Court of Justice shall have jurisdiction in any dispute between the EMI and its servants within the limits and under the conditions laid down in the conditions of employment.

Article 19

Judicial control and related matters

19.1.   The acts or omissions of the EMI shall be open to review or interpretation by the Court of Justice in the cases and under the conditions laid down in this Treaty. The EMI may institute proceedings in the cases and under the conditions laid down in this Treaty.

19.2.   Disputes between the EMI, on the one hand, and its creditors, debtors or any other person, on the other, shall fall within the jurisdiction of the competent national courts, save where jurisdiction has been conferred upon the Court of Justice.

19.3.   The EMI shall be subject to the liability regime provided for in Article 215 of this Treaty.

19.4.   The Court of Justice shall have jurisdiction to give judgment pursuant to any arbitration clause contained in a contract concluded by or on behalf of the EMI, whether that contract be governed by public or private law.

19.5.   A decision of the EMI to bring an action before the Court of Justice shall be taken by the Council of the EMI.

Article 20

Professional secrecy

20.1.   Members of the Council of the EMI and the staff of the EMI shall be required, even after their duties have ceased, not to disclose information of the kind covered by the obligation of professional secrecy.

20.2.   Persons having access to data covered by Community legislation imposing an obligation of secrecy shall be subject to such legislation.

Article 21

Privileges and immunities

The EMI shall enjoy in the territories of the Member States such privileges and immunities as are necessary for the performance of its tasks, under the conditions laid down in the Protocol on the Privileges and Immunities of the European Communities annexed to the Treaty establishing a Single Council and a Single Commission of the European Communities.

Article 22

Signatories

The EMI shall be legally committed to third parties by the President or the Vice-President or by the signatures of two members of the staff of the EMI who have been duly authorized by the President to sign on behalf of the EMI.

Article 23

Liquidation of the EMI

23.1.   In accordance with Article 109*l* of this Treaty, the EMI shall go into liquidation on the establishment of the ECB. All assets and liabilities of the EMI shall then pass automatically to the ECB. The latter shall liquidate the EMI according to the provisions of this Article. The liquidation shall be completed by the beginning of the third stage.

23.2.   The mechanism for the creation of ECUs against gold and US dollars as provided for by Article 17 of the EMS Agreement shall be unwound by the first day of the third stage in accordance with Article 20 of the said Agreement.

23.3.   All claims and liabilities arising from the very short-term financing mechanism and the short-term monetary support mechanism, under the Agreements referred to in Article 6.1, shall be settled by the first day of the third stage.

23.4.   All remaining assets of the EMI shall be disposed of and all remaining liabilities of the EMI shall be settled.

23.5.   The proceeds of the liquidation described in Article 23.4 shall be distributed to the national central banks in accordance with the key referred to in Article 16.2.

23.6.   The Council of the EMI may take the measures necessary for the application of Articles 23.4 and 23.5.

23.7.   Upon the establishment of the ECB, the President of the EMI shall relinquish his office.

PROTOCOL
ON THE EXCESSIVE DEFICIT PROCEDURE

THE HIGH CONTRACTING PARTIES,

DESIRING to lay down the details of the excessive deficit procedure referred to in Article 104c of the Treaty establishing the European Community,

HAVE AGREED upon the following provisions, which shall be annexed to the Treaty establishing the European Community:

Article 1

The reference values referred to in Article 104c(2) of this Treaty are:

-   3% for the ratio of the planned or actual government deficit to gross domestic product at market prices;

– 60% for the ratio of government debt to gross domestic product at market prices.

Article 2

In Article 104c of this Treaty and in this Protocol:

– government means general government, that is central government, regional or local government and social security funds, to the exclusion of commercial operations, as defined in the European System of Integrated Economic Accounts;

– deficit means net borrowing as defined in the European System of Integrated Economic Accounts;

– investment means gross fixed capital formation as defined in the European System of Integrated Economic Accounts;

– debt means total gross debt at nominal value outstanding at the end of the year and consolidated between and within the sectors of general government as defined in the first indent.

Article 3

In order to ensure the effectiveness of the excessive deficit procedure, the governments of the Member States shall be responsible under this procedure for the deficits of general government as defined in the first indent of Article 2. The Member States shall ensure that national procedures in the budgetary area enable them to meet their obligations in this area deriving from this Treaty. The Member States shall report their planned and actual deficits and the levels of their debt promptly and regularly to the Commission.

Article 4

The statistical data to be used for the application of this Protocol shall be provided by the Commission.

PROTOCOL
ON THE CONVERGENCE CRITERIA REFERRED TO IN ARTICLE 109j OF THE TREATY ESTABLISHING THE EUROPEAN COMMUNITY

THE HIGH CONTRACTING PARTIES,

DESIRING to lay down the details of the convergence criteria which shall guide the Community in taking decisions on the passage to the third stage of economic and monetary union, referred to in Article 109j(1) of this Treaty,

HAVE AGREED upon the following provisions, which shall be annexed to the Treaty establishing the European Community:

Article 1

The criterion on price stability referred to in the first indent of Article 109j(1) of this Treaty shall mean that a Member State has a price performance that is sustainable and an average rate of inflation, observed over a period of one year before the examination, that does not exceed by more than $1\frac{1}{2}$ percentage points that of, at most, the three best performing Member States in terms of price stability. Inflation shall be measured by means of the consumer price index on a comparable basis, taking into account differences in national definitions.

Article 2

The criterion on the government budgetary position referred to in the second indent of Article 109j(1) of this Treaty shall mean that at the time of the examination the Member State is not the subject of a Council decision under Article 104c(6) of this Treaty that an excessive deficit exists.

Article 3

The criterion on participation in the exchange-rate mechanism of the European Monetary System referred to in the third indent of Article 109j(1) of this Treaty shall mean that a Member State has respected the normal fluctuation margins provided for by the exchange-rate mechanism of the European Monetary System without severe tensions for at least the last two years before the examination. In particular, the Member State shall not have devalued its currency's bilateral central rate against any other Member State's currency on its own initiative for the same period.

Article 4

The criterion on the convergence of interest rates referred to in the fourth indent of Article 109j(1) of this Treaty shall mean that, observed over a period of one year before the examination, a Member State has had an average nominal long-term interest rate that does not exceed by more than two percentage points that of, at most, the three best performing Member States in terms of price stability. Interest rates shall be measured on the basis of long-term government bonds or comparable securities, taking into account differences in national definitions.

Article 5

The statistical data to be used for the application of this Protocol shall be provided by the Commission.

Article 6

The Council shall, acting unanimously on a proposal from the Commission and after consulting the European Parliament, the EMI or the ECB as the case may be, and the Committee referred to in Article 109c, adopt appropriate provisions to lay down the details of the convergence criteria referred to in Article 109j of this Treaty, which shall then replace this Protocol.

PROTOCOL
AMENDING THE PROTOCOL ON THE PRIVILEGES AND IMMUNITIES OF THE EUROPEAN COMMUNITIES

THE HIGH CONTRACTING PARTIES,

CONSIDERING that, in accordance with Article 40 of the Statute of the European System of Central Banks and of the European Central Bank and Article 21 of the Statute of the European Monetary Institute, the European Central Bank and the European Monetary Institute shall enjoy in the territories of the Member States such privileges and immunities as are necessary for the performance of their tasks,

HAVE AGREED upon the following provisions, which shall be annexed to the Treaty establishing the European Community:

Sole Article

The Protocol on the Privileges and Immunities of the European Communities, annexed to the Treaty establishing a Single Council and a Single Commission of the European Communities, shall be supplemented by the following provisions:

"Article 23

This Protocol shall also apply to the European Central Bank, to the members of its organs and to its staff, without prejudice to the provisions

of the Protocol on the Statute of the European System of Central Banks and the European Central Bank.

The European Central Bank shall, in addition, be exempt from any form of taxation or imposition of a like nature on the occasion of any increase in its capital and from the various formalities which may be connected therewith in the State where the Bank has its seat. The

activities of the Bank and of its organs carried on in accordance with the Statute of the European System of Central Banks and of the European Central Bank shall not be subject to any turnover tax.

The above provisions shall also apply to the European Monetary Institute. Its dissolution or liquidation shall not give rise to any imposition."

PROTOCOL
ON DENMARK

THE HIGH CONTRACTING PARTIES,

DESIRING to settle certain particular problems relating to Denmark,

HAVE AGREED upon the following provisions, which shall be annexed to the Treaty establishing the European Community:

The provisions of Article 14 of the Protocol on the Statute of the European System of Central Banks and of the European Central Bank shall not affect the right of the National Bank of Denmark to carry out its existing tasks concerning those parts of the Kingdom of Denmark which are not part of the Community.

PROTOCOL
ON PORTUGAL

THE HIGH CONTRACTING PARTIES,

DESIRING to settle certain particular problems relating to Portugal,

HAVE AGREED upon the following provisions, which shall be annexed to the Treaty establishing the European Community:

1. Portugal is hereby authorized to maintain the facility afforded to the Autonomous

Regions of the Azores and Madeira to benefit from an interest-free credit facility with the Banco de Portugal under the terms established by existing Portuguese law.

2. Portugal commits itself to pursue its best endeavours in order to put an end to the abovementioned facility as soon as possible.

PROTOCOL
ON THE TRANSITION TO THE THIRD STAGE OF ECONOMIC AND MONETARY UNION

THE HIGH CONTRACTING PARTIES,

Declare the irreversible character of the Community's movement to the third stage of economic and monetary union by signing the new Treaty provisions on economic and monetary union.

Therefore all Member States shall, whether they fulfil the necessary conditions for the adoption of a single currency or not, respect the will for the Community to enter swiftly into the third stage, and therefore no Member State shall prevent the entering into the third stage.

If by the end of 1997 the date of the beginning of the third stage has not been set, the Member States concerned, the Community institutions and other bodies involved shall expedite all preparatory work during 1998, in order to enable the Community to enter the third stage irrevocably on 1 January 1999 and to enable the ECB and the ESCB to start their full functioning from this date.

This Protocol shall be annexed to the Treaty establishing the European Community.

PROTOCOL
ON CERTAIN PROVISIONS RELATING TO THE UNITED KINGDOM OF GREAT BRITAIN AND NORTHERN IRELAND

THE HIGH CONTRACTING PARTIES,

RECOGNIZING that the United Kingdom shall not be obliged or committed to move to the third stage of economic and monetary union without a separate decision to do so by its government and Parliament,

NOTING the practice of the government of the United Kingdom to fund its borrowing requirement by the sale of debt to the private sector,

HAVE AGREED the following provisions, which shall be annexed to the Treaty establishing the European Community:

1. The United Kingdom shall notify the Council whether it intends to move to the third stage before the Council makes its assessment under Article 109j(2) of this Treaty.

   Unless the United Kingdom notifies the Council that it intends to move to the third stage, it shall be under no obligation to do so.

   If no date is set for the beginning of the third stage under Article 109j(3) of this

Treaty, the United Kingdom may notify its intention to move to the third stage before 1 January 1998.

2. Paragraphs 3 to 9 shall have effect if the United Kingdom notifies the Council that it does not intend to move to the third stage.

3. The United Kingdom shall not be included among the majority of Member States which fulfil the necessary conditions referred to in the second indent of Article 109j(2) and the first indent of Article 109j(3) of this Treaty.

4. The United Kingdom shall retain its powers in the field of monetary policy according to national law.

5. Articles 3a(2), 104c(1), (9) and (11), 105(1) to (5), 105a, 107, 108, 108a, 109, 109a(1) and (2)(b) and 109l(4) and (5) of this Treaty shall not apply to the United Kingdom. In these provisions references to the Community or the Member States shall not include the United Kingdom and ref-

erences to national central banks shall not include the Bank of England.

6. Articles 109e(4) and 109h and i of this Treaty shall continue to apply to the United Kingdom. Articles 109c(4) and 109m shall apply to the United Kingdom as if it had a derogation.

7. The voting rights of the United Kingdom shall be suspended in respect of acts of the Council referred to in the Articles listed in paragraph 5. For this purpose the weighted votes of the United Kingdom shall be excluded from any calculation of a qualified majority under Article 109k(5) of this Treaty.

The United Kingdom shall also have no right to participate in the appointment of the President, the Vice-President and the other members of the Executive Board of the ECB under Articles 109a(2)(b) and 109l(1) of this Treaty.

8. Articles 3, 4, 6, 7, 9.2, 10.1, 10.3, 11.2, 12.1, 14, 16, 18 to 20, 22, 23, 26, 27, 30 to 34, 50 and 52 of the Protocol on the Statute of the European System of Central Banks and of the European Central Bank ("the Statute") shall not apply to the United Kingdom.

In those Articles, references to the Community or the Member States shall not include the United Kingdom and references to national central banks or shareholders shall not include the Bank of England.

References in Articles 10.3 and 30.2 of the Statute to "subscribed capital of the ECB" shall not include capital subscribed by the Bank of England.

9. Article 109l(3) of this Treaty and Articles 44 to 48 of the Statute shall have effect, whether or not there is any Member State with a derogation, subject to the following amendments:

(a) References in Article 44 to the tasks of the ECB and the EMI shall include those tasks that still need to be performed in the third stage owing to any decision of the United Kingdom not to move to that stage.

(b) In addition to the tasks referred to in Article 47 the ECB shall also give advice in relation to and contribute to the preparation of any decision of the Council with regard to the United Kingdom taken in accordance with paragraphs 10(a) and 10(c).

(c) The Bank of England shall pay up its subscription to the capital of the ECB as a contribution to its operational costs on the same basis as national central banks of Member States with a derogation.

10. If the United Kingdom does not move to the third stage, it may change its notification at any time after the beginning of that stage. In that event:

(a) The United Kingdom shall have the right to move to the third stage provided only that it satisfies the necessary conditions. The Council, acting at the request of the United Kingdom and under the conditions and in accordance with the procedure laid down in Article 109k(2) of this Treaty, shall decide whether it fulfils the necessary conditions.

(b) The Bank of England shall pay up its subscribed capital, transfer to the ECB foreign reserve assets and contribute to its reserves on the same basis as the national central bank of a Member State whose derogation has been abrogated.

(c) The Council, acting under the conditions and in accordance with the procedure laid down in Article 109l(5) of this Treaty, shall take all other necessary decisions to enable the United Kingdom to move to the third stage.

If the United Kingdom moves to the third stage pursuant to the provisions of this Protocol, paragraphs 3 to 9 shall cease to have effect.

11. Notwithstanding Articles 104 and 109e(3) of this Treaty and Article 21.1 of the Statute, the government of the United Kingdom may maintain its "ways and means" facility with the Bank of England if and so long as the United Kingdom does not move to the third stage.

PROTOCOL
ON CERTAIN PROVISIONS RELATING TO DENMARK

THE HIGH CONTRACTING PARTIES,

DESIRING to settle, in accordance with the general objectives of the Treaty establishing the European Community, certain particular problems existing at the present time,

TAKING INTO ACCOUNT that the Danish Constitution contains provisions which may imply a referendum in Denmark prior to Danish participation in the third stage of economic and monetary union,

HAVE AGREED on the following provisions, which shall be annexed to the Treaty establishing the European Community:

1. The Danish Government shall notify the Council of its position concerning participation in the third stage before the Council makes its assessment under Article 109j(2) of this Treaty.

2. In the event of a notification that Denmark will not participate in the third stage, Denmark shall have an exemption. The effect of the exemption shall be that all Articles and provisions of this Treaty and the Statute of the ESCB referring to a derogation shall be applicable to Denmark.

3. In such case, Denmark shall not be included among the majority of Member States which fulfil the necessary conditions referred to in the second indent of Article 109j(2) and the first indent of Article 109j(3) of this Treaty.

4. As for the abrogation of the exemption, the procedure referred to in Article 109k(2) shall only be initiated at the request of Denmark.

5. In the event of abrogation of the exemption status, the provisions of this Protocol shall cease to apply.

PROTOCOL
ON FRANCE

THE HIGH CONTRACTING PARTIES,

DESIRING to take into account a particular point relating to France,

HAVE AGREED upon the following provisions, which shall be annexed to the Treaty establishing the European Community:

France will keep the privilege of monetary emission in its overseas territories under the terms established by its national laws, and will be solely entitled to determine the parity of the CFP franc.

PROTOCOL
ON SOCIAL POLICY

THE HIGH CONTRACTING PARTIES,

NOTING that 11 Member States, that is to say the Kingdom of Belgium, the Kingdom of Denmark, the Federal Republic of Germany, the Hellenic Republic, the Kingdom of Spain, the

French Republic, Ireland, the Italian Republic, the Grand Duchy of Luxembourg, the Kingdom of the Netherlands and the Portuguese Republic, wish to continue along the path laid down in the 1989 Social Charter; that they have adopted among themselves an Agreement to this end; that this Agreement is annexed to this Protocol; that this Protocol and the said Agreement are without prejudice to the provisions of this Treaty, particularly those relating to social policy which constitute an integral part of the *acquis communautaire:*

1. Agree to authorize those 11 Member States to have recourse to the institutions, procedures and mechanisms of the Treaty for the purposes of taking among themselves and applying as far as they are concerned the acts and decisions required for giving effect to the abovementioned Agreement.

2. The United Kingdom of Great Britain and Northern Ireland shall not take part in the deliberations and the adoption by the Council of Commission proposals made on the basis of this Protocol and the abovementioned Agreement.

By way of derogation from Article 148(2) of the Treaty, acts of the Council which are made pursuant to this Protocol and which must be adopted by a qualified majority shall be deemed to be so adopted if they have received at least 44 votes in favour. The unanimity of the members of the Council, with the exception of the United Kingdom of Great Britain and Northern Ireland, shall be necessary for acts of the Council which must be adopted unanimously and for those amending the Commission proposal.

Acts adopted by the Council and any financial consequences other than administrative costs entailed for the institutions shall not be applicable to the United Kingdom of Great Britain and Northern Ireland.

3. This Protocol shall be annexed to the Treaty establishing the European Community.

AGREEMENT ON SOCIAL POLICY CONCLUDED BETWEEN THE MEMBER STATES OF THE EUROPEAN COMMUNITY WITH THE EXCEPTION OF THE UNITED KINGDOM OF GREAT BRITAIN AND NORTHERN IRELAND

The undersigned 11 HIGH CONTRACTING PARTIES, that is to say the Kingdom of Belgium, the Kingdom of Denmark, the Federal Republic of Germany, the Hellenic Republic, the Kingdom of Spain, the French Republic, Ireland, the Italian Republic, the Grand Duchy of Luxembourg, the Kingdom of the Netherlands and the Portuguese Republic (hereinafter referred to as "the Member states"),

WISHING to implement the 1989 Social Charter on the basis of the *acquis communautaire,*

CONSIDERING the Protocol on social policy,

HAVE AGREED as follows:

Article 1

The Community and the Member States shall have as their objectives the promotion of employment, improved living and working conditions, proper social protection, dialogue between management and labour, the development of human resources with a view to lasting high employment and the combating of exclusion. To this end the Community and the Member States shall implement measures which take account of the diverse forms of national practices, in particular in the field of contractual relations, and the need to maintain the competitiveness of the Community economy.

Article 2

1. With a view to achieving the objectives of Article 1, the Community shall support and complement the activities of the Member States in the following fields:

– improvement in particular of the working environment to protect workers' health and safety;

- working conditions;
- the information and consultation of workers;
- equality between men and women with regard to labour market opportunities and treatment at work;
- the integration of persons excluded from the labour market, without prejudice to Article 127 of the Treaty establishing the European Community (hereinafter referred to as "the Treaty").

2. To this end, the Council may adopt, by means of directives, minimum requirements for gradual implementation, having regard to the conditions and technical rules obtaining in each of the Member States. Such directives shall avoid imposing administrative, financial and legal constraints in a way which would hold back the creation and development of small and medium-sized undertakings.

The Council shall act in accordance with the procedure referred to in Article 189c of the Treaty after consulting the Economic and Social Committee.

3. However, the Council shall act unanimously on a proposal from the Commission, after consulting the European Parliament and the Economic and Social Committee, in the following areas:

- social security and social protection of workers;
- protection of workers where their employment contract is terminated;
- representation and collective defence of the interests of workers and employers, including co-determination, subject to paragraph 6;
- conditions of employment for third-country nationals legally residing in Community territory;
- financial contributions for promotion of employment and job-creation, without prejudice to the provisions relating to the Social Fund.

4. A Member State may entrust management and labour, at their joint request, with the implementation of directives adopted pursuant to paragraphs 2 and 3.

In this case, it shall ensure that, no later than the date on which a directive must be transposed in accordance with Article 189, management and labour have introduced the necessary measures by agreement, the Member State concerned being required to take any necessary measure enabling it at any time to be in a position to guarantee the results imposed by that directive.

5. The provisions adopted pursuant to this Article shall not prevent any Member State from maintaining or introducing more stringent protective measures compatible with the Treaty.

6. The provisions of this Article shall not apply to pay, the right of association, the right to strike or the right to impose lock-outs.

Article 3

1. The Commission shall have the task of promoting the consultation of management and labour at Community level and shall take any relevant measure to facilitate their dialogue by ensuring balanced support for the parties.

2. To this end, before submitting proposals in the social policy field, the Commission shall consult management and labour on the possible direction of Community action.

3. If, after such consultation, the Commission considers Community action advisable, it shall consult management and labour on the content of the envisaged proposal. Management and labour shall forward to the Commission an opinion or, where appropriate, a recommendation.

4. On the occasion of such consultation, management and labour may inform the Commission of their wish to initiate the process provided for in Article 4. The duration of the procedure shall not exceed nine months, unless the management and labour concerned and the Commission decide jointly to extend it.

Article 4

1. Should management and labour so desire, the dialogue between them at Community level may lead to contractual relations, including agreements.

2. Agreements concluded at Community level shall be implemented either in accordance with the procedures and practices specific to management and labour and the Member States or, in matters covered by Article 2, at the joint request of the signatory parties, by a Council decision on a proposal from the Commission.

The Council shall act by qualified majority, except where the agreement in question contains one or more provisions relating to one of the areas referred to in Article 2(3), in which case it shall act unanimously.

Article 5

With a view to achieving the objectives of Article 1 and without prejudice to the other provisions of the Treaty, the Commission shall encourage cooperation between the Member States and facilitate the coordination of their action in all social policy fields under this Agreement.

Article 6

1. Each Member State shall ensure that the principle of equal pay for male and female workers for equal work is applied.

2. For the purpose of this Article, "pay" means the ordinary basic or minimum wage or salary and any other consideration, whether in cash or in kind, which the worker receives directly or indirectly, in respect of his employment, from his employer.

Equal pay without discrimination based on sex means:

(a) that pay for the same work at piece rates shall be calculated on the basis of the same unit of measurement;

(b) that pay for work at time rates shall be the same for the same job.

3. This Article shall not prevent any Member State from maintaining or adopting measures providing for specific advantages in order to make it easier for women to pursue a vocational activity or to prevent or compensate for disadvantages in their professional careers.

Article 7

The Commission shall draw up a report each year on progress in achieving the objectives of Article 1, including the demographic situation in the Community. It shall forward the report to the European Parliament, the Council and the Economic and Social Committee.

The European Parliament may invite the Commission to draw up reports on particular problems concerning the social situation.

DECLARATIONS

1. Declaration on Article 2(2)

The 11 High Contracting Parties note that in the discussions on Article 2(2) of the Agreement it was agreed that the Community does not intend, in laying down minimum requirements for the protection of the safety and health of employees, to discriminate in a manner unjustified by the circumstances against employees in small and medium-sized undertakings.

2 Declaration on Article 4(2)

The 11 High Contracting Parties declare that the first of the arrangements for application of the agreements between management and labour at Community level — referred to in Article 4(2) — will consist in developing, by collective bargaining according to the rules of each Member State, the content of the agreements, and that consequently this arrangement implies no obligation on the Member States to apply the agreements directly or to work out rules for their transposition, nor any obligation to amend national legislation in force to facilitate their implementation.

PROTOCOL
ON ECONOMIC AND SOCIAL COHESION

THE HIGH CONTRACTING PARTIES,

RECALLING that the Union has set itself the objective of promoting economic and social progress, *inter alia*, through the strengthening of economic and social cohesion,

RECALLING that Article 2 of the Treaty establishing the European Community includes the task of promoting economic and social cohesion and solidarity between Member States and that the strengthening of economic and social cohesion figures among the activities of the Community listed in Article 3,

RECALLING that the provisions of Part Three, Title XIV, on economic and social cohesion as a whole provide the legal basis for consolidating and further developing the Community's action in the field of economic and social cohesion, including the creation of a new fund,

RECALLING that the provisions of Part Three, Title XII on trans-European networks and Title XVI on environment envisage a Cohesion Fund to be set up before 31 December 1993,

STATING their belief that progress towards economic and monetary union will contribute to the economic growth of all Member States,

NOTING that the Community's structural Funds are being doubled in real terms between 1987 and 1993, implying large transfers, especially as a proportion of GDP of the less prosperous Member States,

NOTING that the European Investment Bank is lending large and increasing amounts for the benefit of the poorer regions,

NOTING the desire for greater flexibility in the arrangements for allocations from the structural Funds,

NOTING the desire for modulation of the levels of Community participation in programmes and projects in certain countries,

NOTING the proposal to take greater account of the relative prosperity of Member States in the system of own resources,

REAFFIRM that the promotion of economic and social cohesion is vital to the full development and enduring success of the Community, and underline the importance of the inclusion of economic and social cohesion in Articles 2 and 3 of this Treaty,

REAFFIRM their conviction that the structural Funds should continue to play a considerable part in the achievement of Community objectives in the field of cohesion,

REAFFIRM their conviction that the European Investment Bank should continue to devote the majority of its resources to the promotion of economic and social cohesion, and declare their willingness to review the capital needs of the European Investment Bank as soon as this is necessary for that purpose,

REAFFIRM the need for a thorough evaluation of the operation and effectiveness of the structural Funds in 1992, and the need to review, on that occasion, the appropriate size of these Funds in the light of the tasks of the Community in the area of economic and social cohesion,

AGREE that the Cohesion Fund to be set up before 31 December 1993 will provide Community financial contributions to projects in the fields of environment and trans-European networks in Member States with a per capita GNP of less than 90% of the Community average which have a programme leading to the fulfilment of the conditions of economic convergence as set out in Article 104c,

DECLARE their intention of allowing a greater margin of flexibility in allocating financing from the structural Funds to specific needs not covered under the present structural Funds regulations,

DECLARE their willingness to modulate the levels of Community participation in the context of programmes and projects of the structural Funds, with a view to avoiding excessive increases in budgetary expenditure in the less prosperous Member States,

RECOGNIZE the need to monitor regularly the progress made towards achieving economic and social cohesion and state their willingness to study all necessary measures in this respect,

DECLARE their intention of taking greater account of the contributive capacity of individual Member States in the system of own resources, and of examining means of correcting, for the less prosperous Member States, regressive elements existing in the present own resources system,

AGREE to annex this Protocol to the Treaty establishing the European Community.

PROTOCOL
ON THE ECONOMIC AND SOCIAL COMMITTEE AND THE COMMITTEE OF THE REGIONS

THE HIGH CONTRACTING PARTIES,

HAVE AGREED upon the following provision, which shall be annexed to this Treaty establishing the European Community:

The Economic and Social Committee and the Committee of the Regions shall have a common organizational structure.

PROTOCOL
ANNEXED TO THE TREATY ON EUROPEAN UNION AND TO THE TREATIES ESTABLISHING THE EUROPEAN COMMUNITIES

THE HIGH CONTRACTING PARTIES,

HAVE AGREED upon the following provision, which shall be annexed to the Treaty on European Union and to the Treaties establishing the European Communities:

Nothing in the Treaty on European Union, or in the Treaties establishing the European Communities, or in the Treaties or Acts modifying or supplementing those Treaties, shall affect the application in Ireland of Article 40.3.3. of the Constitution of Ireland.

FINAL ACT

1. The Conferences of the Representatives of the Governments of the Member States convened in Rome on 15 December 1990 to adopt by common accord the amendments to be made to the Treaty establishing the European Economic Community with a view to the achievement of political union and with a view to the final stages of economic and monetary union, and those convened in Brussels on 3 February 1992 with a view to amending the Treaties establishing respectively the European Coal and Steel Community and the European Atomic Energy Community as a result of the amendments envisaged for the Treaty establishing the European Economic Community have adopted the following texts:

I
The Treaty on European Union

II
Protocols

1. Protocol on the acquisition of property in Denmark

2. Protocol concerning Article 119 of the Treaty establishing the European Community

3. Protocol on the Statute of the European System of Central Banks and of the European Central Bank

4. Protocol on the Statute of the European Monetary Institute

5. Protocol on the excessive deficit procedure

6. Protocol on the convergence criteria referred to in Article 109j of the Treaty establishing the European Community

7. Protocol amending the Protocol on the privileges and immunities of the European Communities

8. Protocol on Denmark

9. Protocol on Portugal

10. Protocol on the transition to the third stage of economic and monetary union

11. Protocol on certain provisions relating to the United Kingdom of Great Britain and Northern Ireland

12. Protocol on certain provisions relating to Denmark.

13. Protocol on France

14. Protocol on social policy, to which is annexed an agreement concluded between the Member States of the European Community with the exception of the United Kingdom of Great Britain and Northern Ireland, to which two declarations are attached

15. Protocol on economic and social cohesion

16. Protocol on the Economic and Social Committee and the Committee of the Regions

17. Protocol annexed to the Treaty on European Union and to the Treaties establishing the European Communities

The Conferences agreed that the Protocols referred to in 1 to 16 above will be annexed to the Treaty establishing the European Community and that the Protocol referred to in 17 above will be annexed to the Treaty of European Union and to the Treaties establishing the European Communities.

2. At the time of signature of these texts, the Conferences adopted the declarations listed below and annexed to this Final Act:

III
Declarations

1. Declaration on civil protection, energy and tourism

2. Declaration on nationality of a Member State

3. Declaration on Part Three, Titles III and VI, of the Treaty establishing the European Community

4. Declaration on Part Three, Title VI, of the Treaty establishing the European Community

5. Declaration on monetary cooperation with non-Community countries

6. Declaration on monetary relations with the Republic of San Marino, the Vatican City and the Principality of Monaco

7. Declaration on Article 73d of the Treaty establishing the European Community

8. Declaration on Article 109 of the Treaty establishing the European Community

9. Declaration on Part Three, Title XVI, of the Treaty establishing the European Community

10. Declaration on Articles 109, 130r and 130y of the Treaty establishing the European Community

11. Declaration on the Directive of 24 November 1988 (Emissions)

12. Declaration of the European Development Fund

13. Declaration on the role of national Parliaments in the European Union

14. Declaration on the Conference of the Parliaments

15. Declaration on the number of members of the Commission and of the European Parliament

16. Declaration on the hierarchy of Community Acts

17. Declaration on the right of access to information

18. Declaration on estimated costs under Commission proposals

19. Declaration on the implementation of Community law

20. Declaration on assessment of the environmental impact of Community measures

21. Declaration on the Court Auditors

22. Declaration of the Economic and Social Committee

23. Declaration on cooperation with charitable associations

24. Declaration on the protection of animals

25. Declaration on the representation of the interests of the overseas countries and territories referred to in Article 227(3) and (5)(a) and (b) of the Treaty establishing the European Community

26. Declaration on the outermost regions of the Community

27. Declaration on voting in the field of the common foreign and security policy

28. Declaration on practical arrangements in the field of the common foreign and security policy.

29. Declaration on the use of languages in the field of the common foreign and security policy

30. Declaration on Western European Union

31. Declaration on asylum

32. Declaration on police cooperation

33. Declaration on disputes between the ECB and the EMI and their servants

Done at Maastricht this seventh day of February in the year one thousand nine hundred and ninety-two

DECLARATION
ON CIVIL PROTECTION, ENERGY AND TOURISM

The Conference declares that the question of introducing into the Treaty establishing the European Community Titles relating to the spheres referred to in Article 3(t) of that Treaty will be examined, in accordance with the procedure laid down in Article N(2) of the Treaty on European Union, on the basis of a report which the Commission will submit to the Council by 1996 at the latest.

The Commission declares that Community action in those spheres will be pursued on the basis of the present provisions of the Treaties establishing the European Communities.

DECLARATION
ON NATIONALITY OF A MEMBER STATE

The Conference declares that, wherever in the Treaty establishing the European Community reference is made to nationals of the Member States, the question whether an individual possesses the nationality of a Member State shall be settled solely by reference to the national law of the Member State concerned. Member States may declare, for information, who are to be considered their nationals for Community purposes by way of a declaration lodged with the Presidency and may amend any such declarations when necessary.

DECLARATION
ON PART THREE, TITLES III AND VI, OF THE TREATY ESTABLISHING THE EUROPEAN COMMUNITY

The Conference affirms that, for the purposes of applying the provisions set out in Part Three, Title III, Chapter 4 on capital and payments, and Title VI on economic and monetary policy, of this Treaty, the usual practice, according to which the Council meets in the composition of Economic and Finance Ministers, shall be continued, without prejudice to Article 109j(2) to (4) and Article 109k(2).

DECLARATION
ON PART THREE, TITLE VI, OF THE TREATY ESTABLISHING THE EUROPEAN COMMUNITY

The Conference affirms that the President of the European Council shall invite the Economic and Finance Ministers to participate in European Council meetings when the European Council is discussing matters relating to economic and monetary union.

DECLARATION
ON MONETARY COOPERATION WITH NON-COMMUNITY COUNTRIES

The Conference affirms that the Community shall aim to contribute to stable international monetary relations. To this end the Community shall be prepared to cooperate with other European countries and with those non-European countries with which the Community has close economic ties.

DECLARATION
ON MONETARY RELATIONS WITH THE REPUBLIC OF SAN MARINO, THE VATICAN CITY AND THE PRINCIPALITY OF MONACO

The Conference agrees that the existing monetary relations between Italy and San Marino and the Vatican City and between France and Monaco remain unaffected by the Treaty establishing the European Community until the introduction of the ECU as the single currency of the Community.

The Community undertakes to facilitate such renegotiations of existing arrangements as might become necessary as a result of the introduction of the ECU as a single currency.

DECLARATION
ON ARTICLE 73d OF THE TREATY ESTABLISHING THE EUROPEAN COMMUNITY

The Conference affirms that the right of Member States to apply the relevant provisions of their tax law as referred to in Article 73d(1)(a) of this Treaty will apply only with respect to the relevant provisions which exist at the end of 1993. However, this Declaration shall apply only to capital movements between Member States and to payments effected between Member States.

DECLARATION
ON ARTICLE 109 OF THE TREATY ESTABLISHING THE EUROPEAN COMMUNITY

The Conference emphasizes that use of the term "formal agreements" in Article 109(1) is not intended to create a new category of international agreement within the meaning of Community law.

DECLARATION
ON PART THREE, TITLE XVI, OF THE TREATY ESTABLISHING THE EUROPEAN COMMUNITY

The Conference considers that, in view of the increasing importance of nature conservation at national, Community and international level, the Community should, in exercising its powers under the provisions of Part Three, Title XVI, take account of the specific requirements of this area.

DECLARATION
ON ARTICLES 109, 130r AND 130y of THE TREATY ESTABLISHING THE EUROPEAN COMMUNITY

The Conference considers that the provisions of Article 109(5), Article 130r(4), second subparagraph, and Article 130y do not affect the principles resulting from the judgment handed down by the Court of Justice in the AETR case.

DECLARATION
ON THE DIRECTIVE OF 24 NOVEMBER 1988
(Emissions)

The Conference declares that changes in Community legislation cannot undermine the derogations granted to Spain and Portugal until 31 December 1999 under the Council Directive of 24 November 1988 on the limitation of emissions of certain pollutants into the air from large combustion plants.

DECLARATION
ON THE EUROPEAN DEVELOPMENT FUND

The Conference agrees that the European Development Fund will continue to be financed by national contributions in accordance with the current provisions.

DECLARATION
ON THE ROLE OF NATIONAL PARLIAMENTS IN THE EUROPEAN UNION

The Conference considers that it is important to encourage greater involvement of national parliaments in the activities of the European Union.

To this end, the exchange of information between the national parliaments and the European Parliament should be stepped up. In this context, the governments of the Member States will ensure, *inter alia*, that national parliaments receive Commission proposals for legislation in good time for information or possible examination.

Similarly, the Conference considers that it is important for contacts between the national parliaments and the European Parliament to be stepped up, in particular through the granting of appropriate reciprocal facilities and regular meetings between members of Parliament interested in the same issues.

DECLARATION
ON THE CONFERENCE OF THE PARLIAMENTS

The Conference invites the European Parliament and the national parliaments to meet as necessary as a Conference of the Parliaments (or "Assises").

The Conference of the Parliaments will be consulted on the main features of the European Union, without prejudice to the powers of the European Parliament and the rights of the national parliaments. The President of the European Council and the President of the Commission will report to each session of the Conference of the Parliaments on the state of the Union.

DECLARATION
ON THE NUMBER OF MEMBERS OF THE COMMISSION
AND OF THE EUROPEAN PARLIAMENT

The Conference agrees that the Member States will examine the questions relating to the number of members of the Commission and the number of members of the European Parliament no later than at the end of 1992, with a view to reaching an agreement which will permit the establishment of the necessary legal basis for fixing the number of members of the European Parliament in good time for the 1994 elections. The decisions will be taken in the light, *inter alia*, of the need to establish the overall size of the European Parliament in an enlarged Community.

DECLARATION
ON THE HIERARCHY OF COMMUNITY ACTS

The Conference agrees that the Intergovernmental Conference to be convened in 1996 will examine to what extent it might be possible to review the classification of Community acts with a view to establishing an appropriate hierarchy between the different categories of act.

DECLARATION
ON THE RIGHT OF ACCESS TO INFORMATION

The Conference considers that transparency of the decision-making process strengthens the democratic nature of the institutions and the public's confidence in the administration. The Conference accordingly recommends that the Commission submit to the Council no later than 1993 a report on measures designed to improve public access to the information available to the institutions.

DECLARATION
ON ESTIMATED COSTS UNDER COMMISSION PROPOSALS

The Conference notes that the Commission undertakes, by basing itself where appropriate on any consultations it considers necessary and by strengthening its system for evaluating Community legislation, to take account in its legislative proposals of costs and benefits to the Member States' public authorities and all the parties concerned.

DECLARATION
ON THE IMPLEMENTATION OF COMMUNITY LAW

1. The Conference stresses that it is central to the coherence and unity of the process of European construction that each Member State should fully and accurately transpose into national law the Community Directives addressed to it within the deadlines laid down therein.

    Moreover, the Conference, while recognizing that it must be for each Member State to determine how the provisions of Community law can best be enforced in the light of its own particular institutions, legal system and other circumstances, but in any event in compliance with Article 189 of the Treaty establishing the European Community, considers it essential for the proper functioning of the Community that the measures taken by the different Member States should result in Community law being applied with the same effectiveness and rigour as in the application of their national law.

2. The Conference calls on the Commission to ensure, in exercising its powers under Article 155 of this Treaty, that Member States fulfill their obligations. It asks the Commission to publish periodically a full report for the Member States and the European Parliament.

DECLARATION ON ASSESSMENT OF THE ENVIRONMENTAL
IMPACT OF COMMUNITY MEASURES

The Conference notes that the Commission undertakes in its proposals, and that the Member States undertake in implementing those proposals, to take full account of their environmental impact and of the principle of sustainable growth.

DECLARATION
ON THE COURT OF AUDITORS

The Conference emphasizes the special importance it attaches to the task assigned to the Court of Auditors by Articles 188a, 188b, 188c and 206 of the Treaty establishing the European Community.

It requests the other Community institutions to consider, together with the Court of Auditors, all appropriate ways of enhancing the effectiveness of its work.

DECLARATION
ON THE ECONOMIC AND SOCIAL COMMITTEE

The Conference agrees that the Economic and Social Committee will enjoy the same independence with regard to its budget and staff management as the Court Auditors has enjoyed hitherto.

DECLARATION
ON COOPERATION WITH CHARITABLE ASSOCIATIONS

The Conference stresses the importance, in pursuing the objectives of Article 117 of the Treaty establishing the European Community, of cooperation between the latter and charitable associations and foundations as institutions responsible for social welfare establishments and services.

DECLARATION
ON THE PROTECTION OF ANIMALS

The Conference calls upon the European Parliament, the Council and the Commission, as well as the Member States, when drafting and implementing Community legislation on the common agricultural policy, transport, the internal market and research, to pay full regard to the welfare requirements of animals.

DECLARATION
ON THE REPRESENTATION OF THE INTERESTS OF THE OVERSEAS COUNTRIES AND TERRITORIES REFERRED TO IN ARTICLE 227(3) AND (5)(a) AND (b) OF THE TREATY ESTABLISHING THE EUROPEAN COMMUNITY

The Conference, noting that in exceptional circumstances divergences may arise between the interests of the Union and those of the overseas countries and territories referred to in Article 227(3) and (5)(a) and (b), agrees that the Council will seek to reach a solution which accords with the position of the Union. However, in the event that this proves impossible, the Conference agrees that the Member State concerned may act separately in the interests of the said overseas countries and territories, without this affecting the Community's interests. The Member State concerned will give notice to the Council and the Commission where such a divergence of interests is likely to occur and, when separate action proves unavoidable, make it clear that it is acting in the interests of overseas territory mentioned above.

This declaration also applies to Macao and East Timor.

DECLARATION
ON THE OUTERMOST REGIONS OF THE COMMUNITY

The Conference acknowledges that the outermost regions of the Community (the French overseas departments, Azores and Madeira and Canary Islands) suffer from major structural backwardness compounded by several phenomena (remoteness, island status, small size, difficult topography and climate, economic dependence on a few products), the permanence and combination of which severely restrain their economic and social development.

It considers that, while the provisions of the Treaty establishing the European Community and secondary legislation apply automatically to outermost regions, it is nonetheless possible to adopt specific measures to assist them inasmuch and as long as there is an objective need to take such measures with a view to the economic and social development of those regions. Such measures should have their aim both the completion of the internal market and a recognition of the regional reality to enable the outermost regions to achieve the average economic and social level of the Community.

DECLARATION ON VOTING IN THE FIELD OF
THE COMMON FOREIGN AND SECURITY POLICY

The Conference agrees that, with regard to Council decisions requiring unanimity, Member States will, to the extent possible, avoid preventing a unanimous decision where a qualified majority exists in favour of that decision.

DECLARATION ON PRACTICAL ARRANGEMENTS IN THE
FIELD OF THE COMMON FOREIGN AND SECURITY POLICY

The Conference agrees that the division of work between the Political Committee and the Committee of Permanent Representatives will be examined at a later stage, as will the practical arrangements for merging the Political Cooperation Secretariat with the General Secretariat of the Council and for cooperation between the latter and the Commission.

DECLARATION ON THE USE OF LANGUAGES IN THE
FIELD OF THE COMMON FOREIGN AND SECURITY POLICY

The Conference agrees that the use of languages shall be in accordance with the rules of the European Communities.

For COREU communications, the current practice of European political cooperation will serve as a guide for the time being. All common foreign and security policy texts which are submitted to or adopted at meeting of the European Council and of the Council as well as all texts which are to be published are immediately and simultaneously translated into all the official Community languages.

DECLARATION
ON WESTERN EUROPEAN UNION

The Conference notes the following declarations:

I. DECLARATION

by Belgium, Germany, Spain, France, Italy, Luxembourg, the Netherlands, Portugal and the United Kingdom of Great Britain and Northern Ireland, which are members of the Western European Union and also members of the European Union
on
THE ROLE OF THE WESTERN EUROPEAN UNION AND ITS RELATIONS WITH THE EUROPEAN UNION AND WITH THE ATLANTIC ALLIANCE

Introduction

1. WEU Member States agree on the need to develop a genuine European security and defence identity and a greater European responsibility on defence matters. This identity will be pursued through a gradual process involving successive phases. WEU will form an integral part of the process of the development of the European Union and will enhance its contribution to solidarity within the Atlantic Alliance. WEU Member States agree to strengthen the role of WEU, in the longer term perspective of a common defence, compatible with that of the Atlantic Alliance.

2. WEU will be developed as the defence component of the European Union and as a means to strengthen the European pillar of the Atlantic Alliance. To this end, it will formulate common European defence policy and carry forward its concrete implementation through the further development of its own operational role.

WEU Member States take note of Article J.4 relating to the common foreign and security policy of the Treaty on European Union which reads as follows:

> *"1.   The common foreign and security policy shall include all questions related to the security of the Union, including the eventual framing of a common defence policy, which might in time lead to a common defence.*

> *2.   The Union requests the Western European Union (WEU), which is an integral part of the development of the Union, to elaborate and implement decisions and actions of the Union which have defence implications. The Council shall, in agreement with the institutions of the WEU, adopt the necessary practical arrangements.*

> *3.   Issues having defence implications dealt with under this Article shall not be subject to the procedures set out in Article J.3.*

> *4.   The policy of the Union in accordance with this Article shall not prejudice the specific character of the security and defence policy of certain Member States and shall respect the obligations of certain Member States under the North Atlantic Treaty and be compatible with the common security and defence policy established within that framework.*

> *5.   The provisions of this Article shall not prevent the development of closer cooperation between two or more Member States on a bilateral level, in the framework of the WEU and the Atlantic Alliance, provided such cooperation does not run counter to or impede that provided for in this Title.*

> *6.   With a view to furthering the objective of this Treaty, and having in view the date of 1998 in the context of Article XII of the Brussels Treaty, the provisions of this Article may be revised as provided for in Article N(2) on the basis of a report to be presented in 1996 by the Council to the European Council, which shall include an evaluation of the progress made and the experience gained until then."*

A — WEU's relations with European Union

3. The objective is to build up WEU in stages as the defence component of the European Union. To this end, WEU is prepared, at the request of the European Union, to elaborate and implement decisions and actions of the Union which have defence implications.

To this end, WEU will take the following measures to develop a close working relationship with the Union:

- as appropriate, synchronization of the dates and venues of meetings and harmonization of working methods;

- establishment of close cooperation between the Council and Secretariat-General of WEU on the one hand, and the Council of the Union and General Secretariat of the Council on the other;

- consideration of the harmonization of the sequence and duration of the respective Presidencies;

- arranging for appropriate modalities so as to ensure that the Commission of the European Communities is regularly informed and, as appropriate, consulted on WEU activities in accordance with the role of the Commission in the common foreign and security policy as defined in the Treaty on European Union;

- encouragement of closer cooperation between the Parliamentary Assembly of WEU and the European Parliament.

The WEU Council shall, in agreement with the competent bodies of the European Union, adopt the necessary practical arrangements.

B — WEU's relations with the Atlantic Alliance

4. The objective is to develop WEU as a means to strengthen the European pillar of the Atlantic Alliance. Accordingly WEU is prepared to develop further the close working links between WEU and the Alliance and to strengthen the role, responsibilities and contributions of WEU Member States in the Alliance. This will be undertaken on the basis of the necessary transparency and complementarity between the emerging European security and defence identity and the Alliance. WEU will act in conformity with the positions adopted in the Atlantic Alliance.

- WEU Member States will intensify their coordination on Alliance issues which represent an important common interest with the aim of introducing joint positions agreed in WEU into the process of consultation in the Alliance which will remain the essential forum for consultation among its members and the venue for agreement on policies bearing on the security and defence commitments of Allies under the North Atlantic Treaty.

- Where necessary, dates and venues of meetings will be synchronized and working methods harmonized.

- Close cooperation will be established between the Secretariats-General of WEU and NATO.

C — Operational role of WEU

5. WEU's operational role will be strengthened by examining and defining appropriate missions, structures and means, covering in particular:

- WEU planning cell;

- closer military cooperation complementary to the Alliance in particular in the fields of logistics, transport, training and strategic surveillance;

- meetings of WEU Chiefs of Defence Staff;

- military units answerable to WEU.

Other proposals will be examined further including:

- enhanced cooperation in the field of armaments with the aim of creating a European armaments agency;

- development of the WEU Institute into a European Security and Defence Academy.

Arrangements aimed at giving WEU a stronger operational role will be fully compatible with the military dispositions necessary to ensure the collective defence of all Allies.

D — Other measures

6. As a consequence of the measures set out above, and in order to facilitate the strengthening of WEU's role, the seat of the WEU Council and Secretariat will be transferred to Brussels.

7. Representation of the WEU Council must be such that the Council is able to exercise its functions continuously in accordance with Article VIII of the modified Brussels Treaty. Member States may draw on a double-hatting formula, to be worked out, consisting of their representatives to the Alliance and to the European Union.

8. WEU notes that, in accordance with the provisions of Article J.4(6) concerning the common foreign and security policy of the Treaty on European Union, the Union will decide to review the provisions of this Article with a view to furthering the objective to be set by it in

accordance with the procedure defined. The WEU will re-examine the present provisions in 1996. This re-examination will take account of the progress and experience acquired and will extend to relations between WEU and the Atlantic Alliance.

II. DECLARATION

by Belgium, Germany, Spain, France, Italy, Luxembourg, the Netherlands, Portugal and the United Kingdom of Great Britain and Northern Ireland which are members of the Western European Union

*"The Member States of WEU welcome the development of the European security and defence identity. They are determined, taking into ac-*count the role of WEU as the defence component of the European Union and as the means to strengthen the European pillar of the Atlantic Alliance, to put the relationship between WEU and the other European States on a new basis for the sake of stability and security in Europe. In this spirit, they propose the following:*

States which are members of the European Union are invited to accede to WEU on conditions to be agreed in accordance with Article XI of the modified Brussels Treaty, or to become observers if they so wish. Simultaneously, other European Member States of NATO are invited to become associate members of WEU in a way which will give them the possibility of participating fully in the activities of WEU.

The Member States of WEU assume that treaties and agreements corresponding with the above proposals will be concluded before 31 December 1992."

DECLARATION
ON ASYLUM

1. The Conference agrees that, in the context of the proceedings provided for in Articles K.1 and K.3 of the provisions on cooperation in the fields of justice and home affairs, the Council will consider as a matter of priority questions concerning Member States' asylum policies, with the aim of adopting by the beginning of 1993, common action to harmonize aspects of them, in the light of the work programme and timetable contained in the report on asylum drawn up at the request of the European Council meeting in Luxembourg on 28 and 29 June 1991.

2. In this connection, the Council will also consider, by the end of 1993, on the basis of a report, the possibility of applying Article K.9 to such matters.

DECLARATION
ON POLICE COOPERATION

The Conference confirms the agreement of the Member States on the objectives underlying the German delegations's proposals at the European Council meeting in Luxembourg on 28 and 29 June 1991.

For the present, the Member States agree to examine as a matter of priority the drafts submitted to them, on the basis of the work programme and timetable agreed upon in the report drawn up at the request of the Luxembourg European Council, and they are willing to envisage the adoption of practical measures in areas such as those suggested by the German delegation, relating to the following functions in the exchange of information and experience:

- support for national criminal investigation and security authorities, in particular in the coordination of investigations and search operations;

- creation of data bases;

- central analysis and assessment of information in order to take stock of the situation and identify investigative approaches;

- collection and analysis of national prevention programmes for forwarding to Member States and for drawing up Europe-wide prevention strategies;

- measures relating to further training, research, forensic matters and criminal records departments.

Member States agree to consider on the basis of a report, during 1994 at the latest, whether the scope of such cooperation should be extended.

DECLARATION
ON DISPUTES BETWEEN THE ECB AND THE EMI
AND THEIR SERVANTS

The Conference considers it proper that the Court of First Instance should hear this class of action in accordance with Article 168a of the Treaty establishing the European Community. The Conference therefore invites the institutions to adapt the relevant rules accordingly.

Done at Maastricht on the seventh day of February one thousand nine hundred and ninety two.

[Editor's note: the above sentence appears in all 10 languages. The signatures follow.]

REACTIONS TO THE TREATY OF MAASTRICHT

1. European Parliament

Resolution on the results of the intergovernmental conferences, 7 April 1992

The European Parliament,

- having regard to the Treaty on European Union signed in Maastricht on 7 February 1992,
- having regard to the European Parliament's proposals submitted to the IGCs.[1]
- having regard to the Final Declaration adopted by the Conference of the Parliaments of the European Community in Rome in November 1990 and submitted to the IGCs,
- having regard to the proposal from President Mitterrand and Chancellor Kohl to establish European Union,
- having regard to the report of its Committee on Institutional Affairs and the opinions of the Committees on Economic and Monetary Affairs and Industrial Policy as well as all its other standing committees (A 3-0123/92),

A. whereas the European Parliament defined the essential elements of European Union as being:

- economic and monetary union with a single currency and an autonomous central bank;
- a common foreign policy, including joint consideration of the issues of peace, security and arms control;
- a completed single market with common policies in all the areas in which the economic integration and mutual interdependence of the Member States require common action notably to ensure economic and social cohesion and a balanced environment;

- elements of common citizenship and a common framework for protecting basic rights;
- an institutional system which is sufficiently efficient to manage these responsibilities effectively and which is democratically structured, notably by giving the European Parliament a right of initiative, of co-decision with the Council on Community legislation, the right to ratify all constitutional decisions requiring the ratification of the Member States also and the right to elect the President of the Commission;[2]

B. whereas the Treaty of Maastricht contains provisions which are inconsistent with regard to the above requirements and whereas although some progress has been achieved on EMU, common policies and citizenship, the institutional system contains shortcomings to the extent that it is doubtful whether the European Union will be able to achieve its proclaimed objectives, especially if its membership is enlarged, and whereas it has not eliminated the parliamentary democratic deficit;

C. whereas the IGCs themselves recognized the insufficiency of their achievements in that they provided in the Treaty for a new IGC in 1996;

D. whereas, at the intergovernmental conference, a temporary mandate was given for further improvements to be made by the end of 1992 and a decision was taken to create a cohesion fund;

---

[1] Notably its resolutions of 11 July 1990 (OJ No C 231, 17.9.1990, p. 97), 22 November 1990 (OJ No C 324, 24.12.1990, p. 219), 16 May 1990 (OJ No C 149, 18.6.1990, p. 66) and 10 October 1990 (OJ No C 284, 12.11.1990, p. 62).
[2] Its abovementioned resolution of 11 July 1990, paragraph 3.

In general

1. Urges the national parliaments to ratify the Treaty of Maastricht, and at the same time commit their respective governments to redress at the earliest opportunity its major shortcomings summed up in this resolution in accordance with the final declaration of the Conference of Parliaments of the European Community;

2. Draws attention to the following major shortcomings in the new treaty which:

(a) is based on a "pillar" structure that:

    – leaves the common foreign and security policy outside the European Community Treaty (with, therefore, a lesser role for the Commission and for Parliament and no possibility for legal redress at the Court of Justice) and will confuse the rest of the world with the "Union" (represented by the Presidency of Council) acting in some areas and the "Community" (represented by the Commission) acting in others;

    – leaves cooperation in the spheres of justice and home affairs outside the European Community Treaty thus escaping parliamentary and judicial control in an area in which citizens' rights are directly affected with no democratic procedures for decision-taking in this matter;[3]

    – provides for defence matters to be delegated to WEU without providing for appropriate parliamentary control of the activities of this organization;

(b) fails to provide any economic policy authority with adequate democratic legitimacy to counterbalance the autonomous monetary policy authority of the European Central Bank and lays down specific procedures for economic policy decisions which derogate in Council's favour from traditional Community procedures;

(c) does not provide a real co-decision procedure, which would have meant that the EP and the Council would have had the same decision-making powers over any legislative act, since the Council is allowed to act unilaterally in the absence of an agreement with the EP, and also applies this procedure only to a limited area;

(d) fails to provide for parliamentary assent for future treaty changes, for the modification of own resources or for additional measures concerning citizenship;

(e) retains procedures requiring unanimity in Council for a very wide range of decision-taking and legislative procedures, including remarkably, two areas in which the procedure of Article 189b applies, and areas of vital interest to the Community such as many aspects of social and environmental policy and taxation;

(f) implies, with regard to the ACP–EEC Convention, that decision-making will continue to be largely intergovernmental, with the result that in the field of development cooperation Parliament will exercise different powers according to whether it is dealing with ACP–EEC matters, Asia, Latin America or the Mediterranean;

(g) contains altogether such a variety of legislative procedures, mostly with variants, that overall transparency and clarity is lacking, and conflict over legal bases is inevitable;

(h) provides for only a limited increase in the scope of Community action in the field of social policy, even among the 11 Member States committed to making progress in this field, particularly where issues to do with social security and the nationals of third countries are concerned, these matters still being subject to a unanimous vote by the Council, and the right of association which is excluded from the protocol; but welcomes the fact that the social dimension has been strengthened by the agreement of the 11 Member States on social policy on the basis of Community law;

(i) does not stipulate that members of the Committee of the Regions must be democratically elected representatives of regional or local bodies;

(j) introduces a provision allowing Council unilaterally to repeal international agreements to which both Parliament and Council had previously given their assent, and to adopt sanctions without Parliament's approval;

(k) contains in the Protocols, annexed to the Treaty, provisions that set out in detail the principle of equal treatment laid down in Article 119 of the EEC Treaty;

(l) fails sufficiently to develop the concept

---

[3] However, this "pillar" cannot remove from the Community the competences that it already has in this field, notably those accepted in the White Paper on completing the internal market (paragraph 24–31 and 47–56) and those provided for in the EEC Treaty (Articles 100a and 235).

of citizenship and protection for fundamental rights and freedoms, and, in particular, fails to institute a charter of fundamental rights and freedoms on the basis of Parliament's resolution of 12 April 1989[4] adopting the Declaration of fundamental rights and freedoms;

(m) fails to address the issue of the classification and hierarchy of Community acts, thus maintaining the lack of distinction between legislative and executive acts, or the related issue of the procedures for delegating implementing measures to the Commission (commitology procedures) which remain unsatisfactory;

(n) in budgetary matters, formally incorporates the principle that not all expenditure should be included in the budget; maintains the imbalance in relations between the two arms of the Budgetary Authority, notably by granting the Parliament, with regard to own resources, no more than a right of consultation and by maintaining the obsolete distinction between compulsory and non-compulsory expenditure; fails to incorporate any of the procedural advances which have been made in recent years;

(o) keeps the EDF outside the EC budget, contrary to the wishes of Parliament and the Commission;

(p) fails to merge the EAEC and ECSC treaties with the EEC Treaty or even to adjust their legislative procedures in order to bring them into line with the EEC Treaty;

(q) fails to adjust the number of members of the European Parliament to take account of German unity;

(r) fails to lay down specific provisions concerning energy, civil protection and tourism, although these are now added to the list of Community activities specified in Article 3 of the EEC Treaty;

(s) fails to modify the procedures for appointing members of the Court of Justice and the Court of Auditors in order to involve confirmation by the European Parliament and enhance their independence;

(t) fails to recognize Parliament as having equivalent rights to initiate and participate in proceedings before the Court of Justice as the other political institutions and the Member States of the Community;

(u) ought to have stated that the Council, when enacting legislation, will meet publicly;

regrets that only the Council has the power to reject or approve the agreements between management and labour and stresses that the position of the European Parliament may not be weakened in relation to the other institutions; emphasizes, therefore, that any amendment by the Council to the agreements between management and labour must be put through the Community legislative procedure;

deplores the use of a protocol to a treaty reforming the institutions of the European Community to deny European citizens the right to receive an opinion on the interpretation of a point of law from the European Court of Justice in the case of the "Barber Judgment", since such use of retrospective legislation potentially places the executive above the law;

3. Recognizes, nevertheless, the positive elements included in the new Treaty, all of which were requested before the IGCs by the EP, notably:

(a) the commitment to establish economic and monetary union with a single currency and central bank;

(b) the wider scope of Community competences with the addition of new titles and articles to the EEC Treaty concerning, notably, consumer protection, public health, culture, education, industry, development and trans-European networks;

(c) the inclusion in the Treaty of the principle of subsidiarity in defence of national and, especially, regional powers;

(d) the commitment to a common foreign and security policy — though Parliament regrets that this is not covered by the institutional Community system and therefore by Parliament's supervision and political initiative – including a common defence policy;

(e) the enhanced commitment to the principles of economic and social cohesion, ecologically sustainable growth, and a high level of employment;

(f) the enlargement, albeit small, of the domain of qualified majority voting;

(g) the new procedure for the appointment of the Commission which involves the European

4 OJ No C 120, 16.5.1989, p. 51.

Parliament and which links the term of office of the Commission to that of Parliament;

(h) the extension of the legislative powers of the European Parliament in certain areas;

(i) the extension or confirmation of certain powers of control of the European Parliament and certain obligations of the Commission regarding the implementation of the budget, the establishment of committees of inquiry, the right of petition, the recognition of sound financial management as a formal criterion for budgetary control;

(j) the recognition of a right of initiative for the European Parliament, albeit limited;

(k) the citizenship provisions, in particular those providing for voting rights in the Member State of residence for European and local elections:

(l) the obligation on the Member States to prosecute infringements of the Community's financial interests and to coordinate their activities, and the consequent need to promulgate an EC–wide judicial basis to harmonize national judicial systems in this area;

(m) the granting to the Court of Justice of the right to impose penalties on Member States failing to comply with its judgements;

(n) the creation of a consultative Committee of the Regions, on which according to the Maastricht Treaty, the regional and local bodies of all the Member States are to be jointly represented;

(o) provisions encouraging cooperation between national parliaments and the European Parliament without creating new superfluous institutions;

(p) the strengthened role of management and labour at Community level in the context of the social dialogue;

4. Also welcomes other elements introduced into the Treaty, including the appointment by the European Parliament of a European Ombudsman and consular protection for Community citizens in third countries;

5. Regrets the attitude of the current British government that led to special provisions for the UK regarding monetary union and social policy; welcomes, however, the fact that the other Member States were not willing to be blocked by the negative attitude of a single national government; expects that the opt-out clause regarding EMU will, in practice, never be used and considers that the derogation from

parts of social policy is not sustainable and should be rectified as soon as possible;

As regards economic and monetary union

6. Welcomes the historic decision taken by the Maastricht European Council to introduce a single currency by 1999 at the latest and by 1997 at the earliest, a decision which implies the conduct of a monetary policy and the establishment of an independent European System of Central Banks, and urges the governments to coordinate their budgetary policy efforts to the utmost, with a view to minimizing the adverse effects and instability inherent in a lengthy transitional period, since the implementation of the convergence programmes will have an undesirable economic and social impact, in particular in certain Member States;

7. Regrets that EMU appears to be exclusively geared to stability; while acknowledging the importance of stability, calls for deflationary effects to be prevented when Member States not yet meeting the strict convergence criteria gear their policy to those criteria; calls for the objectives of responsible growth and a high level of employment and social protection to be taken equally seriously, even though there is no provision as yet in the Treaty for specific binding measures in this regard;

8. Deplores the marked similarity between the management structure chosen for the European Monetary Institute and that of the Committee of Governors and the EMCF; this is not sufficient to ensure the independence of the EMI *vis-à-vis* the current central banks and *vis-à-vis* national governments;

9. Deplores the fact that, when economic policy-making takes effect, the scope for parliamentary influence will suffer at national and European level, since national parliaments will lose their ability to discipline national governments because the Council will act by a qualified majority, while the European Parliament will only be notified after the event; is shocked by the provision that recommendations to individual Member States will normally not be disclosed, even to the parliament of the Member State concerned;

10. Regrets that the blueprint for economic policy outlined in the Treaty makes redundant the democratic control exercised hitherto by the national parliaments; such a loss, whether

direct or indirect, is evident in the following areas:

(a) the economic policy guidelines traditionally established by democratic control of their budgets;

(b) safeguard measures *vis-à-vis* third countries;

(c) financial assistance from one Member State to another;

(d) the right to ask their governments to make a recommendation in the areas referred to in Article 109d of the EC Treaty;

this loss has not been offset by transferring equivalent democratic control to the European Parliament;

11. Calls, with a view to reducing this democratic deficit, and prior to being in a position to include the abovementioned issues in the forthcoming amendments to the Treaty, for an interinstitutional agreement between the Council, the Commission and the European Parliament on the basis of which these institutions can cooperate with Parliament, particularly in the areas mentioned in the preceding paragraph and in the following areas:

(a) the penalties imposed by the Council on a Member State which fails to comply with a decision concerning the reduction of an excessive deficit;

(b) international agreements concerning monetary or foreign exchange regime matters;

(c) the appointment of the chairman, the vice-chairman and the other members of the Executive Board of the European Central Bank;

(d) the Council directives or decisions laying down the terms and conditions for mutual assistance for a Member State threatened with balance of payments difficulties;

(e) the abrogation of a derogation granted to a Member State concerning the introduction of the ECU as the single currency;

(f) the assessment of convergence programmes;

12. Demands that, in order to tighten up Article 109g on the status of the ECU and to facilitate the conversion of the ECU basket into the ECU single currency, a large number of Community initiatives are taken during the first stage of EMU;

13. Deplores the fact that the Maastricht European Council made no provision for the decisions concerning tax harmonization to be taken by a majority in the Council in co-decision with Parliament. Considers it strange that Article 115 was revised rather than simply deleted. Also regrets that the contribution of the new cohesion fund to financing trans-European networks has been limited under Article 130d of the Treaty to transport infrastructures instead of being extended to cover telecommunications and energy infrastructures;

14. Welcomes the inclusion of Title XIII on industry, but considers that the only way to compensate for the weakness of European industry would be to endow the Community with powers and financial resources equal to the task of overcoming the handicaps in order to face up to the intensification of international competition. Also regrets that the decisions to be taken by the Council on the basis of these articles remain subject to the unanimity rule, and that Parliament's role is confined to delivering a non-binding opinion;

Conclusions

15. Express its determination, as with the Single European Act[5] to:

– exploit to the very limit the possibilities offered by the Treaty of Maastricht;

– to pursue its endeavours to obtain a democratic and effective European Union of federal type;

16. In this light:

(a) invites the national parliaments, when ratifying the Treaty, to call on their respective governments:

– to prepare the next IGC in order to eliminate the shortcomings of the Treaty of Maastricht in particular as regards the remaining democratic deficit and the efficiency of the decision-making process;

– to undertake not to make use in Council of the provisions of paragraph 6 of Article 189b which allows Council to act unilaterally in the event of conciliation failing to reach agreement, and not to adopt in Council any legisla-

[5] Resolution of 16 January 1986, OJ No C 36, 17.2.1986, p. 142.

tive act which Parliament has earlier rejected by absolute majority;

- to relaunch the strategy worked out of the Conference of the Parliaments of the Community, with particular regard to the need to transform the network of relations between the peoples and member countries into a European union on a federal basis based on a draft constitution drawn up by the European Parliament in cooperation with the national parliaments;

(b) invites the Council and the Commission, as in the past, to enter into interinstitutional agreements with the Parliament to ensure that new treaties are applied in the most constructive and democratic way possible;

(c) invites the governments of the Member States to involve Parliament, before the European Council meeting in Lisbon, in the designation of the President and members of the next Commission of the European Communities, whose term of office will take effect on 1 January 1993 and which will exercise the powers conferred upon it by the Maastricht Treaty; declares here and now that it will consider the submission of the Commission's programme of work as an opportunity to pass a vote of confidence or no confidence in the Commission;

(d) invites the Commission, wherever legally possible, to choose for its proposals legal bases that require the co-decision and expects the Commission to withdraw its proposals where, under that procedure, Council and Parliament fail to reach agreement in the conciliation committee or where, under the consultation and cooperation procedures, Parliament rejects a text;

(e) invites the Council to make use of the "passerelle' provided for in Article K.9 of the Treaty of Maastricht and thereby transfer matters concerning justice and home affairs to the field of competence of the European Community;

(f) instructs the responsible parliamentary organs to prepare a reform of Parliament's working methods that will enable it to make full use of the new procedures and to take the necessary measures within their field of responsibility, bearing in mind the obligation imposed by Article F (3) of the Maastricht Treaty for the Union to "provide itself with the means necessary to attain its objectives and carry through its policies";

(g) undertakes to begin already preparations for a new revision of the treaties which should aim to eliminate the shortcomings of the Treaty of Maastricht; believes that many of the issues must be addressed before the IGC scheduled in 1996, in particular because treaty amendments are necessary:

- to adjust the number of members of the European Parliament for German unity;
- to allow the accession of new Member States which requires a significant improvement in decision-taking procedures, notably as regards Parliament's right of co-decision and the functioning of Council;
- to remedy the democratic deficit;

(h) stresses that it will not be able to agree to the accession of new Member States unless further reforms are adopted in addition to the Maastricht Treaty, in particular concerning the elimination of the democratic deficit and the consolidation of the principles and aims on which Political Union is based;

(i) instructs its committee responsible to complete its preparation of a draft constitution as set out in its resolution of 11 July 1990 on the European Parliament's guidelines for a draft constitution for the European Union through procedures involving the national parliaments as provided for in the Final Declaration of the Conference of the parliaments of the European Community of November 1990 in Rome;

17. Instructs its President to forward this resolution and the report of the Committee on Institutional Affairs to the Commission, the Council, the Court of Justice, the Court of First Instance, the Court of Auditors, the Economic and Social Committee and the governments and parliaments of the Member States.

2. Danish Referendum

Statement by the twelve Foreign Ministers following the Danish Referendum,
4 June 1992

The Ministers heard a report by the Danish Foreign Minister on the outcome of the referendum in Denmark, at which they all expressed regret.

The Ministers noted that 11 Member States have expressed the desire for European Union involving all the Member States. They rule out any renegotiation of the text signed at Maastricht.

The ratification procedure will continue in the Member States on the basis of the existing text and in accordance with the schedule agreed on, before the end of the year.

They all agree that the door should be left open for Denmark to participate in the Union.

3. European Council

Birmingham Declaration: A Community close to its Citizens, adopted on 16 October 1992

1. We reaffirm our commitment to the Maastricht Treaty: We need to ratify it to make progress towards European Union if the Community is to remain an anchor of stability and prosperity in a rapidly changing continent, building on its success over the last quarter of a century.

2. As a community of democracies, we can only move forward with the support of our citizens. We are determined to respond to the concerns raised in the recent public debate. We must:

   – demonstrate to our citizens the benefits of the Community and the Maastricht Treaty;

   – make the Community more open, to ensure a better informed public debate on its activities;

   – respect the history, culture and traditions of individual nations, with a clearer understanding of what Member States should do and what needs to be done by the Community;

   – make clear that citizenship of the Union brings our citizens additional rights and protection without in any way taking the place of their national citizenship.

3. Foreign Ministers will suggest ways, before the Edinburgh European Council, of opening up the work of the Community's institutions, including the possibility of some open Council discussions – for example on future work programmes. We welcome the Commission's offer to consult more widely before proposing legislation which could include consultation with all the Member States and a more systematic use of consultation documents (Green Papers). We ask the Commission to complete by early next year its work in improving public access to the information available to it and to other Community institutions. We want Community legislation to become simpler and clearer.

4. We stress the European Parliament's important role in the democratic life of the Community and we welcome the growing contacts between national parliaments and the European Parliament. We reaffirm that national parliaments should be more closely involved in the Community's activities. We shall discuss this with our Parliaments. We welcome the Commission's readiness to respond positively to requests from national parliaments for explanations of its proposals. We underline the importance we attach to the Conference of Parliaments and to the Committee of the Regions.

5. We reaffirm that decisions must be taken as closely as possible to the citizen. Greater unity can be achieved without excessive centralization. It is for each Member State to decide how its powers should be exercised domestically. The Community can only act where Member States have given it the power to do so in the treaties. Action at the Community level should happen only when proper and necessary: the Maastricht Treaty provides the right framework and objectives for this. Bringing to life this principle — "subsidiarity", or "nearness" — is essential if the Community is to develop with the support of its citizens. We look forward to decisions at Edinburgh on the basis of reports on:

   – adapting the Council's procedures and practices — as the Commission for its part has already done — so that the principle becomes an integral part of the Community's decision-making, as the Maastricht Treaty requires;

   – guidelines for applying the principle in practice, for instance by using the lightest possible form of legislation, with maximum freedom for Member States on how best to achieve the objective in question. Community legislation must be implemented and enforced effectively, and without interfering unnecessarily in the daily life of our citizens;

We shall also have a look at the first fruits of the Commission's review of past Community legislation with examples.

6. Making the principle of subsidiarity work should be a priority for all the Community institutions, without affecting the balance between them. We will seek an agreement about this with the European Parliament.

7. The Maastricht Treaty will bring direct benefits to individual citizens. All of us — Council, Commission and Parliament — must do more to make this clear.

8. The European Council in conformity with the responsibilities given to it by the Treaty will ensure that the fundamental principles of the European Union will be fully observed.

4. European Council and the arrangements for Denmark

Conclusions of the Edinburgh meeting, 11–12 December 1992 (extracts)

General

Introduction

1. The European Council met in Edinburgh on 11–12 December 1992 to discuss the central problems on the Community's agenda. The meeting was preceded by an exchange of views between the members of the European Council and the President of the European Parliament on the various issues on the agenda.

2. The European Council agreed on solutions to a very wide range of issues which are essential to progress in Europe. This paves the way for a return to confidence by its citizens in European construction which will contribute to the recovery of the European economy.

In particular the European Council reached agreement on the following major issues:

- The problems raised by Denmark in the light of the outcome of the Danish referendum on 2 June 1992 on the Maastricht Treaty,

- Guidelines to implement the subsidiarity principle and measures to increase transparency and openness in the decision-making process of the Community,

- The financing of Community action and policies during the rest of this decade,

- The launching of enlargement negotiations with a number of EFTA countries,

- The establishment of a plan of action by the Member States and the Community to promote growth and to combat unemployment.

Treaty on European Union — state of the ratification process

3. The members of the European Council reaffirmed their commitment to the Treaty on European Union. Ratification is necessary to make progress towards European Union and for the Community to remain an anchor of stability in a rapidly changing continent, building on its success over the last four decades.

4. Having reviewed the state of the ratification process the European Council agreed to the texts set out in Part B of these Conclusions concerning the issues raised by Denmark in its memorandum "Denmark in Europe" of 30 October 1992. This will create the basis for the Community to develop together, on the basis of the Maastricht Treaty, while respecting, as the Treaty does, the identity and diversity of Member States.

Subsidiarity

5. On the basis of a report from Foreign Ministers the European Council agreed the overall approach, set out in Annex 1, to the application of the subsidiarity principle and the new Article 3b. The European Council invited the Council to seek an inter-institutional agreement between the European Parliament, the Council and the Commission on the effective application of Article 3b by all institutions. The European Council discussed this aspect with the President of the European Parliament. It welcomed the ideas in the draft of an Inter-Institutional Agreement presented by the European Parliament.

6. The European Council received a report from the President of the Commission on the first fruits of the Commission's review of existing and proposed legislation in the light of the subsidiarity principle. These examples are set out in Annex 2. The European Council noted the Commission's intention to withdraw or amend certain proposals and to make proposals for the amendment of items of existing legislation. It looks forward to the final report on the review of existing legislation, which the Commission will prepare for the European Council in December 1993.

Openness and transparency

7. The European Council reaffirmed its commitment at Birmingham to a more open Community and adopted the specific measures set out in Annex 3.

The conclusion with regard to access to the work of the Council will be reviewed at the end of 1994.

The European Council welcomed the measures the Commission has recently decided to take in the field of transparency. These include producing the annual work programme in October, to allow for wider debate, including in national parliaments; seeking closer consultation with the Council on the annual legislative programme; wider consultation before making proposals, including the use of green papers; making Commission documents public in all Community languages; and attaching higher priority to consolidation and codification of legal texts.

The European Council reconfirmed its invitation at Birmingham for the Commission to complete by early next year its work resulting from the declaration in the Maastricht Treaty on improving access to the information available to it and to other Community Institutions.

Accession of new Member States to the Union

8. The European Council in Lisbon agreed that official negotiations with EFTA countries seeking membership of the Union will be opened immediately after the Treaty on European Union is ratified and the agreement has been achieved on the Delors II package.

Given the agreement reached on future financing and the prospects for early ratification of the Treaty on European Union by all Member States, the European Council agreed that enlargement negotiations will start with Austria, Sweden and Finland at the beginning of 1993. These negotiations will be based on the general negotiation framework of which the General Affairs Council took note on 7 December. They will be transformed into negotiations under Article O of the Treaty on European Union once it enters into force, and can only be concluded once the Treaty on European Union has been ratified by all Member States. The conditions of admission will be based on the acceptance in full of the Treaty on European Union and the "acquis", subject to possible transitional measures to be agreed in the negotiations. The European Council invited the Council of Ministers to take decisions on the opening of negotiations on the same basis with Norway as soon as the Commission's opinion on its application is available. Negotiations will to the extent possible be conducted in parallel.

It invited the Commission, in preparing its Opinion on the Swiss application, to take into account the views of the Swiss authorities following the 6 December referendum on the EEA agreement. It welcomes the contacts now underway with the EFTA countries to identify the next steps in proceeding with the agreement.

GATT

9. The European Council welcomed the resumption of negotiations in Geneva on the GATT Uruguay Round. It reaffirmed its commitment at Birmingham to an early, comprehensive and balanced agreement and called on all the parties to complete the negotiations accordingly. It noted that the final package must be judged as a whole.

Promoting economic recovery in Europe

10. The European Council heard a report from the President of the Commission about the economic situation. It discussed the prospects for growth and the rise in unemployment. It agreed to carry forward the action and initiatives set out in the declaration in Annex 4.

Internal Market

11. The European Council noted with particular satisfaction that the White Paper programme for creating the Internal Market will in all essential respects be successfully completed by 31 December 1992. This is a historical moment for the Community, marking the fulfilment of one of the fundamental objectives of the Treaty of Rome. The large Single Market is an irreversible achievement. It will offer consumers more choice and lower prices; it will help job creation and will sharpen the international competitiveness of business in Europe. The Community will remain open to world trade and investment.

12. The European Council noted that since 1985 over 500 internal market measures have been agreed, including nearly all those in the original White Paper. It paid tribute to the vital role played by the Commission in initiating this programme and to the constructive cooperation on it between the Council and the European Parliament. The decision-making procedures introduced by the Single European Act have proved indispensable for the timely completion of the programme.

13. Work on the Single Market programme has covered a wide canvas, opening up public purchasing, liberalizing transport and financial services, improving Community-wide acceptance of product standards, removing non-tariff barriers, and making it easier for people to work throughout the Community.

***

Size of the European Parliament

26. The European Council agreed — on the basis of the proposal of the European Parliament — on the following numbers of members of the European Parliament, from 1994, to reflect German unification and in the perspective of enlargement:

Belgium	25
Denmark	16
Germany	99
Greece	25
Spain	64
France	87
Ireland	15
Italy	87
Luxembourg	6
Netherlands	31
Portugal	25
United Kingdom	87
Total	567

The necessary legal texts will be prepared for adoption in due course.

Seats of the Institutions

27. On the occasion of the European Council Member States reached agreement on the seats of the European Parliament, the Council, the Commission, the Court of Justice and the Court of First Instance, the Economic and Social Committee, the Court of Auditors, and the European Investment Bank. The formal decision is set out in Annex 6.

Overall approach to the application by the Council of the Subsidiarity Principle and Article 3b of the Treaty on European Union

I.   Basic principles

European Union rests on the principle of subsidiarity, as is made clear in Articles A and B of title I of the Treaty on European Union. This principle contributes to the respect for the national identities of Member States and safeguards their powers. It aims at decisions within the European Union being taken as closely as possible to the citizen.

1. Article 3b of the EC Treaty[1] covers three main elements:

- a strict limit on Community action (first paragraph);
- a rule (second paragraph) to answer the question "Should the Community act?". This applies to areas which do not fall within the Community's exclusive competence;
- a rule (third paragraph) to answer the question: "What should be the intensity or nature of the Community's action?". This applies whether or not the action is within the Community's exclusive competence.

2. The three paragraphs cover three distinct legal concepts which have historical antecedents in existing Community Treaties or in the case-law of the Court of Justice:

(i)   The principle that the Community can only act where given the power to do so — implying that national powers are the rule and the Community's the exception — has always been a basic feature of the Community legal order. (The principle of attribution of powers.)

(ii) The principle that the Community should only take action where an objective can better be attained at the level of the Community than at the level of the individual Member States is present in embryonic or implicit form in some provisions of the ECSC Treaty and the EEC Treaty; the Single European Act spelled out the principle in the environment field. (The principle of subsidiarity in the strict legal sense).

[1] Article 3b, as introduced in the EC Treaty by the Treaty on European Union, reads as follows:
"The Community shall act within the limits of the powers conferred upon it by this Treaty and of the objectives assigned to it therein.
   In areas which do not fall within its exclusive competence, the Community shall take action, in accordance with the principle of subsidiarity, only if and insofar as the objectives of the proposed action cannot be sufficiently achieved by the Member States and can therefore, by reason of the scale or effects of the proposed action, be better achieved by the Community.
   Any action by the Community shall not go beyond what is necessary to achieve the objectives of this Treaty."

(iii) The principle that the means to be employed by the Community should be proportional to the objective pursued is the subject of a well-established case-law of the Court of Justice which, however, has been limited in scope and developed without the support of a specific article in the Treaty. (The principle of proportionality or intensity.)

3. The Treaty on European Union defines these principles in explicit terms and gives them a new legal significance

- by setting them out in Article 3b as general principles of Community law;
- by setting out the principle of subsidiarity as a basic principle of the European Union;[2]
- by reflecting the idea of subsidiarity in the drafting of several Treaty articles.[3]

4. The implementation of Article 3b should respect the following basic principles

- Making the principle of subsidiarity and Article 3b work is an obligation for all the Community institutions, without affecting the balance between them.

- An agreement shall be sought to this effect between the European Parliament, the Council and the Commission, in the framework of the interinstitutional dialogue which is taking place among these Institutions.

- The principle of subsidiarity does not relate to and cannot call into question the powers conferred on the European Community by the Treaty as interpreted by the Court. It provides a guide as to how those powers are to be exercised at the Community level, including in the application of Article 235. The application of the principle shall respect the general provisions of the Maastricht Treaty, including the "maintaining in full of the acquis communautaire", and it shall not affect the primacy of Community law nor shall it call into question the principle set out in Article F(3) of the Treaty on European Union, according to which the Union shall provide itself with the means necessary to attain its objectives and carry through its policies.

- Subsidiarity is a dynamic concept and should be applied in the light of the objectives set out in the Treaty. It allows Community action to be expanded where circumstances so require, and conversely, to be restricted or discontinued where it is no longer justified.

- Where the application of the subsidiarity test excludes Community action, Member States would still be required in their action to comply with the general rules laid down in Article 5 of the Treaty, by taking all appropriate measures to ensure fulfilment of their obligations under the Treaty and by abstaining from any measure which could jeopardize the attainment of the objectives of the Treaty.

- The principle of subsidiarity cannot be regarded as having direct effect; however, interpretation of this principle, as well as review of compliance with it by the Community institutions, are subject to control by the Court of Justice, as far as matters falling within the Treaty establishing the European Community are concerned.

- Paragraphs 2 and 3 of Article 3b apply only to the extent that the Treaty gives to the institution concerned the choice whether to act and/or a choice as to the nature and extent of the action. The more specific the nature of a Treaty requirement, the less scope exists for applying subsidiarity. The Treaty imposes a number of specific obligations upon the Community institutions, for example concerning the implementation and enforcement of Community law, competition policy and the protection of Community funds. These obligations are not affected by Article 3b: in particular the principle of subsidiarity cannot reduce the need for Community measures to contain adequate provision

---

[2] See Articles A and B of the Treaty on European Union.
[3] Articles 118a, 126, 127, 128, 129, 129a, 129b, 130 and 130g of the EC Treaty, Article 2 of the Agreement on social policy.
Furthermore, Article K.3(2)b directly incorporates the principle of subsidiarity.

for the Commission and the Member States to ensure that Community law is properly enforced and to fulfil their obligations to safeguard Community expenditures.

- Where the Community acts in an area falling under shared powers the type of measures to apply has to be decided on a case by case basis in the light of the relevant provisions of the Treaty.[4]

II. Guidelines

In compliance with the basic principles set out above, the following guidelines — specific to each paragraph of Article 3b — should be used in examining whether a proposal for a Community measure conforms to the provisions of Article 3b.

First paragraph (Limit on Community action)

Compliance with the criteria laid down in this paragraph is a condition for any Community action.

In order to apply this paragraph correctly the institutions need to be satisfied that the proposed action is within the limits of the powers conferred by the Treaty and is aimed at meeting one or more of its objectives. The examination of the draft measure should establish the objective to be achieved and whether it can be justified in relation to an objective of the Treaty and that the necessary legal basis for its adoption exists.

Second paragraph (Should the Community act?)

(i) This paragraph does not apply to matters falling within the Community's exclusive competence.
For Community action to be justified the Council must be satisfied that both aspects

of the subsidiarity criterion are met: the objectives of the proposed action cannot be sufficiently achieved by Member States' action and they can therefore be better achieved by action on the part of the Community.

(ii) The following guidelines should be used in examining whether the above-mentioned condition is fulfilled:

- the issue under consideration has transnational aspects which cannot be satisfactorily regulated by action by Member States; and/or

- actions by Member States alone or lack of Community action would conflict with the requirements of the Treaty (such as the need to correct distortion of competition or avoid disguised restrictions on trade or strengthen economic and social cohesion) or would otherwise significantly damage Member States' interests; and/or

- the Council must be satisfied that action at Community level would produce clear benefits by reason of its scale or effects compared with action at the level of the Member States.

(iii) The Community should only take action involving harmonization of national legislation, norms or standards where this is necessary to achieve the objectives of the Treaty.

(iv) The objectives of presenting a single position of the Member States vis-à-vis third countries is not in itself a justification for internal Community action in the area concerned.

(v) The reasons for concluding that a Community objective cannot be sufficiently achieved by the Member States but can be better achieved by the Community must be substantiated by qualitative or, wherever possible, quantitative indicators.

---

[4] The new Articles 126 to 129 of the EC Treaty in the areas of education, vocational training and youth, culture and public health will explicitly rule out harmonization of laws and regulations of Member States. It follows that the use of Article 235 for harmonization measures in pursuit of the specific objectives laid down in Articles 126 to 129 will be ruled out. This does not mean that the pursuit of other Community objectives through Treaty articles other than 126 to 129 might not produce effects in these areas. Where Articles 126, 128 and 129 refer to "incentive measures", the Council considers that this expression refers to Community measures designed to encourage cooperation between Member States or to support or supplement their action in the areas concerned, including where appropriate through financial support for Community programmes or national or cooperative measures designed to achieve the objectives of these articles.

Third paragraph (Nature and extent of Community action)

(i) This paragraph applies to all Community action, whether or not within exclusive competence.

(ii) Any burdens, whether financial or administrative, falling upon the Community, national governments, local authorities, economic operators and citizens, should be minimized and should be proportionate to the objectives to be achieved;

(iii) Community measures should leave as much scope for national decision as possible, consistent with securing the aim of the measure and observing the requirements of the Treaty. While respecting Community law, care should be taken to respect well established national arrangements and the organization and working of Member States' legal systems. Where appropriate and subject to the need for proper enforcement, Community measures should provide Member States with alternative ways to achieve the objectives of the measures.

(iv) Where it is necessary to set standards at Community level, consideration should be given to setting minimum standards, with freedom for Member States to set higher national standards, not only in the areas where the Treaty so requires (118a, 130t) but also in other areas where this would not conflict with the objectives of the proposed measure or with the Treaty.

(v) The form of action should be as simple as possible, consistent with satisfactory achievement of the objective of the measure and the need for effective enforcement. The Community should legislate only to the extent necessary. Other things being equal, directives should be preferred to regulations and framework directives to detailed measures. Non-binding measures such as recommendations should be preferred where appropriate. Consideration should also be given where appropriate to the use of voluntary codes of conduct.

(vi) Where appropriate under the Treaty, and provided this is sufficient to achieve its objectives, preference in choosing the type of Community action should be given to encouraging cooperation between Member States, coordinating national action or to complementing, supplementing or supporting such action.

(vii) Where difficulties are localized and only certain Member States are affected, any necessary Community action should not be extended to other Member States unless this is necessary to achieve an objective of the Treaty.

III. Procedures and practices

The Treaty on European Union obliges all institutions to consider, when examining a Community measure, whether the provisions of Article 3b are observed.

For this purpose, the following procedures and practices will be applied in the framework of the basic principles set out under paragraph II and without prejudice to a future interinstitutional agreement.

(a) Commission

The Commission has a crucial role to play in the effective implementation of Article 3b, given its right of initiative under the Treaty, which is not called into question by the application of this article.

The Commission has indicated that it will consult more widely before proposing legislation, which could include consultation with all the Member States and a more systematic use of consultation documents (green papers). Consultation could include the subsidiarity aspects of a proposal. The Commission has also made it clear that, from now on and according to the procedure it already established in accordance with the commitment given at the European Council in Lisbon, it will justify in a recital the relevance of its initiative with regard to the principle of subsidiarity. Whenever necessary, the explanatory memorandum accompanying the proposal will give details on the considerations of the Commission in the context of Article 3b.

The overall monitoring by the Commission of the observance of the provisions of Article 3b in all its activities is essential and measures have been taken by the Commission in this respect. The Commission will submit an annual report to the European Council and the European Parliament through the General Affairs Council on the application of the Treaty in this area. This report will be of value in the debate on the annual report which the European Council has to submit to the European Parliament on progress achieved by the Union (see Article D in the Treaty on European Union).

(b) Council

The following procedure will be applied by the Council from the entry into force of the Treaty. In the meantime it will guide the work of the Council.

The examination of the compliance of a measure with the provisions of Article 3b should be undertaken on a regular basis; it should become an integral part of the overall examination of any Commission proposal and be based on the substance of the proposal. The relevant existing Council rules, including those on voting, apply to such examination.[5] This examination includes the Council's own evaluation of whether the Commission proposal is totally or partially in conformity with the provisions of Article 3b (taking as a starting point for the examination the Commission's recital and explanatory memorandum) and whether any change in the proposal envisaged by the Council is in conformity with those provisions. The Council decision on the subsidiarity aspects shall be taken at the same time as the decision on substance and according to the voting requirements set out in the Treaty. Care should be taken not to impede decision-making in the Council and to avoid a system of preliminary or parallel decision-making.

The Article 3b examination and debate will take place in the Council responsible for dealing with the matter. The General Affairs Council will have responsibility for general questions relating to the application of Article 3b. In this context the General Affairs Council will accompany the annual report from the Commission (see (a) above) with any appropriate considerations on the application of this Article by the Council.

Various practical steps to ensure the effectiveness of the Article 3b examination will be put into effect including:

- working group reports and COREPER reports on a given proposal will, where appropriate, describe how Article 3b has been applied,

- in all cases of implementation of the Article 189b and 189c procedure, the European Parliament will be fully informed of the Council's position concerning the observance of Article 3b, in the explanatory memorandum which the Council has to produce according to the provisions of the Treaty. The Council will likewise inform the Parliament if it partially or totally rejects a Commission proposal on the grounds that it does not comply with the principle of Article 3b.

Transparency — Implementation of the Birmingham Declaration

- Access to the work of the Council
- Information on the role of the Council and its decisions
- Simplification of and easier access to Community legislation

Access to the work of the Council

The process of opening up the work of the Council will start in the following areas:

(a) Open Debates on Work Programme and on Major Initiatives of Community Interest

(i) Open orientation debates on relevant Presidency or Commission work programmes, in both the General Affairs Council and the ECOFIN Council. The timing will be for decision by the Presidency.

(ii) There should be regular open debates on major issues of Community interest. It will be for the Presidency, any Member States or the Commission to propose issues for open debates. The decision will be taken by the Council on a case by case basis.

(b) Legislation

Major new legislative proposals will, whenever appropriate, be the subject of a preliminary

---

[5] In the course of this examination, any Member State has the right to require that the examination of a proposal which raises Article 3b issues be inscribed on the provisional agenda of a Council in accordance with Article 2 of the Council's rules of procedure. If such examination, which will include all relevant points of substance covered by the Commission proposal, shows that the majority required for the adoption of the act does not exist, the possible outcomes include amendments of the proposal by the Commission, continued examination by the Council with a view to putting it into conformity with Article 3b or a provisional suspension of discussion of the proposal. This does not prejudice Member States or Commission rights under Article 2 of the Council's rules of procedure nor the Council obligation to consider the opinion of the European Parliament.

open debate, in the relevant Council, on the basis of the Commission's legislative proposal. It will be for the Presidency, any Member State or the Commission to propose specific subjects for a debate. The decision will be taken by the Council on a case by case basis. Negotiations on legislation in the framework of the Council shall remain confidential.

(c) Publication of Voting Records

When a formal vote is taken in Council, the record of the vote (including explanations of vote where delegations request these) shall be published.

(d) The decision on holding an open debate on a specific item under point (a)(ii) and (b) shall be taken by unanimity

(e) "Public access" shall be achieved by televising the debate for viewing in the press area of the Council building

Information on the role of the Council

A. *Transparency on the Council's decisions*
  - Extension to all Council formations of the practice, established over the years in most Councils, of publishing a full description in the Press release of the conclusions reached by the Council (exceptions being made for cases where such information would damage the interests of the Member States, the Council, or the Community – e.g. negotiating mandates). More systematic emphasis on publication of explanatory summaries concerning important "A" points adopted at the Council. Greater efforts to be made when drafting conclusions to make them understandable to the public.

  - Better background information on Council decisions (e.g. objective, history, link to other subjects) to be made available, if possible for distribution at pre-Council press briefings, in the form of background notes prepared by the Secretariat in user-friendly terms. This initiative could be extended in the future to cover matters relating to Common Foreign and Security policy and Internal and Justice Affairs, taking into account the specific need for confidentiality in some areas.

  - Systematic background pre-Council press briefings by Presidency, assisted by Council Secretariat (today not all Presidencies hold such briefings and often they are limited to the national Press corps).

  - Publication of the common positions established by the Council under the procedures of Articles 189b and 189c and the explanatory memorandum accompanying them.

  - It is important to make all information material available rapidly in all Community languages.

B. *Increase in general information on the role and the activities of the Council*
  - The annual report, which is currently published after long delays, to be published from now on early in the new year on the responsibility of the Secretary-General. Aim to make it more interesting and more understandable to the public — and complementary to, rather than duplicating — the Commission's annual report. There should also be a short summary aimed at broad circulation.

  - Increase in the Council's information activities in general including a reinforcement of the Press Service. Stepping up of the already quite intensive information activity (group visits) performed by the services of the Secretariat. Establishing a programme for visits of journalists — particularly EC news editors — not based in Brussels (in cooperation with the Commission).

C. *Cooperation and more rapid transmission of material*
  - Activating the existing Information Group of the Council and extending it to the other Institutions with a view to developing coordinated information strategies;

  - Cooperation between Member States and Community Institutions in the information field.

  - Use of new communication technologies: data bases, electronic mail for making information available outside Council meeting places (Brussels/Luxembourg).

*Simplification of and easier access to
Community legislation*

*I Making new Community legislation clearer
and simpler*

While the technical nature of most texts and the
need to compromise among the various national
positions often complicate the drafting process,
practical steps should nevertheless be taken to
improve the quality of Community legislation,
such as the following:

(a) guidelines for the drafting of Community
legislation should be agreed upon, containing
criteria against which the quality of drafting of
legislation would have to be checked;

(b) delegations of Member States should
endeavour, at all levels of the Council proceedings, to check more thoroughly the quality
of legislation;

(c) the Council Legal Service should be
requested to review draft legislative acts on a
regular basis before they are adopted by the
Council and make suggestions where necessary
for appropriate redrafting in order to make such
acts as simple and clear as possible;

(d) the Jurist-Linguist Group, which does the
final legal editing of all legislation before it is
adopted by the Council (with the participation
of national legal experts), should give suggestions for simplifying and clarifying the language
of the texts without changing their substance.

*II Making existing Community legislation
more accessible*

Community legislation can be made more readily accessible in a concise and intelligible form
through a speedier and more organized use of
consolidation or codification; an improvement
of the CELEX-database system should also be
considered.

*(1) Improving and organizing consolidation
or codification of Community legislation*

The two possible approaches — unofficial consolidation and official codification[6] — must be
pursued in parallel.

(a) The Office for Official Publications of the
European Communities has an important role
to play in respect of *unofficial consolidation*.
Planning of this began some time ago and a
new system will be operated as from 1993
on, whereby the consolidated version of all
Community legislation undergoing amendments
can be made automatically available following
any such amendment; two years later, the system should be able to cover the whole of
Community legislation (including past legislation) provided that there is adequate funding.
Consolidated legislation should be immediately
published (in the C-series of the Official Journal), possibly after adding the recitals, and/or
made available through CELEX.

(b) *Official codification* is important because
it provides legal security as to the law which
is applicable at a certain moment concerning a
specific issue.

Since official codification can only be done
through the relevant legislative procedures, priorities need to be established and an accelerated working method agreed upon between
the three institutions which have legislative
powers.

(i)   Official codification should take place on
the basis of agreed priorities. The Commission will propose such priorities in its work
programme after appropriate consultation;

(ii) A jointly acceptable accelerated working
method should be sought allowing codified
Community law, (replacing existing legislation without changing its substance) to be
adopted in a speedy and efficient way; a
consultative group composed of the legal
services of the Commission, the Council
and the Parliament would help to carry out
the necessary ground work to permit the
adoption of codified Community legislation
as rapidly as possible under the Community's normal decision-making procedure.

---

[6] A clear distinction must be made between
–   *unofficial consolidation* which consists in editorial assembling, outside any legislative procedure, of the
scattered parts of legislation on a specific issue, which has no legal effect and which leaves all such parts in
force (see for instance the consolidated text of the Financial Regulation, OJ C 80 of 25.03.1991, p. 1);
–   *official codification* which is achieved through the adoption of a formal legislative Community act through
the relevant procedures, while repealing all pre-existing texts (see, for instance, the Council Regulation
on the common organisation of the market in fishery products, OJ L 354 of 23.12.1991 p. 1).

(2) Strengthening the CELEX data system[7]
CELEX should be improved with a view to
  (a) catching up with the delay as to
    – existing legislation,
    – feeding the database in the Greek, Spanish and Portuguese languages;
  (b) making the system more user-friendly and accessible to the public.

The necessary financial means should be made available.

Denmark and the Treaty on European Union

The European Council recalled that the entry into force of the Treaty signed in Maastricht requires ratification by all the twelve Member States in accordance with their respective constitutional requirements, and reaffirmed the importance of concluding the process as soon as possible, without reopening the present text, as foreseen in Article R of the Treaty.

The European Council noted that Denmark has submitted to Member States on 30 October a document entitled *Denmark in Europe* which sets out the following points as being of particular importance:

  – the defence policy dimension,
  – the third stage of Economic and Monetary Union,
  – citizenship of the Union,
  – cooperation in the fields of justice and home affairs,
  – openness and transparency in the Community's decision-making process,
  – the effective application of the principle of subsidiarity,
  – promotion of cooperation between the Member States to combat unemployment.

Against this background, the European Council has agreed on the following set of arrangements, which are fully compatible with the Treaty, are designed to meet Danish concerns, and therefore apply exclusively to Denmark and not to other existing or acceding Member States:

  (a) Decision concerning certain problems raised by Denmark on the Treaty on European Union (Annex 1). This Decision will take effect on the date of entry into force of the Treaty on European Union;
  (b) the declaration in Annex 2.

The European Council has also taken cognizance of the unilateral declarations in Annex 3, which will be associated with the Danish act of ratification of the Treaty on European Union.

Annex 1: Decision of the Heads of State and Government, meeting within the European Council, concerning certain problems raised by Denmark on the Treaty on European Union

The Heads of State and Government, meeting within the European Council, whose Governments are signatories of the Treaty on European Union, which involves independent and sovereign States having freely decided, in accordance with the existing Treaties, to exercise in common some of their competences,

  – desiring to settle, in conformity with the Treaty on European Union, particular problems existing at the present time specifically for Denmark and raised in its memorandum *Denmark in Europe* of 30 October 1992,
  – having regard to the conclusions of the Edinburgh European Council on subsidiarity and transparency,
  – noting the declarations of the Edinburgh European Council relating to Denmark,
  – taking cognizance of the unilateral declarations of Denmark made on the same occasion which will be associated with its act of ratification,
  – noting that Denmark does not intend to make use of the following provisions in such a way as to prevent closer cooperation and action among Member States compatible with the Treaty and within the framework of the Union and its objectives,

---

(7) The Celex system (automated documentation on Community law) was set up in 1970 as an interinstitutional computerized documentation system and was made available to the public in 1981; it contains the entire body of EC law.
On 13 November 1991, the Council adopted a resolution on the reorganization of the operating structures of CELEX with a view to enhancing its effectiveness (OJ No C 308 of 28.11.91, p. 2).

Have agreed on the following decision:

Section A: Citizenship

The provisions of Part Two of the Treaty establishing the European Community relating to citizenship of the Union give nationals of the Member States additional rights and protection as specified in that Part. They do not in any way take the place of national citizenship. The question whether an individual possesses the nationality of a Member State will be settled solely by reference to the national law of the Member State concerned.

Section B: Economic and Monetary Union

1. The Protocol on certain provisions relating to Denmark attached to the Treaty establishing the European Community gives Denmark the right to notify the Council of the European Communities of its position concerning participation in the third stage of Economic and Monetary Union. Denmark has given notification that it will not participate in the third stage. This notification will take effect upon the coming into effect of this decision.

2. As a consequence, Denmark will not participate in the single currency, will not be bound by the rules concerning economic policy which apply only to the Member States participating in the third stage of Economic and Monetary Union, and will retain its existing powers in the field of monetary policy according to its national laws and regulations, including powers of the National Bank of Denmark in the field of monetary policy.

3. Denmark will participate fully in the second stage of Economic and Monetary Union and will continue to participate in exchange-rate cooperation within the European Monetary System (EMS).

Section C: Defence Policy

The Heads of State and Government note that, in response to the invitation from the Western European Union (WEU), Denmark has become an observer to that organization. They also note that nothing in the Treaty on European Union commits Denmark to become a member of the WEU. Accordingly, Denmark does not participate in the elaboration and the implementation of decisions and actions of the Union which have defence implications, but will not prevent the development of closer cooperation between Member States in this area.

Section D: Justice and Home affairs

Denmark will participate fully in cooperation on Justice and Home Affairs on the basis of the provisions of Title VI of the Treaty on European Union.

Section E: Final provisions

1. This decision will take effect on the date of entry into force of the Treaty on European Union; its duration shall be governed by Article Q and N(2) of that Treaty.

2. At any time Denmark may, in accordance with its constitutional requirements, inform other Member States that it no longer wishes to avail itself of all or part of this decision. In that event, Denmark will apply in full all relevant measures then in force taken within the framework of the European Union.

Annex 2: Declarations of the European Council

Declaration on social policy, consumers, environment, distribution of income

1. The Treaty on European Union does not prevent any Member State from maintaining or introducing more stringent protection measures compatible with the EC Treaty:

- in the field of working conditions and in social policy (Article 118A(3) of the EC Treaty and Article 2(5) of the Agreement on social policy concluded between the Member States of the European Community with the exception of the United Kingdom),

- in order to attain a high level of consumer protection (Article 129A(3) of the EC Treaty),

- in order to pursue the objectives of protection of the environment (Article 130T of the EC Treaty).

2. The provisions introduced by the Treaty on European Union, including the provisions on Economic and Monetary Union, permit each Member State to pursue its own policy with regard to distribution of income and maintain or improve social welfare benefits.

Declaration on defence

The European Council takes note that Denmark will renounce its right to exercise the Presidency of the Union in each case involving the elaboration and the implementation of decisions and actions of the Union which have defence implications. The normal rules for replacing the President, in the case of the President being indisposed, shall apply. These rules will also apply with regard to the representation of the Union in international organizations, international conferences and with third countries.

Annex 3: Unilateral declarations of Denmark, to be associated to the Danish Act of Ratification of the Treaty on European Union and of which the eleven other member states will take cognizance

Declaration on citizenship of the union

1. Citizenship of the Union is a political and legal concept which is entirely different from the concept of citizenship within the meaning of the Constitution of the Kingdom of Denmark and of the Danish legal system. Nothing in the Treaty on European Union implies or foresees an undertaking to create a citizenship of the Union in the sense of citizenship of a nation-state. The question of Denmark participating in any such development does, therefore, not arise.

2. Citizenship of the Union in no way in itself gives a national of another Member State the right to obtain Danish citizenship or any of the rights, duties, privileges or advantages that are inherent in Danish citizenship by virtue of Denmark's constitutional, legal and administrative rules. Denmark will fully respect all specific rights expressly provided for in the Treaty and applying to nationals of the Member States.

3. Nationals of the other Member States of the European Community enjoy in Denmark the right to vote and to stand as a candidate at municipal elections, foreseen in Article 8b of the European Community Treaty. Denmark intends to introduce legislation granting nationals of the other Member States the right to vote and to stand as a candidate for elections to the European Parliament in good time before the next elections in 1994. Denmark has no intention of accepting that the detailed arrangements foreseen in paragraphs 1 and 2 of this Article could lead to rules detracting from the rights already given in Denmark in that matter.

4. Without prejudice to the other provisions of the Treaty establishing the European Community, Article 8e requires the unanimity of all the Members of the Council of the European Communities, i.e. all Member States, for the adoption of any provision to strengthen or to add to the rights laid down in Part Two of the EC Treaty. Moreover, any unanimous decision of the Council, before coming into force, will have to be adopted in each Member State, in accordance with its constitutional requirements. In Denmark, such adoption will, in the case of a transfer of sovereignty, as defined in the Danish Constitution, require either a majority of $5/6$ of Members of the Folketing or both a majority of the Members of the Folketing and a majority of voters in a referendum.

Declaration on cooperation in the fields of justice and home affairs

Article K9 of the Treaty on European Union requires the unanimity of all the Members of the Council of the European Union, i.e. all Member States, to the adoption of any decision to apply Article 100C of the Treaty establishing the European Community to action in areas referred to in Article K1(1) to (6). Moreover, any unanimous decision of the Council before coming into force, will have to be adopted in each Member State, in accordance with its constitutional requirements. In Denmark, such adoption will, in the case of a transfer of sovereignty, as defined in the Danish Constitution, require either a majority of $5/6$ of members of the Folketing or both a majority of the Members of the Folketing and a majority of voters in a referendum.

Final declaration

The Decision and Declarations above are a response to the result of the Danish referendum of 2 June 1992 on ratification of the Maastricht Treaty. As far as Denmark is concerned, the objectives of that Treaty in the four areas mentioned in sections A to D of the Decision are to be seen in the light of these documents, which are compatible with the Treaty and do not call its objectives into question.

5. UK: European Communities (Amendment) Act 1993 (The Maastricht Act)

The following is the Maastricht Act as adopted by the UK Parliament. The italicized sections were all introduced by way of amendment. The original Maastricht Bill introduced by the government consisted only of the sections that are not in italics.

An Act to make provision consequential on the Treaty on European Union signed at Maastricht on 7th February 1992.

[20th July 1993]

BE IT ENACTED by the Queen's most Excellent Majesty, by and with the advice and consent of the Lords Spiritual and Temporal, and Commons, in this present Parliament assembled, and by the authority of the same, as follows:

1.(1) In section 1(2) of the European Communities Act 1972, in the definition of "the Treaties" and "the Community Treaties", after paragraph (j) (inserted by the European Communities (Amendment) Act 1986) there shall be inserted the words "and

(k) Titles II, III and IV of the Treaty of European Union signed at Maastricht on 7th February 1992, together with the other provisions of the Treaty so far as they relate to those Titles, and the Protocols adopted at Maastricht on that date and annexed to the Treaty establishing the European Community *with the exception of the Protocol on Social Policy on page 117 of Cm 1934*".

(2) For the purpose of section 6 of the European Parliamentary Elections Act 1978 (approval of treaties increasing the Parliament's powers) the Treaty on European Union signed at Maastricht on 7th February 1992 is approved.

2. No notification shall be given to the Council of the European Communities that the United Kingdom intends to move to the third stage of economic and monetary union (in accordance with the Protocol on certain provisions relating to the United Kingdom adopted at Maastricht on 7th February 1992) unless a draft of the notification has first been approved by Act of Parliament *and unless Her Majesty's Government has reported to Parliament on its proposals for the co-ordination of economic policies, its role in the European Council of Finance Ministers (ECOFIN) in pursuit of the objectives of Article 2 of the Treaty establishing the European Community as provided for in Articles 103 and 102a, and the work of the European Monetary Institute in preparation for economic and monetary union.*

3. In implementing Article 108 of the Treaty establishing the European Community, and ensuring compatibility of the statutes of the national central bank, Her Majesty's Government shall, by order, make provision for the Governor of the Bank of England to make an annual report to Parliament, which shall be subject to approval by a Resolution of each House of Parliament.

4. In implementing the provisions of Article 103(3) of the Treaty establishing the European Community, information shall be submitted to the Commission from the United Kingdom indicating performance on economic growth, industrial investment, employment and balance of trade, together with comparisons with those items of performance from other Member States.

5. Before submitting the information required in implementing Article 103(3) of the Treaty establishing the European Community, Her Majesty's Government shall report to Parliament for its approval an assessment of the medium-term economic and budgetary position in relation to public investment expenditure and to the social, economic and environmental goals set out in Article 2, which report shall form the basis of any submission to the Council and Commission in pursuit of their responsibilities under Articles 103 and 104c.

6. A person may be proposed as a member or alternate member for the United Kingdom of the Committee of the Regions constituted under Article 198a of the Treaty establishing the European Community only if, at the time of the proposal, he is an elected member of a local authority.

7. This Act shall come into force only when each House of Parliament has come to a Resolution on a motion tabled by a Minister of the Crown considering the question of adopting the Protocol on Social Policy.

8. This Act may be cited as the European Communities (Amendment) Act 1993.

INDEX

Page numbers higher than 96 refer to the documentation section of the book